REAL-LIFE HANDICAPPING

AN ECLECTIC HORSEPLAYER'S YEAR AT THE TRACK

by Dave Litfin

City Miner Books • Berkeley, California

Book and Cover Design: Dayna Goforth

Published by City Miner Books, 1997
P.O. Box 176
Berkeley, CA 94701
ISBN 0-933944-18-7

Printed in United States of America

First Edition   10 9 8 7 6 5 4 3 2 1

On the cover: Thunder Gulch springs into action at the start of the Travers Stakes
at Saratoga. The photograph appeared on the front page of the *Daily Racing Form's*
edition of Wednesday, August 23, 1995, and earned photographer Michael J. Marten
an Eclipse Award.

For Addy, Marne, and Samuel

Also by Dave Litfin:

Dave Litfin's *Expert Handicapping*

What the experts are saying about Dave Litfin's *Expert Handicapping:*

"...good reading for good handicappers who want to get better.
A fine book by an "expert" public handicapper. I heartily recommend it."
—Steve Davidowitz, author of *Betting Thoroughbreds*

"The most insightful public handicapper in the business...joins the leaders in
the current crop of turf writers. Aside from the challenging content of this book,
the reader will be comforted by Litfin's unassuming, non-congratulatory style.
The book reads like a fireside chat...encourages us not to follow a guru but
to become independent thinkers."
—*The Cramer–Olmsted Report*, December 1995

"One of the most respected names in thoroughbred betting circles has written his
first book, and it's a wire-to-wire winner...a gold mine of information...
a very good 8 rating."
—*Phillips Racing Newsletter*, October 1995

"...brings a new voice and fresh perspectives to the greatest game in town.
It's a winner!"
—James Quinn, author of nine handicapping books,
including *The Handicapper's Stakes Festival and Figure Handicapping.*

"...the most consistent public handicapper in America."
—Nick Zito,
trainer of Kentucky Derby winners Strike the Gold and Go for Gin.

Contents

Starting Off

IF I HAD IT TO DO over again, I suppose my first book might've been titled something else besides *Dave Litfin's Expert Handicapping*.

"Such a generic title," observed Mark Cramer in his review for the December, 1995 issue of the Cramer-Olmsted Report. "The world 'expert' is too vague, too clinical. I would've called the book something like 'The Art and Science of Handicapping'."

Frankly, I was stymied when it came to giving my first book a title because of the fragmented manner in which it was written: nearly three years passed from the time I began gathering material until the first rough manuscript reached an editor. During that time I stopped and started the manuscript repeatedly, so the material didn't flow as smoothly from one topic to the next as it might have under different circumstances. I'm an introspective person by nature, preferring to blend in with my surroundings, so the fact that my name wound up in the title led to an anxiety attack or two, as you might imagine.

Oh well. For horseplayers, coping with adversity is a way of life. We pick up the broken pieces of our shattered dreams and move on.

Those of you familiar with my handicapping columns and race-analyses in the *Daily Racing Form* realize that I have the utmost respect for the game's ever-fascinating complexity. You evidently feel the same way, otherwise you wouldn't have picked up this book in the first place.

Therefore, I am assuming that, for the majority of my readers here, handicapping is much more than a mere hobby — it is a burning passion. Especially at today's book prices.

In other words, you're the type who thinks nothing of venturing out in snowstorms to pick up a *Daily Racing Form* — even if you're not planning on making any bets—because you still need the result charts. Am I right? I'd also wager that you annually purchase *Maiden Stats* from Bloodstock Research, and *Sire Ratings* from Mike Helm to gain an edge with first time-starters or lightly-raced runners switching to grass or a wet track for the first time. Not only do you know what Tomlinson ratings *are*, you can quote numbers for a dozen or so common look-up sires. Of course, you probably subscribe to the *National Charts Weekly* too.

Real-life Handicapping chronicles a year of playing the horses full-time on the New York circuit. It begins in the fall of 1994 at Belmont Park, continues through a winter and early spring at Aqueduct, moves back to Belmont again in May, and concludes in August with the 1995 Saratoga meet. Along the way a great many subtleties come into play, nuances and wrinkles likely to resurface season after season. Those with a nose for detail should pick up some effective and profitable research techniques. And don't worry: no sheet-style figures (well, there is *one* example of how the sheets can be helpful, but it has little to do with speed figures, per se).

Why not begin such a journey on January 1st, why the first week in September? The reason for the quirky start-up time is simple. I had wrapped up the manuscript for *Expert Handicapping* at the end of the 1994 Saratoga meeting, only to find that in the coming weeks, without consciously trying, enough worthwhile material played itself out on the racetrack to merit another collection. By the time New Year's Day of 1995 rolled around this project was off and running with a life-force all its own.

The discussions that follow revolve around races that I actually played (whether or not I "picked" these races exactly the same way in my published pre-race *Form* analyses). Every effort has been made to recreate the insights, inspirations, conditions and betting decisions as accurately and vividly as possible. It will be as if you are sitting right next to me by the front window in the press box, as we take in everything that's going on around us.

Enjoy. I hope the subject matter points you toward many future winners or at least provides ample food for thought, no matter what circuit you call home.

And at least, this time, I like the title.

Dave Litfin
Belmont Park, Fall 1996

Autumn

IT'S NOT A GOOD IDEA to force things at the beginning of a race-meeting, especially when you've just arrived home from a hot, hectic summer of intensive horseplaying at Saratoga. Better to sit back, observe, and let things unfold a little bit at a time. This is always sound counsel, and particularly useful to remember when racing shifts back downstate to Belmont Park for what was once known as the "fall championship meet."

The barns on the picturesque backstretch of Saratoga are filled with several different kinds of thoroughbreds: stakes runners from all divisions, of course, dozens of fashionably bred 2-year-olds, and a bevy of long-winded grass horses. The low-to-mid priced claimers that are New York racing's bread and butter during the remaining forty-six weeks of the year get the leftovers; many of these cheap platers have been campaigned hard through the spring and early summer, so many stables use Saratoga's six-week session as a timely freshening period. As a result, during the opening stages of Belmont in the fall, players must cope with a steady influx of horses who've been on the sidelines since July, or who perhaps vanned up the thruway for one shot at a Saratoga purse.

Also complicating matters is the dramatic change in the playing fields, most notably insofar as the respective dirt tracks are concerned. Saratoga's main track measures a mile and an eighth in circumference, and saving ground on the relatively sharp turns is usually a prerequisite for success. Off-the-pace horses can win, but only if they get an "inside out" kind of trip: no more than two to three paths out from the rail on the far turn before easing out for a clear run through the stretch; Pat Day, I might add, is a master at this maneuver. Horses caught four or five paths out from the rail going into a Saratoga turn invariably are ten or eleven wide coming out of it , and they practically never win.

Belmont Park's main track, AKA "Big Sandy", is a completely different story. At a mile and a half around, it is the biggest racetrack in the country and once in a while even the most experienced rider can lose his bearings on the gradual, sweeping turns that seemingly go on forever. Horses traveling wide on the far turn at Belmont are at no great disadvantage (unless, of course, an inside bias is present); the move is so commonplace, it has its own nickname: The Belmont Balcony Move.

At any rate, by the time Labor Day weekend is over with, I'm pretty much burned out for a couple of weeks, what with getting the kids back to school and going through six weeks of accumulated junk mail, so I make it a point to take it easy at the windows; as Chauncy Gardener said in *Being There*, "I like to watch." There's nothing like watching a race while completely neutral; instead of the tunnel-vision that comes from focusing in on **The Bet**, one gets a wide-angle view of the race, and usually the eye will zoom in and out on the action at various intervals, as the development of the race warrants.

While I subscribe to the belief that handicapping is not a deterministic science (that is to say, there is no absolute outcome foreordained for any given race), I always strive to wait until an exceptionally value-rich opportunity presents itself at the beginning of a new meeting, in order to give myself a good chance of starting off on the right foot.

MARAUD, turning back from exceptional on-the-pace efforts in routes to a six and a half-furlong sprint, was worth a prime bet on September 7. As mentioned, it's okay to take a closer sprinting on Belmont dirt. Sometimes, that's the best option when a race is as top-heavy with early speed as this one was:

Belmont Park

6

6½ Furlongs **(1:14^3) CLAIMING. Pursee $20,000. 3–year–olds and upward. Weights: 3–year–olds, 118 lbs. Older, 122 lbs. Non–winners of two races since August 1, allowed 3 lbs. Of a race since then, 5 lbs. Claiming price $35,000, for each $2,500 to $30,000, allowed 2 lbs. (Races when entered to be claimed for $25,000 or less not considered.)**

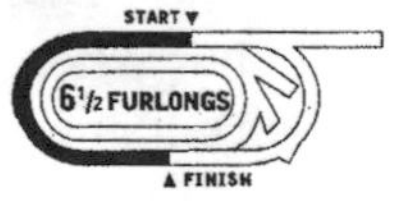

Coupled – Game Wager and Maraud

Carrnac

Own: Boto Stable

SMITH M E (22 5 1 1 .23) **$35,000**

B. c. 4
Sire: Carr de Naskra (Star de Naskra)
Dam: Empire Beauty (On to Glory)
Br: BOTO Thoroughbreds Inc (NY)
Tr: Kelly Timothy D (—)

119

Lifetime Record:	**10**	**4**	**3**	**1**	**$62,110**		
1994	2 1 0 0				**$16,800**	**Turf** 0 0 0 0	
1993	5 2 2 1				**$33,710**	**Wet** 4 2 1 0	**$34,360**
Bel	2 2 0 0				**$21,600**	**Dist** 1 0 0 0	

15Aug94–6Sar	my	6f	:22	$:45^2$	$:57^3$	$1:10^2$	3↑ [S]Alw 28000N1X	**86**	8	5	3½	1^{hd}	1½	1^{hd}	Smith M E	117 b	2.50	89–13	Carrnac117^{hd} Pro On Ice117^{8½} Windy Target112^{1½}	Driving 12
5Aug94–9Sar	my	6f	$:22^2$	$:46^2$	$:58^4$	$1:11^1$	Clm 20000	**79**	9	1	3½	1^{hd}	3^{1½}	6^{7¼}	Santos J A	114 b	4.00	78–19	OcenSplsh117^1 PeerlessPerformer115^3 BenAli'sRullh108^{2½}	Dueled, tired 9
20Oct93–6Aqu	sly	6f	$:22^1$	$:45^4$	:58	$1:10^4$	3↑ [S]Alw 28000N1X	**80**	2	2	3^{5½}	2^1	1^{1½}	2^{hd}	Santos J A	114 b	*.70	88–13	Raise A Rumpus114^{hd} Carrnac114½ African Wish116^6	Just missed 6
22Sep93–6Bel	sly	6f	$:22^3$	:46	$:58^3$	$1:11^4$	Clm 35000	**80**	10	8	4^2	2^{hd}	1½	1^1	Santos J A	117 b	9.20	81–26	Carrnac117^1 The Mechanic117^{nk} Lucky Favorite113^{hd}	Wide, driving 10
12Sep93–2Bel	fst	6f	$:22^3$	$:46^1$	$:58^2$	$1:10^4$	Clm 22500	**89**	8	5	2½	2^1	1^{hd}	1^{1¼}	Santos J A	115 fb	3.10	86–17	Carrnac115^{1¼} Tricky Catman115^5 Freeze Dry119^{no}	Driving 8
23Aug93–9Sar	fst	7f	$:22^2$	:45	$1:09^4$	$1:22^2$	Clm 22500	**75**	4	7	3½	1^{hd}	2^{hd}	3^7	Santos J A	115 fb	4.60	86–08	Green Thoughts115^{5¾} Wet Reel117^{1¼} Carrnac115^{hd}	Bid, weakened 11
12Aug93–10Sar	fst	6f	$:22^2$	$:45^3$	$:57^4$	$1:10^2$	Clm 20000	**73**	9	5	1^{hd}	1½	2^1	2^4	Santos J A	113 fb	11.30	86–11	Super Forbes117^4 Carrnac113^{hd} Lost Pan117^{1¼}	Gamely 12
22Dec92–3Aqu	fst	6f [•]	$:22^3$	$:46^2$	$:59^1$	$1:12^2$	Clm 35000	**74**	2	6	5^{8¼}	4^{4½}	2^{hd}	1^1	Grana P M^5	107 b	21.50	81–16	[D]Carrnac107^1 Mainmanbuddy117^{1¾} Fired On117^{1¾}	Erratic stretch, drvg 7
Disqualified and placed second																				
18Nov92–9Aqu	fst	6f	$:22^4$	:47	$:59^4$	$1:13^1$	Md 30000	**58**	1	2	2½	2^{hd}	1^{hd}	1^{nk}	Grana P M^{10}	104 b	44.10	75–16	Carrnac104^{nk} Joe Hartwick114^4 Everything's Fine118	Driving 12
22Oct92–3Aqu	fst	6½f	$:23^3$	:48	$1:12^1$	$1:18^4$	[S]Md Sp Wt	**11**	7	5	7^{4½}	7^{13}	7^{23}	7^{33}	Lidberg D W	118	13.10	51–18	Itaka118^{1¼} Koluctoo Jimmy Al118^{3¼} Bold Doer118	Outrun 7

WORKOUTS: ●Sep 3 Bel tr.t 3f fst $:35^2$ B *1/9* Aug 28 Sar 5f fst 1:04 B *12/14* Aug 13 Sar 3f fst $:35^4$ H *3/26* Jly 30 Sar 5f fst 1:06 B *40/44* Jly 25 Sar 4f fst $:48^1$ Hg*8/73* Jun 29 Bel tr.t 4f fst $:50^1$ B *5/9*

Game Wager

Own: Hauman Eugene E

MIGLIORE R (11 0 3 0 .00) **$32,500**

B. g. 6
Sire: Pass the Line (Pas Seul)
Dam: Miami Game (Crozier)
Br: Hooper Fred W (Fla)
Tr: Hushion Michael E (1 0 0 0 .00)

115

Lifetime Record:	**57**	**15**	**6**	**7**	**$261,675**		
1994	6 0 1 1				**$11,100**	**Turf** 5 1 0 0	**$10,895**
1993	10 5 2 0				**$95,655**	**Wet** 6 1 2 1	**$25,530**
Bel	15 6 2 3				**$115,730**	**Dist** 5 0 0 2	**$5,530**

Entered 5Sep94– 2 BEL

24Aug94–7Sar	fst	6f	$:22^2$	$:45^2$	$:57^3$	$1:10^1$	3↑ Clm 35000	**85**	5	6	6^{12}	6^7	6^{3¾}	4^{3¼}	Migliore R	117 f	2.00	87–13	AssemblyDancer117¾ Gallpit'sMoment117½ FightingDddy117^2	Late gain 6
7Aug94–5Sar	fst	7f	$:22^3$	$:44^4$	$1:09^1$	$1:21^4$	3↑ Alw 40000N$Y	**84**	3	5	5^{11}	5^{12}	5^5	4^9	Migliore R	115 f	4.60	87–03	Brunswick115^2 Jack Livingston115^2 Corma Ray119^5	Broke awkwardly 5
24Jly94–2Sar	wf	6f	$:22^2$	$:45^1$	$:57^1$	$1:09^3$	Clm 45000	**94**	1	5	6^{5½}	5^{3¾}	2^{1½}	2^{3¼}	Migliore R	113 f	3.40	90–13	Senor Cielo117^{3¼} Game Wager113^{3¼} Chief Master115½	Second best 7
19Jun94–3Bel	fst	6½f	$:22^4$	$:45^3$	$1:09^4$	1:16	Clm 35000	**95**	7	6	6^{5¾}	6^{2¾}	5¾	3^{nk}	Migliore R	117 f	*1.60e	93–12	Zeezaroo117^{hd} Danzig's Dance117^{no} Game Wager117^{hd}	Belated rally 7
28May94–2Bel	gd	1$\frac{1}{16}$ [T]	$:23^3$	$:47^1$	$1:11^3$	$1:42^2$	Clm 45000	**62**	4	2	1½	3^1	7^8	8^{16½}	Davis R G	113 f	9.80	68–21	Palace Line117¾ [D]Known Ranger115^3 Cranshaw'sCorner117^{no}	Gave way 8
13May94–8Bel	fst	6½f	$:22^3$	$:45^4$	1:10	$1:16^2$	3↑ Alw 40000N$Y	**71**	5	7	8^{12}	8^7	8^{8½}	7^{11¾}	Migliore R	115 f	9.30	79–14	Fabersham117^{hd} Key Contender108^{hd} Strikany119^{no}	No factor 8
1Oct93–7Bel	fst	7f	$:22^3$	$:45^2$	1:11	1:24	3↑ Alw 40000N$Y	**86**	2	3	2½	2^{hd}	1½	2^3	Migliore R	119 f	2.70	80–20	Roman Chorus119^3 Game Wager119½ Jacksonport117^1	Gamely 7
18Sep93–4Bel	sly	6f	$:22^2$	$:45^1$	:57	$1:09^2$	3↑ Fall Hwgt H-G2	**68**	3	9	9^{10}	9^{9½}	9^{9¾}	9^{16¼}	Migliore R	129 f	7.70e	77–14	FlySoFree135½ DemalootDemashoot126^{1½} TkeMeOut134^3	Bumped break 10
30Aug93–6Sar	fst	6f	$:22^2$	:45	$:56^4$	1:09	3↑ Alw 40000N$Y	**103**	3	5	6^7	6^2	4¾	1^{2¼}	Migliore R	117 f	*1.60	97–06	Game Wager117^{2¼} Strikany112^{no} Detox117^{3¼}	Going away 6
19Aug93–1Sar	fst	6f	$:22^1$	$:44^4$	$:56^2$	$1:08^1$	3↑ Clm 70000	**101**	7	4	6^{4½}	4^3	4^{2½}	1^1	Migliore R	115 f	2.30e	101–06	Game Wager115^1 Quickest Blade113^{nk} Reappeal108^{nk}	Driving 7

WORKOUTS: Jly 12 Bel tr.t 3f fst $:39^2$ B *13/14* Jly 5 Bel tr.t 3f fst $:39^1$ B *5/6* Jun 15 Bel tr.t 4f fst $:49^4$ B *3/5* Jun 9 Bel [T] 4f fm $:52^2$ B (d) *12/12*

Line Pro

Own: Brida Dennis J
Dk. b or br g. 4
Sire: Allen's Prospect (Mr. Prospector)
Dam: Going Line (Rambunctious)
Br: Landry Harry L (Md)
Tr: Brida Dennis J (—)

PEZUA J M (11 0 0 0 .00) $32,500   115

Lifetime Record: 18 6 4 4 $106,375

1994	4 1 1 1	$28,560	Turf	0 0 0 0
1993	14 5 3 3	$77,815	Wet	3 1 1 1	$22,605
Bel	2 1 1 0	$16,360	Dist	1 1 0 0	$11,700

29Mar94–6Aqu	sly	6f	:221 :452 :572 1:10		Alw 30000N3X	84	3	2	1hd	221	35	391	Graell A	117	4.10	83–15	Tropical Illusion1177 Bushman1192½ Line Pro1171½	Dueled, weakened 6
26Feb94–3Aqu	fst	6f	:231 :47 :59 1:11		Clm 70000	82	5	1	1½	1½	3½	47½	Graell A	113	3.70	81–23	Senor Cielo115¹ Triodet113½ Club De Noche1135½	Drifted, tired 6
10Feb94–6Aqu	fst	6f	:231 :47 :59 1:11		Alw 30000N3X	98	3	3	11	11	12½	21	Graell A	119	3.90	82–30	King Ruckus1171 Line Pro1193 Clever Knave1177	Bid, weakened 5
20Jan94–4Aqu	fst	6f	:233 :473 :593 1:122		Alw 28000N2X	88	5	1	1½	11½	11½	13	Graell A	117	4.40	81–23	Line Pro1173 Six Thirty Two1122½ Slew's Ghost1177	Driving 5
29Dec93–4Aqu	fst	6f	:231 :471 :593 1:122		Clm 50000	90	3	1	12	11½	13½	133	Graell A	117	4.50	81–22	Line Pro1173½ ⑩Dernier's Lass117hd Fly One1191½	Driving 9
3Dec93–4Aqu	fst	6f	:231 :461 :582 ⁴:104		Clm 70000	88	1	4	64½	64½	54	53½	Chavez J F	115	5.50	85–19	Yeckley113½ Six Thirty Two108¹½ Tanako113½	No threat 6
24Nov93–7Aqu	fst	6f	:222 :46	1:112	3↑	Alw 30000N2X	81	6	1	22	31	34	Graell A	120	2.90	81–20	Richmond Runner120³ Lukie's Pop115¹ Line Pro120½	No late bid 7
5Nov93–7Aqu	sly	6f	:222 :454 :581 1:113	3↑	Alw 28000N1X	90	9	2	3½	2hd	1½	15½	Graell A	115	3.20	84–18	Line Pro1175½ Graydon Pool1172 Rise To Rule1222½	Driving 10
14Oct93–6Bel	fst	6f	:222 :454 :58 1:102	3↑	Alw 28000N1X	85	2	1	1½	1hd	2hd	2³½	Graell A	114	3.10	84–10	Man's Hero1143½ Line Pro1143½ Swindle1173½	Gamely 9
29Sep93–4Aqu	fst	6f	:222 :46	1:103		Clm c–25000	98	1	1	1hd	21	1½	1½	Graell A	117	*2.20	87–19	Line Pro1172½ Dam Shot1154 Aye Doo Da1175	Driving 7

Claimed from Davis Barbara J, Moschera Gasper S Trainer

WORKOUTS: Aug 17 Sar tr.t 4f fst :51² B 13/29

Le Risky

Own: Davis Barbara J
Dk. b or br h. 5
Sire: Lejoli (Cornish Prince)
Dam: Frisky and Risky (Cormorant)
Br: Cuomo Michael (NY)
Tr: Moschera Gasper S (3 0 0 0 .00)

SELLERS S J (—) $35,000   117

Lifetime Record: 50 8 2 11 $165,708

1994	14 2 1 5	$51,220	Turf	2 0 0 0
1993	18 3 1 5	$62,655	Wet	8 2 0 2	$37,146
Bel	10 0 0 5	$16,230	Dist	3 0 0 1	$3,890

29Aug94–1Sar	fst	7f	:221 :442 1:092 1:231	3↑	Alw 32000N3X	87	5	6	89½	815	75½	73½	Day P	117 b	4.60	85–13	Barodet113hd Well Known Fun114no Fighting Daddy1171	Outrun 8
13Jly94–4Bel	fst	6f	:221 :45 1:101 1:231		Clm 47500	89	2	6	61²	711	54½	32½	Smith M E	115	*1.40e	83–15	Boss Soss117¾ Senor Cielo117³ Le Risky1152½	Mild rally 6
6Jly94–8Bel	fst	1⅛	:242 :48 1:12 1:42³	3↑	⑤Evan Shpmn H53k	74	4	2	31	52	571	515½	Krone J A	110	9.40	74–23	RichmondRunner116½ CrftyCoventry116² Prospctor'sFlg1173	Gave way 5
21Jun94–6Bel	fst	6f	:224 :452 1:092 1:223		Clm 50000	89	8	7	84½	63½	56	34	Smith M E	117	4.20e	86–11	Senor Cielo1242 Quickest Blade113² Le Risky117nk	Late gain 9
12Jun94–9Bel	fst	6f	:221 :452 1:101 1:352		Clm 50000	93	6	6	65½	62½	42	32½	Smith M E	117	3.50	84–14	O'star1171½ Birdie's Fly117¾ Le Risky117hd	Four wide 6
17May94–6Bel	my	6f	:221 :451 :574 1:10		Clm c–35000	93	3	5	511	65½	34½	1½	Chavez J F	119	3.00	87–17	Nowhere Man115² Top The Record115² Le Risky1192½	Late gain 6

Claimed from Scuderi Vincent S or, Parisella John Trainer

1May94–7Aqu	fst	1	:223 :45 1:09 1:344		Alw 31000N2X	95	6	4	31½	31½	31	1nk	Chavez J F	117	3.30	94–10	Le Risky117nk Giant Leap117nk Peace Baby1173½	Wide, driving 6
23Apr94–7Aqu	fst	7f	:223 :443 1:093 1:23		Alw 31000N2X	90	3	4	32½	44	32½	33	Chavez J F	117 f	3.80e	86–12	Six Thirty Two112²¼ Peace Baby1171½ Le Risky1172	Saved ground 7
16Apr94–2Aqu	sly	6f	:213 :451 :572 1:10		Clm 70000	76	4	6	710	77	76	610½	Chavez J F	113 f	8.50	82–09	GoldnCloud113²½ TropiclIllusion115² QuickstBld113½	Broke slowly, wide 7
7Apr94–2Aqu	my	7f	:223 :454 1:114 1:251		Clm 45000	92	3	1	54½	53¾	42	1½	Chavez J F	113 f	5.80	78–23	Le Risky113½ The Great M. B.1172½ Sparkling Sky113½	Wide, driving 5

WORKOUTS: ● Aug 9 Sar tr.t 4f fst :494 B 1/19

Gallapiat's Moment

Own: Ferriola Ingrid A
B. g. 4
Sire: Gallapiat (Buckpasser)
Dam: Timeless Reason (Timeless Moment)
Br: Harrison Dale (Fla)
Tr: Ferriola Peter (1 0 0 0 .00)

FROST G C (4 1 0 1 .25) $35,000   117

Lifetime Record: 34 8 9 4 $149,004

1994	11 3 2 1	$48,180	Turf	0 0 0 0
1993	18 3 7 3	$74,556	Wet	6 1 2 0	$20,412
Bel	4 2 0 0	$21,420	Dist	2 0 0 2	$5,126

24Aug94–7Sar	fst	6f	:222 :452 :57³ 1:10¹	3↑	Clm 35000	91	4	3	32½	33½	31½	2²	Frost G C	117 fb	22.50	89–13	AssemblyDancer117³ Gallpit'sMoment117½ FightingDddy117²	Willingly 6
1Aug94–1Sar	fst	6f	:22 :45 :572 1:10		Clm 35000	83	7	5	64½	72½	63½	55½	Luzzi M J	117 fb	7.40	85–12	Gold Candy Too1172 Fighting Daddy117no Maraud1151½	No factor 7
16Jly94–1Bel	fst	6f	:224 :453 :573 1:102		Clm c–25000	94	6	7	53	2½	1hd	1no	Santos J A	117 fb	6.00	89–12	Gallapiat's Moment117no Sand Kicker1174 Clever Knave1171	Hard drive 8

Claimed from Kimmel Caesar P, Kimmel John C Trainer

25Jun94–4Bel	fst	6f	:223 :452 :572 1:093		Clm 25000	71	2	4	42	51½	55½	48½	Luzzi M J	119 fb	4.60	84–12	Gold Candy Too1175 Six Thirty Two1172 Maraud112½	Saved ground 7
12Jun94–6Bel	fst	6f	:223 :451 :571 1:094		Clm 35000	86	4	3	52½	54	5½	511	Luzzi M J	117 fb	10.00	85–12	Memorized110nk Wonder Carr115¾ Ocean Splash115¹½	Lacked rally 7
21May94–2Bel	fst	7f	:221 :451 1:10 1:232		Clm 25000	86	1	4	2½	22½	21½	1hd	Luzzi M J	117 fb	4.10	86–13	Gallapiat's Moment117hd Wonder Carr115² Roman Chorus1152½	Driving 7
24Apr94–3Aqu	fst	6f	:21 :443 :57 1:094	3↑	Alw 31000N3X	72	7	7	710	74½	74½	711½	Migliore R	117 fb	13.90	82–12	Boundary117²¾ Carsey's Pal1171 Contarito117nk	Outrun 7
29Mar94–6Aqu	sly	6f	:222 :452 :572 1:10		Alw 30000N3X	68	4	5	46	59	515½	Migliore R	119 fb	3.40	76–15	Tropical Illusion1177 Bushman1192½ Line Pro1171½	No factor 6
6Mar94–7Aqu	fst	6f	:222 :46 1:10		Alw 28000N2X	98	3	4	34	31	31	1½	Migliore R	117 fb	13.40	91–13	Gallapiat's Moment117½ Peace Baby117¾ Unreal Mot117¹½	Driving 5
13Feb94–6Aqu	wf	6f	:221 :452 :574 1:103		Clm 25000	93	1	4	33	31	2hd	12	Leon F5	112 fb	4.80	90–16	⑥Gllpt'sMomnt112² NorthrnCrush1172 UnrlMot117½	Drifted in, driving 5

Disqualified and placed second

WORKOUTS: Aug 16 Sar tr.t 4f fst :53¹ B 39/40   Aug 9 Sar 5f fst 1:03¹ B 12/16   Jly 28 Sar tr.t① 3f sf :39³ B 1/1   Jly 11 Bel tr.t 5f fst 1:04² B 5/5

Insured Winner

Own: Oxenberg Beatrice
Dk. b or br g. 4
Sire: Baldski (Nijinsky II)
Dam: La Chaposa (Ups)
Br: Fabry W A & Johnson Jeffrey E (Fla)
Tr: Hough Stanley M (1 0 0 1 .00)

BAILEY J D (20 3 2 2 .15) $30,000   113

Lifetime Record: 22 4 3 2 $75,630

1994	5 2 1 0	$21,800	Turf	2 0 0 0
1993	10 0 2 0	$12,820	Wet	7 3 0 0	$36,060
Bel	7 1 2 2	$23,990	Dist	2 0 1 0	$5,320

26Aug94–9Sar	my	6f	:214 :451 :574 1:11	3↑	Clm 22500	87	1	1	1½	1½	12½	1½	Bailey J D	115 b	7.00	86–17	Insured Winner115½ Pension Fraud1172½ Moby Jak117½	Driving 9
5Aug94–9Sar	my	6f	:222 :462 :584 1:111		Clm 25000	56	6	2	2½	2hd	84½	816½	Bailey J D	117 b	*2.40	69–19	OcenSplsh1171 PeerlessPerformer115³ BenAli'sRullh1082½	Used in pace 9
18Jly94–4Bel	sly	7f	:223 :454 1:11 1:234		Clm 17500	94	3	2	11½	12	14	19	Bailey J D	117 b	*2.20	84–20	Insured Winner1179 Ben Ali's Rullah113² Prioritizer1154	Ridden out 6
8Jly94–1Bel	fst	6f	:221 :452 :574 1:103		Clm 17500	88	5	3	21½	21	2½	2½	Bailey J D	117 b	9.00	87–15	Revolt1179½ Insured Winner117hd Six Thirty Two117hd	Gamely 8
12Jan94–7GP	sly	6f	:221 :453 :582 1:114		Clm 20000	75	2	7	54½	651	75	65½	Bailey J D	117 b	3.40	77–19	Man O' Smoke1171 Gallapiat's Song117hd StrikeMeDown117¹	Weakened 7
23Dec93–9Crc	fst	6f	:22 :46 :582 1:104		Clm 35000	65	1	6	43	54½	46	47	Douglas R R	115 b	3.50	84–14	FlyBirdieFly115¾ WinthropRoad1176 Mnny'nBuck112nk	Early foot inside 7
14Nov93–1Aqu	fst	7f	:23 :46 1:104 1:24		Clm 35000	67	2	12	42½	42½	51¾	710	Perret C	117	4.40	74–17	TheMechanic1105½ OutForGold117¾ FiveStarGeneral1131½	Checked break 12
22Sep93–6Bel	sly	6f	:223 :45 1:10 1:171		Clm 45000	77	6	3	31½	31½	32½	41½	Bailey J D	117	3.60	80–13	Carnac117¹ The Mechanic117nk Lucky Favorite113hd	Mild gain 10
9Sep93–4Bel	fst	6½f	:221 :451 1:103 1:171		Clm 45000	76	3	4	2½	21½	53¾	53¾	Bailey J D	113	6.00	83–13	Blum Gone117nk Slews Gold117²¼ Gravel King115nk	Flattened out 7
22Aug93–1Sar	fst	6f	:223 :451 :571 1:094		Clm 45000	65	3	2	54½	510½		Bailey J D	117 b	8.20	82–07	Super Forbes113² Mr Rocky113¹ Six Thirty Two1131½	Tired 6

WORKOUTS: Sep 3 Bel 4f fst :48 B 12/50   ● Aug 17 Sar tr.t 4f fst :484 H 1/29   Jly 30 Sar tr.t 4f fst :492 B 3/62   Jly 16 Bel 4f fst :472 H 5/66   ● Jun 29 Bel 5f fst 1:00 Hg 1/28   Jun 22 Bel 6f fst 1:144 H 1/3

Maraud

Own: Hauman Eugene E
Ch. h. 5
Sire: Sunny's Halo (Halo)
Dam: Alpha Flight (Oxford Flight)
Br: Wolff A Don (WV)
Tr: Hushion Michael E (1 0 0 0 .00)

MIGLIORE R (11 0 3 0 .00) $32,500   115

Entered 5Sep94– 2 BEL

Lifetime Record: 41 8 2 14 $136,051

1994	12 3 1 5	$46,400	Turf	1 0 0 0	$350
1993	12 1 1 4	$32,910	Wet	6 1 0 1	$17,311
Bel	8 1 0 4	$20,640	Dist	1 0 0 0	

17Aug94–4Sar	fst	1⅛	:463 1:114 1:373 1:573	3↑	Clm 32500	88	6	1	1½	11	3nk	36	Migliore R	115 f	*3.00	85–15	Ambush Alley117¾ Decoder1175¾ Maraud115¹½	Weakened 7
6Aug94–10Sar	fst	1⅛	:47 1:114 1:374 1:511		Clm 32500	88	8	2	21	11	11½	22½	Migliore R	115	6.00	79–17	A Call To Rise117hd Maraud115² Carney's Kid117³	Couldn't last 9
1Aug94–1Sar	fst	6f	:22 :451 :572 1:10		Clm 32500	92	4	4	1½	11	1hd	3½	Migliore R	115 f	4.00e	89–12	Gold Candy Too1172 Fighting Daddy117no Maraud115¹½	Bid, weakened 7
6Jly94–2Bel	fst	7f	:223 :462 1:112 1:234		Clm 22500	86	3	2	1hd	1hd	11½	14	Migliore R	115 f	3.30	86–12	Maraud1154 Carney's Kid1191 Saratoga Ridge110no	Driving 7
25Jun94–4Bel	fst	6f	:223 :452 :572 1:093		Clm 25000	76	4	5	521	411	45½	37	Luttrell M G5	112 f	3.30	86–12	Gold Candy Too1175 Six Thirty Two117² Maraud112½	No threat 7
4May94–2Bel	fst	6f	:23 :452 1:091 1:354		Clm 25000	85	3	3	33½	31½	11½	1½	Migliore R	117 f	*1.80	81–16	Bushman113²½ The Mechanic112nk Maraud1172	No late bid 9
17Apr94–9Aqu	fst	6f	:22 :46 1:093 1:351		Clm 25000	87	4	2	1hd	1½	11	1½	Migliore R	117 f	*3.00	92–18	Maraud117½ Northern Witness1171½ Vet Jet1174	Driving 9
30Mar94–6Aqu	my	6f	:221 :473 :593 1:113	3↑	Alw 36000N$Y	40	4	5	54½	561	611	625	Migliore R	115 f	20.90	72–08	Strikany122nk Nowhere Man115¾ Golden Cloud1225½	Outrun 6
24Mar94–1Aqu	fst	6f	:231 :473 :593 1:113		Clm 22500	90	6	3	1½	1½	14½	191	Migliore R	115 f	2.30	84–20	Maraud1154½ Northern Witness1131½ The Ronald1173½	Mild drive 9
2Mar94–3Aqu	fst	6f	:232 :462 :583 1:112		Clm 17500	80	1	7	54	32½	31½	Migliore R	117 f	*2.30	84–20	Midnight Sunny117no Alex's Candy112¹½ Maraud1172	Steadied 9/16 pl 7

WORKOUTS: Jun 24 Bel 3f fst :374 B 18/30

Boss Soss
Own: Rottkamp John R
CHAVEZ J F (19 1 4 3 .05) $35,000
B. c. 4
Sire: Sauce Boat (Key to the Mint)
Dam: Nuryette (Nureyev)
Br: Hermitage Farm Inc (Ky)
Tr: Odintz Jeff (1 0 0 0 .00)
117

Lifetime Record:	19	4	1	3	$149,048						
1994	9	2	0	2	$52,361	Turf	2	0	0	0	
1993	5	0	0	1	$17,500	Wet	3	1	0	0	$22,776
Bel	2	1	0	1	$17,760	Dist	2	0	0	0	$4,441

5Aug94-4Sar my 7f :23 :463 1:112 1:241 Clm c-30000 78 1 4 2hd 2½ 54 68½ Bailey J D 119 2.40 76-19 Quickest Blade113¾ Dibbs N' Dubbs113¾ Cold Colony117hd Dueled inside 6
Claimed from Lewis Robert B, Lukas D Wayne Trainer
13Jly94-4Bel fst 7f :221 :45 1:101 1:231 Clm 50000 97 1 3 31½ 31½ 2½ 1¾ Bailey J D 117 2.60 87-15 Boss Soss117¾ Senor Cielo1173 Le Risky1152¼ Driving 8
2Jun94-5Bel fst 7f :231 :463 1:102 1:223 Clm 70000 99 6 1 11 11½ 2½ 3¾ Bailey J D 113 7.00 89-08 Richmond Runner113nk Nymphist113½ Boss Soss1136¾ Weakened 6
6May94-6CD wf 6½f :224 :462 1:11 1:172 3↑ Alw 32070N$Y 86 5 4 32½ 31½ 33 43½ Smith M E L 122 *2.40 89-09 Arabica117nk Stellar Tower1223 Rare Taste122hd Flattened out 8
15Apr94-7Kee sly 7f :223 :462 1:113 1:241 Alw 33300N$Y 104 11 2 33 22½ 1½ 1½ Smith M E L 113 8.40 80-25 Boss Soss113½ Stellar Tower1181 Dread Me Not1153 Hard drive 12
10Mar94-3SA fst 7f :222 :443 1:091 1:22 Alw 41000N3L 79 1 5 3nk 3nk 4¾ 44¾ McCarron C J LB 116 11.30 87-10 Gavel Gate1161 Crafty1162½ I'm Checkin' Out1171¼ Rode rail 5
11Feb94-6SA fst 1 :224 :46 1:10 1:353 Alw 50000N3X 85 5 4 4¾ 64 66 59½ Valenzuela P A LB 117 25.60 81-19 Kingdom Found1162 Mojave Gold116½ TurbulentKris1166½ Flattened out 7
2Feb94-8SA fst 6f :214 :444 :57 1:09 Alw 46000N3X 70 5 3 3nk 3nk 64¾ 610¾ Valenzuela P A LB 117 7.80 81-13 Mister Jolie1162 Cimply A Winner1172 Prince Wild1162 Dueled, tired 7
14Jan94-8SA fst 1 :23 :463 1:10 1:341 Alw 50000N3X 93 6 1 2½ 3nk 34½ 36¼ Valenzuela P A LB 117 27.40 92-12 Bossanova1162¾ Tinners Way1163½ Boss Soss117hd Weakened 8
17Nov93-6Hol fm 1 Ⓣ :231 :463 1:104 1:353 Clm 62500 65 9 5 63½ 85¾ 108½ 108¾ Flores D R LB 116 8.50 78-14 Minks Law116nk Easy Access116no Niner Bush117no Wide trip 10
WORKOUTS: Aug 21 Sar tr.t 3f fst :393 B *10/11* Jly 31 Sar tr.t 5f fst 1:031 B *3/11* Jly 25 Sar tr.t 4f fst :514 B *25/43* Jly 8 Bel 5f fst 1:012 H *5/16* Jun 21 Bel 3f fst :36 H *3/24* Jun 14 Bel 4f fst :51 B *47/68*

Ocean Splash
Own: Sommer Viola
ALVARADO F T (9 1 1 0 .11) $35,000
Dk. b or br h. 5
Sire: Clever Trick (Icecapade)
Dam: Rain Gauge (Sauce Boat)
Br: Farish W S (Ky)
Tr: Martin Frank (2 1 0 0 .50)
117

Lifetime Record:	36	5	3	12	$96,710						
1994	9	3	0	2	$28,240	Turf	0	0	0	0	
1993	13	0	2	5	$25,830	Wet	5	1	0	4	$21,240
Bel	9	0	0	4	$11,280	Dist	1	0	0	0	$1,140

22Aug94-9Sar my 7f :23 :46 1:11 1:24 3↑ Clm c-25000 82 6 6 610 69 33 34 Sellers S J 119 fb *2.20 81-17 Giant Leap117½ Exolever1123½ Ocean Splash1192 Rallied wide 7
Claimed from Wong Fei K, Sciacca Gary Trainer
5Aug94-9Sar my 6f :222 :462 :584 1:111 Clm 25000 97 7 8 912 85½ 41½ 11 Sellers S J 117 fb 5.30 85-19 OcenSplsh1171 PeerlessPerformer1153 BenAli'sRullh1082½ Wide, driving 9
12Jly94-4Bel fst 6f :23 :463 :582 1:102 Clm 30000 75 1 6 67½ 63½ 64¾ 67¼ Smith M E 113 fb 3.60 82-16 DibbsN'Dubbs115hd Zeezroo119hd PensionFrud1152¼ Broke slowly, outrun 6
19Jun94-3Bel fst 6½f :224 :453 1:094 1:16 Clm 32500 94 4 7 76¾ 74½ 71½ 4nk Smith M E 115 b 2.60 93-12 Zeezaroo117hd Danzig's Dance117no Game Wager117hd Drifted, rallied 7
7Jun94-6Bel fst 6f :223 :451 :571 1:094 Clm 32500 91 7 8 810 85 74¾ 31 McCauley W H 115 b 6.80 91-13 Memorized110nk Wonder Carr115¾ Ocean Splash1151½ Checked break 8
21May94-1Bel fst 7f :224 :452 1:094 1:23 Clm c-25000 78 2 5 55½ 68 66¾ 65¾ Luzzi M J 117 b 3.80 82-13 Bushman119¾ Pencil1171½ Northern Witness117no No factor 7
Claimed from Rudlein Stable, Bond Harold James Trainer
26Mar94-10Hia fst 6f :214 :45 :571 1:102 Clm 25000 92 4 6 812 87½ 65¾ 11¼ Sellers S J 119 b 7.70 93-16 DH Ocean Splash119 DH My Boy Cary1171¼ Sam's Sunny Hour1174 9
Extremely wide top str, driving
10Mar94-8GP fst 6f :213 :443 :563 1:09 Alw 30000N2X 68 8 10 1014 87¾ 710 610¾ Sellers S J 119 b 16.20 85-09 Corma Ray1192¾ Plano Pleasure1194¾ Inside Connection122½ Belated bid 10
6Feb94-5GP fst 6f :213 :44 :564 1:094 Clm 20000 89 6 9 98½ 810 64¾ 1nk Sellers S J 117 b 17.30 92-11 Ocean Splash117nk Gallapiat's Song1172 Tahiti Boy117½ 10
Six wide leaving bkstr, eight wide top str, driving
25Nov93-4Aqu fst 6f :231 :473 1:00 1:13 3↑ Clm 35000 71 3 6 66 66 65½ 59¾ Velazquez J R 117 b 20.00 67-20 Triodet1196½ Tropical Illusion115nk Reappeal1121 Checked break 6
WORKOUTS: ●Sep 2 Bel 4f fst :461 H *1/36* Jly 31 Bel 3f fst :371 B *3/6* ●Jly 4 Aqu 4f fst :47 H *1/4*

Imaging
Own: Jewel-E Stables
SANTOS J A (16 3 2 1 .19) $35,000
B. g. 4
Sire: Crafty Prospector (Mr. Prospector)
Dam: Anthonize (Silver Buck)
Br: Carlesimo John (Ky)
Tr: Friedman Mitchell (3 2 1 0 .67)
117

Lifetime Record:	19	4	4	3	$89,351						
1994	11	2	1	2	$50,670	Turf	1	0	0	0	
1993	8	2	3	1	$38,681	Wet	3	1	1	0	$22,964
Bel	5	2	0	1	$43,200	Dist	3	0	1	1	$9,466

24Jly94-2Sar wf 6f :222 :451 :571 1:093 Clm c-30000 83 3 3 41½ 43½ 53 57¼ Bailey J D 117 2.80 86-13 Senor Cielo1173¼ Game Wager1133¼ Chief Master115½ Lacked rally 7
Claimed from Hough Stanley M, Hough Stanley M Trainer
7Jly94-6Bel fst 6½f :23 :461 1:10 1:162 3↑ Clm 75000 91 6 3 2hd 3nk 21½ 43 Bailey J D 112 6.00 88-12 Farmonthefreeway1152¾ Rocking Josh112hd Fabersham112nk Dueled, tired 7
23Jun94-4Bel fm 1 Ⓣ :222 :444 1:09 1:332 Clm 75000 — 7 7 711 911 1029 — Santos J A 117 5.70 — 10 Bill Of Rights113nk Say Dance119hd Stubass1159 Outrun, eased 10
12Jun94-7Bel fst 7f :23 :46 1:10 1:221 3↑ Alw 34000N4X 87 5 2 21 31 32 36½ Santos J A 122 5.50 86-11 Richmond Runner119hd Golden Tent1196¼ Imaging122½ Weakened 7
30May94-1Bel fst 7f :222 :452 1:101 1:23 3↑ Alw 32000N3X 99 5 2 32½ 42½ 2½ 1¾ Santos J A 119 9.80 88-16 Imaging119¾ Corma Ray1195 I'm No Quacker119nk Driving 6
17May94-7Bel my 7f :221 :45 1:102 1:232 3↑ Alw 30000N2X 95 1 5 21½ 21½ 2hd 1hd Bailey J D 119 1.90 86-17 Imaging119hd Danzig's Dance1121 Whitney Tower1122½ Wide, driving 6
3May94-2Bel fst 6f :223 :453 :572 1:093 Clm 50000 94 2 6 42 31½ 3½ 51¼ Bailey J D 117 2.60 92-14 Nymphist117nk Memorized108½ Senor Cielo117nk Flattened out 7
27Feb94-6GP fst 6f :22 :444 :57 1:10 Clm c-50000 74 10 3 107½ 87¾ 99¾ 77¾ Sellers S J 117 7.90 83-13 Ocala Flame115hd Solid Sunny115¾ Tar Men1151 11
Extremely wide top str, no threat Claimed from Fortuna Stable Inc, Hennig John K Trainer
9Feb94-6GP fst 6f :212 :434 :56 1:083 Alw 27000N2X 69 11 2 97 65¾ 77½ 610½ Maple E L 119 4.40 87-04 AdventureRoad1194¼ GentlePatrick1191¼ Reloction1191½ Failed to menace 11
27Jan94-7GP gd 7f :22 :443 1:091 1:224 Alw 28400N2X 84 7 1 21½ 43½ 33 32 Santos J A L 119 2.40 87-13 Callme Guy B1191¾ Imtoocool122hd Imaging119¾ 7
Seven wide str, drifted in, rallied
WORKOUTS: Aug 29 Sar tr.t 4f fst :523 B *30/31* Aug 17 Sar tr.t 4f fst :521 B *17/29* Aug 8 Sar tr.t 4f fst :512 B *9/21* ●Jly 21 Sar tr.t 3f fst :36 H *1/8* Jly 2 Bel 4f fst :491 B *20/48* Jun 20 Bel 4f fst :49 B *16/37*

After a careful read of a race's conditions, the two questions handicappers must ask are:

1) What is the overall pace complexion?
2) How does the favorite stack up; does he figure to be comfortable with demands made upon him in terms of class, distance, footing and the probable pace?

This race was packed with early speed, and most of the horses who projected to be battling on the front-end didn't inspire much confidence. Carrnac had won two of four starts against 3-year-old claiming sprinters a year ago, but he had succumbed first time against older, tougher claiming competition after dueling for half a mile when returned from a long layoff; ten days later he had been life-and-death to defeat preliminary New York bred allowance horses. Line Pro had not been out since the end of March and showed next to nothing in the way of workout activity — a solitary, slow breeze in :51 2/5 three weeks ago. Insured Winner's two victories as a 4-year-old had come in slop and mud when able to secure a clear lead at the pre-stretch call. Boss Soss also had speed, but at 2-1 he had to be considered a vulnerable favorite because of the suspicious $15,000 drop in price first time off the claim. Some trainers win with this move occasionally, but the logic should be pretty clear: any horse claimed for $50,000 a month ago and offered for $35,000 on its very first start for the new connections is damaged goods. Imaging showed the identical pattern and thus could be considered a vulnerable second choice at 5-1.

With knocks on several early pace combatants and the first two betting choices deemed vulnerable, this race cried out to be played.

Even though Maraud had been on the lead at the pre-stretch call in each of his last four races, he didn't figure to be contesting the early pace in this match up. Maraud was different than any other horse in the race because he'd been routing in his last two starts whereas everyone else had been racing at six or seven furlongs, and those relatively slow-paced routes to which Maraud had become accustomed meant that he'd likely be somewhere off the leaders early.

Maraud figured to have a good conditioning foundation, plenty of "bottom," after those routes. Many trainers do very well with the route-to-sprint switch: Bill Badgett Jr. and Carl Domino in New York, Mary Eppler in Maryland, Neil Howard in the midwest being some of the most well-known examples. The routes tend to relax horses mentally so that they're very tractable in terms of rating off the pace when shortened up. Plus, Maraud had shown repeatedly that he was a versatile, hard-knocking type around one turn: his three wins earlier in the year had come at six furlongs, seven furlongs, and a mile; he had won by stalking the early pace on two occasions, and he had been unfazed by a prolonged head-and-head duel enroute to a four-length score in his most recent sprint at Belmont.

As stated earlier, both of Maraud's route performances in August had been exceptional, and essentially, this is what made him such an attractive play at nearly 7-1. Even though I do not calculate numerical pace ratings (the pitfalls of such procedures are discussed at length in *Expert Handicapping*), there are other ways of gauging the strength of what a horse did in past races in terms of the pace.

One of the handiest tools is the "instant variant," as so described by Mark Cramer in his landmark book, *Thoroughbred Cycles*: "When doing daily variants, numbers file by in an abstract parade. By doing instant variants, numbers become vibrant images."

To use the concept of instant variants for a real-life evaluation of Maraud's current form was simple: merely consult the Form's result charts for August 6 and August 17 to see how other routes compared with Maraud's:

TENTH RACE
Saratoga
AUGUST 6, 1994

1⅛ MILES. (1.47) CLAIMING. Purse $20,000. 4-year-olds and upward. Weight, 122 lbs. Non-winners of two races at a mile or over since July 1, allowed 3 lbs. Of such a race since then, 5 lbs. Claiming price $35,000, for each $2,500 to $30,000, allowed 2 lbs. (Races when entered to be claimed for $25,000 or less not considered.)

Value of Race: $20,000 Winner $12,000; second $4,400; third $2,400; fourth $1,200. Mutuel Pool $302,949.00 Exacta Pool $278,929.00 Triple Pool $301,835.00

Last Raced	Horse	M/Eqt.	A.	Wt	PP	St	¼	½	¾	Str	Fin	Jockey	Cl'g Pr	Odds $1
27Jly94 ^{4}Sar^{2}	A Call To Rise	f	6	117	7	4	5^{2}	5^{2}	$3^{\frac{1}{2}}$	$2^{\frac{1}{2}}$	$1^{\frac{3}{4}}$	Luzzi M J	35000	4.80
1Aug94 ^{1}Sar^{3}	Maraud		5	115	8	5	2^{4}	$2^{2\frac{1}{2}}$	1^{2}	$1^{1\frac{1}{2}}$	2^{2}	Migliore R	32500	6.00
27Jly94 ^{4}Sar^{4}	Carney's Kid	b	5	117	9	9	$8^{\frac{1}{2}}$	8^{24}	$4^{1\frac{1}{2}}$	3^{1}	3^{3}	Chavez J F	35000	13.60
28Jun94 ^{2}Bel^{1}	Iron Gavel		4	117	1	1	3^{hd}	$3^{\frac{1}{2}}$	5^{1}	$4^{2\frac{1}{2}}$	4^{7}	Alvarado F T	35000	1.80
25Jly94 ^{4}Sar^{4}	Turk's Hero	bf	4	113	3	2	$1^{\frac{1}{2}}$	1^{1}	2^{hd}	5^{2}	5^{5}	Carr D	30000	29.70
25Jly94 ^{1}Sar^{2}	Art History		4	117	5	8	7^{6}	7^{1}	6^{2}	7^{2}	6^{nk}	Davis R G	35000	10.00
17Jly94 ^{10}ElP^{3}	Burlingame	b	4	117	2	3	$6^{\frac{1}{2}}$	6^{hd}	8	6^{hd}	7^{4}	Day P	35000	8.00
22Jly94 ^{9}Sar^{8}	Slews Gold	b	4	108	4	6	$4^{\frac{1}{2}}$	4^{hd}	7^{1}	8	8	Luttrell M G^{5}	30000	26.10
24Jly94 ^{5}Sar^{2}	Border Cat		5	117	6	7	9	9	—	—	—	Sellers S J	35000	3.80

Border Cat:Eased

OFF AT 6:05 Start Good. Won driving. Time, :23^{1}, :47, 1:11^{4}, 1:37^{4}, 1:51^{1} Track fast.

$2 Mutuel Prices:

10–(J)–A CALL TO RISE	11.60	5.20	4.00
11–(L)–MARAUD		6.40	4.80
12–(M)–CARNEY'S KID			7.20

$2 EXACTA 10–11 PAID $77.00 $2 TRIPLE 10–11–12 PAID $217.00

B. g, by Poles Apart–A Bugle Command, by Command Control. Trainer Friedman Mitchell. Bred by Manfuso John A (Md).

A CALL TO RISE settled in the middle of the pack for five furlongs, gained between horses on the turn then wore down MARAUD in the final sixteenth. MARAUD forced the early pace from outside, opened a clear advantage on the far turn, continued on the front while drifting out in midstretch, then weakened late. CARNEY'S KID outrun for a half, after breaking slowly, rallied three wide on the turn then finished willingly to gain a share. IRON GAVEL raced just off the pace while saving ground then tired in the drive. TURK'S HERO was used up setting the early pace. ART HISTORY was never a factor. BURLINGAME never reached contention. SLEWS GOLD faded after going six furlongs. BORDER CAT was never close and was eased in the stretch. PRIVATE PLAN was injured in the gate prior to the start and was scratched by the stewards on the advice of the track veterinarian. All monies wagered on PRIVATE PLAN in the mutuel, exacta and triple pools were refunded and a consolation double was paid. MARAUD and CARNEY'S KID wore mud caulks.

Owners— 1, Jewel-E Stables; 2, Hauman Eugene E; 3, Paraneck Stable; 4, Joques Farm; 5, Morrell Samuel F; 6, Lerman Roy S; 7, Danehy Jack; 8, Garren Murray M; 9, Ackerley Bros Farm

Trainers—1, Friedman Mitchell; 2, Hushion Michael E; 3, Sweigert Laura; 4, Moschera Gasper S; 5, Engel Charles F; 6, Lerman Roy S; 7, Lauer Michael E; 8, Garren Murray M; 9, Lake Robert P

Scratched— Sparkling Sky (8Jly94 ^{6}BEL^{1}), Private Plan (16Jly94 ^{1}CRC^{1}), Ambush Alley (23Jly94 ^{10}DEL^{8}), Studley Do Right (27Jly94 ^{4}SAR^{1})

$2 Daily Double (6–10) Paid $81.80; Consolation Daily Double (6–6) Paid $9.20; Daily Double Pool $461,250.

On August 6, Maraud had forced the pace and taken a clear lead past midstretch in the tenth and final race on the card; the fractions for this claiming route carrying a $20,000 purse were :23 1/5, :47, 1:11 4/5, and 1:37 4/5, with a final time of 1:51 1/5.

A race earlier, Thunder Rumble, the 1992 Travers winner, had blown apart the Saratoga Cup Handicap with a spectacular performance at the same nine-furlong distance:

NINTH RACE
Saratoga
AUGUST 6, 1994

1⅛ MILES. (1.47) 77th Running of THE SARATOGA CUP HANDICAP. Purse $250,000 added. 3-year-olds and upward. By subscription of $250 each which should accompany the nomination; $1,250 to pass the entry box; $1,250 to start. The purse to be divided 60% to the winner, 22% to second, 12% to third and 6% to fourth. Weights Monday, August 1. Starters to be named at the closing time of entries. Trophies will be presented to the winning owner, trainer and jockey. Closed Wednesday July 20, with 28 nominations.

Value of Race: $250,000 Winner $150,000; second $55,000; third $30,000; fourth $15,000. Mutuel Pool $615,463.00 Exacta Pool $603,115.00 Triple Pool $521,663.00

Last Raced	Horse	M/Eqt.	A.	Wt	PP	St	¼	½	¾	Str	Fin	Jockey	Odds $1
20Jly94 ^{6}Bel^{1}	Thunder Rumble	f	5	112	6	2	2^{hd}	$2^{1\frac{1}{2}}$	$2^{2\frac{1}{2}}$	$1^{\frac{1}{2}}$	1^{4}	Migliore R	3.30
20Jly94 ^{8}Bel^{1}	West by West		5	113	4	5	6^{1}	6^{hd}	$7^{\frac{1}{2}}$	4^{hd}	2no	Day P	2.90
4Jly94 ^{8}Bel^{4}	Wallenda		4	117	7	6	8	8	8	5^{1}	3^{nk}	Perret C	3.30
20Jly94 ^{8}Bel^{2}	Itaka		4	112	8	8	1^{2}	1^{4}	$1^{1\frac{1}{2}}$	$2^{3\frac{1}{2}}$	$4^{1\frac{1}{2}}$	Sellers S J	28.80
16Jly94 ^{11}Crc^{4}	Pistols and Roses		5	115	3	3	3^{4}	3^{4}	3^{4}	3^{1}	5^{7}	Smith M E	6.70
30May94 ^{8}Bel^{8}	Colonial Affair		4	120	1	4	7^{5}	7^{3}	6^{1}	6^{2}	$6^{1\frac{1}{2}}$	Santos J A	5.00
23Jun94 ^{8}Bel^{2}	Miner's Mark		4	117	5	7	4^{hd}	$5^{1\frac{1}{2}}$	5^{hd}	7^{hd}	$7^{\frac{1}{2}}$	Bailey J D	5.80
4Jly94 ^{8}Bel^{3}	Federal Funds	b	5	111	2	1	$5^{3\frac{1}{2}}$	4^{hd}	4^{1}	8	8	Carr D	52.60

OFF AT 5:30 Start Good. Won driving. Time, :23^{3}, :47, 1:11^{1}, 1:35^{4}, 1:48^{2} Track fast.

$2 Mutuel Prices:

6–(F)–THUNDER RUMBLE	8.60	4.40	3.00
4–(D)–WEST BY WEST		4.20	2.80
7–(G)–WALLENDA			2.80

$2 EXACTA 6–4 PAID $40.20 $2 TRIPLE 6–4–7 PAID $161.00

Dk. b. or br. h, by Thunder Puddles–Lyphette, by Lyphard. Trainer O'Connell Richard. Bred by Widmer Konrad (NY).

THUNDER RUMBLE settled just behind the early pacesetter, closed the gap on the turn, accelerated to the front in midstretch then drew away under strong left hand encouragement. WEST BY WEST raced well back for six furlongs, split horses to launch his bid at the quarter pole, then outfinished WALLENDA for the place. WALLENDA trailed to the turn, circled four wide into the stretch then closed late in the middle of the track to gain a share. ITAKA rushed up after breaking slowly, opened a wide gap along the backstretch, continued on the front into midstretch then weakened in the final eighth. PISTOLS AND ROSES raced just off the early pace, angled out while within striking distance on the turn then tired in the drive. COLONIAL AFFAIR taken in hand on the first turn, lodged a mild rally while three wide entering the stretch then flattened out. MINER'S MARK reserved for six furlongs while between horses, dropped back approaching the stretch, then lacked a further response. FEDERAL FUNDS gave way on the turn.

Owners— 1, Braeburn Farm; 2, Peace John H; 3, Dogwood Stable; 4, Brophy Stable; 5, Willis Family Stable; 6, Centennial Farms; 7, Phipps Ogden; 8, Garren Murray M

Trainers—1, O'Connell Richard; 2, Arnold George R II; 3, Alexander Frank A; 4, Domino Carl J; 5, Gianos George; 6, Schulhofer Flint S; 7, McGaughey Claude III; 8, Garren Murray M

Overweight: Itaka (3), Federal Funds (1).

Noteworthy are the fractions for the $250,000 stake: slower than Maraud's race through the first quarter, exactly the same after a half, and just three ticks faster at the six-furlong split. That the Saratoga Cup went on to finish in a time nearly three full seconds faster than the claiming race is a given: after all, that's why the stakes horses competed for twelve and a half times as much purse money. The important thing was that Maraud held to finish a clear second after contesting early splits comparable to those of a stakes run just half an hour earlier.

What about Maraud's most recent route, August 17?

FOURTH RACE
Saratoga
AUGUST 17, 1994

$1\frac{3}{16}$ MILES. (1.54^{3}) CLAIMING. Purse $20,000. 3–year–olds and upward. Weights: 3–year–olds, 117 lbs. Older, 122 lbs. Non–winners of two races at a mile or over since July 15, allowed 3 lbs. Of such a race since then, 5 lbs. Claiming price $35,000, for each $2,500 to $30,000, allowed 2 lbs. (Races when entered to be claimed for $25,000 or less not considered.)

Value of Race: $20,000 Winner $12,000; second $4,400; third $2,400; fourth $1,200. Mutuel Pool $321,824.00 Exacta Pool $510,522.00 Quinella Pool $113,587.00

Last Raced	Horse	M/Eqt.	A.	Wt	PP	St	¼	½	¾	Str	Fin	Jockey	Cl'g Pr	Odds $1
23Jly94 ^{10}Del^{8}	Ambush Alley	b	4	117	5	6	$6^{1/2}$	$6^{1/2}$	$4^{1/2}$	2^{hd}	1^{hd}	Krone J A	35000	10.90
4Aug94 ^{4}Sar^{5}	Decoder	f	4	117	2	4	3^{3}	3^{6}	3^{3}	1^{hd}	$2^{5\frac{3}{4}}$	Day P	35000	4.70
6Aug94 ^{10}Sar^{2}	Maraud	f	5	115	6	5	1^{2}	$1^{1/2}$	1^{1}	3^{2}	$3^{1\frac{1}{4}}$	Migliore R	32500	*3.00
12Aug94 ^{9}Sar^{9}	Yaros	b	5	117	3	1	$5^{1/2}$	4^{hd}	5^{4}	4^{hd}	$4^{3\frac{1}{2}}$	Luzzi M J	32500	6.10
6Aug94 ^{10}Sar^{3}	Carney's Kid	b	5	117	1	3	$2^{1/2}$	2^{hd}	2^{hd}	5^{4}	$5^{3\frac{3}{4}}$	Chavez J F	35000	4.10
27Jly94 ^{4}Sar^{1}	Studley Do Right	b	5	115	4	2	7	7	6^{1}	6^{hd}	$6^{3\frac{3}{4}}$	Smith M E	30000	3.00
19Jly94 ^{4}Bel^{1}	Akiko	f	5	117	7	7	4^{1}	$5^{1/2}$	7	7	7	Velazquez J R	35000	7.30

***—Actual Betting Favorite.**

OFF AT 2:33 Start Good. Won driving. Time, :23^{3}, :47^{3}, 1:11^{4}, 1:37^{3}, 1:57^{3} Track fast.

$2 Mutuel Prices:

5–(F)–AMBUSH ALLEY	23.80	8.80	4.40
3–(B)–DECODER		5.80	3.60
6–(G)–MARAUD			3.40

$2 EXACTA 5–3 PAID $133.80 $2 QUINELLA 3–5 PAID $58.00

Ch. g, by Gulch–Shamaritan, by Sham. Trainer Eppler Mary E. Bred by Brant Peter & Wofram Shannon A (Ky).

AMBUSH ALLEY reserved for six furlongs while between horses, swung out to launch his bid on the turn, rallied four wide into the stretch then outgamed DECODER in a hard drive. DECODER forced the pace between horses to the top of the stretch, surged to the front in midstretch, fought heads apart along the inside into deep stretch and yielded grudgingly. MARAUD angled to the inside while taking the lead on the first turn, set the pace along the inside into upper stretch then tired in the final eighth. YAROS pinched back in the early stages, failed to threaten thereafter. CARNEY'S KID was used up forcing the early pace. STUDLEY DO RIGHT steaided between horses on the first turn and was never close thereafter. AKIKO was finished early. MARAUD wore mud caulks.

Owners— 1, Rogers Samuel H Jr; 2, Dogwood Stable; 3, Hauman Eugene E; 4, Jewel-E Stables; 5, Paraneck Stable; 6, Davis Barbara J; 7, Sommer Viola

Trainers—1, Eppler Mary E; 2, Vestal Peter M; 3, Hushion Michael E; 4, Friedman Mitchell; 5, Sweigert Laura; 6, Moschera Gasper S; 7, Martin Frank

Scratched— A Call To Rise (6Aug94 ^{10}SAR^{1})

Running for a purse of $20,000, Maraud had set fractions of :23 3/5, :47 3/5, and 1:11 4/5 before surrendering the lead through a mile in 1:37 3/5 and a mile and three-sixteenths in 1:57 3/5.

Four races later, overnight handicap males running for a $50,000 purse ran as follows:

EIGHTH RACE
Saratoga
AUGUST 17, 1994

1⅛ MILES. (1.47) HANDICAP. Purse $50,000. 3–year–olds and upward. Weights Saturday, August 13. Declarations by 10:00 A.M. Sunday, August 14. Closed Saturday, August 13, with 10 nominations.

Value of Race: $50,000 Winner $30,000; second $11,000; third $6,000; fourth $3,000. Mutuel Pool $331,585.00 Exacta Pool $484,332.00 Minus Show Pool $501.96

Last Raced	Horse	M/Eqt.	A.	Wt	PP	St	¼	½	¾	Str	Fin	Jockey	Odds $1
31Jly94 ^{5}Sar^{1}	Key Contender	b	6	119	4	5	1^{hd}	$1^{1/2}$	1^{hd}	$2^{2\frac{1}{2}}$	1^{1}	Bailey J D	1.00
30Jly94 ^{8}AP^{4}	Grand Jewel	bf	4	120	1	3	3^{hd}	3^{hd}	$2^{2\frac{1}{2}}$	1^{hd}	2^{3}	Day P	1.50
6Aug94 ^{9}Sar^{8}	Federal Funds	b	5	114	6	6	6	6	6	4^{hd}	$3^{5\frac{1}{2}}$	Luzzi M J	a-8.50
13Mar94 ^{8}Aqu^{3}	Michelle Can Pass	bf	6	120	5	2	4^{2}	4^{3}	4^{2}	5^{2}	4^{hd}	Velazquez J R	4.30
31Jly94 ^{5}Sar^{4}	Jacksonport	b	5	111	3	1	2^{2}	$2^{1/2}$	3^{hd}	3^{1}	5^{5}	Chavez J F	a-8.50
12Aug94 ^{6}Sar^{5}	Classi Envoy	b	4	114	2	4	5^{6}	5^{7}	5^{5}	6	6	Migliore R	22.90

a–Coupled: Federal Funds and Jacksonport.

OFF AT 4:38 Start Good. Won driving. Time, :25, :48^{4}, 1:12^{3}, 1:37, 1:50 Track fast.

$2 Mutuel Prices:

4–(D)–KEY CONTENDER	4.00	2.40	2.10
2–(A)–GRAND JEWEL		2.60	2.10
1A–(F)–FEDERAL FUNDS (a–entry)			2.10

$2 EXACTA 4–2 PAID $8.80

Ch. h, by Fit to Fight–Key Witness, by Key to the Mint. Trainer Miller MacKenzie. Bred by Mellon Paul (Va).

KEY CONTENDER dueled for the early lead outside JACKSONPORT, shook off that one on the far turn, battled inside GRAND JEWEL into the stretch, relinquished the lead in midstretch then fought back to draw clear in the late stages. GRAND JEWEL settled just outside the early leaders, made a run to challenge entering the stretch, gained a slim lead in midstretch, bobbled slightly inside the furlong marker, then weakened late. FEDERAL FUNDS far back for seven furlongs, rallied belatedly. MICHELLE CAN PASS raced within striking distance four wide to the turn then lacked a strong closing bid. JACKSONPORT hustled up on the first turn, battled inside the winner for five furlongs, tired. CLASSI ENVOY was never a factor. KEY CONTENDER wore mud caulks.

Owners— 1, Rokeby Stables; 2, Farish William S; 3, Garren Murray M; 4, Jay Cee Jay Stable; 5, Garren Murray M; 6, Sabine Stable
Trainers—1, Miller Mackenzie; 2, Howard Neil J; 3, Garren Murray M; 4, Destefano John M Jr; 5, Garren Murray M; 6, Barbara Robert
Overweight: Classi Envoy (2).

Going a *shorter* route, Key Contender had posted a front-running win through easy fractions of :25, :48 4/5, and 1:12 3/5. Based on what he'd run earlier on the card, Maraud would've enjoyed a four-length lead midway on the far turn had he been in the pricey overnight handicap!

So, even without benefit of pace ratings, a real-life analytical comparison of what Maraud's route efforts had been like was indeed possible, and yielded the conclusion that he had performed above and beyond the call of duty in comparatively fast-paced races.

Evidently, trainer Michael Hushion (among the most astute claiming trainers in New York) felt confident of Maraud's chances off the turnback to a sprint as well: he scratched his other entrant, Game Wager.

SIXTH RACE
Belmont
SEPTEMBER 7, 1994

6½ FURLONGS. (1.14^{3}) CLAIMING. Pursee $20,000. 3–year–olds and upward. Weights: 3–year–olds, 118 lbs. Older, 122 lbs. Non–winners of two races since August 1, allowed 3 lbs. Of a race since then, 5 lbs. Claiming price $35,000, for each $2,500 to $30,000, allowed 2 lbs. (Races when entered to be claimed for $25,000 or less not considered.)

Value of Race: $20,000 Winner $12,000; second $4,400; third $2,400; fourth $1,200. Mutuel Pool $261,355.00 Exacta Pool $452,321.00

Last Raced	Horse	M/Eqt.	A.	Wt	PP	St	¼	½	Str	Fin	Jockey	Cl'g Pr	Odds $1
17Aug94 4Sar3	Maraud	f	5	115	6	7	$7^{3\frac{1}{2}}$	$7^{1\frac{1}{2}}$	1^{hd}	$1^{2\frac{3}{4}}$	Migliore R	32500	6.80
22Aug94 9Sar3	Ocean Splash	bf	5	117	8	9	8^{1}	9	5^{hd}	2^{2}	Alvarado F T	35000	6.20
15Aug94 6Sar1	Carrnac	b	4	119	1	5	5^{hd}	6^{hd}	$6^{\frac{1}{2}}$	$3^{\frac{3}{4}}$	Smith M E	35000	11.40
24Jly94 2Sar5	Imaging		4	117	9	4	6^{1}	$5^{\frac{1}{2}}$	2^{hd}	4^{nk}	Santos J A	35000	5.10
5Aug94 4Sar6	Boss Soss		4	117	7	2	$4^{\frac{1}{2}}$	$4^{\frac{1}{2}}$	$3^{\frac{1}{2}}$	5^{nk}	Chavez J F	35000	2.00
24Aug94 7Sar2	Gallapiat's Moment	bf	4	117	4	6	3^{hd}	3^{hd}	$4^{\frac{1}{2}}$	6no	Frost G C	35000	8.30
29Aug94 1Sar7	Le Risky		5	117	3	8	9	8^{hd}	$7^{\frac{1}{2}}$	7^{4}	Sellers E	35000	11.70
29Mar94 6Aqu3	Line Pro	f	4	115	2	1	2^{2}	2^{hd}	8^{1}	$8^{2\frac{1}{2}}$	Pezua J M	32500	6.30
26Aug94 9Sar1	Insured Winner	b	4	113	5	3	$1^{\frac{1}{2}}$	1^{1}	9	9	Bailey J D	30000	19.60

OFF AT 3:30 Start Good. Won driving. Time, :22^{4}, :46, 1:10, 1:16 Track fast.

$2 Mutuel Prices:

1A–(G)–MARAUD	15.60	8.20	4.00
8–(I)–OCEAN SPLASH		7.20	4.40
2–(A)–CARRNAC			6.60

$2 EXACTA 1–8 PAID $126.20

Ch. h, by Sunny's Halo–Alpha Flight, by Oxford Flight. Trainer Hushion Michael E. Bred by Wolff A Don (WV).

MARAUD reserved early, waited patiently while behind a wall of horses on the turn, angled out in upper stretch, then unleashed a strong late run to win going away. OCEAN SPLASH trailed for a half, circled five wide into the stretch, then finished well in the middle of the track to gain the place. CARRNAC settled just behind the leaders while saving ground, then finished willingly to gain a share. IMAGING lodged a bid four wide to threaten on the turn, remained a factor into midstretch and weakened. BOSS SOSS split horses to reach contention at the top of the stretch, then lacked a strong closing bid. GALLAPIAT'S MOMENT checked in tight at the start, stalked the pace while three wide into upper stretch, tired. LE RISKY saved ground to the turn, angled out in upper stretch and lacked a strong closing bid. LINE PRO and INSURED WINNER were used up battling for the early lead. MARAUD wore mud caulks. INSURED WINNER wore an aluminum pad.

Owners— 1, Hauman Eugene E; 2, Sommer Viola; 3, Boto Stable; 4, Jewel-E Stables; 5, Rottkamp John R; 6, Ferriola Ingrid A; 7, Davis Barbara J; 8, Brida Dennis J; 9, Oxenberg Beatrice

Trainers—1, Hushion Michael E; 2, Martin Frank; 3, Kelly Timothy D; 4, Friedman Mitchell; 5, Odintz Jeff; 6, Ferriola Peter; 7, Moschera Gasper S; 8, Brida Dennis J; 9, Hough Stanley M

Scratched— Game Wager (5Sep94 2BEL9)

Maraud settled nicely while the early battle raged up front, waited patiently behind horses on the turn, and exhibited his superior "bottom" by overpowering his rivals in the stretch.

Summing up, then, and with a couple of additional points: First, this route-to-sprint play works best with horses who have shown early speed in their most recent routes, and who have previously shown the ability to win or finish up close in sprints. Second, sprints of six and a half furlongs and seven furlongs are the ideal stomping ground for the maneuver; that extra sixteenth or eighth of a mile can be the difference between getting up in time or running out of racetrack. Third, there is the question of Maraud's front bandages. How does one deal with front wraps, which can be a sign of trouble? The answer lies in knowing your trainers. Hushion, for instance, uses front wraps virtually without exception; with other trainers, front bandages may very well have more ominous implications.

THE ROUTE-TO-SPRINT angle is most potent when the pace projects to be contested by two or more horses, thus giving the turnback horse dead aim at tiring speed, but the move is also effective against a lone front runner provided there is cause to view the potential target suspiciously. Some weeks later, the following situation presented itself:

4 Aqueduct

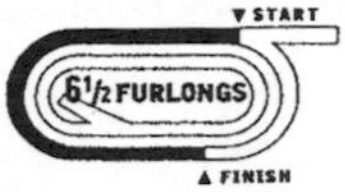

6½ Furlongs **(1:15) CLAIMING. Purse $26,000. 3-year-olds and upward. Weights: 3-year-olds, 119 lbs. Older, 122 lbs. Non-winners of two races since October 1, allowed 3 lbs. Of a race since then, 5 lbs. Claiming price $50,000, for each $2,500 to $45,000, allowed 2 lbs. (Races when entered to be claimed for $40,000 or less not considered.)**

Nowhere Man

Own: Perroncino John S

AGOSTO R (9 2 0 0 .22) **$45,000**

Ch. g. 5
Sire: Fountain of Gold (Mr. Prospector)
Dam: Sister Aggie (Great Above)
Br: Matthews Karen & P (Fla)
Tr: Terracciano Neal (6 2 0 0 .33)

1067

Lifetime Record:	35	9	4	6	$143,628						
1994	9	3	2	0	$47,700	Turf	1	0	0	0	
1993	7	1	0	0	$7,200	Wet	8	3	2	2	$46,838
Aqu	4	1	1	0	$34,140	Dist	4	1	0	1	$12,390

20Oct94-8Aqu gd	6f		:22	:452	:574	1:104	3↑ Handicap50k	76	4	1	1½	2½	44½	510	Lydon P J	112 fb	6.80	78-18	Primitive Hall116¾ Golden Pro1132½ Rizzi1156½	Used up	5
17May94-6Bel my	6f		:221	:453	:574	1:10	Clm 32500	103	2	1	1½	12½	12	12	McCauley W H	115 b	*1.70	91-17	Nowhere Man1152 Top The Record1152 Le Risky1192½	Driving	6
3May94-2Bel fst	6f		:223	:453	:572	1:093	Clm 45000	94	4	4	1½	1hd	2hd	41	Luttrell M G5	108 fb	2.90	92-14	Nymphist117nk Memorized108½ Senor Cielo117nk	Broke awkwardly	7
16Apr94-2Aqu sly	6f		:213	:45	:572	1:10	Clm 70000	87	6	1	11	1½	2½	46	Graell A	113 fb	2.70	86-09	Golden Cloud1132½ Tropical Illusion1152 Quickest Blade1131½	Tired	7
30Mar94-6Aqu my	6f		:221	:451	:564	1:09	Alw 36000N$Y	104	3	1	11	1hd	2½	2nk	Graell A	115 fb	5.90	97-08	Strikany122nk Nowhere Man1155½ Golden Cloud1225½	Gamely	6
20Mar94-7Aqu fst	6f	⊡	:23	:462	:584	1:112	Alw 36000N$Y	94	3	2	12½	11	11	21¼	Graell A	115 fb	11.40	85-21	Won Song1151¼ Nowhere Man1151½ Farmonthefreeway115no	Weakened	5
11Mar94-2Aqu gd	6f	⊡	:232	:463	:583	1:104	Clm 25000	93	1	4	11	13½	14	15	Graell A	117 fb	*1.30	89-17	Nowhere Man1175 Baypark1153½ Jessup North117nk	Driving	6
21Feb94-4Aqu fst	6f	⊡	:232	:47	:592	1:121	Clm c-17500	75	8	4	2hd	3nk	62¾	72½	Graell A	117 b	4.80	79-20	Exploding Rainbow119no Ben Ali's Rullah117¾ RedHotRed117no	Four wide	9
Claimed from Davis Barbara J, Moschera Gasper S Trainer																					
12Feb94-2Aqu fst	6f	⊡	:231	:463	:583	1:11	Clm 14000	82	6	3	12	12	13	14	Graell A	117 b	*1.30	88-16	Nowhere Man1174 Family Tries117½ Alyjandro1142¼	Driving	9
30Dec93-2Aqu fst	6f	⊡	:23	:471	1:001	1:132	3↑ Clm c-17500	44	4	4	32	41½	56	616¼	Migliore R	117 fb	1.80	60-24	Ben Ali's Rullah117no With It117¾ Exploding Rainbow1176	Tired	7
Claimed from Schwartz Barry K, Hushion Michael E Trainer																					

WORKOUTS: Oct 16 Aqu 5f fst 1:024 B *1/2* ●Oct 9 Aqu 4f fst :472 H *1/5* ●Sep 30 Aqu 4f fst :474 H *1/16* Sep 21 Aqu 3f fst :37 B *2/4* Sep 8 Aqu 3f fst :39 B *7/7*

O'star

Own: Lamarque Ronald M

CHAVEZ J F (47 8 5 6 .17) **$50,000**

B. c. 4
Sire: Risen Star (Secretariat)
Dam: Twofold (Timeless Moment)
Br: Lamarque Ronnie (Ky)
Tr: Badgett William Jr (6 0 2 1 .00)

117

Lifetime Record:	29	5	4	3	$114,391						
1994	10	2	0	2	$40,501	Turf	2	0	0	0	
1993	12	3	2	1	$63,410	Wet	5	0	0	0	$660
Aqu	3	0	0	1	$5,760	Dist	0	0	0	0	

3Sep94-9Bel fst	1 1/16		:232	:461	1:101	1:421	3↑ Clm 50000	89	1	1	2hd	2½	2½	41	Chavez J F	117	4.00	90-12	ACallToRise113nk SprklingSky117no Ptsyprospect109¾	Dueled, weakened	9
23Jly94-6Sar my	1⅛	⊗	:47	1:12	1:383	1:514	Clm 75000	84	5	1	2hd	2hd	4½	55	Chavez J F	117	5.00	72-27	Correntino117hd Senor Tomas1174 Patriot Strike113¾	Dueled, tired	5
12Jun94-9Bel fst	1		:224	:452	1:101	1:352	Clm 50000	97	8	1	21	2hd	1½	11½	Chavez J F	117	4.70	86-14	O'star1171½ Birdie's Fly117¾ Le Risky117hd	Driving	8
2Jun94-7Bel fm	1¼	Ⓣ	:481	1:122	1:37	2:001	3↑ Alw 36000N4X	42	6	3	2hd	83¼	814	827¼	Perret C	119 b	3.70e	62-13	Sentimental Moi1191¾ Correntino1191½ Turk Passer1193	Gave way	8
19May94-8Bel sly	1 1/16		:222	:45	1:092	1:421	3↑ Alw 44000N$mY	73	2	3	22½	23	46½	514	Smith M E	115 b	4.60	77-14	Say Dance1176½ Jacksonport1155½ I Like To Win1171½	Gave way	6
15Apr94-8Aqu fst	1		:224	:444	1:083	1:34	Alw 35000N4X	88	6	4	43	31	33½	36½	Velazquez J R	117	12.20	91-14	Stop And Listen119¾ Dominant Prospect1175¾ O'star1173	Tired	8
19Mar94-7FG fst	1 1/16		:23	:461	1:10	1:42	Alw 30000N$Y	89	1	3	32½	33	43½	49½	Martin E M Jr	L 117	3.30	95 —	Pie In YourEye1174½ PremierAdvocate1173½ SpeakNoEvil1171½	Inside trip	6
27Feb94-10FG fst	1 1/16		:234	:472	1:112	1:422	Whirlaway H51k	90	2	5	52¾	43½	44	45½	Poyadou B E	L 111	8.80	97-11	Cool Quaker1141 Dixie Poker Ace1211½ Dixieland Heat1143	Outrun	6
14Feb94-9FG fst	140		:233	:46	1:103	1:39	Alw 22000N$Y	90	1	5	58½	68	53½	35¾	Day P	L 122	*2.10	97-12	Cool Quaker119nk Speak No Evil1175½ O'star122no	Mild close	8
5Jan94-9FG fst	1 1/16		:231	:463	1:121	1:462	Alw 19500N4L	86	8	5	53¼	42½	2hd	2no	Martin E M Jr	L 117	*1.50	83-19	[D]Tea Box117no O'star1171½ No Name Dancer1142		12
Lugged in break, 4-wide rally, bumped deep stretch Placed first through disqualification.																					

WORKOUTS: Oct 17 Bel 5f fst 1:014 H *3/19* Oct 11 Bel 4f fst :48 B *7/38* Oct 3 Bel 5f fst 1:042 B *32/35* Sep 26 Bel 5f fst 1:02 B *10/19* Sep 12 Bel 5f fst 1:01 B *5/25* Aug 7 Sar 5f fst 1:014 H *11/36*

Nowhere Man was the dominant early speed among six sprinters going six and a half furlongs, and he was also the 9-5 favorite. There were several knocks against the one-dimensional speedball: his best Beyer Speed Figures had been delivered on muddy tracks, his effort nine days earlier, his first start in five months, had been less than inspiring (though he had been ambitiously spotted). Most notably, there was the matter of that additional sixteenth. Nowhere Man had won at the distance, yes, but had earned the bulk of his fortunes at six furlongs.

The extra sixteenth played right into the hands (hooves?) of O'Star, the lone entrant turning back from a dirt route. The colt hadn't started in nearly two months but had worked five furlongs at regularly-spaced intervals, an ample sign of current fitness in this age of year-round racing. Unlike Nowhere Man, whose wins during the year had come for claiming tags of $14,000, $25,000 and $32,500, O'Star had already won at today's $50,000 level, scoring in a one-turn mile at Belmont after forcing a quick pace.

O'Star had engaged in a long duel for command when last seen on September 3 in a one-turn route at Belmont, and held to finish fourth, beaten a length. An instant variant check revealed the following:

NINTH RACE
Belmont
SEPTEMBER 3, 1994

1 1/16 MILES. (1.39^{4}) CLAIMING. Purse $28,000. 3-year-olds and upward. Weights: 3-year-olds, 118 lbs. Older, 122 lbs. Non-winners of two races at a mile or over since August 1, allowed 3 lbs. Of such a race since then, 5 lbs. Claiming price $50,000, for each $2,500 to $45,000, allowed 2 lbs. (Races when entered to be claimed for $40,000 or less not considered.)

Value of Race: $28,000 Winner $16,800; second $6,160; third $3,360; fourth $1,680. Mutuel Pool $279,291.00 Exacta Pool $390,440.00 Triple Pool $588,327.00

Last Raced	Horse	M/Eqt.	A.	Wt	PP	St	¼	½	¾	Str	Fin	Jockey	Cl'g Pr	Odds $1
6Aug94 10Sar1	A Call To Rise		6	113	2	9	6hd	5hd	5½	51	1nk	Luzzi M J	45000	9.60
8Jly94 6Bel1	Sparkling Sky	bf	5	117	5	6	2½	1hd	1½	1½	2no	Migliore R	50000	6.20
13Jly94 2Bel1	Patsyprospect	f	3	109	7	1	88	82	71	4½	3¾	Frost G C	45000	25.40
23Jly94 6Sar5	O'star		4	117	1	5	1hd	21½	21	22½	41½	Chavez J F	50000	4.00
21Aug94 4Sar2	Dibbs N' Dubbs	bf	6	115	4	7	43	41½	32½	31	51¼	Maple E	47500	4.30
5Aug94 5Sar4	Mc Comas	b	4	117	6	8	5hd	61½	4½	62½	61½	Krone J A	50000	2.00
21Aug94 5Mth6	Commander Evander	bf	6	112	8	3	7½	71	82	74	76½	Beckner D V5	50000	11.60
17Aug94 7Sar2	Regal Mike	b	6	117	9	2	9	9	9	82	85½	Leon F	50000	9.50
6Aug94 4Sar5	Brush Full	b	3	113	3	4	3½	3hd	6hd	9	9	Mojica R Jr	50000	18.50

OFF AT 5:17 Start Good. Won driving. Time, :23^{2}, :46^{1}, 1:10^{1}, 1:35^{2}, 1:42^{1} Track fast.

$2 Mutuel Prices:			
2-(B)-A CALL TO RISE	21.20	9.60	6.20
6-(G)-SPARKLING SKY		7.20	5.80
8-(I)-PATSYPROSPECT			11.80

$2 EXACTA 2-6 PAID $118.40 $2 TRIPLE 2-6-8 PAID $1,592.00

B. g, by Poles Apart–A Bugle Command, by Command Control. Trainer Friedman Mitchell. Bred by Manfuso John A (Md).

A CALL TO RISE reserved for six furlongs while saving ground, closed strongly along the rail to get up in the final strides. SPARKLING SKY alternated for the lead from outside into the stretch, shook off O'STAR in upper stretch, continued on the front into deep stretch and yielded grudgingly. PATSYPROSPECT outrun for six furlongs, closed strongly from outside but could not get up. O'STAR dueled along the rail into midstretch and weakened. DIBBS N' DUBBS raced in close contention to the top of the stretch and lacked a strong closing bid. MC COMAS was never a serious threat. COMMANDER EVANDER was never a factor. REGAL MIKE never reached contention. BRUSH FULL was finished after going a half.

Owners— 1, Jewel-E Stables; 2, Finkelstein Morty; 3, Entenmann Robert; 4, Lamarque Ronald M; 5, Sommer Viola; 6, Paulson Madeleine; 7, Last State Stable; 8, Davidson Herbert S; 9, Buckland Farm

Trainers—1, Friedman Mitchell; 2, Imperio Joseph; 3, Riley Willie; 4, Badgett William Jr; 5, Martin Frank; 6, Mott William I; 7, Alvarez Luis C; 8, Wendel Arthur; 9, Cordero Angel Jr

Scratched— Ambush Alley (17Aug94 4SAR1), Iron Gavel (13Aug94 4SAR5)

O'Star dueled through splits of :23 2/5, :46 1/5, 1:10 1/5, and 1:35 2/5. Compare those fractions with the only other dirt route on the card:

FIRST RACE
Belmont
SEPTEMBER 3, 1994

1⅛ MILES. (1.45^{2}) CLAIMING. Purse $19,000. 3-year-olds and upward. Weights: 3-year-olds, 118 lbs. Older, 122 lbs. Non-winners of two races at a mile or over since August 1, allowed 3 lbs. Of such a race since then, 5 lbs. Claiming price $25,000; for each $2,500 to $20,000, 2 lbs. (Races when entered to be claimed for $18,000 or less not considered.) (Day 2 of a 39 Day Meet. Clear. 72.)

Value of Race: $19,000 Winner $11,400; second $4,180; third $2,280; fourth $1,140. Mutuel Pool $214,828.00 Exacta Pool $410,797.00

Last Raced	Horse	M/Eqt.	A.	Wt	PP	St	¼	½	¾	Str	Fin	Jockey	Cl'g Pr	Odds $1
17Aug94 4Sar7	Akiko	f	5	117	6	3	2½	21	2½	11	11½	Krone J A	25000	4.60
17Aug94 4Sar4	Yaros	b	5	117	3	6	4½	3½	31	2½	2nk	Migliore R	25000	2.40
16Jly94 1Crc1	Private Plan	f	4	117	8	1	3½	4hd	51½	52½	3½	Luzzi M J	25000	2.80
10Aug94 4Sar5	Red Scamper	b	9	115	4	5	61	51	41	4hd	41¼	Smith M E	22500	4.60
19Aug94 10Sar3	Established Lie		5	117	5	?	1½	1½	11	31½	52½	Velazquez J R	25000	15.60
29Jly94 1Sar4	Devoted Glory		5	115	1	8	8	7½	6hd	61	62½	Alvarado F T	22500	12.70
19Aug94 10Sar2	Charming Buck		7	115	2	7	5hd	6hd	71	710	711	Santos J A	22500	6.10
29Jly94 6Atl2	Too Wild		4	117	7	4	71	8	8	8	8	Cruz E F	25000	31.10

OFF AT 1:00 Start Good. Won driving. Time, :24^{2}, :48^{3}, 1:13^{1}, 1:36^{4}, 1:49^{1} Track fast.

$2 Mutuel Prices:			
7-(I)-AKIKO	11.20	5.40	3.20
1-(C)-YAROS		3.80	2.40
9-(K)-PRIVATE PLAN			2.40

$2 EXACTA 7-1 PAID $39.20

Ch. h, by Strawberry Road–Campechito, by Olden Times. Trainer Martin Frank. Bred by Pauslon Allen E (Ky).

AKIKO forced the pace from outside into upper stretch, took charge in midstretch then edged away under brisk urging. YAROS raced in close contention along the inside into the stretch then held well for the place. PRIVATE PLAN reserved for five furlongs while saving ground, angled out in upper stretch then closed late to gain a share. PRIVATE PLAN reserved for fire furlongs while saving ground, angled out in upper stretch then closed late to gain a share. RED SCAMPER gradually gained while four wide on the turn then lacked a strong closing bid. ESTABLISHED LIE was used up setting the early pace. DEVOTED GLORY was never a factor after breaking slowly. CHARMING BUCK never reached contention. TOO WILD was outrun. TOO WILD wore mud caulks.

Owners— 1, Sommer Viola; 2, Jewel-E Stables; 3, Young Scott; 4, Joques Farm; 5, Caputo John; 6, Corrado Fred L; 7, J M Dee Stable; 8, Condren William J

Trainers—1, Martin Frank; 2, Friedman Mitchell; 3, Gianos George; 4, Moschera Gasper S; 5, Schettino Dominick A; 6, Debonis Robert; 7, Odintz Jeff; 8, Zito Nicholas P

Scratched— Pension Fraud (26Aug94 9SAR2), Stately Wager (22Aug94 9SAR4), Sorabosia (29Jly94 1SAR1)

Quite a difference! Akiko had won by pressing a slow early pace, the six-furlong split three seconds slower than in O'Star's race.

O'Star didn't have the kind of sprint-speed to stay with Nowhere Man down the backstretch but he was certainly no plodder, having contested the pace in his three most recent races, including that fast-paced effort of September 3rd. O'Star had enough positional speed to stay within range, and because he was accustomed to longer races he figured to have considerably more gas left in the tank than Nowhere Man, whose best game was six furlongs.

FOURTH RACE
Aqueduct
OCTOBER 29, 1994

6½ FURLONGS. (1.15) CLAIMING. Purse $26,000. 3-year-olds and upward. Weights: 3-year-olds, 119 lbs. Older, 122 lbs. Non-winners of two races since October 1, allowed 3 lbs. Of a race since then, 5 lbs. Claiming price $50,000, for each $2,500 to $45,000, allowed 2 lbs. (Races when entered to be claimed for $40,000 or less not considered.)

Value of Race: $26,000 Winner $15,600; second $5,720; third $3,120; fourth $1,560. Mutuel Pool $241,891.00 Exacta Pool $430,435.00 Quinella Pool $90,273.00

Last Raced	Horse	M/Eqt.	A.	Wt	PP	St	¼	½	Str	Fin	Jockey	Cl'g Pr	Odds $1
3Sep94 9Bel4	O'star		4	117	2	2	2 1½	23	1hd	1 1¼	Chavez J F	50000	4.60
20Oct94 8Aqu5	Nowhere Man	bf	5	107	1	4	15	15	23	2 1½	Agosto R7	45000	1.80
29Aug94 1Sar8	Danzig's Dance	b	5	115	4	5	4 1½	3½	32	3 4¼	Luzzi M J	47500	5.00
18Oct94 7Aqu7	Birdie's Fly	bf	4	117	6	1	510	510	4½	4 2½	Luttrell M G	50000	10.80
4Oct94 2Bel2	Bill Of Rights		5	115	5	6	6	6	6	5hd	Samyn J L	47500	4.90
16Oct94 2Bel5	Boss Soss		4	117	3	3	3hd	4 1½	52	6	Smith M E	50000	2.85

OFF AT 1:54 Start Good. Won driving. Time, :22, :444, 1:101, 1:17 Track fast.

$2 Mutuel Prices:			
2-(B)-O'STAR	11.20	4.70	4.00
1-(A)-NOWHERE MAN		3.90	3.00
4-(D)-DANZIG'S DANCE			3.50

$2 EXACTA 2-1 PAID $46.40 $2 QUINELLA 1-2 PAID $19.20

B. c, by Risen Star–Twofold, by Timeless Moment. Trainer Badgett William Jr. Bred by Lamarque Ronnie (Ky).

O'STAR settled just behind the early pacesetter, closed the gap in upper stretch then wore down NOWHERE MAN to win going away. NOWHERE MAN sprinted clear in the early stages, set the pace along the inside into midstretch and weakened in the final eighth. DANZIG'S DANCE unhurried for a half, failed to threaten with a mild late rally. BIRDIE'S FLY never reached contention. BILL OF RIGHTS was never a factor. BOSS SOSS gave way after going a half. NOWHERE MAN and DANZIG'S DANCE wore mud caulks.

Owners— 1, Lamarque Ronald M; 2, Perroncino John S; 3, Zablowitz Karen S; 4, Ferriola Ingrid A; 5, Boketo Stable; 6, Kimmel Caesar P & Nicholson Ronald

Trainers—1, Badgett William Jr; 2, Terracciano Neal; 3, Parisella John; 4, Ferriola Peter; 5, Kelly Timothy D; 6, Toner James J

Overweight: Nowhere Man (1).

O'Star wore down Nowhere Man to win going away.

A POTENT EARLY PACE scenario that players should always be prepared to exploit is the maiden dropping into claiming company after displaying a flash of ability, such as a brief but noticeable burst of speed, at the special-weight level. The maiden special to maiden claiming class drop, as has been explained ever since the days of James Quinn's *Handicapper's Condition Book*, is among the most powerful class drops in racing; when the dropper also appears capable of dominating the early pace, it's time for an enthusiastic wager.

1 **Belmont Park**

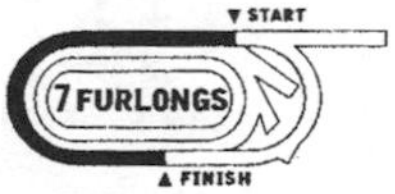

7 Furlongs **(1:201) MAIDEN CLAIMING. Purse $12,000. 3-year-olds and upward. Weights: 3-year olds, 119 lbs. Older, 122 lbs. Claiming price $35,000, for each $2,500 to $30,000, allowed 2 lbs.**

Kent Clark
Own: Lundy & McRich Stables & Sardo
PEZUA J M (104 6 6 9 .06) $30,000
Dk. b or br g. 3 (Apr)
Sire: Instrument Landing (Grey Dawn II)
Dam: Gate Lady (Noble Nashua)
Br: Paccione Stella (NY)
Tr: Lundy Sarah A (7 0 0 0 .00)
115

Lifetime Record:	7 M 0 0	$0		
1994	7 M 0 0		Turf	2 0 0 0
1993	0 M 0 0		Wet	2 0 0 0
Bel	4 0 0 0		Dist	1 0 0 0

4Oct94-9Bel fst 1 1/16	:233 :472 1:131 1:461 3+ [S]Md Sp Wt	26	6	10	109¾	78½	710	721	Pezua J M	119		56.80	50-29	Landing Pad1195 Sir Noble1195 Baer Affair1192	Checked break 10
14Sep94-3Bel fm 1 1/16 [T]	:233 :472 1:12 1:423 3+ Md Sp Wt	35	10	8	1012	1012	1013	1021½	Pezua J M	118	b	92.90	61-14	Yokohama1182 Super Twenty Five1181¾ Hawkeye Bay1183	Outrun 10
2Sep94-1Bel fm 1 1/16 [T]	:241 :474 1:121 1:434 3+ [S]Md Sp Wt	54	10	10	1013	1010	99	87½	Pezua J M	118		25.40	70-17	Crooked Heels1181½ Lord Basil118nk Al's Rose118hd	No factor 10
Placed 7th through disqualification.															
5Aug94-3Sar my 1 3/16 ⊗	:491 1:151 1:411 2:003 3+ [S]Md Sp Wt	34	8	4	47	59	521	530	Luttrell M G5	112	b	49.40	46-28	Little Fran1171 Grave Dancer11711 Ace The Test1227	No threat 8
17Jly94-1Bel fst 1 1/16	:242 :481 1:13 1:453 3+ [S]Md Sp Wt	34	4	1	32	55½	611	618½	Caldwell D A7	109	b	36.00	55-23	Thor Thors1061½ Rogersdividends1168 Little Fran1166½	Done early 6
2Jly94-3Bel fst 6f	:222 :453 :581 1:111 3+ [S]Md Sp Wt	45	8	10	912	912	911	914½	Caldwell D A5	111	b	71.40	71-13	Night Trap1162¼ Elocat's Banner1114¾ Rogersdividends116¾	Outrun 10
19May94-9Bel sly 7f	:224 :454 1:11 1:24 3+ [S]Md Sp Wt	-0	1	8	88½	819	729	761¼	Santos J A	115		15.00	— 15	Milbrook1086½ Coshio1156 Thor Thors1157¾	Outrun 8

WORKOUTS: Sep 30 Bel 5f fst 1:024 B *29/44* Sep 25 Bel tr.t 4f gd :523 B *34/36* Sep 12 Bel 4f fst :494 B *20/29* Aug 29 Sar 5f fst 1:023 H *13/21* Aug 24 Sar 5f fst 1:041 B *35/39* Aug 15 Sar tr.t[T] 5f sf 1:052 B (d) *17/17*

Crown Pearl
Own: Juddmonte Farms
VELAZQUEZ J R (134 13 17 19 .10) $30,000
Ch. c. 3 (May)
Sire: Cox's Ridge (Best Turn)
Dam: Bethamane (Wajima)
Br: Juddmonte Farms (Ky)
Tr: Mott William I (56 15 7 9 .27)
115

Lifetime Record:	4 M 0 1	$3,000			
1994	4 M 0 1	$3,000	Turf	0 0 0 0	
1993	0 M 0 0		Wet	2 0 0 1	$3,000
Bel	2 0 0 0		Dist	0 0 0 0	

30Sep94-3Bel fst 1	:231 :464 1:114 1:373 3+ Md 35000	52	6	7	67	65¾	512	516	Perez R M5	113	4.40	59-29	Fifth Set11410 High Regent1133 Dependableness1181¼	No factor 7
21Sep94-9Bel fst 1	:23 :461 1:112 1:373 3+ Md 32500	59	12	11	95½	74¼	77¼	58	Perez R M5	111	3.70	67-19	Canheski1187 Iain's Storm118½ Facetious Buck114nk	Lacked rally 12
14Aug94-2Sar sly 1⅛	:483 1:131 1:382 1:511 3+ Md Sp Wt	51	7	4	65½	66	710	722	Smith M E	117	2.90	58-22	Private Cody1177 Timeless Dream117½ Libertine1174	Wide, outrun 7
29Jly94-3Sar my 6f	:222 :462 :584 1:122 3+ Md Sp Wt	73	2	1	57½	53	44	33¾	Smith M E	116	3.50	75-19	Its A Star1161¾ Ball's Bluff1162 Crown Pearl116nk	Late gain 6

WORKOUTS: Oct 11 Bel 4f fst :513 B *36/38* Sep 15 Sar tr.t 6f fst 1:173 B *1/1* Sep 9 Sar 5f fst 1:052 B *1/1* Sep 2 Sar tr.t 5f fst 1:051 B *1/2* Aug 28 Sar 4f fst :492 B *4/13* Aug 9 Sar 3f fst :371 B *3/5*

Fog Storm
Own: Buxton Anne K
BROWN T M (1 0 0 0 .00) $30,000
Dk. b or br g. 3 (May)
Sire: Our Native (Exclusive Native)
Dam: Hard Hearted Hanna (Dancer's Image)
Br: Thomas E W (Ky)
Tr: Buxton Anne K (—)
1087

Lifetime Record:	0 M 0 0	$0		
1994	0 M 0 0		Turf	0 0 0 0
1993	0 M 0 0		Wet	0 0 0 0
Bel	0 0 0 0		Dist	0 0 0 0

WORKOUTS: ●Oct 10 Med 3f fst :36 B *1/6* Sep 9 Med 5f fst 1:023 Bg *7/7* Sep 2 Atl 4f fst :512 B *5/6* Aug 20 Atl 5f fst 1:02 H *5/16*

Inside News

Own: Gayno Stables

LUZZI M J (143 19 13 16 .13) **$30,000**

Ch. c. 3 (Mar)
Sire: Meadowlake (Hold Your Peace)
Dam: Restless Doggie (Restless Wind)
Br: Brylynn Farm (Fla)
Tr: Dupps Kristina (3 0 0 2 .00)

115

Lifetime Record:	4 M 1 0	$5,500			
1994	3 M 1 0	$5,500	Turf	1 0 0 0	
1993	1 M 0 0		Wet	0 0 0 0	
Bel	2 0 1 0	$5,500	Dist	2 0 0 0	

29Jun94-9Bel	fst	7f	:231 :463 1:111 1:233	3↑ Md Sp Wt	46	1	3	21	74	812	820	Luttrell M G5	109	20.20	65-16	Inside The Beltway1142¼ [D]Crafty Mist1143 Ball's Bluff1142¾	Brief speed	9
10Jun94-1Bel	fm	1 1/16 [T]	:234 :48 1:113 1:414	3↑ Md Sp Wt	42	1	5	54½	77	79	613¼	Velazquez J R	114	5.70	74-10	No Storm1141 Staire To Heaven1144 Top Trader1141	Stumbled break	8
25May94-5Bel	fst	6f	:222 :462 :584 1:111	3↑ Md Sp Wt	63	1	4	32	42	43½	26½	Velazquez J R	122	18.60	78-15	Pauliano1226½ Inside News122nk Dr. Guida1221	Willingly	8
4Nov93-5Aqu	fst	7f	:23 :461 1:113 1:244	Md Sp Wt	39	7	2	1½	21	612	719½	Guerra W A	118	28.20	60-17	I'm Very Irish1181¼ Plutonius1188 Signal Tap118½	Tired	8

WORKOUTS: Oct 4 Bel 6f fst 1:153 B *3/4* Sep 28 Bel 5f sly 1:042 B (d)*3/3* Sep 22 Bel 4f fst :491 B *21/53* ●Sep 16 Bel 3f fst :361 H *1/12*

Charlie Cush

Own: Pokoik Lee

CHAVEZ J F (166 25 23 20 .15) **$35,000**

B. g. 3 (Apr)
Sire: Believe It (In Reality)
Dam: Flying Damsel (Damascus)
Br: Carrion Jaime S (Fla)
Tr: Sciacca Gary (73 8 6 10 .11)

119

Lifetime Record:	7 M 1 3	$9,900			
1994	4 M 1 2	$7,080	Turf	0 0 0 0	
1993	3 M 0 1	$2,820	Wet	2 0 0 1	$3,000
Bel	4 0 1 2	$6,900	Dist	1 0 0 0	

20Oct94-1Bel	gd	6f	:224 :454 :581 1:11	3↑ Md 30000	67	2	1	1½	1½	1hd	22	Chavez J F	115	4.00	84-14	Plutonius1192 Charlie Cush115½ Level Land1146	Held place	6
25Sep94-9Bel	gd	6f	:222 :453 :574 1:103	3↑ Md 35000	61	8	3	42	3½	23	35¼	Chavez J F	118	*2.50	83-12	Dialed For Running114nk O'my Gy1095 Charlie Cush1181½	Four wide	9
29Aug94-9Sar	fst	7f	:22 :451 1:11 1:241	3↑ Md Sp Wt	27	1	6	1½	43	1181½	1126½	Chavez J F	117 b	10.30	58-13	Silver Fox117nk Andover Road11711 Iron Mountain1175	Gave way	11
21Aug94-1Sar	sly	6½f	:222 :46 1:12 1:182	3↑ Md Sp Wt	47	3	8	43½	44	44½	313½	Chavez J F	117 b	5.20	69-20	Spanos1179½ Runaway Brian1174 Charlie Cush117hd	Pinched break	8
19Sep93-1Bel	sly	6f	:222 :462 :59 1:112	Md 50000	18	1	1	1½	1½	67	622½	Antley C W	118 b	2.00	60-20	Sir Wollaston1144 Twilight Classic114no Jido1147	Used in pace	7
28Aug93-3Sar	fst	6f	:22 :46 :582 1:114	Md Sp Wt	45	4	4	41½	53	64½	68	Perret C	118	6.50	75-14	Squire Jones118½ Turnbull Creek1181½ Personal Escort1183	Tired	7
16May93-3Bel	fst	5f	:223 :462 :592	Md Sp Wt	54	4	3	1hd	2hd	21½	33¼	Antley C W	118	4.50	81-15	Gliding Arrow1183 Lahint118nk Charlie Cush118no	Dueled, weakened	7

WORKOUTS: Sep 21 Bel 4f fst :481 H *7/36* Sep 16 Bel 3f fst :384 B *11/12* Sep 10 Bel 3f fst :37 B *12/25* ●Aug 13 Sar tr.t 3f fst :361 H *1/14* Aug 7 Sar 3f fst :36 Hg*2/22* Jly 18 Bel 4f fst :471 H *3/45*

Loyal Todd

Own: Krohn Nat

RODRIGUEZ O (20 2 0 2 .10) **$30,000**

B. g. 5
Sire: B. K. Todd (Quack)
Dam: Loyal Diplomat (Diplomat Way)
Br: Krohn Nat (Fla)
Tr: Krohn Nat (2 0 0 0 .00)

1117

Lifetime Record:	3 M 0 0	$0		
1994	1 M 0 0		Turf	0 0 0 0
1993	2 M 0 0		Wet	1 0 0 0
Bel	3 0 0 0		Dist	0 0 0 0

18May94-5Bel	fst	6f	:224 :463 :59 1:114	3↑ Md 30000	–0	1	4	66	88	827	831½	Alvarado F T	120 f	48.30	50-16	Dixie Reef1171 Premium Value1131¾ Cleft1082½	Outrun	8
24Sep93-3Bel	my	6f	:224 :464 :59 1:112	3↑ Md 30000	–0	8	4	21	75	815	839¾	Leon F5	113	69.90	43-24	Eternal Friend1149½ Vintage Book118½ Pilfer1144¼	Brief speed	8
11Jly93-3Bel	fst	6f	:223 :453 :574 1:103	3↑ Md 30000	–0	10	11	1010	1115	1116	1137½	Pezua J M	118	88.70	49-12	GllntPip1181½ Shootthemessngr1151½ CrowndKnight1181	Steadied break	11

WORKOUTS: Oct 5 Bel tr.t 5f fst 1:031 B *2/3* Sep 20 Bel tr.t 3f fst :371 B *6/8* Sep 14 Bel tr.t 4f fst :494 B *4/5* Sep 8 Bel tr.t 4f fst :50 B *7/14* Sep 1 Bel tr.t 3f fst :36 H *6/16* Aug 11 Bel 3f fst :373 B *5/5*

High Regent

Own: Condren William & Cornacchia Joseph

SMITH M E (169 35 28 18 .21) **$35,000**

B. c. 3 (Mar)
Sire: Vice Regent (Northern Dancer)
Dam: Barkerville Belle (Ruthie's Native)
Br: Franks John (Ont-C)
Tr: Zito Nicholas P (66 7 8 7 .11)

119

Lifetime Record:	9 M 4 0	$12,720		
1994	8 M 4 0	$12,720	Turf	1 0 0 0
1993	1 M 0 0		Wet	0 0 0 0
Bel	8 0 4 0	$12,720	Dist	0 0 0 0

11Oct94-1Bel	fst	1 1/16	:233 :47 1:121 1:451	3↑ Md 35000	70	7	3	1hd	1hd	21	26	Beckner D V5	114	3.50	70-24	Cherokee Hill1196 High Regent1145 Blazon Skates119hd	No match	8
30Sep94-3Bel	fst	1	:231 :464 1:114 1:373	3↑ Md 35000	64	7	2	31	2hd	25	210	Beckner D V5	113	*1.60	65-29	Fifth Set11410 High Regent1133 Dependableness1181¼	Held place	7
21Sep94-9Bel	fst	1	:23 :461 1:112 1:373	3↑ Md 35000	57	2	2	1½	2hd	34	69½	Davis R G	118	*1.60	66-19	Canheski1187 Iain's Storm118½ Facetious Buck114nk	Dueled, tired	12
9Sep94-1Bel	fst	1 1/16	:232 :472 1:123 1:441	3↑ Md 35000	83	8	4	42	3nk	1hd	2hd	Davis R G	118	*2.20	81-17	Libertine118hd High Regent1189 Robber Baron1135¾	Second best	10
12Aug94-3Sar	fm	1 1/16 [T]	:231 :471 1:121 1:424	3↑ Md Sp Wt	67	2	2	35	54½	42	56	Luzzi M J	117	10.60	79-10	Artemus Hawk117nk Andover Road1171¼ Super Twenty Five1173	Tired	10
12Jly94-9Bel	fst	1	:232 :47 1:133 1:403	3↑ Md 35000	65	2	5	31½	1hd	1½	2nk	Alvarado F T	116	5.40	60-24	Blue Eyed Bob112nk High Regent1164 Robber Baron1112	Gamely	12
17Jun94-9Bel	fst	6f	:221 :452 :58 1:11	3↑ Md Sp Wt	64	8	4	42	43	86¼	97¼	Luzzi M J	114	19.50	79-15	Thru 'n Thru1141¼ [D]Ball's Bluff1141¼ Changing Rahy114nk	Gave way	10
25May94-5Bel	fst	6f	:222 :462 :584 1:111	3↑ Md Sp Wt	59	6	8	2½	1hd	32¼	47¾	Luzzi M J	122	13.50	77-15	Pauliano1226½ Inside News122nk Dr. Guida1221	Dueled inside	8
23Jun93-3Bel	fst	5½f	:214 :451 :581 1:052	Md Sp Wt	37	5	9	710	79½	79½	712¼	Perret C	118	25.70	76-14	Gusto Z1181¼ Wire Squire1183½ Arrival Time118¾	Broke slowly	9

WORKOUTS: Sep 3 Bel 4f fst :50 B *37/50* ●Aug 27 Bel tr.t 5f fst 1:012 H *1/12* Aug 7 Bel 4f fst :482 B *4/25* Jly 31 Bel 4f fst 48 H *3/33* Jly 23 Bel 4f fst :492 B *5/18*

Strike For Life

Own: Yorkes Arthur F

BECKNER D V (156 18 20 24 .12) **$30,000**

Ch. g. 3 (May)
Sire: Strike the Anvil (Bolinas Boy)
Dam: Tour En Voiture (Large as Life)
Br: Pilcher Docia & Hubert (Fla)
Tr: Reynolds Patrick L (9 1 0 2 .11)

1105

Lifetime Record:	12 M 0 1	$3,920			
1994	12 M 0 1	$3,920	Turf	5 0 0 0	$1,620
1992	0 M 0 0		Wet	1 0 0 0	
Bel	5 0 0 1	$2,160	Dist	1 0 0 0	

21Sep94-9Bel	fst	1	:23 :461 1:112 1:373	3↑ Md 30000	47	11	7	5¾	52¼	910	814½	Rydowski S R	114	40.60	60-19	Canheski1187 Iain's Storm118½ Facetious Buck114nk	Four wide	12
5Sep94-5Bel	fm	1¼ [T]	:472 1:123 1:374 2:012	3↑ Md Sp Wt	55	3	5	86¼	104¾	89¾	811¼	Pezua J M	118	37.90	72-13	Watrals Sea Trip1181¼ Ace The Test117¾ Winterton118nk	No factor	12
12Aug94-3Sar	fm	1 1/16 [T]	:231 :471 1:121 1:424	3↑ Md Sp Wt	66	10	6	56½	2½	62¾	66¼	Beckner D V5	112	36.70	78-10	Artemus Hawk117nk Andover Road1171¼ Super Twenty Five1173	Bid, tired	10
17Jly94-5Bel	fm	1 1/16 (T)	:233 :463 1:10 1:414	3↑ Md Sp Wt	49	6	6	64½	78	78	616¼	Leon F	116	18.20	73-09	Staire To Heaven1162¾ Royce Joseph1115 Rana Sanga1166	No menace	12
6Jly94-9Bel	fm	1¼ [T]	:472 1:113 1:364 2:014	3↑ Md Sp Wt	65	8	2	31	1½	21½	44¾	Mickens T J5	111	52.30	76-16	Halo Care1161¾ Ace The Test122no Risk Your Wealth1163	Bid, tired	12
26Jun94-5Bel	fm	1 (T)	:23 :46 1:094 1:34	3↑ Md Sp Wt	68	9	7	74½	85	78	611¼	Leon F	114	117.50	81-16	Holy Mountain1146½ Dole Raider1141¾ Haagbah1141¼	No threat	12
15Jun94-3Bel	fst	1 1/16	:232 :464 1:114 1:423	3↑ Md 30000	38	2	6	65½	79	517	428½	Beckner D V7	103	10.10	60-11	Poets Pistol11010 Charmed Prospect1143 Grand Chef11815	No threat	9
3Jun94-1Bel	fst	1 1/16	:233 :471 1:123 1:444	3↑ Md 32500	61	8	2	31½	3½	3½	37	Beckner D V7	105	46.00	71-20	Mean Pancho1141 Charmed Prospect1146 StrikeForLife1051¾	Weakened	8
24May94-1Bel	fst	1⅛	:47 1:123 1:394 1:532	3↑ Md 30000	32	6	3	31½	42½	87	815½	Graell A	111	50.40	48-24	Mike N Chris1113½ Mean Pancho115½ Tetlie1152½	Tired	10
8May94-9Bel	my	7f	:223 :453 1:10 1:23	3↑ Md 35000	15	6	7	73¾	713	718	728½	Chavez J F	115	4.00	59-09	Panico1143 Charmed Prospect1115 Facetious Buck1133	Wide, outrun	8

WORKOUTS: Oct 6 Aqu 4f fst :50 B *6/9* Sep 17 Aqu 4f fst :513 B *5/6* Aug 28 Sar 4f fst :513 B *11/13* Aug 9 Sar (T) 3f fm :363 B *1/1*

Manna Manna

Own: Tam Ping W

PEREZ R M (96 15 10 11 .16) **$30,000**

B. g. 3 (Feb)
Sire: Simply Majestic (Majestic Light)
Dam: Light Frost (Bold Ambition)
Br: Oxley John T (Ky)
Tr: Lake Robert P (26 2 3 7 .08)

1105

Lifetime Record:	4 M 0 0	$0		
1994	2 M 0 0		Turf	1 0 0 0
1993	2 M 0 0		Wet	0 0 0 0
Bel	1 0 0 0		Dist	0 0 0 0

20Oct94-1Bel	gd	6f	:224 :454 :581 1:11	3↑ Md 30000	43	3	2	2½	44½	66¼	611½	Beckner D V5	110	35.70	74-14	Plutonius1192 Charlie Cush115½ Level Land1146	Forced pace, tired	6
1Jan94-9Aqu	fst	6f [•]	:23 :472 1:004 1:142	Md 20000	36	7	5	83	96¼	79¼	79¾	Mojica R Jr	118 f	45.60	61-27	Outlaw Angel1081½ Spicy Hi113½ Fast Fiji1184½	No factor	12
26Aug93-3Sar	fst	6f	:22 :453 :581 1:11	Md 45000	–0	3	9	1014	1018	1015	1026½	Frost G C	114 f	39.70	60-10	IcingOnTheCake1183 [DH]TwilightClssic114 [DH]SirWollston1142½	Outrun	10
22Jly93-5Bel	fm	7f (T)	:234 :474 1:112 1:231	Md Sp Wt	—	6	7	78	712	723	—	Davis R G	118	14.80	— 12	Kitten'sFirst115no CheckRid11810 DynmitLugh1182	Checked break, eased	7

WORKOUTS: Oct 10 Bel 3f fst :36 H *3/13* Sep 22 Aqu (T) 6f fm 1:202 B (d) *1/2* Sep 17 Aqu 6f fst 1:163 B *2/2* Sep 10 Aqu 5f fst 1:051 B *6/7* Sep 4 Aqu 4f fst :482 H *2/8* Aug 24 Sar tr.t (T) 4f gd :494 B *9/14*

Iain's Storm
Own: Turchiarelli Anthony & Yvonne
MOJICA R JR (84 5 6 14 .06) — $35,000

B. c. 3 (Mar)
Sire: Obligato (Northern Dancer)
Dam: Quiet Glory (Cavamore)
Br: Turchiarelli Mr & Mrs Anthony (NY)
Tr: Weiss Richard M (7 0 1 1 .00)

119

Lifetime Record:	8 M 1 1	$8,800			
1994	6 M 1 1	$8,800	Turf	0 0 0 0	
1993	2 M 0 0		Wet	1 0 0 0	
Bel	3 0 1 0	$4,660	Dist	1 0 0 0	$1,380

4Oct94-9Bel	fst	1 1/16	:233	:472	1:131	1:461	3↑ SMd Sp Wt	12	8	6	32	2½	54½	412	Mojica R Jr	119 b	5.60	59-29	Landing Pad1195 Sir Noble1195 Baer Affair1192	No late bid 10
21Sep94-9Bel	fst	1	:23	:461	1:112	1:373	3↑ Md 35000	61	5	3	3½	3nk	23	27	Mojica R Jr	118 b	51.50	68-19	Canheski1187 Iain's Storm118½ Facetious Buck114nk	Held place 12
17Jly94-9Bel	fst	6f	:222	:453	:581	1:113	3↑ Md 35000	34	7	8	813	812	513	517¾	Rydowski S R	116 b	38.20	65-16	Lightnin' Cat112nk Stantorian1137 Super Twenty Five1165½	No factor 8
22Mar94-7Aqu	fst	7f	:233	:482	1:143	1:28	SMd Sp Wt	49	1	10	21	41	41½	43	Nelson D	122	15.90	61-26	Gus' Pop122no Song Of David1222 The Real Cool Gang1221	Saved ground 10
9Mar94-5Aqu	fst	6f ⊡	:232	:47	:592	1:121	SMd Sp Wt	25	4	7	813	79½	617	619½	Nelson D	122	7.20	62-19	All Man11710 Yarborough1221 He Will Do It1221	Pinched break 8
21Feb94-6Aqu	fst	6f ⊡	:231	:463	:592	1:131	SMd Sp Wt	42	6	10	98½	812	714	310¼	Carr D	122	40.50	67-20	Fini Cassette1229¼ Yarborough1221 Iain's Storm1222	Checked break 11
30Nov93-7FL	my	5½f	:224	:463	1:00	1:07	SMd Sp Wt	18	3	6	614	619	622	510½	Faine C	121	34.60	69-17	Fuzzy Thinking1212 Tropic Zone121½ Tonawanda News121½	Outrun 6
21Nov93-5FL	gd	5½f	:232	:474	1:014	1:082	SMd Sp Wt	19	7	5	713	713	615	610½	Faine C	120	22.60	63-22	Step Lord1202 Tropic Zone120¾ Sky's Romance120hd	Showed nothing 7

WORKOUTS: Sep 30 Aqu 4f fst :52 B *15/16* ●Sep 16 Aqu 3f fst :36 H *1/6* Sep 7 Aqu 6f fst 1:163 B *1/1* Aug 15 Bel tr.t 4f my :54 B *3/3*

Whirlaroo
Own: Hobeau Farm
WYNTER N A (9 1 0 1 .11) — $35,000

B. g. 3 (Feb)
Sire: Buckaroo (Buckpasser)
Dam: Swirlaway (Sir Ivor)
Br: Hobeau Farm (Fla)
Tr: Jerkens H Allen (51 14 7 5 .27)

119

Lifetime Record:	1 M 0 0	$0		
1994	1 M 0 0		Turf	0 0 0 0
1993	0 M 0 0		Wet	0 0 0 0
Bel	1 0 0 0		Dist	0 0 0 0

30Sep94-5Bel	fst	6f	:222	:454	:58	1:11	3↑ Md Sp Wt	53	1	3	11	2½	65½	711½	Wynter N A	118	2.90e	74-14	Expressed1181½ Get Behind Me1181 Cozy Prospect1184½	Used early 8

WORKOUTS: Oct 11 Bel tr.t 3f fst :373 B *1/2* ●Sep 17 Bel tr.t 6f fst 1:143 B *1/5* Sep 14 Bel 5f fst 1:02 H *13/23* Sep 10 Bel tr.t 6f fst 1:194 B *3/5* Aug 31 Bel 5f fst 1:032 B *32/38*

The opener on October 14 was a maiden claimer at seven furlongs that attracted a field of 11 — all of them 3-year-olds except for a poor soul named Loyal Todd, who had never finished in front of another horse in his life.

The 8-5 favorite was High Regent. Whenever players spot a favorite with this kind of profile, bells should go off. Start looking for an overlay somewhere else in the field! High Regent had raced against $35,000 maiden claimers five times and had managed to finish second in four of them, twice blowing photos after having the lead at the stretch call. He was favored because his established form was obviously better than anyone else's; players are strongly cautioned here that a series of close recent finishes from a maiden claimer can best be described as fool's gold. The more times they get close without winning, the less likely they are to find the winner's circle; invariably, some lightly-raced horse improves enough to win.

The dominant early pace in the race was Whirlaroo, who was being dropped into a claimer by Allen Jerkens after debuting at the special-weight level in a six-furlong sprint. A scan of the raw fractional times does not tip off Whirlaroo's early supremacy, which helps to explain whey the Hobeau Farm gelding was a generous 5-1. Some others in the race had shown some early zip: High Regent was cutting back in distance after contesting the lead at the pre-stretch call of his last four starts; Inside News was dropping to claimers after racing within a length of :23 1/5 quarter last time out; and 4-1 second choice Charlie Cush had dueled from start to midstretch in splits of :22 4/5 and :45 4/5 less than two weeks ago.

But although Charlie Cush and Whirlaroo were emerging from races that featured identical half-miles of :45 4/5 and both of those races had been run over Belmont main tracks with an identical variant of 14, there was no comparison between the two. It so happened that September 30 was one of those early autumn days that lets you know summer is really over; the temperature never made it out of the 60s, and steady winds of 25 miles per hour put a real chill in the air; those winds blew against the fields down the backstretch (as any player could tell by looking at the infield flags), so that a half in :45 4/5 on this particular day truly was something extraordinary.

Examine the charts of the four sprints run on the card, and you'll see the effect the wind had on the early fractions; also note the conditions of each race:

FIRST RACE **6 FURLONGS. (1.07^4) MAIDEN CLAIMING. Purse $12,000. Fillies and mares, 3-year-olds and upward. Weights: 3-year-olds, 118 lbs. Olde., 122 lbs. Claiming price $35,000, for each $2,500 to $30,000, allowed 2 lbs. (Day 25 of a 39 Day Meet. Clear. 67.)**

Belmont

SEPTEMBER 30, 1994

Value of Race: $12,000 Winner $7,200; second $2,640; third $1,440; fourth $720. Mutuel Pool $107,613.00 Exacta Pool $232,900.00

Last Raced	Horse	M/Eqt.	A.	Wt	PP	St	¼	½	Str	Fin	Jockey	Cl'g Pr	Odds $1
	Flippy		3	111	5	4	$2^{1/2}$	$1^{1/2}$	1^3	1^3	Rosario V^7	35000	1.90
	Learn To Hope		3	118	4	5	5^2	$4^{1/2}$	2^1	2^3	Davis R G	35000	2.40
22Sep94 ^{5}Bel^3	Yul Babe		3	109	1	3	$3^{1/2}$	3^2	3^2	3^4	Lantz J A^5	30000	4.20
	Weekend Leave	f	3	114	6	6	6	5^1	5^4	$4^{8 1/2}$	Velazquez J R	30000	2.30
7Jun94 ^{9}Bel^{12}	Allaspin	b	3	114	3	1	1^{hd}	2^1	4^{hd}	5^3	Graell A	30000	21.10
15Sep94 ^{9}Bel^8	Sondra P.		3	108	2	2	4^3	6	6	6	Martin J V^{10}	35000	23.50

OFF AT 1:00 Start Good. Won driving. Time, :23, :47, :59^2, 1:12^3 Track fast.

$2 Mutuel Prices:			
5-(E)-FLIPPY	5.80	3.20	2.20
4-(D)-LEARN TO HOPE		3.40	2.20
1-(A)-YUL BABE			2.20

$2 EXACTA 5-4 PAID $15.40

Dk. b. or br. f, (Apr), by Chas Conerly–Flip's Pleasure, by Flip Sal. Trainer Jerkens H Allen. Bred by Hobeau Farm (Fla).

FLIPPY broke awkwardly then checked while veering out at the start, rushed up from outside to contest the early pace, took charge while drifting out in upper stretch, then drew off under pressure. LEARN TO HOPE checked at the start, was unhurried for a half then finished willingly to best the others. YUL BABE raced in close contention along the inside into the stretch, drifted out briefly in midstretch, then lacked a strong closing bid. WEEKEND LEAVE checked while being carried out at the start and failed to threaten thereafter. ALLASPIN battled inside the winner into upper stretch and tired. SONDRA P. was finished early. YUL BABE wore mud caulks.

Owners— 1, Hobeau Farm; 2, Jones Joseph M Jr; 3, My Samsara Stables; 4, Glencrest Farm; 5, Corrado Fred L; 6, Galvin Neal & Patrick David

Trainers—1, Jerkens H Allen; 2, Dunham Bob G; 3, Nocella Vincent R; 4, Levine Bruce N; 5, Debonis Robert; 6, Magnier Paul

Scratched— Dante's Brew (29Sep94 ^{5}BEL^5)

Flippy cut a half in :47 winning the first race, a $35,000 maiden claimer for 3-year-old fillies.

FIFTH RACE **6 FURLONGS. (1.07^4) MAIDEN SPECIAL WEIGHT. Purse $28,000. 3-year-olds and upward. Weights: 3-year-olds, 118 lbs. Older, 122 lbs.**

Belmont

SEPTEMBER 30, 1994

Value of Race: $28,000 Winner $16,800; second $6,160; third $3,360; fourth $1,680. Mutuel Pool $210,023.00 Exacta Pool $399,764.00

Last Raced	Horse	M/Eqt.	A.	Wt	PP	St	¼	½	Str	Fin	Jockey	Odds $1
11Sep94 ^{1}Bel^2	Expressed	b	4	118	6	2	$3^{1/2}$	$1^{1/2}$	1^3	$1^{1 1/2}$	Santos J A	1.70
	Get Behind Me		3	118	2	8	$7^{1/2}$	$6^{1/2}$	$2^{1/2}$	2^1	Krone J A	a-2.90
11Sep94 ^{1}Bel^3	Cozy Prospect		3	118	4	1	2^1	3^{hd}	3^1	$3^{4 1/2}$	Smith M E	4.50
10Aug94 ^{10}Sar^4	Acqua Santa	b	3	118	5	7	8	$7^{1 1/2}$	5^{hd}	4^4	Maple E	17.20
18Sep94 ^{3}Bel^3	Wild Surmise		3	118	3	6	4^1	$4^{2 1/2}$	4^1	5^{nk}	Davis R G	6.20
29Jly94 ^{2}Sar^5	Darien Cowboy	f	3	118	8	5	6^3	5^1	7^4	6^{nk}	Alvarado F T	4.60
	Whirlaroo		3	118	1	3	1^1	2^1	6^1	7^7	Wynter N A	a-2.90
2Sep94 ^{5}Bel^{10}	Tyler's Time	b	3	118	7	4	$5^{2 1/2}$	8	8	8	Velazquez J R	24.80

a-Coupled: Get Behind Me and Whirlaroo.

OFF AT 2:55 Start Good. Won driving. Time, :22^2, :45^4, :58, 1:11 Track fast.

$2 Mutuel Prices:			
5-(F)-EXPRESSED	5.40	2.80	2.20
1A-(B)-GET BEHIND ME (a-entry)		3.20	2.20
3-(D)-COZY PROSPECT			2.40

$2 EXACTA 5-1 PAID $19.60

Dk. b. or br. g, by Valid Appeal–Oedipus Rex, by Rexson. Trainer Domino Carl J. Bred by Mangurian Harry T Jr (Fla).

EXPRESSED never far back, rallied three wide to take the lead on the turn, extended his advantage in upper stretch then held sway under intermittent urging. GET BEHIND ME hit the side of the gate at the start, raced well back for a half, rallied between horses leaving the turn, angled to the middle of the track in upper stretch then closed steadily but could not get up. COZY PROSPECT forced the early pace between horses, dropped back slightly on the turn then finished willingly to gain a share. ACQUA SANTA was never a factor. WILD SURMISE raced in traffic on the far turn, angled out on the turn then lacked the needed response when called upon. DARIEN COWBOY saved ground to no avail. WHIRLAROO rushed up along the rail to gain the early lead then gave way leaving the turn. TYLER'S TIME was outrun. GET BEHIND ME and WHIRLAROO wore mud caulk

Owners— 1, Kinsman Stable; 2, Hobeau Farm; 3, Blue Goose Stable & Miller Leverett; 4, Leahy Thomas & Meriwether John W; 5, Old Lane Stable; 6, Andrews Edwin C; 7, Hobeau Farm; 8, Phillips John W

Trainers—1, Domino Carl J; 2, Jerkens H Allen; 3, Kelly Thomas J, 4, Freeman Willard C; 5, Penna Angel Jr; 6, Arnold George R II; 7, Jerkens H Allen; 8, Skiffington Thomas J

According to the chart of the fifth, Whirlaroo rushed up along the rail to get clear by a length after the first quarter and was within half a length of the lead after a half-mile in :45 4/5. Note also that he was one of *two* first time-starters saddled by Jerkens, and that the other, Get Behind Me, had springboarded off the early duel to finish second; could it be that Whirlaroo had been employed as a "rabbit," ensuring an honest pace for his stretch-running stablemate?

The sixth was a claimer for older, multiple winners:

SIXTH RACE
Belmont
SEPTEMBER 30, 1994

6 FURLONGS. (1.07^4) CLAIMING. Purse $14,500. 4-year-olds and upward. Weight, 122 lbs. Non-winners of two races since September 1, allowed 3 lbs. Of a race since then, 5 lbs. Claiming price $17,500, for each $1,000 to $15,500, allowed 2 lbs. (Races when entered to be claimed for $14,000 or less not considered)

Value of Race: $14,500 Winner $8,700; second $3,190; third $1,740; fourth $870. Mutuel Pool $209,963.00 Exacta Pool $408,275.00

Last Raced	Horse	M/Eqt.	A.	Wt	PP	St	¼	½	Str	Fin	Jockey	Cl'g Pr	Odds $1
17Sep94 2Bel12	Panico		4	115	3	1	11½	11½	12	12	Velazquez J R	16500	2.90
11Sep94 9Bel12	Game Wager	f	6	117	2	3	3½	2½	23	22½	Migliore R	17500	2.00
11Sep94 9Bel5	Border Cat	b	5	117	1	4	53½	56	3½	32½	Pezua J M	17500	6.30
20Sep94 9Bel7	Appealing Tracy	bf	5	113	6	5	43½	42	4½	41¾	Chavez J F	15500	3.80
20Jly94 9Bel1	Paraco	b	4	115	4	2	2½	31	55	55	Mojica R Jr	16500	3.00
18Jly94 6Bel7	Litigation Rex	bf	4	115	5	6	6	6	6	6	Graell A	16500	27.00

OFF AT 3:24 Start Good. Won driving. Time, $:23^3$, $:46^4$, $:58^2$, $1:10^3$ Track fast.

$2 Mutuel Prices:

1A-(D)-PANICO	7.80	3.60	2.60
3-(B)-GAME WAGER		3.40	2.60
2-(A)-BORDER CAT			3.20

$2 EXACTA 1-3 PAID $29.40

B. g, by Exclusive Era-Arusha Belle, by African Sky. Trainer Brida Dennis J. Bred by Dr & Mrs Bruce C Wells (Md).

PANICO outsprinted rivals for the early advantage, raced uncontested on the lead for a half then turned back GAME WAGER under brisk urging. GAME WAGER raced just off the pace to the top of the stretch but couldn't gain on the winner while best of the others. BORDER CAT reserved for a half while saving ground, failed to threaten with a mild late rally. APPEALING TRACY raced within striking distance while four wide to the turn then faded. PARACO was used up trying to keep the early pace. LITIGATION REX checked at the start, and was never close thereafter. GAME WAGER wore mud caulks.

Owners— 1, Payne C Beale; 2, Hauman Eugene E; 3, Ackerley Bros Farm & Ackerley R G; 4, Thor John; 5, Jewel-E Stables; 6, Cohen Max R

Trainers—1, Brida Dennis J; 2, Hushion Michael E; 3, Lake Robert P; 4, Sciacca Gary; 5, Friedman Mitchell; 6, Meittinis Louis N

Scratched— Line Pro (16Sep94 2BEL3), Nauset Flash (16Sep94 6MED5)

Panico wired the field through splits of :23 3/5 and :46 4/5, more than a full second slower at each call than Whirlaroo's race half an hour earlier.

The featured eighth, a $42,000 classified allowance, was the icing on the cake:

EIGHTH RACE
Belmont
SEPTEMBER 30, 1994

6½ FURLONGS. (1.14^3) ALLOWANCE. Purse $42,000. 3-year-olds and upward which have not won a race of $25,000 since May 1. Weights: 3-year-olds, 118 lbs; Older, 122 lbs. Non-winners of a race of $21,000 since August 1, allowed 3 lbs. Of such a race since June 1, 5 lbs. (Maiden, claiming, starter and restricted races not considered.)

Value of Race: $42,000 Winner $25,200; second $9,240; third $5,040; fourth $2,520. Mutuel Pool $182,875.00 Exacta Pool $281,867.00

Last Raced	Horse	M/Eqt.	A.	Wt	PP	St	¼	½	Str	Fin	Jockey	Odds $1
18Sep94 8Bel5	Rizzi	b	3	108	2	3	12½	12½	12	17½	Beckner D V5	2.30
29Aug94 4Sar2	Chief Desire	f	4	117	4	4	5	5	21½	22	Chavez J F	2.20
29Aug94 4Sar5	Won Song	b	4	117	3	1	42½	3hd	31	3¾	Santagata N	11.90
5Sep94 7Bel3	Lost Soldier		4	117	1	5	3hd	4hd	5	4nk	Velazquez J R	1.30
28Aug94 8Pha3	R. D. Wild Whirl	f	6	117	5	2	22	2½	4hd	5	Migliore R	10.50

OFF AT 4:22 Start Good For All But LOST SOLDIER. Won driving. Time, $:23^1$, $:46^2$, 1:10, 1:16 Track fast.

$2 Mutuel Prices:

2-(B)-RIZZI	6.60	3.80	3.60
4-(D)-CHIEF DESIRE		3.20	2.80
3-(C)-WON SONG			4.00

$2 EXACTA 2-4 PAID $21.00

B. c, (Feb), by Afleet-Top Wish, by Topsider. Trainer Jerkens H Allen. Bred by Kinghaven Farms Limited (Ont-C).

RIZZI sprinted clear in the early stages, raced uncontested on the lead into the stretch then drew off with authority. CHIEF DESIRE trailed for a half, rallied four wide to reach contention on the turn but was no match for the winner. WON SONG raced within striking distance between horses into upper stretch and lacked a strong closing bid. LOST SOLDIER stumbled at the start, rallied along the inside on the turn then flattened out. R. D. WILD WHIRL sat just behind the winner to the turn, faded. RIZZI, CHIEF DESIRE and WON SONG wore mud caulks.

Owners— 1, Hobeau Farm; 2, Hagedorn Charles G; 3, Anchel Edward & Judith; 4, Mohammed Al Maktoum; 5, Dommelf Robert W

Trainers—1, Jerkens H Allen; 2, Hushion Michael E; 3, Laboccetta Frank; 4, Mott William I; 5, Rowan Steve E

Scratched— Dalhart (7Aug94 8SAR6)

Rizzi, who also happened to call Jerkens' shedrow home, went wire-to-wire in :23 1/5 and :46 2/5 — splits that were each several ticks slower than Whirlaroo's race!

Whirlaroo's quarter of :22 2/5 had been the fastest of the day by several ticks, and he had been just half a length behind a :45 4/5 half mile that was faster by three lengths than any other sprint on the card, including the classified allowance. Whirlaroo figured to be loose on the lead through the opening half mile, and that's usually all it takes to win a maiden-claiming sprint.

The betting was fairly predictable. Since the crowd places its greatest emphasis on finish positions, beaten lengths and final time speed ratings, High Regent was their clear-cut favorite.

Whirlaroo had faded to finish seventh after being involved in that super-quick pace, so his resulting Beyer Speed Figure of 53 was 17 points less than what High Regent had earned on October 11. (Note that High Regent's route race on the same day as Whirlaroo's debut found him a length off a half mile split in :46 4/5, making his time approximately :47, which projected to put him several lengths behind Whirlaroo, who had run his half in slightly under :46.)

The fact that Whirlaroo had missed fifth by a pair of necks was known only to those who kept a file of result charts; a "5" as his official finish position instead of a "7" might very well have knocked his price down a point or two.

I reasoned that if Hobeau Farm and Allen Jerkens had been able to upset Kelso three times with Beau Purple, and had twice taken the measure of Secretariat (with Onion in the Whitney and Prove Out in the Woodward), they could beat High Regent with Whirlaroo.

FIRST RACE

Belmont

OCTOBER 14, 1994

7 FURLONGS. (1.20¹) MAIDEN CLAIMING. Purse $12,000. 3–year–olds and upward. Weights: 3–year–olds, 119 lbs. Older, 122 lbs. Claiming price $35,000, for each $2,500 to $30,000, allowed 2 lbs. (Day 37 of a 39 Day Meet. Clear. 64.)

Value of Race: $12,000 Winner $7,200; second $2,640; third $1,440; fourth $720. Mutuel Pool $166,677.00 Exacta Pool $350,264.00

Last Raced	Horse	M/Eql. A.Wt	PP	St	¼	½	Str	Fin	Jockey	Cl'g Pr	Odds $1
30Sep94 5Bel⁷	Whirlaroo	3 119	11	7	1¹½	12½	12½	1²	Wynter N A	35000	5.10
	Fog Storm	f 3 115	3	9	2½	2½	2⁴	2¹	Nelson D†	30000	5.80
21Sep94 9Bel⁸	Strike For Life	b 3 110	8	6	7ʰᵈ	4²	3¹	3⁵	Beckner D V⁵	30000	30.10
11Oct94 1Bel²	High Regent	b 3 119	7	1	3³	3⁵	4³	4²½	Smith M E	35000	1.60
29Jun94 9Bel⁸	Inside News	3 115	4	8	9²	8¹½	6ʰᵈ	5ⁿᵏ	Luzzi M J	30000	9.90
4Oct94 9Bel⁴	Iain's Storm	b 3 119	10	5	6ʰᵈ	5¹	5¹½	6⁶½	Mojica R Jr	35000	9.70
2Oct94 1Bel²	Charlie Cush	3 119	5	2	4ʰᵈ	6¹½	7³	7¹½	Chavez J F	35000	4.00
4Oct94 9Bel⁷	Kent Clark	3 115	1	11	11	11	8½	8ⁿᵏ	Pezua J M	30000	45.80
30Sep94 3Bel⁵	Crown Pearl	3 115	2	10	10⁸	10⁵	9½	9⁶½	Velazquez J R	30000	14.60
2Oct94 1Bel⁶	Manna Manna	3 110	9	4	5½	7¹	10⁸	10⁷½	Perez R M⁵	30000	53.30
18May94 5Bel⁸	Loyal Todd	bf 5 111	6	3	8²	9ʰᵈ	11	11	Rodriguez O⁷	30000	114.70

OFF AT 1:00 Start Good. Won driving. Time, :22², :45³, 1:11¹, 1:25 Track fast.

$2 Mutuel Prices:

11–(K)–WHIRLAROO	12.20	8.80	6.20
3–(C)–FOG STORM		8.20	5.80
8–(H)–STRIKE FOR LIFE			8.40

$2 EXACTA 11–3 PAID $135.00

B. g, (Feb), by Buckaroo–Swirlaway, by Sir Ivor. Trainer Jerkens H Allen. Bred by Hobeau Farm (Fla).

WHIRLAROO sprinted clear in the early stages, set the pace along the inside into the stretch then held sway under steady pressure. FOG STORM chased the winner the entire way but couldn't gain on that one while holding for the place. STRIKE FOR LIFE unhurried early, rallied four wide on the turn then closed steadily to gain a share. HIGH REGENT raced in close contention from outside to the turn and tired. INSIDE NEWS failed to threaten while improving his position in the stretch. IAIN'S STORM raced wide. CHARLIE CUSH was finished early while saving ground. KENT CLARK checked at the start, and was never close thereafter. CROWN PEARL never reached contention. MANNA MANNA was never a factor. LOYAL TODD steadied between horses at the half mile pole then was outrun. WHIRLAROO and FOG STORM wore mud caulks.

Owners— 1, Hobeau Farm; 2, Buxton Anne K; 3, Yorkes Arthur J; 4, Condren William & Cornacchia Joseph; 5, Gayno Stables & Gaylord Edward L; 6, Turchiarelli Anthony & Yvonne; 7, Pokoik Lee; 8, Lundy & McRich Stables & Sardo; 9, Juddmonte Farms; 10, Tam Ping W; 11, Krohn Nat

Trainers— 1, Jerkens H Allen; 2, Buxton Anne K; 3, Reynolds Patrick L; 4, Zito Nicholas P; 5, Dupps Kristina; 6, Weiss Richard M; 7, Sciacca Gary; 8, Lundy Sarah A; 9, Mott William I; 10, Lake Robert P; 11, Krohn Nat

†Apprentice Allowance Waived: Fog Storm (7).

Whirlaroo sprinted clear early and was under a steady drive to maintain a safe margin over Fog Storm, a first-timer from obscure connections who had attracted considerable support on the tote board.

Significantly, Whirlaroo was breaking toward the outside, which is ideally where handicappers want their potential winning frontrunners positioned in one-turn races. Horses with natural speed who break from outside posts are able to avoid getting shuffled back in the mad scramble for early position, and their jockeys are able to see the race developing in front of them: if they outbreak the field, a clear lead from whichever is deemed the most resilient path on the track is assured; if they break a step slow, or if others are sent hard for the lead, the outside breakers can settle into a stalking trip free and clear of traffic, avoiding a debilitating pace duel.

Of course, two-turn routes featuring short runs to the first bend are an entirely different matter. Under such conditions, saving ground is paramount, so the mad scramble usually takes place among horses breaking from the outside posts, as they scurry to avoid being fanned out to the parking lot.

An additional point regarding interpretation of odds is also called for here. Everything is relative. A maiden entered for a $30,000 tag by Shug McGaughey that is going of at 5-1 is being shunned like the plague by the cognoscenti. On the other hand, owner/trainer Anne K. Buxton was a virtual unknown in New York, so when she brought the unfashionably-bred Fog Storm into town off a handful of workouts at Atlantic City and the Meadowlands, the price of 5-1 was a signal that someone had an inkling about him. Evidently, they bet him to win, because the exacta on the third and fourth betting choices in the race came back an inflated $135.

Like the Ogden Phipps/Shug McGaughey barn, the Hobeau Farm/Allen Jerkens outfit is top shelf. Hobeau is owned by Jack Dreyfus, founder of the Dreyfus Mutual Fund, and Jerkens, at the age of 45, was the youngest trainer ever inducted into the Hall of Fame. Still, these guys are willing to drop lightly-raced horses into maiden claimers if they think that's what is required:

Candy Cone
Own: Hobeau Farm

B. g. 3 (Jan)
Sire: Chas Conerly (Big Burn)
Dam: Tandelee (Menocal)
Br: Hobeau Farm (Fla)
Tr: Jerkens H Allen 37 12 7 6 .32)

WYNTER N A (12 2 1 1 .17)

123

Lifetime Record:	8 4 2 1	$95,154
1995	5 2 2 1	$72,354	Turf	0 0 0 0
1994	3 2 0 0	$22,800	Wet	1 0 0 0
Aqu	2 2 0 0	$36,000	Dist	1 1 0 0	$20,400

2Apr95-6Aqu fst 1⅛	:48³ 1:13¹ 1:38⁴ 1:52¹	Alw 30940N2X	86 3 1 1¹ 1¹ 1⁵ 1⁵	Wynter N A	112	0.95	79−23	Candy Cone112⁵ Husky Harry118⁶ Skipsilver115	Handily 3
4Mar95-8Aqu fst 6f	:23¹ :46⁴ :59 1:11¹	Best Turn-G3	83 1 6 6⁵ 6⁴ 4⁶ 3⁶	Wynter N A	117	7.90	81−24	Da Hoss117³ Pat N Jac115³ Candy Cone117½	In traffic, drifted 9
24Feb95-8Aqu fst 1¹⁄₁₆	:24¹ :48³ 1:13⁴ 1:45³	Alw 34000N2X	77 7 3 2½ 2¹ 2⁴ 2⁷	Wynter N A	117	2.20	70−29	Guadalcanal119⁷ Candy Cone117² Larchmont117ʰᵈ	Willingly 7
5Feb95-7Aqu fst 6f	:23¹ :48 1:00³ 1:13⁴	FredCaposela53k	78 2 4 4⁴ 4³½ 3⁵ 2³	Wynter N A	117	2.60	71−28	Angle Of Pursuit114³ Candy Cone117⁷ Pat N Jac115½	Mild gain 5
11Jan95-7Aqu fst 6f	:23⁴ :48 1:00 1:12²	Alw 42000N$Y	82 4 5 2³ 2¹ 1ʰᵈ 1¹½	Wynter N A	115	*1.30	81−22	Candy Cone115¹½ Criminal Bundle115⁵½ Husky Harry115ⁿᵏ	Drifted in late 8
3Dec94-9Aqu fst 6f	:22³ :46³ :59 1:12	Clm 45000	85 6 3 3¹ 1² 1³ 1¹½	Wynter N A	113	*1.85	82−24	Candy Cone113½ Firm Decree117⁴½ Chute Boss117¹½	Driving 8
29Sep94-9Bel fst 6f	:22⁴ :46¹ :58⁴ 1:11³	Md 30000	70 8 3 2½ 1½ 1⁴ 1⁹	Wynter N A	114	3.40	83−15	Candy Cone114⁹ Suprise World118¹½ Firstontherun113½	Mild drive 10
23Sep94-3Bel my 6f	:22¹ :46¹ :58⁴ 1:12	Md 45000	41 1 6 5³½ 4²½ 5⁵ 5⁸½	Wynter N A	114	4.10	72−14	Hi Time Ruler115³ Dr. Shenanigans114² Pay Buddy109½	Saved ground 7

WORKOUTS: Apr 13 Bel tr.t 5f my 1:02 B 1/2 Mar 31 Bel tr.t 3f fst :36⁴ H 9/16 Mar 24 Bel tr.t 1 fst 1:43 B 1/1 Feb 23 Bel tr.t 3f fst :37³ B 5/13 Feb 17 Bel tr.t 7f fst 1:29² B 1/1 ●Feb 2 Bel tr.t 3f fst :34⁴ H 1/18

Two weeks prior to Whirlaroo's win, they dropped Candy Cone down to $30,000 for a lengthy score, also with Noel Wynter up.

THE PREDICTABLE TRIUMPHS of Maraud, O'Star and Whirlaroo were living, breathing attestation to James Quinn's advice; "Pace analysis beats pace ratings." To find such pace standouts, it isn't necessary to compile or subscribe to numerical ratings, which is not to say that doing so is wrong, just that there is more than one way to skin the pace cat.

But spot plays can be few and far between, the greatly expanded betting menus brought about by the simulcast explosion of the 1990s notwithstanding. A player's course of action isn't often so cut-and-dried at the racetrack (or at the satellite wagering facility, to be high-technically correct) as it is when the Whirlaroos of the world are involved, or at least it shouldn't be. For every Whirlaroo deserving a maximum bet as a most likely winner at 5-1, there are dozens of situations shaded in varying degrees of ambiguity.

One of the things that first attracted most of us to the game is that, with the rare exception of, say, a Secretariat in the Belmont Stakes, or a Spectacular Bid galloping around the track in a Woodward-walkover, there is no deterministic "right" answer to picking winners. Swarming all around us is uncertainty, confusion, and misconception. Ultimately, success comes when players learn to accept and function through the chaos and begin to consider their options in color, instead of searching for absolute choices in black-and-white.

Complex, competitive races offer flexible and creative players many different avenues of exploration; all that is required is a little common sense, some imagination, and the ability to think on one's feet.

As races go, handicappers will be hard-pressed to find a more complex, competitive event than the 17th running of the Flower Bowl Invitational handicap on Saturday, September 24.

Belmont Park

9

1¼ MILES. **(Inner Turf). (1:57^3) 17th Running of THE FLOWER BOWL INVITATIONAL HANDICAP. Purse $200,000. Grade I. Fillies and mares, 3–year–olds and upward. By invitation only with no subscription fees. The Purse to be divided 60% to the winner, 22% to second, 12% to third and 6% to fourth. The New York Racing Association Inc. will select a field of fourteen (14) invitees by Saturday, September 10. The assignment of weights for these invitees will be published on Wednesday, September 14. The owners and/or trainers of these (14) selected horses will be required to notify the New York Racing Association Inc. of their intentions of running or not, no later than Saturday, September 17. A list of alternates and their weight assignments will be published on Monday, September 19. The New York Racing Association Inc. reserves the right to reassign weight to any horse after the weights have been published. Starters to be named at the closing time of entries. Trophies will be presented to the winning owner, trainer and jockey. This race will be limited to 14 starters and alternates (High weights preferred). The New York Racing Association Inc. reserves the right to transfer this race to the main track.**

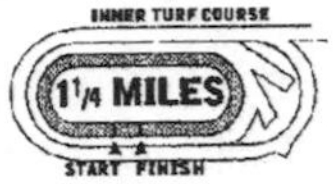

Mutuel field – Saratoga Source, Twice The Vice

Midnight Heights (GB)

Own: Team Valor Stables
SAMYN J L (37 6 2 5 .16)

B. f. 4
Sire: Persian Heights (Persian Bold)
Dam: Midnight Music (Midsummer Night II)
Br: Peacock Mrs R D & Swettenham Stud (GB)
Tr: Hennig Mark (13 3 1 1 .23)

112

Lifetime Record:	18 5 3 1	$132,611			
1994	5 0 0 1	$14,638	Turf	18 5 3 1	$132,611
1993	11 5 3 0	$117,973	Wet	0 0 0 0	
Bel [T]	0 0 0 0		Dist [T]	9 2 3 1	$89,906

29Aug94–7Sar fm 1⅜ [T] :50^1 1:15^3 1:40^3 2:16^4 3↑ ⒻWaya55k 92 5 6 5^5 3^3 4^{1¼} 4^{1¼} Bailey J D 113 5.30 81–18 SrtogSource113^{nk} Tiffny'sTylor113½ MrketBoostr122½ In traffic stretch 7
16Jly94◆ Newmarket(GB) gd 1½ [T]RH 2:31 3↑ ⒻAphrodite Stakes (Listed) Hcp 25700 7^{7½} Ryan W 130 8.00 Wandesta116^{1¾} Darrery128^2 Moon Carnival128^{no} 11 *Held up towards rear, never a factor*
Tr: John Dunlop
25Jun94◆ Curragh(Ire) gd 1¼ [T]RH 2:10^3 3↑ ⒻPretty Polly Stakes-G2 Stk 76400 4^{3¼} Roche C 132 6.00 Del Deya132^{nk} Ballykett Nancy120½ Kayfa132^{2½} 8 *Tracked leader, ridden 3f out, weakened inside final furlong*
12Jun94◆ San Siro(Ity) hy *1¼ [T]RH 2:07^2 3↑ ⒻPremio Legnano-G3 Stk 78200 3^3 Carson W 127 2.80 Alpride115^{2¾} Arkona127¾ Midnight Heights127^{1¼} 11 *Rated in 7th, improved 3f out, one-paced final furlong*
19May94◆ Goodwood(GB) yl 1¼ [T]RH 2:12^1 3↑ Festival Stakes (Listed) Stk 30500 5^{5¾} Munro A 122 10.00 Alderbrook124½ Wagon Master124^5 Instant Affair119^{hd} 12 *Rated in mid-pack, mild late gain. Only Royale 8th*
19Oct93◆ San Siro(Ity) hy *1½ [T]RH 2:44^2 3↑ ⒻPremio Giovanni Falck (Listed) Stk 50600 1¾ Munro A 120 *2.00 Midnight Heights120¾ Guest Harbour118^{2½} Seattle Jey118^{1½} 8 *Well placed in 3rd, rallied to lead 100y out*
26Sep93◆ Capannelle(Ity) sf *1¼ [T]RH 2:04^1 3↑ ⒻPremio Lydia Tesio-G2 Stk 114000 2^{1¼} Ryan W 120 *.90 Pracer120^{1¼} Midnight Heights120^{hd} Forthwith120^{nk} 7 *Reserved in 5th, bid 1-1/2f out, finished well w/o threatening*
12Sep93◆ Capannelle(Ity) gd *1¼ [T]RH 2:02^1 3↑ ⒻPremio Archidamia (Listed) Stk 52600 1^4 Ryan W 116 2.50 Midnight Heights116^4 Rose Violet116^{2¾} Dama Grande121^{1½} 9 *Tracked in 4th, led 2f out, easily clear*
18Aug93◆ York(GB) gd *1$\frac{5}{16}$ [T]LH 2:12^2 3↑ Fulford Rated Handicap Hcp 26100 13^{49½} Williams T 113 6.00 Stoney Valley118¾ Alberbrook124^{nk} Cumbrian Challenge123^{no} 13 *Unruly gate,chased in mid-pack, weakened 4f out, tailed off*
30Jly93◆ Goodwood(GB) yl 1¼ [T]RH 2:13^4 Spitfire Handicap Hcp 78000 2^{nk} Munro A 117 14.00 Western Cape124^{nk} Midnight Heights117^1 Al Senafi117½ 18 *Well placed in 5th,hard ridden 2f out,finishd well under pressure*

WORKOUTS: Sep 19 Bel 5f fst 1:02^1 B *23/35* Sep 13 Bel 4f fst :52 B *22/24* Aug 27 Sar tr.t 3f fst :37^2 B *5/13*

Danish (Ire)

Own: McCalmont H
KRONE J A (77 21 7 12 .27)

B. f. 3 (Apr)
Sire: Danehill (Danzig)
Dam: Tea House (Sassafras)
Br: McCalmont Major V (Ire)
Tr: Hammond John (1 0 1 0 .00)

113

Lifetime Record:	9 3 1 2	$54,074			
1994	4 2 0 2	$39,839	Turf	9 3 1 2	$54,074
1993	5 1 1 0	$14,235	Wet	0 0 0 0	
Bel [T]	0 0 0 0		Dist [T]	1 0 0 1	$7,409

28Aug94◆ Deauville(Fr) yl *1¼ [T]RH 2:14^4 ⒻPrix de la Nonette-G3 Stk 62900 3^1 Dubroeucq G 128 25.00 Grafin128½ Maidment128½ Danish128^{1½} 7 *Led to 150y out, no answer to first two*
27Jly94◆ La Teste(Fr) fm *1 [T]RH ⒻPrix La Sorellina (Listed) Stk 31500 1^{hd} Dubroeucq G 119 3.50 Danish119^{hd} Fire and Sword119^{1½} Amy Ride119½ 9 *Led after 1f, held gamely. Time not taken*
21Jun94◆ Saint-Cloud(Fr) gd *1 [T]LH 1:41^4 Prix Bosalino Alw 26900 1^{1½} Marcus B 120 4.80 Danish120^{1½} White Girl120½ Most Beautiful117^{nk} 9 *Wire to wire, driving*
23May94◆ Wissembourg(Fr) gd *7½f [T]LH Prix Martine Lutz Alw 7100 3^{4½} Gruhn D 123 Sigismond138^4 Son Brondo136½ Danish123½ 11 *Time not taken*
28Aug93◆ Curragh(Ire) gd 1 [T]Str 1:41^2 EBF Futurity Stakes-G3 Stk 34800 7^8 Hughes R 119 10.00 Cois Na Tine122¾ Ballykett Nancy119^2 City Nights122^{2½} 7 *Trailed throughout*
Tr: Michael Kauntze
14Aug93◆ Curragh(Ire) yl 7f [T]Str 1:31^2 EBF Tyros Stakes (Listed) Stk 20700 4^{3½} Gilson P ✓ 123 8.00 Majestic Role120¾ Gothic Dream123^2 Via Condotti123¾ 11 *Tracked leader, bid 2f out, dueled 1f out, faded late*
18Jly93◆ Naples(Ity) gd *7½f [T]LH 1:29 ⒻPremio FIA Breeders' Cup(Lstd) Stk 51200 7^{11} Supple W J 120 5.00 Michelle Hicks120^{2½} Suspiria120^{1½} Sopran Armony120¾ 8 *Always towards rear*
8Jun93◆ Leopardstwn(Ire) gd 6f [T]Str 1:13^2 ⒻSilver Flash EBF Stakes (Lstd) Stk 22400 2^1 O'Connor W J 122 *2.50 Las Meninas122^1 Danish122^1 Common Rumpus122^{nk} 9 *Dueled for a half, finished well under pressure*
14May93◆ Leopardstwn(Ire) sf 6f [T]Str 1:20^3 ⒻGoodbodys Stockbrokers EBF Mdn Maiden 12000 1¾ O'Connor W J 122 8.00 Danish122¾ Bassmaat122¾ Astronave122^{hd} 10 *Tracked in 3rd,led 1-1/2f out,drftd left,dueled briefly,prevailed*

Dahlia's Dreamer

Own: Paulson Madeleine

CHAVEZ J F (77 8 10 11 .10)

Ch. m. 5
Sire: Theatrical (Nureyev)
Dam: Dahlia (Vaguely Noble)
Br: Paulson Allen E (Ky)
Tr: Mott William I (28 5 5 5 .18)

112

Lifetime Record:	18 4 7 2	$188,538			
1994	7 1 3 1	$80,818	Turf	16 3 6 2	$174,678
1993	11 3 4 1	$107,720	Wet	1 0 1 0	$3,060
Bel Ⓣ	8 1 3 1	$98,078	Dist Ⓣ	4 0 3 0	$65,938

3Sep94-6Bel fm 1 1/16 [T] :25 :48 1:111 1:404 3↑ⒻAlw 38000N4X 100 1 1 11½ 1½ 1½ 2nk Velazquez J R 117 *.50 92-14 Irving's Girl117nk Dahlia's Dreamer11710 La Turka117¾ Gamely 5
10Jly94-8Bel fm 1¼ [T] :484 1:122 1:361 1:593 3↑ⒻNew York H-G2 99 4 1 11 11 1½ 2nk Velazquez J R 112 18.50 92-14 You'd Be Surprised118nk Dahlia's Dreamer1124½ Aquilegia1153 Gamely 6
9Jun94-8Bel fm 1 1/16 Ⓣ :243 :472 1:111 1:41 3↑ⒻAlw 36000N4X 79 3 3 2½ 1hd 52½ 78 Maple E 119 *2.40 85-07 La Piaf1193¼ Blazing Kadie119¾ Irving's Girl1192 Steadied, rank early 10
8May94-10Hia fm 1⅛ Ⓣ 1:463 3↑ⒻColumbiana H100k 92 1 3 32½ 22 22½ 36½ Day P L 114 1.60 98-08 Alice Springs1142½ Camiunch1144 Dahlia's Dreamer1142 Weakened 9
17Apr94-11Hia fm 1⅛ Ⓣ 1:481 3↑ⒻBlk Helen H-G3 94 2 1 11 11 1hd 32¾ Maple E L 113 10.60 95-10 Aquilegia113¾ ViaBorghese1161½ [D]Dhli'sDremer113hd Drifted in deep str 9
Disqualified and placed 4th
14Mar94-9GP fm *1 1/16 Ⓣ :233 :471 1:11 1:414+ ⒻAlw 33000N3X 95 2 2 21½ 2½ 12 12½ Smith M E L 116 *.60 108 — Dahlia's Dreamer1162½ Verbal Volley1161¾ La Turka116nk Ridden out 10
9Feb94-7GP fm *1 1/16 Ⓣ :241 :471 1:11 1:462+ ⒻAlw 30000N3X 91 1 1 1hd 11½ 21½ 24½ Smith M E L 116 *.70 80-17 Track Gossip1164½ Dahlia's Dreamer1165½ Fly So High1161½ Best of others 8
30Oct93-8Bel sf 1⅜ [T] :471 1:123 1:382 2:17 3↑ⒻAthenia H-G3 88 5 1 11½ 11 35 39¼ Velazquez J R 110 3.20e 57-32 Trampoli1171½ KirovPremiere1108 Dahlia'sDremer1103 Speed, weakened 8
11Sep93-8Bel sf 1¼ [T] :492 1:142 1:391 2:034 3↑ⒻFlowr Bwl H-G1 97 4 1 12½ 1½ 2hd 2½ Velazquez J R 110 14.00 70-24 Far Out Beast111½ Dahlia's Dreamer110½ Lady Blessington1183¾ Gamely 10
27Aug93-6Sar fm 1 1/16 Ⓣ :233 :464 1:104 1:412 3↑ⒻAlw 32500N3X 87 9 3 31 31½ 3½ 22 Krone J A 117 *.80 85-12 Tiffny'sTylor1172 Dhli'sDrmr117½ LifIsDlcous1142½ Steadied, rank, block 9

WORKOUTS: Sep 22 Bel 4f fst :48 B 4/52 Sep 14 Bel 4f fst :49 B 17/39 Sep 1 Bel 4f fst :493 B 20/26 Aug 24 Bel tr.t 7f fst 1:28 B 1/1 ●Aug 16 Bel tr.t 5f fst 1:003 H 1/13 ●Aug 7 Bel 4f fst :471 H 1/25

Irish Linnet

Own: Delaney Austin

VELAZQUEZ J R (76 6 5 12 .08)

B. m. 6
Sire: Seattle Song (Seattle Slew)
Dam: Royal Slip (Royal Match)
Br: Delaney Austin (NY)
Tr: O'Brien Leo (42 4 5 3 .10)

116

Lifetime Record:	50 14 14 7	$859,226			
1994	8 3 3 1	$207,398	Turf	45 13 12 6	$831,026
1993	10 2 3 1	$155,648	Wet	0 0 0 0	
Bel Ⓣ	13 6 3 2	$260,026	Dist Ⓣ	1 0 0 0	

10Sep94-8Bel fm 1 1/16 [T] :233 :462 1:102 1:392 3↑ⒻNobleDamselHG3 107 2 3 32 3nk 15 16½ Velazquez J R 117 4.20 99-11 Irish Linnet1176½ Statuette1131 Cox Orange117¾ Driving 10
17Aug94-9Sar fm 1⅛ [T] :464 1:10 1:334 1:462 3↑Ⓕ[S]Yaddo H86k 103 6 4 43 31½ 22 11 Velazquez J R 123 *1.50 95-10 Irish Linnet1231 It's Personal1115 All Tango1105 Driving 10
27Jly94-9Sar yl 1 1/16 Ⓣ :233 :473 1:122 1:433 3↑ⒻSar Bud BCH155k 93 1 1 1½ 1hd 31 54¾ Velazquez J R 117 5.60 71-24 WeekendMdness115¾ You'dBeSurprised120nk Hd1103 Dueled, weakened 8
19Jun94-6Pen fm 1 1/16 Ⓣ 1:391 3↑ⒻPen Bud BCH76k 100 2 6 69 62½ 31½ 11 Velazquez J R 122 *1.20 96-09 Irish Linnet1221 Sh Bang115no Highland Crystal1181½ Closed well inside 7
5Jun94-8Bel fm 1⅜ [T] :47 1:11 1:351 2:113 3↑ⒻShpshdBay H-G3 101 2 1 11½ 11½ 11½ 2½ Velazquez J R 115 12.40 95-08 Market Booster114½ Irish Linnet1151 Fairy Garden120hd Gamely 9
20May94-8GS yl *1⅛ Ⓣ :48 1:131 1:393 1:501+ 3↑ⒻVineland H-G3 97 2 4 43½ 42 32 31 Santos J A 117 2.30 86-17 Cox Orange116½ Highland Crystal113½ Irish Linnet1176¾ Good try 6
30Apr94-8Aqu fm 1 1/16 Ⓣ :241 :483 1:122 1:431 3↑ⒻBeaugay H-G3 98 3 4 31½ 31 2½ 2½ Chavez J F 116 *1.20 92-07 Cox Orange112½ Irish Linnet116¾ Statuette1162½ Steadied early 5
21Apr94-8Aqu yl 1 1/16 Ⓣ :243 :501 1:151 1:464 3↑ Handicap46k 99 1 3 42 41¾ 2½ 21½ Chavez J F 115 3.60 74-28 Personal Draw1141½ Irish Linnet115no River Majesty122½ Took up 1/8 pl 6
13Nov93-8Crc sf 7½f Ⓣ 1:311 3↑ⒻMiss Trpcl H50k 81 3 9 77¼ 66 66½ 55½ Vasquez J 119 *1.00 — Chickasha1132 Drina1151¾ Northern Nation110no Belated bid 11
23Oct93-8Aqu sf 1 Ⓣ :23 :472 1:131 1:391 3↑ⒻAqu Bdw B C157k 97 10 10 910 96 77 32 Migliore R 116 6.00 78-20 One Dreamer1162 Ecnie MeenieMiney111no IrishLinnet116nk Belated rally 10

WORKOUTS: Sep 4 Bel 5f fst 1:014 B 22/36 Aug 11 Sar tr.t 4f fst :513 B 15/24 Jly 19 Sar tr.t 4f fst :492 B 2/6 Jly 12 Bel 5f fst 1:014 B 12/40 Jly 3 Bel 5f fst 1:002 H 4/21

Agathe

Own: Wildenstein Daniel

SMITH M E (97 20 12 9 .21)

Ch. f. 3 (Jan)
Sire: Manila (Lyphard)
Dam: Albertine (Irish River)
Br: Allez France Stables Ltd (Ky)
Tr: Fabre Andre (—)

117

Lifetime Record:	6 1 2 2	$171,363			
1994	4 1 1 1	$160,040	Turf	6 1 2 2	$171,363
1993	2 M 1 1	$11,323	Wet	0 0 0 0	
Bel Ⓣ	0 0 0 0		Dist Ⓣ	1 1 0 0	$36,880

6Aug94♦ Deauville(Fr) gd *1¼ ⓉRH 2:073 ⒻPrix de Psyche-G3 Stk 62700 1nk Peslier O 123 *1.00e Agathe123nk Truly a Dream128hd My Trim123no 9
Led after 1-1/2f,gamely held off simultaneous late challenges
12Jun94♦ Chantilly(Fr) gd *1 5/16 ⓉRH 2:074 ⒻPrix de Diane (French Oaks)-G1 Stk 424000 32½ Peslier O 128 5.20 East of the Moon128hd Her Ladyship1282½ Agathe128½ 9
Led,2nd after 3f,bid over 1f out,outfinished
15May94♦ Longchamp(Fr) gd *1 ⓉRH 1:37 ⒻPoule d'Essai des Pouliches-G1 Stk 296000 21½ Peslier O 128 7.20e East of the Moon1281½ Agathe128nk Belle Argentine1282½ 8
3rd along rail,in tight over 1f out,held 2nd
24Apr94♦ Longchamp(Fr) fm *1 ⓉRH 1:38 ⒻPrix de la Grotte-G3 Stk 58900 42½ Peslier O 128 4.50 Flagbird1281 East of the Moon1281 Belle Argentine128nk 8
Rated in 6th, finished well without threatening
28Sep93♦ Saint-Cloud(Fr) sf *1 ⓉLH 1:492 ⒻPrix Seria Alw 29700 2¾ Jarnet T 128 *1.00 Three Angels128¾ Agathe1281 Zapata Beauty128nk 8
Rank in 3rd, led 1f out, headed 100y out
7Sep93♦ Longchamp(Fr) fm *1 ⓉRH 1:404 ⒻPrix de la Cascade Mdn (FT)29600 3½ Jarnet T 128 *.70e Sail Storm128½ Three Angels128hd Agathe1281½ 6
Tracked in 3rd, lacked room 1f out, finished well

Grafin

Own: Salman Fahd

MIGLIORE R (56 6 11 5 .11)

Ch. f. 3 (Mar)
Sire: Miswaki (Mr. Prospector)
Dam: Reigning Countess (Far North)
Br: Robertson Corbin J (Ky)
Tr: Boutin Francois (—)

114

Lifetime Record:	5 3 1 1	$84,947			
1994	5 3 1 1	$84,947	Turf	5 3 1 1	$84,947
1993	0 M 0 0		Wet	0 0 0 0	
Bel Ⓣ	0 0 0 0		Dist Ⓣ	1 1 0 0	$37,048

28Aug94♦ Deauville(Fr) yl *1¼ ⓉRH 2:144 ⒻPrix de la Nonette-G3 Stk 62900 1½ Head F 128 6.20 Grafin128½ Maidment128½ Danish1281½ 7
Tracked in 4th,bid 1f out,hard ridden to lead final 16th,held
4Aug94♦ Deauville(Fr) gd *1 ⓉRH 1:412 ⒻPrix de la Calonne (Listed) Stk 38600 11 Asmussen C 123 *.70e Grafin1231 Moivouloirtoi1231½ Sarmatie1234 9
Well placed in 3rd, led 70y out, driving
3Jly94♦ Saint-Cloud(Fr) gd *7f ⓉLH 1:241 ⒻPrix Amandine (Listed) Stk 38700 32½ Asmussen C 128 *1.50e Shamaniya1281 Blue Burgee1281½ Grafin128hd 9
Unruly pre-start,3rd on rail,evenly late
16Jun94♦ Longchamp(Fr) gd *1 ⓉRH 1:41 ⒻPrix Fould Alw 30200 11½ St-Martin E 128 *1.50 Grafin1281½ Terney123hd Athykaneyev128¾ 6
Unhurried in 5th,bid 1-1/2f out, led 1f out,driving
12May94♦ Longchamp(Fr) gd *1 ⓉRH 1:432 ⒻPrix des Ternes Alw 29400 21 Asmussen C 123 8.20 Gravure Bleue1231 Grafin123hd Pink Shade1281 14
Close up early,7th halfway,rallied between horses,up for 2nd

Trampoli

Own: Salman Fahd

QUINN T R (—)

Dk. b or br m. 5
Sire: Trempolino (Sharpen Up-GB)
Dam: Luth de Saron (Luthier)
Br: Mayland Stud (Ky)
Tr: Clement Christophe (20 5 2 2 .25)

120

Lifetime Record:	19 9 2 2	$594,821			
1994	4 3 0 0	$237,600	Turf	19 9 2 2	$594,821
1993	8 4 1 1	$250,040	Wet	0 0 0 0	
Bel Ⓣ	8 6 0 0	$273,840	Dist Ⓣ	7 4 0 0	$118,868

13Sep94-8Bel fm 1¼ [T] :482 1:124 1:364 2:001 3↑ⒻAlw 46000N$mY 97 4 2 23 2½ 11 1½ Smith M E 117 *.70 89-12 Trampoli117½ Saratoga Source1223½ Silky Feather1176 Driving 4
5Jun94-8Bel fm 1⅜ [T] :47 1:11 1:351 2:113 3↑ⒻShpshdBay H-G3 84 6 5 612 43½ 74½ 810 Smith M E 123 2.70 86-08 MarketBooster114½ IrishLinnet1151 FairyGarden120hd Bid, flattened out 9
16Mar94-8GP fm 1½ Ⓣ :474 1:122 2:01 2:252 3↑ⒻOrchid H-G2 103 7 5 53½ 2hd 1½ 11½ Smith M E 121 *.50 93-08 Trampoli1211½ GoodMorningSmile110¾ NorthernEmerld1121½ Ridden out 7
1Jan94-10Crc fm 1½ Ⓣ :491 1:133 2:032 2:28 3↑ⒻLaPrvntInvH-G2 103 9 7 63½ 42½ 1hd 12½ Smith M E 120 *1.40 90-10 Trampoli1202½ Putthepowdertoit1151½ Adoryphar1121½ 14
Steadied final turn, drew clear
17Oct93-8Bel sf 1½ Ⓣ :512 1:164 2:07 2:312 3↑ⒻLong Islnd HG2 103 1 4 42 1½ 1½ 1nk Smith M E 119 *1.10 65-35 Trampoli119nk Bright Generation1144¾ Northern Emerald10811 Driving 5
30Oct93-8Bel sf 1⅜ [T] :471 1:123 1:382 2:17 3↑ⒻAthenia H-G3 105 6 6 66 21 11½ 11½ Smith M E 117 2.70 66-32 Trampoli1171½ Kirov Premiere1108 Dahlia's Dreamer1103 Driving 8
7Aug93-9Sar gd 1½ [T] :473 1:13 2:051 2:301 3↑ Swrd Dncr H-G1 — 7 4 68½ 917 — — Samyn J L 111 12.20 — 27 Spectacular Tide1122¾ Square Cut112¾ Dr. Kiernan117½ Tired, eased 9
17Jly93-8Bel fm 1⅜ [T] :50 1:143 1:384 2:14 3↑ⒻShpshd Bay HG3 98 1 4 43 42½ 3½ 1hd 1nk Smith M E 116 *1.60 81-16 Trampoli116nk Aquilegia116no Revasser1141 Driving 4
19Jun93-8Bel fm 1¼ [T] :471 1:111 1:35 1:59 3↑ⒻNew York H-G2 92 5 8 47 3½ 42 54 Smith M E 118 b *2.80 91-11 Aquilegia114no Via Borghese117¾ Ginny Dare1083 Pinched break 11
13May93-1Bel fm 1¼ [T] :483 1:13 1:37 2:003 3↑ⒻHandicap46k 97 6 5 55½ 52½ 31½ 1½ Smith M E 122 *.50 87-13 Trampoli122½ Ginny Dare111no Mckaymackenna1182½ Driving 6

WORKOUTS: Sep 22 Bel [T] 4f fm :503 B (d)6/17 Sep 10 Bel 3f fst :36 H 4/25 Sep 3 Bel 4f fst :502 B 42/50 Aug 24 Sar tr.tⓉ 4f gd :484 B 2/14 Aug 22 Sar tr.tⓉ 3f sf :38 B (d)1/3

Via Borghese

Own: Parrish Malcolm E

SANTOS J A (84 10 11 6 .12)

B. m. 5
Sire: Seattle Dancer (Nijinsky II)
Dam: Angela Serra (Arctic Tern)
Br: Bedford Farms & Panama Foreign Traders (Ky)
Tr: Penna Angel Jr (7 1 0 1 .14)

117

Lifetime Record:	20 11 4 1	$630,304			
1994	5 2 1 0	$157,210	Turf	20 11 4 1	$630,304
1993	9 5 3 0	$404,797	Wet	0 0 0 0	
Bel ⓣ	1 0 1 0	$27,412	Dist ⓣ	4 0 2 0	$136,888

14Aug94-9Sar sf 1⅛ Ⓣ :501 1:143 1:392 1:52 3+ ⒻDiana H-G2 104 2 1 1¹ 1¹ 1½ 1² Santos J A 115 4.90 75-25 Via Borghese115² Blazing Kadie110¹ Coronation Cup108⁵ Driving 7
30Jly94-6Atl fm 1³⁄₁₆ ⓣ :484 1:122 1:372 1:551 3+ ⒻMatchmaker-G2 93 2 5 54½ 52¾ 53 45¼ Santos J A L 115 3.60 80-14 Alice Springs118¾ Hero's Love118½ Cox Orange118nk Rallied late 8
17Apr94-11Hia fm 1⅛ ⓣ 1:481 3+ ⒻBlk Helen H-G3 97 9 4 31½ 31½ 31 2¾ Smith M E L 116 *1.50 96-10 Aquilegia113¾ Via Borghese116½ ⒹDahlia's Dreamer113hd Gamely 9
12Mar94-4GP fm 1⅛ ⓣ :231 :461 1:10 1:392 + 3+ ⒻBuckrm Oak HG3 94 6 4 31⁶ 41⁵ 52½ 55¾ Bailey J D L 119 *.90 93-02 Marshua's River115⁵½ Sheila's Revenge117no Tango Charlie115nk 7
Late rally between horses
26Feb94-8GP fm *1 ⓣ :23 :462 1:103 1:37 ⒻAlw 42000N$mY 99 5 7 76½ 54½ 1½ 1nk Bailey J D L 114 *.50 95-11 Via Borghese114nk Topsa114¾ Too Loud116⁴ 10
Steadied top str, driving inside
23Oct93-10Lrl yl 1⅛ ⓣ :482 1:132 1:383 1:512 3+ ⒻAll Along-G2 102 2 4 45½ 45½ 31½ 2no Velasquez J L 118 *.70 73-32 Lady Blessington116no Via Borghese118hd Logan's Mist116½ Gamely 5
28Aug93-9AP gd 1³⁄₁₆ ⓣ :492 1:133 1:38 1:553 3+ ⒻBeverly D-G1 102 4 4 42½ 31½ 31 3nk Velasquez J L 123 7.00 88-11 ⒹLet's Elope123no Flawlessly123nk Via Borghese123no Crowded late 7
Placed second through disqualification.
8Aug93-10Rkm fm *1⅛ ⓣ 1:464 3+ ⒻSpcy Lvng H-G3 103 2 5 56 44½ 31 1² Velasquez J LB 121 *.70 100-08 Via Borghese121² Ginny Dare112¹ Saratoga Source114¹ Driving 9
4Jly93-11Rkm fm 1¹⁄₁₆ ⓣ :231 :473 1:114 1:43 3+ ⒻRkm BC H104k 103 6 4 54 53 12½ 12¾ Velasquez J L 115 *.60 98-10 Via Borghese115²¾ Navarra113² Miss Otis110¹ Mild drive 9
19Jun93-8Bel fm 1¼ Ⓣ :471 1:111 1:35 1:59 3+ ⒻNew York H-G2 101 3 3 36½ 2hd 2½ 2no Velasquez J 117 3.80 95-11 Aquilegia114no Via Borghese117¾ Ginny Dare108³ Sharp try 11

WORKOUTS: Sep 21 Bel 5f fst 1:023 B 22/31 Sep 16 Bel Ⓣ 6f fm 1:134 H 1/1 Sep 10 Bel 6f fst 1:141 H 3/12 Sep 4 Bel 4f fst :491 B 27/40 Aug 26 Sar tr.tⓣ 4f sf :521 B (d) 9/9 Aug 9 Sar 5f fst 1:032 B 13/16

Empress Club (Arg)

Own: Jaffee Laurence

DAVIS R G (71 10 9 13 .14)

Dk. b or br m. 6
Sire: Farnesio (Good Manners)
Dam: Elysee (El Gran Capitan)
Br: Haras Abolengo (Arg)
Tr: Pinnell Charles (—)

116

Lifetime Record:	25 16 2 1	$1,146,906			
1994	5 1 0 1	$74,500	Turf	25 16 2 1	$1,146,906
1993	6 3 0 0	$305,280	Wet	0 0 0 0	
Bel ⓣ	0 0 0 0		Dist ⓣ	5 2 1 0	$456,845

3Sep94-6BM fm 1¹⁄₁₆ ⓣ :233 :47 1:104 1:423 3+ ⒻHillsbrgh H-G3 95 3 5 54½ 54 3½ 1¹ Chapman T M B 119 6.00 95-07 Empress Club119¹ Ask Anita116hd Zoonaqua114nk Rallied far wide 7
29Jly94-3Dmr fm 1¹⁄₁₆ ⓣ :25 :494 1:134 1:441 3+ ⒻAlw 55000N$mY 90 3 3 42½ 42½ 52¾ 32¼ Delahoussaye E B 122 3.60 83-14 User Friendly115¹½ Lyphard's Delta122¹ Empress Club122½ Up for 3rd 5
3Jly94-8Hol fm 1⅛ ⓣ :48 1:111 1:35 1:472 + 3+ ⒻBevrlyHllsH-G1 89 5 1 1hd 2hd 31 66 Black C A B 116 24.10 81-14 Corrazona119nk HollywoodWildcat124no Flwlessly124¹ Dueled, weakened 7
12Jun94-8Hol fm 1⅛ ⓣ :464 1:10 1:341 1:462 + 3+ ⒻGamely H-G1 99 1 5 54½ 42 62¾ 45¼ Black C A B 118 8.30 87-10 Hollywood Wildcat122²½ Mz.ZillBear114²¾ Flawlessly124nk 4 wide into lane 6
21May94-4Hol fm 1 ⓣ :234 :463 1:101 1:343 ⒻⓇConvenienceH62k 90 2 6 66½ 76½ 74 61¾ Gonzalez S Jr B 121 3.60 89-10 Camilla Blu114hd Dis Moi Tout117nk ⒹⒽCargo118 Late bid 8
31Jly93♦ Clairwood(SAf) gd *1⅛ ⓣRH 1:52 3+ Mainstay International Hcp-G2 Stk 148000 95 Marcus A 127 *1.40 Secret Rites118 Flaming Rock128 Seal Ring116 17
Tr: A T Millard *Chased in 6th, one-paced last quarter*
3Jly93♦ Greyville(SAf) gd *1¼ ⓣRH 2:131 3+ Rothmans July Handicap-G1 Stk 300000 72½ Coetzee F 128 3.00 Dancing Duel114 Gaelic Find118 Flaming Rock128 19
Mid-pack for over a mile, in tight, mild late gain
27Mar93♦ Gosforth Pk(SAf) gd *1¼ ⓣLH 2:043 3+ Administrator's Cup-G1 Stk 393000 75½ Coetzee F 128 *.40 Cardinal Fury118no Please Be True117¹ Gaelic Find119 15
Tracked in 4th, briefly 3rd over 2f out, faded
6Mar93♦ Turffontein(SAf) yl *1 ⓣRH 1:39 3+ First National Bank 1600-G3 Stk 130000 12½ Marcus A 122 *.15 Empress Club122²½ Please Be True122½ Queen's Gold127 13
Well placed in 4th, led over 2f out, drew clear
30Jan93♦ Kenilworth(SAf) gd *1¼ ⓣLH 2:022 3+ Metropolitan Stakes-G1 Stk 259000 11¾ Marcus A 122 *.60 Empress Club122¹¾ Flaming Rock128 Secret Rites119 20
Rated in 7th, 3rd 2f out, rallied to lead approaching final furlong

WORKOUTS: Sep 22 Bel Ⓣ 4f fm :54 B (d) 17/17 ●Sep 14 SLR tr.t 4f fst :472 B 1/4 Aug 29 SLR tr.t 4f fst :493 H 8/8 ●Aug 23 SLR tr.t 5f fst :591 H 1/6 Aug 10 SLR tr.t 4f fst :472 H 1/2 Jly 20 SLR tr.t 5f fst 1:011 H 2/7

Alywow

Own: Kinghaven Farms

PENNA D (—)

B. f. 3 (Feb)
Sire: Alysheba (Alydar)
Dam: Triple Wow (Coastal)
Br: Kinghaven Frms Ltd. & Kinghaven Mngmnt Inc. (Ont-C)
Tr: Attfield Roger L (—)

114

Lifetime Record:	12 6 2 3	$312,103			
1994	6 3 0 2	$207,009	Turf	5 5 0 0	$211,882
1993	6 3 2 1	$105,094	Wet	2 1 1 0	$52,650
Bel ⓣ	0 0 0 0		Dist ⓣ	0 0 0 0	

10Sep94-7WO fm 1¹⁄₁₆ ⓣ :224 :45 1:091 1:394 3+ ⒻCan BCH-G1C 96 6 9 10¹⁰ 85½ 3nk 1² Penna D L 115 *.80 98-02 Alywow115² Bold Ruritana116½ Myrtle Irene120² Strong wide rally 10
3Aug94-9Sar yl 1¹⁄₁₆ ⓣ :231 :48 1:123 1:434 ⒻNijana-G3 101 6 9 96½ 53 41 13½ Smith M E 121 2.80 75-25 Alywow121³½ Irish Forever121no Knocknock114² Wide, driving 9
Run in divisions
19Jun94-9WO fst 1⅛ :472 1:12 1:371 1:493 ⒻⓈCanadianOaksG1 90 2 9 109½ 75½ 45 33 Penna D L 121 3.35e 95-12 Plenty Of Sugar121³ Mysteriously121no Alywow121½ 10
Broke step slowly, advanced three wide final turn, gave best stretch
5Jun94-10WO fst 1¹⁄₁₆ :23 :471 1:114 1:431 ⒻSelene-G1C 86 5 7 79 68 49 37½ Penna D L 123 3.85 93-08 Holly Regent116½ Stellarina113⁶ Alywow123⁶ 7
Five wide final turn, finished well
20May94-9Pim fst 1⅛ :47 1:114 1:374 1:51 ⒻBlackEydSsn-G2 78 10 13 12¹³ 12¹⁴ 71⁴ 510¼ Pino M G L 119 f 6.30 79-24 Calipha114²½ Bunting114⁷ Golden Braids114¹ No threat 13
30Apr94-11Pim fm 1¹⁄₁₆ ⓣ :233 :483 1:123 1:434 ⒻLady Dean55k 75 1 8 81⁰ 86½ 11½ 13¾ Pino M G 119 f 2.40 82-17 Alywow119³¾ Night Fax114³ Premier Mombo119no Wide, driving 10
16Oct93-9WO sly 1¹⁄₁₆ :232 :471 1:123 1:454 ⒻPr Elzabth-G1C 72 5 4 51¹ 56 34½ 2⁴ Seymour D J 119 *.95 83-10 Term Limits119⁴ Alywow119no Blushing Blond119⁵½ 6
Couldn't handle track, widest, game effort for place
18Sep93-7WO fm 1 Ⓣ :233 :481 1:14 1:394 ⒻNatalma-G1C 70 7 7 76¾ 52½ 2² 1½ Seymour D J 116 *1.10 78-18 Alywow116½ Quiet Cheer116⁴ Seymoura Mary114¹½ 9
Five wide final turn, driving. Run in divisions
4Sep93-3WO my 7f ⊗ :223 :452 1:103 1:242 ⒻAlw 33200NC 73 7 1 45 46 35 1² Seymour D J 114 2.75 89-11 Alywow114² Lets Be Alert116½ Do It Fast114²½ Driving outside 7
13Aug93-4WO fm *7f Ⓣ :243 :483 1:144 1:264 ⒻMd Sp Wt 60 2 3 21½ 21½ 21 11½ Seymour D J 117 *1.40 85-15 Alywow117¹½ Seymoura Mary117½ Quiet Cheer117¹¾ Good late response 10

WORKOUTS: ●Sep 20 WO tr.t 5f fst 1:01 B 1/6 Sep 4 WO tr.t Ⓣ 6f fm 1:132 B (d) 2/11 Aug 29 WO 5f fst 1:01 B 2/29 Aug 17 Sar 4f fst :474 H 6/70 Aug 13 Sar 4f fst :482 B 3/35 ●Jly 29 Sar tr.tⓣ 5f sf 1:012 H 1/15

Market Booster

Own: Moyglare Stud

LUZZI M J (81 12 8 7 .15)

B. m. 5
Sire: Green Dancer (Nijinsky II)
Dam: Final Figure (Super Concorde)
Br: Moyglare Stud Farm Ltd (Ky)
Tr: Lukas D Wayne (6 3 1 1 .50)

115

Lifetime Record:	25 6 4 3	$517,698			
1994	8 1 0 2	$82,584	Turf	21 6 4 2	$508,698
1993	5 1 1 0	$189,775	Wet	2 0 0 0	
Bel ⓣ	2 1 0 0	$66,960	Dist ⓣ	6 2 1 0	$235,395

29Aug94-7Sar fm 1⅜ Ⓣ :501 1:153 1:403 2:164 3+ ⒻWaya55k 93 2 1 2½ 1¹ 3nk 3¾ Santos J A 122 b 3.40 81-18 Saratoga Source113nk Tiffany's Taylor113½ Market Booster122½ Gamely 7
10Jly94-8Bel fm 1¼ Ⓣ :484 1:122 1:361 1:593 3+ ⒻNew York H-G2 70 2 2 21 42½ 67½ 613¾ Santos J A 116 b 5.70 78-14 You'd Be Surprised118nk Dahlia's Dreamer112⁴½ Aquilegia115³ Tired 6
5Jun94-8Bel fm 1⅜ Ⓣ :47 1:11 1:351 2:113 3+ ⒻShpshdBay H-G3 102 9 3 36½ 33½ 21½ 1½ Santos J A 114 b 21.00 96-08 Market Booster114½ Irish Linnet115¹ Fairy Garden120hd Driving 9
6May94-7CD wf 1¹⁄₁₆ :24 :48 1:122 1:433 3+ ⒻLouisvlBdBCHG2 80 4 2 21½ 44½ 71⁴ 715¼ Day P L 111 b 13.70 81-10 One Dreamer115⁴ Kalita Melody117³ Added Asset114³ Gave way 7
6Mar94-8SA fst 1⅛ :464 1:104 1:36 1:49 ⒻS Margrita HG1 84 5 1 1hd 2hd 65½ 71² Day P LB 114 41.20 76-18 Paseana123²¾ Kalita Melody117hd Stalcreek119² Inside duel 9
12Feb94-8SA fst 1¹⁄₁₆ :231 :471 1:11 1:414 ⒻS Maria H-G1 91 4 3 51½ 52½ 67 67½ Solis A LB 116 b 26.70 79-14 Supah Gem116no Paseana124no Alysbelle116½ Saved ground 7
27Jan94-8SA fst 1¹⁄₁₆ :232 :462 1:102 1:42 ⒻAlw 58500N$mY 89 1 3 43½ 43½ 41¾ 31¾ Solis A LB 119 4.90 83-16 Thirst For Peace117½ Party Cited121½ MarketBooster119⁴ Finished well 4
9Jan94-8SA fm 1⅛ ⓣ :47 1:11 1:352 1:473 ⒻS Grgonio H-G2 84 6 7 63¾ 64 108½ 97¾ McCarron C J LB 120 4.70 73-19 Hero's Love119½ Skimble118½ Miss Turkana118¾ Gave way 10
14Nov93-8SA fm 1¼ ⓣ :50 1:144 1:382 2:024 3+ ⒻYel Rbn Inv-G1 90 4 7 74¾ 52½ 87 94¾ Kinane M J LB 122 8.50f 68-27 PossiblyPerfect118¹½ Tribulation118hd Miatuschk122no Bumped hard start 13
3Oct93♦ Longchamp(Fr) hy *1½ ⓣRH 2:374 3+ Prix de l'Arc de Triomphe-G1 Stk 1500000 108½ Kinane M J 127 77.00 Urban Sea127nk White Muzzle123½ Opera House130¾ 23
Tr: Dermot K Weld *Well placed in 5th, weakening when bumped 1-1/2f out*

WORKOUTS: Sep 21 Bel 4f fst :502 B 27/35 Sep 15 Bel Ⓣ 5f fm 1:032 B (d) 12/13 Sep 8 Bel Ⓣ 4f fm :504 B (d) 11/11 Aug 22 Sar tr.tⓣ 6f sf 1:18 B (d) 1/3 Aug 15 Sar tr.tⓣ 5f sf 1:021 B (d) 6/17 Aug 7 Sar tr.t 5f fst 1:041 B 7/1

Saratoga Source
Own: Augustin Stables
MAPLE E (46 5 8 3 .11)

Ch. m. 5
Sire: Saratoga Six (Alydar)
Dam: Exotic Source (The Minstrel)
Br: Smith Sarah L (Va)
Tr: Sheppard Jonathan E (5 0 1 0 .00)

113

Lifetime Record:	21	6	6	2	$265,366						
1994	4	1	2	0	$54,571	Turf	21	6	6	2	$265,366
1993	8	2	2	1	$119,953	Wet	0	0	0	0	
Bel Ⓣ	2	0	1	0	$10,120	Dist Ⓣ	5	1	3	0	$67,678

13Sep94-8Bel	fm	1¼	🅃	:482 1:124 1:364 2:001	3↑ ⒻAlw 46000N$mY	96	2	3	33½	31	21	2½	Krone J A	122	2.70	88-12	Trampoli117½ Saratoga Source1223½ Silky Feather1176	Willingly 4
29Aug94-7Sar	fm	1⅜	🅃	:501 1:153 1:403 2:164	3↑ ⒻWaya55k	94	7	3	1½	21	1hd	1nk	Krone J A	113	*1.20	82-18	Saratoga Source113nk Tiffany's Taylor113½ Market Booster122½	Driving 7
27Jly94-9Sar	yl	1 1/16	Ⓣ	:233 :473 1:122 1:433	3↑ ⒻSar Bud BCH155k	94	7	7	73½	83½	62¼	44	Santos J A	114	17.30	72-24	WeekendMdness115¾ You'dBSurprisd120nk Hd1103	Stead, shuffled turn 8
17Jly94-8Pen	yl	5f	Ⓣ	:561	3↑ ⒻAlw 12573N2Y	78	1	8	86¼	65¾	34½	21½	Canary T K	L 115f	2.80	94-04	Sweet Poison1191½ Saratoga Source1151 Dream For Me1192¼	Full of run 8
11Sep93-8Bel	sf	1¼	🅃	:492 1:142 1:391 2:034	3↑ ⒻFlowr Bwl H-G1	77	6	5	55	85	77½	79¾	Santos J A	113	5.00	61-24	Far Out Beast111½ Dahlia's Dreamer110½ Lady Blessington1183¾	Tired 10
23Aug93-8Sar	fm	1⅜	🅃	:492 1:15 1:391 2:154	3↑ ⒻWaya54k	97	2	3	43	31½	2½	11¼	Krone J A	119	2.30e	87-16	Saratoga Source1191¼ Adoryphar117no Far Out Beast117¾	Driving 6
8Aug93-10Rkm	fm	*1⅛	Ⓣ	1:464	3↑ ⒻSpcy Lvng H-G3	96	1	7	78	56	53¾	33	Cruguet J	L 114	3.60	97-08	Via Borghese1212 Ginny Dare1121 Saratoga Source1141	Gamely 9
14Jly93-7Atl	fm	1 1/16	Ⓣ	:493 1:134 1:384 1:574	3↑ ⒻMatchmaker-G2	90	1	6	34	42¼	42¼	2nk	Krone J A	L 118	2.90	71-21	FairyGarden120nk SartogSource118hd Logn'sMist1183	Brushed str,closed 8
4Jly93-11Rkm	fm	1 1/16	Ⓣ	:231 :473 1:114 1:43	3↑ ⒻRkm BC H104k	90	5	6	43	32	54¾	45¾	Jones S R	L 111	4.80	92-10	Via Borghese1152¾ Navarra1132 Miss Otis1101	Checked near stretch 9
13Jun93-6Pen	fm	1 1/16	Ⓣ	1:383	3↑ ⒻPen Bud B C77k	98	6	5	54	53¼	31½	12½	Jones S R	L 112	4.70	104-01	Saratoga Source1122½ Words Of War1191¾ Tango Charlie114no	Driving 7

WORKOUTS: Aug 26 Sar tr.t Ⓣ 4f sf :51 B (d) *6/9* Aug 25 Sar tr.t Ⓣ 5f fm 1:04 B *7/9* Jly 11 Del 6f fst 1:174 B *1/1* Jly 5 Del 5f fst 1:033 B *3/4*

Twice The Vice
Own: Lewis Robert B
STEVENS G L (—)

Ch. f. 3 (Apr)
Sire: Vice Regent (Northern Dancer)
Dam: Double Set (Resurgent)
Br: Angus M. MacLean (Ky)
Tr: Bell Thomas R II (—)

113

Lifetime Record:	6	4	1	0	$198,375						
1994	3	2	1	0	$130,800	Turf	2	1	1	0	$108,250
1993	3	2	0	0	$67,575	Wet	0	0	0	0	
Bel Ⓣ	0	0	0	0		Dist Ⓣ	0	0	0	0	

21Aug94-8Dmr	fm	1⅛	Ⓣ	:461 1:102 1:352 1:473	ⒻDMR Oaks-G1	100	1	6	66	64½	31½	1nk	Stevens G L	LB 120	3.40	98-04	Twice The Vice120nk Malli Star1201½ Pharma1203	Brushed, gamely 6
27Jly94-8Dmr Run in divisions	fm	1	Ⓣ	:223 :472 1:121 1:36	ⓇOceanside67k	97	3	5	52½	63¼	53¼	21	Delahoussaye E	LB 116	5.60	89-10	Saltgrass1141 Twice The Vice116½ ⒹOcean Crest114hd	4 wide into lane 10
4Jly94-8Hol	fst	6f		:213 :443 :571 1:092	3↑ ⒻAlw 41000N2X	94	6	4	42½	32	1½	12	Delahoussaye E	LB 116	4.00	93-11	Twice The Vice1162 Dancing Ovation118no Bawl For Beulah1167½	Driving 9
5Nov93-7SA	fst	7f		:221 :45 1:102 1:224	ⒻAnoakia82k	86	7	4	3½	3½	11	14½	Delahoussaye E	LB 116	3.60	89-17	Twice The Vice1164½ Private Persuasion1191 Roget's Fact1155½	Driving 9
11Oct93-6SA	fst	1		:222 :453 1:102 1:363	ⒻMd Sp Wt	85	7	4	42½	21	1hd	1½	Delahoussaye E	B 116	*1.60	87-07	Twice The Vice116½ Besar1165½ Starlit Bronze1164½	Game inside 9
28Aug93-5Dmr	fst	6f		:22 :453 :58 1:102	ⒻMd Sp Wt	70	7	9	128	98	66½	46¼	Delahoussaye E	B 117	4.10	81-12	Cee's Maryanne117½ Besar1174½ Mostly Overcast1171¼	Wide early 12

WORKOUTS: Sep 22 Bel 3f fst :38 B *12/21* Sep 17 SA 1 fst 1:381 H *1/2* Sep 10 Hol 7f fst 1:261 H *1/2* Sep 3 Hol 4f fst :474 H *7/31* Aug 15 Dmr Ⓣ 5f fm 1:024 H (d) *4/4* Aug 9 Dmr 4f fst :502 H *35/40*

The contention ran so deep that Twice The Vice, winner of the Grade 1 Del Mar Oaks with a Beyer Speed Figure of 100 — one of the top three last-out figures in the field — was part of the mutual field along with Saratoga Source, herself a stakes winner little more than three weeks earlier.

Scan the records from top to bottom. Does anyone pretend to have zeroed in on a definitive "right answer?"

When I originally looked the race over, Agathe seemed a safe choice for the simple purpose of writing something insightful about the race in the *Form* on a 48-hour deadline. Her trainer was Andre Fabre, who had pulled off the biggest upset in Breeders' Cup history less than a year earlier when Arcangues won the Classic at on-track odds of 133-1; Fabre had a long history of success at the Belmont fall meeting as well, having imported several French horses to win major stakes in recent years, including the Breeders" Cup Turf with In The Wings, and the Long Island Handicap with Peinture Bleue on consecutive afternoons in October of 1990. The latter, like Agathe, had been a Daniel Wildenstein-owned 3-year-old filly taking on older rivals.

But a price of 2-1 on Agathe was no bargain considering that she was fresh off a maiden win (albeit in a Group 3 stake) and pitted against some mares with pretty impressive credentials: Irish Linnet had run a Beyer of 107 winning for the 14th time in her career a fortnight earlier, and was the field's leading money-earner with the exception of Empress Club, who had made her million in South Africa; Trampoli was a four-time winner at the distance and showed two wins from as many starts over Belmont turf courses labeled "soft," as the course would be today; Alywow had won all five of her grass races, four of them stakes, and seemed able to handle any kind of footing (except for dry dirt); and while Dahlia's Dreamer at first glance seemed ambitiously placed, a thorough inspection of her record showed she had nearly wired the Flower Bowl's 1993 renewal over soft turf at 14-1, right after blowing a conditioned "three other than" allowance at odds-on in her prior start — as she had similarly done on September 3.

With so much talent crammed into the starting gate, it didn't make sense to take 2-1 on a filly who was a virtual unknown. Granted, Fabre was a genius at importing to Belmont; he knew that the relatively short flight to the East Coast, the cool autumn climate and Belmont's immense and gentle turns all worked to his advantage, because these conditions out of all the racing venues in the United States most closely resembled the European game. The fact that recent rains had rendered the course soft was icing on the cake. But while Agathe might have headed the list as a lukewarm favorite on a trainer-handicapper's personal betting line, odds of 2-1 are always tough to swallow when a large, competitive field is muscling its way for position around two turns; this is the kind of race where trips and racing luck figure to influence the outcome.

And besides, Agathe wasn't the only "Dame from Deauville". Danish had won three races overseas to Agathe's one, and though she hadn't won a graded stakes, she'd won three times including a Listed stake, and her three victories had come in Ireland as well as France, at three different venues: a win over a straight course at Leopardstown; a win over a left-handed course (American style) at Saint-Cloud; and a win over a right-handed course at La Teste. Danish, if nothing else, was a good traveler who was adaptable to just about any course layout, and her most recent effort, a close-up third in a Group 3 at Deauville, indicated she could handle the Flower Bowl's mile and a quarter over "off" turf as well. Plus, John Hammond may not have been as well-known as Fabre, the "French Fox", but his preparations of import Dear Doctor for the Arlington Million and assaults on Belmont's Turf Classic and Man O'War Stakes earlier in the 1990s had been first-rate.

But while Agathe's price of 2-1 left little to the imagination, Danish was blinking at 30-1 on the board and thus opened up all kinds of possibilities for creative across-the-board wagering. Instead of the traditional win-place-show, however, which only scores big when the horse wins, bets can be structured through the exotic pools so that returns are maximized when the long shot runs well enough to finish in the money. For example, an across-the-board wager on Danish that took advantage of the potential for big payoffs offered by exotics might've been constructed like this:

- Win bet on Danish
- Exacta-savers with Danish in second slot under contenders
- Trifecta-savers with Danish in third slot under contenders

NINTH RACE
Belmont
SEPTEMBER 24, 1994

1¼ MILES. (Inner Turf)(1.57³) 17th Running of THE FLOWER BOWL INVITATIONAL HANDICAP. Purse $200,000. Grade I. Fillies and mares, 3-year-olds and upward. By invitation only with no subscription fees. The Purse to be divided 60% to the winner, 22% to second, 12% to third and 6% to fourth. The New York Racing Association Inc. will select a field of fourteen (14) invitees by Saturday, September 10. The assignment of weights for these invitees will be published on Wednesday, September 14. The owners and/or trainers of these (14) selected horses will be required to notify the New York Racing Association Inc. of their intentions of running or not, no later than Saturday, September 17. A list of alternates and their weight assignments will be published on Monday, September 19. The New York Racing Association Inc. reserves the right to reassign weight to any horse after the weights have been published. Starters to be named at the closing time of entries. Trophies will be presented to the winning owner, trainer and jockey. This race will be limited to 14 starters and alternates (High weights preferred). The New York Racing Association Inc. reserves the right to transfer this race to the main track.

Value of Race: $200,000 Winner $120,000; second $44,000; third $24,000; fourth $12,000. Mutuel Pool $413,643.00 Exacta Pool $484,942.00 Triple Pool $563,941.00

Last Raced	Horse	M/Eqt.	A.Wt	PP	¼	½	¾	1	Str	Fin	Jockey	Odds $1
3Sep94 6Bel2	Dahlia's Dreamer		5 112	3	1³	1½	1¹	1³	1⁸	1¹³	Chavez J F	12.70
10Sep94 7WO1	Alywow		3 114	9	7hd	8hd 10½	9½	5²	2nk	Penna D	6.00
28Aug94 Dea3	Danish-IR		3 113	2	2¹	2¹	4¹½	2¹½	2½	3nk	Krone J A	29.50
6Aug94 Dea1	Agathe		3 117	5	8¹½	7¹½ 5hd	4hd	3²½	4³	Smith M E	2.10
14Aug94 9Sar1	Via Borghese		5 117	7	3½	5hd 9½	8hd	6¹	5½	Santos J A	5.70
21Aug94 8Dmr1	Twice The Vice		3 113	12	9hd	9¹½ 7hd	3hd	4½	6²	Stevens G L	f-6.90
10Sep94 8Bel1	Irish Linnet		6 116	4	4½	6² 3hd	6½	7²½	7⁶	Velazquez J R	5.30
13Sep94 8Bel1	Trampoli		5 120	6	10¹	10½ 8½	10²	8½	8nk	Migliore R	9.80
29Aug94 7Sar3	Market Booster	b	5 115	10	6½	3hd 6¹	7hd	9⁶	9⁹	Santagata N	46.70
29Aug94 7Sar4	Midnight Heights-GB		4 112	1	12	12 12	11¹½	11³	10⁶½	Samyn J L	28.90
13Sep94 8Bel2	Saratoga Source		5 113	11	11½	11½ 11½	12	12	11nk	Maple E	f-6.90
3Sep94 6BM1	Empress Club-AR		6 116	8	5½	4¹ 2¹	5¹	10hd	12	Davis R G	16.10

f-Mutuel Field: Twice The Vice and Saratoga Source.

OFF AT 5:15 Start Good. Won ridden out. Time, :23³, :49, 1:14¹, 1:40¹, 2:05² Course soft.

$2 Mutuel Prices:

3-(C)-DAHLIA'S DREAMER	27.40	13.40	10.40
10-(J)-ALYWOW		8.20	6.60
2-(B)-DANISH-IR			14.40

$2 EXACTA 3-10 PAID $302.40 $2 TRIPLE 3-10-2 PAID $6,557.00

Ch. m, by Theatrical-Dahlia, by Vaguely Noble. Trainer Mott William I. Bred by Paulson Allen E (Ky).

DAHLIA'S DREAMER sprinted clear in the early stages, set the pace under pressure along the backstretch, shook off DANISH to get clear on the turn, opened a wide gap in upper stretch then drew away to a lengthy score while being ridden out. ALYWOW far back for six furlongs, steadied in traffic on the far turn, moved up rapidly between horses entering the stretch/then outfinished DANISH for the place. DANISH stalked the pace while three wide along the backstretch, made a run to threaten on the far turn, was unable to stay with the winner approaching the stretch, then weakened in the final eighth. AGATHE under a snug hold while in traffic on the first turn, worked her way forward along the backstretch, made a run between horses to reach contention on the turn then lacked a strong closing bid. VIA BORGHESE up close early, fell back considerably along the backstretch, raced well back to the turn, circled six wide into the stretch then failed to threaten while improving her position with a late run in the middle of the track. TWICE THE VICE unhurried for six furlongs, rallied four wide to threaten at the quarter pole, then flattened out. IRISH LINNET settled in the middle of the pack while saving ground, steadied along the inside leaving the far turn, took up while lacking room at the quarter pole, and was never close thereafter. TRAMPOLI was never a factor. MARKET BOOSTER raced within striking distance from outside for seven furlongs then steadied between horses while tiring on the turn. MIDNIGHT HEIGHTS steadied along the rail on the first turn and was never close thereafter. SARATOGA SOURCE never reached contention. EMPRESS CLUB moved up between to contest the pace on the far turn then gave way nearing the quarter pole.

Players who envisioned Dahlia's Dreamer running back to her Flower Bowl of a year ago certainly could've used the well-connected mare as a saver, and Alywow at 5-for-5 on grass was a must-use.

When Dahlia's Dreamer galloped the field silly on the front-end under the ever-aggressive Jorge Chavez, and Alywow kicked in late to get second, and Danish managed to hold off Agathe for the show spot, the trifecta came back a whopping $6,557, which is much more fun to cash in than an across-the-board ticket worth $14.40 to show.

In fact, three scenarios offered potential rewards in the Flower Bowl. Those who believed in the form pattern of Dahlia's Dreamer strongly enough, and who liked the idea of a horse loose on the lead and carrying lightweight on soft turf, cashed on a win bet at better than 12-1; those who thought 6-1 on a filly with a strong closing punch who was unbeaten on grass an ample reward cashed on a $302.40 exacta-saver by keying her underneath the pacesetter; and backers of Danish who keyed the grossly underbet 29-1 shot in the third position of trifectas as a "show" bet happily filled out I.R.S. forms.

EXACTLY ONE WEEK later, the feature was the $100,000-added Rare Perfume Handicap, and handicappers again had an opportunity to tackle graded stakes fillies (this time strictly 3-year-olds) on soft turf:

8 Belmont Park

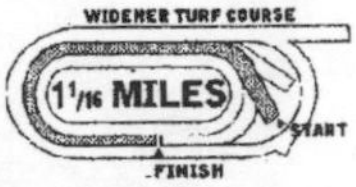

1 1/16 MILES. (Turf). (1:39¹) 16th Running of THE RARE PERFUME HANDICAP. Purse $100,000 Added. Grade II. Fillies, 3-year-olds. By subscription of $100 each which should accompany the nomination; $500 to pass the entry box: $500 to start with $100,000 added. The added money and all fees to be divided 60% to the winner, 22% to second, 12% to third and 6% to fourth. Weights Tuesday, September 27. Starters to be named at the closing time of entries. Trophies will be presented to the winning owner, trainer and jockey. The New York Racing Association Inc. reserves the right to transfer this race to the main track. Closed Wednesday, September 14, with 35 nominations.

Grafin

Own: Mohammed al Maktoum

PERRET C (29 1 4 8 .03)

Ch. f. 3 (Mar)
Sire: Miswaki (Mr. Prospector)
Dam: Reigning Countess (Far North)
Br: Robertson Corbin J (Ky)
Tr: Boutin Francois (—)

122

Lifetime Record: 5 3 1 1 $84,947

1994	5	3	1	1	$84,947	Turf	5	3 1 1		$84,947
1993	0	M	0	0		Wet	0	0 0 0		
Bel Ⓣ	0	0	0	0		Dist Ⓣ	0	0 0 0		

28Aug94♦ Deauville(Fr) yl *1¼ ⓉRH 2:14⁴ ⒻPrix de la Nonette-G3 Stk 62900 1½ Head F 128 6.20 Grafin128½ Maidment128½ Danish1281½ 7
Tracked in 4th,bid 1f out,hard ridden to lead final 16th,held

4Aug94♦ Deauville(Fr) gd *1 ⓉRH 1:41² ⒻPrix de la Calonne (Listed) Stk 38600 1¹ Asmussen C 123 *.70e Grafin123¹ Moivouloirtoi1231½ Sarmatie123⁴ 9
Well placed in 3rd, led 70y out, driving

3Jly94♦ Saint-Cloud(Fr) gd *7f ⓉLH 1:24¹ ⒻPrix Amandine (Listed) Stk 38700 32½ Asmussen C 128 *1.50e Shamaniya128¹ Blue Burgee1281½ Grafin128hd 9
Unruly pre-start,3rd on rail,evenly late

16Jun94♦ Longchamp(Fr) gd *1 ⓉRH 1:41 ⒻPrix Fould Alw 30200 11½ St-Martin E 128 *1.50 Grafin1281½ Terney123hd Athykaneyev128½ 6
Unhurried in 5th,bid 1-1/2f out, led 1f out,driving

12May94♦ Longchamp(Fr) gd *1 ⓉRH 1:43² ⒻPrix des Ternes Alw 29400 2¹ Asmussen C 123 8.20 Gravure Bleue123¹ Grafin123hd Pink Shade128¹ 14
Close up early,7th halfway,rallied between horses,up for 2nd

WORKOUTS: Sep 23 Bel 3f sly :39⁴ B 4/6

Avie's Fancy

Own: Smith Stanton J Jr

FERRER J C (1 0 0 0 .00)

Dk. b or br f. 3 (Feb)
Sire: Lord Avie (Lord Gaylord)
Dam: Fancy Pan (Paavo)
Br: Gunsmith Stables (NJ)
Tr: Perlsweig Mark (—)

120

Lifetime Record: 13 7 1 2 $177,509

1994	6	4	0	0	$111,870	Turf	5	3	1 0	$97,600
1993	7	3	1	2	$65,639	Wet	2	2	0 0	$47,160
Bel Ⓣ	0	0	0	0		Dist Ⓣ	2	2	0 0	$69,000

5Sep94-9Med fm 1 1/16 Ⓣ :23 :47¹ 1:11¹ 1:41² ⒻBoilngSprngHG3 98 5 1 1¹ 1¹ 1³ 1³ Ferrer J C 119 2.60 94–12 Avie's Fancy119³ Teasing Charm1131¼ Knocknock1151¾ Mild drive 7
21Aug94-6Mth gd 1 1/16 Ⓣ :23² :47¹ 1:12 1:44¹+ ⒻThomsJMalley40k 96 8 4 35½ 1hd 1³ 1⁶ Ferrer J C 121 6.30 77–27 Avie's Fancy121⁶ Cavada121¾ Accountinquestion116nk Driving 9
30Jly94-11Mth sly 1 1/16 ⊗ :23⁴ :47⁴ 1:12³ 1:45¹ ⒻLittleSilver35k 85 2 1 1² 1½ 1¹ 13¾ Ferrer J C 116 f *1.00 79–14 Avie's Fancy1163¾ Tj's Tuff As Nails1125¾ Sea Ditty112⁶ Driving 7
2Jly94-9AP gd 1⅛ Ⓣ :46³ 1:11¹ 1:36⁴ 1:49¹ ⒻPucker Up-G3 71 12 5 42½ 4³ 8¹⁰ 811½ Ferrer J C 116 29.30 80–17 Work The Crowd118½ Irish Forever1163¼ Looking For Heaven116hd Faded 14
11Jun94-9Mth fm 1 Ⓣ :22⁴ :45³ 1:09⁴ 1:35⁴ 3↑ ⒻRevidere35k 87 5 6 4⁵ 41¾ 3½ 1² Ferrer J C 112 6.90 87–13 Avie's Fancy112² In My Heart112¹ Uncharted Waters112no Driving 9
27Apr94-6GS fst 5½f :22⁴ :46 :58¹ 1:04⁴ 3↑ ⒻAlw 14500N3X 56 3 3 2¹ 3³ 48½ 49½ Castillo R E 109 2.90 85–10 My Sister Juliet111nk Sophistique Pine1196¾ Angel Top1192½ Tired 5
13Nov93-9Med fst 6f :22 :45 :58³ 1:11³ Ⓕ[S]NJ Futy57k 53 8 2 3¹ 42¼ 4³ 3⁶ Ferrer J C 119 2.60 77–15 Donna Doo119⁵ Aspiring Proof119¹ Avie's Fancy119½ Mild rally 8
31Oct93-8Pha sly 7f :22¹ :45³ 1:11⁴ 1:26¹ ⒻSchuylkill43k 65 8 3 2hd 2hd 1hd 11¼ Ferrer J C 114 *1.40 75–21 Avie's Fancy1141¼ Cavada114no Jake's Sister1141½ Drifted out, driving 8
16Oct93-4Bel fst 1 :22⁴ :45¹ 1:10 1:35² ⒻFrizette-G1 51 4 2 3½ 74¼ 69½ 622¾ McCarron C J 119 39.90 68–12 Heavenly Prize119⁷ Facts Of Love1194¾ Footing1192½ Used early 7
24Sep93-5Med yl 1 Ⓣ :22¹ :48¹ 1:14² 1:40³ ⒻSalem County40k 75 1 1 1½ 11½ 15½ 2² Ferrer J C 117 5.40 68–28 Irish Forever120² Avie's Fancy117¹² Normandy Belle117⁴ Best of rest 9

WORKOUTS: ●Sep 26 Mth 5f fst 1:01 H 1/20 Sep 19 Mth 6f fst 1:14³ B 1/3 Sep 4 Mth 3f fst :35¹ B 2/8 Aug 20 Mth 3f fst :35² B 3/24 Aug 14 Mth 5f my 1:04¹ B 5/5 Jly 23 Mth 5f fst 1:02² B 8/34

Golden Tajniak (Ire)

Own: Perez Robert

PEREZ R M (51 8 7 6 .16)

B. f. 3
Sire: Thatching (Thatch)
Dam: Tajniak (Irish River)
Br: A J Poulton (Epping) Ltd (Ire)
Tr: Callejas Alfredo (10 0 1 1 .00)

114

Lifetime Record: 16 3 4 6 $142,945

1994	6	1	0	2	$54,977	Turf	15	3	4 6	$142,945
1993	10	2	4	4	$87,968	Wet	0	0	0 0	
Bel Ⓣ	3	1	0	0	$38,235	Dist Ⓣ	2	1	0 1	$48,072

2Sep94-8Bel fm 1 Ⓣ :22⁴ :46¹ 1:10¹ 1:34 ⒻPebbles69k 67 11 2 2½ 2hd 31½ 812¼ Perret C 118 7.20 80–17 Saxuality114no Lady Affirmed1182¼ Tensie's Pro1183¼ Dueled, tired 11
3Aug94-7Sar yl 1 1/16 Ⓣ :23³ :47⁴ 1:12² 1:43⁴ ⒻNijana-G3 81 2 3 32½ 5³ 4⁴ 3⁹ Perret C 118 2.30 66–25 Coronation Cup114⁵ Stretch Drive114⁴ Golden Tajniak118¹ Lacked rally 7
Run in divisions
3Jly94-7Bel fm 7f Ⓣ :23¹ :46 1:09¹ 1:21² 3↑ ⒻDruintop55k 90 5 4 5³ 52½ 41¾ 42¾ Bailey J D 112 5.80 92–09 Lady Affirmed108¹ Statuette119nk Sh Bang1141½ Four wide 6
12Jun94-8Bel fst 1⅛ :45¹ 1:08³ 1:33² 1:46² ⒻMotherGoose-G1 — 1 4 4³ 6¹⁶ 6³⁹ — Bailey J D 121 17.70 — 14 Lakewy1214¼ CinnmonSugr121⁶ InsideInformtion121nk Broke slow, eased 6
22May94-8Bel gd 1 1/16 Ⓣ :24 :47⁴ 1:12² 1:44 ⒻTanya58k 94 1 4 41½ 4¾ 11½ 12¾ Bailey J D 114 11.30 78–24 Golden Tajniak1142¾ Polar Princess112nk Petiteness112nk Driving 12
20Mar94♦ Capannelle(Ity) gd *7½f ⓉRH 1:33³ ⒻPremio Ceprano Alw 26900 3⁵ Ferrer J 123 6.00 Secret Nymph1233½ Carmen The Best1231½ Golden Tajniak123³ 8
Tr: G Fratini
Always well placed, outfinished

1Dec93♦ Capannelle(Ity) hy *1 ⓉRH 1:46 ⒻPremio Dobrowa Alw 26100 3⁴ Luongo A 126 3.30 Tablet1212½ Secret Nymph1261½ Golden Tajniak1261½ 11
Close up, lacked finishing bid

16Nov93♦ Capannelle(Ity) hy *7½f ⓉRH 1:40¹ ⒻPremio Approval Alw 26900 21¼ Luongo A 126 .90 Secret Nymph1211¼ Golden Tajniak1263½ Paris Texas121¹⁰ 5
Tracked in 3rd, bid 2f out, not good enough

1Nov93 Capannelle(Ity) sf *7f ⓉRH 1:26² ⒻCriterium Femminile (Listed) Stk 49000 2¾ Holland D 123 2.80 Giselle Penn120¾ Golden Tajniak123nk Secret Nymph123¹ 10
Held up in rear, finished strongly, gaining at line

10Oct93♦ San Siro(Ity) hy *1 ⓉStr 1:50⁴ ⒻPremio Dormello-G3 Stk 78000 310¼ Holland D 123 42.00 Alpride123nk Sensazione123¹⁰ Golden Tajniak123¾ 13
Tracked in 4th, lacked rally

WORKOUTS: Sep 22 Bel [T] 5f fm 1:02⁴ B (d) 10/13 Sep 12 Bel 4f fst :47² H 3/29 Aug 29 Bel tr.t 5f fst 1:02³ B 11/15 Aug 21 Sar 4f fst :49 B 15/52 Aug 1 Sar 4f fst :48 H 6/37 Jly 26 Sar Ⓣ 4f gd :53 B (d) 18/18

Saxuality

Own: Alexander Leslie

KRONE J A (96 25 7 17 .26)

Dk. b or br f. 3 (May)
Sire: Dynaformer (Roberto)
Dam: She Skates (Overskate)
Br: Meadowview Farm (Ky)
Tr: Terrill William V (24 4 5 7 .17)

117

Lifetime Record: 6 5 0 0 $110,580

1994	6	5	0	0	$110,580	Turf	1	1	0 0	$41,580
1993	0	M	0	0		Wet	2	1	0 0	$18,000
Bel Ⓣ	1	1	0	0	$41,580	Dist Ⓣ	0	0	0 0	

2Sep94-8Bel fm 1 Ⓣ :22⁴ :46¹ 1:10¹ 1:34 ⒻPebbles69k 94 7 11 105½ 83¼ 52¼ 1no Krone J A 114 4.50 92–17 Saxuality114no Lady Affirmed1182¼ Tensie's Pro1183¼ Driving 11
8Aug94-4Sar fst 6½f :23¹ :46¹ 1:10² 1:16⁴ 3↑ ⒻAlw 32000N3X 91 6 1 3¹ 3½ 1hd 1hd Krone J A 112 2.10 91–15 Saxuality112hd Footing1134½ Imah117nk Wide, driving 6
23Jly94-9Sar sly 7f :22¹ :44² 1:09 1:22 ⒻTest-G1 69 4 6 53½ 56½ 77½ 716¾ Davis R G 112 25.20 78–12 Twist Afleet114¹ Penny's Reshoot118² Heavenly Prize121¹⁰ Wide turn 8
18May94-9Bel wf 6f :21⁴ :45 :58 1:11¹ 3↑ ⒻAlw 30000N2X 85 2 3 3⁵ 3² 2½ 1hd Santos J A 114 *.70 85–16 Saxuality114hd Firstflagtofly111⁴ Lady Hunter1101½ Driving 7
29Apr94-6Aqu fst 6½f :22¹ :45¹ 1:10¹ 1:16⁴ ⒻAlw 27000N1X 92 4 2 2½ 1½ 1⁴ 19½ Santos J A 116 *.40 97–11 Saxuality1169½ Divine1164½ Fawn's Angel109¹¹ Ridden out 5
14Mar94-6GP fst 6f :22³ :46¹ :58² 1:11 ⒻMd Sp Wt 81 8 4 1hd 1¹ 1⁵ 1¹⁰ Santos J A 121 4.80 86–13 Saxuality121¹⁰ Mistletoe And Ivy121nk Our Miz Waki1211½ Driving 11

WORKOUTS: Sep 22 Bel [T] 6f fm 1:15³ B (d) 3/7 ●Sep 15 Bel [T] 6f fm 1:12³ H (d) 1/4 ●Aug 24 Sar tr.t Ⓣ 5f gd :59² H 1/15 Aug 17 Sar tr.t Ⓣ 5f fm 1:00² H 4/20 ●Aug 6 Sar tr.t 5f gd 1:02 H 1/4 ●Jly 17 Bel 5f fst :58¹

Casa Eire

Own: Connaughton Bernard

MARQUEZ C H JR (—)

B. f. 3 (Apr)
Sire: Compliance (Northern Dancer)
Dam: Casarette (Upper Case)
Br: Spielman Michael (NY)
Tr: O'Brien Leo (50 5 5 3 .10)

117

	Lifetime Record:	20 4 3 1	$242,820
1994	8 2 0 0	$90,120	Turf	9 2 2 0	$133,790
1993	12 2 3 1	$152,700	Wet	2 0 1 0	$24,356
Bel ⊤	5 1 1 0	$96,444	Dist ⊤	5 0 1 0	$29,964

16Sep94-7Med fm 5f ⊤ :224 :46 :581	ⒻEgret35k	83 1 8 8½ 9¹⁰ 64½ 1½	Marquez C H Jr	121	5.00e	88-12	Casa Eire121½ Grab112¾ Shamrock Angel112nk	Driving 12
2Sep94-8Bel fm 1 ⊤ :231 1:01 1:34	ⒻPebbles69k	70 1 5 7³½ 72½ 7⁷½ 6¹⁰½	Velazquez J R	121	12.70	81-17	Sexuality114no Lady Affirmed118²½ Tensie's Pro1183½	Steadied 1/4 pl 11
11Aug94-8Sar fm 1 ⊤ :231 :461 1:101 1:403	ⒻAlw 34000N3X	83 1 3 31⁰ 42½ 32½ 59½	Migliore R	113	12.20	85-08	Gray Mood117²½ Open Toe117¾ New Wave114²½	Tired 8
3Aug94-9Sar yl 1¹⁄₁₆ ⊤ :231 :48 1:123 1:434	ⒻNijana-G3	59 8 6 85½ 74 87½ 8¹⁹	McCauley W H	121	13.00	56-25	Alywow121³½ Irish Forever121no Knocknock114²	No menace 9
Run in divisions							
25Jun94-8Bel fm 1⅛ ⊤ :224 :452 1:083 1:394	Hill Prince-G3	63 2 7 75¾ 85½ 810 916½	Velazquez J R	117	21.50	83-11	Pennine Ridge112²½ Check Ride119²½ Add The Gold114¹½	Done early 9
25May94-7Bel fm 1¹⁄₁₆ ⊤ :224 :46 1:10 1:404 3+	ⒻAlw 44000N$mY	68 4 3 3¹½ 42 44½ 41½²	Beckner D V⁷	108	5.40	79-12	You'd Be Surprised121²½ Sh Bang12¹⁵ Park Dream121⁸	No threat 5
14May94-8Bel fm 1 ⊤ :23 :452 :47 23 1nk	Saranac-G3	92 4 4 47 43 2½ 1nk	Bravo J	114	17.50	89-20	Casa Eire114nk Warn Me114nk Presently117¹	Driving 6
24Apr94-6Aqu fst 1 :23 :462 1:111 1:37	ⒻⓇNY Stallion65k	40 3 6 64½ 54½ 513 523½	Santos J A	121	3.80	59-14	Minetonightsfirst116¹½ Come On Joy116¹⁰ Tensie's Pro116¹⁰	No factor 7
14Nov93-4Aqu yl 1 ⊤ :233 :492 1:16 1:41	ⒻⓈEast View74k	65 3 10 10⁸¼ 85 33 23	Santos J A	118	*1.20e	67-29	Great Triumph118⁴ Casa Eire118³½ All For Fitness116³	Rallied wide 11
31Oct93-7Aqu sly 6f :23 :47 :592 1:122	ⒻⓇNY Stlln80k	66 8 5 7³½ 42 2½ 2½	Santos J A	116	*1.20e	79-18	Princess J V116½ Casa Eire116⁶ Kiss The Pro1143½	Rallied wide 10
Fillies division							

WORKOUTS: Aug 25 Sar tr.t 4f fst :50 B 3/19 • Jly 28 Sar 4f my :492 H 1/14 Jly 20 Sar tr.t 4f fst :522 B 4/7 Jly 12 Bel 5f fst 1:02 B 16/40

Jade Flush

Own: Condren & Cornacchia & Paulson

DAVIS R G (90 13 14 14 .14)

Ch. f. 3 (Apr)
Sire: Jade Hunter (Mr. Prospector)
Dam: Royal Strait Flush (Seattle Slew)
Br: Paulson Allen E (Ky)
Tr: Zito Nicholas P (44 4 4 3 .09)

111

	Lifetime Record:	14 4 2 2	$112,770
1994	10 3 1 2	$91,070	Turf	0 0 0 0	
1993	4 1 1 0	$21,700	Wet	2 1 0 1	$26,400
Bel ⊤	0 0 0 0		Dist ⊤	0 0 0 0	

4Sep94-8Bel fst 1⅛ :461 1:101 1:35 1:471	ⒻGazelle H-G1	59 5 3 42½ 59½ 521 527½	Bailey J D	115	11.10	68-05	Heavenly Prize123⁶½ Cinnamon Sugar118¹½ SovereignKitty118¹	Gave way 5
21Aug94-5Sar sly 1⅛ :47 1:121 1:37 1:493 3+	ⒻAlw 34000N3X	116 1 1 1³½ 17 118 126½	Bailey J D	112	*.50e	88-25	Jade Flush112²⁶ Dahar's Best114¹⁶ Open Toe117¹½	Handily 5
13Aug94-8Sar fst 1¼ :48 1:12 1:372 2:031	ⒻAlabama-G1	68 5 6 6⁵ 6¹² 519 529½	Bailey J D	121	40.20	59-23	Heavenly Prize121⁷ Lakeway121¹¹ Sovereign Kitty121½	No factor 7
27Jly94-7Sar wf 1⅛ :464 1:104 1:364 1:502	ⒻAlw 50000NC	86 4 4 44 42½ 42 33	Sellers S J	116	6.20	81-19	Sovereign Kitty116⁴ Brighter Course116¹ Jade Flush116³½	Lacked rally 4
12Jun94-2Bel fst 1 :231 :461 1:111 1:371 3+	ⒻAlw 30000N2X	78 2 2 2½ 1½ 1³ 1⁴½	Santos J A	114	*.80	77-14	Jade Flush114⁴½ Fittin Purrfect111½ Dancer's Gate119nk	Driving 4
22May94-6Bel fst 7f :222 :452 1:101 1:234 3+	ⒻAlw 30000N2X	73 5 5 2½ 31 43½ 44½	Santos J A	114	2.70	80-19	Brighter Course113⁴ UnrealCupcake119nk SafeAtHome112no	Forced pace 5
5Mar94-10GP fst 1½ :231 :462 1:111 1:423	ⒻBonnie Miss-G2	88 2 3 51½ 41½ 31 33	Bravo J	114	8.60	93-06	Inside Information114²½ Cinnamon Sugar113nk Jade Flush114⁴	Late rally 10
19Feb94-6GP gd 1⅛ :234 :48 1:132 1:46	ⒻAlw 27000N1X	86 2 4 31 1½ 15 15½	Bravo J	118	*1.30	80-19	Jade Flush118⁵½ Return Of Mom118³ Carey's Visit118no	11
Ducked in upper str, checked to avoid rail, handily							
23Jan94-7GP fst 1⅛ :223 :462 1:11 1:423	ⒻAlw 24000N1X	84 10 6 53½ 21½ 21½ 23½	Bravo J	120	7.70	93-04	Cinnamon Sugar117³½ Jade Flush120⁸ Sgian Dubh117½	Best of others 12
5Jan94-7GP fst 1⅛ :232 :473 1:13 1:453	ⒻAlw 23000N2L	71 7 2 2½ 21 33 43½	Bravo J	117	11.80	79-21	My Lady T. J114nk Scent Of A Rose114¹½ Chalynn114¹½	Weakened 10

WORKOUTS: Sep 26 Bel 5f fst 1:02½ B 12/19 Sep 19 Bel 5f fst 1:03 B 30/35 Sep 11 Bel 4f fst :50³ B 38/60 Aug 28 Sar tr.t 5f fst 1:04½ B 8/18 Aug 6 Sar 3f gd :39² B 6/7 Jly 12 Bel 5f fst 1:03⁴ B 35/40

Uncharted Waters

Own: Steinberg Philip & Teinowitz Wm

SAMYN J L (43 8 2 5 .19)

B. f. 3 (May)
Sire: Blushing John (Blushing Groom)
Dam: Forever Waving (Hoist the Flag)
Br: Foxfield (Ky)
Tr: Schulhofer Flint S (33 7 1 5 .21)

110

	Lifetime Record:	9 2 1 2	$47,915
1994	6 0 1 2	$14,730	Turf	7 1 1 2	$30,215
1993	3 2 0 0	$33,185	Wet	0 0 0 0	
Bel ⊤	3 0 1 0	$3,840	Dist ⊤	4 0 1 0	$7,040

7Sep94-7Bel fm 1⅛ ⊤ :243 :48 1:114 1:413 3+	ⒻAlw 34000N2X	75 7 3 52 62½ 67½	Santos J A	113	4.10	83-15	Arctic Aazia117³ Running On E1174 Aucilla113¹½	Faded 9
24Aug94-6Sar gd 1⅛ ⊤ :242 :481 1:123 1:433 3+	ⒻAlw 32000N2X	88 6 6 55½ 5³ 3½ 2½	Krone J A	112	12.70	75-22	Knocknock112¾ UnchrtedWtrs112½ Kris'sKiss117½	Wide, drifted stretch 9
3Aug94-9Sar yl 1¹⁄₁₆ ⊤ :231 :48 1:123 1:434	ⒻNijana-G3	79 3 7 65 95½ 74½ 7¹⁰	Santos J A	114	25.30	65-25	Alywow121³½ Irish Forever121no Knocknock114²	No factor 9
Run in divisions							
25Jun94-8Bel fm 1 ⊤ :221 :451 1:094 1:333 3+	ⒻAlw 32000N2X	74 9 6 43 41½ 36½ 312½	Santos J A	111	5.20	81-11	Dayflower119⁶ Jiving Around119³½ UnchartedWaters111²	Bid, weakened 9
11Jun94-9Mth fm 1 ⊤ :224 :453 1:094 1:354 3+	ⒻRevidere35k	80 1 5 55½ 52½ 53 33	Bravo J	112	4.10	84-15	Avie's Fancy112² In My Heart112½ Uncharted Waters112no	Late gain 9
22May94-8Bel gd 1¹⁄₁₆ ⊤ :24 :474 1:12 1:44	ⒻTanya58k	68 11 9 94½ 82½ 107½ 1012½	Santos J A	114	5.40	66-24	Golden Tajniak114²½ Polar Princess112½ Petiteness112nk	Wide trip 12
15Oct93-4Kee fm 1 ⊤ :222 :464 1:123 1:38	ⒻAlw 24415N2L	72 9 8 64½ 63½ 21½ 1³	Day P	121	*.70	80-15	Uncharted Waters121³ Fred's Affair118¹½ Bedroom Blues118⁴	9
Stumbled, start, swerved out, ridden out							
29Sep93-3Bel fst 1 :24 :481 1:134 1:40	ⒻMd Sp Wt	64 1 1 1³½ 1½ 1¹½ 1¹½	Santos J A	117	*1.00	68-23	Uncharted Waters117² Izara117¹½ A Day To Remember117²	Driving 5
5Sep93-3Bel fst 7f :233 :472 1:111 1:234	ⒻMd Sp Wt	52 8 1 2hd 21 43½ 413½	Santos J A	117	7.50	71-15	Sovereign Kitty117¹½ Return Of Mom117hd Sky Flasher117³½	Forced pace 9

WORKOUTS: Sep 26 Bel tr.t 4f fst :50 B 17/35 • Sep 21 Bel 5f fst :59⁴ H 1/31 Sep 16 Bel 4f fst :49² H 14/35 • Sep 3 Bel 4f fst :46⁴ H 1/50 Aug 21 Sar 4f fst :50³ B 36/52 Aug 16 Sar 4f fst :48⁴ B 8/22

Knocknock

Own: Oh Tony Stable

MCCAULEY W H (1 0 0 0 .00)

Dk. b or br f. 3 (Feb)
Sire: Dynaformer (Roberto)
Dam: Bonnie Empress (Young Emperor)
Br: Schwartz Herbert T (Ky)
Tr: Schwartz Scott M (4 0 1 0 .00)

114

	Lifetime Record:	13 3 2 4	$95,442
1994	9 2 2 3	$77,562	Turf	10 3 2 3	$93,762
1993	4 1 0 1	$17,880	Wet	0 0 0 0	
Bel ⊤	5 1 2 1	$35,040	Dist ⊤	5 2 0 2	$58,722

5Sep94-9Med fm 1⅛ ⊤ :23 :471 1:111 1:412	ⒻBoilngSprngHG3	89 1 5 64½ 42½ 34 34½	Santagata N	115	6.40	90-12	Avie's Fancy119³ Teasing Charm113¹½ Knocknock115¹½	Mild bid 7
24Aug94-6Sar gd 1⅛ ⊤ :242 :481 1:123 1:433 3+	ⒻAlw 32000N2X	90 7 4 43 31½ 2hd 1½	Day P	112	*1.60	76-22	Knocknock112½ Uncharted Waters112½ Kris's Kiss117½	Driving 9
3Aug94-9Sar yl 1¹⁄₁₆ ⊤ :231 :48 1:123 1:434	ⒻNijana-G3	93 5 3 33 85 51½ 33½	Day P	114	22.60	71-25	Alywow121³½ Irish Forever121no Knocknock114²	Willingly 9
Run in divisions							
7Jly94-7Bel fm 1¼ ⊤ :501 1:142 1:381 2:014 3+	ⒻAlw 32000N2X	85 3 4 42½ 52½ 54½ 33½	Smith M E	116	6.00	78-16	Teasing Charm114nk Jiving Around117³ Knocknock116¹½	Mild rally 7
21Jun94-8Bel fm 1⅜ ⊤ :493 1:151 1:393 2:163 3+	ⒻAlw 30000N1X	82 6 2 21 42 2½ 1hd	Smith M E	111	4.30	72-23	Knocknock111hd Miss Carmella119³½ Petiteness111nk	Driving 8
29May94-2Bel fm 1⅛ ⊤ :49 1:13 1:372 2:021 3+	ⒻAlw 30000N2L	81 5 1 1½ 21 31 24	Smith M E	114	2.30	75-19	Adored Slew121nk Knocknock114⁴ Sistermarymargaret121nk	Up for place 9
13May94-7Bel fm 1¼ ⊤ :492 1:13 1:392 2:04 3+	ⒻAlw 30000N1X	78 4 2 2hd 2½ 2² 24	Smith M E	112	3.00	69-24	Caroline Of Kent114½ Knocknock112³ Reflection119²	Gamely 9
4May94-7Bel fm 1 ⊤ :231 :46 1:103 1:351 3+	ⒻAlw 30000N1X	72 7 2 2½ 2hd 2¹ 86½	McCauley W H	112 fb	7.70	79-15	Basic Assumption113²½ Doc's Josephine119² Whisling Song119no	Tired 12
24Apr94-7Aqu gd 1¹⁄₁₆ ⊤ :231 :47 1:112 1:424 3+	ⒻAlw 30000N1X	69 1 2 1½ 1hd 441 461	Davis R G	112 fb	6.60	74-20	New Wave114¹½ Royal Pilkinow114¹½ Letscapade112⁴	Tired 10
11Nov93-2Aqu yl 1 ⊤ :243 :502 1:162 1:50	ⒻMd Sp Wt	66 4 1 1½ 1hd 1½ 1nk	Velazquez J R	117 b	29.90	61-34	Knocknock117nk Petiteness117½ Gossamer117³	Driving 9

WORKOUTS: • Sep 22 Aqu ⊤ 5f fm 1:02 H (d) 1/6 • Sep 1 Aqu ⊤ 5f fm 1:02¹ H (d) 1/5 Aug 19 Sar tr.t 5f sf 1:05 B (d) 2/5 Jly 29 Sar tr.t 5f sf 1:04 H 9/15 Jly 22 Sar tr.t 4f sf :50 H 8/15 Jly 18 Sar 5f fst 1:04¹ B 9/

Lady Affirmed

Own: Harbor View Farm

CHAVEZ J F (109 18 13 15 .17)

Ro. f. 3 (Mar)
Sire: Affirmed (Exclusive Native)
Dam: Festivity (Spectacular Bid)
Br: Harbor View Farm (Ky)
Tr: Jerkens H Allen (29 6 4 3 .21)

117

	Lifetime Record:	8 4 1 1	$107,076
1994	7 4 1 1	$107,076	Turf	5 3 1 0	$87,996
1993	1 M 0 0		Wet	0 0 0 0	
Bel ⊤	5 3 1 0	$87,996	Dist ⊤	1 1 0 0	$18,000

15Sep94-7Bel fm 1 ⊤ :232 :461 1:092 1:331 3+	ⒻAlw 36000N3X	97 8 8 85½ 63 2½ 14	Chavez J F	113	*.80	96-13	Lady Affirmed113⁴ Jiving Around117no Manila Lila117²½	Wide, mild drive 10
2Sep94-8Bel fm 1 ⊤ :224 :461 1:101 1:34	ⒻPebbles69k	94 6 7 52½ 4½ 11½ 2no	Chavez J F	118	*1.80	92-17	Sexuality114no Lady Affirmed118²½ Tensie's Pro1183½	Wide, lost bob 11
16Jly94-7Bel fm 1 ⊤ :231 :451 1:084 1:331 3+	ⒻAlw 34000N3X	82 1 2 1hd 11 31 58½	Chavez J F	111	1.80	87-06	Dayflower119⁵ Sky Feather117no Light And Love114½	Dueled, tired 6
3Jly94-8Bel fst 7f :221 :45 1:093 1:221 3+	ⒻDrumtop55k	96 6 3 2½ 21½ 1hd 1⁴	Chavez J F	108	6.60	95-09	Lady Affirmed108³ Statuette118nk Sh Bang114¹½	Driving 6
24Jun94-8Bel fst 1¹⁄₁₆ :233 :47 1:112 1:424 3+	ⒻAlw 34000N2X	89 4 4 2½ 2½ 1hd 35½	Chavez J F	111	5.50	81-14	Link River112²½ Persnickity111²½ Lady Affirmed111²½	Bid, weakened 6
3Jun94-8Bel fm 1¹⁄₁₆ ⊤ :232 :46 1:111 1:423 3+	ⒻAlw 30000N2L	86 3 6 41½ 2hd 1½ 1½	Chavez J F	111	2.70	88-13	Lady Affirmed111½ Last Blood119hd Venetian Red119no	Driving 8
11May94-1Bel fst 7f :221 :453 1:103 1:24 3+	ⒻMd Sp Wt	84 4 1 1½ 1½ 1hd 1½	Luttrell M G⁵	110	13.20	83-17	Lady Affirmed110¹½ Jade Birld115nk Pretty Treaty115⁹	Driving 7
29Aug93-6Sar fst 6f :22 :453 :574 1:11	ⒻMd Sp Wt	— 8 7 11¹⁶	Maple E	117	5.20e	— 09	Lady Hunter117⁴ Defer West117¹¼ Brighter Course117²	Pulled up 12

WORKOUTS: Sep 27 Bel 7f sly 1:37 B 1/1 Sep 10 Bel tr.t 3f fst :37³ B 6/8 Sep 1 Bel 5f fst 1:03 B 6/16 Aug 29 Bel 6f fst 1:30¹ B 1/1 • Aug 20 Sar 4f my :46 H 1/12 Aug 16 Sar 7f fst 1:33 B 2/2

The crowd was having difficulty separating three entrants. The slight favorite was French import Grafin, trained by the legendary Francois Boutin; she had beaten Danish in the Prix de la Nonette last time out, notching her third win in five starts, and she had been scratched from the Flower Bowl to await this. Also attracting strong support were Lady Affirmed and Saxuality, who had finished noses apart in the Pebbles Stakes a month ago; since then, Lady Affirmed had returned for an extremely impressive allowance victory.

None among the trio was an especially enticing proposition at the odds. Grafin was conceding anywhere from five to twelve pounds and was unfamiliar with her surroundings — acceptable traits at generous mutuels, but liabilities at 2-1. Neither Lady Affirmed nor Saxuality possessed any experience whatsoever on soft turf; all their turf racing had been done during the summer months, when the courses play much harder and faster than during the cool, wet weather of autumn.

For all intents and purposes, this put Lady Affirmed and Saxuality on "equal footing" with Jade Flush, who had never raced on soft turf ... or on any kind of turf, for that matter. Normally, horses with suitable pedigrees switch to grass most readily in the maiden and preliminary allowance conditions, where they meet opponents similarly experienced (and often of questionable talent). For every Prized who successfully makes the switch to grass against graded stakes company, there surely are dozens who fail miserably.

But racing is a game of exceptions, and the rewards are generous for the handicapper who can spot them. The first thing to spot in the record of Jade Flush is that Beyer of 116 two races back. It's hard to miss, isn't it, sandwiched as it is between a 68 and a 59?

At Saratoga on August 21, Jade Flush encountered slop for the first time, and she had taken to the water like Esther Williams, splashing her way to an effortless 26-length win against allowance fillies. Significantly, her Beyer of 116 wasn't some kind of subjective projection, because there had been another nine-furlong race for fillies and mares on the card: the Grade 1 John A. Morris, which was won by Link River in time several ticks slower than what Jade Flush had required.

While the 116 was legit from a technical standpoint, it seemed a perfect illustration of the adage concerning what often happens when a horse shakes loose and wins without facing any challenges: the horse will be hard-pressed to put forth the same type of effort next time out. Indeed, that's exactly what happened: Jade Flush was entered in the Grade 1 Gazelle and promptly had her head handed to her, finishing a distant last of five.

The question now before handicappers is this: what are the chances of Jade Flush running that 116 (or anything close to it, since that would also be good enough to win) back again on soft turf? Perhaps she was a sore-footed individual who appreciated a surface that didn't sting quite as much as a hard, fast dirt track. At least she had already shown the ability to rebound from a drubbing, having been far up the track in the Alabama just eight days before hanging up that 116. At 11-1, handicappers might take a calculated gamble on her...especially after consulting *Maiden Stats* to get some idea of whether or not she was bred for grass.

	SIRE INFO								DAM INFO										SIBLING INFO		YRLG SALES INFO		
Horse	# wnr/str	2yo wnr/str	% 1st	awd	Mud w%/sts	Turf w%/sts	% 1stT	Spl	prf	Dpl	# fls	# wnr/str	# sw	2yo wnr/str	awd	Mud w%/sts	Turf wnr/str	Dosage Index	Top Sibling	/Earn$	Price/Sire avg	# Rnk/sld	Stud Fee
ADE FLUSH	12/ 26	9/ 23	17	6.7	0/ 8	25/ 8	20	3.91	ur	3.09	6	4/ 4	2	2/ 3	8.5	33/ 3	2/ 3	3.57	Tenga	/$ 50k			
DE FRAICHE	12/ 26	9/ 23	17	6.7	0/ 8	25/ 8	20	3.91	w	0.63	3	2/ 2	0	1/ 1	8.5	0/ 0	0/ 1	1.60	Fleur De Chine	/$ 36k			
DE GLADE	12/ 26	9/ 23	17	6.7	0/ 8	25/ 8	20	3.91	ur	2.40	12	6/10	3	2/ 5	8.5	100/ 1	2/ 3	1.46	Dom Donizetti (Ire)	/$244k			
FFAROO	182/ 242	67/ 158	12	7.0	14/ 618	6/ 249	4	2.73	sw		1							1.35					
GABOW									ur	0.26	4	1/ 2	0	0/ 2	6.5	0/ 4	0/ 0	4.78	Mr. Magistrate	/$ 6.2k	$ 6.0k/$ 6.[illegible]k	2/ 6	2.5k

To quickly bring the uninitiated up to speed, *Maiden Stats* is an annual publication available every April from the Kentucky-based Bloodstock Research Information Services. The book resembles a telephone directory in size and scope, and indeed, provides "numbers" for well over 30,000 thoroughbreds of each generation. Statistical categories include: mud and turf capability, dosage indices, stud fees, sire and dam stats, public auction history and top sibling information.

That Jade Flush's young sire, Jade Hunter, was getting first-time-turf winners at a 20 percent clip was not significant as yet, because his statistical sample — only 26 starters overall — was still quite limited; what was noteworthy, however, was that her dam, Royal Strait Flush, had thrown two previous grass-winners from three runners who had tried the green stuff. So, Jade Flush had "license" to handle the footing. And she had already shown two starts back that she was capable of great things when the footing pleased her:

EIGHTH RACE
Belmont
OCTOBER 1, 1994

$1\frac{1}{16}$ MILES. (Inner Turf)(1.39¹) 16th Running of THE RARE PERFUME HANDICAP. Purse $100,000 Added. Grade II. Fillies, 3-year-olds. By subscription of $100 each which should accompany the nomination; $500 to pass the entry box: $500 to start with $100,000 added. The added money and all fees to be divided 60% to the winner, 22% to second, 12% to third and 6% to fourth. Weights Tuesday, September 27. Starters to be named at the closing time of entries. Trophies will be presented to the winning owner, trainer and jockey. The New York Racing Association Inc. reserves the right to transfer this race to the main track. Closed Wednesday, September 14, with 35 nominations.

Value of Race: $111,900 Winner $67,140; second $24,618; third $13,428; fourth $6,714. Mutuel Pool $275,851.00 Exacta Pool $375,315.00 Triple Pool $341,012.00

Last Raced	Horse	M/Eqt.	A.	Wt	PP	St	¼	½	¾	Str	Fin	Jockey	Odds $1
4Sep94 8Bel5	Jade Flush		3	111	5	3	1^1	1^1	$1^{1\frac{1}{2}}$	$1^{2\frac{1}{2}}$	$1^{6\frac{1}{2}}$	Davis R G	11.50
15Sep94 7Bel1	Lady Affirmed		3	117	8	8	8	7^1	$2^{\frac{1}{2}}$	2^2	$2^{\frac{3}{4}}$	Chavez J F	2.30
2Sep94 8Bel1	Saxuality		3	117	3	2	$7^{\frac{1}{2}}$	$5^{\frac{1}{2}}$	4^1	$3^{\frac{1}{2}}$	3no	Krone J A	2.90
5Sep94 9Med3	Knocknock		3	114	7	6	3^1	3^1	3^{hd}	4^2	4^3	Santagata N	9.00
2Sep94 8Bel8	Golden Tajniak-IR		3	114	2	1	4^1	$4^{\frac{1}{2}}$	7^1	5^1	5^3	Perez R M	17.00
16Sep94 7Med1	Casa Eire		3	117	4	4	2^{hd}	2^{hd}	$5^{\frac{1}{2}}$	$6^{1\frac{1}{2}}$	6no	Marquez C H Jr	19.30
28Aug94 Dea1	Grafin		3	122	1	5	5^{hd}	6^{hd}	$6^{\frac{1}{2}}$	7^8	$7^{12\frac{1}{2}}$	Perret C	2.00
7Sep94 7Bel6	Uncharted Waters		3	110	6	7	6^2	8	8	8	8	Samyn J L	23.90

OFF AT 5:15 Start Good. Won driving. Time, :24³, :49, 1:14¹, 1:40, 1:46³ Course soft.

$2 Mutuel Prices:			
6-(F)-JADE FLUSH	25.00	10.00	6.00
9-(I)-LADY AFFIRMED		4.40	3.60
4-(D)-SAXUALITY			3.40

$2 EXACTA 6-9 PAID $95.00 $2 TRIPLE 6-9-4 PAID $269.00

Ch. f, (Apr), by Jade Hunter–Royal Strait Flush, by Seattle Slew. Trainer Zito Nicholas P. Bred by Paulson Allen E (Ky).

JADE FLUSH sprinted clear in the early stages, raced uncontested on the front for five furlongs, dug in when challenged at the top of the stretch then drew away under steady right hand encouragement. LADY AFFIRMED trailed for nearly a half, moved up rapidly while four wide to threaten approaching the stretch, but was no match for the winner while outfinishing SAXUALITY for the place. SAXUALITY unhurried early, launched a rally between horses leaving the far turn, made a run to reach contention on the turn then lacked a strong closing bid. KNOCKNOCK raced in close contention along the inside for seven furlongs then finished evenly. GOLDEN TAJNIAK raced just behind the early leaders, steadied along the inside on the far turn and failed to threaten thereafter. CASA EIRE prompted the pace between horses for five furlongs and tired. GRAFIN raced in traffic along the backstretch, angled out on the turn then lacked the needed response when called upon. UNCHARTED WATERS was never a factor.

Owners— 1, Condren & Cornacchia & Paulson; 2, Harbor View Farm; 3, Alexander Leslie; 4, Oh Tony Stable; 5, Perez Robert; 6, Connaughton Bernard; 7, Mohammed Al Maktoum; 8, Steinberg Philip & Teinowitz W

Trainers—1, Zito Nicholas P; 2, Jerkens H Allen; 3, Terrill William V; 4, Schwartz Scott M; 5, Callejas Alfredo; 6, O'Brien Leo; 7, Boutin Francois; 8, Schulhofer Flint S

Scratched— Avie's Fancy (5Sep94 9MED1)

$2 Pick-6 (7-6-3-14-2-6) 6 Correct 7 Tickets Paid $8,174.00; 5 Correct 189 Tickets Paid $100.00; Pick-6 Pool $101,730.

Much like Dahlia's Dreamer the week before, Jade Flush fell out on a clear lead, and never looked back. While it is true that, generally speaking, finishing ability is paramount to success on grass, this much is also true: it is much more difficult for horses to accelerate when the going is soft and laboring, and weight also has more of an effect under such conditions than it does on harder, more resilient surfaces. Horses lightly weighted and capable of setting the pace with an even rate of energy distribution are a formidable presence on soft turf.

Jade Flush could not be considered a "standout" selection, but there were enough positives in her record to make odds of 11-1 an acceptable risk; perhaps not along the lines of a prime bet, but certainly a flyer who rated a "chance at a price."

Jade Flush was in good form going into the Rare Perfume, but that fact was partially hidden by a poor last-race finish. Returned to a surface she liked, and allowed to get brave on a clear lead as had been the case at Saratoga, she responded with a romping win at 11-1. Jade Flush was erratic, but was capable of murderous performances under adverse conditions many horses do not like: slop and soft turf. Whatever the reason, be it conformation, soreness soothed by cushy ground, the mechanics of her stride, Jade Flush moved up many lengths when the ground was to her liking.

It wasn't long before another situation came along where a subtle and positive read about a horse's footing preference proved to be the key:

6 Belmont Park

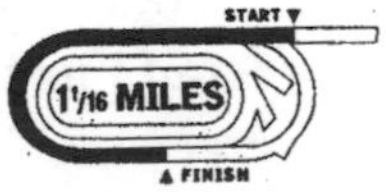

1 1/16 MILES. (1:394) ALLOWANCE. Purse $32,000. 3-year-olds and upward which have not won a race other than maiden, claiming or starter. Weights: 3-year-olds, 119 lbs. Older, 122 lbs. Non-winners of a race other than claiming at a mile or over since September 15, allowed 3 lbs. Of such a race since September 1, 5 lbs.

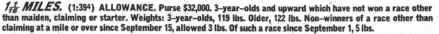

Pleasant Dancer

Own: Buckland Farm
MIGLIORE R (73 8 16 6 .11)

B. c. 3 (Mar)
Sire: Pleasant Colony (His Majesty)
Dam: Dance Review (Northern Dancer)
Br: T. M. Evans (Va)
Tr: Campo John P (5 1 0 0 .20)

114

Lifetime Record:	10 1 2 1	$29,815			
1994	6 0 2 0	$11,745	Turf	0 0 0 0	
1993	4 1 0 1	$18,070	Wet	3 0 1 0	$6,600
Bel	3 0 0 0	$1,680	Dist	2 0 0 0	

15Sep94-6Bel	fst	1⅛	:472 1:113 1:361 1:483	3↑ Alw 32000N1X	70	6	4	3½	31	68½	612¾	Santos J A	113	5.80	75-11	Peace Negotiations113½ Absent Minded1136½ Concoctor1133½	Gave way	6
22Aug94-7Sar	my	1⅛	:471 1:121 1:381 1:512	3↑ Alw 30000N1X	77	1	1	32½	53½	33	25½	Sellers S J	112	10.10	73-23	Wayfarer1175½ PleasantDancer112no PeaceNegotiations112nk	Up for place	7
31Jly94-8Sar	fst	1⅛	:472 1:113 1:363 1:493	Jim Dandy-G2	78	1	4	59	515	512	518	Sellers S J	112	29.00	70-13	Unaccounted For1141 Tabasco Cat1265 Ulises11412	No factor	5
13Jly94-5Bel	fst	6f	:223 :46 :584 1:114	3↑ Alw 28000N1X	67	4	1	65¾	67½	53½	43¾	Alvarado F T	114	13.50	78-15	Thru 'n Thru1131½ Timeless Endeavor114no The Jogger1132¼	Outrun	6
13Mar94-7Lrl	fst	7½f	:232 :471 1:121 1:304	Alw 16800N1X	85	7	5	43½	21½	23	23¼	Skinner K	115	8.30	— —	Mr. Meadow1153¼ Pleasant Dancer1151¼ Curriamo1202¼	Held place	7
22Jan94-5Aqu	fst	170 ⊡	:234 :474 1:132 1:441	Count Fleet54k	64	4	3	31	4¾	66	612¼	Guerra W A	113	13.00	65-24	Sonny's Bruno1131¼ Cape Verde1131 Hussonet1133	Tired	7
11Dec93-8Aqu	sly	1 1/16 ⊡	:222 :463 1:114 1:463	Nashua-G3	60	5	—	—	—	—	614¼	Guerra W A	114	20.40	58-31	Popol's Gold114no Personal Merit1171¼ Sonny's Bruno1143½	Snow	11
27Nov93-2Aqu	fst	1	:233 :472 1:13 1:392	Md Sp Wt	74	4	2	2½	1½	1hd	1nk	Guerra W A	118	5.10	67-31	Pleasant Dancer118nk Chockie Mountain1181¾ Signal Tap1186½	Driving	10
3Nov93-1Med	fst	1	:233 :471 1:121 1:384	Md Sp Wt	62	2	7	65½	57	55½	35¾	Guerra W A	118	3.90	76-17	Jericho Blaise1183¾ Barge In1182 Pleasant Dancer1182	Mild rally	9
19Sep93-5Bel	my	7f	:23 :462 1:112 1:243	Md Sp Wt	41	5	2	1hd	42½	77½	515¾	Cruguet J	118	7.70	64-20	Personal Escort1182¼ Turnbull Creek1182 Red Mcfly1189½	Used up	8

WORKOUTS: Sep 30 Bel tr.t 5f fst 1:011 H *3/10* Sep 9 Bel tr.t 5f fst 1:02 B *2/8* Sep 3 Bel tr.t 3f fst :373 B *7/9* Aug 20 Sar tr.t 3f fst :371 B *3/16* ●Aug 12 Sar tr.t 5f fst 1:023 B *1/6* Jly 25 Sar 5f fst 1:02 H *26/64*

Timeless Dream

Own: Cooper Audrey Hastings
PEREZ R M (64 11 7 7 .17)

Ch. g. 3 (Mar)
Sire: Timeless Native (Timeless Moment)
Dam: Daydream (Believe It)
Br: Lucy G. Bassett (Ky)
Tr: O'Brien Leo (56 6 5 4 .11)

1095

Lifetime Record:	8 1 2 1	$32,470			
1994	6 1 2 0	$28,240	Turf	0 0 0 0	
1993	2 M 0 1	$4,230	Wet	2 0 2 0	$11,440
Bel	3 1 0 0	$18,210	Dist	0 0 0 0	

Entered 4Oct94- 6 BEL

25Sep94-5Bel	gd	1	:23 :453 1:093 1:351	3↑ Alw 32000N1X	65	4	3	41	53¾	510	512	Velazquez J R	113	4.50	75-15	Free Agent1131 Concoctor113½ Absent Minded1133	Tired	5
11Sep94-1Bel	fst	6f	:223 :46 :574 1:10	3↑ Md Sp Wt	82	6	7	56½	3½	11	13	Velazquez J R	118	*1.80	91-08	Timeless Dream1183 Expressed1223 Cozy Prospect1181¾	Drew off	7
14Aug94-2Sar	sly	1⅛	:483 1:131 1:382 1:511	3↑ Md Sp Wt	76	2	2	21½	22	2½	27	Santos J A	117	*1.30	73-22	PrivateCody1177 TimelessDrem117½ Libertine1174	Not pushed final 1/16	7
29Jly94-2Sar	my	6f	:222 :453 :574 1:103	3↑ Md Sp Wt	94	6	5	79	76½	37	25½	Chavez J F	116	8.40	82-19	Scherbo1165½ TimelessDream1166 AprilChristms1161¾	Wide, belated rally	7
15Feb94-5Aqu	fst	6f ⊡	:231 :463 :591 1:122	Md Sp Wt	59	8	6	63¼	53¾	44½	57	Velazquez J R	122	2.90	74-22	Cosa Diavolo122½ Approximate1224 Showiz122no	Bumped early	11
4Feb94-7Aqu	fst	6f ⊡	:223 :462 :592 1:123	Md Sp Wt	57	2	8	98¾	96½	97½	57¾	Leon F5	117	*2.10	72-21	Hi Jinxer1224 Lulu's Little Boy1221½ Copper Mount122¾	Dull effort	10
28Jly93-3Sar	fst	5f	:214 :451 :573	Md Sp Wt	77	4	3	53½	52	3½	31¾	Velazquez J R	118	4.10	95-08	Goodbye Doeny1181¾ Hussonet118no Timeless Dream1182¾	Willingly	7
8Jly93-5Bel	fst	5f	:214 :451 :58	Md Sp Wt	63	1	2	2hd	1hd	41½	44¾	Velazquez J R	110	15.60	86 09	The Jogger118¾ Explored1182 Frisco Gold1182	Dueled inside	8

WORKOUTS: Sep 22 Bel Ⓣ 4f fm :513 B (d) *13/17* Sep 10 Bel 3f fst :384 B *18/25* ●Aug 31 Sar tr.t 5f fst 1:033 B *1/4* Aug 25 Sar tr.t 4f fst :501 B *6/19* Aug 8 Sar tr.t 3f fst :392 B *13/15* Jly 25 Sar tr.t 5f fst 1:023 B *2/13*

Golden Plover

Own: Ardboe Stable
SANTOS J A (106 14 15 10 .13)

B. c. 3 (Mar)
Sire: Storm Bird (Northern Dancer)
Dam: Aliata (Mr. Prospector)
Br: Moseley Mr & Mrs James (Ky)
Tr: Schulhofer Flint S (38 7 1 5 .18)

114

Lifetime Record:	8 1 1 1	$15,295			
1994	8 1 1 1	$15,295	Turf	4 0 1 0	$6,770
1993	0 M 0 0		Wet	1 0 0 1	$1,100
Bel	0 0 0 0		Dist	1 0 0 0	$825

13Sep94-6Bel	fm	1⅜ Ⓣ	:47 1:12 1:364 2:132	3↑ Alw 32000N1X	68	7	1	1½	1hd	21	88¾	Santos J A	114 b	6.00	78-12	BestOfMusic1132½ BewreTheQuest113¾ ThWildIrishmn1171¼	Used in pace	12
25Aug94-7Sar	fm	1 3/16 ⓣ	:472 1:121 1:371 1:564	3↑ Alw 30000N1X	82	4	4	32	31½	21½	22	Maple E	112 fb	38.00	79-25	Henry S.1122 Golden Plover1121¼ Stayed Too Long117nk	Checked 1/16 pl	11
15Aug94-8Sar	yl	1⅛ Ⓣ	:493 1:141 1:384 1:513	3↑ Alw 30000N2L	69	11	7	74	74¾	67¾	69¼	Krone J A	112 fb	34.10	68-21	Trevelyan112nk Inside The Beltway1121¾ Rugged Bugger1121¼	No threat	11
3Jly94-4Mth	fm	1 1/16 ⓣ	:241 :474 1:12 1:431	3↑ Alw 17000N1X	66	8	3	42½	41¾	62¾	58	Santagata N	113 fb	18.10	80-14	Hero's Warning1162 MyBrotherGary1081½ RaiseYourBlade1164	Bid, tired	10
22Jun94-7Mth	fst	1 1/16	:224 :471 1:122 1:461	3↑ Alw 16500N2L	66	4	7	63¾	35	310	419½	Thomas D B	113 f	13.80	54-30	Love Song1082 Precious Link11214 Blue Dan You1143	Jostled start	8
30May94-7Suf	fst	6f	:221 :452 :581 1:12	3↑ Alw 11760N2L	47	2	8	43½	36½	510	812½	Gambardella C	B 114 f	3.10	75-17	Bronx Boy1223¾ Fearless Devil1141½ Brassy Loopie1161	Stum st, stopped	8
11May94-8Suf	fst	6f	:223 :471 1:002 1:141	3↑ Md Sp Wt	63	4	7	31½	1½	14	14½	Gambardella C	B 122 f	*1.40	77-23	Golden Plover1224½ Holme Room1224½ Kaltondori1223½	2w, ridden out	10
1May94-6Suf	wf	6f	:224 :464 1:001 1:144	3↑ Md Sp Wt	54	8	4	21	2½	21½	32½	Caraballo J C	B 118 f	*.60	71-27	Del'sLittleMan1221¾ WindsweptGoal114¾ GoldenPlover1184½	2 wide, tired	8

WORKOUTS: Oct 1 Bel 4f fst :492 B *24/50* Sep 26 Bel 4f fst :47 H *2/50* Sep 21 Bel 4f fst :493 B *20/36* ●Sep 9 Bel 4f fst :464 H *1/22* Aug 8 Sar tr.t ⓣ 4f fm :483 H *17/28*

Canheski
Own: Sullimar Stable
SAMYN J L (48 8 4 5 .17)

B. g. 3 (Jan)
Sire: Baldski (Nijinsky II)
Dam: Candy Castle (Habitat)
Br: Sullivan Mary A (Fla)
Tr: Johnson Philip G (31 4 3 4 .13)

114

Lifetime Record :	5 1 1 0	$10,535			
1994	5 1 1 0	$10,535	Turf	1 0 0 0	
1993	0 M 0 0		Wet	1 0 0 0	
Bel	2 1 1 0	$10,440	Dist	0 0 0 0	

21Sep94-9Bel	fst	1	:23	:461	1:112	1:373	3↑ Md 35000	72	8	5	4¾	4¾	13	17	Samyn J L	118 b	5.20	75-19	Canheski1187 Iain's Storm118½ Facetious Buck114nk	Wide, driving 12
7Sep94-5Bel	fst	6f	:221	:452	:581	1:11	3↑ Md 30000	72	5	5	813	712	47	22½	Samyn J L	114 b	48.50	83-14	Speedy Harry1182½ Canheski114nk Stantorian1134½	Belated rally 10
24May94-5Bel	fm	1 1/16 Ⓣ	:232	:464	1:111	1:431	3↑ Md Sp Wt	33	2	6	42	75	79¼	817½	Hernandez R	115 b	5.90	62-23	Price Rise115nk Jacsonzac1171¼ Thirty Good Ones115nk	Steadied far turn 10
10Apr94-9Aqu	wf	6f	:22	:452	:581	1:113	Md 45000	32	9	6	107¾	1010	1011	813½	Leon F	118	13.40	70-11	You The Man118nk Spicy Promises1181 Approximate1221	Outrun 10
20Mar94-12Hia	fst	7f	:23	:46	1:112	1:243	Md 50000	47	8	10	108½	1013	912	711½	Samyn J L	122	11.60	74-11	Mighty Bowl1221½ Parella Fella1173½ Request A Star118¾	Mild bid 12

WORKOUTS: Sep 30 Bel tr.t 3f fst :364 B 5/19 Sep 16 Bel tr.t 4f fst :512 B 8/10 Sep 2 Bel tr.t 3f fst :364 B 2/12 Aug 27 Sar tr.t 5f fst 1:043 B 4/5 Aug 21 Sar tr.t 6f fst 1:172 B 2/5 Aug 16 Sar tr.t 4f fst :504 B 13/40

Absent Minded
Own: Cohen Robert B
MAPLE E (61 6 10 6 .10)

B. g. 3 (Apr)
Sire: Polish Navy (Danzig)
Dam: Wimbledon Star (Hoist the Flag)
Br: Brushwood Stable (Pa)
Tr: Shapoff Stanley R (27 4 4 2 .15)

114

Lifetime Record :	7 1 3 1	$39,331			
1994	7 1 3 1	$39,331	Turf	1 0 0 0	
1993	0 M 0 0		Wet	1 1 0 0	$16,200
Bel	3 0 2 1	$17,920	Dist	1 0 1 0	$7,040

25Sep94-5Bel	gd	1	:23	:453	1:093	1:351	3↑ Alw 32000N1X	85	3	1	2hd	1hd	2½	31½	Maple E	113 b	2.20	85-15	Free Agent1131 Concoctor113½ Absent Minded1133	Dueled, weakened 5
15Sep94-6Bel	fst	1⅛	:472	1:113	1:361	1:483	3↑ Alw 32000N1X	90	4	2	2hd	1½	11½	2½	Maple E	113 b	4.40	87-11	Peace Negotiations113½ Absent Minded1136½ Concoctor1133½	Gamely 6
2Sep94-6Bel	fst	1 1/16	:232	:464	1:11	1:422	3↑ Alw 32000N1X	84	9	2	2½	2hd	2hd	22½	Maple E	113 b	14.80	87-10	Kerfoot Corner1132½ Absent Minded113nk Per Pop1174¾	Gamely 9
25Aug94-7Sar	fm	1 3/16 Ⓣ	:472	1:121	1:371	1:564	3↑ Alw 30000N1X	62	3	3	43	42½	97	811	Smith M E	114 b	7.50	70-25	HenryS.1122 GoldenPlover1121¼ StayedTooLong117nk	Check 1/16 pl, tired 11
23Jly94-2Sar	my	1⅛ ⊗	:464	1:114	1:391	1:524	3↑ Md Sp Wt	84	7	3	1½	11	12	11¾	Day P	116 b	*.90	72-27	Absent Minded1161¾ Ace The Test1225 Tenochtitlan11616	Driving 8
19Jun94-5CD	fst	7f	:223	:461	1:112	1:233	3↑ Md Sp Wt	84	7	3	42½	2½	21½	23	Romero R P	113 fb	8.70	89-12	Inflate1123 Absent Minded1133 Rocket City112½	Bid, second best 12
28May94-6CD	fst	7f	:224	:461	1:111	1:241	3↑ Md Sp Wt	75	1	9	52¼	41¾	56½	46½	Sellers S J	113 fb	4.00	82-11	BlzngBsqu1104½ BondByHonor1121 LookForTrobl1121	No late response 12

WORKOUTS: Oct 3 Bel tr.t 4f fst :494 B 16/26 Sep 22 Bel tr.t 4f fst :483 H 8/18 Sep 11 Bel 6f fst 1:122 H 2/4 Sep 1 Bel tr.t 3f fst :352 H 2/16 Aug 21 Sar 6f fst 1:142 H 2/4 Aug 17 Sar tr.t Ⓣ 6f fm 1:18 B 6/6

At first glance, the sixth race on October 6 didn't seem to hold much promise from a wagering point-of-view. The preliminary allowance route was a one-turn affair (all races up to and including a mile and an eighth require only one turn on Belmont's massive main track) at a mile and a sixteenth, and drew a field of five after scratches including a 2-5 favorite, Absent Minded.

A cursory examination of the past performances suggested Absent Minded would be tough to beat. His two previous one-turn routes at Belmont on fast tracks had earned him Beyers of 90 and 84; of the others, Pleasant Dancer's 78, earned at Saratoga, represented the best Beyer in a route run over a fast track, and that colt had been a dozen lengths behind Absent Minded when they met at Belmont on September 15.

If things were that simple, however, we would all simply wait for 2-5 shots like Absent Minded to come along, bet everything we had, and slowly but surely amass our fortunes; indeed there are a handful of bettors who fit that description: that rare breed known as "bridgejumpers."

Real life doesn't work that way, especially at the racetrack, where one of the basic guidelines for success is to minimize risk while maximizing profits. For a 2-5 to be legitimate, it must look like a mortal cinch from every conceivable angle, and even then it's only worthwhile use is as a single in the Pick 6. A picky player (the best kind to be) could poke a few holes in Absent Minded's record: his only victory had come in the mud, and he had lost ground through the final furlong in all three allowance starts on dirt at Belmont, notably blowing a clear midstretch lead two races back.

The horse with a profile slightly different from the others was Golden Plover, who was returning to dirt after four races on grass (over four different layouts at varying distances) at Monmouth, Saratoga and Belmont. Golden Plover was the distant second choice at 5-1.

Golden Plover had never raced on Belmont's main track, but all indications were that he liked it very, very much. To recall, I stated earlier that this book would probably be best-received by those who would go forth in a snowstorm for a *Form* just to get the charts. I amend that statement here, to add that you're just as concerned about maintaining a chronological file of the *Form's* workout tabs as well. If not, you should be. The few seconds that it takes to file the tabs away is time well spent, because the importance and relevance of the information contained therein is often underestimated, and underbet, by the Beyer-crazed crowd.

Taking a look now at Golden Plover's workout line, note that in his two workouts termed "handily" by the clockers (both works on the main track), the colt had shown nothing less than exceptional speed. (As an aside, it puzzles me that the term "handily" has two entirely different meanings in describing horses' performances: during the afternoon in actual competition, "handily" describes an easy winner, noticeably more authoritative than "driving" and "ridden out", but not quite as effortless as "easily," which describes a horse who is being eased up under the wire. The handy winner is neither being whipped, nor subjected to urging through the jockey's hands, which remain motionless as the horse wins "in hand." But for morning workouts, "breezing" conveys the same thing "handily" means in a race, while workouts termed "handily" mean the horse was asked more aggressively for a strenuous effort).

In any event, Golden Plover's drill of September 9 was best-of-22, and a check of the actual tab itself revealed how impressive it was:

BELMONT PARK — Track Fast

Three Furlongs							
Bronze Willow	:37¹ B	Trailblazer	:37⁴ B	Promising Rainbow	:48¹ H	Secret Weapon	1:02 B
Canadian Halo	:37⁴ B	Valid Impression	:37 Hg	Saucy Relic	:50 B	Spire	1:01³ H
Chenin Blanc	:39 B	**Four Furlongs**		Scoop The Gold	:51 B	Toomuchpleasure	1:02² Hg
Criminal Bundle	:36 B	Clear Mandate	:49² B	Skipper	:47² H	**Six Furlongs** 1:07⁴	
Criminal Speedy	:36⁴ Bg	Cool Change	:49² B	Tabloid Tattle	:49⁴ B	As Indicated	1:12¹ H
Detached	:37¹ Hg	D'moment	:48 H	Tidal Wavy	:48³ B	Napper Tandy	1:17³ Bg
Dr. Alfoos	:34¹ H	Francis Marion	:47 H	Transient Trend	:50³ Bg	Seeking Regina	1:15⁴ B
England Expects	:36² B	Gliding Lark	:54 B	Vega's Secret	:48⁴ H	Vigorous Princess	1:15⁴ H
Facula	:36 B	Golden Plover	:46⁴ H	Volatility	:48 H	West Point Mint	1:14 H
Father Shea	:36² H	Johnny North	:49¹ B	**Five Furlongs** :56¹		Wild Surmise	1:16 B
Johnnys Glory	:36 H	Justfortherecord	:48 H	Alytune	1:01¹ H	**Seven Furlongs** 1:20¹	
Passive Aggresive	:37¹ Hg	Kerfoot Corner	:47⁴ H	Conduit Street	1:02 B	Blarneystone Lass	1:28 B
Pastures New	:38¹ B	Merciful Judge	:48 H	Garendare(GB)	1:02¹ B	Outlaw	1:28³ B
Seminole Storm	:37¹ Hg	Nobody Picked Six	:53 B	Kentucky Blush	1:01¹ H		
Share The Fun	:37 B	Odawa Moon	:48⁴ B	Little Fran	1:02² H		
		Out From Under	:49 B	Missymooiloveyou	1:01⁴ H		

GOLDEN PLOVER (4f) pulled up in :58 4/5. AS INDICATED (6f) is steadily progressing.

According to the comment at the bottom, Golden Plover had *pulled up* in :58 4/5, which was roughly a dozen lengths faster than the best listed five-furlong workout on the tab!

After an easy breeze on September 21, Golden Plover was again asked for speed five days later, and responded with a :47 that was second-best of 50 at the distance. (In the days before the *Form* listed workout-rankings, this information would've been pure gold, for there was no "bullet" to attract attention to a work that had been faster than 48 others) A look at the full September 26 tab:

Monday   September 26, 1994

ARLINGTON — Track Muddy   (Dogs Up)

Three Furlongs						
Little Toi Soldier	:38 B	Flying Ten	:53² B	Shotgun Slew	:51² Bg	I M Redrum	1:04 Bg
M C's Pearl	:39⁴ B	For Brentton	:52³ B	Swift Dispersal	:54 B	Kuma	1:02³ B
Midway Queen	:36³ Bg	Hair Cut	:54 B	Tow Zone	:51² Bg	Level Sands	1:03 B
Young Sprout	:36² Bg	King And Hart	:54⁴ B	Wild Runner	:54⁴ B	Majesty M. D.	1:06⁴ B
Four Furlongs		Lite Touch	:51 B	Five Furlongs	:57¹	Mickey C.	1:06² B
Alyrivo	:51⁴ B	Major Power	:53 B	Adarec	1:01⁴ B	Pantano	1:03³ B
Budman Dude	:54⁴ B	Miss Blushable	:51² B	Bossman Dude	1:03³ Bg	Steel Rain	1:05¹ B
D's Moment	:54⁴ B	Our Gatsby	:51² B	Della Deluxa	1:06⁴ B	Western Cowgirl	1:01³ H
Double Jeopardy	:52 B	Our Onother	:54⁴ B	Denouncer	1:06⁴ B	Six Furlongs	1:08
Eskimo Slush	:53² B	Rising Of The Moon	:49³ B	Dr. Cardia	1:06⁴ B	Pleasure's Diamond	1:16 B
		Round The Mountain	:49³ B	Fit Dancer	1:06⁴ B		

BELMONT PARK — Track Fast

Three Furlongs						
Advanced Placement	:34³ H	Brite Guy	:50⁴ B	Learning The Ropes	:48⁴ B	Chostah	1:03 B
Apolda	:38 B	Cigar	:49⁴ B	Lost Soldier	:48⁴ B	Dahar's Best	1:01¹ B
Devilicious	:36⁴ B	Colonal Hart	:49⁴ B	Merci'ocain	:50 B	Date Stone	1:03 B
Figgity Feet	:39 B	Colonial Affair	:47³ H	Miss Prospector	:48 B	Flying Cherub	1:02 B
Found Money	:37³ B	Cosa Diavolo	:48⁴ B	Montreal Red	:49⁴ B	Homah Naskra	1:01³ B
Funny Wild	:37 B	Crafty Lady	:51 B	Moonlight Dancer	:48⁴ B	Jade Flush	1:02¹ B
Gem Seeker	:36² B	Crowned Crane	:48 B	Mr Market	:48 B	Madame Adolphe	1:01² B
Kerfoot Corner	:38² B	D'moment	:48³ B	Prenup	:49³ B	Miss Carolina(PR)	1:03 B
Prayer Warrior	:36⁴ B	Demon Damon	:49¹ B	Promising Rainbow	:48⁴ D	O'star	1:02 B
She's Fine	:38 B	Fifth Set	:48 B	Red Rosio	:51 B	Parmelina	1:01² B
Golden Plover	:47 H	Golden Plover	:47 H	Reflection	:51² B	Poulet Chasseur	1:01² B
Shepherd's Moon	:36⁴ B	Golden Pro	:49 B	Rient	:51 B	Quant	1:01² B
Stauder	:35³ H	Gray Mood	:49 B	So Sterling	:48⁴ B	Scoop The Gold	1:00³ H
Trusted Friend	:39 B	Green Gaitor	:48¹ B	Spirited Player	:48³ B	Signal Tap	1:00 H
Whitney Tower	:38 B	High Talent	:49³ B	Symphony Lady	:51 B	Star Standard	1:03⁴ B
Four Furlongs		Hollie	:49³ B	Tabloid Tattle	:50⁴ B	Venetian Red	1:03³ B
A Call To Rise	:49¹ B	Inside The Beltway	:46³ H	Talb	:50 B	Six Furlongs	1:07⁴
Aly Tigress	:48⁴ B	Iron Lady	:51³ B	Volatility	:50¹ B	Conduit Street	1:14⁴ H
Anzac Native	:49⁴ B	Irving's Girl	:48³ B	Wicked And Wild	:50⁴ B	Gala Star	1:13³ H
Axe Creek	:49² B	Ivor's Chukka	:49² B	Five Furlongs	:56¹	Johnnys Glory	1:16 B
Aztec Hill	:50 B	Kelbey	:48 B	Adams Trail	1:01 B		
Baling Wire	:48⁴ B	Lady Trilogy	:49² B	Aspen Gal	1:03 B		
Boynton Canyon	:53 B	Lawman	:49⁴ B	Cayman Slough	1:03 B		

STAUDER (3f) is sharp. MONTREAL RED (4f) holds his good form. SIGNAL TAP (5f) galloped out 3/4's in 1:12 3/5.

Golden Plover's time had been two ticks off the best of the morning. Just as significantly, his time of :47 was at least a full second faster than every other half-mile work on the tab...with the exception of his stablemate, Colonial Affair, whom he'd "only" outworked by three lengths. A month earlier, Scotty Schulhofer had sent Colonial Affair out to win the Grade 1 Whitney Handicap (he would go on to win the Jockey Club Gold Cup before being retired due to injury in the final days leading up to the Breeder's Cup Classic).

Golden Plover had been racing on turf, yes, but there was nothing in his record to suggest that he was, in fact, a turf horse. And his recent workouts literally shouted that he was getting over the Belmont strip with all due haste. After all, his maiden victory had come on dirt, and at the time *someone* must've believed he could handle it, for he was dispatched at 3-5 and 7-5 for his first two starts at Suffolk Downs. After being roughed up at the start of his next two dirt races the colt had spent the entire summer on the grass, and hadn't raced too shabbily on that surface, either, though his good form was nicely camouflaged.

After racing evenly from the extreme outside post over yielding ground while making his first start in six weeks August 15, he had finished nine lengths in front of Absent Minded on the main turf course ten days later, pressing the pace throughout and holding for second despite checking a sixteenth from the wire. His most recent race of September 13 served to throw many bettors off the scent, thanks to an ugly-looking eighth place finish and a low Beyer of 68. The number by itself is meaningless. Many figure-makers, whether they are concerned with fractional or final time, will not even try to rate races at a mile and three-eighths, where the effects of pace can and often do throw things way out of whack. And even if you were going to rate Golden Plover off that race, it would be prudent to have a look at his position at the stretch call, a point at which he was running second, just a length from the lead — after having engaged in a prolonged duel. Especially noteworthy is the fact that, in races at a mile and three-eighths, the stretch call makes note of horses' respective positions after they have traveled a mile and a quarter — *after they have run 10 of the race's 11 furlongs, or 90.9 percent of the race!* It goes without saying, then, that horses who lose considerable ground in the final furlong of these marathons often go postward at generous odds when cut back to shorter routes.

With none of the others striking fear into handicapper's hearts, Golden Plover, a horse with recent, hidden good form who was tearing up the track in the mornings, was 5-1 against Absent Minded, a gelding who already had managed to come out second best in three of his seven career starts.

Make that four out of eight:

	SIXTH RACE													

SIXTH RACE
Belmont
OCTOBER 6, 1994

1¼ MILES. (1.394) ALLOWANCE. Purse $32,000. 3–year–olds and upward which have not won a race other than maiden, claiming or starter. Weights: 3–year–olds, 119 lbs. Older, 122 lbs. Non–winners of a race other than claiming at a mile or over since September 15, allowed 3 lbs. Of such a race since September 1, 5 lbs.

Value of Race: $32,040. Winner $19,200; second $7,040; third $3,840; fourth $1,920. Mutuel Pool $181,876.00 Exacta Pool $360,509.00 Minus Show Pool $9,253.93

Last Raced	Horse	M/Eqt. A.Wt	PP	St	¼	½	¾	Str	Fin	Jockey	Odds $1
13Sep94 9Bel9	Golden Plover	3 114	3	2	2²	1hd	1½	11½	12¾	Santos J A	5.00
25Sep94 5Bel3	Absent Minded	b 3 114	5	1	4¹	5	2¹	22½	2³	Maple E	0.40
25Sep94 5Bel5	Timeless Dream	3 109	2	5	5	4½	3hd	34	3⁹	Perez R M5	6.60
21Sep94 9Bel1	Canheski	b 3 114	4	3	3½	3hd	4½	42	43¼	Samyn J L	7.20
15Sep94 6Bel6	Pleasant Dancer	b 3 114	1	4	1½	22½	5	5	5	Migliore R	10.70

OFF AT 3:30 Start Good. Won driving. Time, :24, :47³, 1:11³, 1:36², 1:42⁴ Track fast.

$2 Mutuel Prices:	4–(D)–GOLDEN PLOVER	12.00	3.40	2.10
	6–(F)–ABSENT MINDED		2.40	2.10
	3–(C)–TIMELESS DREAM			2.10

$2 EXACTA 4–6 PAID $26.00

B. c, (Mar), by Storm Bird–Aliata, by Mr. Prospector. Trainer Schulhofer Flint S. Bred by Moseley Mr & Mrs James (Ky).

GOLDEN PLOVER forced the early pace from outside, took charge on the far turn, dug in when challenged by ABSENT MINDED approaching the stretch then drew clear under pressure. ABSENT MINDED reserved early, rallied three wide to challenge on the turn but was no match for the winner. TIMELESS DREAM lodged a mild rally between horses on the turn then flattened out. CANHESKI raced just off the pace between horses, checked inside ABSENT MINDED on the turn, then tired. PLEASANT DANCER set the early pace along the inside then gave way after going a half.

Owners— 1, Ardboe Stable; 2, Cohen Robert B; 3, Cooper Audrey Haslings; 4, Sullimar Stable; 5, Buckland Farm

Trainers—1, Schulhofer Flint S; 2, Shapoff Stanley R; 3, O'Brien Leo; 4, Johnson Philip G; 5, Campo John P

Scratched— O' Lucky Star (18Sep94 3BEL 1)

Golden Plover, who had an excellent conditioning foundation ("bottom") thanks to his series of longer turf routes, had been sharpened to a fine edge in his workouts on the main track, and ran right to those works by widening his lead on Absent Minded at each call following an easy opening pace. Note the third quarter was run in :24, identical to the first quarter — a race shape inhospitable to Absent Minded after he had somehow been taken back to last by Eddie Maple, who just happens to be one of Andy Beyer's favorite riders of all time.

Somewhat ironically, Golden Plover received considerably more respect at the windows when, three weeks later, he sought to parlay his successful turf-to-dirt switch into another victory at the next level of allowances. He ran very well this time, too, finishing a clear second; unfortunately, he had the misfortune to run into someone else who adapted readily to a change in surface from turf to dirt:

Cigar
Own: Paulson Allen E
BAILEY J D (—)

B. h. 5
Sire: Palace Music (The Minstrel)
Dam: Solar Slew (Seattle Slew)
Br: Paulson Allen E (Md)
Tr: Mott William I (—)

LB 124

Lifetime Record :	20	9	2	4	$1,579,815						
1995	5	5	0	0	$1,309,800	Turf	11	1	2	4	$82,015
1994	6	2	0	2	$180,840	Wet	0	0	0	0	
Suf	0	0	0	0		Dist	2	2	0	0	$630,000

13May95-10Pim	fst	1 3/16	:48 1:112 1:351 1:533	Pim Spec H-G1	**114**	1	1	1 1½	1 1½	15	12¼	Bailey J D	L 122	*.40	106-02	Cigar1222¼ Devil His Due1212¾ Concern1214½	Ridden out 6
15Apr95-9OP	fst	1⅛	:462 1:104 1:352 1:471	Oaklawn H-G1	**121**	4	4	45	41½	1hd	12½	Bailey J D	L 120	*1.70	103-13	Cigar1202½ Silver Goblin1194 Concern1221	7
Bumped, hit by opponents' whip, driving																	
5Mar95-9GP	fst	1¼	:472 1:114 1:364 2:024	3↑ Gulf Park H-G1	**116**	9	4	45	1hd	15	17½	Bailey J D	L 118	*.50	87-19	Cigar1187½ Pride Of Burkaan1141 Mahogany Hall1132	11
Six wide bkstr, six wide top str, ridden out																	
11Feb95-9GP	fst	1⅛	:462 1:103 1:363 1:493	3↑ Donn H-G1	**114**	4	1	12	1hd	1½	15½	Bailey J D	L 115	4.00	89-13	Cigar1155½ Primitive Hall1121½ Bonus Money1123½	9
Five wide top str, drifted out driving																	
22Jan95-10GP	fst	1 1/16	:231 :464 1:112 1:431	Alw 33000N4X	**108**	5	1	1hd	11	1 1½	12	Bailey J D	L 122	*.50	92-13	Cigar1222 Upping The Ante1198¾ Chasin Gold1221	8
Crowded, bumped start, driving																	
26Nov94-8Aqu	fst	1	:223 :454 1:111 1:36	3↑ NYRA Mile H-G1	**115**	6	4	42	1 1½	17	17	Bailey J D	111	8.90	88-28	Cigar1117 Devil His Due1242¼ Punch Line1121	Wide, ridden out 12
28Oct94-6Aqu	fst	1	:222 :443 1:094 1:353	3↑ Alw 34000N2X	**104**	6	2	12	13	16	18	Smith M E	117	3.50	90-23	Cigar1178 Golden Plover1193½ Gulliviegold1092	Handily 6
7Oct94-8Bel	fm	1 1/16 Ⓣ	:232 :463 1:104 1:412	3↑ Alw 36000N3X	**79**	2	4	35	2½	34½	38½	Krone J A	117	3.40	80-15	Unaccounted For1142½ Same Old Wish1198 Cigar117½	Flattened out 6
16Sep94-7Bel	fm	1 Ⓣ	:23 :452 1:083 1:33	3↑ Alw 34000N2X	**76**	10	8	77¼	45	66¾	78½	Bailey J D	117	*1.90	89-13	Jido1082½ Bermuda Cedar1142 Limited War1132	Wide, flattened out 11
8Aug94-1Sar	fm	1⅛ Ⓣ	:472 1:12 1:363 1:483	3↑ Alw 34000N3X	**86**	1	4	43½	42	3½	33	Smith M E	117	3.20	89-11	My Mogul1191½ Next Endeavor1191½ Cigar117nk	Lacked room stretch 8

WORKOUTS: May 31 Bel 5f fst 1:024 B *28/37* May 24 Bel 5f fst 1:041 B *13/13* May 10 Bel 4f fst :504 B *13/23* May 4 Bel 6f fst 1:132 B *5/11* Apr 26 Bel 4f fst :53 B *23/23* Apr 12 OP 4f gd :482 B *2/17*

Cigar had been floundering on turf, winning just one of his 11 starts, and trainer Bill Mott just happened to pick this day to see if a change might pick up the head of this under-achieving colt. Poor Golden Plover couldn't possibly have known what he was getting into!

POSITION AND BEATEN lengths at the finish, and, by inference, last-out Beyer figures, are greatly over-emphasized by the wagering public. This is a good thing, since positive-expectation situations arise for players willing to exercise the greatest computer ever invented (their brains) and delve beyond the obvious. Golden Plover's recent races, when looked at carefully, combined with his workout lines, supplemented with the fuller picture painted by the workout tabs, shouted to all who would listen that here was a horse in terrific form. Most didn't hear the message. The exposed and obvious form of Absent Minded was much easier to pick up on.

The October 6 card was rich with potential for those willing to spend the time and energy to read between past performance lines. An hour or so prior to Golden Plover's victory, handicappers were confronted with a field of eight 3-year-olds sprinting six and a half furlongs. There was no shortage of ugly-looking running lines:

4 Belmont Park

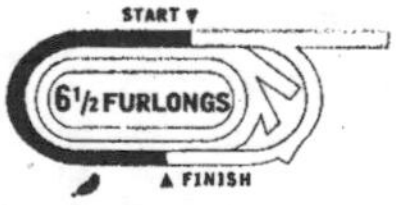

6½ Furlongs **(1:143) CLAIMING. Purse $14,500. 3-year-olds. Weight, 122 lbs. Non-winners of two races since September 1, allowed 3 lbs. Of a race since then, 5 lbs. Claiming price $17,500, for each $1,000 to $15,500, allowed 2 lbs. (Races when entered to be claimed for $14,000 or less not considered.)**

Ibis Baba
Own: Shivmangal Doodnauth
MOJICA R JR (59 4 5 9 .07) **$17,500**

Dk. b or br g. 3 (Mar)
Sire: Waquoit (Relaunch)
Dam: Princess Mistletoe (Reindeer)
Br: Landry Harry L (Md)
Tr: Shivmangal Doodnauth (1 0 0 0 .00)

117

Lifetime Record :	17	1	3	1	$18,800						
1994	15	1	3	1	$18,800	Turf	0	0	0	0	
1993	2	M	0	0		Wet	2	0	1	0	$4,060
Bel	4	0	0	0	$1,200	Dist	0	0	0	0	

27Sep94-6Bel	sly	6f	:221 :45 :57 1:10†	Clm 30000	**54**	3	3	38½	48½	410	414	Perez R M5	109 fb	7.30	76-18	Catchin Air1153 Matthew RedDog1179½ TimelessEndeavor1171½	No factor 4
18May94-4Bel	fst	1 1/16 ⊗	:23 :461 1:113 1:45	Clm 35000	**24**	7	4	66¾	78	79	723¾	Beckner D V7	110 fb	11.20	53-16	Lucky Eight1171¼ Promising Rainbow1174 Curious Jeb1173	Done early 7
1May94-2Aqu	fst	1	:222 :443 1:101 1:363	Clm 45000	**39**	3	5	514	59	516	524½	Alvarado F T	114 b	8.50	60-10	MediclPro11710 Tnksfornotcomlng1178 PlnetryCircle1174	Broke slowly 5
20Apr94-4Aqu	fst	1	:233 :464 1:12 1:371	Alw 29000N1X	**47**	6	5	52½	66	610	618	Alvarado F T	117 fb	11.20	64-16	Gifted Son117nk Final Clearance1171½ Cosa Diavolo1174	Outrun 6
9Apr94-2Aqu	fst	1	:23 :46 1:112 1:381	Clm 25000N2L	**68**	5	7	42½	22	2½	2½	Alvarado F T	117 fb	20.20	76-14	Churkin119½ Ibis Baba117½ Fortunate Tumble1136	Gamely 12
1Apr94-6Aqu	fst	6f	:223 :464 :59 1:121	Clm 25000N2L	**35**	8	4	55	53½	76¾	614¼	Smith M E	117 fb	4.60	67-16	Prince Louder1131¼ Fortunate Move1171 United Congress1144	Five wide 8
20Mar94-2Aqu	fst	6f ⊡	:233 :474 1:002 1:131	Clm 25000	**40**	1	4	33½	32	36	311	Alvarado F T	119 fb	2.00	66-21	Master Dooley1175 Eager Carnie1176 Ibis Baba1197½	Tired 4
10Mar94-1Aqu	sly	6f ⊡	:224 :46 :58 1:102	Clm 25000N2L	**67**	2	6	21	22	24	27	Santagata N	122 fb	4.40	84-13	Solar Win1137 Ibis Baba1223½ Just Feathers113½	No match 7
6Mar94-2Aqu	fst	6f ⊡	:223 :452 :573 1:102	Alw 26000N1X	**72**	3	5	64½	76	76¾	68	Mickens T J7	110 fb	30.00	83-11	Prank Call1174½ Cosa Diavolo119½ Kitty's Stage117hd	No factor 7
21Feb94-2Aqu	fst	6f ⊡	:234 :474 1:003 1:14	Md 30000	**57**	8	1	2½	2½	1½	11½	Alvarado F T	118 fb	3.10	73-20	Ibis Baba1181½ Facetious Buck117no The Real Cool Gang118¾	Driving 10

WORKOUTS: Sep 22 Aqu Ⓣ 4f fm :50 B (d)*2/3* Sep 15 Aqu Ⓣ 3f fm :404 B (d)*2/2* Sep 10 Aqu 5f fst 1:03 B *4/7* Sep 3 Aqu 5f fst 1:022 Hg*3/4* Aug 21 Bel tr.t 3f fst :37 B *4/9*

Colonel Slade

Own: Due Process Stable

SMITH M E (125 28 19 13 .22) **$17,500**

Dk. b or br g. 3 (Feb)
Sire: Deputy Minister (Vice Regent)
Dam: Flash Prancer (Mr. Prospector)
Br: Due Process Stables (Ky)
Tr: Nobles Reynaldo H (16 1 1 3 .06)

117

Lifetime Record:	12 1 4 3		$34,695			
1994	8 1 2 2	$21,205	Turf	0 0 0 0		
1993	4 M 2 1	$13,490	Wet	1 0 0 0		
Bel	3 0 1 1	$7,240	Dist	0 0 0 0		

21Sep94- 2Bel fst 6f :22² :45³ :57³ 1:10⁴ Clm 17500 74 2 2 6³ 7⁴½ 5⁷½ 3³¾ Smith M E 117 4.90 84-17 Sky Cry114³ Full Of Sauce113nk Colonel Slade117¹½ 9
Steadied 3/8 pl, blocked 1/4 pl
19Aug94- 5Mth fst 6f :21⁴ :45³ :58³ 1:12¹ Clm 20000 69 6 3 6⁹¾ 6⁷ 4⁴½ 3¾ Rivera L Jr L 116 *2.30 77-21 Pacific War116¾ Sunny's Bullet114no Colonel Slade116nk Finished fast 7
27Jly94- 4Mth fst 6f :21³ :44³ :57¹ 1:10³ Clm 18000 73 4 7 6⁴½ 6⁶ 5⁴½ 2² Rivera L Jr L 114 6.70 84-12 MagicalProspect116² ColonelSlade114¹½ Chrmin'Merlin119¾ Closed well 11
4Jly94- 5Mth fst 6f :21⁴ :45¹ :58 1:11 Alw 16500N2L 38 2 5 7⁴½ 8⁸½ 8¹¹ 8¹⁸½ Velez J A Jr L 120 2.80 65-21 Direct Delight116³ Shananie's Boss116² Trial Team116½ Dull effort 8
14Jun94- 6Mth fst 6f :21⁴ :45² :58 1:10⁴ 3↑ Md Sp Wt 92 4 4 3¹½ 2hd 1hd 1³¾ Velez J A Jr L 115 2.80 85-22 Colonel Slade115³¾ Buffalo Dan115³½ Six Twenty Six115⁸½ Driving 7
16Feb94- 3GP fst 6f :22 :45 :57¹ 1:09⁴ Md Sp Wt 71 2 1 2½ 2½ 3³½ 4⁸ Douglas R R 122 1.70 84-12 A Firm Mister122¹¾ Ten Star Fleet122⁶½ Chasin Gold122no Weakened 7
5Feb94- 6GP fst 7f :22 :45 1:10³ 1:24² Md Sp Wt 76 6 1 4² 4¹½ 2³ 2⁵½ Douglas R R 120 2.10 75-16 Theater Of War120⁵½ Colonel Slade120¹ Expansionist120¾ Gamely 9
8Jan94- 6GP fst 6f :22 :45 :57¹ 1:09⁴ Md Sp Wt 77 7 2 5³ 5⁴½ 4⁴½ 4⁶½ Douglas R R 120 *.90e 86-09 Kyle's Code120²¼ Meadow Monster120³½ Magic Caver120¾ No excuse 11
19Sep93- 5Bel my 7f :23 :46² 1:11² 1:24³ Md Sp Wt 35 3 1 2hd 1½ 4⁵½ 6¹⁸¾ McCarron C J 118 b *1.10 61-20 Personal Escort118²¼ Turnbull Creek118² Red Mcfly118⁹½ Dueled, tired 8
4Sep93- 5Bel fst 7f :23¹ :46² 1:10³ 1:23¹ Md Sp Wt 79 1 1 1hd 1hd 1hd 2¾ Davis R G 118 b *.70 86-14 Changing Breeze118¾ Colonel Slade118¹³ Alydawn118¹ Gamely 6

WORKOUTS: Sep 16 Mdl 4f fst :49 B 1/1 Sep 10 Mdl 5f fst 1:02 B 1/1 ●Aug 13 Mdl 4f fst :48 B 1/4 Jly 22 Mdl 4f fst :49² B 2/5

Ken's Landing

Own: Lazer Two Stable

MIGLIORE R (73 8 16 6 .11) **$17,500**

Ch. g. 3 (May)
Sire: Prosperous (Mr. Prospector)
Dam: Fay Goldberg (Superbity)
Br: Kennedy Louis J (Fla)
Tr: Klesaris Robert P (18 1 5 2 .06)

117

Lifetime Record:	13 3 3 2		$50,161			
1994	6 2 0 1	$28,000	Turf	0 0 0 0		
1993	7 1 3 1	$22,161	Wet	0 0 0 0		
Bel	2 1 0 0	$14,400	Dist	2 0 2 0	$6,920	

21Sep94- 1Med fst 6f :22 :45 :57 1:09³ Clm 25000 55 3 8 8¹⁰ 8¹⁰ 7¹³ 5¹⁴ Nelson D 116 f 8.20 79-16 Heroic Pursuit116⁷ Offender116¹½ Fabulous Force116½ No factor 8
28May94- 1Bel fst 6f :23¹ :47 :58⁴ 1:10⁴ Clm 70000 34 2 4 6⁴½ 6²½ 6⁶½ 6²² Migliore R 114 f *2.40 65-14 Catchin Air115⁷ Windy Target115¾ Francis Marion117²½ Dull try 6
5May94- 6Bel fst 6f :22 :45² :58 1:11 Clm 50000 79 1 4 7⁸½ 5² 1½ 1³½ Migliore R 117 f 6.30 86-18 Ken's Landing117³½ Cape Verde110¹½ Index Fund117¾ Wide, driving 7
15Mar94- 3GP fst 6f :22 :45³ :58² 1:11² Clm c-32000 73 4 4 5⁶½ 4⁵ 2² 1²½ Chapman K L5 112 f 4.10 84-15 Ken's Landing112²½ Fortunate Move117no Powerful Patch117nk Driving 9
Claimed from Kimran Stable, Toner James J Trainer
21Feb94- 5GP fst 7f :22¹ :45² 1:10² 1:23² Clm 25000 78 4 8 3¹½ 1¹ 1³ 3¹ Chapman K L5 112 f 6.20 85-13 Grateful Appeal119nk Talktomylawyer117¾ Ken'sLanding112²½ Weakened 10
21Jan94- 7GP fst 6f :22 :45¹ :57² 1:10¹ Clm 50000 51 3 8 6⁴½ 8⁸½ 8¹² 10¹²¾ Santos J A 117 14.70 77-11 Ultimate Don117nk Maudlin's Sunny117¾ Honest Colors117²½ Stopped 10
28Nov93- 7Grd gd 6½f :24¹ :47³ 1:13⁴ 1:20⁴ Alw 18000N2L 72 3 3 3⁴ 3⁴½ 3²½ 2hd David D J 119 *1.20 77-23 All My Effort119hd Ken's Landing119³ Groveland117¹½ Stalked duel turn 5
20Nov93- 9Grd fst 1 :23 :47¹ 1:12⁴ 1:41¹ Alw 31000NC 60 3 4 4²½ 3² 5⁶½ 4¹⁰ Montpellier C 116 9.10 62-25 YongeCstlefield124⁵ WinterRenegde116¹½ BoldShot115³½ Two path turns 7
12Nov93- 8Grd fst 6½f :23¹ :47² 1:13⁴ 1:20⁴ Clm 37500 66 2 7 6⁶½ 3³½ 3⁴ 2¹½ David D J 118 4.95 75-25 Top End122¹½ Ken's Landing118³ J J Liberty116¹¾ 7
Clumsy early, closed steadily
28Oct93- 6Grd fst 7f :23 :47 1:13 1:26³ Clm 47500 57 5 8 6⁵½ 7⁴½ 4³½ 3³½ Duross A C5 111 13.15 81-15 BldAndAmzng122¹ JJLbrty116²½ Kn'sLndng111¾ Rallied between horses 8

WORKOUTS: Sep 17 Bel tr.t 4f fst :50¹ B 19/22 Sep 10 Bel tr.t 5f fst 1:03³ B 6/6 Sep 3 Bel tr.t 4f fst :49⁴ B 8/20 Aug 28 Bel tr.t 4f fst :47² H 2/11 Aug 21 Sar tr.t 4f fst :52⁴ B 32/37 Aug 13 Sar tr.t 3f fst :37⁴ B 7/14

Full Of Sauce

Own: Vogel Hortense & Marcus

PEZUA J M (88 5 4 7 .06) **$15,500**

Ch. c. 3 (Mar)
Sire: Sauce Boat (Key to the Mint)
Dam: Playful Hooky (Master Derby)
Br: Vogel Hortense & Marcus (Ky)
Tr: Barrera Luis (9 2 1 0 .22)

113

Lifetime Record:	26 1 5 6		$28,970			
1994	19 1 5 5	$26,990	Turf	0 0 0 0		
1993	7 M 0 1	$1,980	Wet	0 0 0 0		
Bel	10 1 2 1	$14,190	Dist	0 0 0 0		

21Sep94- 2Bel fst 6f :22² :45³ :57³ 1:10⁴ Clm 15500 74 4 9 8⁵½ 6³¾ 4⁷ 2³ Pezua J M 113 35.20 84-17 Sky Cry114³ Full Of Sauce113nk Colonel Slade117¹½ Broke slowly,m wide 9
2Sep94- 9Bel fst 7f :22⁴ :45³ 1:10³ 1:23⁴ Clm 16500 56 7 8 8¹⁰ 9⁷½ 7⁷½ 6¹⁰ Pezua J M 115 36.00 74-12 Bomb Free117⁴½ Creston House117nk Harry Sherman113²½ No factor 10
15Jly94- 9Bel fst 6f :22² :45³ :58 1:11¹ Clm 15500 54 10 6 8⁶½ 7⁵½ 7⁵¾ 7⁹½ Leon F 113 29.90 76-18 Sky Cry114nk Zeal Brown112³½ Magic's Cause117¹½ No threat 11
6Jly94- 3Bel fst 6f :22² :46¹ :58⁴ 1:12 Clm 17500 46 6 7 7⁷½ 6³½ 7⁵ 7¹¹½ Beckner D V5 112 5.60 70-16 Sky Cry112³ Always There117½ Magic's Cause117²½ Checked break 7
19Jun94- 1Bel fst 6f :22 :45¹ :57⁴ 1:10³ Clm 22500 60 1 4 6⁸½ 5⁴½ 6³ 5⁶½ Leon F 117 9.70 82-12 Nostrudance117¹½ Tun N' It Up110nk Always There113² Checked 1/4 pl 6
1Jun94- 1Bel fst 6f :22⁴ :46⁴ :59¹ 1:12² Clm 17500 63 7 8 4³½ 2½ 2hd 2¾ Leon F 119 8.60 78-20 Captain Moonlight117¾ FullOfSauce119¾ June'sPistol106² Broke slowly 8
25May94- 1Bel fst 6f :22 :45² :58² 1:11³ Clm 25000 60 1 7 6⁷ 4⁴½ 4³ 4⁵ Beckner D V7 112 23.60 78-15 Tea In MyEye117hd Moment'sGlory119²½ ProudRambler112² Lacked rally 8
18May94- 3Bel fst 6f :22² :46¹ :59¹ 1:12² 3↑ Md 35000 54 6 6 5³½ 4¹½ 2hd 1½ Luttrell M G5 110 5.50 79-16 Full Of Sauce110½ Shininlikediamonds113¹½ Lightnin' Cat115² Driving 8
4May94- 9Bel fst 6f :22³ :46 :58² 1:11³ 3↑ Md 35000 57 10 6 5⁷ 4³ 4²½ 3⁴½ Luttrell M G5 110 7.10 79-11 Approximate115⁴ Showiz115nk Full Of Sauce110⁴ Mild rally 10
28Apr94- 9Aqu fst 6f :22⁴ :46³ :59¹ 1:12¹ 3↑ Md 25000 47 9 9 5⁴½ 5⁴ 3⁶ 3¹⁰ Sindab P7 109 7.10 71-19 Captain Moonlight115⁶ Ramazan117⁴ Full Of Sauce109no Four wide 11

WORKOUTS: Oct 4 Bel tr.t 4f fst :49¹ B 9/24 Sep 29 Bel tr.t 4f fst :49⁴ B 23/37 Sep 15 Bel tr.t 4f fst :50 B 6/9 Sep 9 Bel tr.t 4f fst :50⁴ B 9/12 Aug 30 Bel tr.t 4f fst :49¹ B 7/21 Aug 24 Bel tr.t 4f fst :49 H 11/30

Brush Full

Own: Buckland Farm

RODRIGUEZ O (10 0 0 1 .00) **$17,500**

Dk. b or br c. 3 (Mar)
Sire: Broad Brush (Ack Ack)
Dam: Full Song (Stop the Music)
Br: T. M. Evans (Ky)
Tr: Cordero Angel Jr (8 2 1 1 .25)

107[10]

Lifetime Record:	9 1 1 1		$24,520			
1994	5 0 1 1	$9,520	Turf	0 0 0 0		
1993	4 1 0 0	$15,000	Wet	3 0 0 0		
Bel	5 1 1 1	$24,520	Dist	1 0 1 0	$6,160	

3Sep94- 9Bel fst 1⅟₁₆ :23² :46¹ 1:10¹ 1:42¹ 3↑ Clm 50000 60 3 3 3¹½ 6⁵ 9¹⁴ 9¹⁷½ Mojica R Jr 113 b 18.50 74-12 A Call To Rise113nk Sparkling Sky117no Patsyprospect109¾ Finished early 9
6Aug94- 4Sar wf 7f :22³ :46¹ 1:11 1:23⁴ Clm 75000 52 4 2 2² 3¹½ 5⁴½ 5¹⁹ Mojica R Jr 117 b 8.60 68-16 Gifted Son117³ Tomorrow's Comet113¹ Medical Pro113¹⁰ Tired 5
23Jly94- 7Sar sly 7f :22¹ :45¹ 1:09¹ 1:21⁴ 3↑ Alw 28000N1X 55 3 3 2¹ 4⁴ 5¹¹ 5²⁵ Mojica R Jr 111 b 9.00 71-22 Prenup117¾ Skyphone111⁵ A Track Attack111⁸½ Used up 6
3Jly94- 3Bel fst 6½f :23² :46³ 1:10⁴ 1:16⁴ 3↑ Alw 28000N1X 85 3 1 2hd 2hd 2hd 2⁴½ Mojica R Jr 113 b 3.50 84-13 Party Manners113⁴½ Brush Full113² Stoney Wolf119¹½ Dueled, weakened 5
21Jun94- 7Bel fst 6f :22⁴ :46 :57¹ 1:09² 3↑ Alw 28000N2L 86 6 5 2½ 2½ 3²½ 3³ Mojica R Jr 112 b 14.90 91-11 Secret Savings113hd Saratoga Shark112³ Brush Full112³ Forced pace 7
17Oct93- 5Bel fst 6f :22² :45⁴ :58² 1:11⁴ Md Sp Wt 75 1 1 1½ 1½ 1²½ 1⁶ Mojica R Jr 118 b 24.90 81-14 Brush Full118⁶ Plutonius118½ Beasleyathisbest118² Driving 10
25Sep93- 2Bel fst 1 :22⁴ :45⁴ 1:11³ 1:38³ Md Sp Wt 43 6 1 2hd 3²½ 6⁹½ 6²⁰½ Velasquez J 118 b 27.20 54-31 Able Buck118¹½ Palance118⁵¾ Jo Ran Express118nk Dueled, tired 8
25Aug93- 3Sar my 7f :22 :44⁴ 1:10 1:23³ Md Sp Wt 59 1 7 5⁴ 6⁴½ 6⁴½ 6⁶ Velasquez J 118 13.90 81-08 Personal Favor118¹¾ Peace Negotiations118¾ Arrovente118²½ No factor 8
7Aug93- 5Sar gd 5f :21³ :45 :57³ Md Sp Wt 64 4 9 8¹¹ 8⁹½ 6⁴¾ 8⁴½ Krone J A 118 13.90 90-08 Upping The Ante118½ Youthful Legs118nk Frisco Gold118² Greenly 10

WORKOUTS: Sep 22 Bel 3f fst :38⁴ B 18/21 Aug 24 Sar tr.t 4f fst :53⁴ B 21/23 Jly 17 Bel 4f fst :50² B 38/57

Bomb Free

Own: Willis Sheldon

BAILEY J D (122 22 21 16 .18) **$15,500**

Ch. c. 3 (May)
Sire: Explodent (Nearctic)
Dam: Trouble Free (Nodouble)
Br: Goodwood Thoroughbreds (Ky)
Tr: Gianos George (8 3 0 1 .38)

115

Lifetime Record:	17 2 3 3		$33,595			
1994	15 2 2 3	$31,505	Turf	1 0 0 0	$155	
1993	2 M 1 0	$2,090	Wet	4 0 1 1	$7,590	
Bel	2 1 0 0	$8,700	Dist	0 0 0 0		

21Sep94- 2Bel fst 6f :22² :45³ :57³ 1:10⁴ Clm 17500 60 9 7 5²½ 4²½ 6⁷½ 7⁸½ Bailey J D 119 f 3.30 78-17 Sky Cry114³ Full Of Sauce113nk Colonel Slade117¹½ Wide, tired 9
2Sep94- 9Bel fst 7f :22⁴ :45³ 1:10³ 1:23⁴ Clm 17500 77 10 1 5³½ 2² 1²½ 1⁴½ Bailey J D 117 f 8.90 84-12 Bomb Free117⁴½ Creston House117nk Harry Sherman113²½ Drifted, driving 10
24Aug94- 2Sar fst 1⅛ :46⁴ 1:12 1:38² 1:51⁴ Clm 25000 57 9 2 1½ 1hd 5²½ 7¹³ Bailey J D 117 f 20.00 64-23 C. Lenny Runn117¹½ Churkin117³½ Creston House117² Dueled, tired 9
14Aug94- 1Sar sly 1⅛ :48⁴ 1:13 1:39 1:52³ Clm 30000 52 5 2 1½ 3²½ 4³ 4¹⁴½ Alvarado F T 113 f 3.00 59-22 PromisingRainbow117nk ATrackAttck117¹⁰ Lightnin'Ct113⁴ Used in pace 5
29Jly94- 4Sar my 1⅛ ⊗ :49² 1:14² 1:40² 1:53⁴ Clm 35000 80 2 1 1½ 1½ 1hd 2nk Davis R G 117 f 7.40 67-30 Brett's Jet112nk Bomb Free117¹⁰ Burn The Toast117hd Gamely 6
17Jly94- 8Crc fm 1⅟₁₆ ⓣ :23 :47 1:10⁴ 1:41⁴ 3↑ Alw 17200N1X 51 8 2 2½ 6⁴½ 7⁹ 7¹⁴ Ramos W S L 115 f 4.20 77-09 Simpleton112³½ Bright Arrow119¾ Back Bay119¾ Tired 8
4Jly94- 9Crc fst 1⅟₁₆ ⊗ :23² :47² 1:13⁴ 1:47³ Alw 17200N1X 39 8 4 4²½ 7¹¹ 7¹⁹ 7²⁵¾ Ramos W S L 121 f 5.00 55-13 Bonbon D'or118¹½ Personal Prince118³½ Simpleton118² 8
Broke inward start, gave way
18Jun94-10Crc gd 1 :23⁴ :47⁴ 1:13³ 1:41¹ Alw 17200N1X 75 4 2 2²½ 1hd 1¹ 5³ Castillo H Jr L 122 f 22.10 78-19 Runaway Witness119¹¾ CimarronSecret119¾ TomTerrific119½ Weakened 12
5Jun94-11Crc fst 1⅛ ⊗ :49⁴ 1:15⁴ 1:42⁴ 1:55⁴ 3↑ Md Sp Wt 62 4 1 1½ 1½ 1⁴ 1¹⁰½ Ramos W S L 115 f *1.30 74-18 Bomb Free115¹⁰ Sea Carmen122nk Frere Jack115⁷ Ridden out 8
23Apr94-12Hia sly 1⅟₁₆ ⊗ :23² :47¹ 1:13³ 1:48 Md Sp Wt 36 7 2 1½ 1² 2hd 3⁵½ Castillo H Jr 122 *1.50 70-11 Riverdale122¹¾ Henry S.122⁴ Bomb Free122⁸ Weakened 7

Cleft
Own: Harvey Ardale
WYNTER N A (7 1 0 1 .14) $17,500

B. g. 3 (Jan)
Sire: Gulch (Mr. Prospector)
Dam: All About Style (Raja Baba)
Br: Heronwood Farm Inc (Va)
Tr: Armstrong Dale (3 0 0 0 .00)

117

Lifetime Record:	7 1 0 1	$8,760		
1994	7 1 0 1	$8,760	Turf	0 0 0 0
1993	0 M 0 0		Wet	0 0 0 0
Bel	6 1 0 1	$8,760	Dist	0 0 0 0

21Sep94-2Bel	fst	6f	:222 :453 :573 1:104	Clm 17500	51	3 3 2½ 22 89¼ 912¼	Wynter N A	117 b	59.40	75-17	Sky Cry1143 Full Of Sauce113nk Colonel Slade1171½	Forced pace	9
15Jly94-9Bel	fst	6f	:222 :453 :58 1:111	Clm 17500	45	11 5 63½ 95½ 96¾ 912¾	Chavez J F	119 b	16.50	72-18	Sky Cry114nk Zeal Brown1123½ Magic's Cause1171¼	Wide trip	11
6Jly94-3Bel	fst	6f	:222 :461 :584 1:12	Clm 17500	59	7 5 43 41½ 32½ 46	Chavez J F	119 b	11.60	75-16	Sky Cry1123 Always There117½ Magic's Cause1172½	Wide, tired	7
26Jun94-3Bel	fst	6f	:223 :462 :59 1:123	3↑ Md 30000	70	6 2 22 2hd 1½ 11	Chavez J F	110 b	3.30	78-16	Cleft1101 Premium Value1101¾ Spicy Promises1121¼	Driving	13
26May94-9Bel	fst	6f	:222 :46 :583 1:12	3↑ Md 35000	44	8 1 1hd 31 74¾ 88	Santos J A	115 b	5.60	73-15	Showiz115nk Premier Pierre111nk Shininlikediamonds1132¼	Used in pace	10
18May94-5Bel	fst	6f	:224 :463 :59 1:114	3↑ Md 35000	56	4 2 21½ 2½ 3½ 32¾	Beckner D V7	108 b	4.10	79-16	Dixie Reef1171 Premium Value1131¾ Cleft1082½	Dueled wide, tired	8
30Apr94-9Aqu	fst	6f	:214 :452 :581 1:104	3↑ Md Sp Wt	54	5 3 66½ 66 55½ 611½	Chavez J F	115	4.70	76-15	Bold Spector1153½ King Protea1155 Dixie Reef117½	No factor	10

WORKOUTS: Oct 1 Aqu 5f fst 1:041 B *6/6* Sep 15 Aqu ⓣ 5f fm 1:044 B (d) *2/4* Sep 8 Aqu ⓣ 4f fm :503 H (d) *1/3*

Planetary Circle
Own: Zablowitz Karen S
CHAVEZ J F (127 20 18 16 .16) $17,500

B. g. 3 (Mar)
Sire: Secret Prince (Cornish Prince)
Dam: Miss Tunaiik Bay (Poker)
Br: Empert Carol & Richard (NY)
Tr: Parisella John (10 1 1 2 .10)

117

Lifetime Record:	16 2 1 5	$52,360			
1994	10 2 1 4	$49,360	Turf	1 0 0 0	
1993	6 M 0 1	$3,000	Wet	2 1 0 0	$15,000
Bel	2 0 0 0	$1,200	Dist	0 0 0 0	

18May94-4Bel	fst	1 1/16 ⊗	:23 :461 1:113 1:45	Clm 35000	51	4 2 3½ 2hd 42½ 48¼	Luzzi M J	117 fb	*.80	69-16	Lucky Eight1171¼ Promising Rainbow1174 Curious Jeb1173	5 wide, tired	7
1May94-2Aqu	fst	1	:222 :443 1:101 1:363	Clm 50000	51	2 2 22 24 311 318	Luzzi M J	117 b	1.80	67-10	Medical Pro11710 Tanksfornotcoming1178 Planetary Circle1174	Used up	5
14Apr94-6Aqu	gd	7f	:223 :454 1:111 1:24	Clm 55000	66	4 5 2½ 2½ 33 39¼	Luzzi M J	113 b	3.40	75-19	Ben's Jet117¾ Talktomylawyer1178½ Planetary Circle113nk	Tired	8
1Apr94-1Aqu	fst	1	:233 :471 1:123 1:373	Clm c-40000	74	3 2 2½ 2hd 23 24½	Velazquez J R	117 b	*1.50	75-25	Talktomylawyer1174½ PlanetryCircle1172¾ OutFromUnder11711	Held place	5
Claimed from Ledgemere Farm, O'brien Leo Trainer													
16Mar94-2Aqu	fst	6f ⊡	:23 :47 :592 1:124	Clm 35000	75	6 7 64¼ 72¾ 34 3¾	Velazquez J R	115 b	7.00	78-22	Six Peak117nk N Dever117½ Planetary Circle1155	Steadied, alt course	7
26Feb94-7Aqu	fst	1 1/16 ⊡	:24 :482 1:141 1:473	[S]Alw 28000N1X	78	5 4 32 2hd 2hd 1no	Chavez J F	119 b	4.10	67-33	Planetary Circle119no To Ta Roo11711 Commodore Admiral1176	Driving	6
17Feb94-5Aqu	fst	6f ⊡	:232 :47 :593 1:122	[S]Alw 26000N1X	56	3 5 31 41½ 55½ 510½	Chavez J F	119 b	11.40	70-26	Boldly Brave117nk Mccullough110¾ Memories Of Linda1175½	Used up	6
5Feb94-4Aqu	fst	6f ⊡	:231 :47 :593 1:123	[S]Alw 26000N1X	72	5 4 43 51¾ 42 31	Chavez J F	122 b	13.50	79-16	More To Tell117½ To Ta Roo117½ Planetary Circle1221	Mild bid, wide	7
29Jan94-1Aqu	sly	1 1/16 ⊡	:23 :48 1:14 1:471	[S]Md Sp Wt	67	4 1 1½ 1½ 1½ 1½	Chavez J F	122 b	4.30	69-25	Planetary Circle122½ Promising Rainbow1228 Air Gunner122½	Driving	12
5Jan94-5Aqu	fst	6f ⊡	:231 :474 1:004 1:14	[S]Md Sp Wt	36	2 11 99½ 810 812 711¼	Vega H	122	24.50	62-26	Iclaimit122nk Raja's Charter1226¾ Russian Love1221½	Outrun	12

WORKOUTS: Sep 27 Aqu 3f sly :38 B *3/3*

Lets practice reading between the lines, shall we? Start with the 3-2 favorite, Colonel Slade: study his pp's until you can spot the hidden message — the one that says, I AM A MONEY BURNER. It's right there in the odds column, which notes that the gelding has lost as the favorite on four previous occasions, and that during the past 13 months he's a seven-time loser at odds lower than 3-1.

How about Ken's Landing, the co-second choice at 9/2? If you look carefully you'll see where his pp's say, I HURT MYSELF. What else but physical injury could have precipitated what happened after his big win of May 5: a 22-length drubbing as the favorite three weeks later, followed by a layoff of nearly four months, and an uninspiring return two weeks ago at the $25,000 level — half the price he had won so impressively for just three starts ago. If you want to give this gelding the benefit of the doubt and include him as a back-up in Pick 6s, or on top in an exacta as protection for a win bet on someone else, fine, but he's no bargain standing on his own.

These basement-level claiming races for 3-year-olds ($17,500 down to $15,500 is the lowest rung at which sophomores compete on the New York circuit) can be approached in much the same way as maiden claimers: the best profile is a horse with speed dropping down in class, a horse who isn't already a proven loser at the low end of the totem pole.

Examining the race in that light, begin by throwing out Colonel Slade. Not only is he a money-burning fool, he's being overbet in this spot because of the trouble line "Steadied 3/8 pl, blocked 1/4 pl" last time out. There is no wager-value in this kind of a trip. Anyone who can read is aware of what happened, and they will bet accordingly. How about looking at it this way: cheap horses usually find themselves in trouble because they lack sufficient positional speed and/or athleticism to avoid getting into a blindswitch in the first place. Moreover, Colonel Slade was defeated in his last race by Full Of Sauce, who is already a five-time loser sprinting at this class level.

Throw out Ibis Baba, whose only decent performance since a maiden win in February came against "non winners of two lifetimes" claimers six months ago. And throw out the 5-1 shot Planetary Circle on the grounds that a single, solitary three-furlong breeze of :38 is hardly an encouraging workout line for a horse who hasn't been out since May.

We're left with Brush Full, Bomb Free and Cleft, and the latter pair were both up the track behind proven loser Full Of Sauce and sucker-horse Colonel Slade last time out — although Bomb Free could prove dangerous if able to reproduce his big win when dropped to $17,500 for the first time on September 2.

But it was Brush Full who was the most interesting prospect, despite the fact that he'd lost his three most recent starts by an aggregate 61 lengths and beaten home the grand total of one horse. But as Einstein said, everything is relative, and that theory is just as valid for handicappers as it is for nuclear physicists.

Consider the extenuating circumstances of Brush Full's last three defeats. In his most recent race of September 3, he competed for $50,000, three brackets upward from $17,500 on the New York claiming hierarchy; not only that, he'd tangled with *older* $50,000 horses, at a distance beyond his previous capabilities. Despite those obstacles he raced within a length and a half of the :46 1/5 half-mile split, and within five lengths after six furlongs in 1:10 1/5. Two races back, competing at the $75,000 level in his first start for a tag, he prompted the pace to upper stretch before fading. Three races back, he pressed Prenup through an opening quarter of :22 1/5 in the slop at Saratoga. Prenup had come back to wire Belmont's Grade 1 Jerome Handicap over the Labor Day weekend!

In short, Brush Full had recently faced competition *light years* tougher than today's. Earlier in his campaign, Brush Full's first two races as a 3-year-old had been strong showings in preliminary allowances, against a pair of regally bred tigers from the Ogden PhippsShug McGaughey Juggernaut; Party Manners, in fact, had ripped through the rest of his allowance conditions as the summer unfolded.

Not only was Brush Full dropping sharply in class, and not only did he possess enough speed to get to the front, he was repeating a previously successful form-pattern. To wit: Weaken in two sprints at Saratoga; flash speed and finish far back when brought back to Belmont in a route; cut back to a sprint second time over the track.

Brush Full was in the same final stage of a winning form-pattern he had carried out almost exactly a year ago. Those interested in form patterns who have not yet read Mark Cramer's *Thoroughbred Cycles* are strongly advised to do so.

FOURTH RACE
Belmont
OCTOBER 6, 1994

6½ FURLONGS. (1.14^{3}) CLAIMING. Purse $14,500. 3–year–olds. Weight, 122 lbs. Non–winners of two races since September 1, allowed 3 lbs. Of a race since then, 5 lbs. Claiming price $17,500, for each $1,000 to $15,500, allowed 2 lbs. (Races when entered to be claimed for $14,000 or less not considered.)

Value of Race: $14,500 Winner $8,700; second $3,190; third $1,740; fourth $870. Mutuel Pool $195,190.00 Exacta Pool $364,964.00 Quinella Pool $89,506.00

Last Raced	Horse	M/Eqt.	A.	Wt	PP	St	¼	½	Str	Fin	Jockey	Cl'g Pr	Odds $1
3Sep94 ^{9}Bel^{9}	Brush Full		3	107	5	1	1^{2}	1^{3}	1^{3}	1^{1}	Rodriguez O^{10}	17500	5.00
21Sep94 ^{1}Med^{5}	Ken's Landing	f	3	117	3	7	7^{hd}	$4^{\frac{1}{2}}$	$2^{1\frac{1}{2}}$	2^{3}	Migliore R	17500	4.90
21Sep94 ^{2}Bel^{3}	Colonel Slade		3	117	2	2	5^{hd}	7^{1}	$4^{1\frac{1}{2}}$	$3^{4\frac{1}{4}}$	Smith M E	17500	1.50
27Sep94 ^{6}Bel^{4}	Ibis Baba	bf	3	117	1	6	8	8	6^{1}	$4^{\frac{1}{2}}$	Mojica R Jr	17500	31.60
21Sep94 ^{2}Bel^{7}	Bomb Free	f	3	115	6	4	2^{1}	$2^{1\frac{1}{2}}$	$3^{\frac{1}{2}}$	$5^{2\frac{1}{4}}$	Bailey J D	15500	4.50
18May94 ^{4}Bel^{4}	Planetary Circle	b	3	117	8	3	$3^{\frac{1}{2}}$	3^{1}	$5^{\frac{1}{2}}$	$6^{\frac{3}{4}}$	Chavez J F	17500	5.80
21Sep94 ^{2}Bel^{2}	Full Of Sauce		3	113	4	8	6^{1}	$5^{\frac{1}{2}}$	$7^{2\frac{1}{2}}$	$7^{6\frac{1}{2}}$	Pezua J M	15500	8.30
21Sep94 ^{2}Bel^{9}	Cleft	b	3	117	7	5	$4^{1\frac{1}{2}}$	6^{1}	8	8	Wynter N A	17500	54.20

OFF AT 2:29 Start Good. Won driving. Time, :22^{3}, :45^{4}, 1:11^{1}, 1:18 Track fast.

$2 Mutuel Prices:			
5–(E)–BRUSH FULL	12.00	6.60	4.20
3–(C)–KEN'S LANDING		6.00	3.40
2–(B)–COLONEL SLADE			2.40

$2 EXACTA 5–3 PAID $71.80 $2 QUINELLA 3–5 PAID $34.80

Dk. b. or br. c, (Mar), by Broad Brush–Full Song, by Stop the Music. Trainer Cordero Angel Jr. Bred by T. M. Evans (Ky).

BRUSH FULL sprinted clear in the early stages, raced uncontested on the lead into the stretch, and was never threatened while being kept to the task. KEN'S LANDING away a bit slowly, raced while far back for a half, closed the gap while saving ground on the turn, then finished with good energy for the place. COLONEL SLADE outrun for a half while between horses, failed to threaten with a mild late rally. IBIS BABA trailed for a half then passed mostly tiring horses. BOMB FREE raced up close for a half then gave way. PLANETARY CIRCLE raced wide and tired. FULL OF SAUCE was never a factor after being pinched back at the start. CLEFT was finished early.

Owners— 1, Buckland Farm; 2, Lazer Two Stable; 3, Due Process Stable; 4, Jimpat Stble & Shivmangal Doodnauth; 5, Willis Sheldon; 6, Zablowitz Karen S; 7, Vogel Hortense & Marcus; 8, Harvey Ardale

Trainers—1, Cordero Angel Jr; 2, Klesaris Robert P; 3, Nobles Reynaldo H; 4, Shivmangal Doodnauth; 5, Gianos George; 6, Parisella John; 7, Barrera Luis; 8, Armstrong Dale

Ken's Landing was claimed by Nicholson Ronald; trainer, Toner James J.,
Colonel Slade was claimed by Sommer VIola; trainer, Martin Frank.
Scratched— Strike For Life (21Sep94 ^{9}BEL^{8})

Under 10-pound apprentice Omar Rodriguez (who was most assuredly advised about the benefits of early speed by former riding great turned trainer Angel Cordero Jr.), Brush Full broke on top and was never headed. (If you re going to back a horse being ridden by a triple bug, speed types offer the least risk, since all the kid has to do is hang on for dear life)

Cordero, by the way, has proven to be just as crafty with a horse under a shedrow as he was in the saddle. Less than two weeks later, at Aqueduct, Libertine, who most recently had pressed the pace against older claimers, dropped back in with 3-year-olds while moving down to $17,500 for the first time, and delivered a thoroughly predictable score:

Libertine
Own: Evans Robert S
SANTOS J A (84 10 12 15 .12) **$17,500**

B. c. 3 (Jan)
Sire: Cherokee Colony (Pleasant Colony)
Dam: Lusty Lady (Star de Naskra)
Br: Evans R S (Fla)
Tr: Cordero Angel Jr (13 3 2 2 .23)

117

Lifetime Record :	**9**	**2**	**0**	**1**	**$21,960**						
1994	**8**	**2**	**0**	**1**	**$21,960**	**Turf**	**1**	**0**	**0**	**0**	
1993	**1**	**M**	**0**	**0**		**Wet**	**2**	**0**	**0**	**1**	**$3,240**
Aqu	**2**	**1**	**0**	**0**	**$9,300**	**Dist**	**0**	**0**	**0**	**0**	

18Oct94-1Aqu	fst	1⅛	:482	1:13	1:392	1:53		Clm 17500	**82**	3	3	21	2½	11½	15	Santos J A	117 b	2.85	71-21	Libertine1175 Churkin1171½ Montedora1135½	Driving	7
21Sep94-6Bel	fst	1 1/16	:24	:471	1:113	1:43	3↑	Clm 25000	**73**	9	4	51¼	43¼	87¾	810½	Velazquez J R	115 b	29.10	77-19	Studley Do Right117hd Lightning Runner1121¾ Mc Comas1121	Tired	9
9Sep94-1Bel	fst	1 1/16	:232	:472	1:123	1:441	3↑	Md 35000	**83**	7	5	32	1hd	2hd	1hd	Santos J A	118 b	3.00	81-17	Libertine118hd High Regent1189 Robber Baron1135¾	Driving	10
25Aug94-5Sar	fst	1⅛	:482	1:13	1:384	1:521	3↑	Md Sp Wt	**64**	4	6	64½	76½	67½	48¼	Santos J A	117 b	2.60e	67-25	Free Agent1174 Cherokee Hill1172¼ Walsh1172	Wide turn	9
14Aug94-2Sar	sly	1⅛	:483	1:131	1:382	1:511	3↑	Md Sp Wt	**75**	4	6	43½	55½	34½	37½	Day P	117 b	13.20	72-22	Private Cody1177 Timeless Dream117½ Libertine1174	Mild gain	7
6Aug94-1Sar	wf	1⅛	:493	1:143	1:40	1:522	3↑	Md Sp Wt	**55**	6	6	63	52	59½	515¼	Rodriguez O10	107 b	24.50	59-17	Wayfarer1174¾ Private Cody117¾ Glitterati1172¾	Wide, bore out turn	6
17Jly94-5Bel	fm	1 1/16 Ⓣ	:233	:463	1:10	1:414	3↑	Md Sp Wt	**37**	4	5	84¾	99¾	1111	1021¾	Velazquez J R	116 b	*2.00e	67-09	Staire To Heaven1162¾ Royce Joseph1115 Rana Sanga1166	Steadied turn	12
29Jun94-9Bel	fst	7f	:231	:463	1:111	1:233	3↑	Md Sp Wt	**58**	5	7	42	21	78½	714½	Velazquez J R	114 b	25.40	71-16	Inside The Beltway1142¼ [D]CraftyMist1143 Ball'sBluff1142¾	Flattened out	9
19Nov93-3Aqu	fst	6f	:223	:462	:582	1:104		Md Sp Wt	**64**	8	6	76¼	85½	77	69½	Velazquez J R	118 b	18.30	78-19	Secret Savings118nk Meritocrat1182¼ Tempt The Devil1184	No factor	8

WORKOUTS: Nov 5 **Bel 4f fst :483 H** *8/49* Oct 8 **Bel 3f fst :36 H** *2/15* Sep 4 **Bel 4f fst :474 H** *10/40*

NORMAL PEOPLE MARK the passing of the seasons by the calendar. but most New York horseplayers, of course, are not normal, and they aren't fully convinced that another summer is really over until the scene shifts nine miles west on the Belt Parkway to Aqueduct, in the heart of beautiful South Ozone Park, Queens.

While some racetracks are nestled in the foothills of majestic mountain ranges, others are lined with palm trees, and still others can be found where the surf meets the turf, Aqueduct resembles Alcatraz more than anything else, situated as it is between Jamaica Bay, John F. Kennedy International Airport, and the Home Depot that now sits on what used to be part of the track's parking lot on Rockaway Boulevard. The move back to the Big A can be a bit depressing at first, because you know you're going to be there through some nasty weather for seven long months. But it only takes a winner or two to make a horseplayer feel like he's come to the right place.

As things developed, I didn't have to wait long. The third day of the meet brought typical Aqueduct weather: a dishwater-gray sky and a persistent drizzle that turned into heavier showers as the card wore on. The main track was labeled good, but had been floated and really was closer to muddy. (Maintenance crews "float" a track by towing heavy raft-like boards that compress the surface and bring excess moisture up to the top, where it can run off through the drainage system.)

Scratches peppered the card, as is often the case when inclement weather strikes, so that by the time post time for the feature rolled around, only five sprinters were left to contest a $50,000 overnight handicap at six furlongs:

8 Aqueduct

6 Furlongs (1:08) HANDICAP. Purse $50,000. 3-year-olds and upward. Weights Sunday, October 16. Declarations by 10:00 A.M. Tuesday, October 18. Closed with 8 nominations.

▼START 6 FURLONGS ▲FINISH

Worldwide (Ire)

Own: Perez Robert
BAILEY J D (3 1 1 1 .33)

Dk. b or br h. 5
Sire: Sayyaf (Habitat)
Dam: Yoko (Gay Mecene)
Br: Dabaghi M (Ire)
Tr: Callejas Alfredo (—)

115

Lifetime Record: 35 11 0 1 $187,337
1994 8 4 0 0 $66,371 | Turf 35 11 0 1 $187,337
1993 15 3 0 0 $26,255 | Wet 0 0 0 0
Aqu 0 0 0 0 | Dist 0 0 0 0

30Aug94♦ Deauville(Fr) gd *5f ⓉStr :59 3↑ Prix du Cercle (Listed) Stk 38800 52½ Peslier O 130 7.70 Cyrano Storme123nk Ya Malak121hd Wessam Prince121¾ 9 *Well placed in 3rd, one-paced late*
Tr: Francesco Flachi
19Jun94♦ San Siro(Ity) gd *5f ⓉStr :572 3↑ Premio Bersaglio (Listed) Stk 51100 4¾ Planard M 123 – Palacegate Episode120nk Late Parade117½ Imprevedibile123hd 9 *Tracked in 3rd, bid 1f out, not good enough*
2Jun94♦ Chantilly(Fr) gd *5f ⓉStr :583 3↑ Prix du Gros-Chene-G2 Stk 90300 64¼ Cesandri M 124 10.00 Spain Lane118nk Blue Siren117½ Way West1241½ 10 *Led for 2f, chased in 4th, weakened inside final furlong*
1May94♦ San Siro(Ity) gd *5f ⓉStr :581 3↑ Premio Certosa (Listed) Stk 68000 1nk Planard M 126 3.70 Worldwide126nk Arranvanna1261 Imprevedibile1262¼ 10 *Well placed in 3rd, led 1f out, held well*
1Apr94♦ Marseille-PV(Fr) gd *7½f ⓉLH 3↑ Prix des Tamaris Alw 15500 11 Cesandri M 130 2.20 Worldwide1301 Master Blaser1263½ Kriegspiel1285 8 *Led throughout, driving. Time not taken*
13Mar94♦ Marseille-PV(Fr) gd *7½f ⓉLH 3↑ Prix Bright Dover Alw 13900 1¾ Hureau S 128 6.40 Worldwide128¾ Master Blaser1322½ Lou Noble121½ 14 *Led throughout, repelled late challenge. Time not taken*
4Feb94♦ Cagnes-sr-Mr(Fr) hy *5f ⓉStr 1:032 3↑ Prix Sky Lawyer Alw 17600 13½ Hureau S 132 6.10 Worldwide1323½ Run and Gun1266 Hundredfold1321½ 15 *Quickly away, led throughout, clear halfway*
19Jan94♦ Cagnes-sr-Mr(Fr) hy *5f ⓉStr 1:042 3↑ Prix Paul Bufnoir Alw 19400 52¾ Hureau S 132 9.00 Shakadari132nk Run and Gun126no Irish Shoal132no 19 *Mid-pack for a half, finished well without threatening*
13Dec93♦ Marseille-PV(Fr) sf *7½f ⓉLH 3↑ Prix de Canoubier Hcp 17100 87 Hureau S 140 – Gay Native1201 Lawra1101 Tallino1221½ 13 *Towards rear early, never threatened. Time not taken*
10Nov93♦ Evry(Fr) sf *6f ⓉStr 1:20 3↑ Prix Contessina (Listed) Stk 35600 77¾ Mosse G 123 17.00 Huron Warrior1231½ Lit de Justice123½ Way West1232 11 *Never a factor*

WORKOUTS: Oct 16 Bel tr.t 3f fst :384 B *3/3*

Golden Pro

Own: Double R Stable & Iselin & Kaufman
SMITH M E (6 0 1 1 .00)

Dk. b or br c. 4
Sire: Distinctive Pro (Mr. Prospector)
Dam: Solicitous (Cutlass)
Br: Gerald Gallo (Fla)
Tr: Serpe Philip M (1 0 0 1 .00)

113

Lifetime Record: 12 4 2 2 $73,660
1994 3 0 1 1 $13,420 | Turf 0 0 0 0
1993 9 4 1 1 $60,240 | Wet 1 0 0 0 $250
Aqu 0 0 0 0 | Dist 7 3 2 1 $57,580

6Oct94-8Bel fst 6f :22 :444 :564 1:09 3↑ Alw 36000N4X 103 2 2 47 44½ 32½ 21 Smith M E 117 9.00 95-14 Man's Hero1191 Golden Pro1172½ Unreal Mot1172½ Willingly 6
15Sep94-8Bel fst 6f :224 :454 :572 1:091 3↑ Alw 42000N$Y 88 2 5 43 52 54 54¾ Smith M E 115 3.70 90-12 Golden Tent115nk Senor Cielo1152 Rocking Josh1151 Tired 7
4Jan94-8GP fst 6f :221 :451 :572 1:093 3↑ Hallandale H50k 98 10 3 76 43 53½ 34 Smith M E L 113 12.50 89-14 Binalong116½ I Can't Believe1133½ Golden Pro113nk Lacked late response 12
16Nov93-9Med fst 6f :221 :45 :571 1:10 3↑ Alw 23000N3X 91 3 4 32½ 3½ 11½ 11½ Smith M E 114 *.80 91-15 Golden Pro1141½ Sans Souci Slew1162 Freeze Dry1143¾ Handily 5
25Sep93-4Bel fst 6½f :223 :453 1:102 1:164 3↑ Alw 32000N3X 97 3 4 32½ 43 3½ 31¾ Smith M E 113 9.10 87-19 Strikany1131 Apprentice113¾ DH Golden Pro113 Evenly 6
23Jly93-9Mth fst 170 :224 :463 1:112 1:422 3↑ Alw 19000N3X 75 3 4 44½ 55½ 57 46¼ Bravo J -110 *1.40 82-21 Royal N Gold116½ Sans Souci Slew1165½ Fling116nk Fract. gate 7
29Jun93-8Mth fst 6f :22 :45 :573 1:104 3↑ Alw 20000N2X 95 7 2 51¼ 31 2hd 12½ Bravo J 109 *1.20 85-24 Golden Pro1092½ Dances With Dice1142¾ Sweet Beast1103 Driving 7
5Jun93-7Bel fst 7f :222 :45 1:091 1:231 Riva Ridge-G3 63 4 9 74 86 912 1016¾ Ferrer J C 115 45.20 70-13 Montbrook1172 As Indicated1222 Forever Whirl122hd Outrun 10
30Apr93-8Hia fst 7f :233 :464 1:112 1:24 Alw 18000N2L 99 9 1 31 2hd 13½ 18 Ferrer J C 116 *.70 89-18 Golden Pro1168 L's Golden Knight116nk Distinctive Gem1161½ Ridden out 10
20Mar93-2GP sly 7f :222 :454 1:104 1:233 Alw 25000N1X 68 6 8 52½ 42½ 68½ 510¼ Krone J A 115 *1.40 75-12 Sweet Beast1124 The Vid1131½ Inside Connection1204¾ Weakened 10

WORKOUTS: Oct 16 Bel 4f fst :483 B *5/20* Oct 1 Bel 5f fst 1:033 B *45/50* Sep 26 Bel 4f fst :49 B *21/51* Sep 13 Bel 3f fst :37 B *4/14* Sep 9 Bel tr.t 7f fst 1:30 B *1/1* Sep 3 Bel 5f fst 1:004 Hg*9/29*

Rizzi

Own: Hobeau Farm
VELAZQUEZ J R (2 0 0 0 .00)

B. c. 3 (Feb)
Sire: Afleet (Mr. Prospector)
Dam: Top Wish (Topsider)
Br: Kinghaven Farms Limited (Ont-C)
Tr: Jerkens H Allen (—)

115

Lifetime Record: 14 5 1 3 $163,783
1994 9 3 0 1 $104,103 | Turf 1 0 0 0
1993 5 2 1 2 $59,680 | Wet 2 1 0 1 $52,365
Aqu 4 1 1 2 $61,885 | Dist 7 2 1 1 $97,483

9Oct94-8Bel fst 6f :22 :444 :563 1:09 3↑ Boojum H-G2 84 8 5 54 73¾ 86 711¾ Beckner D V 112 b 8.10 84-11 Meritocrat1131 Birdonthewire1174½ Lite The Fuse1101 No factor 8
30Sep94-8Bel fst 6½f :231 :462 1:10 1:16 3↑ Alw 42000N$Y 110 2 3 12½ 12½ 12 17½ Beckner D V5 108 b 2.30 93-14 Rizzi1087½ Chief Desire1172 Won Song117¾ Drew off 5
18Sep94-8Bel yl 1 Ⓣ :232 :47 1:104 1:35 Jamaica H-G2 70 2 2 23 21 57½ 513½ Beckner D V 110 b *2.10e 73-22 Pennine Ridge1183¾ Holy Mountain1166¾ I'm Very Irish113hd No late bid 7
16Jly94-8Bel fst 6f :221 :444 :57 1:093 3↑ TrueNorth H-G2 103 9 6 11½ 1½ 1hd 41¼ Beckner D V 109 b 3.40e 92-12 Friendly Lover114no Boundary1171 Birdonthewire119nk Weakened 9
24Jun94-7Bel fst 7f :214 :441 1:084 1:221 3↑ Alw 32000N3X 107 2 2 1½ 11½ 16 15 Beckner D V7 104 b 3.00 92-17 Rizzi1045 Kyoko1195 Carsey's Pal119nk Driving 7
7May94-6Bel fst 7f :213 :441 1:092 1:214 3↑ Alw 32000N3X 80 3 4 2½ 2hd 41¾ 311½ Samyn J L 112 b 1.90 82-06 Aztec Empire11910 Carsey's Pal1191½ Rizzi112no Dueled, tired 5
16Apr94-8Aqu sly 6f :213 :441 :562 1:091 Best Turn-G3 103 3 2 1hd 12 13 15 Samyn J L 117 b 11.00 96-09 Rizzi1175 Mr. Shawklit1172½ Memories Of Linda1151 Driving 7
26Jan94-6GP fst 7f :214 :442 1:092 1:23 Alw 39000N$Y 52 3 5 2½ 2hd 56 613 Smith M E 115 b 1.40 75-12 Exclusive Praline1144 Smart Enough115no DefenseWitness1083½ Faltered 7
5Jan94-8GP fst 6f :23 :462 :583 1:101 Spec Bid BC74k 59 7 3 52½ 64¾ 612 615 Smith M E 117 b *1.50 75-14 Halo'sImage1143¾ DistinctRelity119nk SenorConquistdor1131¼ Wide, tired 7
4Dec93-7Aqu fst 6f ⊡ :221 :45 :574 1:104 Perpetuate54k 89 4 6 76½ 65 32½ 1nk Smith M E 117 b 5.00 89-16 Rizzi117nk End Sweep1197½ Mr. Flintlock119nk Driving 7

WORKOUTS: ●Oct 7 Bel tr.t 3f fst :343 H *1/11* Sep 14 Bel tr.t 1 fst 1:414 B *1/1* Sep 10 Bel tr.t 7f fst 1:283 B *2/3* Sep 5 Bel tr.t 6f fst 1:131 H *1/1* Aug 29 Bel tr.t 4f fst :51 B *15/18* Aug 24 Bel tr.t 3f fst :372 B *4/15*

Nowhere Man

Own: Perroncino John S
PEZUA J M (2 0 0 0 .00)

Ch. g. 5
Sire: Fountain of Gold (Mr. Prospector)
Dam: Sister Aggie (Great Above)
Br: Matthews Karen & P (Fla)
Tr: Terracciano Neal (1 0 0 0 .00)

112

Lifetime Record: 34 9 4 6 $143,628
1994 8 3 2 0 $47,700 | Turf 1 0 0 0
1993 7 1 0 0 $7,200 | Wet 8 3 2 2 $46,838
Aqu 3 1 1 0 $34,140 | Dist 27 8 4 5 $130,978

17May94-6Bel my 6f :221 :453 :574 1:10 Clm 32500 103 2 1 1½ 12½ 12 12 McCauley W H 115 b *1.70 91-17 Nowhere Man1152 Top The Record1152 Le Risky1192½ Driving 6
3May94-2Bel fst 6f :223 :453 :572 1:093 Clm 45000 94 4 4 1½ 1hd 2hd 41 Luttrell M G5 108 fb 2.90 92-14 Nymphist117nk Memorized108½ Senor Cielo117nk Broke awkwardly 7
16Apr94-2Aqu sly 6f :213 :45 :572 1:10 Clm 70000 87 6 1 11 1½ 2½ 46 Graell A 113 fb 2.70 86-09 Golden Cloud1132½ Tropical Illusion1152 Quickest Blade1131½ Tired 7
30Mar94-6Aqu my 6f :221 :451 :564 1:09 Alw 36000N$Y 104 3 1 11 1hd 2½ 2nk Graell A 115 fb 5.90 97-08 Strikany122nk Nowhere Man1155½ Golden Cloud1225½ Gamely 6
20Mar94-7Aqu fst 6f ⊡ :23 :462 :584 1:112 Alw 36000N$Y 94 3 2 12½ 11 11 21¼ Graell A 115 fb 11.40 85-21 Won Song1151¼ Nowhere Man1151½ Farmonthefreeway115no Weakened 5
11Mar94-2Aqu gd 6f ⊡ :232 :463 :583 1:104 Clm 25000 93 1 4 11 13½ 14 15 Graell A 117 fb *1.30 89-17 Nowhere Man1175 Baypark1153½ Jessup North117nk Driving 6
21Feb94-4Aqu fst 6f ⊡ :232 :47 :592 1:121 Clm c-17500 75 8 4 2hd 3nk 62¾ 72½ Graell A 117 b 4.80 79-20 Exploding Rainbow119no Ben Ali's Rullah117¾ RedHotRed117no Four wide 9
Claimed from Davis Barbara J, Moschera Gasper S Trainer
12Feb94-2Aqu fst 6f ⊡ :231 :463 :583 1:11 Clm 14000 82 6 3 12 12 13 14 Graell A 117 b *1.30 88-16 Nowhere Man1174 Family Tries117½ Alyjandro1142¼ Driving 9
30Dec93-2Aqu fst 6f ⊡ :23 :471 1:001 1:132 3↑ Clm c-17500 44 4 4 32 41½ 56 616¼ Migliore R 117 fb 1.80 60-24 Ben Ali's Rullah117no With It117¾ Exploding Rainbow1176 Tired 7
Claimed from Schwartz Barry K, Hushion Michael E Trainer
15Dec93-1Aqu my 6f ⊡ :23 :462 :584 1:12 3↑ Clm 14000 84 6 3 11½ 11½ 13 13½ Migliore R 117 fb 4.00 83-21 Nowhere Man1173½ Wonder Carr117nk Red Hot Red1172 Driving 8

WORKOUTS: Oct 16 Aqu 5f fst 1:024 B *1/2* ●Oct 9 Aqu 4f fst :472 H *1/5* ●Sep 30 Aqu 4f fst :474 H *1/16* Sep 21 Aqu 3f fst :37 B *2/4* Sep 8 Aqu 3f fst :39 B *7/7*

Primitive Hall
Own: Lawrie Peter D

BRAVO J (3 0 1 0 .00)

B. g. 5
Sire: Dixieland Band (Northern Dancer)
Dam: Dame Avie (Lord Gaylord)
Br: Sharp Bayard (Pa)
Tr: Lewis Wilfred J (—)

116

Lifetime Record:	14	4	4	3	$150,465						
1994	4	0	2	0	$35,788	Turf	2	0	0	1	$5,055
1993	9	3	2	3	$103,742	Wet	3	0	1	1	$25,440
Aqu	1	0	0	1	$14,040	Dist	2	2	0	0	$24,300

27Mar94-9Pha sly	1		:23^4	:46^4	1:11^2	1:37^1	3↑ Alw 22170N3m	100	1	1	1^{hd}	1^{hd}	1$1\frac{1}{2}$	2$\frac{1}{2}$	Molina V H	116	*.80	91-23	Mandy's Lad119$\frac{1}{2}$ Primitive Hall116$3\frac{1}{2}$ Accession116^2	Drifted, just failed	7
13Mar94-8Aqu fst	1⅛	⊡	:47^3	1:11^1	1:36^1	1:49^2	3↑ Grey Lag BCHG3	101	1	1	2^{hd}	1^{hd}	2$2\frac{1}{2}$	4$4\frac{1}{4}$	Molina V H	113	22.80	85-21	As Indicated127$3\frac{1}{4}$ Federal Funds110$\frac{3}{4}$ MichelleCanPass119^{nk}	Dueled, tired	10
21Feb94-9Lrl my	7f		:22^2	:45^2	1:10	1:22^4	3↑ Gen George-G2	91	12	9	7$9\frac{1}{2}$	6$8\frac{1}{2}$	6$7\frac{1}{2}$	5$9\frac{1}{4}$	Molina V H	118	28.80	86-20	Blushing Julian118$4\frac{1}{2}$ Chief Desire123$3\frac{1}{2}$ Who Wouldn't118^1	Wide	12
1Jan94-8Aqu fst	1$\frac{1}{16}$	⊡	:24	:47^3	1:12^2	1:45^3	3↑ Aqueduct H-G3	95	4	3	4$2\frac{1}{4}$	2$1\frac{1}{2}$	2^5	2^5	Molina V H	113	14.40	72-33	As Indicated121^5 Primitive Hall113$6\frac{1}{2}$ Jacksonport112$2\frac{1}{4}$	Best of rest	6
4Dec93-8Aqu fst	1$\frac{1}{16}$	⊡	:23^4	:47^3	1:12	1:44^1	3↑ Qns County HG3	93	8	2	2^1	2$\frac{1}{2}$	2^2	3$1\frac{3}{4}$	Molina V H	113	6.80	82-30	Repletion111$1\frac{1}{4}$ Dibbs N' Dubbs111$\frac{1}{2}$ Primitive Hall113$\frac{3}{4}$	Gamely	8
6Nov93-3Aqu sly	1⅛		:47^1	1:12^4	1:38^1	1:51	3↑ Stuyvsnt H-G3	100	4	1	1^{hd}	1^{hd}	2^{hd}	3$1\frac{3}{4}$	Molina V H	113	13.20	79-20	Michelle Can Pass115^{nk} KeyContender115$1\frac{1}{2}$ PrimitiveHall113$2\frac{3}{4}$	Weakened	8
9Oct93-9Pha fst	1⅛		:48^2	1:12	1:37	1:50^1	3↑ Norristown HG3	95	3	1	2^{hd}	2^{hd}	1$\frac{1}{2}$	1$\frac{3}{4}$	Molina V H	109	3.90	87-18	Primitive Hall109$\frac{3}{4}$ Gala Spinaway116^{nk} Sand Lizard117$1\frac{3}{4}$	Driving	7
3Sep93-8Bel fm	1$\frac{1}{16}$	Ⓣ	:24^4	:47^3	1:11^1	1:41^1	3↑ Alw 34000N3X	87	1	4	4^8	3^4	4^1	3^3	Santos J A	117	6.80	87-10	River Majesty117^2 Happy Trails117^1 Primitive Hall117^{nk}	Mild rally	6
15Aug93-6Mth fst	1		:23	:46^1	1:10^2	1:36^3	3↑ Alw 28000N$mY	93	5	2	2$\frac{1}{2}$	2^1	2$4\frac{1}{2}$	2^5	Bravo J	117	3.20	84-25	Dusty Screen122^5 Primitive Hall117^5 Dr. Zoom122$4\frac{3}{4}$	Second best	6
26Jly93-8Pha fst	7f		:22^1	:44^1	1:08^4	1:22	3↑ Alw 21400N3X	85	3	5	4$3\frac{1}{2}$	4$3\frac{1}{2}$	3^6	2$6\frac{1}{2}$	Molina V H	122	3.00	89-18	Jest Punching111$6\frac{1}{2}$ Primitive Hall122$3\frac{1}{4}$ Swiss Road116^{nk}	Second best	7

WORKOUTS: Oct 13 Bel 6f fst 1:14^3 H *4/8* ●Oct 6 Bel tr.t 5f fst 1:01^4 H *1/5* Sep 30 Bel tr.t 4f fst :49^2 B *12/29* Sep 26 Mth 5f fst 1:04^3 B *14/20* Sep 15 Mth 3f fst :35 H *2/17* ●Sep 9 Mth 3f fst :35^3 B *1/12*

The 3-5 favorite was Rizzi. To recall, the Allen Jerkens-trained colt had cleared to the lead through comparatively slow fractions on September 30, a few races after stablemate Whirlaroo sped though considerably quicker splits in a maiden dash. Allowed to gallop along, Rizzi had literally been blown down the Belmont homestretch by those blustery blasts, and had come home his final sixteenth in :06 seconds — a most favorable set of circumstances, indeed.

While the natural inclination was to forgive Rizzi his distant seventh place drubbing in the Grade 2 Boojum Handicap most recently, there was cause for skepticism even though he was dropping back in with apparently less-formidable sprinters. Three races prior to the Boojum, Rizzi had set the pace to midstretch in the True North Handicap — also Grade 2 — and had wound up fourth, beaten slightly more than a length for the win. That race made it more difficult to explain away his subsequent lackluster performance in the Boojum, a race where he never contended at any point. Moreover, Rizzi had a history of running his best races when fresh: his first triple-digit Beyer had come in the Best Turn Stakes when brought back from a layoff of nearly three months; his next big race had been delivered on June 24 following a seven-week absence and he had been shelved a race later, following the big try in the True North; his wind-blown Beyer of 110 two races ago had been his first dirt outing in two and a half months. Now, however, Rizzi was starting for the fourth time in his current form cycle, and it was possible he might be, as they say in Europe, "over the top," or past his peak.

One could apply the same theory to Golden Pro, who was emerging from a career-best Beyer of 103. Following a route attempt in July of his 3-year-old campaign, the colt had compiled a spotty attendance record, starting only twice the remainder of 1993 and once during the first week of 1994 before going to the bench yet again. Returned after another extended absence he had run well at Belmont, but this would be his third start in five weeks. Was he sufficiently recovered from his injuries to withstand the rigors of consistent training? And even if that was the case, it was possible he'd be a bit muscle-sore following that strenuous exertion only two weeks ago.

Getting a read on how Rizzi and Golden Pro would handle their regimens of recent racing was tricky, and so too was gauging the readiness of the remaining three contestants, because Worldwide, Nowhere Man and Primitive Hall were all returning from layoffs.

Worldwide had been a useful sort overseas, winning 11 of 35 on the turf, but how the 5-year-old would handle a muddy dirt track was anyone's guess — especially since his pedigree was strictly oriented toward turf; too, the lonely-looking workout in :38 4/5 was a sign he would be short of top condition.

Nowhere Man appeared a bit on the cheap side for these, having started in claiming races for as little as $14,000 earlier in the year. But he did have tremendous early speed and had run his best races on muddy tracks, including a Beyer of 104 in a classified allowance on this surface in March. Rizzi would not get an easy lead with this guy drawn directly to his outside.

If Golden Pro could run back to his last race, he might enjoy a tactical edge if Nowhere Man and Rizzi hooked up in a speed duel.

Such a pace scenario would also work to the benefit of Primitive Hall, who *was* advantageously drawn outside so that Joe Bravo could see how the race developed inside before committing to a course of action.

At first glance handicappers might've dismissed Primitive Hall as a router ironing out the kinks in his first race in nearly seven months; as a matter of fact, most players did toss him at first glance, because at 8-1 he was no more highly regarded than Worldwide.

For horses to be taken seriously first time back from a layoff, they cannot show a workout line such as Worldwide's. The line should consist of a series of drills at regularly-spaced intervals, designed to enhance stamina and sharpen speed, and should contain at least one workout at least five furlongs in length. There is no better example of such a line than the one displayed by Primitive Hall.

In addition to workouts that pass muster, the returnee should be able to boast one or more of the following three traits:

- Won or ran close-up, beaten in a photo as a first time-starter
- Won or ran close-up first time back from a previous layoff.
- Trainer has history of having layoff horses cranked and ready.

Primitive Hall's current past performances showed only one layoff start: a wide-trip fifth in the Grade 2 General George on a muddy track at Laurel back in February. While that race was probably better than it looked (he finished in front of seven horses, missing third by just a length and a quarter), it did not provide handicappers with a very clear picture of what to expect today, although some deductive reasoning suggested that he had run well fresh in the past: his current 10-race record showed only one of four career wins, so the other three must have come in the four starts not shown; based on his career totals, two of those wins had come at today's distance.

This is why it's so important to go out in snowstorms to get your copy of the *Form*. Four starts back, Primitive Hall had run second in the Aqueduct Handicap; by digging out my *Form* from that New Year's Day event, I was able to see the horse's record from day one:

4 Primitive Hall

Own: Lawrie Peter D
MOLINA V H (1 0 0 1 .00)

B. g. 5
Sire: Dixieland Band (Northern Dancer)
Dam: Dame Avie (Lord Gaylord)
Br: Sharp Bayard (Pa)
Tr: Lewis Wilfred J (1 0 0 1 .00)

113

Lifetime Record :	10	4	2	3	$114,677					
1993	9	3	2	3	$103,742	Turf	2	0	0	1	$5,055
1992	1	1	0	0	$10,935	Wet	1	0	0	1	$14,040
Aqu [•]	1	0	0	1	$10,602	Dist	1	0	0	1	$10,602

4Dec93-8Aqu	fst	1 1/16	[•]	:234	:473	1:12	1:441	3↑ Qns County HG3	93	8	2	21	2½	22	31¾	Molina V H	113	6.80	82-30	Repletion1111¼ Dibbs N' Dubbs111½ Primitive Hall113¾	Gamely	8
6Nov93-3Aqu	sly	1⅛		:471	1:124	1:381	1:51	3↑ Stuyvsnt H-G3	100	4	1	1hd	1hd	2hd	31¾	Molina V H	113	13.20	79-20	Michelle Can Pass115nk KeyContender1151½ PrimitiveHall1132¾	Weakened	8
9Oct93-9Pha	fst	1⅛		:482	1:12	1:37	1:501	3↑ Norristown HG3	95	3	1	2hd	2hd	1½	1¾	Molina V H	109	3.90	87-18	Primitive Hall109¾ Gala Spinaway116nk Sand Lizard1171¾	Driving	7
3Sep93-8Bel	fm	1 1/16	[T]	:244	:473	1:111	1:411	3↑ Alw 34000N3X	87	1	4	48	34	41	33	Santos J A	117	6.80	87-10	River Majesty1172 Happy Trails1171 Primitive Hall117nk	Mild rally	6
15Aug93-6Mth	fst	1		:23	:461	1:102	1:363	3↑ Alw 28000N$mY	93	5	2	2½	21	24½	25	Bravo J	117	3.20	84-25	Dusty Screen1225 Primitive Hall1175 Dr. Zoom1224¾	Second best	6
26Jly93-8Pha	fst	7f		:221	:441	1:084	1:22	3↑ Alw 20000N3X	85	3	5	43½	43½	36	26½	Molina V H	122	3.00	89-18	Jest Punching1116½ Primitive Hall1223¼ Swiss Road116nk	Second best	7
7Jly93-9Mth	fst	1		:233	:471	1:112	1:374	3↑ Alw 18500N3L	92	3	1	1hd	2hd	11½	14¾	Molina V H	120	2.30	83-24	Primitive Hall1204¾ Mighty Avanti1103½ Forty Nine Smiles1203		6
Broke thru gate, drew out																						
18Jun93-9Mth	fm	*1⅛	(T)	:46	1:111	1:35	1:482+	3↑ Alw 19500N3L	82	5	2	2½	21½	31	43	Molina V H	121	3.10	103-02	Abduct113½ Main Bid117¾ Senor Appeal1171¾	Tired late	7
7Jun93-9Pha	fst	6f		:22	:452	:58	1:104	3↑ [S]Alw 22275N1X	89	8	7	31	1hd	13½	19	Molina V H	116	*1.20	87-24	PrimitiveHll1169 RuggedAttitude1143 ChimneySwepJo1081½	Ridden out	10
25May92-6Pha	fst	6f		:222	:453	:573	1:102	[S]Md Sp Wt	86	4	4	11	11½	15	18½	Molina V H	122	4.30	89-11	Primitive Hall1228½ Pressman122¾ Tedstarossa122	Handily	10

WORKOUTS: Dec 28 Pha 3f fst :35 H *3/17* Dec 19 Pha 5f fst 1:014 B *4/6* Dec 1 Pha 3f fst :373 B *4/9* ●Oct 29 Pha 5f fst :583 H *1/18* Oct 1 Mth 6f fst 1:15 B *2/2*

Primitive Hall had won his career debut, and also won when brought back from a lay-off of more than a year for his second start. Both victories came at six furlongs.

Primitive Hall classed up, having raced competitively in six straight graded stakes prior to the layoff, and the fact that those first two career wins were hidden from the crowd made him a wolf in sheep's clothing.

EIGHTH RACE
Aqueduct
OCTOBER 20, 1994

6 FURLONGS. (1.08) HANDICAP. Purse $50,000. 3-year-olds and upward. Weights Sunday, October 16. Declarations by 10:00 A.M. Tuesday, October 18. Closed with 8 nominations.

Value of Race: $50,000 Winner $30,000; second $11,000; third $6,000; fourth $3,000. Mutuel Pool $143,955.00 Exacta Pool $284,355.00

Last Raced	Horse	M/Eqt. A.Wt	PP	St	¼	½	Str	Fin	Jockey	Odds $1
27Mar94 9Pha²	Primitive Hall	5 116	5	2	4²	1½	1²	1½	Bravo J	8.00
6Oct94 8Bel²	Golden Pro	4 113	2	3	5	4ʰᵈ	2½	2²½	Smith M E	2.75
9Oct94 8Bel⁷	Rizzi	b 3 115	3	5	3½	3¹	3¹	3⁶½	Velazquez J R	0.65
30Aug94 Dea⁵	Worldwide-IR	5 115	1	4	2³½	5	5	4ⁿᵏ	Bailey J D	8.30
17May94 6Bel¹	Nowhere Man	bf 5 112	4	1	1½	2²½	4²	5	Lydon P J	6.80

OFF AT 3:43 Start Good. Won driving. Time, :22, :45², :57⁴, 1:10⁴ Track good.

$2 Mutuel Prices:
6-(F)-PRIMITIVE HALL	18.00	5.40	2.40
3-(C)-GOLDEN PRO		3.60	2.30
4-(D)-RIZZI			2.10

$2 EXACTA 6-3 PAID $63.50

B. g, by Dixieland Band-Dame Avie, by Lord Gaylord. Trainer Lewis Wilfred J. Bred by Sharp Bayard (Pa).

PRIMITIVE HALL reserved early, rapidly gained to take the lead on the turn, opened a clear advantage in upper stretch then turned back GOLDEN PRO under brisk urging. GOLDEN PRO checked slightly in the early stages, raced well back to the turn then closed steadily from outside but could not get up. RIZZI settled just behind the leaders for a half and lacked a strong closing bid. WORLDWIDE showed only brief speed. NOWHERE MAN set the pace to the turn and gave way. RIZZI wore mud caulks.

Owners— 1, Lawrie Peter D & Lewis Wilfred J; 2, Double R Stable & Iselin & Kaufman; 3, Hobeau Farm; 4, Perez Robert; 5, Perroncino John S

Trainers— 1, Lewis Wilfred J; 2, Serpe Philip M; 3, Jerkens H Allen; 4, Callejas Alfredo; 5, Terracciano Neal

Scratched— Who Wouldn't (10ct94 7LRL²), Friendly Lover (90ct94 8BEL⁴), Golden Tent (10ct94 7LRL³)

Bᴜʀʀᴏᴡɪɴɢ ᴛʜʀᴏᴜɢʜ ᴀ sᴛᴀᴄᴋ of old *Forms* to look back on the early stages of horses' careers, as with Primitive Hall, often provides valuable insights about what can be expected today. So too, can looking *forward* especially when it comes to lightly-raced horses.

Handicappers are dealing with a veritable gold mine here, for when these unproved runners go to the grass, or stretch out to routes, or catch wet tracks for the first time, the ones with backgrounds and preparations suitable to the new conditions are often over-looked and offer some of the most lucrative opportunities in the game.

Likewise, lightly-raced horses that don't pan out when asked to do something new can, and often do, rebound when returned to more favorable conditions. Case in point, the sev-enth race of November 16:

7

Aqueduct

6 Furlongs (1:08) ALLOWANCE. Purse $30,000. 2-year-olds which have not won a race other than maiden or claiming. Weight, 122 lbs. Non-winners of a race other than claiming since November 1, allowed 3 lbs. Of such a race since October 15, 5 lbs.

Robby Two
Own: Cohen Robert B

MAPLE E (43 7 7 5 .16)

B. c. 2 (May)
Sire: Kris S. (Roberto)
Dam: Cassowary (Cormorant)
Br: C. P. Beler (NY)
Tr: Shapoff Stanley R (21 2 7 2 .10)

117

Lifetime Record :	4 1 0 0		$21,300
1994	4 1 0 0	$21,300	Turf 0 0 0 0
1993	0 M 0 0		Wet 1 1 0 0 $16,800
Aqu	0 0 0 0		Dist 2 0 0 0

15Oct94–4Bel fst 1¹⁄₁₆	:23⁴ :47² 1:13 1:45¹	Ⓢ SleepyHollow75k	56 4 3 1½ 1ʰᵈ 37½ 417	Chavez J F	115 b *1.90 59–21 Outlaw115² Moonlight Dancer115¹³ Atrebla115²	Dueled, tired 10
28Sep94–5Bel my 7f	:22⁴ :46¹ 1:11 1:23²	Ⓢ Md Sp Wt	86 3 4 1ʰᵈ 1¹ 1⁴ 1¹²	Chavez J F	118 b 4.30e 86–14 Robby Two118¹² Demon Damon118²¾ Revolutionary Era118⁴	Ridden out 7
16Sep94–3Bel fst 6f	:22⁴ :46³ :58⁴ 1:11¹	Ⓢ Md Sp Wt	46 4 7 76½ 73½ 64½ 69½	Maple E	118 – 13.50 76–10 Crusader's Story118ⁿᵒ Porphyry118ⁿᵏ Thunder Gulch118¹½	No threat 8
5Sep94–3Bel fst 6f	:23² :47¹ :59² 1:11³	Ⓢ Md Sp Wt	54 3 6 3¹½ 1ʰᵈ 3² 6⁷	Maple E	118 4.00e 76–14 Larchmont118² Billy The Bid118¹ Demon Damon118ⁿᵏ	Bid, tired 13

WORKOUTS: Nov 13 Bel tr.t 4f fst :48¹ H 4/34 Nov 10 Bel tr.t 4f sly :50¹ B 1/2 Nov 4 Bel 4f fst :49 B 5/36 Oct 27 Bel tr.t 4f fst :47³ H 2/23 Oct 10 Bel 1 fst 1:40² H 1/2 ●Oct 5 Bel tr.t 6f fst 1:14¹ H 1/4

Testability

Own: Hooper Fred W

BAILEY J D (56 10 9 13 .18)

B. c. 2 (Apr)
Sire: Copelan (Tri Jet)
Dam: Fleetest (Cutlass)
Br: F. W. Hooper (Fla)
Tr: Serpe Philip M (8 1 2 1 .13)

117

Lifetime Record :	2 1 1 0	$21,600			
1994	2 1 1 0	$21,600	Turf	0 0 0 0	
1993	0 M 0 0		Wet	0 0 0 0	
Aqu	0 0 0 0		Dist	1 0 1 0	$6,600

21Sep94-5Bel	fst	6f	:231	:462	:581	1:11	Alw 30000N1X	79	5	5	23	1hd	2hd	2½	Bailey J D	117	*.70	85-17	Ross Creek117½ Testability117hd Chute Boss1171	Broke slowly	5
2Jun94-3Bel	fst	5½f	:231	:464	:584	1:051	Md Sp Wt	67	2	1	1½	11	16	18¾	Bailey J D	115	*.60	89-08	Testability1158¾ Silver Medalist1153 Spoon Bend1152	Handily	6

WORKOUTS: ●Nov 12 Bel 5f fst 1:001 H 1/45 Nov 6 Bel 3f fst :37 B 5/8 Oct 6 Bel 5f fst 1:001 H 3/29 Oct 1 Bel 4f fst :484 B 16/52 ●Sep 14 Bel 5f fst :584 H 1/23 Sep 8 Bel 5f fst :583 H 2/21

Our Exuberant Lad

Own: Filosa Richard & Hills Timothy A

DAVIS R G (72 11 13 10 .15)

Ch. g. 2 (Feb)
Sire: Exuberant (What a Pleasure)
Dam: Catalina Lass (Exclusive Ribot)
Br: Kathryn A. Stromberger (Fla)
Tr: Hills Timothy A (2 0 0 0 .00)

117

Lifetime Record :	2 1 0 0	$16,800			
1994	2 1 0 0	$16,800	Turf	0 0 0 0	
1993	0 M 0 0		Wet	2 1 0 0	$16,800
Aqu	1 0 0 0		Dist	1 1 0 0	$16,800

23Oct94-8Aqu	my	7f	:222	:454	1:111	1:243	Cowdin-G2	52	3	7	2½	22	45	715	Davis R G	122	4.20	66-19	Old Tascosa1222½ Thunder Gulch1221½ Adams Trail1222¼	Forced pace, tired	8
27Sep94-3Bel	sly	6f	:221	:452	:574	1:111	Md Sp Wt	79	2	1	13½	12½	13	13	Perret C	118	4.30	85-18	Our Exuberant Lad1183 Churka118¾ Stauder1182½	Ridden out	4

WORKOUTS: Nov 11 Bel 5f fst 1:001 Hg2/10 ●Oct 19 Bel 3f fst :354 B 1/16 ●Oct 13 Bel 6f fst 1:141 H 1/8 Oct 7 Bel 3f fst :37 B 5/16 Sep 22 Bel 4f fst :48 H 4/53 Sep 16 Bel 6f fst 1:14 Hg2/5

Mr. Greeley

Own: Condren William & Cornacchia Joseph

BECKNER D V (111 15 17 21 .14)

Ch. c. 2 (May)
Sire: Gone West (Mr. Prospector)
Dam: Long Legend (Reviewer)
Br: Herman Sarkowsky (Ky)
Tr: Zito Nicholas P (32 5 1 5 .16)

112[5]

Lifetime Record :	5 1 2 0	$29,000			
1994	5 1 2 0	$29,000	Turf	0 0 0 0	
1993	0 M 0 0		Wet	2 0 2 0	$11,000
Aqu	0 0 0 0		Dist	0 0 0 0	

8Oct94-8Bel	fst	1 1/16	:232	:461	1:111	1:44	Champagne-G1	52	3	4	1hd	3½	1113	1128	Krone J A	122	27.80	54-17	Timber Country122½ Sierra Diablo1226½ On Target122nk	Dueled inside	11
22Sep94-7Bel	fst	1 1/16	:232	:472	1:113	1:433	Alw 32000N1X	67	1	1	11	1hd	52½	59	Krone J A	122	2.70	75-27	Flitch117¾ Reality Road1172 Tony Riccio1171¼	Gave way	5
8Sep94-3Bel	fst	1	:224	:47	1:121	1:38	Md Sp Wt	75	6	1	11	13	15	16	Krone J A	118	*.40	73-27	Mr. Greeley1186 Arezzano1189½ Flame Keeper1184	Handily	6
19Aug94-5Sar	sly	7f	:23	:462	1:104	1:231	Md Sp Wt	77	5	3	31½	1½	1½	21¾	Krone J A	118	3.40e	87-09	Top Account1181¾ Mr. Greeley11811 Jackson1182½	Gamely	8
27Jly94-5Sar	wf	5f	:22	:461		:594	Md Sp Wt	47	4	7	79¼	52½	32	21¼	Krone J A	118	3.60	83-12	L' Aquilon1181¼ Mr. Greeley1183¼ Valid Motion1185¼	Broke slowly	7

WORKOUTS: ●Nov 9 Bel 5f fst :591 H 1/22 Nov 1 Bel 5f gd 1:023 B 5/18 Oct 25 Bel 5f fst 1:014 B 4/17 Oct 17 Bel 5f fst 1:062 B 20/20 ●Oct 7 Bel 3f fst :352 H 1/16 ●Sep 30 Bel 6f fst 1:103 H 1/10

Pat N Jac

Own: Sabine Stable

CHAVEZ J F (117 18 14 12 .15)

B. c. 2 (May)
Sire: Pentelicus (Fappiano)
Dam: Arts and Clover (Arts and Letters)
Br: Rustlewood Farm Inc. (Fla)
Tr: Barbara Robert (22 5 1 1 .23)

117

Lifetime Record :	3 1 0 0	$18,720			
1994	3 1 0 0	$18,720	Turf	0 0 0 0	
1993	0 M 0 0		Wet	1 0 0 0	
Aqu	2 0 0 0	$1,920	Dist	1 1 0 0	$16,800

8Nov94-7Aqu	fst	1	:224	:46	1:112	1:381	Alw 32000N1X	64	5	4	42	41½	34½	47½	Chavez J F	117	8.90	69-20	Stauder1122¾ Churka1174½ Jackson117nk	Checked 1/2 pl	7
23Oct94-8Aqu	my	7f	:222	:454	1:111	1:243	Cowdin-G2	44	5	8	76½	75½	812	819	Luzzi M J	122	24.75	62-19	OldTascosa1222½ ThunderGulch1221½ AdmsTril1222¼	Broke slowly, outrun	8
4Oct94-5Bel	fst	6f	:223	:454	:584	1:121	Md Sp Wt	64	3	6	65¾	33	2hd	1nk	Smith M E	118	8.20	80-14	Pat N Jac118nk Judge Me Not118no Sosa1181	Driving	9

WORKOUTS: Nov 5 Bel 5f fst 1:012 H 5/22 Oct 18 Bel 5f fst 1:013 B 2/15 Oct 12 Bel 4f fst :474 H 5/50 Sep 29 Bel tr.t 5f fst 1:01 H 4/13 Sep 22 Bel 5f fst 1:014 Hg21/41 Sep 16 Bel 5f fst 1:022 Hg15/26

Silver Midnight

Own: Harris Charles E

PEREZ R M (85 12 9 13 .14)

Dk. b or br c. 2 (Mar)
Sire: Silver Deputy (Deputy Minister)
Dam: Pococurante (Nain Bleu)
Br: Lucille Wakefield (Ont-C)
Tr: Jolley Leroy (7 0 1 0 .00)

112[5]

Lifetime Record :	4 1 0 1	$18,000			
1994	4 1 0 1	$18,000	Turf	0 0 0 0	
1993	0 M 0 0		Wet	0 0 0 0	
Aqu	0 0 0 0		Dist	1 0 0 1	$3,000

7Sep94-7WO	fst	7f	:222	:451	1:093	1:223	[R]Simcoe-G3C	55	4	4	2hd	1hd	412	619	Penna D	117 b	5.15	79-10	Saints Leader12211 Heaven's Wish117nk All Firmed Up1176	Early speed	7
11Aug94-5Sar	fst	5f	:222	:46		:591	Md Sp Wt	70	6	7	11½	12	13	11½	Bailey J D	118 b	5.30	87-14	SilverMidnight1181½ Admiralty1183 AdamsTril118hd	Broke slowly, driving	8
1Jly94-5Bel	fst	6f	:222	:463	:594	1:123	Md Sp Wt	46	1	1	1½	1½	31	310	McCauley W H	115	4.40	68-15	Flitch1158 Ross Creek1152 Silver Midnight1159	Dueled inside	6
10Jun94-3Bel	fst	5f	:214	:45		:573	Md Sp Wt	47	5	6	64½	65¼	65½	611¼	Santos J A	115	8.90	82-09	Jump The Shadow1154½ Furious Folly1152 Ago1152½	Drifted wide, green	6

WORKOUTS: Nov 14 Bel 4f fst :484 B 5/22 Oct 26 Bel 4f fst :481 H 9/38 Oct 7 Bel 4f fst :48 H 8/39 Sep 5 WO 3f fst :354 B 4/16 Aug 24 Sar 5f fst 1:004 H 8/39

Chute Boss

Own: Wet Beak Stable

LUZZI M J (101 17 12 13 .17)

Ch. g. 2 (Jan)
Sire: Who's Fleet (Villamor)
Dam: Chinkers (Master Derby)
Br: Kurbanali Steve (Fla)
Tr: Tesher Howard M (12 1 0 1 .08)

117

Lifetime Record :	7 1 0 2	$17,304			
1994	7 1 0 2	$17,304	Turf	0 0 0 0	
1993	0 M 0 0		Wet	1 0 0 0	
Aqu	1 0 0. 0		Dist	1 0 0 1	$3,600

23Oct94-8Aqu	my	7f	:222	:454	1:111	1:243	Cowdin-G2	63	8	1	88½	53½	66	510	Chavez J F	122 b	7.50	71-19	OldTascosa1222½ ThunderGulch1221½ AdamsTrail1222¼	Wide, flattened out	8
11Oct94-7Bel	fst	7f	:231	:471	1:131	1:271	Alw 30000N1X	44	2	3	51¾	41½	43½	46¾	Velazquez J R	117 b	*1.30	60-21	AdmsTril1223¾ FortunteErrol117no MercifulJudge1193	Steadied, boxed in	6
21Sep94-5Bel	fst	6f	:231	:462	:581	1:11	Alw 30000N1X	78	2	1	33½	4¾	3½	3½	Chavez J F	117 b	13.70	85-17	Ross Creek117½ Testability117hd Chute Boss1171	Rallied inside	5
19Jly94-3Mth	fst	5½f	:221	:453	:574	1:041	Alw 17000N1X	40	4	2	54½	55	56½	616½	Bravo J	117 b	5.00	77-17	Enlighten1176¾ Culinary Delight120nk Akiba1171½	Gave way	7
19Jun94-9Hou	fst	5f	:22	:46		:59	Hou Juvenile29k	61	7	4	74½	75¼	63¾	43	Brown D E	117 b	33.10	— —	Gallant Talent1172 Baha Mirimba117½ Tricuit122½	Improved position	13
8Jun94-6Hou	fst	5f	:22	:463		:594	Md Sp Wt	55	9	1	51½	71¾	2½	1¾	Norwood J K	118 b	24.50	— —	Chute Boss118¾ Good Heaven's Boy118½ Alit1182¾	Drew clear	12
25May94-5Hou	fst	5f	:221	:462		:594	Md Sp Wt	33	2	6	88¼	87	78½	36¾	Norwood J K	118 b	35.90	— —	BhMirimb1185¾ GoodHeven'sBoy1181 ChuteBoss1181¼	Improved position	9

WORKOUTS: Nov 13 Bel 4f fst :49 B 8/32 Nov 6 Bel tr.t 3f fst :362 B 5/15 Oct 31 Bel 4f fst :49 H 9/31 Oct 20 Bel 4f fst :494 B 16/37 Oct 1 Bel 4f fst :494 B 31/52 Sep 14 Bel 4f fst :48 H 7/39

Manila Thriller

Own: Dogwood Stable

SANTOS J A (84 10 12 15 .12)

B. c. 2 (Feb)
Sire: Manila (Lyphard)
Dam: Promising Risk (Exclusive Native)
Br: Humphrey G Watts Jr & Louise I etal (Ky)
Tr: Alexander Frank A (12 3 0 1 .25)

117

Lifetime Record :	6 1 2 1	$34,980			
1994	6 1 2 1	$34,980	Turf	4 0 1 1	$13,280
1992	0 M 0 0		Wet	1 1 0 0	$16,200
Aqu	0 0 0 0		Dist	1 0 1 0	$5,500

28Oct94-9Med	yl	1 1/16	(T)	:223	:463	1:112	1:431	Yng America-G3	70	6	7	74½	52½	55	56¾	Santos J A	115 b	8.60	78-14	MissUnionAvenue116nk GreenMensGo113nk MneIngredint1223	No factor	9
10Sep94-2Bel	fm	1	(T)	:23	:46	1:101	1:343	Alw 32000N1X	72	2	4	42	32	23	26¾	Santos J A	117 b	*2.20	82-11	Diplomatic Jet1176¾ Manila Thriller1175 Reality Road1172¼	No match	7
21Aug94-3Sar	sly	7f	⊗	:221	:452	1:112	1:253	Md Sp Wt	68	6	3	1hd	13½	14	11½	Santos J A	118 b	*2.20	77-20	Manila Thriller1181½ Noble 'n Heart1185 Banquet1185½	Driving	8
7Aug94-3Sar	gd	1	[T]	:23	:473	1:122	1:38	Md Sp Wt	72	1	6	64	52¼	33½	31¼	Perret C	118	*2.40	86-18	HoustonConnection118no Noble'nHrt1181¼ MnilThrillr1183	Checked 3/8 pl	10
15Jly94-3Bel	gd	6f	⊗	:23	:464	:593	1:124	Md Sp Wt	50	8	4	2½	2hd	2hd	21½	Perret C	115	*.80	75-18	Spanish Halo1151½ Manila Thriller1153 Boyonette1157¾	Gamely	8
4Jly94-3Bel	fm	6f	(T)	:221	:46	:574	1:094	Md Sp Wt	64	9	9	67	42½	43½	45¼	McCauley W H	115	2.90	82-13	Diplomatic Jet115nk Blues Fan1152 Banquet1153	Pinched break, wide	11

WORKOUTS: Nov 8 Bel 4f fst :493 B 8/26 ●Oct 20 Bel 6f fst 1:124 H 1/6 Oct 12 Bel 5f fst 1:023 B 12/19 Oct 6 Bel 5f fst 1:014 H 5/29 ●Sep 29 Bel tr.t 4f fst :48 H 1/37 Sep 6 Bel tr.t 5f fst 1:021 B 2/7

Ft. Stockton

Own: New Farm

SMITH M E (94 23 22 11 .24)

B. c. 2 (Apr)
Sire: Cure the Blues (Stop the Music)
Dam: Tai the Devil (Tai)
Br: Kathy Brown (Tex)
Tr: Perkins Benjamin W (2 0 1 0 .00)

117

Lifetime Record :	1 1 0 0	$7,500			
1994	1 1 0 0	$7,500	Turf	0 0 0 0	
1993	0 M 0 0		Wet	1 1 0 0	$7,500
Aqu	0 0 0 0		Dist	0 0 0 0	

26May94-1GS	sly	5f	:221	:464		:593	Md Sp Wt	59	8	4	1hd	1½	11½	13¼	Wilson R	118	*.30	90-07	Ft. Stockton1183¼ I Request More118¾ Striking Lord1182	Driving	8

WORKOUTS: Nov 12 NwF 5f fst 1:022 B 1/2 Nov 1 NwF 4f fst :512 Bg2/3 ●Oct 25 NwF 5f fst 1:02 B 1/4 Oct 19 NwF 4f fst :502 B 5/8 ●Sep 19 Mth 5f fst :592 Hg1/27 Sep 13 Mth 5f fst 1:022 B 3/12

For the most part, trying to anticipate what these 2-year-olds will do today is an exercise in futility. Only three — Our Exuberant Lad, Pat N Jac and Chute Boss — have raced at Aqueduct, and of those, Pat N Jac is the only one who was lucky enough to catch a fast track. Looking at their Beyer Speed Figures is like trying to follow a ping-pong match: they're all over the place. Robby Two's three fast track races received figures of 54, 46 and 56, but he shot to an 86 when able to shake loose in the mud; Our Exuberant Lad earned a 79 winning in the slop at Belmont, but fell off to a 52 in the mud at Aqueduct; Chute Boss earned figures ranging from 33 to 61 in his first four starts, returned from a two-month layoff with a leap to 78, then produced a 44 and a 63.

Moreover, since healthy and upwardly-mobile horses typically improve in relatively big jumps as they mature through their 2-year-old seasons, it would be short-sighted to judge a colt such as Ft. Stockton on the basis of a single Beyer of 59 earned in a sloppy track maiden win almost six months ago.

With so much uncertainty surrounding this field, I had channeled my handicapping energies the previous evening to the more predictable races on the card; this race might yet prove playable, but that would depend on late-breaking factors such as the odds and post parade appearances.

Midway through the betting Testability was established as a clear-cut favorite, with several others, Ft. Stockton, Mr. Greeley, Pat N Jac, and Our Exuberant Lad, offered between 4-1 and 8-1. It was easy to see why the crowd was betting this way. Both of Testability's races had been good, a reassuring trait in a race containing several inconsistent runners; plus, his most recent Beyer of 79 was the best last-out-number by a wide margin. The connections of Ft. Stockton were highly respected due to their documented history of success with shippers to New York, so he was the second choice even though many bettors shied away from a figure standpoint, since every other horse had run a Beyer superior to that 59 from May. The three others below 10-1 were deemed to have some kind of a chance, but it was hard to get a handle on what they might do in this spot.

Given the volatility of 2-year-old form, and the fact that their preferences are as yet unformed for the most part, it's silly to accept 7-5 on horses like Testability based on what they've shown in only one or two prior races. Playing devil's advocate (something players should make it a practice to do with short-priced horses), Testability doesn't make it to the races much, and the month-long gap in workout activity from October 6 to November 6 begs attention. Lightly raced horses in good form don't spend a month in the barn without racing or working out unless something is amiss.

Mr. Greeley boasted *two* dirt Beyers competitive with Testability's 79, and he was the only member of the field about whom that could be said. But Nick Zito's colt had not beaten a horse in his two most recent starts, so it was hard to know what to expect in this spot...or was it? The colt's connections had accounted for two of the last four Kentucky Derby winners, Strike the Gold and Go For Gin. After Mr. Greeley's handy maiden victory they could be forgiven if visions of another run for the roses danced in their heads. But what happened after that must've been a rude awakening for owners Bill Condren and Joe Cornacchia, and most of all for Zito. The racy-looking chestnut folded his tent after carving out the early pace in a preliminary allowance at a mile and a sixteenth, and had then stopped miserably after slugging it out on the front-end in the Champagne against Timber Country, who had parlayed that performance into a Breeders' Cup Juvenile victory, and a lock on the 2-year-old championship.

Judging from those last two races, if Mr. Greeley was going to kill the world he certainly wasn't going to do it in routes. He had never raced at today's distance, skipping from five to seven furlongs at Saratoga, but his workout in 1:10 3/5 on September 30 indicated that six furlongs was right up his alley. Significantly, that time was faster than anyone in this field had run in the *afternoons* — including Testability, who had been half a length behind a 1:11 last time out.

BELMONT PARK — Track Fast

Three Furlongs									
Alyinda	:38⁴ Bg	Claudius	:49¹ B	Thayer	:49¹ B	La Quinta Nina	1:05 B
Do Hush	:37 B	Dance Of Sunshine	:51¹ B	Thrilling	:48⁴ B	Lady Lisa	1:06 B
Escarrgot	:37¹ B	Dominant Prospect	:47² H	Thunder Gulch	:48⁴ B	Lahint	1:01 B
Et Vous	:35⁴ H	Easy Does It	:49 B	Trailblazer	:49¹ Bg	Merciful Judge	1:00² H
Full And Fancy	:35⁴ H	Father Shea	:47³ H	Trick Trick	:49 B	My Card	1:04 B
Furious Folly	:35⁴ H	French Steal	:47³ H	Trusted Friend	:50 B	New Wave	1:02³ B
Heed	:36² B	Great All Over	:51⁴ B	Valley Ofthe Jolly	:49³ B	New York Lights	1:02³ B
Ivory Hunter	:35⁴ H	Halo Habit	:48 B	Willful Discovery	:50² B	Non Partisan	1:00³ H
Java Java	:35 H	Henry S.	:50² B	Winloc's Dr. Pete	:49³ B	Northern Centaur	1:01² B
Leagueofherown	:36⁴ B	Home Binder	:53 B	Yolanders Pet	:49² B	Pluckemin	1:00³ H
Lindsey's Laughter	:39² B	Jerry Bomb	:48¹ B	**Five Furlongs** :56¹		Precocious Paris	1:00³ H
Lottsa Talc	:35¹ H	Just You Dare	:49 B	Adored Slew	1:00² H	Pretty Prep	1:03³ B
Mighty Fly	:37² Bg	Justfortherecord	:47 H	Aladans Girl	1:03² B	River Arly (Fr)	1:02⁴ B
Naskra Dance	:39² B	Kerfoot Corner	:49³ B	Alyantis	1:06 B	Safe At Home	:59² H
No Talk	:37² Bg	London Fog	:47³ H	Apollyon	1:02³ B	Silver Spots	1:02³ B
Odawa Moon	:36⁴ Bg	Lukas Comin	:49² B	Baldski's Gamble	1:03 B	Since You Ask	1:05 Bg
Passive Aggresive	:37² Bg	Manor Queen	:48⁴ B	Bella Dawn	1:00³ H	Sosa	1:00 H
Principality	:36¹ B	Mcfanny	:48⁴ Bg	Ben's Moment	1:01 B	Southern Forest	1:02³ B
Social Approval	:39⁴ Bg	Missymooiloveyou	:47³ H	Change The Tune	1:02³ B	Stormy Blues	1:00³ B
Tetlie	:36⁴ B	Monte Lucho (Arg)	:50 B	Cooperstown	1:02¹ B	War Victor	1:04 B
The Romerator	:39⁴ Bg	**Moroccan Magic**	:46¹ H	Crimson Guard	1:00³ H	**Six Furlongs** 1:07⁴
Time's Arrow	:35² H	Nobody Picked Six	:48² H	Distinct Manner	1:01⁴ B	Easy Miner	1:13³ H
Tolltally Light	:38⁴ Bg	Not For Love	:50³ B	Dynamic Storm	1:02¹ B	King Of The City	1:16³ B
Vega's Secret	:36⁴ Hg	Once Wild Ski	:49 B	Flag Down	1:01³ B	Lure	1:11⁴ H
Winds	:37⁴ Bg	Quick To Finish	:47⁴ H	Fraise	1:03 B	Mr. Greeley	1:10³ H
Ziggyberries	:37 B	Robbers Gold	:49 B	Gambler's Phantasy	1:03 B	Our Dear Dana	1:19 H
Four Furlongs		Sandy's Image	:49² B	Gifted Son	1:05 B	Outlaw	1:13² H
Alygitter	:51 Bg	Scannapieco	:49 B	Gliding Arc	1:01³ B	Paradise Creek	1:19 B
Annie Bonnie	:50² B	Shahra Bay	:48⁴ B	Glorious Purple	1:05 B	Rara Avis	1:16³ B
Blitzz U S A	:50¹ B	Shepherd's Moon	:50² B	Gulpha Gorge	1:02 B	Record Level	1:18³ Bg
Bon James	:51 B	Shine On Steinlen	:48⁴ B	Hodgman	1:05 Bg	Storm In Sight	1:18 B
Canadian Halo	:49¹ Bg	Statuette	:48 B	Hollywood Flash	1:02 B	**Seven Furlongs** 1:20¹
Chenin Blanc	:52² B	Swing So High	:49 B	Kapok	1:02 B	Lulu's Little Boy	1:27³ B
		Tara Roma	:50 B	Kent Clark	1:02⁴ B		

Workout corrections: Flys On Kris and Flies On Kris should read MIGHTY FLY; Holy Knowly should read BON JAMES. STORMY BLUES (5f) holds form. LURE (6f) is in top form. MR. GREELEY (6f) opened eyes.

A look at the work tab shows the track hadn't been abnormally fast on the morning of September 30, when, according to the clocker's comment, Mr. Greeley "opened eyes." The second-fastest workout at six furlongs belonged to Lure, a track record-holder going five furlongs at Belmont who was training toward the Breeders' Cup Mile, an event he had won each of the previous two years; Lure had gone more than a full second slower than Mr. Greeley, and the other works had ranged anywhere from 1:13 2/5 to 1:19.

Mr. Greeley's latest work, a bullet :59 1/5 a week ago, was also much faster than the next-fastest time:

Wednesday November 9, 1994

AQUEDUCT — Track Fast

Three Furlongs							
Cirastaire	:39 B	Adkin's Park	:493 B	Pops Is Tops	:511 B	Wheal D'or	:482 H
Dynamic Brett	:40 B	Critical Crew	:493 B	Royal Sir	:51 B	Woo La La	:514 B
Uncle Jimmy And I	:373 B	Lilly's Moment	:492 B	Runaway Dude	:493 Bg	**Five Furlongs** :57	
Four Furlongs		Little Arturo	:502 B	Sammi De	:504 B	Corkibu	1:023 B
		Miss Fix It	:494 B	Slate Six	:483 H	In Accordance	1:013 H

Workout correction: 11/6/94 Pure Vintage should read (5f) 1:04 3/5b.

BELMONT PARK — Track Fast

Three Furlongs							
A J Philbar	:384 Bg	Swamp Cat	:383 B	Shahra Bay	:501 B	**Mr. Greeley**	**:591 H**
Ard Righ Mocroi	:374 B	Tara Roma	:363 H	Tabloid Tattle	:493 B	Parmelina	1:005 H
Bianco D'oro	:38 Bg	Thunderlake	:363 H	Terrorist	:49 B	Pluckemin	1:01 H
Brighter Course	:351 H	With Approval	:372 Bg	Tintinnabular	:493 Hg	Raymond Angelo	1:03 B
Children's Rights	:38 Hg	**Four Furlongs**		Trusted Friend	:502 Bg	Senor Rex	1:002 H
Chip Shortage	:383 B	Concoctor	:501 B	**Five Furlongs** :561		She's Fine	1:014 H
Daunting Era	:36 H	Criminal Rose	:50 B	Attractive Missile	1:011 H	Trailblazer	1:004 H
Diggers Well	:38 Bg	Darlin Danika	:494 B	Australasia	1:02 B	Turk Passer	1:003 H
For Sport	:372 B	**Gold Toes**	:473 H	Country Cat	1:022 B	Willful Defiance	1:024 Hg
Get Approval	:382 Bg	Joy Of Ireland	:503 B	Elocat's Banner	1:01 H	Yolande's Pet	1:031 B
Jah	:363 B	Linda's Crusade	:494 B	Hazy	1:013 H	Zimmerman	1:01 H
Kristen's Baby	:373 B	Martha's Vineyard	:493 B	Intriguing	1:033 B	**Six Furlongs** 1:074	
Limited War	:372 B	My Spring Love	:501 B	Kresa	1:021 H	Arrovente	1:161 B
My Saratoga Yacht	:372 Bg	Naval Talk	:502 Bg	Little Fran	1:021 B	**1 Mile** 1:323	
Red Planet	:352 H	Pretty Prep	:49 H	Maple Creek	1:032 B	Winterton	:1.45 B
Retain Earnings	:39 B	Royal Marine	:502 Bg	Metalmark	1:024 B		
		Said Privately	:49 B	Miss Halo Country	1:02 H		

BRIGHTER COURSE (3f) finished full of run and galloped out in :46 4/5. GOLD TOES (4f) went his 1/4 in :24 1/5. MR. GREELEY (5f) showed a high turn of speed.

"Showing a high turn of speed," his :59 1/5 was the only time that came close to breaking 1:00.

Mr. Greeley had not exactly been a paragon of consistency thus far, but his recent workouts indicated he was rounding to the good form he'd shown in late summer, even if it wasn't apparent from his two most recent races. He looked a picture in the post parade and prerace warm-ups and was being offered at 6-1. He was certainly no mortal cinch, but considering his connections, his workouts, and the ability he'd displayed at distances up to a mile, he was worth keying in exactas — especially if you wanted to toss Testability because of the constant layoffs and the month's gap between workouts.

SEVENTH RACE
Aqueduct
NOVEMBER 16, 1994

6 FURLONGS. (1.08) ALLOWANCE. Purse $30,000. 2-year-olds which have not won a race other than maiden or claiming. Weight, 122 lbs. Non-winners of a race other than claiming since November 1, allowed 3 lbs. Of such a race since October 15, 5 lbs.

Value of Race: $30,000 Winner $18,000; second $6,600; third $3,600; fourth $1,800. Mutuel Pool $217,610.00 Exacta Pool $433,720.00

Last Raced	Horse	M/Eqt. A.Wt	PP	St	1/4	1/2	Str	Fin	Jockey	Odds $1
8Oct94 8Bel11	Mr. Greeley	2 112	4	1	31	11½	15	13	Beckner D V5	6.10
26May94 1GS1	Ft. Stockton	2 117	9	2	41	2hd	23	29	Smith M E	4.10
28Oct94 9Med5	Manila Thriller	b 2 117	8	7	62	51½	3½	32	Santos J A	12.30
8Nov94 7Aqu4	Pat N Jac	b 2 117	5	3	5½	4hd	4hd	42	Chavez J F	7.20
15Oct94 4Bel4	Robby Two	bf 2 117	1	9	9	9	6½	51½	Maple E	18.70
21Sep94 5Bel2	Testability	2 117	2	8	1½	31½	52	62	Bailey J D	1.40
23Oct94 8Aqu7	Our Exuberant Lad	b 2 117	3	4	2hd	6hd	71	7no	Davis R G	7.60
23Oct94 8Aqu5	Chute Boss	b 2 117	7	5	83½	81	81½	83½	Luzzi M J	15.80
7Sep94 7WO6	Silver Midnight	2 112	6	6	7hd	7½	9	9	Perez R M5	24.75

OFF AT 3:13 Start Good. Won driving. Time, :223, :462, :581, 1:102 Track fast.

$2 Mutuel Prices:	4—(D)—MR. GREELEY	14.20	7.80	5.10
	9—(I)—FT. STOCKTON		6.20	4.40
	8—(H)—MANILA THRILLER			5.40

$2 EXACTA 4-9 PAID $91.50

Ch. c, (May), by Gone West–Long Legend, by Reviewer. Trainer Zito Nicholas P. Bred by Herman Sarkowsky (Ky).

MR. GREELEY forced the early pace while three wide, opened a clear advantage on the turn then drew away under steady right hand encouragement. FT. STOCKTON never far back, rallied four wide leaving the turn but was no match for the winner while clearly second best. MANILA THRILLER reserved for a half while four wide, failed to threaten while improving his position in the stretch. PAT N JAC raced within striking distance along the inside for a half and lacked a strong closing bid. ROBBY TWO bumped soundly at the start, never reached contention. TESTABILITY bumped at the start, set the pace along the rail to the turn and gave way. OUR EXUBERANT LAD bumped with TESTABILITY at the start, forced the early pace between horses then gave way on the far turn. CHUTE BOSS was never a factor. SILVER MIDNIGHT was outrun.

Owners— 1, Condren William & Cornacchia Joseph; 2, New Farm; 3, Dogwood Stable; 4, Sabine Stable; 5, Cohen Robert B; 6, Hooper Fred W; 7, Filosa Richard & Hills Timothy A; 8, Wet Beak Stable; 9, Harris Charles E

Trainers—1, Zito Nicholas P; 2, Perkins Benjamin W; 3, Alexander Frank A; 4, Barbara Robert; 5, Shapoff Stanley R; 6, Serpe Philip M; 7, Hills Timothy A; 8, Tesher Howard M; 9, Jolley Leroy

After stalking Testability to the turn, Mr. Greeley forged to the lead and quickly drew clear when that rival faltered, and maintained a comfortable margin over Ft. Stockton, who in turn was nine lengths clear of the others. The exacta linking the second and third betting choices was worth a generous $91.50.

Mr. Greeley's Beyer for the race came in at a 99, a 22-point jump from his previous high. The most talented 2-year-olds take such moves in stride, and Mr. Greeley confirmed the number by winning the Spectacular Bid Stakes at Gulfstream in his next start, again earning a 99. That race also confirmed that Mr. Greeley was at his best in sprints.

"I think we got a little ahead of ourselves in the fall," Zito told Joe Hirsch a few days after the Spectacular Bid. "Mr. Greeley was always an exciting prospect, and when he broke his maiden by six lengths at Belmont Park in September, we asked too much too soon by running him in the Champagne Stakes. He wasn't ready for Grade 1 competition, and it showed. So we backed away from him briefly and didn't run him again for five weeks. It was time well spent, and he ran a big race to win at Aqueduct. He also had a long interval between that race and the Spectacular Bid. If a fellow takes his time with a horse and doesn't get too excited, they'll both feel a lot better, and will be better off."

Zito's patience and perceptiveness with Mr. Greeley paid off during the colt's 3-year-old season. After winning the Spectacular Bid, he placed in the Hutcheson despite bleeding, then won the Swale and the Lafayette on Lasix:

Mr. Greeley
Own: Condren William & Cornacchia Joseph

Ch. c. 3 (May)
Sire: Gone West (Mr. Prospector)
Dam: Long Legend (Reviewer)
Br: Herman Sarkowsky (Ky)
Tr: Zito Nicholas P (—)

Lifetime Record :	10	5	3	0	$203,252						
1995	4	3	1	0	$156,252	Turf	0	0	0	0	
1994	6	2	2	0	$47,000	Wet	2	0	2	0	$11,000
	0	0	0	0		Dist	0	0	0	0	

12Apr95-8Kee	gd	7f	:22^3	:44^4	1:09	1:21^2	Lafayette-G3	**107**	4	3	2^{hd}	$1^{2\frac{1}{2}}$	1^2	$1^{1\frac{1}{2}}$	Krone J A	L 121	*1.20	94-06	Mr. Greeley$121^{1\frac{1}{2}}$ Peaks And Valleys118^3 Tethra$121^{1\frac{1}{2}}$	Sharp, ridden out	7
11Mar95-11GP	fst	7f	:22^4	:45^3	1:09	1:22	Swale-G3	**103**	1	4	$2^{\frac{1}{2}}$	$1^{\frac{1}{2}}$	1^1	$1^{\frac{3}{4}}$	Krone J A	L 114	*1.00	93-11	Mr. Greeley$114^{\frac{3}{4}}$ Devious Course$119^{1\frac{3}{4}}$ Pyramid Peak114^2	Driving	6
28Jan95-9GP	fst	7f	:21^3	:44	1:09^1	1:23^2	Hutcheson-G2	**90**	2	4	$1^{1\frac{1}{2}}$	$1^{1\frac{1}{2}}$	1^1	$2^{3\frac{1}{4}}$	Bailey J D	117	*1.10	83-16	Valid Wager$119^{3\frac{1}{4}}$ Mr. Greeley$117^{2\frac{1}{2}}$ Don Juan A$114^{\frac{3}{4}}$		7
Broke inward, bumped start, rushed, bled																					
4Jan95-8GP	fst	6f	:22^3	:45^3	:58^2	1:10^3	Spec Bid BC-G3	**99**	1	7	$1^{1\frac{1}{2}}$	1^2	1^5	$1^{6\frac{1}{4}}$	Krone J A	112	*.60	88-19	Mr. Greeley$112^{6\frac{1}{4}}$ Make Me$112^{\frac{3}{4}}$ Sea Emperor119^1		7
Bobbled start, saved ground																					
16Nov94-7Aqu	fst	6f	:22^3	:46^2	:58^1	1:10^2	Alw 30000N1X	**99**	4	1	$3^{\frac{1}{2}}$	$1^{1\frac{1}{2}}$	1^5	1^3	Beckner D V5	112	6.10	90-14	Mr. Greeley112^3 Ft. Stockton117^9 Manila Thriller117^2	Driving	9
8Oct94-8Bel	fst	$1\frac{1}{16}$	:23^2	:46^1	1:11^1	1:44	Champagne-G1	**52**	3	4	1^{hd}	$3^{\frac{1}{2}}$	11^{13}	11^{28}	Krone J A	122	27.80	54-17	Timber Country$122^{\frac{1}{2}}$ Sierra Diablo$122^{6\frac{1}{2}}$ On Target122^{nk}	Dueled inside	11
22Sep94-7Bel	fst	$1\frac{1}{16}$	:23^2	:47^2	1:11^3	1:43^3	Alw 32000N1X	**67**	1	1	1^1	1^{hd}	$5^{2\frac{1}{2}}$	5^9	Krone J A	122	2.70	75-27	Flitch$117^{\frac{3}{4}}$ Reality Road117^2 Tony Riccio$117^{1\frac{1}{4}}$	Gave way	5
8Sep94-3Bel	fst	1	:22^4	:47	1:12^1	1:38	Md Sp Wt	**75**	6	1	1^1	1^3	1^5	1^6	Krone J A	118	*.40	73-27	Mr. Greeley118^6 Arezzano$118^{9\frac{1}{2}}$ Flame Keeper118^4	Handily	6
19Aug94-5Sar	sly	7f	:23	:46^2	1:10^4	1:23^1	Md Sp Wt	**77**	5	3	$3^{1\frac{1}{2}}$	$1^{\frac{1}{2}}$	$1^{\frac{1}{2}}$	$2^{1\frac{3}{4}}$	Krone J A	118	3.40e	87-09	Top Account$118^{1\frac{3}{4}}$ Mr. Greeley118^{11} Jackson$118^{2\frac{1}{2}}$	Gamely	8
27Jly94-5Sar	wf	5f	:22	:46^1		:59^4	Md Sp Wt	**47**	4	7	$7^{9\frac{1}{4}}$	$5^{2\frac{1}{2}}$	3^2	$2^{1\frac{1}{4}}$	Krone J A	118	3.60	83-12	L' Aquilon$118^{1\frac{1}{4}}$ Mr. Greeley$118^{3\frac{1}{4}}$ Valid Motion$118^{5\frac{1}{4}}$	Broke slowly	7

WORKOUTS: **Apr 24 CD 5f sly 1:01^1 B** *2/12* **Apr 7 Kee 5f fst 1:02^1 B** *16/23* **Mar 28 GP 5f fst 1:03^1 B** *16/23* **Mar 21 GP 5f fst 1:04^3 B** *18/21* **Mar 4 GP 5f fst 1:01^3 B** *8/40* **●Feb 24 GP 5f fst :59 H** *1/32*

In the fall, Mr. Greeley finished second, beaten a neck, in the Breeder's Cup Sprint. Ft. Stockton became a stakes-winning sprinter as well.

Winter

MACKENZIE MILLER, who trained a legendary list of champions for Paul Mellon's Rokeby Stable, including Kentucky Derby winner Sea Hero, once remarked, "As far as I'm concerned, the racing season begins in May and ends in November." Because the thoroughbred industry is such a significant source of revenue for the New York State treasuries, however, racing has been conducted continuously in the state ever since the installation of Aqueduct's winterized inner dirt track in 1975. That's more than two decades of racing without a break, with no end in sight other than the usual dark days or weather-related cancellations. Nevertheless, it is important to bear in mind that the season Miller referred to does, for all intents and purposes, effectively end in New York right around Thanksgiving, when the last turf race has been run and the main track is bundled up tight against the elements.

At this time, a dramatic change takes place in the local equine population. Many of the top stables migrate to Florida for the winter, and in their place comes a sudden influx of horses from the Meadowlands in New Jersey; Woodbine, which is Canada's major venue; day-trippers from the nearby Maryland, Pennsylvania and New England circuits; and New York-breds from Finger Lakes.

Although the quality of New York's product necessarily suffers during the winter, there are still plenty of opportunities available to horseplayers who know what to look for. Whereas Belmont's main track is a mile and a half around and horses can, generally speaking, win from anywhere on its sweeping turns, Aqueduct's inner track is only a mile in circumference, so that horses with early speed and inside position have a built-in edge on the tight-turned layout. Inside speed is particularly dangerous in two-turn races: handicappers will probably make more winning sprint-to-route stretchout plays from December through mid-March than they will during the rest of the year.

The winter game also provides players with a much-needed break of sorts, thanks to its relative simplicity. Six furlongs is the only sprint distance available; practically all the routes are run at either a mile and 70 yards, a mile and a sixteenth, or a mile and an eighth; there is no turf racing to be concerned with; there is no 2-year-old racing until April; horses breaking from inside posts going two turns have a big advantage; and a relatively small percentage of capable claiming trainers win a large percentage of the races.

As far as my handicapping was concerned, the first horse that qualified as a legitimate standout was a 3-year-old filly entered against five rivals in a $35,000 claimer at a mile and 70 yards, who enjoyed advantages in terms of class, form cycle, and early pace.

Examine the field for the sixth race, December 9:

6 Aqueduct

INNER DIRT COURSE — 1 MILE 70 YDS — START FINISH

1 MILE 70 YARDS. **(Inner Dirt). (1:39³) CLAIMING. Purse $21,000. Fillies, 3-year-olds. Weight, 121 lbs. Non-winners of two races at a mile or over since November 1, allowed 3 lbs. Of such a race since then, 5 lbs. Claiming price $35,000, for each $2,500 to $30,000, allowed 2 lbs. (Races when entered to be claimed for $25,000 or less not considered.)**

Believe In Doris

Own: Wilson Charles T Jr

MADRID A JR (11 0 3 1 .00) — $35,000

Ro. f. 3 (Apr)
Sire: Vigors (Grey Dawn II)
Dam: Some Believe (Believe It)
Br: Wilson Charles T Jr (Ky)
Tr: Hernandez Ramon M (20 2 5 2 .10)

116

Lifetime Record: 18 3 0 5 $46,440										
1994	13	3	0	2	$40,980	Turf	6	1	0	1	$15,720
1993	5	M	0	3	$5,460	Wet	3	0	0	1	$2,580
Aqu [•]	4	1	0	2	$11,280	Dist	3	1	0	2	$10,440

11Nov94-4Aqu	fst	1 ⊗	:242 :481 1:133 1:39	3↑ Ⓕ Clm 45000	50	1	5	59½	56¾	47	412¼	Rodriguez O7	104 b	14.80	61-21	PrncssPckl1172 MssPocktCort1138½ BnnShppr1131¾	Broke slowly, outrun	5
29Oct94-9Aqu	fm	1⅛ Ⓣ	:483 1:123 1:374 1:503	3↑ Ⓕ Clm 50000	70	8	5	610	79½	910	79¼	Rodriguez O7	107 b	36.75	78-13	Spectaculaire1132¼ Louisville Lu1171 Miss Pocket Court1131	No threat	10
9Oct94-6Bel	fm	1 1/16 Ⓣ	:232 :464 1:112 1:433	Ⓕ Clm 35000	74	4	10	106¾	105¼	44	1½	Rodriguez O7	109 b	7.80	80-21	BelieveInDoris109½ SugarFootin111½ RockfordPeach1162	Wide, driving	10
24Sep94-2Bel	my	6f	:222 :451 :573 1:101	3↑ Ⓕ Clm 35000	61	3	5	611	66½	66	58	Maple E	113 b	16.30	82-13	Unreal Cupcake1175 Nikki's Rose1101 Tuesday Edition113½	No factor	6
2Jly94-4Bel	fm	1 1/16 [T]	:25 :494 1:141 1:434	Ⓕ Clm 45000	64	1	9	96¾	73	96	98½	Hernandez R	112 b	14.40	68-15	Aucilla1161½ Skip One1142 Caroline Of Kent112no	Outrun	9
14Jun94-7Bel	fm	1 1/16 Ⓣ	:232 :461 1:10 1:413	Ⓕ Clm 50000	68	9	10	1010	712	47½	37¼	Alvarado F T	116 b	7.00	83-09	SkipOne1143 SunshineLindjn1114¼ BlivInDoris1165½	Checked break, wide	11
5Jun94-4Bel	fm	1 1/16 [T]	:231 :464 1:104 1:403	Ⓕ Clm 70000	64	6	8	63½	52¼	89¾	814	Hernandez R	112 b	23.70	79-08	New Wave1167½ Sunshine Lindajane109hd Safe At Home116¾	Gave way	8
7May94-5Bel	fm	1 Ⓣ	:223 :452 1:094 1:343	3↑ Ⓕ Alw 30000N1X	67	7	7	67½	74¾	56½	510½	Hernandez R	113 b	6.00	78-13	Teasing Charm1103 Watrals Charm1193 Sum Attack110½	No threat	9
8Apr94-7Aqu	fst	1	:233 :464 1:121 1:38	Ⓕ Alw 29000N1X	60	4	4	44½	42½	54½	48¾	Alvarado F T	116 b	4.30	69-24	Netka1165½ Skip One109nk Shouldnt Say Never1163	No threat	5
25Mar94-1Aqu	fst	7f	:23 :464 1:131 1:264	Ⓕ Clm 37500	71	6	3	610	68	32½	13½	Alvarado F T	116 b	10.40	70-26	Believe In Doris1163½ Pucker Lips1183 May Ropido112½	Driving	6

WORKOUTS: Oct 19 Bel tr.t 5f fst 1:05 B *10/11* Sep 11 Bel tr.t 5f fst 1:02 H *2/9*

Delta West

Own: Lilley Bert

VELAZQUEZ J R (106 10 10 10 .09) — $35,000

B. f. 3 (Feb)
Sire: Tank's Prospect (Mr. Prospector)
Dam: Delta Daiquiry (Delta Flag)
Br: John W. Rooker (Ky)
Tr: O'Connell Richard (32 1 3 4 .03)

116

Lifetime Record: 8 2 1 1 $18,590										
1994	8	2	1	1	$18,590	Turf	1	0	0	0	$90
1993	0	M	0	0		Wet	1	0	0	1	$1,100
Aqu [•]	0	0	0	0		Dist	1	0	1	0	$3,800

23Nov94-2Aqu	fst	6f	:23 :47 :593 1:123	Ⓕ Clm 47500	57	1	8	58	89½	78½	710	Smith M E	114	17.60	69-21	Wonderlan1141¼ Runaway Fling1144 Jackie Ramos116½	Outrun	8
12Nov94-1Aqu	fst	7f	:234 :471 1:12 1:25	Ⓕ Clm 45000	62	7	1	52½	62¾	74¼	65½	Santos J A	114	2.60e	73-19	Runaway Fling1121½ Sapor119¾ Skip One1161	No factor	7
24Jun94-7Atl	fm	*1⅛ Ⓣ	:504 1:151 1:414 1:544	3↑ Ⓕ Alw 9000N2X	50	6	2	2½	21½	59	69½	Pennisi F A	112 f	5.80	65-25	No Fat Chicks116no Melrose Abbey1162 Aglory Gold1165¼	Tired	6
31May94-8Mth	fst	1 1/16	:234 :49 1:134 1:471	3↑ Ⓕ Alw 19000N2X	71	6	2	22½	21	23½	22½	Pennisi F A	112 f	5.80	66-33	Sugar Raised1182½ Delta West112no Shouldnt Say Never1136	Willingly	6
21Apr94-7GS	fst	1	:242 :481 1:123 1:382	3↑ Ⓕ Alw 12500N1X	67	1	1	1½	1hd	1hd	1½	Pennisi F A	112 f	6.00	90-13	Delta West112½ Flower Fair116hd K. C.'s Highlandia1161¼	Driving	6
2Apr94-3GS	fst	1	:24 :481 1:133 1:402	3↑ Ⓕ Md Sp Wt	61	1	1	1hd	11	14	16	Pennisi F A	112 f	3.70	80-17	Delta West1126 Yamasee122nk Leaping Fame1132	Driving	8
10Mar94-3GS	my	6f	:232 :473 1:00 1:121	Ⓕ Md Sp Wt	35	9	2	2½	21½	37½	310	Pennisi F A	122 f	42.10	71-15	Palm Hearts1223½ Louisa's A Pro1226½ Delta West1221¾	No late rally	10
18Feb94-3GS	fst	5½f	:223 :464 :593 1:062	Ⓕ Md Sp Wt	27	6	9	1010	1013	812	89	Pennisi F A	119 f	21.50	78-15	Fit To Flirt119hd Affirmed Peach119¾ Steel And Lace1191¾	Outrun	11

WORKOUTS: Nov 8 Bel tr.t 5f fst 1:03 B *7/14* Nov 3 Bel tr.t 5f fst 1:021 B *3/7* Oct 28 Bel tr.t 5f fst 1:003 H *2/14* Oct 23 Bel 5f fst 1:023 Hg *7/17* Oct 17 Bel tr.t 5f fst 1:034 B *5/6* Oct 12 Bel tr.t 4f fst :50 B *10/12*

A Day To Remember

Own: Sigel Marshall E

CHAVEZ J F (209 32 25 20 .15) — $35,000

B. f. 3 (Mar)
Sire: Over the Rainbow (Alydar)
Dam: Delightful Spring (Francis S.)
Br: Sigel Marshall E (NY)
Tr: Picou James E (8 0 1 0 .00)

116

Lifetime Record: 36 2 1 5 $76,968										
1994	22	1	0	4	$42,240	Turf	9	1	0	0	$26,298
1993	14	1	1	1	$34,728	Wet	3	0	0	0	$1,680
Aqu [•]	6	0	0	2	$10,200	Dist	7	0	0	3	$16,080

27Nov94-9Aqu	fst	1	:24 :483 1:142 1:402	Ⓕ Clm 35000	53	3	9	107¾	107¾	911	713½	Rydowski S R	116 b	36.00	52-33	Cherry Glow1164 Fawn's Angel112nk Fighting Feather1162	No factor	10
9Nov94-1Aqu	fst	6½f	:23 :464 1:121 1:19	Ⓕ Clm 35000	42	6	3	75¼	75½	78¾	715¾	Santagata N	116	28.75	70-14	Jupiter Assembly116nk Wonderlan1161¼ Cherry Glow1162½	Outrun	7
20Oct94-7Aqu	gd	1	:233 :47 1:124 1:391	3↑ Ⓕ [S] Alw 34000N2X	59	2	4	65	54	64¾	69	Bravo J	114	9.70	63-27	Alkris1174 New York Flag117hd Shiani1173	No threat	8
15Oct94-7Bel	fm	1 1/16 [T]	:25 :483 1:112 1:403	3↑ Ⓕ [S] TiconderogaH75k	52	4	8	98½	98½	1016	1121	Chavez J F	109	31.80	72-05	Putthepowdertoit1155 Great Triumph1121½ Irish Linnet1261	Outrun	11
25Sep94-4Bel	gd	1 1/16	:24 :472 1:12 1:434	3↑ Ⓕ [S] Alw 34000N2X	69	5	7	64	4¾	31	42½	Perret C	113	20.80	80-15	Lois' Flag1091½ [D] New York Flag112¾ Willspynow113nk		8
Checked, struck with whip 1/8 pl Placed third through disqualification.																		
20Sep94-7Bel	gd	1 1/16 [T]	:251 :484 1:122 1:432	Ⓕ Clm 75000	33	7	10	109½	109	1016	1022½	Chavez J F	118	14.90	57-20	Skip One1121¼ Jupiter Assembly112hd Glorious Purple1122¼	Outrun	10
4Sep94-6Bel	fm	1 Ⓣ	:224 :46 1:101 1:344	3↑ Ⓕ [S] Alw 34000N2X	78	8	9	85¾	62½	73¼	42	Perret C	118	27.40	86-10	Dinner Diamond117¾ High Talent1171 Leo N' Me117nk	Rallied wide	12
27Aug94-9Sar	gd	1 1/16 Ⓣ	:23 :471 1:124 1:46	3↑ Ⓕ [S] Alw 30000N1X	77	9	8	99¼	44	22½	1no	Chavez J F	112	12.30	64-29	A Day To Remember112no ThroughTheTulips1142½ Dilettante117nk	Driving	11
1Aug94-2Sar	fst	6f	:221 :453 :574 1:11	Ⓕ Clm 35000	50	2	3	64	53	48½	413½	Chavez J F	116	6.90	72-12	Princess J V116½ Indian Paradise11610 Braided Way1162½	Wide trip	6
25Jly94-9Sar	fm	1⅛ [T]	:472 1:113 1:37 1:494	3↑ Ⓕ [S] Alw 30000N1X	65	3	2	22	21½	42½	69	Carr D	111	18.40	77-15	Royal Pelliknow1125 Lost Era1171 Winalot Bonnie117nk	Tired	12

WORKOUTS: Dec 5 Bel tr.t 4f sly :483 H *2/7* Nov 20 Bel 7f fst 1:314 B *1/1* Nov 5 Bel 4f fst :484 H *11/49* Oct 29 Bel 4f fst :502 B *20/39* Oct 13 Bel [T] 3f fm :361 H (d) *1/2* Oct 5 Bel 6f fst 1:174 B *1/1*

Ogy's Threat

Own: Davis Barbara J

PEREZ R B (187 32 22 31 .17) — $30,000

Dk. b or br f. 3 (Apr)
Sire: Ogygian (Damascus)
Dam: Threat (Ack Ack)
Br: August Moon Farm (Ky)
Tr: Moschera Gasper S (98 25 15 26 .26)

107⁵

Lifetime Record: 16 3 1 0 $24,470										
1994	16	3	1	0	$24,470	Turf	6	1	0	0	$7,230
1993	0	M	0	0		Wet	3	0	0	0	$180
Aqu [•]	0	0	0	0		Dist	5	1	1	0	$13,520

27Nov94-9Aqu	fst	1	:24 :483 1:142 1:402	Ⓕ Clm 32500	57	1	6	52¼	62¾	67½	611	Chavez J F	114 f	10.90	55-33	Cherry Glow1164 Fawn's Angel112nk Fighting Feather1162	No threat	10
9Nov94-7Aqu	fst	1	:231 :463 1:124 1:394	3↑ Ⓕ Alw 32000N1X	53	3	8	79	76½	68	69½	Smith M E	115	9.60	59-33	VigorousPrincess1102½ SugarFootin1151 SilverVictory1081½	Broke slowly	8
1Nov94-4Aqu	sly	1	:241 :473 1:124 1:383	Ⓕ Clm c-22500	51	4	5	74¾	76½	78	612¼	Velazquez J R	114 f	17.90	63-33	CherryGlow114½ BlazingClearance1161¾ SunshineLindjne1161½	No factor	8
Claimed from Sanchez John P, Hough Stanley M Trainer																		
20Oct94-9Aqu	gd	1 1/16 Ⓣ	:24 :483 1:134 1:461	Ⓕ Clm 35000	68	1	8	68	86	77¾	76¼	Velazquez J R	116 f	9.00	72-15	May Ropido1161 Maggie's Loveboat1181½ Sudana1161½	No factor	10
14Oct94-4Bel	fst	1 1/16	:234 :473 1:13 1:473	Ⓕ Clm 17500	74	1	5	42¼	21	1hd	14	Velazquez J R	116 f	*2.10	64-36	Ogy's Threat1164 Monster Order111¾ Fire Attack112nk	Driving	8
30Sep94-4Bel	fst	1 1/16	:234 :474 1:132 1:472	Ⓕ Clm 16500	71	6	5	52½	32½	23½	2no	Velazquez J R	114 f	7.10	65-29	CountryRedNeck111no Ogy'sThreat1141 CleningHouse1169	Rallied wide	7
14Sep94-7Med	fm	1 1/16 Ⓣ	:224 :464 1:111 1:422	Ⓕ Clm 30000	57	5	6	54	52	67½	68½	Beckner D V5	106 f	25.70	80-11	Proud Angela115¾ Da Bounboun1163½ Nose For Gold1143¼	Even trip	8
28Jly94-4Sar	sly	1⅛ ⊗	:471 1:133 1:402 1:534	Ⓕ Clm 35000	27	7	10	919	810	811	827	Chavez J F	116 f	13.20	40-17	Proud Angela116½ Chaines Cowgirl1166 Neon Fairytale1116	No menace	11
9Jly94-6Bel	fm	1¼ [T]	:503 1:15 1:394 2:043	3↑ Ⓕ Alw 30000N1X	64	7	1	12	1hd	75¾	99½	Velazquez J R	111	18.60	57-19	Mrs. Marcos117nk Petiteness1111 Crandall117nk	Used up	11
5Jun94-4Bel	fm	1 1/16 [T]	:231 :464 1:104 1:403	Ⓕ Clm 70000	71	3	4	43	83¾	79¼	711	Chavez J F	112 f	19.80	82-08	NewWave1167½ SunshineLindajane109hd SafeAtHome116¾	Checked, tired	8

WORKOUTS: Oct 29 Bel 4f fst :491 B *10/39* Oct 9 Bel 5f fst 1:02 H *10/15* Sep 11 Bel 3f fst :372 B *5/9*

Fighting Feather
Own: Solano Rafael

SOMSANITH N (1 0 0 1 .00) — $35,000

Ch. f. 3 (May)
Sire: Fit to Fight (Chieftain)
Dam: Traipsin Lady (Laomedonte)
Br: Kaster Mr & Mrs Richard S (Ky)
Tr: Solano Rafael (1 0 0 1 .00)

116

Lifetime Record: 27 5 4 5 $72,897										
1994	17	3	2	4	$54,922	Turf	1	0	0	0 $350
1993	10	2	2	1	$17,975	Wet	5	0	2	1 $10,147
Aqu ⊡	3	0	0	0	$2,820	Dist	2	0	0	0 $1,800

27Nov94-9Aqu fst 1	:24	:483	1:142	1:402	ⒻClm 35000	69	4	3	31	4¾	34½	34¼	Somsanith N	116	6.10	62-33	Cherry Glow1164 Fawn's Angel112nk Fighting Feather1162	Willingly	10
12Nov94-3Med fst 1	:233	:47	1:113	1:38	3↑ⒻAlw 26000N3X	69	3	4	2hd	3nk	44	64	Beitia A O	L 113	9.80	82-14	Nose For Gold114¾ Lu Lu's Lullaby116no Ruth's Revenge1122¾	Tired	6
6Nov94-6Pha fst 7f	:221	:443	1:094	1:223	3↑ Alw 18500N3X	78	5	3	44½	42	53	54¼	Bisono J	L 110	11.70	89-19	Zeno Fon116¾ War Leader114nk D'baja116nk	Very wide	7
21Oct94-8Pha fst 7f	:223	:46	1:112	1:244	3↑ⒻAlw 18500N3X	66	7	3	44	52½	44	32	Bisono J	L 112 f	11.20	80-18	Surely Kris116no Z Rated1162 Fighting Feather112nk	Evenly	8
27Sep94-3Med sly 6f	:222	:451	:582	1:112	ⒻClm 35000	59	4	5	53¾	53	55½	47	Beitia A O	L 115	7.70	77-18	Lookingtoyou118nk La La Honey1144½ Cut The Spending1182¼	No factor	7
3Aug94-8Mth fst 1 ⊗	:233	:472	1:132	1:404	ⒻClm 35000	43	7	7	73½	76½	610	613	Beitia A O	L 114	4.40	55-30	Majahuitas114½ Lill's Cutlass114½ Aca Rose1161¾	No factor	9
16Jly94-2Bel fst 6½f	:223	:46	1:104	1:171	ⒻClm 45000	68	2	2	43	63¾	45½	38	Beitia A O	116	11.00	79-12	Susan Valley1165 Mastina1163 Fighting Feather1163	No threat	6
4Jly94-5Bel fst 1	:224	:46	1:113	1:382	ⒻClm 35000	72	5	6	56	41½	2hd	11¼	Beitia A O	116	6.20	71-24	Fighting Feather1161¼ LifeBoat1162 CountryRedNeck1119	Wide, driving	7
25Jun94-2Bel fst 6f	:222	:452	:573	1:102	ⒻClm 60000	67	4	5	54½	65½	66	56¾	Beitia A O	112	10.80	82-12	Exquisite Star1142 Heather's Apparel1121¼ Princess J V114¾	No factor	6
11Jun94-9Mth fm 1 Ⓣ	:224	:453	1:094	1:354	3↑ⒻRevidere35k	9	8	9	911	917	924	935½	Beitia A O	L 114	90.70	51-13	Avie's Fancy1122 In My Heart1121 Uncharted Waters112no	No factor	9

Dancing Lacey
Own: Reinacher Robert J Jr

MAPLE E (96 11 12 13 .11) — $35,000

Ch. f. 3 (May)
Sire: Sword Dance (Nijinsky II)
Dam: White Lace (Whitesburg)
Br: Frontiere Dominic (Ky)
Tr: Reinacher Robert Jr (19 2 3 1 .11)

116

Lifetime Record: 12 3 0 3 $31,170										
1994	9	2	0	1	$19,280	Turf	0	0	0	0
1993	3	1	0	2	$11,890	Wet	2	0	0	0 $575
Aqu ⊡	0	0	0	0		Dist	2	1	0	0 $9,600

27Nov94-9Aqu fst 1	:24	:483	1:142	1:402	ⒻClm 30000	66	6	8	85¾	86½	56½	46¼	Maple E	113	15.60	60-33	Cherry Glow1164 Fawn's Angel112nk Fighting Feather1162	No threat	10
16Aug94-9Del fst 1	:23	:474	1:14	1:40	3↑ⒻAlw 9000N3L	74	2	5	33½	1hd	15	115½	Petersen J L	L 114	2.00	83-27	DancingLcey11415 Shesurecnexplode1132½ Amnd'sSilver113hd	Going away	7
24Jly94-8Pha gd 7f	:222	:444	1:093	1:22	3↑ⒻAlw 17000N4L	62	8	8	88	99½	910	710¾	Elliott S	L 115	29.90	85-10	Anna's Gal1163½ Woodman's Girl116½ Sophisticatedblend122nk	Wide	11
24Jun94-10Pha fst 1 1/16	:232	:481	1:142	1:474	ⒻAlw 16000N2L	57	5	8	87½	54	22	1½	Black A S	L 116	11.90	73-27	Dancing Lacey116½ Taine1227¾ Giana1144½	Driving	12
3Jun94-8Pha fst 1	:243	:492	1:152	1:431	ⒻAlw 16616N2L	52	2	6	67½	46½	48½	45½	Hampshire J F Jr	116	3.70	56-38	Silver Galore116nk Native Falcon1091 Carnavalesca1224¼	Swung wide	6
16Apr94-8Pha sly 170	:222	:483	1:153	1:463	ⒻBryn Mawr26k	39	4	4	54	63¾	611	619¼	Aguila G E	118 fb	26.10	48-30	AskShananie12212 FmilyEffort1183¼ LoftyExpression1201½	No real threat	7
2Apr94-9Pha fst 7f	:231	:461	1:123	1:263	ⒻDaffodil27k	60	2	7	89½	813	64½	65	Aguila G E	118 fb	24.20	68-21	Fighting Feather118¾ DH Dance A Go Go118 DH Rasputin120½	No factor	8
7Mar94-5Pha gd 6f	:214	:452	:584	1:114	ⒻAlw 13500N1X	51	4	7	77¾	76¾	54	35½	Aguila G E	119 b	13.00	76-20	Fighting Feather1164 Nose For Gold1161½ Dancing Lacey119¾	Wide	9
13Jan94-3GS sly 1	:232	:471	1:14	1:432	ⒻAlw 11500N1X	45	7	8	815	515	413	410¼	Hampshire J F Jr	114	11.50	55-34	Shananie Lane1141½ Tira Me Sue1145¼ Lasting Shore1203½	Some gain	8
12Dec93-2Pha fst 6f	:223	:462	:592	1:121	ⒻMd Sp Wt	42	6	3	57	58½	43	11½	Hampshire J F Jr	122	5.70	80-20	Dancing Lacey1221½ Glen Cara Lassie1171 Hidden Crest1221¾	Driving	9

WORKOUTS: Dec 4 Bel tr.t 4f fst :484 B 4/20 Nov 24 Bel 4f fst :52 B 9/9 Nov 18 Bel 5f fst 1:02 B 8/17 Nov 12 Bel tr.t 5f fst 1:051 B 20/20 Nov 5 Bel 5f fst 1:022 H 12/22 Oct 27 Bel 4f fst :501 B 24/35

While I tend to agree for the most part with decision-oriented players when they argue that handicapping is not a deterministic science, and that any given match up of horses offers a myriad of possible outcomes, Delta West, in my mind, had a stranglehold on this race from several angles.

To begin with, Delta West had never raced this cheaply. This can be a significant factor standing alone, and is especially potent with 3-year-olds in November and December because, for purposes of official age classification in race-conditions, January 1 is the universal birthday of the thoroughbred. By mid-December, time is running out on 3-year-olds before they have to face older, tougher competition, so their connections are looking to earn whatever purses they can, and drop the horses in class. The risk of losing these 3-year-olds via the claim-box is minimal, because most rival horsemen will prefer to take a wait-and-see approach as to where the horses fit in the class hierarchy; typically, most "newly-turned 4s" will require a considerable drop in claiming price to compete effectively.

Besides the class drop, Delta West showed the quintessential pattern for a router being brought back from a layoff: two sprints, followed by the stretchout. The same pattern had produced Delta West's maiden win in her third career start back in April at Garden State, and she had come back to repeat with a wire-to-wire score in a preliminary allowance. Following a willing finish for second at the non-winners of two level on May 31 — her third solid performance from as many attempts in routes on dirt — she gave way after prompting the pace in a turf race on June 24, and went to the shelf for the entire summer and most of the fall.

After half a dozen workouts spaced apart like clockwork every five or six days (the last five at five furlongs), Delta West returned to competition on November 12 in a $50,000-to-$45,000 claiming sprint, and was up fairly close to the pace in what had been a tightly-bunched field (a mere two and a half lengths separated five runners at the first call, and the spread was roughly the same at the second call). Back at the same level less than two weeks later, Delta West received her second sprint tune-up and ran exactly as expected, finishing next-to-last at 17-1.

Now, Delta West was stretching back to two turns, conditions under which she has run well in all three previous starts (against non-claiming company); she was dropping to her lowest level yet; and in a field containing several bona-fide plodders, she also projected as controlling early speed almost certain to secure a ground-saving trip from post 2. She had been first or second at the first call in each of her three dirt routes, demonstrating in her allowance win the willingness, determination and rating ability to withstand a prolonged challenge for the lead.

As the card progressed toward the sixth race, there was the question of how to take advantage of Delta West's supremacy. Although she probably wouldn't be an overwhelming favorite (the fact that every other filly had a Beyer Speed Figure superior to her previous best of 71 helped in that regard), the fact that this soon-to-be 4-year-old had been carefully pointed for this opportunity was fairly obvious to anyone who inspected her past performances. In a short field, she figured to go off at no better than 2-1 or so, and those odds are just not my cup of tea as far as win-betting is concerned.

Thankfully, the sixth race was the middle leg of Aqueduct's late Pick 3, which required bettors to select the winners of the fifth, sixth and seventh races. Delta West wasn't terribly exciting as a win bet at 2-1, but she was a rock-solid single for purposes of the Pick 3. Hopefully, the other two legs wouldn't be as cut-and-dried as the sixth; if that was the case, the Pick 3 would have terrific payoff potential because, while Delta West wouldn't be much higher than 2-1, she wouldn't be 3-5, either...and she wouldn't be *everyone's* single in the Pick 3.

THE FIFTH RACE basically clinched the idea of shooting for a score in Pick 3s. This was one of the bread-and-butter races of winter — a claiming route at nine furlongs for relatively cheap $17,500-to-$15,500 older platers. With five minutes to post, a grizzled 6-year-old veteran of the claiming wars by the name of Commander Evander was odds-on in the wagering. Can you play devil's advocate with this 4-5 shot?

5 **Aqueduct**

1⅛ MILES. **(Inner Dirt). (1:471) CLAIMING. Purse $15,500. 4-year-olds and upward. Weight, 122 lbs. Non-winners of two races at a mile or over since November 1, allowed 3 lbs. Of such a race since then, 5 lbs. Claiming price $17,500, for each $1,000 to $15,500, allowed 2 lbs. (Races when entered to be claimed for $14,000 or less not considered.)**

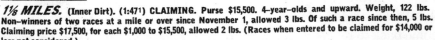

Eire Power
Own: Miron Stephen E
MADRID A JR (11 0 3 1 .00) $17,500

B. h. 5
Sire: Irish Tower (Irish Castle)
Dam: Exploding Wind (Explodent)
Br: Miron Julie (Ky)
Tr: Debonis Robert (35 4 5 4 .11)

117

Lifetime Record:	53	8	6	11	$148,970						
1994	12	2	2	2	$44,540	Turf	18	2	2	3	$45,010
1993	16	3	1	5	$35,570	Wet	13	4	0	4	$53,220
Aqu ⊡	10	3	2	2	$55,460	Dist	10	2	2	0	$23,740

30Nov94- 1Aqu fst 1⅛ :481 1:133 1:394 1:53 Clm c-14000 65 7 8 810 78 57 512¾ Rydowski S R 117 b 8.20 58-27 Stately Wager117½ Sea Baba1174 Power Bolt1151¼ No factor 8
Claimed from Rottkamp John R, Odintz Jeff Trainer
20Nov94- 2Aqu fst 1 :23 :464 1:122 1:392 Clm 14000 60 4 5 610 46 46½ 36½ Rydowski S R 117 b 6.30 64-25 Devoted Glory117¾ Jason Dean1125¾ Eire Power1172 No threat 6
6Nov94- 4Aqu wf 1 :224 :451 1:102 1:373 Clm 17500 62 2 7 711 75½ 89¼ 810½ Rydowski S R 117 b 8.60e 70-18 Charming Buck117nk Devoted Glory1152½ Callisto113hd Outrun 9
15Jun94- 1Bel fst 1⅛ :472 1:113 1:36 1:482 Clm 22500 68 7 5 73¾ 63¼ 66¾ 714½ Alvarado F T 115 fb 3.40 75-11 Iron Gavel117hd Northern T.1131¾ Slews Gold1173¾ No factor 7
4Mar94- 4Aqu sly 170 ⊡ :234 :474 1:124 1:421 Clm c-25000 81 6 5 55½ 42½ 42½ 32½ Davis R G 117 fb 2.00 84-22 Crackedbell1171¾ Yaros117¾ Eire Power1173½ Rallied wide 6
Claimed from G Lack Farms, Hernandez Sandino Trainer
25Feb94- 4Aqu fst 1 1/16 ⊡ :234 :473 1:114 1:432 Alw 32000N3X 88 4 3 54¼ 33 35 46 Alvarado F T 119 fb 9.60 82-16 Swindle1191 Aye Doo Da1175 Crafty Coventry119hd Saved ground 7
17Feb94- 3Aqu fst 1⅛ ⊡ :493 1:141 1:401 1:532 Clm 30000 85 2 8 86 86 53½ 23 Alvarado F T 115 fb 4.40 66-37 Sorabosia1123 Eire Power115nk All Canadian115¾ Finished well 9
12Feb94- 6Aqu fst 1 1/16 ⊡ :233 :474 1:121 1:434 Alw 40000N$mY 83 1 5 66 67 49½ 47¾ Alvarado F T 115 fb 5.90 78-24 Jacksonport1151½ CommanderEvnder115nk SprklingSky1156 Lacked rally 6
29Jan94- 5Aqu sly 170 ⊡ :231 :472 1:123 1:421 Alw 30000N2X 91 10 10 97½ 74½ 41¾ 1¾ Alvarado F T 117 10.50 87-25 EirPowr117¾ CrftyCovntry1171 SilngOnApryr117¾ Broke slowly, driving 10
22Jan94- 1Aqu fst 170 ⊡ :242 :482 1:134 1:442 Clm c-17500 59 4 4 32 42 48 714 Alvarado F T 122 b 2.90 62-24 Green Thoughts1154 True Slew1131 Hudlam's Sidekick1086½ Tired 10
Claimed from Pollard Damon, Pollard Damon Trainer

WORKOUTS: Oct 30 Aqu 4f fst :494 Hg 3/14 Oct 19 Aqu 4f fst :50 B 3/7 Oct 13 Aqu 4f fst :514 B 6/6 Oct 6 Aqu 4f fst :494 B 5/9

Studley Do Right

Own: Davis Barbara J

ALVARADO F T (158 29 21 23 .18) $17,500

Dk. b or br g. 5
Sire: At the Threshold (Norcliffe)
Dam: Goalsteen (Baldski)
Br: Franks John (Fla)
Tr: Moschera Gasper S (98 25 15 26 .26)

117

Lifetime Record: 48 12 8 7 $183,590
1994 14 3 2 2 $50,970 Turf 23 5 4 1 $64,750
1993 16 4 4 2 $69,520 Wet 6 1 0 5 $24,740
Aqu 0 0 0 0 Dist 8 4 0 2 $56,530

16Nov94-2Aqu fst 1 1/8 :49 1:14 1:394 1:524 3+ Clm 25000 77 4 5 56 43 4½ 44¾ Alvarado F T 117 b 1.65e 67-24 CountrySky117no RedScmper1173 Pl'sMemory1171½ Bobbled break, wide 7
13Oct94-1Bel fst 1 1/16 :233 :464 1:112 1:422 3+ Clm 25000 78 5 9 99½ 75 78¾ 612 Alvarado F T 119 b *1.50e 78-16 Lightning Runner112¾ Electrojet1171½ Akiko1174¾ No factor 9
21Sep94-6Bel fst 1 1/16 :24 :471 1:113 1:43 3+ Clm 25000 91 6 5 71¾ 84¾ 43 1hd Alvarado F T 117 b *2.60 87-19 StdlyDoRght117hd LghtnngRnnr1121¾ McCms1121 Shuff back, wide, drvg 9
10Sep94-1Bel fst 1 1/16 :242 :482 1:124 1:422 3+ Clm 25000 86 4 3 52 51½ 42 25 Alvarado F T 117 b 4.80 85-10 PrivatePlan1175 StudleyDoRight1172½ MobyJk1171½ Blocked, altered crs 7
17Aug94-4Sar fst 1 3/16 :473 1:114 1:373 1:573 3+ Clm 30000 75 4 7 77¾ 68½ 66½ 614½ Smith M E 115 b 3.00 77-15 Ambush Alley117hd Decoder1175¾ Maraud1151½ Steadied 1st turn 7
27Jly94-4Sar wf 1 1/8 :47 1:113 1:373 1:504 Clm 30000 88 2 4 48½ 43½ 11 1nk Alvarado F T 113 b *.80e 82-19 Studley Do Right113nk A Call To Rise1174½ Electrojet115no Driving 5
22Jun94-1Bel fst 1 1/16 :233 :464 1:11 1:423 Clm 35000 87 8 2 42 41½ 42 43¾ Luzzi M J 117 b 3.60e 85-11 Carney's Kid115hd Sparkling Sky117no Yaros1133½ No late bid 8
25May94-9Bel fm 1 1/16 Ⓣ :233 :481 1:112 1:414 Clm 35000 69 2 3 52½ 65½ 47 49¾ Smith M E 117 b 2.60 77-12 Polaris Star1177 Deja1172 Class Hat110¾ No threat 10
5May94-4Bel fm 1 1/16 Ⓣ :25 :482 1:123 1:421 Clm 50000 64 3 7 79 74¾ 811 815 Santagata N 117 b 10.30 70-14 Zee Buck113nk Cranshaw's Corner117nk Palace Line1172½ Outrun 9
16Apr94-1Aqu sly 1 1/8 :48 1:122 1:381 1:512 Clm 50000 87 4 2 2hd 31 42½ 34½ Davis R G 117 fb *1.60 74-19 Electrojet1131¼ ACallToRise1133¼ StudleyDoRight117½ Dueled, weakened 6

WORKOUTS: Dec 2 Bel tr.t 4f fst :501 B 13/23 Nov 8 Bel 4f fst :50 B 9/26 Oct 31 Bel tr.t 3f fst :362 B 4/12 Oct 11 Bel 4f fst :483 B 17/38 Oct 5 Bel tr.t 4f fst :491 B 7/22 Sep 19 Bel 4f fst :472 H 6/65

Out Of The Realm

Own: West Point Stable

VELAZQUEZ J R (106 10 10 10 .09) $15,500

Ch. h. 5
Sire: Exile King (Exclusive Native)
Dam: Prize Amber (Ambernash)
Br: Wood Alexander (NY)
Tr: Johnstone Bruce (20 1 2 1 .05)

113

Lifetime Record: 38 6 5 3 $198,395
1994 6 0 0 0 Turf 20 4 2 1 $81,240
1993 16 3 2 2 $66,790 Wet 7 0 1 2 $25,870
Aqu 3 0 0 0 Dist 7 1 1 1 $96,400

8Nov94-6Aqu fm 1 1/16 Ⓣ :233 :483 1:124 1:44 3+ Clm 45000 75 2 6 75½ 52½ 66 66 Velazquez J R 113 14.70 83-13 So Sterling1131½ Clover City113hd Known Ranger1142 No threat 8
18Oct94-4Aqu fm 1 1/16 Ⓣ :23 :472 1:111 1:422 3+ Clm 35000 83 9 8 89½ 64½ 53¾ 51 Velazquez J R 117 20.10 96-03 SmilingAndDancin117nk CloverCity119¾ Cranshw'sCorner112no Mild rally 10
5Oct94-1Bel gd 1 1/16 Ⓣ :241 :481 1:124 1:431 3+ Clm 35000 72 5 5 59 56½ 66½ 66¾ Velazquez J R 117 11.90 73-21 So Sterling117nk Possibilities1121½ Rubber Matt1071¾ No factor 7
16Sep94-4Bel fm 1¼ Ⓣ :483 1:123 1:36 2:003 3+ Clm 35000 80 12 9 1011 109 68 64¾ Velazquez J R 117 10.50 82-13 Clover City1191½ Two Wise112nk Alpstein117nk No threat 12
25Aug94-2Sar fm 1 3/16 Ⓣ :463 1:122 1:371 1:553 3+ Clm 45000 77 5 9 919 64 55 58½ Velazquez J R 117 24.80 79-25 Tidy Colony1174 Ijtihaad113¾ Up In Front113½ Improved position 11
4Aug94-4Sar gd 1 1/8 Ⓣ :491 1:132 1:38 1:501 Clm 35000 76 7 5 43 31½ 84 87 Smith M E 117 14.80 69-24 Bye Union Ave.119¾ Marabella Star1171½ Cranshaw's Corner1171 Faded 9
31Dec93-6Aqu fst 1 5/8 ⊡ :483 1:412 2:071 2:482 3+ Handicap48k 66 6 7 711 517 522 533 Luzzi M J 110 26.90 54-31 Michelle Can Pass1241½ Federal Funds11116 Hugatag1139 Outrun 7
11Dec93-7Aqu sly 1 1/8 ⊡ :482 1:131 1:384 1:504 3+ Handicap48k 42 1 6 626 629 641 637¾ Davis R G 115 11.60 51-31 Liver Stand1196 Land Grant122¾ Sylvester Stone1122 Outrun 6
12Nov93-8Aqu yl 1 3/8 Ⓣ :502 1:161 1:414 2:213 3+ Handicap48k 81 6 7 713 77¾ 74¾ 67½ Perret C 112 4.70 68-26 Reggae1161¾ Asserche1162½ Deja1101 No factor 7
11Oct93-8Bel fm 1 1/16 Ⓣ :24 :463 1:10 1:401 3+ ⓈAshly Cole H73k 79 10 10 109½ 108½ 86¾ 610½ Velasquez J 114 4.90 84-12 Preporant1174 Scott The Great116¾ Forlibend1134 No factor 10

WORKOUTS: Dec 4 Bel tr.t 4f fst :504 B 16/20 Nov 23 Bel tr.t 4f fst :493 B 18/31 Nov 4 Bel 4f fst :50 B 21/36 Oct 13 Bel Ⓣ 6f fm 1:162 B (d) 3/7 Oct 3 Bel 4f fst :512 B 30/32 Sep 15 Bel Ⓣ 4f fm :53 B (d) 10/10

Commander Evander

Own: Riccio James A

LUZZI M J (200 33 27 25 .17) $15,500

Ch. g. 6
Sire: Top Command (Bold Ruler)
Dam: Mom's Mia (Great Mystery)
Br: Fuller Peter (Ky)
Tr: Parisella John (39 10 8 8 .26)

113

Lifetime Record: 67 12 12 3 $249,480
1994 13 3 2 2 $59,670 Turf 3 0 0 0
1993 17 4 1 0 $70,630 Wet 8 2 0 0 $20,700
Aqu 17 4 4 0 $106,760 Dist 11 4 3 0 $68,780

27Nov94-4Aqu fst 1 :24 :473 1:131 1:392 Clm 17500 85 2 2 1½ 1½ 1½ 2½ Luzzi M J 117 fb *.90 70-33 DevotdGlory117½ CommndrEvndr1174½ SilingOnApryr1173½ Couldn't last 6
10Nov94-1Aqu sly 1 1/8 :474 1:131 1:391 1:52 Clm 14000 93 2 2 2½ 1½ 17 17¾ Luzzi M J 117 fb *1.30 76-32 CommanderEvnder1177¾ SylvesterStone115¾ McComs11712 Kept to drive 8
28Oct94-4Aqu fst 1 :23 :462 1:12 1:384 Clm 15500 80 5 1 1½ 1hd 31 31½ Luzzi M J 113 fb 3.30 72-23 RedScamper1171 DevotedGlory110½ CommanderEvnder113¾ Weakened 6
21Sep94-6Bel fst 1 1/16 :24 :471 1:113 1:43 3+ Clm c-25000 63 2 2 31 95½ 910 916 Davis R G 117 fb 4.20 71-19 Studley Do Right117hd Lightning Runner1121¾ Mc Comas1121 Done early 9
Claimed from Last State Stable & Marx Joseph, Alvarez Luis C Trainer
3Sep94-9Bel fst 1 1/16 :232 :461 1:101 1:421 3+ Clm 50000 82 8 7 74¾ 86 78 75½ Beckner D V5 112 fb 11.60 86-12 A Call To Rise113nk Sparkling Sky117no Patsyprospect109¾ No factor 9
21Aug94-5Mth fst 1 70 :223 :454 1:103 1:412 3+ Alw 30000N$mY 64 5 5 613 613 610 616½ Marquez C H Jr L 115 fb 3.80 77-07 Key To Manhattan1154 Island Edition115no Conveyor1221¾ Outrun 6
19May94-8Bel sly 1 1/16 :222 :45 1:092 1:421 3+ Alw 44000N$mY 70 5 5 69½ 69 69½ 616 Mojica R Jr 115 fb 3.00 75-14 Say Dance1176½ Jacksonport1155½ I Like To Win1171½ Outrun 6
28Apr94-4Aqu fst 7f :224 :46 1:094 1:222 Clm 70000 99 7 1 2½ 21½ 53 43 Mickens T J7 106 fb 12.10 89-19 Fabersham117nk Tropical Illusion1132½ Rocking Josh113nk Forced pace 7
8Apr94-1Aqu fst 1 :24 :473 1:122 1:373 Clm 70000 93 1 2 1½ 2hd 3½ 31 Rojas R I 113 fb *1.80 79-24 Tanako113¾ Rocking Josh113hd Commander Evander1133½ Dueled inside 6
13Mar94-8Aqu fst 1 1/8 ⊡ :473 1:111 1:361 1:492 3+ GreyLag BCH-G3 86 6 4 54 64 910 813½ Rojas R I 109 fb 32.00 75-21 As Indicated1273½ Federal Funds110¾ Michelle Can Pass119nk Wide, tired 10

WORKOUTS: Oct 25 Aqu 3f fst :39 B 5/6 Sep 16 Aqu 5f fst 1:00 H 1/3

Mc Comas

Own: G LaCk Farms

CHAVEZ J F (209 32 25 20 .15) $17,500

Ch. g. 4
Sire: Strawberry Road (Whiskey Road)
Dam: Galafest (Cornish Prince)
Br: Paulson Allen E (Ky)
Tr: Martin Gregory F (3 1 0 2 .33)

117

Lifetime Record: 26 3 3 6 $111,088
1994 13 1 1 3 $36,950 Turf 7 1 1 0 $28,600
1993 11 2 1 3 $67,838 Wet 3 1 0 1 $24,088
Aqu 0 0 0 0 Dist 3 0 1 1 $8,800

10Nov94-1Aqu sly 1 1/8 :474 1:131 1:391 1:52 Clm c-14000 79 5 8 511 45½ 38 38½ Smith M E 117 b 2.25 67-32 Commander Evander1177¾ Sylvester Stone115¾ McComas11712 No threat 8
Claimed from Paulson Madeleine, Mott William I Trainer
13Oct94-1Bel fst 1 1/16 :233 :464 1:112 1:422 3+ Clm 25000 74 2 4 42 52½ 58½ 714½ Perez R B5 112 b 2.80 76-16 Lightning Runner112¾ Electrojet1171½ Akiko1174¾ Gave way 9
21Sep94-6Bel fst 1 1/16 :24 :471 1:113 1:43 3+ Clm 25000 88 8 7 82½ 63¾ 53½ 32 Perez R B5 112 b 4.20 85-19 Studley Do Right117hd Lightning Runner1121¾ Mc Comas1121 9
Steadied turn, wide, checked late
11Sep94-9Bel fm 1 1/16 Ⓣ :231 :461 1:101 1:403 3+ Clm 35000 65 12 8 86½ 95½ 87½ 711 Perez R B5 112 b 12.90 84-09 Clover City1172½ Known Ranger1172 Golden Explosive1172¾ No factor 12
3Sep94-9Bel fst 1 1/16 :232 :461 1:101 1:421 3+ Clm 50000 84 6 5 63½ 44 65½ 63¾ Krone J A 117 b *2.00 87-12 A Call To Rise113nk Sparkling Sky117no Patsyprospect109¾ No threat 9
5Aug94-5Sar my 1 1/8 :492 1:141 1:384 1:512 3+ Alw 34000N3X 83 2 4 42½ 42¾ 45½ 410 Krone J A 117 7.10 69-28 Party Manners114no Signal Tap1141 St. Elias1179 Tired 4
5Jun94-6Bel fst 1 1/16 :233 :463 1:11 1:423 3+ Alw 32000N2X 92 3 4 43½ 41½ 2hd 14¾ Krone J A 119 b 3.40 89-11 Mc Comas1194¾ Peace Baby1191½ Danzig's Dance119nk Alt course, driving 5
4May94-4Bel fm 1¼ Ⓣ :484 1:122 1:363 2:01 3+ Alw 32000N2X 77 7 4 42½ 43 53 59 Smith M E 119 b 4.90 76-15 Majesty's Darby1191½ Noble Sheba1194¾ Peter And119no Faded 7
22Apr94-7Aqu yl 1 1/16 Ⓣ :241 :483 1:14 1:461 3+ Alw 31000N2X 81 3 8 67½ 64 64½ 64 Davis R G 119 b *1.70 74-22 VictoryCross1191 TunbridgeWells119½ GallopingThunder119hd No threat 10
13Mar94-9GP fst 1 1/16 :234 :473 1:113 1:424 Alw 34700N2X 90 4 5 43 43 4¾ 42½ Smith M E L 119 b 7.50 94-06 Pride Prevails119¾ Bull Inthe Heather1191½ Hooterville Three119no 9
Lacked racing room leaving final turn, late rally

WORKOUTS: Nov 27 Bel tr.t 5f fst 1:02 H 2/13 Nov 3 Bel 5f fst 1:021 B 11/25 Oct 27 Bel 4f fst :50 B 22/35 Oct 7 Bel 4f fst :50 B 26/39

Dixieland Music

Own: MacMillan William C Jr

MARTIN G J (39 3 5 4 .08) $17,500

B. g. 5
Sire: Dixieland Band (Northern Dancer)
Dam: Illiterate (Arts and Letters)
Br: Southeast Associates (Pa)
Tr: Shapoff Stanley R (39 4 10 4 .10)

107 10

Lifetime Record: 36 2 7 4 $53,605
1994 13 1 4 2 $25,855 Turf 2 0 0 1 $2,115
1993 12 0 1 2 $8,805 Wet 3 0 1 0 $3,120
Aqu 0 0 0 0 Dist 0 0 0 0

26Nov94-3Aqu fst 1 :234 :471 1:13 1:383 3+ Clm 25000 56 1 1 2hd 52 712 721¼ Bailey J D 117 7.10 54-28 Akiko1122 Decoder1171½ Giant Leap1177½ Used in pace 7
1Nov94-8Lrl my 7f :223 :454 1:112 1:242 3+ Alw 15000N1X 44 6 4 1½ 1hd 44 1018½ Carle J D L 117 5.90 68-12 Banditback1151½ Kahli Kisu1171¾ Don's Boy Ben1171¾ Gave way 10
15Oct94-7Lrl fst 6f :23 :462 :582 1:104 3+ Alw 15000N1X 72 10 4 97¾ 1012 910 86½ Hamilton S D L 117 2.90 79-14 Lucky Quadrant1141 Play By Ear114½ Mary's Buckaroo1191¾ Outrun 10
30Sep94-4Lrl fst 7f :223 :454 1:101 1:224 3+ Clm 25000 84 2 1 11 11½ 2hd 23 Carle J D L 117 8.00 92-14 Wood Fox1173 Dixieland Music1171¾ Bucknell117hd Weakened 8
16Sep94-8Pim fst 1 1/16 :233 :461 1:104 1:453 3+ Alw 18500N1X 57 1 1 112 115 13 58½ Carle J D L 117 *.70 71-21 Baederman1176 Gold Quoit1171½ Royal Thyme117hd Tired 8
2Sep94-7Tim fst 4f :23 :462 3+ Alw 12000N2Y 66 5 4 52¾ 54¾ 31½ Thornton J E L 117 14.00 91-16 Mur Wick119¾ Got Everything117½ Dixieland Music1171 Carried wide 6
29Jly94-6Pim fst 1 1/16 :231 :462 1:102 1:44 3+ Clm 18500N2L 83 3 1 14 16 16 13¾ Carle J D L 117 3.10 87-21 Dixieland Music1173¾ Mo Valay1105½ Lovem 'n Leavem1146½ Driving 7
1Jly94-2Lrl fst 1 1/16 :242 :491 1:141 1:464 3+ Clm 18500N2L 63 8 2 2½ 1hd 1½ 31 Carle J D L 122 2.90 75-29 Electric Slide114¾ Double Ridder113nk Dixieland Music122nk Weakened 8
11Jun94-5Pim fst 5½f :222 :453 :583 1:05 3+ Alw 16500N1X 70 6 5 52½ 43 64¾ 53½ Carle J D L 117 7.40 94-13 Hagley's Hero1171½ Powerful Pursuader115¾ Lusty Bidder117no Wide 11
21May94-4Pim fst 6f :23 :461 :59 1:121 3+ Alw 16500N1X 70 3 3 43 43½ 43 44½ Carle J D L 117 4.40 82-15 Hrundle117¾ AlgebrHendrson1171½ SynthSummr1171¾ Lacked needed bid 7

WORKOUTS: ●Nov 24 Bel tr.t 4f fst :48 H 1/7 Sep 24 Pim 4f fst :492 B 3/14 Sep 13 Pim 4f fst :49 B 3/13

```
Live Like Royalty                      B. g. 6                                                  Lifetime Record :  48  8  7  4    $95,291
Own: Tramutola Thomas                  Sire: Dauphin Fabuleux (Le Fabuleux)                1994  14 4 1 2   $35,911  Turf  0 0 0 0
                                       Dam: Lyphards Karma (Lyphard)                       1993  15 2 4 1   $25,084  Wet   5 1 0 1  $12,036
MIGLIORE R (133 28 19 26 .21)  $17,500 Br: Sam Son Farms (Ont-C)                     117   Aqu ⊡  0 0 0 0           Dist  1 0 0 0     $426
                                       Tr: Hushion Michael E (35 6 5 8 .17)
29Oct94-7WO fst 7f      :23   :452  1:102 1:24  3↑ Alw 19800N1X   65 6 3 43  69   69¼ 511   Luciani D   L 118 b 20.90 80-15 Bold Demon1187 T. P.'s Way1121¼ World Famous115½          Showed little 6
21Oct94-2WO fst 1 1/16  :243  :482  1:124 1:45  3↑ Alw 21800N1X   60 4 3 42  44   59½ 514¾  Hawley S    L 118 b  3.45 76-19 Domino's Whip1132½ Steady Heart1124 Mactaquac1152¾                Tired 5
9Oct94-9WO  fst 1 3/16  :493  1:141 1:401 2:00  3↑ Alw 21800N1X   76 2 1 14  12   21  35    Hawley S    L 116 b  3.05 82-21 Arctic Grail1165 Park Gate114hd Live Like Royalty116¾          Weakened 7
9Sep94-8WO  fst 1 1/16  :244  :481  1:123 1:452 3↑ Alw 21800N1X   69 1 1 11½ 42   46  45    Hawley S    L 116 b  4.20 84-19 DnceTower109no ColonlNicholson1162½ WorldOfMgic1112½   Weakened rail 6
2Sep94-4WO  fst 1 1/16  :24   :481  1:131 1:461 3↑ Clm c-12000    81 6 4 2hd 1hd  12  14    Lauzon J M  L 116 b *1.95 85-14 LivLikRoylty1164 WorldOfMgc1111½ PublcOpnon1212   Driving three path 6
   Claimed from Schickedanz Bruno, Wright Michael W Trainer
18Aug94-5WO fst 1¼      :472  1:13  1:384 2:05  3↑ Clm 9500       81 7 5 64  3nk  1hd 2½    Lauzon J M  L 117    *3.75 86-13 Housey'sRpids116½ LiveLikRoylty117½ ArcticGril1154   Bid strongly turn 10
6Aug94-1WO  fst 1 1/16  :241  :482  1:122 1:441 3↑ Clm 8000       83 5 2 2½  2½   2hd 1hd   Luciani D5  L 119 b  2.45 95-06 Live Like Royalty119hd Dorsan118hd World Of Magic1181¼       Hard ridden 7
14Jly94-7WO fst 1 1/16  :234  :473  1:124 1:454 3↑ Clm 9500       79 2 1 14  14   12  11    Hawley S    L 116 b  7.65 87-17 LiveLikeRoylty1161 KnightlyTruce1165½ TheMlynoDsrt118½    Good rating 7
2Jly94-3WO  fst 7f      :231  :454  1:112 1:244 3↑ Clm 8000N1Y    69 3 9 52¼ 43   33½ 1no   Lauzon J M  L 121 b  8.20 87-13 Live Like Royalty121no Cool Run119hd Royal Mansfield1181½                13
   Inside, just up between horses
12Jun94-3WO fst 7f      :22   :442  1:102 1:234 3↑ Clm 10000      53 6 5 53¼ 67¾  710 611¾  Platts R    L 118 b  5.90 80-07 French Escapade1183½ Play On The Ice1161¼ Runaway Chris1161½                9
   Well placed backstretch
WORKOUTS: Dec 1 Bel 4f fst :48 H 2/25  Nov 21 Bel 6f fst 1:152 B 4/7  Sep 29 WO 6f my 1:15 B 1/2  Sep 19 WO 5f fst 1:023 H 11/27
```

For starters, Commander Evander owned the track record for a mile and 70 yards, having run the distance in 1:39 3/5 back in January of 1993. The following winter, as shown toward the bottom of his past performances, he had been good enough to merit a chance in a graded stake. He had missed by a hard-fought length when entered to be claimed for $70,000 on April 8. Shelved after a last place finish in the slop in mid-May, he finished last in two of his three starts when returned in late summer, and was claimed for $25,000 by John Parisella, who at the time was among the top win-percentage trainers in New York, and who had a reputation for successfully moving his newly-acquired stock up the ladder. But Parisella couldn't move this horse up — in fact, he didn't even try! After the claim, Commander Evander stayed in the barn for over five weeks, and showed only a three-furlong breeze in a very slow :39 when his new handlers ran him for the first time...for $10,000 less than what they paid. The message is clear: Parisella, who is a real "sharpie," does not give anything away. By offering Commander Evander for $15,500, he's telling players, in not so many words, that the horse is damaged goods, and not worth the $25,000 he paid for it. Even when the gelding managed to shake loose in the slop and win under a drive when dropped another notch to $14,000 on November 10, and came back to narrowly miss at 9-10 back at the $17,500 level last time out, the fact remains he is on a downward spiral, or at least those closest to him believe that to be true. To make matters worse, Commander Evander's best recent races have come on the lead, and the presence in this field of the one-dimensional speedball Dixieland Music, who has superior early foot, relegates him to the role of pace-prompter.

What of the others? Studley Do Right is a viable contender off the drop to $17,500 for the first time, along with a 4-for-8 record at the distance. Although his one-run style can be a drawback on the inner track, it isn't as much of a liability at nine furlongs as it would be in the shorter routes.

Mc Comas is fresh off a claim, and shows some back races that would make him competitive on a top try. Live Like Royalty is a Woodbine shipper getting a trainer-change to Mike Hushion, one of the top claiming trainers in New York.

Being totally overlooked at 17-1 was Eire Power, a three-time winner on the inner track who was making his fourth start back from a layoff. The 5-year-old had been claimed last time out by Bob DeBonis on behalf of owner Stephen Miron, and I recalled that they had campaigned the horse before. Rummaging through *Forms* from earlier in the year, I came across some Eire Power pp's that looked like this:

Eire Power
Own: G Lack Farms
ALVARADO F T (143 21 11 26 .15)

B. h. 5
Sire: Irish Tower (Irish Castle)
Dam: Exploding Wind (Explodent)
Br: Miron Julie (Ky)
Tr: Hernandez Sandino (17 7 3 0 .41)

119

Lifetime Record: 47 8 6 9 $143,330									
1994	6	2	2	0	$38,900	Turf	18 2 2 3	$45,010	
1993	16	3	1	5	$35,570	Wet	11 4 0 3	$51,060	
Aqu ⊡	8	3	2	1	$51,380	Dist	10 2 1 3	$40,320	

17Feb94- 3Aqu fst 1⅛ ⊡ :493 1:141 1:401 1:532	Clm 30000	81 2 8 86 86 53¼ 23	Alvarado F T	115 fb 4.40	66–37	Sorabosia1123 Eire Power115nk All Canadian115¾	Finished well	9
12Feb94- 6Aqu fst 1 1/16 ⊡ :233 :474 1:121 1:434	Alw 40000N$mY	80 1 5 66 67 49½ 47¾	Alvarado F T	115 fb 5.90	78–24	Jacksonport1151½ CommanderEvnder115nk SprklingSky1156	Lacked rally	6
29Jan94- 5Aqu sly 170 ⊡ :231 :472 1:123 1:421	Alw 30000N2X	89 10 10 97½ 74½ 41¾ 1¾	Alvarado F T	117 10.50	87–25	EirPowr117¾ CrftyCovntry1171 SilngOnApryr117¾	Broke slowly, driving	10
22Jan94- 1Aqu fst 170 ⊡ :242 :482 1:134 1:442	Clm c-17500	57 4 4 32 42 48 714	Alvarado F T	122 b 2.90	62–24	Green Thoughts1154 True Slew1131 Hudlam's Sidekick1086½	Tired	10
Claimed from Pollard Damon, Pollard Damon Trainer								
13Jan94- 3Aqu my 1 1/16 ⊡ :48 1:143 1:44 2:061	Clm 20000	84 5 4 49½ 45½ 11½ 12¾	Alvarado F T	114 b 4.10	43–58	Eire Power1142¾ Sanfran1174½ Easy Spender1173	Driving	7
1Jan94- 4Aqu fst 1 1/16 ⊡ :241 :484 1:133 1:472	Clm 17500	85 4 5 43 33 33 2¾	Alvarado F T	119 b 2.70	67–33	Callisto117¾ Eire Power1192 Brucon1139½	Finished well	7
22Dec93- 1Aqu fst 1⅛ ⊡ :474 1:132 1:41 1:543 3↑	Clm 16500	78 11 8 76½ 52½ 1½ 12¼	Alvarado F T	115 b 19.90	70–28	Eire Power1152¼ Cost Too Much117½ Hudlam's Sidekick117no	Driving	11
21Nov93- 1Aqu fst 1⅛ :492 1:143 1:413 1:552 3↑	Clm c-12500	74 5 6 52 31½ 2hd 22	Alvarado F T	117 b 3.40	57–37	Nake The Snake1172 Eire Power1171 Fun Escort1082½	Willingly	8
Claimed from Miron Stephen E, Debonis Robert Trainer								
10Nov93- 9Aqu fst 1 :233 :473 1:134 1:403 3↑	Clm 12500	67 6 9 93 52 41½ 31¾	Alvarado F T	117 b 2.30	59–38	Blitz The Pass113no Nake The Snake1171¾ EirePower1172	Checked 3/16 pl	11
21Oct93- 4Aqu sly 1⅛ :491 1:13 1:372 1:494 3↑	Clm 17500	58 4 7 78 78½ 512 721½	Alvarado F T	117 b 9.30	65–22	Sylvester Stone1176¾ Runaway Storm11911 Carrdiographer117no	Outrun	7

WORKOUTS: Dec 15 Bel tr.t 4f sly :52 B *7/8*

Miron and DeBonis had lost Eire Power right before the start of inner track racing last winter, and he had racked up three wins and a placing at ascending class levels from his first five starts on the surface. With winter fast approaching, Miron and DeBonis reclaimed Eire Power for $14,000 on November 30. They had no intention of watching this horse go on another tear for someone else.

The stretch-running Eire Power was in a good spot in terms of the pace, which projected to be set by the unrateable Dixieland Music, and pressed by a physically-suspect favorite.

THE FINAL LEG of this all-route Pick 3 was the seventh race, a race that also had a clear cut pacesetter and a vulnerable favorite:

7 Aqueduct

INNER DIRT COURSE — 1 1/16 MILES — START FINISH

1 1/16 MILES. **(Inner Dirt). (1:41) CLAIMING. Purse $28,000. 3-year-olds and upward. Weights: 3-year-olds, 120 lbs. Older, 122 lbs. Non-winners of two races at a mile or over since November 1, allowed 3 lbs. Of such a race since then, 5 lbs. Claiming price $50,000, for each $2,500 to $45,000, allowed 2 lbs. (Races when entered to be claimed for $40,000 or less not considered.)**

Alpstein
Own: Marinos Jane E
PEREZ R B (187 32 22 31 .17) **$45,000**

Ch. g. 4
Sire: Raconteur (The Minstrel)
Dam: Cunning Vixen (Provante)
Br: Nuesch Felix J (NY)
Tr: Moschera Gasper S (98 25 15 26 .26)

108⁵

Lifetime Record: 30 5 3 6 $114,470								
1994	17	4	2	4	$84,120	Turf	10 3 0 3	$57,780
1993	13	1	1	2	$30,350	Wet	3 0 3 0	$15,320
Aqu ⊡	6	0	0	1	$4,800	Dist	3 0 1 0	$4,620

25Nov94- 4Aqu fst 1⅛ :482 1:123 1:38 1:511 3↑	Clm 45000	93 4 1 1½ 1½ 21 31½	Alvarado F T	114 b 2.80e	79–13	Electrojet110¾ Ambush Alley113½ Alpstein1144	Weakened	7
17Nov94- 8Aqu gd 1⅛ Ⓣ :474 1:131 1:383 1:51 3↑	Alw 36000N3X	84 4 10 77 52 43 44½	Davis R G	117 b 15.20	80–15	ChiefMster112hd Presently1152½ GrndContinentl1152	Pinched break, wide	11
4Nov94- 4Aqu fst 1 :232 :461 1:103 1:352 3↑	Clm 45000	83 5 3 32½ 31 33½ 59¾	Alvarado F T	114 b 13.60	81–14	Danzig's Dance1155 Decoder1131½ A Call To Rise1171½	Flattened out	6
20Oct94- 4Aqu fst 1⅛ :51 1:151 1:40 1:522 3↑	Clm 45000	— 3 — — — — —	Perez R B5	108 b 5.50	— 27	Private Plan113hd A Call To Rise117½ Sparkling Sky113nk		7
Clipped heels, lost rider								
23Sep94- 6Bel my 1 1/16 ⊗ :233 :471 1:111 1:42 3↑	Clm c-35000	92 4 2 2½ 1½ 11 21½	Bailey J D	117 b 1.80	90–10	T. Barone1171½ Alpstein117hd Pension Fraud1126	Weakened	5
Claimed from Larson Stables, Parisella John Trainer								
16Sep94- 4Bel fm 1¼ Ⓣ :483 1:123 1:36 2:003 3↑	Clm 35000	87 4 1 11 12½ 12 31½	Bailey J D	117 b 2.70	85–13	Clover City1191½ Two Wise112nk Alpstein117nk	Weakened	12
12Aug94- 9Sar fm 1 1/16 Ⓣ :461 1:102 1:35 1:533 3↑	Clm 35000	88 3 4 42½ 3½ 13½ 1hd	Bailey J D	119 b 3.00	97–10	Alpstein119hd No Fumar1172 Turtle Beach117nk	Wide, driving	11
24Jly94- 5Sar fst 1⅛ ⊗ :481 1:122 1:371 1:51	Clm 35000	91 1 1 11½ 12½ 13½ 11½	Bailey J D	117 b *1.10	81–19	Alpstein1171½ Border Cat1174½ Telegrapher1171	Driving	5
28Jun94- 1Bel fm 1 1/16 Ⓣ :232 :46 1:10 1:411	Clm 35000	74 2 8 78¾ 75½ 75 79½	Bailey J D	117 b 7.80	83–12	Crnshw'sCorner1172 SoSterling1171 NorthrnWitnss1172½	Checked break	10
8Jun94- 1Bel fm 1 1/16 Ⓣ :241 :473 1:12 1:413	Clm 35000	85 3 8 67½ 62½ 43 33½	Migliore R	119 b 2.90	85–09	ⒹEbony Magic117nk Jocovitch1173 Alpstein1191½	Mild rally	8

WORKOUTS: Nov 13 Bel 4f fst :48 H *2/32* Oct 31 Bel tr.t 3f fst :37 B *7/12* Oct 11 Bel 5f fst 1:003 H *5/28* Oct 4 Bel tr.t 4f fst :474 H *2/24*

Pension Fraud
Own: Perroncino John S
SANTAGATA N (88 6 10 6 .07) **$45,000**

Dk. b or br g. 6
Sire: Temperence Hill (Stop the Music)
Dam: Peggy's Fling (Delta Judge)
Br: Olsson Sture G (Md)
Tr: Terracciano Neal (35 3 6 2 .09)

113

Lifetime Record: 84 9 21 18 $351,490								
1994	25	2	5	3	$57,340	Turf	11 0 1 3	$17,260
1993	20	2	4	7	$105,190	Wet	19 2 9 3	$88,400
Aqu ⊡	27	4	5	7	$140,080	Dist	18 2 3 5	$73,380

27Nov94- 7Aqu fst 1 :232 :463 1:121 1:381 3↑	Alw 46000N$mY	88 7 3 32½ 31 32 45½	Lumpkins J	115 f 15.20	71–33	Aztec Empire1152½ Sparkling Sky119nk Jacksonport1153	No late bid	7
13Nov94- 2Aqu fst 7f :231 :471 1:121 1:25 3↑	Clm c-25000	88 5 4 56 41½ 21 1hd	Migliore R	117 *2.60	79–22	Pension Fraud117hd Sorabosia1172 Le Risky1172	Driving	6
Claimed from Jewel-e Stables, Friedman Mitchell Trainer								
3Nov94- 4Aqu fst 6f :214 :45 :572 1:10 3↑	Clm 25000	91 4 4 67½ 63½ 42½ 21	Migliore R	117 3.65	91–15	Justfortherecord1121 Pension Fraud117hd Yeckley1173½	Rallied wide	6
20Oct94- 1Aqu fst 7f :23 :454 1:104 1:233 3↑	Clm 25000	91 4 5 32 33 1hd 21	Santos J A	117 5.20	85–18	Ocean Splash1171 Pension Fraud117¾ Le Risky112½	Held place	8
7Oct94- 1Bel fst 6f :224 :461 :58 1:10 3↑	Clm 25000	88 4 3 64¾ 62¾ 51½ 42¼	Perez R B5	112 4.10	88–16	The Great M. B.112¾ Current Impact1171¾ Line Pro117no	No threat	6
23Sep94- 6Bel my 1 1/16 ⊗ :233 :471 1:111 1:42 3↑	Clm 35000	92 3 1 1½ 2½ 31 31½	Perez R B5	112 2.30	90–10	T. Barone1171½ Alpstein117hd Pension Fraud1126	Dueled inside	5
16Sep94- 2Bel fst 6f :22 :443 :564 1:092 3↑	Clm 25000	86 9 9 88¾ 86¾ 44½ 44	Santos J A	117 *1.90	90–10	Justfortherecord1093 Cesar B.115½ Line Pro117½	Mild gain	10
5Sep94- 2Bel fst 7f :231 :461 1:102 1:231 3↑	Clm 25000	86 4 4 2hd 2hd 3½ 71¾	Davis R G	117 3.70	85–14	PeerlessPerformer117nk ChngeOfFortune117hd HotSlw117½	Used in pace	9
26Aug94- 9Sar my 6f :214 :451 :574 1:11 3↑	Clm 25000	86 9 5 411 47 43 2½	Santos J A	117 4.30	85–17	Insured Winner115½ Pension Fraud1172½ Moby Jak1171½	Finished well	9
5Aug94- 9Sar my 6f :222 :462 :584 1:111	Clm 25000	79 2 5 56½ 62 21 57½	Migliore R	117 4.60	78–19	OcenSplsh1171 PeerlessPerformer1153 BnAli'sRullh1082½	Flattened out	9

Decoder

Own: Tigri Michael

LUMPKINS J (11 1 4 0 .09) $45,000

Dk. b or br g. 4
Sire: Lost Code (Codex)
Dam: Bald Witch (Baldski)
Br: Lenihan Richard (Ky)
Tr: Barker Edward R (11 0 2 3 .00)

113

Lifetime Record:	29 4 7 1	$96,617		
1994	17 1 5 1	$49,212	Turf 11 2 1 1	$28,582
1993	12 3 2 0	$47,405	Wet 3 0 0 0	$1,506
Aqu ⊡	0 0 0 0		Dist 7 2 0 0	$37,294

4Dec94-6Aqu fst 1 :232 :463 1:114 1:372 3↑ Clm 35000 92 6 4 22 12 1½ 2¾ Lumpkins J 117 8.50 80-34 A Call To Rise117¾ Decoder1171½ The Great M. B.1172 Drifted, weakened 6
26Nov94-3Aqu fst 1 :234 :471 1:13 1:383 3↑ Clm c-25000 91 7 5 55½ 31 21½ 22 Lumpkins J 117 f 4.40 73-28 Akiko1122 Decoder1171½ Giant Leap1177½ Willingly 7
Claimed from Perroncino John S, Terracciano Neal Trainer
17Nov94-8Aqu gd 1⅛ Ⓣ :474 1:131 1:383 1:51 3↑ Alw 36000N3X 68 9 7 109¾ 107¾ 911 912 Pezua J M 117 f 25.50 73-15 Chief Master112hd Presently1152½ Grand Continental1152 No factor 11
4Nov94-4Aqu fst 1 :232 :461 1:103 1:352 3↑ Clm 45000 92 6 4 43½ 43 43½ 25 Pezua J M 113 f 11.50 86-14 Danzig's Dance1155 Decoder1131½ A Call To Rise1171½ Rallied inside 6
14Oct94-9Bel fm 1¼ Ⓣ :472 1:113 1:354 2:003 3↑ Clm 35000 80 5 5 54 21 33 53½ Pezua J M 117 f 14.70 84-14 So Sterling119½ Two Wise112¾ Bewray117hd Flattened out 12
29Sep94-2Bel wf 1⅛ :48 1:131 1:39 1:52 Clm c-17500 63 4 2 21 2hd 55½ 616½ Migliore R 117 fb *2.30 54-22 LightningRunner112½ RedScamper1174½ ChrmingBuck1172 Dueled, tired 6
Claimed from Hauman Eugene E, Hushion Michael E Trainer
9Sep94-8Bel fst 1 :232 :461 1:11 1:362 3↑ Alw 36000N3X 73 2 6 66 61¾ 44 49½ Migliore R 117 f 3.60 71-17 Committee Chairman1122 Famous Fan117½ DirectDelight1137 No threat 6
27Aug94-2Sar gd 1⅜ Ⓣ :472 1:131 1:39 2:173 3↑ Clm c-35000 76 5 7 710 62¾ 64½ 56 Day P 117 f *2.00 72-29 Doctor Disaster117nk Two Wise1122 Power Bolt117nk Evenly 10
Claimed from Dogwood Stable, Vestal Peter M Trainer
17Aug94-4Sar fst 1⅛ :473 1:114 1:373 1:573 3↑ Clm 35000 97 2 3 3½ 31 1hd 2hd Day P 117 f 4.70 91-15 Ambush Alley117hd Decoder1175¾ Maraud1151½ Gamely 7
4Aug94-4Sar gd 1⅛ Ⓣ :491 1:132 1:38 1:501 Clm 35000 82 4 6 64½ 74 62½ 54½ Day P 117 f 7.10 72-24 ByeUnionAve.119¾ MrbellStr1171½ Crnshw'sCorner1171 Broke thru gate 9

WORKOUTS: ●Oct 28 Aqu 4f fst :491 B 1/8 Sep 22 Bel 4f fst :48 H 4/53

Ambush Alley

Own: Rogers Samuel H Jr

DAVIS R G (165 23 31 16 .14) $45,000

Ch. g. 4
Sire: Gulch (Mr. Prospector)
Dam: Shamaritan (Sham)
Br: Brant Peter & Wofram Shannon A (Ky)
Tr: Eppler Mary E (5 0 1 0 .00)

113

Lifetime Record:	34 6 2 7	$118,416		
1994	16 2 1 3	$46,425	Turf 10 0 0 3	$19,741
1993	15 3 1 3	$60,581	Wet 6 2 1 0	$32,230
Aqu ⊡	0 0 0 0		Dist 12 5 0 2	$66,370

25Nov94-4Aqu fst 1⅛ :482 1:123 1:38 1:511 3↑ Clm 45000 94 2 5 55 44 31 2¾ Davis R G 113 b 8.20 79-13 Electrojet110¾ Ambush Alley113½ Alpstein1144 Up for place 7
30Oct94-9Lrl fst 1⅛ :484 1:124 1:363 1:484 3↑ W Haight H50k 83 3 7 711 79½ 510 512½ Carle J D L 108 b 18.40 81-14 Ameri Valay1173½ Richie The Coach1146½ Dixie Hero113no Outrun 7
20Oct94-4Aqu fst 1⅛ :51 1:151 1:40 1:522 3↑ Clm 45000 92 5 6 54 52¾ 41¾ 41 Krone J A 113 b 5.60 73-27 Private Plan113hd A Call To Rise117½ Sparkling Sky113nk No late bid 7
6Oct94-8Lrl fst 1⅛ :472 1:114 1:374 1:50 3↑ Clm 50000 91 2 4 54½ 33½ 43½ 34¾ Rocco J L 117 b 3.60 83-18 Dynamic Brush1172½ Baron Mathew1152½ Ambush Alley1174½ Willingly 7
13Sep94-6Pim fst 1¹⁄₁₆ :233 :473 1:114 1:441 3↑ Clm 50000 92 6 8 87¾ 64¾ 5½ 3nk Rocco J L 117 b 18.60 86-17 Baron Mathew117no Boldly Done117nk Ambush Alley117½ Closed 10
17Aug94-4Sar fst 1⅛ :473 1:114 1:373 1:573 3↑ Clm 35000 97 5 6 67½ 44 2hd 1hd Krone J A 117 b 10.90 91-15 Ambush Alley117hd Decoder1175¾ Maraud1151½ Driving 7
23Jly94-10Del yl *1 Ⓣ :241 :48 1:124 1:392 3↑ Alw 9600N$Y 49 3 8 89 79½ 810 817¾ Prado A J L 116 b 16.00 62-26 Halo Hansom1174½ Northern Front1165 Dixieland Magic1194½ No factor 8
8Jly94-6Bel fst 1¹⁄₁₆ :232 :463 1:104 1:432 Clm 50000 76 7 8 87 76¾ 68½ 59½ Krone J A 117 b 5.20 76-15 Sparkling Sky1131 Aye Doo Da1136¾ A Call To Rise113½ No factor 8
11Jun94-8Pim fst 1¹⁄₁₆ :241 :482 1:13 1:441 3↑ Alw 27000N$Y 92 2 4 32 43½ 43 52½ Rocco J L 120 b 3.60e 83-23 Coringa120no Super Memory1181 Ibex1181½ Weakened 6
30May94-3Mth fst 170 :241 :48 1:114 1:424 3↑ Alw 28000N$mY 69 1 4 41¾ 46¼ 513 517¾ Santagata N L 119 b 9.60 68-25 Slick Horn1172 Storm Tower1178¼ Antartic Wings1172¼ Gave way 5

Lord Beer

Own: Austin Sandra H & Heatherwood Farm

MAPLE E (96 11 12 13 .11) $50,000

Dk. b or br c. 4
Sire: Cormorant (His Majesty)
Dam: Bright Tribute (Barrera)
Br: Nielsen Gerald A (NY)
Tr: Schosberg Richard (37 5 9 1 .14)

117

Lifetime Record:	21 6 0 4	$157,638		
1994	8 2 0 1	$48,102	Turf 0 0 0 0	
1993	10 3 0 3	$95,136	Wet 1 0 0 0	$2,760
Aqu ⊡	12 5 0 3	$131,442	Dist 8 5 0 1	$123,342

27Nov94-7Aqu fst 1 :232 :463 1:121 1:381 3↑ Alw 46000N$mY 75 6 4 64 68½ 610 612¾ Alvarado F T 115 f 15.50 64-33 Aztec Empire1152½ Sparkling Sky119nk Jacksonport1153 No threat 7
2Nov94-8Aqu my 1 ⊗ :23 :462 1:122 1:384 3↑ Alw 46000N$mY 72 5 2 21 53½ 48 410¾ Alvarado F T 115 f 8.30 63-29 SparklingSky1151½ CrftyCoventry1154½ ExcellentTipper1105 Forced pace 5
26Oct94-6Aqu fst 1 :234 :472 1:112 1:363 3↑ Clm 70000 81 2 4 31 32½ 56 59½ Migliore R 114 f 5.30 75-27 Swindle113¾ Dream Prosperous1154½ Toroweap1172 Tired 5
23Mar94-6Aqu fst 1⅛ :482 1:124 1:38 1:504 Alw 40000N$mY 87 2 1 1½ 1½ 24 39½ Migliore R 119 f *1.80 73-24 Double Calvados1157 Correntino1152½ Lord Beer1191½ Speed, tired 5
11Mar94-4Aqu fst 170 ⊡ :231 :47 1:114 1:401 Clm 70000 100 1 1 11 11 14 18 Migliore R 113 f *1.70 97-17 Lord Beer1138 Cranshaw's Corner1131 The Great M. B.1138 Ridden out 7
21Feb94-8Aqu fst 1⅛ ⊡ :464 1:111 1:374 1:504 3↑ Stymie H-G3 93 7 3 33½ 75 85¾ 99½ Davis R G 110 f 15.20 72-35 Koluctoo Jimmy Al1114 Michelle Can Pass1201½ FederalFunds111¾ Tired 11
23Jan94-6Aqu fst 1¹⁄₁₆ ⊡ :234 :473 1:13 1:46 3↑ ⓈKings Pt H55k 82 6 7 73¾ 42½ 56 47½ Davis R G 116 f 3.50 67-31 Double Calvados1102 Classi Envoy1201½ Triodet1124 In tight break 9
9Jan94-4Aqu fst 1¹⁄₁₆ ⊡ :234 :473 1:121 1:441 Alw 34000N4X 96 5 1 11½ 11½ 11½ 1nk Davis R G 117 f 2.20 84-20 Lord Beer117nk Correntino117nk Cranshaw's Corner1173¾ Driving 7
9Dec93-8Aqu fst 1¹⁄₁₆ ⊡ :234 :473 1:12 1:442 Blue Swords54k 82 8 3 34 53½ 77¾ 711¼ Davis R G 122 f 5.40 72-25 Punch Line1226½ Classi Envoy122½ Koluctoo Jimmy Al1192 Tired 9
20Nov93-8Aqu fst 1 :223 :454 1:113 1:384 ⓈJsph A Gimma70k 86 7 5 43½ 31½ 44 46½ Madrid A Jr 119 f 14.90 64-45 Itaka1195½ Koluctoo Jimmy Al122½ Corma Ray113½ Lacked rally 8

WORKOUTS: Oct 19 Bel tr.t 5f fst 1:012 B 2/11 Oct 13 Bel tr.t 4f fst :484 H 5/12 Oct 7 Bel tr.t 4f fst :481 H 3/10 Oct 1 Bel tr.t 3f fst :37 B 2/12

Regal Mike

Own: Davidson Herbert S & Wendel Arthur

LEON F (50 2 2 4 .04) $45,000

B. h. 6
Sire: Regal Embrace (Vice Regent)
Dam: Ray Kay (Nehoc's Brother)
Br: Nolan Howard C (NY)
Tr: Wendel Arthur (9 1 0 1 .11)

113

Lifetime Record:	56 5 7 4	$118,240		
1994	24 3 6 3	$70,600	Turf 2 0 0 0	
1993	15 0 0 0	$2,820	Wet 8 0 2 2	$14,380
Aqu ⊡	13 1 0 0	$17,610	Dist 17 1 1 0	$20,970

15Nov94-5Aqu fst 1⅛ :461 1:104 1:37 1:50 3↑ Alw 36000N3X 66 4 4 421 419 418 522¼ Leon F 117 b 20.90 64-20 Danzig's Dance1173¾ Dream Prosperous1124 Private Plan11711 Outrun 5
30Oct94-9Aqu fst 7f :23 :46 1:114 1:25 3↑ ⓈAlw 32000N2X 77 7 5 76½ 85¼ 41 1hd Leon F 117 b 12.90 79-18 RglMk117hd Cn'tSlowDown1141½ Rgrsdvdnds1161½ Bumped break, driving 8
15Oct94-9Bel fst 1⅛ :454 1:102 1:353 1:49 3↑ ⓈEmpireClsscH75k 76 3 9 913 912 712 619 Leon F 110 b 30.00 67-21 Itaka1242½ Terrorist1127 Patsyprospect1072½ Broke slowly 9
1Oct94-2Bel my 1¹⁄₁₆ :24 :464 1:103 1:431 3↑ ⓈAlw 34000N2X 74 2 5 63 54½ 55½ 510¼ Leon F 117 b 9.20 75-19 AdvncdPlcmnt1171½ MstrchtAccord1172½ FlyngGrom1142½ Checked 3/8 pl 8
18Sep94-4Bel wf 1¼ ⊗ :49 1:134 1:38 2:022 3↑ ⓈAlw 34000N2X 74 2 7 73½ 53½ 52 33 Leon F 117 b 4.40 76-13 Little Fran115no Flying Groom1133 Regal Mike1171½ Mild gain 7
3Sep94-9Bel fst 1¹⁄₁₆ :232 :461 1:101 1:421 3↑ Clm 50000 70 9 9 97¾ 98 812 811¾ Leon F 117 b 9.50 79-12 A Call To Rise113nk Sparkling Sky117no Patsyprospect109¾ Outrun 9
17Aug94-7Sar fst 1⅛ :473 1:122 1:383 1:514 3↑ ⓈAlw 32000N2X 88 7 8 88¼ 76½ 32½ 2½ Leon F 117 b 10.30 76-15 Kristen's Baby112½ Regal Mike117½ More To Tell1139 Willingly 8
18Jly94-7Bel sly 7f :231 :461 1:102 1:233 3↑ ⓈAlw 30000N2X 78 4 4 65½ 63¾ 44½ 24 Leon F 117 b 5.20 81-20 Homah Halo1114 Regal Mike1172½ More To Tell111no 6
Steadied 3/16 pl, lost whip stretch
9Jly94-5Bel fst 1¹⁄₁₆ :223 :454 1:104 1:432 Clm 22500 91 2 9 79 62 32 22 Leon F 115 b 23.50 83-19 Northern T.1152 Regal Mike1153 Our Homeboy1122½ Rallied inside 9
28Jun94-7Bel fm 1¹⁄₁₆ Ⓣ :231 :461 1:103 1:413 3↑ ⓈAlw 32000N2X 54 4 9 1014 1010 811 715½ Leon F 119 b 31.70 74-12 Tunbridge Wells1192½ Crafty Investment1141½ Cinco Rey1142 No menace 10

WORKOUTS: Sep 13 Bel tr.t 4f fst :491 B 6/13

Rocking Josh

Own: Valente Roddy

LUZZI M J (200 33 27 25 .17) $45,000

Ch. g. 5
Sire: Whitesburg (Crimson Satan)
Dam: Cold Carol (Run a Native)
Br: Farrow Edith O (Ky)
Tr: Levine Bruce N (41 5 6 5 .12)

113

Lifetime Record:	48 8 12 7	$204,422		
1994	17 1 5 4	$76,520	Turf 2 0 0 0	$846
1993	19 4 6 2	$85,344	Wet 9 3 2 3	$59,362
Aqu ⊡	6 1 1 1	$25,280	Dist 11 3 2 1	$57,434

22Nov94-6Aqu wf 7f :224 :452 1:103 1:24 3↑ Clm 45000 93 3 3 59½ 58½ 54 3¾ Davis R G 113 f 13.80 83-24 SenorCielo117nk TheGrtM.B.108½ RockingJosh1132 Lacked room stretch 6
9Nov94-4Aqu fst 6f :221 :463 :583 1:111 3↑ Clm 50000 82 2 6 613 64 45½ 25½ Davis R G 117 f 4.10 80-14 Current Impact1145½ Rocking Josh1171¾ ⒹUnreal Mot1173 Up for place 6
21Oct94-2Aqu gd 6½f :233 :47 1:113 1:181 3↑ Clm 70000 81 1 4 2½ 42 41½ 44½ Davis R G 113 f 5.40 86-16 Golden Tent115nk Shining Bid1172 Senor Cielo1192 Checked late 4
6Oct94-8Bel fst 6f :22 :444 :564 1:09 3↑ Alw 36000N4X 88 1 5 512 610 56 56¾ Krone J A 117 f 5.90 89-14 Man's Hero1191 Golden Pro1172¾ Unreal Mot1172½ No threat 6
15Sep94-8Bel fst 6f :224 :454 :572 1:091 3↑ Alw 42000N$Y 94 1 7 64½ 42 32 32¼ Krone J A 115 f 7.20e 93-12 GoldenTent115nk SenorCielo1152 RockingJosh1151 Checked break, wide 7
22Aug94-6Sar my 7f :23 :462 1:104 1:23 3↑ Clm 75000 82 4 2 21 23 34½ 38 Chavez J F 112 f 2.00 82-17 Repletion1224 Vouch For Me1224 Rocking Josh112½ Lacked rally 4
3Aug94-5Sar gd 1⅛ ⊗ :4/2 1:111 1:361 1:50 3↑ Alw 44000N$mY 86 5 4 46 35½ 46½ 410¾ Chavez J F 117 f 6.10e 75-24 Contract Court1177½ Binary Light1173 Excellent Tipper117nk Lacked rally 7
20Jly94-6Bel fst 7f :231 :461 1:103 1:231 3↑ Alw 40000N$Y 88 4 4 42 5¾ 32½ 23½ Chavez J F 117 f 4.20 83-17 Thunder Rumble1173½ Rocking Josh117hd Island Edition1174¾ Late gian 5
7Jly94-6Bel fst 6½f :23 :461 1:10 1:162 3↑ Clm 75000 92 1 4 75 52½ 33 22¾ Chavez J F 112 f 6.00 88-12 Farmonthefreeway1152¾ Rocking Josh112hd Fabersham112nk Up for place 7
12Jun94-7Bel fst 7f :23 :46 1:10 1:221 3↑ Alw 34000N4X 86 2 4 42 41½ 53½ 47 Chavez J F 119 f 4.60 85-11 Richmond Runner119hd Golden Tent1196½ Imaging122½ 7
Steadied, lacked room 1/4 pole

Yeckley
Own: Hauman Eugene E & Schwartz Barry K
MIGLIORE R (133 28 19 26 .21) **$45,000**

Ch. g. 4
Sire: Medieval Man (Noholme II)
Dam: Golden Fingers (Precious Boy)
Br: Zellen Larry (Fla)
Tr: Hushion Michael E (35 6 5 8 .17)

113

Lifetime Record:	29	9	2	3	$130,660						
1994	11	2	0	1	$25,045	Turf	2	0	0	0	$550
1993	12	4	1	2	$68,800	Wet	7	4	0	0	$44,145
Aqu ⊡	3	1	1	1	$26,120	Dist	2	0	1	1	$10,520

29Nov94-2Aqu wf	7f		:232	:47	1:114	1:242	3↑ Clm 35000	90	5	1	11½	1½	12	14	Luzzi M J		117 f	*1.25	82-21	Yeckley1174 Current Impact122hd Birdie's Fly1173	Driving	7
15Nov94-8Aqu fst	6f		:224	:46	:573	1:094	3↑ Alw 42000N$Y	88	3	2	11½	1hd	32½	66¼	Migliore R		115 fb	*1.25e	87-17	Boom Towner115¾ Golden Pro1152½ Golden Tent122½	Used up	6
3Nov94-4Aqu fst	6f		:214	:45	:572	1:10	3↑ Clm c-25000	91	1	6	21	1hd	11½	31	Krone J A		117 fb	3.35	91-15	Justforthrcord1121 PnsionFrud117hd Yckly1173½	Broke slowly, weakened	6
Claimed from Zellen Larry, Goldberg Alan E Trainer																						
21Oct94-4Aqu wf	6f		:221	:461	:581	1:104	Clm 17500	89	7	1	13	11	13	1¾	Chavez J F		117 fb	8.80	88-16	Yeckley117¾ Blum Gone1172 Clever Knave107¾	Driving	8
9Sep94-6Med sly	6f		:214	:45	:574	1:103	3↑ Clm 16000	65	7	2	31	31½	34½	58	Bravo J	L	116 fb	2.60	80-12	Sawmill Run1163¾ Ever So True1161 Sammy From Miami1191¾	Weakened	8
31Aug94-6Mth fst	6f		:213	:442	:573	1:11	3↑ Clm 25000	69	9	1	11	1hd	2hd	85½	Lopez C C	L	116 fb	19.40	79-19	World Island116hd Gallant Step116¾ My Impression1162¼	Weakened	10
12Jly94-7Mth fst	6f		:22	:45	:572	1:103	3↑ Clm 35000	80	6	1	11½	1hd	21	56	Bravo J	L	116 fb	2.80	80-19	Jousting Match1162 Unusual Performer112hd Contarito112nk	Tired	6
2Jly94-6Mth fst	6f		:213	:444	:572	1:102	3↑ Clm 40000	80	2	6	12	11	1hd	56½	Bravo J	L	116 fb	3.70	80-20	Teddy Drone1161½ Bates Return1162 My Impression1221	Tired	8
19Jun94-4Mth fm	5f	Ⓣ	:212	:443		:561	3↑ Clm 50000	65	6	3	41	32½	75¼	78¾	Bravo J	L	116 fb	11.90	84-07	Light Them All112¾ Distinctive Hat1221 Joey's First Jove1161¾	Gave way	7
2Feb94-9GP sly	6f		:222	:461	:582	1:112	Alw 39800N1Y	49	2	3	2½	33	411	521	Bravo J	L	115 fb	2.60	63-34	Linear1154 Tri To Watch1194 Premier Explosion1158½	Stopped	5

WORKOUTS: Oct 15 Mdl 5f fst 1:02 B *1/1* Oct 3 Mdl 4f fst :491 B *1/1*

Yeckley was stuck out in post position 8, but the sprinter owned sufficient speed to clear this route field in the short run to the clubhouse turn. The gelding was in the midst of an upward form cycle: he had won for $17,500 on October 21, had been claimed a fortnight later by Mike Hushion out of a sharp try for $25,000, and had responded with a four-length victory against $35,000 sprinters two starts later. Hushion was spotting him aggressively in this richer route, looking to strike again while the iron was hot.

Yeckley had rateable speed, as evidenced by his most recent performance. After drawing clear through a quarter of :23 2/5, by far the slowest quarter in his current record, Yeckley had let the field come back to him in the second quarter: his lead was whittled to half a length after a slow half in :47. From there, however, he finished with plenty in reserve, widening to a four-length win.

A subtle point: had Yeckley been entered back in a sprint, players might well have downgraded the November 29 victory because he had things all his own way dictating a very deliberate tempo; but such rating ability is quite a desirable trait when sprinters are asked to ration their speed going long.

It also helped that Yeckley had experience going two turns on the inner track, experience not shown in his current record:

2 Yeckley
Own: Zellen Larry
BRAVO J (10 3 3 1 .30) **$50,000**

Ch. g. 3 (Apr)
Sire: Medieval Man (Noholme II)
Dam: Golden Fingers (Precious Boy)
Br: Zellen Larry (Fla)
Tr: Goldberg Alan E (3 0 0 2 .00)

117

Lifetime Record:	16	5	2	2	$76,815						
1993	10	2	1	2	$40,000	Turf	1	0	0	0	$350
1992	6	3	1	0	$36,815	Wet	2	1	0	0	$9,750
Aqu	4	1	1	1	$27,920	Dist	9	3	1	1	$42,845

22Oct93-9Med fst	6f		:22	:444	:563	1:084	Kingland Sta35k	73	6	2	22½	23	26	413¾	Santagata N	L	113 b	6.90	83-15	Jess C's Whirl11510 Gold Candy Too117¾ Greatsilverfleet1172¾	Tired	6
6Sep93-5Med fm	5f	Ⓣ	:212	:444		:572	Mercer35k	65	2	4	73½	45	68	68	Santagata N	L	117 b	7.80	82-10	Sweet Beast1153¾ Joes Slupy113nk Guru Dude1153	Tired	11
24Aug93-7Mth fst	6f		:213	:44	:564	1:102	3↑ Alw 19000N3X	94	2	2	1½	12½	16	12¾	Bravo J	L	111 b	4.30	87-21	Yeckley1112¾ Talc's Boy116no Bandit Corsair116hd	Driving	8
18Jly93-8Pha fst	6f		:214	:45	:58	1:111	Laurel25k	74	3	1	2hd	2hd	2½	66	Black A S		120 b	3.60	79-17	My Impression1222¾ Proxy Contest120½ Splitwindowcoup122½		7
Came out start, raced erratic																						
2Jly93-10Mth wf	6f		:213	:45	:574	1:111	3↑ Alw 21000N3X	77	5	1	2hd	11½	1½	42¾	Bravo J		110 b	*.70	80-24	Forget It116½ Royal N Gold1162¼ Contarito116no	Weakened	7
19Jun93-6Mth fst	6f		:214	:442	:571	1:104	3↑ Alw 20000N2X	92	5	1	1½	12	13½	15¾	Bravo J		109 b	*1.60	85-19	Yeckley1095¾ Gold Candy Too1112 My Max1151	Drew out	6
28May93-1Bel fst	6f		:223	:45	:572	1:093	Clm 50000	89	5	2	3½	1hd	1hd	32½	Antley C W		117 b	10.30	89-14	Chief Desire1132½ Tricky Catman113no Yeckley1177	Willingly	7
8Feb93-7Aqu fst	1 1/16	⊡	:23	:463	1:122	1:451	Clm 75000	64	7	2	21½	2½	34½	310¼	Antley C W		117 b	*1.30	69-20	Silver Key113nk Iron Gavel11310 Yeckley1173½	Tired	9
30Jan93-9Pha fst	7f			:45	1:103	1:234	Patriot25k	—	1	9	—	—	—	—	Verge M E		119 b	4.90	— 18	Chip's Dancer115¾ Blushing Julian1153½ Tri For The Gold119½	Lost rider	9
1/4 of 21 4/5 deleted, beam set off by riderless horse																						
9Jan93-1Aqu fst	170	⊡	:234	:482	1:132	1:422	Clm 80000	88	6	1	11	11	1hd	21¾	Santagata N		114 b	7.60	88-20	Tanako1221¾ Yeckley1144½ Farmonthefreeway117¾	Held place	7

WORKOUTS: Oct 2 Mth 5f fst 1:03 B *7/9* Sep 25 Mth 4f fst :493 B *19/55* Aug 20 Mth 4f fst :484 B *8/35* Aug 10 Mth 4f fst :48 B *3/37*

Two winters ago, Yeckley had finished a very respectable second after setting all the pace, but had moved back to sprints and stayed there following a third place finish on February 8.

This race was by no means a walkover for Yeckley, who, after all, had never actually won a route race. The morning-line favorite was Rocking Josh, a hard-hitting gelding who had lacked room in the stretch when a fast-closing third going seven furlongs last time out.

Rocking Josh would be very dangerous if able to run back to that race, and his overall record of 3-for-11 at the distance suggested he might. But the gelding had started 17 times during 1994 and had managed to win only once. In a competitive race where no less than five horses had earned Beyer figures in the 90s in their most recent starts, Rocking Josh was a contender, but he was also a tenuous favorite.

The first important decisions regarding strategy in the Pick 3 had been reached: spread out, using several contenders in the first and third legs, and key Delta West in the middle. The second phase was to structure an actual play.

One of the major mistakes many bettors make with Pick 3s is that they fail to make any distinctions about the merits of their contenders. Why go 3 x 3 x 3 in the Pick 3, betting equal amounts on each of the 27 different combinations, when surely some horses in the mix are preferred more strongly than others? Players would be much better off employing "key horses" in each leg, and insisting that at least one of them win in order to hit. Say, for example, that the three contenders in each leg are as follows:

$$123 \ / \ 456 \ / \ 789$$

Covering all 27 combinations for $2 each would cost $54, and even if the Pick 3 is hit, 26 losing bets are guaranteed. But what if #1 was most preferred in the first leg, #4 was preferred in the second leg, and #7 was deemed to be the key in the third leg. Instead of one $54 ticket covering 123 with 456 with 789, the bet would be:

1 with 456 with 789
123 with 4 with 789
123 with 456 with 7

This play also contains 27 combinations, but with an important difference: should one of the three keys win, the Pick 3 is hit once; should two keys win, the Pick 3 is hit twice; and if all three keys win, the Pick 3 is hit three times. Of course, when non-keyed contenders win all three legs the bet is lost, so the profitability of this approach depends on players ability to hit some keys with a fair degree of accuracy.

That's what makes horses like Delta West so nice to come by. When a strong enough case can be made for a horse to single it, figuring out how to spread the bets around becomes a much simpler process. Commander Evander was being overbet, so I decided to take three shots to beat him, using Studley Do Right, Mc Comas, and Eire Power. In the third leg, I used all except for Pension Fraud and Regal Mike, making the base play 3 x 1 x 6 = 18 x $2 = $36, and I added on a few extra combinations using the horses I thought would be overlays. If I was right about Commander Evander being vulnerable and Delta West ran as expected, the third leg was practically sewn up, and offered several chances at a good-priced winner.

FIFTH RACE
Aqueduct
DECEMBER 9, 1994

1⅛ MILES. (Inner Dirt)(1.47^{1}) CLAIMING. Purse $15,500. 4-year-olds and upward. Weight, 122 lbs. Non–winners of two races at a mile or over since November 1, allowed 3 lbs. Of such a race since then, 5 lbs. Claiming price $17,500, for each $1,000 to $15,500, allowed 2 lbs. (Races when entered to be claimed for $14,000 or less not considered.)

Value of Race: $15,500 Winner $9,300; second $3,100; third $1,705; fourth $930; fifth $465. Mutuel Pool $182,946.00 Exacta Pool $423,597.00

Last Raced	Horse	M/Eqt.	A.	Wt	PP	St	¼	½	¾	Str	Fin	Jockey	Cl'g Pr	Odds $1
30Nov94 ^{1}Aqu^{5}	Eire Power		5	117	1	2	7	5^{1}	$5^{\frac{1}{2}}$	1^{hd}	1^{nk}	Madrid A Jr	17500	17.10
16Nov94 ^{2}Aqu^{4}	Studley Do Right	b	5	117	2	1	$5^{\frac{1}{2}}$	$6^{\frac{1}{2}}$	6^{4}	$2^{\frac{1}{2}}$	$2^{\frac{3}{4}}$	Alvarado F T	17500	2.60
10Nov94 ^{1}Aqu^{3}	Mc Comas	bf	4	117	5	6	4^{6}	$3^{\frac{1}{2}}$	$2^{\frac{1}{2}}$	$3^{3\frac{1}{2}}$	3^{9}	Chavez J F	17500	6.70
27Nov94 ^{4}Aqu^{2}	Commander Evander	bf	6	113	4	3	2^{2}	$2^{2\frac{1}{2}}$	3^{7}	4^{2}	4^{6}	Luzzi M J	15500	0.80
26Nov94 ^{3}Aqu^{7}	Dixieland Music		5	108	6	5	$1^{3\frac{1}{2}}$	1^{8}	1^{4}	5^{9}	$5^{6\frac{1}{2}}$	Martin G J^{10}	17500	46.75
29Oct94 ^{7}WO^{5}	Live Like Royalty	bf	6	117	7	7	$3^{\frac{1}{2}}$	4^{5}	$4^{\frac{1}{2}}$	$6^{\frac{1}{2}}$	$6^{2\frac{1}{2}}$	Migliore R	17500	6.30
8Nov94 ^{6}Aqu^{6}	Out Of The Realm		5	113	3	4	6^{1}	7	7	7	7	Velazquez J R	15500	22.20

OFF AT 2:12 Start Good. Won driving. Time, :23^{1}, :47, 1:12^{2}, 1:39^{4}, 1:53 Track fast.

$2 Mutuel Prices:

1–EIRE POWER	36.20	10.00	4.20
2–STUDLEY DO RIGHT		3.80	3.00
5–MC COMAS			5.30

$2 EXACTA 1–2 PAID $143.00

B. h, by Irish Tower–Exploding Wind, by Explodent. Trainer Debonis Robert. Bred by Miron Julie (Ky).

EIRE POWER ,unhurried for five furlongs, rapidly gained on the turn, bumped with STUDLEY DO RIGHT while angling out at the quarter pole then outfinished that one in a long drive. STUDLEY DO RIGHT far back for five furlongs, angled four wide while gaining on the turn, battled outside the winner through the lane and yielded grudgingly. MC COMAS settled just off the pace while saving ground, made a run to challenge entering the stretch then weakened in the final eighth. COMMANDER EVANDER raced up close for six furlongs then faded. DIXIELAND MUSIC opened a long lead along the backstretch then gave way at the quarter pole.LIVE LIKE ROYALTY raced within striking distance on the turn then tired. OUT OF THE REALM was never a factor. COMMANDER EVANDER pulled up sore after the finish and was vanned off.

Owners— 1, Miron Stephen E; 2, Davis Barbara J; 3, G Lack Farms; 4, Riccio James A; 5, MacMillan William C Jr; 6, Tramutola Thomas; 7, West Point Stable

Trainers—1, Debonis Robert; 2, Moschera Gasper S; 3, Martin Gregory F; 4, Parisella John; 5, Shapoff Stanley R; 6, Hushion Michael E; 7, Johnstone Bruce

Overweight: Dixieland Music (1).

When the pace collapsed in the fifth and Eire Power outgamed Studley Do Right in a stretch-long drive, it knocked most Pick 3 tickets right out of the box. Now, it was up to Delta West to live up to her role as a stand-alone single:

SIXTH RACE
Aqueduct
DECEMBER 9, 1994

1 MILE 70 YARDS. (Inner Dirt)(1.39^{3}) CLAIMING. Purse $21,000. Fillies, 3-year-olds. Weight, 121 lbs. Non–winners of two races at a mile or over since November 1, allowed 3 lbs. Of such a race since then, 5 lbs. Claiming price $35,000, for each $2,500 to $30,000, allowed 2 lbs. (Races when entered to be claimed for $25,000 or less not considered.)

Value of Race: $21,000 Winner $12,600; second $4,200; third $2,310; fourth $1,260; fifth $630. Mutuel Pool $243,895.00 Exacta Pool $518,443.00

Last Raced	Horse	M/Eqt.	A.	Wt	PP	St	¼	½	¾	Str	Fin	Jockey	Cl'g Pr	Odds $1
23Nov94 ^{2}Aqu^{7}	Delta West		3	116	2	1	$1^{\frac{1}{2}}$	$1^{\frac{1}{2}}$	1^{1}	1^{5}	1^{7}	Velazquez J R	35000	2.30
27Nov94 ^{9}Aqu^{4}	Dancing Lacey		3	116	6	6	2^{1}	$2^{\frac{1}{2}}$	$3^{1\frac{1}{2}}$	2^{2}	$2^{\frac{1}{2}}$	Maple E	35000	2.05
27Nov94 ^{9}Aqu^{3}	Fighting Feather		3	116	5	4	4^{1}	6	$4^{\frac{1}{2}}$	4^{2}	$3^{5\frac{1}{2}}$	Somsanith N	35000	3.10
27Nov94 ^{9}Aqu^{7}	A Day To Remember		3	116	3	[illegible]	6	$3^{\frac{1}{2}}$	$2^{\frac{1}{2}}$	3^{1}	4^{4}	Chavez J F	35000	14.00
11Nov94 ^{4}Aqu^{4}	Believe In Doris	b	3	116	1	[illegible]	$5^{\frac{1}{2}}$	5^{1}	5^{1}	5^{4}	$5^{5\frac{1}{2}}$	Madrid A Jr	35000	5.40
27Nov94 ^{9}Aqu^{6}	Ogy's Threat	f	3	108	4	5	$3^{2\frac{1}{2}}$	$4^{\frac{1}{2}}$	6	6	6	Perez R B^{5}	30000	7.70

OFF AT 2:38 Start Good. Won driving. Time, :24^{4}, :50, 1:15^{1}, 1:40^{3}, 1:44^{3} Track fast.

$2 Mutuel Prices:

3–DELTA WEST	6.60	3.60	2.40
6–DANCING LACEY		3.70	2.30
5–FIGHTING FEATHER			2.30

$2 EXACTA 3–6 PAID $27.40

B. f, (Feb), by Tank's Prospect–Delta Daiquiry, by Delta Flag. Trainer O'Connell Richard. Bred by John W. Rooker (Ky).

DELTA WEST set the pace under pressure for five furlongs, opened a clear advantage on the turn then drew off under mild encouragement. DANCING LACEY, away slowly, forced the pace from outside to the turn but was no match for the winner. FIGHTING FEATHER settled just off the pace while three wide for six furlongs then lacked a strong closing bid. A DAY TO REMEMBER, outrun early, moved up from outside to threaten on the turn and flattened out. BELIEVE IN DORIS was never a serious threat. OGY'S THREAT, up close early while saving ground, faded after going five furlongs.

Owners— 1, Lillie Bert; 2, Reinacher Robert Jr; 3, Solano Rafael; 4, Sigel Marshall E; 5, Wilson Charles T Jr; 6, Davis Barbara J

Trainers—1, O'Connell Richard; 2, Reinacher Robert Jr; 3, Solano Rafael; 4, Picou James E; 5, Hernandez Ramon M; 6, Moschera Gasper S

Overweight: Ogy's Threat (1).

Scratched— Mitey Jenny (7Dec94 ^{7}AQU^{10})

Shaking off Dancing Lacey into the far turn, Delta West drew off under mild urging to win by seven. Now it was up to someone, *anyone* except Pension Fraud or Regal Mike:

SEVENTH RACE
Aqueduct
DECEMBER 9, 1994

1 1/16 MILES. (Inner Dirt)(1.41) CLAIMING. Purse $28,000. 3-year-olds and upward. Weights: 3-year-olds, 120 lbs. Older, 122 lbs. Non-winners of two races at a mile or over since November 1, allowed 3 lbs. Of such a race since November 1, 5 lbs. Claiming price $50,000, for each $2,500 to $45,000, allowed 2 lbs. (Races when entered to be claimed for $40,000 or less not considered.)

Value of Race: $28,000 Winner $16,800; second $5,500; third $3,080; fourth $1,680; fifth $840. Mutuel Pool $243,895.00 Exacta Pool $518,443.00

Last Raced	Horse	M/Eqt. A.Wt	PP	St	1/4	1/2	3/4	Str	Fin	Jockey	Cl'g Pr	Odds $1
29Nov94 2Aqu1	Yeckley	bf 4 113	8	3	1^2	1$^{1\frac{1}{2}}$	1$^{1\frac{1}{2}}$	1^3	1^2	Migliore R	45000	5.60
22Nov94 6Aqu3	Rocking Josh	f .5 113	7	5	3hd	3$\frac{1}{2}$	2^1	2$^{1\frac{1}{2}}$	2nk	Luzzi M J	45000	2.60
25Nov94 4Aqu2	Ambush Alley	b 4 113	4	8	7^4	6$\frac{1}{2}$	5^1	4^2	3^3	Davis R G	45000	3.10
27Nov94 7Aqu4	Pension Fraud	f 6 113	2	1	4$^{1\frac{1}{2}}$	4^1	3$\frac{1}{2}$	3hd	4^6	Santagata N	45000	12.40
4Dec94 6Aqu2	Decoder	4 113	3	4	6$\frac{1}{2}$	5$\frac{1}{2}$	4$\frac{1}{2}$	5^3	5^4	Lumpkins J	45000	7.90
25Nov94 4Aqu3	Alpstein	4 108	1	2	5$\frac{1}{2}$	7^7	6$^{1\frac{1}{2}}$	6^2	6no	Perez R B5	45000	6.70
27Nov94 7Aqu6	Lord Beer	f 4 117	5	6	2$\frac{1}{2}$	2$\frac{1}{2}$	7^5	7^1	7nk	Maple E	50000	4.10
15Nov94 5Aqu5	Regal Mike	b 6 113	6	7	8	8	8	8	8	Leon F	45000	34.75

OFF AT 3:04 Start Good. Won driving. Time, :24¹, :48², 1:12³, 1:37³, 1:44¹ Track fast.

$2 Mutuel Prices:	8–YECKLEY	13.20	7.90	4.80
	7–ROCKING JOSH		4.90	3.40
	4–AMBUSH ALLEY			2.90

$2 EXACTA 8–7 PAID $76.00

Ch. g, by Medieval Man–Golden Fingers, by Precious Boy. Trainer Hushion Michael E. Bred by Zellen Larry (Fla).

YECKLEY sprinted clear in the early stages, was rated on the front into the stretch, opened a comfortable advantage in midstretch then held sway under brisk left hand encouragement. ROCKING JOSH stalked the pace from outside to the top of the stretch but was no match for the winner while holding for the place. AMBUSH ALLEY, in tight at the start, steadied along the inside on the turn, then closed gradually but could not get up. PENSION FRAUD raced in close contention along the inside into upper stretch and lacked a strong closing bid. DECODER raced within striking distance to the turn and tired. ALPSTEIN was never a serious threat. LORD BEER was used up forcing the early pace. REGAL MIKE was outrun. YECKLEY wore mud caulk.

Owners— 1, Hauman Eugene E & Schwartz Barry K; 2, Valente Roddy; 3, Rogers Samuel H Jr; 4, Perroncino John S; 5, Tigri Michael; 6, Marinos Jane E; 7, Austin Sandra H & Heatherwood Farm; 8, Davidson Herbert S & Wendel Arthur

Trainers— 1, Hushion Michael E; 2, Levine Bruce N; 3, Eppler Mary E; 4, Terracciano Neal; 5, Barker Edward R; 6, Moschera Gasper S; 7, Schosberg Richard; 8, Wendel Arthur

Scratched— Iron Gavel (25Nov94 6AQU3)

$2 Pick–3 (1–3–8) Paid $1,331.00; Pick–3 Pool $183,796.

Yeckley bounded out in front and cleared from his outside post, rated kindly on the front-end, and maintained his advantage at a $13.20 mutual. Rocking Josh finished in the money for the 10th time against only one victory during the year.

Because the takeout in Pick 3s is extracted only once instead of three times, as is the case with traditional win parlays, the Pick 3 usually pays more, and this result was no exception. A $2 parlay on Eire Power, Delta West and Yeckley would've been worth $788.40, but the Pick 3 payoff was nearly twice that, at $1,331.

The Pick 3 is not without its drawbacks. You don't get to see potential payoffs until the results of the first two legs are in. You only get to see odds for the first leg. Paddock, post parade and pre-race warmup observations are limited to the first leg as well. Overall, however, the Pick 3 provides players the opportunity to structure bets in such a way as to truly reflect their opinions, and real bonanzas can be reeled in when overbet favorites are out of the mix.

TRAINER HANDICAPPERS uncover more than their fair share of overlaid winners because they have information not available to the general public, and this richer background with a stable's past maneuvers enables them to develop confidence in their opinions instead of merely guessing. The record-keeping approach that packs the most bang for the buck, at least for me, is embarrassingly simple — something along the lines of, "Everything I Ever Needed to Know, I Learned in Kindergarten." All I do is clip the past performances of each day's winners and paste them into an expandable loose-leaf notebook, along with notations of pertinent data not contained in the pp's themselves — the date, race distance, class, mutual payoff, and any other notes concerning blinkers, front bandages, Lasix, and whatever else seems appropriate. The procedure is admittedly low-tech, but the hands-on process of working with the past performances gives one a more intimate relationship with what kind of horses are winning what kind of races — and for whom! — so that without consciously thinking about it, an awareness is cultivated about things that otherwise would go completely unnoticed. This approach has the benefit of capturing a lot of potentially value-rich details that fall through the cracks of computer-generated statistical studies; it's great to know that Joe Backstretch is 0-for-53 with first time-starters at Saratoga over the last five years, but for the most part players will merely wind up making "percentage plays" based on abstract numbers when they should be looking for specific pattern-matches they can really sink their teeth into.

The fourth race on December 16 provides an example of the kinds of insights trainer handicapping can be expected to produce. A field of seven went to the post in this nine-furlong route for 3-year-olds who would soon be turning 4, including an odds-on entry from Gasper Moschera, a high-volume claiming trainer annually among New York's top three in number of winners saddled. The entry is 2-5, and the price seems reasonable considering that Brett's Jet and Churkin have combined to win the staggering total of 15 races during the year.

Scan through the race. Based on established class, earnings-per-start, recent accomplishments, and things of that nature, which horse would logically be the first elimination?

4 Aqueduct

1⅛ MILES. **(Inner Dirt). (1:47¹) CLAIMING. Purse $28,000. 3-year-olds. Weight, 122 lbs. Non-winners of two races at a mile or over since November 15, allowed 3 lbs. Of such a race since then, 5 lbs. Claiming price $50,000, for each $2,500 to $45,000, allowed 2 lbs. (Races when entered to be claimed for $40,000 or less not considered.)**

Coupled - Brett's Jet, Matthew Red Dog and Churkin

Kristen's Baby

Own: Tigri Michael
LUMPKINS J (17 2 6 0 .12) **$50,000**

B. g. 3 (May)
Sire: Chromite (Mr. Prospector)
Dam: No Song (Nostrum)
Br: Martin James C (NY)
Tr: Barker Edward R (12 0 2 3 .00)

117

Lifetime Record:	11 4 2 1	$113,297			
1994	10 4 2 1	$113,297	Turf	0 0 0 0	
1993	1 M 0 0		Wet	2 1 1 0	$36,662
Aqu ⊡	0 0 0 0		Dist	3 1 1 0	$48,860

15Nov94-5Aqu fst 1⅛ :461 1:104 1:37 1:50 3↑ Alw 36000N3X **70** 5 5 527 528 520 419¼ Santos J A 115 5.50 67-20 Danzig's Dance1173¾ Dream Prosperous1124 Private Plan11711 No factor 5
18Oct94-7Aqu fst 7f :231 :46 1:102 1:224 3↑ Alw 34000N3X **75** 7 6 99¾ 88 66½ 611 Migliore R 114 3.95 79-15 Mr. Tyler1142 Golden Larch111nk More To Tell1166 No factor 9
28Sep94-8Bel my 1½ ⊗ :472 1:12 2:024 2:291 LRealizatnH-G3 **92** 8 6 58 43½ 32½ 23 Luzzi M J 111 *2.50 81-22 Personal Merit1133 Kristen's Baby111hd Holy Mountain11611 Up for place 8
27Aug94-9FL fst 1⅛ :453 1:101 1:361 1:484 Ⓢ New York Dby125k **93** 5 5 48½ 35½ 22½ 22 Luzzi M J 119 2.90 108 — Copper Mount1192 Kristen's Baby1195¾ Late Skate1195 Best of rest 5
17Aug94-7Sar fst 1⅛ :473 1:122 1:383 1:514 3↑ Ⓢ Alw 32000N2X **89** 4 6 65 52½ 21½ 1½ Luzzi M J 112 2.80 77-15 Kristen's Baby112½ Regal Mike117½ More To Tell1139 Driving 8
31Jly94-10Sar fst 7f :224 :461 1:111 1:234 3↑ Ⓢ Alw 28000N1X **89** 4 9 96 53 1½ 14½ Luzzi M J 111 2.80 86-16 Kristen's Baby1114½ Fabian111no Concordes Prospect114no Wide, driving 12
18Jly94-2Bel sly 1 1/16 ⊗ :24 :474 1:124 1:443 Clm c-35000 **89** 1 7 46 32 13 14½ Davis R G 117 7.50 79-22 Kristen's Baby1174½ Ben's Jet11711 Critical Mass1174½ Drew off 7
Claimed from Martin James C, Peitz Daniel C Trainer
1Jly94-6CD fst 1 1/16 :24 :473 1:123 1:444 3↑ Clm 25000N2L **83** 12 9 912 710 34½ 33¼ Bisono C V L 111 4.80e 87-11 HolySmokesAndy1203 PersonalFavor110nk Kristen'sBaby1114½ Wide rally 12
16Jun94-3CD fst 6f :22 :462 :591 1:12 3↑ Md 17500 **71** 11 8 84¾ 85¼ 34 1½ Woods C R Jr L 112 7.50 86-15 Kristen'sBby112½ Amightynotion113hd ThereAndBck1182 6-wide, driving 12
14May94-7CD fst 6f :22 :454 :572 1:104 3↑ Md 30000 **51** 4 11 1111 1115 813 78½ Woods C R Jr L 111 8.40 84-10 Flight Pay1074 Crafty Financing1112½ Shaka Rock111hd 11
Sluggish squeezed start

WORKOUTS: Dec 7 Bel tr.t 4f fst :53 B *43/46* Nov 30 Bel 5f fst 1:032 B *12/15* Nov 9 Bel 3f fst :373 B *11/20* Oct 30 Bel tr.t 5f fst 1:032 B *5/6* Sep 22 Bel 5f fst 1:034 B *37/41* Sep 16 Bel 6f fst 1:144 H *4/5*

Brett's Jet

Own: Joques Farm
PEREZ R B (220 36 27 36 .16) **$45,000**

Ch. g. 3 (Mar)
Sire: Little Missouri (Cox's Ridge)
Dam: Lodge Pole (Mehmet)
Br: Audette F J & Joan I (Fla)
Tr: Moschera Gasper S (113 27 19 29 .24)

108⁵

Lifetime Record:	18 8 1 6	$87,835			
1994	17 8 1 6	$87,555	Turf	1 0 0 0	
1993	1 M 0 0	$280	Wet	3 1 0 2	$19,820
Aqu ⊡	1 0 0 1	$3,740	Dist	1 1 0 0	$12,000

11Dec94-7Aqu wf 1 1/16 ⊡ :234 :48 1:122 1:432 3↑ Alw 32980N2X **88** 3 3 48 33½ 38 39½ Alvarado F T 115 b *1.30 78-22 Fanchee1154½ Bull Inthe Heather1175 Brett's Jet1151 No threat 4
4Dec94-9Aqu fst 7f :224 :46 1:103 1:232 3↑ Alw 32000N2X **87** 9 5 87½ 96½ 35 34¼ Alvarado F T 115 b 4.90 82-15 Crafty1173½ Our Emblem1151 Brett's Jet1152¾ Evenly 9
19Nov94-6Aqu wf 1 :23 :462 1:114 1:361 3↑ Alw 34000N2X **82** 3 6 65 52¼ 32½ 37¾ Alvarado F T 115 b 1.60e 79-20 Sky Hero1102¾ Electrojet1125 Brett's Jet1155¾ No late bid 7
12Nov94-5Aqu fst 1 :23 :454 1:104 1:363 Clm 45000 **92** 1 3 33 2½ 13 13½ Alvarado F T 114 b *1.25 85-23 Brett's Jet1143½ Fleet Eagle1137½ Time In The City1175½ Driving 5
30Sep94-7Bel fst 1 1/16 :232 :471 1:124 1:444 Clm 35000 **96** 4 5 63½ 32 13 17 Alvarado F T 117 b 2.50 78-29 Brett's Jet1177 Mean Pancho11211 Heavenwood112nk Wide, driving 7
15Aug94-4Sar yl 1 1/16 Ⓣ :232 :464 1:111 1:424 Clm 70000 **4** 1 10 1024 1027 1032 1040½ Smith M E 113 b 7.30 39-21 Head Trip1172 Best Of Music1137 Natural Fact1171½ Outrun 10
29Jly94-4Sar my 1⅛ ⊗ :492 1:142 1:402 1:534 Clm c-35000 **80** 5 6 52 31 2hd 1nk Luttrell M G5 112 b *1.60 67-30 Brett's Jet112nk Bomb Free11710 Burn The Toast117hd Lugged in, driving 6
Claimed from Alexander Bruce, Alexander Bruce Trainer
10Jly94-8FL fst 1 3/16 :491 1:134 1:383 1:582 3↑ Alw 7500s **72** 1 4 32½ 32 32½ 35 Hulet L 112 b *.90 106-09 North Warning113hd Coby Escapade1134¾ Brett's Jet1124½ No closing bid 6
12Jun94-10Tdn fst 1 :24 :482 1:132 1:392 3↑ Alw 10500N1m **76** 2 6 64 32 12 12¾ Rivera H Jr B 119 b *.30 90-13 Brett'sJet1192¾ ReflectiveLight1161½ BlzingProspector1165½ Hand ridden 6
27May94-7WO fst 1 1/16 :243 :494 1:142 1:453 Clm 37500 **72** 5 5 43½ 3½ 1½ 1½ Landry R C 115 b 2.50 88-13 Brett's Jet115½ Winter Renegade1182½ Mactaquac1153¼ 5
Good move rail into slow pace, held gamely stretch

WORKOUTS: Oct 30 Bel tr.t 4f fst :482 H *4/11* Oct 23 Bel tr.t 4f fst :492 B *7/20* Sep 22 Bel 4f fst :491 B *21/53* Sep 16 Bel tr.t 3f fst :393 B *6/6*

Minute Ryder

Own: Caspa Stable

CHAVEZ J F (235 37 27 26 .16) $45,000

B. g. 3 (May)
Sire: Red Ryder (Raise a Native)
Dam: Minatela (Minnesota Mac)
Br: Estate of Raymond T Pericles (Fla)
Tr: Galluscio Dominic G (29 4 3 2 .14)

113

Lifetime Record: 16 4 4 3 $52,108
1994 16 4 4 3 $52,108 Turf 3 1 1 0 $15,065
1993 0 M 0 0 Wet 3 2 0 1 $25,945
Aqu [•] 1 0 0 0 $630 Dist 1 1 0 0 $12,500

10Dec94-4Aqu fst 170 [•] :241 :491 1:141 1:433 Clm 35000 64 2 7 79 79½ 612 510½ Chavez J F 117 fb *2.10 69-23 Geret's Jewel117hd Cross Ice Pass113nk Mean Pancho115¾ No factor 7
24Oct94-7Crc fm *1½ Ⓣ 2:312 3↑ Hcp 12500s 74 1 4 310 24 22½ 24¼ Toribio A R L 122 fb *.50 82-27 Comme Pink1144¼ Minute Ryder122nk Theorum1128 Gamely 7
16Oct94-5Crc gd *1 1/16 Ⓣ 1:444 Clm 35000 87 8 8 812 910 45½ 1½ Toribio A R L 120 fb 3.00 80-25 Minute Ryder120½ Explosive Date117nk Rupert Spring Fire1151¼ 10
Clipped heels bkstr, stumbled, driving
1Oct94-11Crc sly 1⅛ :48 1:132 1:401 1:533 3↑ Alw 19100N2X 87 1 7 66¾ 33 11 11 Toribio A R L 119 fb *1.50 85-19 Minute Ryder1191 ConfidenceIsHigh1222 NetAbility1194½ Driving, inside 8
23Sep94-9Crc sly 1 1/16 :232 :473 1:132 1:47 3↑ Alw 19100N2X 86 4 5 57½ 31½ 41½ 31 Toribio A R L 118 fb 3.00 83-32 Knight Waltz1191 Net Ability119hd Minute Ryder118½ Rallied 7
12Sep94-8Crc sly 1¼ :494 1:161 1:422 2:082 3↑ Alw 17500N1X 80 10 9 95¼ 41½ 12½ 15¼ Toribio A R L 115 fb 4.70 88-25 Minute Ryder1155¼ March Fifth115¾ ThisSongWillDo115nk Driving, inside 10
3Sep94-7Crc yl *1⅛ Ⓣ 1:52 3↑ Clm 25000 84 6 3 44½ 62½ 4¾ 1no Morales C E L 115 fb 28.40 59-42 [D]Minute Ryder115no Bay Rocket117nk Runabout Bird1171 10
Drifted out lvg furlong pole, drftd in deep str and drftd out fin, dvg Disqualified and placed 5th
15Aug94-2Crc fst 1 :243 :484 1:134 1:411 3↑ Md 25000 69 6 7 63½ 44 2hd 13 Toribio A R L 117 fb *1.80 81-14 Minute Ryder1173 Purple Toe122¾ Windswept Goal117nk Driving 7
28Jly94-10Crc fst 7f :232 :471 1:14 1:28 3↑ Md 12500 51 4 11 88¼ 75¼ 55 2no Toribio A R 117 fb 4.30 72-16 Morriston Flash117no Minute Ryder117hd Vamanosok1171¾ 11
Split horses deep str, brushed, rallied
2Jun94-2Crc fst 1 1/16 :241 :484 1:141 1:48 3↑ Md 12500 58 5 4 44 31 31½ 34½ Toribio A R 115 fb 10.40 74-25 MyMagicTouch1154¼ PhntomChllenger115nk MinuteRyder115¾ Late rally 8

WORKOUTS: Dec 3 Crc 4f sly :493 B (d) *4/43* Nov 22 Crc 5f fst 1:023 B *5/17* Nov 12 Crc 5f fst 1:03 B *10/30* Oct 13 Crc 4f fst :491 B *6/34*

Personnel Director

Own: Casson Helen & Lanzara Ed

LUZZI M J (222 39 28 28 .18) $45,000

Gr. g. 3 (Feb)
Sire: Personal Flag (Private Account)
Dam: Joanie's Hero (King's Bishop)
Br: Curpier Joy E (NY)
Tr: Battles Jake (—)

115

Lifetime Record: 20 5 1 1 $43,444
1994 19 5 1 1 $43,444 Turf 2 0 0 0
1993 1 M 0 0 Wet 5 1 0 0 $4,200
Aqu [•] 8 1 0 0 $8,280 Dist 2 0 1 0 $6,380

21Nov94-9FL fst 170 :232 :464 1:113 1:431 3↑ [S]Alw 10800N2 75 1 6 513 59¾ 32½ 12¾ Cullum W 117 b 3.10 93-14 Personnel Director1172¾ Cannonball Express1192 I'm Tired116¾ Drew off 7
5Nov94-2FL fst 1 :232 :463 1:111 1:384 3↑ Alw 7400N4L 67 3 6 69 38½ 24 11 Cullum W 116 b *1.95 93-03 Personnel Director1161 Tropic Zone1146 Pre Native Lad116nk Driving 8
21Oct94-9FL fst 1 :243 :483 1:13 1:391 3↑ Alw 7400N4L 70 1 4 44 32 34½ 32¼ Cullum W 117 b *2.20 89-15 CollegitePrince116no TropicZone1122¼ PersonnlDirctor1171¼ Reared start 6
1Oct94-9FL sly 1 :234 :472 1:133 1:411 3↑ Alw 7000N3L 66 5 4 44½ 31½ 1½ 11 Cullum W 116 b 7.10 81-24 Personnel Director1161 Duel Zone116no Ichabod Rider1157 Driving 6
18Sep94-5FL fst 170 :234 :473 1:123 1:45 3↑ Alw 7000N3L 61 6 6 610 514 49 47 Cullum W 116 b 4.90 77-16 Ice Covered1161½ Duel Zone1164 Hello Danny1161½ No threat 6
11Sep94-10FL fst 1 :26 :502 1:15 1:41 3↑ [S]Alw 11400N2 67 2 4 2½ 32 35 49¼ Saul D 112 b 3.50 73-27 Amberjack1168 Alibi's Sun1161 Wanna B. Alive116nk Weakened 6
27Aug94-1Sar wf 7f :22 :442 1:092 1:224 Clm 30000 59 7 3 712 717 76 714¼ Leon F 113 33.90 77-11 Fleet Eagle1132 Zeal Brown1121 Commodore Admiral1172½ No factor 8
9Jly94-6FL wf 1 1/16 :231 :463 1:113 1:452 3↑ [S]GenVlyBdrsH25k 72 9 9 910 78½ 53½ 57 Cullum W 108 b 14.20 87-16 Who's Gonna BRite114nk LatinLetters1144¾ Turk'sHero1141 Finished well 9
18Jun94-4Bel fm 1 1/16 [T] :25 :481 1:121 1:424 3↑ [S]Alw 32000N2X 53 4 5 53½ 62¾ 69¼ 615½ Velazquez J R 111 b 26.20 66-13 Clover City119hd Green Gaitor119nk Tamara R.1141¼ No factor 8
12May94-7Bel fm 1 1/16 [T] :242 :482 1:131 1:442 3↑ [S]Alw 32000N2X 75 3 5 54½ 52½ 64 65½ Luttrell M G5 110 b 6.60 68-21 Alpstein1191¼ Island Resort119hd Doctor Disaster1191¼ Checked early 10

WORKOUTS: Nov 30 FL 4f my :54 H *7/7* Nov 14 FL 7f fst 1:312 B *1/1* Oct 13 FL 5f fst 1:06 B *5/5*

Blaze Of The Sun

Own: R Kay Stable

VELAZQUEZ J R (131 14 14 11 .11) $50,000

Dk. b or br c. 3 (Mar)
Sire: Halo (Hail to Reason)
Dam: Sol de Terre (Mr. Prospector)
Br: Overbrook Farm (Ky)
Tr: Araya Rene A (10 1 0 0 .10)

117

Lifetime Record: 3 1 1 0 $13,360
1994 3 1 1 0 $13,360 Turf 0 0 0 0
1993 0 M 0 0 Wet 1 1 0 0 $7,200
Aqu [•] 0 0 0 0 Dist 0 0 0 0

Entered 15Dec94- 4 AQU
19Nov94-5Aqu wf 7f :233 :473 1:123 1:251 3↑ Md c-35000 74 8 4 2½ 1½ 1½ 11½ Perez R B5 115 f *.50 78-21 Blaze Of The Sun1151½ Robber Baron1156½ Poulet Chasseur1111¼ Driving 9
Claimed from Mohammed Al Maktoum, Mott William I Trainer
4Nov94-5Aqu fst 7f :232 :47 1:111 1:234 3↑ Md Sp Wt 84 5 7 31½ 1hd 1hd 2nk Velazquez J R 120 18.60 85-15 Get Behind Me120nk Blaze Of The Sun120¾ Turn West1202¾ Sharp try 7
11May94-3Bel fst 7f :224 :462 1:112 1:24 Md Sp Wt 42 4 7 2½ 31½ 89½ 819½ Velazquez J R 122 14.00 63-17 Waldoboro1223 Pleasant Phoenix1222¾ Chrys1221¾ Forced pace, tired 11

WORKOUTS: ●Dec 9 Bel tr.t 4f fst :462 H *1/66* Oct 31 Bel 4f fst :53 B *29/31* Oct 20 Bel 6f fst 1:15 Bg *2/6* Oct 13 Bel 3f fst :362 B *6/20* Oct 1 Sar tr.t 5f fst 1:032 B *1/3* Sep 22 Sar tr.t 5f fst 1:033 B *1/1*

Churkin

Own: Joques Farm

MIGLIORE R (156 33 20 31 .21) $45,000

Dk. b or br c. 3 (May)
Sire: Allen's Prospect (Mr. Prospector)
Dam: Kahaila (Pitcairn)
Br: Paulson Allen E (Ky)
Tr: Moschera Gasper S (113 27 19 29 .24)

115

Lifetime Record: 23 7 2 2 $94,940
1994 19 7 2 2 $93,530 Turf 1 0 0 0
1993 4 M 0 0 $1,410 Wet 2 1 0 1 $15,000
Aqu [•] 5 1 0 0 $6,600 Dist 5 0 2 1 $12,770

29Nov94-4Aqu wf 1 :223 :453 1:112 1:372 Clm 35000 88 9 6 53½ 1hd 11½ 13 Alvarado F T 117 3.55 81-24 Churkin1173 Geret's Jewel117nk Rogersdividends119nk Driving 9
20Nov94-7Aqu fst 1 :232 :464 1:12 1:372 3↑ Alw 32000N1X 86 1 6 54 42½ 13 13 Alvarado F T 115 11.50 81-25 Churkin1153 Absent Minded1151 Bailadoro110¾ Driving 8
9Nov94-2Aqu fst 1⅛ :481 1:131 1:391 1:524 3↑ Alw 32000N1X 80 1 5 59 56½ 32½ 32¾ Smith M E 115 4.60 69-33 Sophie's Friend1151½ Absent Minded1151¼ Churkin1153½ Mild gain 6
28Oct94-9Aqu fst 1 :224 :454 1:112 1:382 Clm 17500 76 6 10 1010 54¾ 31½ 1½ Smith M E 117 *2.80 76-23 Churkin117½ Montedora113nk Creston House1122 Wide, driving 10
18Oct94-1Aqu fst 1⅛ :482 1:13 1:392 1:53 Clm 17500 74 6 4 610 38½ 34 25 Smith M E 117 *1.70 66-21 Libertine1175 Churkin1171½ Montedora1135½ Wide, up for place 7
15Sep94-4Bel fst 1 1/16 :231 :462 1:111 1:423 Clm 25000 61 6 9 86½ 74¼ 55 415¾ Smith M E 117 *1.60 73-11 Free Agent1196 A Track Attack1177 Creston House1132¾ No factor 9
24Aug94-2Sar fst 1⅛ :464 1:12 1:382 1:514 Clm 25000 76 6 8 911 74¾ 31 21¼ Davis R G 117 3.40 76-23 C. Lenny Runn1171¼ Churkin1173¼ Creston House1172 Rallied 6 wide 9
18Jly94-2Bel sly 1 1/16 ⊗ :24 :474 1:124 1:443 Clm 35000 55 6 4 56½ 42½ 410 420 Smith M E 117 3.90 59-22 Kristen's Baby1174½ Ben's Jet11711 Critical Mass1174½ No threat 7
Awarded third purse money
7Jly94-2Bel fst 1 1/16 :24 :48 1:13 1:453 Clm c-25000 71 2 6 53 41½ 1hd 12¾ Davis R G 117 *1.60 74-26 Churkin1172¾ Ei' Kareem1171¾ Treadstone1171½ Wide, driving 6
Claimed from Condren William J, Zito Nicholas P Trainer
18Jun94-2Bel fst 1 :231 :463 1:112 1:37 Clm 17500 82 6 7 42 31½ 13 17 Davis R G 117 2.90 78-12 Churkin1177 Sean's World1176¾ Fortunate Tumble113hd Driving 7

WORKOUTS: Oct 10 Bel tr.t 4f fst :492 B *8/18* Oct 1 Bel tr.t 4f fst :50 B *13/21*

Island Skater

Own: Entenmann & Sound View & Timber Bay

SANTAGATA N (100 8 10 7 .08) $50,000

Dk. b or br g. 3 (Feb)
Sire: Overskate (Nodouble)
Dam: Prissy Wicks (Cresta Rider)
Br: Timber Bay Farm (NY)
Tr: Entenmann William J (4 1 1 0 .25)

119

Lifetime Record: 7 2 2 0 $34,940
1994 7 2 2 0 $34,940 Turf 3 0 1 0
1993 0 M 0 0 Wet 0 0 0 0
Aqu [•] 1 1 0 0 $19,200 Dist 0 0 0 0

7Dec94-9Aqu fst 1 1/16 [•] :23 :474 1:124 1:453 3↑ [S]Alw 32000N1X 73 4 4 42½ 31½ 1½ 1nk Santagata N 115 *2.60 77-21 Island Skater115nk Uncle Pockets1153 Waki Road115nk Driving 12
12Nov94-6Aqu fst 1 :224 :461 1:114 1:381 3↑ [S]Alw 32000N1X 73 11 3 33 31½ 21 21¼ Santagata N 115 7.60 76-23 Come On Talc1151¼ Island Skater115¾ Landing Pad1173 Held place 11
29Oct94-6Aqu fm 1⅛ Ⓣ :484 1:14 1:392 1:521 3↑ [S]Alw 32000N1X 69 5 1 11½ 1½ 1hd 63½ Santagata N 114 10.00 75-13 Jacsonzac1171 CaptainBainbridge116nk WatralsSeTrip1141¼ Used in pace 12
26Aug94-3Pha fst 1 1/16 :234 :483 1:143 1:502 3↑ Md Sp Wt 63 4 4 2½ 2hd 11½ 14½ Lloyd J S 115 5.20 60-38 Island Skater1154½ Son Of Pearl115nk Harry's Blade1162½ Driving 6
21May94-1Mgo hd *2¼ Hurdles 4:143 3↑ Md Sp Wt — 4 6 58 55½ — — Cooney P 132 - — — Logroller1443 Final Final1444 [DH]Joli's Summer144 Pulled up 7
7May94-6Bro hd *2 Ⓣ 3:35 3↑ Md Sp Wt — 8 6 610 47 43 41 Durnin A 135 - — — Robbie T.147½ Radical Rory149nk King Kazar151hd Lacked a rally 6
2Apr94-1Cam fm *1 Ⓣ 1:431 3↑ Md Sp Wt — 7 3 53½ 31¼ 31 21 Ryan C G 144 - 83 — Grenade1501 Island Skater144½ Paddock Dancer1471½ Gave way 12

WORKOUTS: Oct 26 Fai 4f fst :501 B *2/2* Oct 17 Fai 3f fst :373 B *3/3* Sep 29 Fai 4f fst :504 B *4/4*

Rather quickly, it becomes apparent that Blaze Of The Sun doesn't measure up in terms of established class, seasoning, or anything like that. Fresh from a win against $35,000 maidens, he will be facing a much more difficult task here. Brett's Jet is dropping from allowance company, and has won his last four starts when entered to be claimed; his mate Churkin has won three of his last four races, and his two most recent Beyers show he's never been better.

There were two factors that made Blaze Of The Sun an attractive play, one which could be seen by anyone, and one that required extra-curricular record-keeping.

The first thing the colt had going for him was a tactical advantage as the only early speed of the match up; he had shown natural speed in three prior sprints and now was stretching out to face six rivals who could be classified as stretch-running types.

The second thing was not so easy to see — unless you had access to the past performances of René Araya's eight previous winners:

Cape Verde
Own: R Kay Stable

VELAZQUEZ J R (163 32 28 22 .20)

Dk. b or br c. 3 (Apr)
Sire: Seeking the Gold (Mr. Prospector)
Dam: Dakar (Damascus)
Br: Hidaway Farm & Rosenberg J David (Ky)
Tr: Araya Rene A (22 4 1 1 .18)

117

Lifetime Record : 6 3 2 0 $45,109

1994	1	0	1	0	$12,089	Turf	0	0	0	0	
1993	5	3	1	0	$33,020	Wet	1	0	1	0	$2,420
Aqu ⊡	2	1	1	0	$25,289	Dist	2	1	0	0	$13,200

22Jan94- 5Aqu fst 170 ⊡ :234 :474 1:132 1:441 Count Fleet50k 80 5 1 11 1½ 12½ 21½ Velazquez J R 113 3.90 75–24 Sonny's Bruno1131½ Cape Verde1131 Hussonet1133 Speed, weakened 7
20Dec93- 6Aqu fst 6f ⊡ :224 :462 :584 1:122 Clm 50000 74 3 5 11 11 14 14½ Velazquez J R 117 6.80 81–22 Cape Verde1174½ Lightning Show117nk Sir Wollaston117¾ Driving 9
18Nov93- 2Aqu fst 7f :233 :482 1:144 1:28 Clm c-25000 66 4 7 41 1½ 13 16½ Davis R G 117 *1.40 64–25 CpeVerde1176½ TruConviction1172 CrryARos1136½ Stumbled brk, driving 7
Claimed from Mohammed Al Maktoum, Mott William I Trainer
14Oct93- 3Bel fst 1 :24 :474 1:124 1:39 Md 35000 62 1 1 2½ 1½ 11 11¼ Davis R G 118 *1.30 73–22 Cape Verde1181¼ Sir Noble1115 Promising Rainbow1182¾ Driving 8
22Sep93- 3Bel sly 7f :23 :473 1:133 1:264 Md 35000 56 11 1 1hd 11 1½ 2½ Davis R G 118 5.50 68–26 True Conviction118½ Cape Verde1182¾ King Of Kolchis1183¾ Gamely 12
20Aug93- 4Sar gd 6f :221 :46 :583 1:112 Md Sp Wt 24 8 2 76½ 65 87½ 821¾ Smith M E 118 4.00 63–15 Royal Minister1186 Speedy Harry1182½ Royce Joseph1183 Outrun, wide 8
WORKOUTS: Jan 12 Bel tr.t 5f fst 1:06 B *26/26* Jan 6 Bel tr.t 3f fst :37 B *3/16* Dec 17 Bel tr.t 4f fst :493 B *11/78* ●Nov 30 Bel tr.t 3f fst :343 H *1/22* Nov 10 Bel 5f fst 1:014 H *17/34* Nov 3 Bel 4f fst :523 B *38/39*

A year ago, almost to the day, Araya had claimed Cape Verde, a colt whose profile bore a striking resemblance to Blaze Of The Sun's. Both were well bred cast-offs from the high-powered stable of Mohammed Al Maktoum and trainer Bill Mott; both had shown natural speed in limited opportunities; both were given approximately a month off after the claim; both had recorded a best-of-morning workout in their first listed a.m. activity for Araya; both were ridden by John Velazquez.

Araya is a shrewd, low-profile trainer with a history of making astute claims. He grabbed a young New York-bred filly named McKaymackenna for $35,000 in 1992 and won three stakes with her; and he hadn't done too badly with Cape Verde, who won for $50,000 first time off the claim and then stretched out to nearly wire the Count Fleet Stakes.

A mega-rich owner like Mohammed Al Maktoum and an Eclipse-winning trainer like Bill Mott have barnfulls of the best bloodlines on earth, so they don't have a lot of time to spend on horses like Cape Verde and Blaze Of The Sun when they don't live up to their potential for one reason or another. But a guy like Araya doesn't have 60 head on the Belmont backstretch, he might have half a dozen, and thus he can devote significantly more time and attention to fixing, or at least temporarily patching up whatever problems these horses have.

Blaze Of The Sun was stepping up from maiden claimers, but that didn't have to mean he was outclassed. Just the mere fact that Maktoum and Mott had this horse originally suggests he was cut out to be a nice horse. And if one consulted *Maiden Stats*, the impression was confirmed that Blaze Of The Sun had a touch of class:

	SIRE INFO								DAM INFO												SIBLING INFO		YRLG SALES INFO	
Horse	# wnr/str	2yo wnr/str	% 1st	awd	Mud w%/sts	Turf w%/sts	% 1stT	Spl	prf	Dpl	# fls	# wnr/str	# sw	2yo wnr/str	awd	Mud w%/sts	Turf wnr/str	Dosage Index	Top Sibling	/Earn$	Price/Sire avg	# Rnk/sld
BLAZE ANGEL	17/ 23	8/ 15	33	6.3	11/ 55	0/ 5	0	0.81	w	0.02	3	0/ 1	0	0/ 1	0.0	0/ 0	0/ 0	19.00				
BLAZE AWAY	34/ 47	9/ 27	11	7.4	7/ 27	16/ 67	4	3.79	w	0.31	4	0/ 2	0	0/ 2	0.0	0/ 1	0/ 2	1.67				
BLAZED STAR	73/111	26/ 76	8	7.2	10/ 144	8/ 125	2	1.80	sw		2							3.89				
BLAZEING CLASSIC	46/ 72	17/ 48	7	6.8	6/ 182	3/ 63	0	0.52	ur	0.29	3	1/ 2	0	0/ 2	5.5	0/ 1	0/ 0	0.00	Old English Runner	/$ 5.3k		
BLAZEN CASEY	51/ 69	9/ 29	3	6.8	18/ 120	0/ 3	0	0.49	p		5							2.00				
BLAZE OF OAK	98/167	21/ 81	18	[illegible]	13/ 134	13/ 498	12	1.46	up	0.26	2	0/ 1	0	0/ 1	0.0	0/ 1	0/ 0	2.47			[illegible]	[illegible]
BLAZE OF THE SUN	317/440	94/251	13	7.7	14/ 561	11/ 732	11	4.08	up		3							3.52			$130k/$ 77k	2/ 17
BLAZER VIC	1/ 3	0/ 1	0	8.0	0/ 4	0/ 0	0	0.05	w	0.06	4	1/ 2	0	1/ 2	0.0	0/ 0	0/ 0	0.00	Barton's Bounder	/$ 1.3k		

Blaze Of The Sun was sired by Halo, whose progeny include Kentucky Derby, Preakness and Breeders' Cup Classic winner Sunday Silence, and whose average winning distance (awd) is a stamina-oriented 7.7 furlongs. This supports the assumption that he can stretch out successfully.

Particularly noteworthy is the Yearling Sales Info located on the extreme right. It reveals that, at a price of $130,000, Blaze Of The Sun was the second-most expensive of 17 Halo yearlings sold in 1992.

If one chose to look at Blaze Of The Sun in a positive light due to his pace advantage and the trainer-pattern match, a case could be made that this was an expensive yearling who was bred to handle the added distance, and who might assert his innate class if allowed to get brave on the lead.

FOURTH RACE
Aqueduct
DECEMBER 16, 1994

1⅛ MILES. (Inner Dirt)(1.47^{1}) CLAIMING. Purse $28,000. 3–year–olds. Weight, 122 lbs. Non–winners of two races at a mile or over since November 15, allowed 3 lbs. Of such a race since then, 5 lbs. Claiming price $50,000, for each $2,500 to $45,000, allowed 2 lbs. (Races when entered to be claimed for $40,000 or less not considered.)

Value of Race: $28,000 Winner $16,800; second $5,600; third $3,080; fourth $1,680; fifth $840. Mutuel Pool $185,568.00 Exacta Pool $377,165.00 Quinella Pool $71,627.00

Last Raced	Horse	M/Eqt.	A.	Wt	PP	St	¼	½	¾	Str	Fin	Jockey	Cl'g Pr	Odds $1
19Nov94 ^{5}Aqu^{1}	Blaze Of The Sun		3	117	5	4	1^{3}	1^{1}	1^{1}	1^{2½}	1^{2½}	Velazquez J R	50000	5.60
7Dec94 ^{9}Aqu^{1}	Island Skater		3	119	7	6	6^{4}	6^{5}	5^{hd}	2^{3½}	2^{2½}	Santagata N	50000	12.40
11Dec94 ^{7}Aqu^{3}	Brett's Jet	b	3	109	2	1	5^{2}	4^{hd}	6^{4}	3^{2½}	3^{½}	Perez R B^{5}	45000	a-0.45
15Nov94 ^{5}Aqu^{4}	Kristen's Baby		3	117	1	3	4^{hd}	5^{1½}	4^{hd}	4^{4}	4^{10}	Lumpkins J	50000	6.30
10Dec94 ^{4}Aqu^{5}	Minute Ryder	bf	3	113	3	7	7	7	7	5^{1}	5^{7}	Chavez J F	45000	10.20
21Nov94 ^{9}FL^{1}	Personnel Director	b	3	115	4	2	2^{1½}	2^{½}	3^{1}	7	6^{2}	Luzzi M J	45000	13.10
29Nov94 ^{4}Aqu^{1}	Churkin		3	115	6	5	3^{hd}	3^{½}	2^{hd}	6^{6}	7	Migliore R	45000	a-0.45

a–Coupled: Brett's Jet and Churkin.

OFF AT 1:48 Start Good. Won driving. Time, :24^{1}, :50, 1:15^{3}, 1:40^{2}, 1:52^{4} Track fast.

$2 Mutuel Prices:				
	6–BLAZE OF THE SUN	13.20	10.80	2.10
	7–ISLAND SKATER		14.80	2.10
	1–BRETT'S JET (a–entry)			2.10

$2 EXACTA 6–7 PAID $129.50 $2 QUINELLA 6–7 PAID $64.00

Dk. b. or br. c, (Mar), by Halo–Sol de Terre, by Mr. Prospector. Trainer Araya Rene A. Bred by Overbrook Farm (Ky).

BLAZE OF THE SUN went right to the front, made all the pace while clear, then was kept to a drive to hold sway. ISLAND SKATER rallied five wide into the lane to be clear for the place. BRETT'S JET launched a mild rally from between rivals into the lane to gain a share. KRISTEN'S BABY saved ground, raced in tight quarters into the lane, then finished evenly. A claim of foul by the rider of KRISTEN'S BABY against the rider of BRETT'S JET was not allowed. MINUTE RYDER was outrun. PERSONNEL DIRECTOR tired from his early efforts. CHURKIN raced in contention three wide to the stretch and weakened.

Owners— 1, R Kay Stable; 2, Entenmann & Sound View & Timber Bay; 3, Joques Farm; 4, Tigri Michael; 5, Caspa Stable; 6, Casson Helen G & Lanzara Ed; 7, Joques Farm

Trainers—1, Araya Rene A; 2, Entenmann William J; 3, Moschera Gasper S; 4, Barker Edward R; 5, Galluscio Dominic G; 6, Battles Jake; 7, Moschera Gasper S

Overweight: Brett's Jet (1).

Scratched— Rogersdividends (10Dec94 ^{4}AQU^{6}), Matthew Red Dog (2Dec94 ^{4}AQU^{1})

Along with a win bet, I made sure to use the exacta as a "saver" by protecting with Blaze Of The Sun underneath the entry. But after Araya's claim got loose through a half-mile split of :50 and six furlongs in 1:15 3/5, the race had effectively been turned into a three-furlong sprint, and Blaze Of The Sun had a head-start.

THE DEVELOPMENT OF CONSISTENT work habits in the areas of record-keeping and research are important, and pay off handsomely when a nugget is unearthed that's not obvious to the crowd, such as the hidden sprint form and ability to win off workouts shown by Primitive

Hall, or the remarkably similar backgrounds shared by Cape Verde and Blaze Of The Sun from the beginning of their careers until they were claimed by, and won for, René Araya.

Players are likely to find, however, that the bulk of their insights will probably be triggered through the simple task of maintaining a set of result charts, whether they are used to determine instant variants, as discussed earlier, or for clarifying a myriad of other subtleties.

For example, all five of the sprint races on a given day are won wire-to-wire. Was it due to a speed bias? The mere fact that all the sprints were won by frontrunners is inconclusive standing on its own; players must refer to the charts to see the odds: were the winners favorites or second choices (expected to run well), or were several of them implausible longshots who would've been hard-pressed to hang on under normal conditions? What were the margins of victory? Inordinately large winning margins (such as those often registered by mud larks in the slop) tend to bolster the notion that a bias influenced the results. So too, would the fact that few of the trailing horses changed positions behind the respective winners.

All these details help players gain a sharper focus into the overall picture of what's really going on during a day's races. And if the charts are read carefully enough, players will find a steady source of winners under the realm of trip handicapping.

The first thing to learn about a "tough trip" is that, as with any other piece of handicapping information, its value is directly proportionate to how many bettors know about it. A horse who breaks slowly, checks violently at the quarter pole, and finishes fastest of all when clear to wind up second by a neck is absolutely useless as a "horse to watch" if he receives a big fat trouble line in his past performances. The tough trips that are of wager-value are of a subtler nature: horses trapped on the rail who resented dirt being kicked back in their muzzle; horses forced to run in between rivals most of the way while others in the race ran freely in the clear; horses engaged in sustained battles for the lead who weaken only in the final stages, so that their finish positions and beaten lengths seem unremarkable to a crowd concerned mostly with effects and not with cause.

One of the best descriptions of this principle in action occurred with just seven shopping days until Christmas:

3 Aqueduct

INNER DIRT COURSE START · 6 FURLONGS · FINISH

6 Furlongs (Inner Dirt). (1:08³) CLAIMING. Purse $20,000. 3-year-olds. Weight, 122 lbs. Non-winners of two races since November 15, allowed 3 lbs. Of a race since then, 5 lbs. Claiming price $35,000, for each $2,500 to $30,000, allowed 2 lbs. (Races when entered to be claimed for $25,000 or less not considered.)

Clever Packets
Own: Joques Farm

MIGLIORE R (166 35 22 33 .21) $32,500

Dk. b or br g. 3 (Feb)
Sire: Clever Trick (Icecapade)
Dam: Hour Serenade (Bold Hour)
Br: Allor Fred M & Nancy L (Ky)
Tr: Moschera Gasper S (121 29 19 32 .24)

115

	Lifetime Record :	16 3 1 3	$23,180
1994	10 3 0 1	$19,517	Turf 1 0 0 0
1993	6 M 1 2	$3,663	Wet 1 0 0 0 $412
Aqu▣	1 0 0 0		Dist 6 0 0 2 $3,063

7Dec94- 6Aqu fst 6f ▣ :224 :46 :574 1:10¹ 3+ Alw 30000N1X 54 4 2 5³ 7⁶ 78½ 71³ Perez R B5 110 b 8.70 79 – 12 Vallata Lane115²¾ Expressed117¹ Senor Rex117³ Outrun 7
19Nov94- 1Aqu gd 7f :23 :46² 1:12 1:25 Clm c-22500 67 7 1 11 1² 1½ 44¾ Beckner D V5 110 b 3.15 74 – 21 Ken'sLanding112no MeanPncho112hd CrossIcePss1174½ Drifted, weakened 7
  Claimed from Sanders Melissa I, Parisella John Trainer
9Jly94- 9Pln fst 170 :224 :46⁴ 1:11 1:43 Clm c-12500N2X 61 2 2 2² 2hd 1½ 2² Warren R J Jr LB 115 b 2.60 74 – 20 ▣Go Go Louie115² Clever Packets115² Seymoure Tail115½ Held gamely 6
  Claimed from Crockett Ron, Fierce Fordell Trainer Placed first through disqualification.
10Jun94- 8GG fm 1⅟₁₆ ① :23 :47⁴ 1:12² 1:44⁴ + Clm 20000N1Y 65 2 3 31½ 2² 73½ 87 Espinoza V LB 119 b 10.30 75 – 18 Prince Midnight119hd Teriley119½ Mick's First Night119¹ 9
  Brushed, steadied midstretch
15May94- 4GG fst 1⅟₁₆ :224 :46 1:10⁴ 1:44 Clm 16000 72 1 3 3⁴ 3½ 21½ 33½ Boulanger G LB 117 b 5.40 73 – 12 ThreeStripes117³½ SheerAmbition117no CleverPackets117³½ Wide 2nd turn 7
7May94- 1GG my 1⅟₁₆ :23² :47² 1:11⁴ 1:44² Alw 12500s 64 8 1 11 1hd 35 511½ Boulanger G LB 117 b 5.40 64 – 28 Champagne Shane116⁴¾ T. C. Blue115³¾ Healbequick116nk Gave way 8
31Mar94- 4GG fst 1⅟₁₆ :222 :45⁴ 1:10³ 1:44³ Clm 12500N2L 70 4 1 1³ 1⁴ 1⁴ 1nk Lopez A D LB 119 b 8.40 74 – 26 Clever Packets119nk I Need Air119¹ Healbequick119³ Steady urging 8
5Mar94- 9GG fst 1⅟₁₆ :224 :46³ 1:12 1:45 Md 12500 65 2 1 11½ 1³ 1³ 15 Boulanger G LB 118 b 6.30 72 – 19 Clever Packets118⁵ Prince Midnight118nk Light Storm1133 Ridden out 11
11Feb94- 3GG fst 6f :223 :46¹ :59¹ 1:121 Md 12500 43 1 3 1hd 1hd 2½ 46½ Boulanger G LB 118 fb *.80 71 – 18 Riot Road118no Snow Cheifs Pride118³ Our Little Bubba118³½ Tired 9
12Jan94- 5BM fst 6f :223 :45⁴ :58¹ 1:11 Md 12500 45 9 2 2½ 2hd 3⁴ 511 Baze R A LB 118 b *.90 75 – 16 Avonworth Hi118² Sudden Stride118⁸ Vinnie's Cousin118½ Weakened 11

WORKOUTS: Nov 17 Aqu 3f fst :39 B 2/2

Fleet Call

Own: Mazur Edward

B. g. 3 (Mar)
Sire: Afleet (Mr. Prospector)
Dam: Chic and Sassy (His Majesty)
Br: Meyerhoff Robert E (Md)
Tr: Schaeffer Stephen W Jr (4 0 0 1 .00)

PEZUA J M (117 8 10 16 .07) $30,000 113

Lifetime Record: 13 3 3 3 $54,430											
1994	10	3	2	2	$49,625	Turf	6	2	1	1	$35,235
1993	3	M	1	1	$4,805	Wet	0	0	0	0	
Aqu	0	0	0	0		Dist	1	0	0	1	$1,705

2Dec94-4Aqu fst 1 :23 :461 1:12 1:384 Clm c-22500 60 2 2 2½ 1½ 23 311 Migliore R 115 b 0.95 63-28 Matthew Red Dog1127 Shepskate1134 Fleet Call1154 Bid, faltered 5
Claimed from S Kay S Stable, Seewald Alan Trainer
25Nov94-9Aqu fst 7f :23 :461 1:112 1:242 Clm 17500 84 3 5 2½ 2hd 13 15½ Smith M E 117 b *1.15 82-24 Fleet Call1175½ Creston House1106 Mutuality117nk Driving 9
16Nov94-9Aqu fst 1 :231 :47 1:121 1:381 Clm 17500 77 4 5 51½ 21 23½ 23 Smith M E 117 b 3.55 74-24 Meadowcoaster1123 Fleet Call117½ Brush Full1104 Held place 8
4Oct94-9Med yl 1 1/16 Ⓣ :224 :464 1:121 1:441 3↑ Alw 23000N2X 60 7 6 68 73 57½ 712 McCauley W H L 113 *2.20 68-20 Undue Influence1113 Babe's Honor116hd Wiloso1153½ Outrun 10
21Sep94-9Med fm 1 1/16 Ⓣ :223 :462 1:112 1:43 3↑ Alw 21000N2X 66 8 6 63 41½ 4¾ 68 McCauley W H L 113 *1.30 78-18 Thawabat116nk Knight Course1113½ Undue Influence114½ No rally 9
4Jly94-7Lrl yl 1⅛ Ⓣ :494 1:161 1:421 1:543 Alw 20000N2X 80 6 5 53¾ 63½ 36½ 22½ Seefeldt A J L 117 3.00 55-43 Winsox1172½ Fleet Call117½ Majestico1157 Rallied 7
12Jun94-10Pim fm 1⅛ Ⓣ :464 1:114 1:37 1:494 Royal Vale35k 80 2 5 410 41½ 21 33¾ Seefeldt A J L 114 3.30 82-11 Honorable Flight1221½ Majestico1142½ Fleet Call1145 Wide, hung 7
24May94-5Pim fm 1⅛ Ⓣ :471 1:122 1:382 1:512 Alw 18500N1X 82 6 10 912 88 1hd 11¾ Seefeldt A J L 120 *1.50 78-18 Fleet Call1201¾ Double Ridder1155 Deacon's Lane1151¾ Stumbled, wide 12
7May94-3Bel fm 1¼ Ⓣ :47 1:114 1:371 2:02 3↑ Md Sp Wt 83 4 2 1hd 1½ 13 11½ Seefeldt A J 115 14.10 80-13 Fleet Call1151½ Hawkeye Bay1154 Rain Alert124½ Driving 9
10Apr94-10OP fst 1 1/16 :231 :472 1:123 1:453 3↑ Md Sp Wt 63 10 10 97¾ 95½ 69½ 611¾ Seefeldt A J L 114 18.70 61-25 Maftool1201 Passing Attack1202½ Shebas Ridge114nk Improved position 10

WORKOUTS: ●Dec 13 Bel tr.t 3f fst :362 H 1/18 Nov 13 Med 4f fst :48 H 1/3 ●Oct 23 Med 3f fst :36 B 1/6

Iclaimit

Own: Valente Roddy

Ch. g. 3 (Mar)
Sire: Claim (Mr. Prospector)
Dam: Iorbit (The Pruner)
Br: Just Resting Farm (NY)
Tr: Sciacca Gary (82 7 5 7 .09)

CHAVEZ J F (248 41 27 27 .17) $30,000 113

Lifetime Record: 17 4 2 2 $75,315											
1994	15	4	2	2	$72,315	Turf	1	0	0	0	
1993	2	M	0	0	$3,000	Wet	1	1	0	0	$10,800
Aqu	3	1	0	0	$15,300	Dist	14	4	2	0	$69,795

30Nov94-2Aqu fst 6f :223 :461 :583 1:113 Clm 22500 91 2 1 12½ 12½ 13 13½ Chavez J F 117 b 3.10 84-21 Iclaimit1173½ Ken's Landing1142 Bailadoro112hd Driving 7
8Nov94-6Med fst 6f :22 :45 :574 1:111 Clm 25000 58 6 1 1hd 2hd 51½ 77 Bravo J L 119 b 2.40 78-14 Winz For Three1161½ Always There116hd Dancing Lobo1162½ Weakened 7
2Nov94-9Aqu my 6f :222 :461 :584 1:12 Clm 25000 86 1 2 12 13½ 14 12 Chavez J F 117 b *1.55 82-22 Iclaimit1172 Speedy Harry117no Ken's Landing1127½ Driving 10
18Oct94-9Aqu fst 7f :223 :452 1:104 1:24 Clm 25000 76 2 9 11 11 2hd 33¼ Chavez J F 117 b *2.35 81-15 Fabian1153 Colonel Slade110nk Iclaimit1171 Weakened 9
29Sep94-7Bel fst 6f :22 :45 :572 1:094 3↑ ⓈAlw 32000N2X 71 7 4 35 33 73¾ 69¾ Chavez J F 113 9.20 82-15 More To Tell109¾ Memories Of Linda1143 Raja's Charter1133 Tired 9
24Aug94-10Sar fst 6f :222 :452 :572 1:101 3↑ ⓈAlw 30000N2X 77 7 3 31½ 3½ 42½ 55¼ Chavez J F 113 11.20 84-13 Terrorist112½ Pro On Ice1172½ More To Tell1131½ Tired 12
31Jly94-4Sar fst 6f :222 :46 :58 1:104 3↑ ⓈAlw 30000N2X 86 7 2 43 42½ 3½ 42 Krone J A 113 *2.40 85-16 Nicks Court1141½ Night Trap116nk More To Tell111nk Led, flattened out 8
16Jly94-5Bel fm 1 1/16 Ⓣ :23 :461 1:094 1:401 3↑ ⓈAlw 32000N2X 58 7 4 41½ 32 45½ 515 Mojica R Jr 112 6.60e 82-06 My Mogul117½ Nickel Defense1134 Sunny Deputy1128 Tired 10
29Jun94-4Bel fst 6f :224 :461 :583 1:104 3↑ ⓈAlw 28000N1X 89 2 1 2½ 2½ 11 17 Krone J A 111 2.80 87-16 Iclaimit1117 Alanne117nk Gus' Pop1112 Driving 9
29May94-6Bel fst 6½f :223 :461 1:112 1:174 3↑ ⓈAlw 28000N1X 67 2 7 2½ 2hd 32 38¼ Chavez J F 119 3.90 76-19 To Ta Roo1194 Rock Star1194½ Iclaimit1193 Dueled, tired 8

WORKOUTS: Dec 10 Bel tr.t 3f fst :363 H 3/13 Nov 23 Bel tr.t 3f fst :36 H 3/12 Oct 29 Bel 3f fst :363 B 2/5 ●Oct 14 Bel 3f fst :354 H 1/10 Sep 26 Bel tr.t 4f fst :491 B 12/35

Dancing Lobo

Own: Friedman Leo

B. g. 3 (Apr)
Sire: Masked Dancer (Nijinsky II)
Dam: Larry's Girl (Larry's Reward)
Br: Wolf Thomas W (Pa)
Tr: Rowan Steve E (3 0 0 0 .00)

MCCARTHY M J (—) $30,000 113

Lifetime Record: 16 3 2 5 $43,630											
1994	13	2	2	3	$34,527	Turf	0	0	0	0	
1993	3	1	0	2	$9,103	Wet	2	0	0	1	$2,302
Aqu	0	0	0	0		Dist	10	2	0	5	$23,515

Entered 17Dec94- 7 PHA
4Dec94-7Pha fst 6f :214 :444 :572 1:104 3↑ Alw 17135N2X 73 6 1 2½ 11½ 12½ 3½ Lloyd J S L 114 b 4.30 86-15 Masterful Melody120hd Yukon Willie116½ Dancing Lobo1142 Weakened 10
23Nov94-4Aqu fst 6f :221 :463 :593 1:123 Clm 45000 64 6 2 1½ 1hd 42 77½ Colton R E 113 b 6.50e 72-21 Vallata Lane1174 Francis Marion1132¼ High Justice117nk Dueled inside 7
8Nov94-6Med fst 6f :22 :45 :574 1:111 Clm 25000 73 4 5 51½ 31 2hd 31½ Lloyd J S L 116 fb 27.00 84-14 Winz For Three1161½ Always There116hd Dancing Lobo1162½ Weakened 7
16Oct94-3Pha fst 6f :221 :452 :574 1:104 Clm 16000 74 3 2 3nk 1½ 11½ 11¾ Lloyd J S L 116 b 12.20 87-15 Dancing Lobo1161¾ Jaunty Jake1162½ X'burt119nk Drifted out, driving 7
8Oct94-8Pha fst 6½f :22 :44 1:083 1:153 ⓈPeppy Addy38k 58 4 4 2hd 3½ 56¾ 913¼ Lloyd J S L 115 b 54.60 87-13 Le Grande Pos1173½ Matienzo117½ Cloud Kicker1154 Stopped 9
6Sep94-8Pha fst 7f :222 :45 1:102 1:233 3↑ Alw 16000N3L 62 1 6 5¾ 62¾ 66½ 69 Lloyd J S L 114 b 38.80 79-16 Vigorous Factor1162¾ Loyal Opposition115¾ Rotorua116½ Blocked 1/4 12
27Aug94-8Pha fst 7f :22 :461 1:111 1:25 3↑ Alw 17135N2X 32 4 3 1hd 4½ 814 820 Lloyd J S L 113 b 15.00 61-18 Three Timer113hd Saint Phillip1223 Vigorous Factor116nk Stopped 8
13Aug94-1Sar fst 6f :221 :451 :572 1:10 Clm 45000 49 3 7 86½ 98½ 910 918¾ Rydowski S R 113 b 13.80e 72-09 Mr. Tyler1172½ Medical Pro1125½ Zeal Brown108½ Outrun 9
27Mar94-8Pha sly 6f :214 :452 :581 1:104 Alw 14500N2X 31 6 1 32 22 410 621¼ Molina V H L 122 b 5.00 66-24 Sinceilostmybaby1161½ JacquesAbord1196½ RunningRock1167½ Wide, tired 7
12Mar94-8Pha fst 7f :224 :46 1:114 1:252 Alw 16073N2X 53 1 3 11 1hd 25 29¾ Molina V H L 122 b 4.40 69-22 Catchtheconnection1179¾ DancingLobo1221 Ed'sIrishBoy122¾ No match 6

WORKOUTS: Nov 22 Pha 2f fst :234 B 1/2 ●Nov 4 Pha 4f fst :471 B 1/16 Oct 4 Pha 5f fst 1:011 B 5/16 Sep 22 Pha 4f fst :494 B 13/26

Lord Sage

Own: Reynolds David P

B. g. 3 (Apr)
Sire: Lord Gaylord (Sir Gaylord)
Dam: Foxcroft Finale (Real Value)
Br: Reynolds David P (Md)
Tr: Kelly Timothy D (31 8 5 3 .26)

LOVATO F JR (34 3 1 5 .09) $35,000 117

Lifetime Record: 5 1 0 1 $12,720											
1994	5	1	0	1	$12,720	Turf	0	0	0	0	
1993	0	M	0	0		Wet	2	1	0	1	$11,160
Aqu	3	1	0	0	$9,960	Dist	5	1	0	1	$12,720

21Jun94-7Bel fst 6f :224 :46 :571 1:092 3↑ Alw 28000N2L 60 2 4 42 41½ 57 513 Lovato F Jr 113 f 31.10 81-11 Secret Savings113hd Saratoga Shark1123 Brush Full1123 Tired 7
6Apr94-1Aqu wf 6f :22 :452 :573 1:103 Clm 50000 74 6 2 66 31½ 33 36¾ Lovato F Jr 119 3.50 82-14 Jacksome1173½ Grateful Appeal1173¼ Lord Sage1195½ No late bid 6
17Mar94-4Aqu fst 6f ⊡ :231 :471 1:00 1:13 Alw 26000N1X 77 3 6 65 43 42½ 43½ Lovato F Jr 117 8.50 75-23 ⒹDissterMstr117hd StormStrt1173 Kitty'sSg117nk Stead, pinched break 6
5Mar94-3Aqu my 6f ⊡ :232 :474 1:001 1:123 Md 50000 80 2 5 410 41½ 1hd 14 Lovato F Jr 122 12.80 80-19 LordSge1224 Shininlikedimonds1225¾ FctiousBuck1133 Blocked, driving 6
15Feb94-5Aqu fst 6f ⊡ :231 :463 :591 1:122 Md Sp Wt 38 5 8 53 97 1012 1015¼ Lovato F Jr 122 21.20 66-22 Cosa Diavolo122½ Approximate1224 Showiz122no Bumped early 11

WORKOUTS: Dec 14 Bel tr.t 5f fst 1:041 B 18/27 ●Dec 10 Bel tr.t 3f fst :35 Hg1/13 Dec 3 Bel tr.t 5f fst 1:023 B 5/15 Nov 27 Bel 4f fst :514 B 25/27 Nov 21 Bel tr.t 3f fst :374 B 8/20 Nov 16 Bel 3f fst :37 B 2/5

Lightnin' Cat

Own: Gold Montana Farm

B. g. 3 (Jan)
Sire: Storm Cat (Storm Bird)
Dam: Murlesk (Nashua)
Br: Overbrook Farm (Ky)
Tr: Jerkens Steven T (17 3 1 1 .18)

LEON F (57 2 3 7 .04) $30,000 113

Lifetime Record: 16 3 5 4 $63,960											
1994	14	3	5	4	$61,560	Turf	0	0	0	0	
1993	2	M	0	0	$2,400	Wet	2	0	0	1	$2,400
Aqu	1	0	1	0	$2,900	Dist	10	2	4	2	$42,060

8Dec94-4Aqu fst 6f ⊡ :23 :464 :592 1:122 Clm c-17500 75 6 2 2½ 33 32 2nk Perez R B5 112 1.45 81-18 Frozen Ammo117nk Lightnin' Cat112hd Brush Full1176 Willingly 8
Claimed from Davis Barbara J, Moschera Gasper S Trainer
30Nov94-2Aqu fst 6f :223 :461 :583 1:113 Clm 25000 61 5 2 33 22½ 44½ 512 Migliore R 117 *1.85 72-21 Iclaimit1173½ Ken's Landing1142 Bailadoro112hd Lacked rally 7
10Nov94-2Aqu sly 6½f :224 :47 1:114 1:181 Clm 35000 67 1 3 1½ 1hd 42½ 59¼ Beckner D V5 112 *1.10 80-19 Francis Marion1171¾ Bailadoro112nk Heavenwood1065 Dueled, tired 6
23Oct94-4Aqu fst 6f :221 :452 :573 1:101 Clm 35000 81 5 3 64½ 54 54½ 24¾ Perez R B5 114 3.45 86-11 Catchin Air1154¾ Lightnin' Cat114nk Crafty Harold115½ Up for place 7
7Oct94-2Bel fst 6f :231 :463 :582 1:102 Clm 50000 74 2 1 42 41 43½ 35¾ Perez R B5 114 *1.20 83-16 Heroic Pursuit113¾ Bold Spector1135 Lightnin' Cat114nk Boxed in 6
20Sep94-6Bel fst 6f :223 :46 :58 1:102 3↑ Alw 30000N1X 91 6 2 53½ 31 1hd 11½ Santos J A 114 *.60e 89-19 Lightnin' Cat1141½ Private Cody1131½ I'm Escapin117nk Wide, driving 8
8Sep94-6Bel fst 7f :223 :454 1:103 1:232 3↑ Alw 30000N1X 87 11 1 31 3nk 13 31¾ Beckner D V5 108 7.70 84-15 FiveStarGeneral1171 GoldstarRoad114¾ Lightnin'Ct108¾ Bid, weakened 11
14Aug94-1Sar sly 1⅛ :484 1:13 1:39 1:523 Clm c-30000 59 1 1 2½ 1½ 1hd 310¼ Bailey J D 113 1.90 63-22 PromisingRainbow117nk ATrckAttck11710 Lightnin'Ct1134 Dueled inside 5
Claimed from Tam Ping W, Lake Robert P Trainer
3Aug94-4Sar gd 7f :224 :451 1:101 1:234 Clm c-22500 82 2 5 2½ 2½ 1hd 1no Bailey J D 117 3.30 86-13 Lightnin' Cat117no Sky Cry113¾ Mill Dam1105½ Driving 7
Claimed from Young William T, Lukas D Wayne Trainer
17Jly94-9Bel fst 6f :222 :453 :581 1:113 3↑ Md 30000 79 6 3 32½ 22 21 1nk Bailey J D 112 *1.30 83-16 Lightnin' Cat112nk Stantorian1137 Super Twenty Five1165½ Driving 8

WORKOUTS: Dec 16 Bel tr.t 3f fst :393 B 5/10

Meadowcoaster

Own: Team Wizard Stable

ALVARADO F T (183 32 27 28 .17) $35,000

Ch. g. 3 (May)
Sire: Meadowlake (Hold Your Peace)
Dam: Coastland (Coastal)
Br: Carrion Jamie S (Fla)
Tr: Johnson Philip G (49 8 8 5 .16)

117

Lifetime Record:	15 2 3 2	$22,420			
1994	13 2 3 1	$20,660	Turf	1 0 0 0	$125
1993	2 M 0 1	$1,760	Wet	3 0 0 1	$1,320
Aqu	1 0 0 0	$1,260	Dist	9 1 3 2	$11,590

10Dec94-4Aqu fst 170 :241 :491 1:141 1:433 Clm 35000 80 1 1 1½ 1½ 1½ 41 Davis R G 117 5.40 79-23 Geret's Jewel117hd Cross Ice Pass113nk Mean Pancho115¾ Weakened 7
29Nov94-4Aqu wf 1 :223 :453 1:112 1:372 Clm 35000 78 3 5 42 2hd 32 55½ Luzzi M J 117 13.70 75-24 Churkin1173 Geret's Jewel117nk Rogersdividends119nk Tired 9
16Nov94-9Aqu fst 1 :231 :47 1:121 1:381 Clm 17500 82 7 2 1hd 11 13½ 13 Beckner D V5 112 7.50 77-24 Meadowcoaster1123 Fleet Call117½ Brush Full1104 Drifted, driving 8
22Oct94-7Crc fm *1 1/16 Ⓣ 1:431 3↑ Clm 32000 59 8 2 23½ 53½ 66 811¾ Rivera J A II 114 fb 59.20 76-24 Lucky Rocky1173½ Bruce What Kin1152¼ Wild Forest1151 Stopped 8
13Oct94-7Crc fst 6f :214 :452 :581 1:112 Clm 20000 67 1 4 22 24 25 58 Rivera J A II 117 fb 21.70 82-19 Ultimate Don1191¾ Miron's Gentleman115hd Lunar Force1172½ Weakened 7
1Oct94-9Crc sly 6f :214 :452 :582 1:114 3↑ Alw 17400N1X 66 7 5 64½ 66 65½ 67¾ Rivera J A II 117 fb 52.60 80-13 Ultimate Don1171 Fortuitous1171¼ Turf Star1171 Failed to menace 9
10Sep94-7Crc sly 6f :22 :453 :581 1:112 Clm 20000 68 2 5 44 45½ 37 39½ Rivera J A II 117 fb 21.30 80-17 Bye Guys1173 Third Glory1156½ Meadowcoaster117¾ Lacked response 7
25Aug94-10Crc gd 6f :221 :461 :591 1:13 3↑ Md 12500 70 8 1 2½ 1½ 16 19 Rivera J A II 118 fb *.50 82-15 Meadowcoaster1189 T. T.'s Eskimo1182¼ Gate Warrior1183¾ Ridden out 8
6Aug94-6Crc fst 1 1/16 :234 :483 1:143 1:481 3↑ Md Sp Wt 34 6 3 3½ 31½ 815 921¾ Rivera J A II 117 fb 2.30 56-16 Cool Hand Fluke1175 Regal Royal Bowl1223 Uno Mas Lead1173½ Tired 11
18Jly94-1Crc fst 6f :222 :461 :584 1:111 3↑ Md 32000 67 2 5 31½ 32½ 24 210 Rivera J A II 117 fb 5.70 81-16 LightningSurge11710 Medowcoster1172¾ Gontodrwoods1101¾ Second best 7

WORKOUTS: Nov 12 Bel tr.t 1 fst 1:45 B 2/2 Nov 8 Bel tr.t 4f fst :50 B 9/16

Level Land

Own: Pin Oak Stable

PEREZ R B (234 40 29 37 .17) $35,000

Ro. c. 3 (Apr)
Sire: Gulch (Mr. Prospector)
Dam: Strike a Balance (Green Dancer)
Br: Pin Oak Stud (Ky)
Tr: Mott William I (45 18 10 8 .40)

112[5]

Lifetime Record:	8 2 1 2	$27,700			
1994	8 2 1 2	$27,700	Turf	0 0 0 0	
1993	0 M 0 0		Wet	1 0 0 0	$1,800
Aqu	0 0 0 0		Dist	6 2 0 2	$20,400

2Dec94-6Aqu fst 6f :22 :454 :584 1:124 3↑ Clm 25000N2L 73 10 1 31 31 1½ 1¾ Perez R B5 112 b 3.30 78-21 Level Land112¾ Sunshine Ed113¾ Creston House112nk Driving 10
13Nov94-4Aqu fst 6f :231 :471 :593 1:12 3↑ Clm 25000N2L 74 5 2 22 1½ 21 35 Perez R B5 115 b 3.25 77-22 Public Terms1153¾ Colonel Slade1101¼ Level Land1153½ Bid, weakened 7
3Nov94-9Aqu fst 6f :221 :462 :584 1:114 3↑ Md 35000 69 13 1 4¾ 2hd 13 13 Krone J A 120 b *1.10 83-15 Level Land1203 Connecticut Yankee1166 Acqua Santa1202½ Ridden out 13
20Oct94-1Bel gd 6f :224 :454 :581 1:11 3↑ Md 35000 66 4 6 42 2½ 3½ 32½ Perez R B5 114 b *1.80 83-14 Plutonius1192 Charlie Cush115½ Level Land1146 No late bid 6
24Sep94-1Bel my 1 :224 :454 1:104 1:361 3↑ Md Sp Wt 33 3 2 25 46½ 414 424½ Perez R B5 113 b 2.50 57-20 CrftyTruce1182½ RoyceJosph118hd Kris'Rinbow11822 Bobbled break, tired 4
11Sep94-1Bel fst 6f :223 :46 :574 1:10 3↑ Md Sp Wt 63 7 4 33 2½ 33 47¾ Perez R B5 113 b 2.30 83-08 Timeless Dream1183 Expressed1223 Cozy Prospect1181¾ Bid, tired 7
19Jly94-5Bel fst 7f :224 :454 1:112 1:243 3↑ Md Sp Wt 77 7 1 2½ 2hd 1hd 21¼ Velazquez J R 116 b 10.30 79-19 Crafty Mist1161¼ Level Land1165½ Fleet Stalker1163½ Gamely 9
17Jun94-9Bel fst 6f :221 :452 :58 1:11 3↑ Md Sp Wt 68 6 10 74 74½ 75½ 55¾ Mickens T J7 107 b 23.20 80-15 Thru 'n Thru1141¼ DBall's Bluff1141¼ Changing Rahy114nk No threat 10

WORKOUTS: Dec 15 Bel tr.t 3f fst :382 B 7/11 Nov 30 Bel 3f fst :39 B 5/8 ●Oct 28 Bel 6f fst 1:143 H 1/4 Oct 20 Bel 5f fst 1:032 B 4/7 Oct 14 Bel 3f fst :373 B 7/10 Sep 22 Bel 4f fst :513 B 49/53

Heavenwood

Own: Amrlati John J

SANTAGATA N (107 8 12 9 .07) $30,000

B. g. 3 (May)
Sire: Baederwood (Tentam)
Dam: Failing Light (Cyane)
Br: Manfuso Robert T & Voss Katherine M (Md)
Tr: Ferraro James W (13 1 3 2 .08)

113

Lifetime Record:	18 4 2 3	$51,803			
1994	15 2 1 3	$38,483	Turf	1 0 0 0	
1993	3 2 1 0	$13,320	Wet	2 0 0 1	$3,660
Aqu	0 0 0 0		Dist	3 1 1 0	$7,455

4Dec94-9Aqu fst 7f :224 :46 1:103 1:232 3↑ Alw 32000N2X 75 5 4 52 62¾ 56½ 510½ Valdivia J10 106 b 20.90 77-15 Crafty1173½ Our Emblem1151 Brett's Jet1152¾ Saved ground 9
29Nov94-4Aqu wf 1 :223 :453 1:112 1:372 Clm 32500 82 8 2 21½ 3nk 21½ 43½ Rodriguez O7 108 b 7.60 77-24 Churkin1173 Geret's Jewel117nk Rogersdividends119nk Forced pace, tired 9
10Nov94-2Aqu sly 6½f :224 :47 1:114 1:181 Clm 30000 84 6 1 41 3nk 32 32 Rodriguez O7 106 b 3.15 88-19 Francis Marion1171¾ Bailadoro112nk Heavenwood1065 Wide trip 6
19Oct94-9Aqu fst 7f :223 :453 1:104 1:24 Clm 17500 85 3 7 43½ 3½ 12 14½ Rodriguez O7 110 b 5.90 84-20 Heavenwood1104½ ATrckAttck1175 CrestonHouse117¾ Stead 3/8 pl, drvg 10
30Sep94-7Bel fst 1 1/16 :232 :471 1:124 1:444 Clm 35000 65 6 2 2hd 42 411 318 Beckner D V5 112 b 9.90 60-29 Brett's Jet1177 Mean Pancho11211 Heavenwood112nk Dueled, tired 7
16Sep94-7Bel fm 1 Ⓣ :23 :452 1:083 1:33 3↑ Alw 34000N2X 54 6 4 67 88½ 915 918 Davis R G 113 b 64.00 79-13 Jido1082½ Bermuda Cedar1142 Limited War1132 Done early 11
24Aug94-2Sar fst 1⅛ :464 1:12 1:382 1:514 Clm c-25000 68 3 6 49 62¾ 64 46½ Krone J A 117 b 4.40 70-23 C. Lenny Runn1171¼ Churkin1173½ Creston House1172 Checked turn 9
Claimed from Manfuso Robert T, Voss Katharine M Trainer
9Aug94-7Pim fst 6f :23 :454 :59 1:121 3↑ Alw 18000N2X 63 7 6 57 56½ 66¼ 86 Pino M G L 114 b 4.40 80-13 Hagley's Hero117¾ Algebar Henderson1191 Harundale1171½ Wide 9
16Jly94-8Lrl fst 7f :23 :461 1:104 1:232 RCavalier Cup35k 61 1 6 1½ 1½ 55½ 813½ Pino M G 114 b 11.20 78-12 Canton River1221½ Can't Be Denied1223¼ Foxie G1223¾ Tired 8
28Jun94-6Lrl fst 6f :22 :452 :574 1:104 Clm 30000 82 7 2 24 24 23 21¾ Prado E S 117 b *1.50 84-14 Gallant Impression1151¾ Heavenwood117hd Cache And Carry1172 Closed 7

WORKOUTS: Oct 13 Aqu 3f fst :39 B 2/2

Heavenwood had gone on my "Horses to Bet a Lung On" list on the basis of an excruciatingly difficult trip going a one-turn mile on November 29. But those who hadn't seen the race and/or supplemented their visual impressions with an inspection of the chart would hardly notice a thing, since the comment line for the effort read, "Forced pace, tired," which is about as mundane as a comment line gets.

Handicappers need to know: what kind of pace was it, and what kind of effort was involved in being among the leaders?

The first question was answered easily enough: the $35,000 claimer for 3-year-olds had featured internal splits of :22 3/5, :45 3/5 and 1:11 2/5, and a check of the seven other one-turn races — three each at six and seven furlongs, and one other at a mile — showed that Heavenwood's race had been contested through the fastest quarter-mile on the card, and that the half-mile split was fastest of the day by three ticks. Notably, the older $35,000 claimer Yeckley (refer back to his pp's from earlier in this chapter) had wired his field after carving out a half in :47, and had come back to win a $50,000 claimer off the stretchout.

SECOND RACE
Aqueduct
NOVEMBER 29, 1994

7 FURLONGS. (1.20^{1}) CLAIMING. Purse $20,000. 3-year-olds and upward. Weights: 3-year-olds, 120 lbs. Older, 122 lbs. Non-winners of two races since October 15, allowed 3 lbs. Of a race since then, 5 lbs. Claiming price $35,000, for each $2,500 to $30,000, allowed 2 lbs. (Races when entered to be claimed for $25,000 or less not considered.)

Value of Race: $20,000 Winner $12,000; second $4,400; third $2,400; fourth $1,200. Mutuel Pool $137,577.00 Exacta Pool $274,304.00 Quinella Pool $64,001.00

Last Raced	Horse	M/Eqt.	A.	Wt	PP	St	¼	½	Str	Fin	Jockey	Cl'g Pr	Odds $1
15Nov94 ^{8}Aqu^{6}	Yeckley	f	4	117	5	1	$1^{1\frac{1}{2}}$	$1^{\frac{1}{2}}$	1^{2}	1^{4}	Luzzi M J	35000	1.25
22Nov94 ^{6}Aqu^{6}	Current Impact	bf	4	122	7	2	2^{2}	$2^{1\frac{1}{2}}$	2^{3}	2^{hd}	Migliore R	35000	2.65
22Nov94 ^{7}Aqu^{7}	Birdie's Fly	f	4	117	2	5	$3^{\frac{1}{2}}$	$3^{\frac{1}{2}}$	$3^{\frac{1}{2}}$	3^{3}	Luttrell M G	35000	6.40
25Nov94 ^{4}Aqu^{7}	Berseto		5	113	6	3	5^{3}	$5^{3\frac{1}{2}}$	$4^{\frac{1}{2}}$	$4^{\frac{3}{4}}$	Madrid A Jr	30000	18.10
8Nov94 ^{6}Aqu^{4}	Green Gaitor		5	117	1	6	$4^{\frac{1}{2}}$	4^{hd}	$5^{1\frac{1}{2}}$	5^{1}	Velazquez J R	35000	a-3.40
18Nov94 ^{4}Aqu^{3}	Change of Fortune	b	5	113	3	4	$6^{1\frac{1}{2}}$	6^{2}	6^{5}	$6^{8\frac{1}{2}}$	Davis R G	30000	a-3.40
17Jly94 ^{4}Sar^{6}	Account Number	bf	5	117	4	7	7	7	7	7	Mojica R Jr	35000	11.90

a-Coupled: Green Gaitor and Change of Fortune.

OFF AT 12:55 Start Good. Won driving. Time, :23^{2}, :47, 1:11^{4}, 1:24^{2} Track wet fast.

$2 Mutuel Prices:			
4-(E)-YECKLEY	4.50	3.00	2.60
6-(G)-CURRENT IMPACT		2.80	2.50
2-(B)-BIRDIE'S FLY			3.30

$2 EXACTA 4-6 PAID $12.40 $2 QUINELLA 4-6 PAID $6.90

What kind of an effort had Heavenwood put forth? Take a moment to examine the November 29 chart, paying particular attention to positions and beaten lengths margins at each point of call:

FOURTH RACE
Aqueduct
NOVEMBER 29, 1994

1 MILE. (1.32^{2}) CLAIMING. Purse $21,000. 3-year-olds. Weight, 122 lbs. Non-winners of two races at a mile or over since October 15, allowed 3 lbs. Of such a race since then, 5 lbs. Claiming price $35,000, for each $2,500 to $30,000, allowed 2 lbs. (Races when entered to be claimed for $25,000 or less not considered.)

Value of Race: $21,000 Winner $12,600; second $4,620; third $2,520; fourth $1,260. Mutuel Pool $156,692.00 Exacta Pool $344,624.00 Quinella Pool $75,683.00

Last Raced	Horse	M/Eqt.	A.	Wt	PP	St	¼	½	¾	Str	Fin	Jockey	Cl'g Pr	Odds $1
20Nov94 ^{7}Aqu^{1}	Churkin		3	117	9	2	$6^{1\frac{1}{2}}$	$5^{\frac{1}{2}}$	1^{hd}	$1^{1\frac{1}{2}}$	1^{3}	Alvarado F T	35000	3.55
30Oct94 ^{7}Aqu^{9}	Geret's Jewel	bf	3	117	5	6	9	9	6^{1}	4^{hd}	2^{nk}	Samyn J L	35000	8.00
16Nov94 ^{4}Aqu^{1}	Rogersdividends	b	3	119	6	5	7^{4}	$7^{3\frac{1}{2}}$	5^{1}	$5^{1\frac{1}{2}}$	3^{nk}	Migliore R	35000	6.60
10Nov94 ^{2}Aqu^{3}	Heavenwood	b	3	108	8	1	2^{1}	2^{hd}	$3^{\frac{1}{2}}$	$2^{\frac{1}{2}}$	4^{2}	Rodriguez O^{7}	32500	7.60
16Nov94 ^{9}Aqu^{1}	Meadowcoaster		3	117	3	9	5^{1}	$4^{1\frac{1}{2}}$	2^{hd}	3^{hd}	5^{4}	Luzzi M J	35000	13.70
3Nov94 ^{8}Lrl^{8}	Roaring Times	b	3	115	7	4	$8^{\frac{1}{2}}$	$8^{\frac{1}{2}}$	$7^{1\frac{1}{2}}$	7^{4}	6^{1}	Davis R G	30000	a-1.10
29Oct94 ^{11}Crc^{6}	Free Agent	bf	3	117	2	7	$3^{\frac{1}{2}}$	$1^{1\frac{1}{2}}$	$4^{1\frac{1}{2}}$	$6^{\frac{1}{2}}$	$7^{7\frac{1}{2}}$	Chavez J F	35000	a-1.10
12Nov94 ^{2}Aqu^{1}	Dependableness	b	3	117	1	8	$4^{\frac{1}{2}}$	6^{hd}	9	8^{2}	8	Leon F	35000	57.25
19Nov94 ^{6}Aqu^{7}	Publicized		3	119	4	3	$1^{\frac{1}{2}}$	$3^{\frac{1}{2}}$	$8^{\frac{1}{2}}$	9	—	Maple E	35000	11.80

Publicized:Eased
a-Coupled: Roaring Times and Free Agent.

OFF AT 1:51 Start Good. Won driving. Time, :22^{3}, :45^{3}, 1:11^{2}, 1:37^{2} Track wet fast.

$2 Mutuel-Prices:			
2B-(M)-CHURKIN	9.10	4.90	4.20
7-(G)-GERET'S JEWEL		6.50	6.90
8-(I)-ROGERSDIVIDENDS			5.60

$2 EXACTA 2-7 PAID $71.00 $2 QUINELLA 2-7 PAID $39.00

Dk. b. or br. c, (May), by Allen's Prospect-Kahaila, by Pitcairn. Trainer Moschera Gasper S. Bred by Paulson Allen E (Ky).

CHURKIN settled just off the early pace, rallied four wide on the turn, took the lead in upper stretch, then drew away under brisk urging. GERET'S JEWEL trailed to the turn then rallied belatedly. ROGERSDIVIDENDS unhurried for a half, advanced five wide into the stretch then closed late to gain a share. HEAVENWOOD forced the pace while three wide to the turn then weakened in the drive. MEADOWCOASTER raced in close contention between horses to the top of the stretch and tired. ROARING TIMES was never a factor while racing wide. FREE AGENT moved through along the rail to gain a clear advantage approaching the far turn, gave way after going six furlongs. DEPENDABLENESS was finished early. PUBLICIZED was used up battling for the early and was eased late. ROARING TIMES and PUBLICIZED wore mud caulks.

Owners— 1, Joques Farm; 2, Donaldson Robert; 3, Jewel-E Stables; 4, Amriati John J; 5, Team Wizard Stable; 6, Zimpom Stable; 7, Zimpom Stable; 8, Harbor View Farm; 9, Tam Ping W

Trainers—1, Moschera Gasper S; 2, Ferriola Peter; 3, Friedman Mitchell; 4, Ferraro James W; 5, Johnson Philip G; 6, Barbara Robert; 7, Kelly Michael J; 8, Hernandez Ramon M; 9, Lake Robert P

Corrected weight: Roaring Times (115).

Scratched— Currant Mountain (17Nov94 ^{8}AQU^{10}), Catchin Air (23Nov94 ^{6}AQU^{2}), Matthew Red Dog (24Nov94 ^{4}AQU^{3}), Crooked Heels (22Sep94 ^{6}BEL^{6}), Clever Packets (19Nov94 ^{1}AQU^{4})

Let's begin with the first quarter (especially since, in races at a mile, this call appears merely as a "2" when the past performances are generated). Note that Heavenwood was strongly pressing the split of :22 3/5, just half a length behind Publicized. Using the footnote in tandem with the numbers in the points of call, try to form a mental image of how the race has developed after half a mile, as the field approaches the turn: Heavenwood is still second, but there is a new leader, as Free Agent "...moved through along the rail to gain a clear advantage." Heavenwood has overtaken Publicized by a head, and Publicized is in turn just half a length in front of Meadowcoaster, so four horses are within two lengths of each other on the front. The 3/4 call, a.k.a. the six-furlong call, covers the action around the far turn. At this point, there is *another new leader as* Churkin "...rallied four wide." Meadowcoaster is now a head in front of Heavenwood, and the first three horses are battling heads apart. Free Agent, who had rushed to the lead leaving the backstretch, has begun to tire from his exertions and has dropped to fourth, half a length behind Heavenwood. The stretch call is where Heavenwood earns his stripes: Churkin has swept by to a clear lead, but Heavenwood has *regained* second position from Meadowcoaster. In the final furlong, after a prolonged and grueling fight on the front-end to beat back several challenges, Heavenwood "weakens" to finish fourth, beaten a pair of necks by Geret's Jewel and Rogersdividends, two stretch-running vultures who attacked the exhausted pacesetters to get second and third money in the final strides. Significantly, three horses who were involved in the fight with Heavenwood during various stages of the fastest-paced race of the day, Publicized, Free Agent and Meadowcoaster, all finished well behind our hero.

Wow! Let's bet the ranch next time!

Unfortunately, trainer James Ferraro saddled his charge with an impossible task five days later by throwing him into an exceptionally strong "two other than" allowance with a triple-bug up. Even so, Heavenwood managed to split the field at better than 20-1. The fractions from that $32,000 allowance (:22 4/5, :46 and 1:10 3/5) were comparable to what an overnight handicap field chasing a $46,000 purse had recorded two races earlier:

SEVENTH RACE	7 FURLONGS. (1.20¹) HANDICAP. Purse $46,000. 3-year-olds and upward. Weights Thursday, December 1. Declarations by 10:00 A.M. Friday, December 2. Closed Thursday December 1, with 10 nominations.

Aqueduct
DECEMBER 4, 1994

Value of Race: $46,000 Winner $27,600; second $10,120; third $5,520; fourth $2,760. Mutuel Pool $188,992.00 Exacta Pool $330,765.00

Last Raced	Horse	M/Eqt. A.Wt	PP	St	¼	½	Str	Fin	Jockey	Odds $1
15Oct94 5Bel2	Fabersham	b 6 116	7	3	7²	7⁴	4½	1hd	Migliore R	b-0.00
22Nov94 6Aqu1	Senor Cielo	7 114	4	1	3⁵	2½	1½	2¹	Alvarado F T	b-0.00
15Nov94 8Aqu3	Ⓓ Golden Tent	bf 5 118	1	8	4½	52½	63·	3¾·	Nelson D	*1.55
27Nov94 7Aqu1	Aztec Empire	b 4 115	2	7·	51½	4hd	5hd	4½	Samyn J L	1.55
30Oct94 8Aqu7	Kyoko	4 114	8	4·	8	8	71½	5¾	Madrid A Jr	a-8.70
27Nov94 7Aqu5	Prospector's Flag	4 112	6	2	1²	1½	3½	6nk	Cruz E F	24.25
15Oct94 10Lrl8	Astudillo-IR	4 112	3	5	2½	3⁶	2hd	77½	Maple E ·	a-8.70
30Oct94 8Aqu6	Chief Desire	4 122	5	6	6²	6hd	8	8	Chavez J F	2.50

*—Actual Betting Favorite.
Ⓓ–Golden Tent disqualified and placed 4th.
a–Coupled: Kyoko and Astudillo–IR.
b–Coupled: Fabersham and Senor Cielo.

OFF AT 3:12 Start Good. Won driving. Time, :22⁴, :45³, 1:10⁴, 1:24 Track fast.

$2 Mutuel Prices:
4–(B)–AZTEC EMPIRE	5.10	2.80	2.10
3–(A)–GOLDEN TENT		2.60	2.20
1A–(I)–KYOKO (a-entry)			2.30

$2 EXACTA 4-3 PAID $12.80

I bet $20 win & place in the rather unlikely event he was sharp enough to pull off a real stunner. Needless to say, I was thrilled to see him back in against 3-year-old $35,000 claimers two weeks later. The morning-line favorite was Iclaimit, and players are encouraged to check out his Beyer Speed Figure pattern. The in-and-outer is fresh from a big win with a figure of 91, and we can see three previous instances where he bounced immediately following similar good efforts: from an 89 to a 58 (excusable perhaps, since the 58 came on turf); from an 86 to a 77 (with no apparent mishap); and from an 86 to a 58 at the Meadowlands (perhaps he didn't respond well to Lasix, and/or competing "under the lights"). One thing for sure is that we shouldn't have to make all kinds of excuses to explain away several bad races from 8-5 shots, particularly when they appear ready to bounce. Plus, Iclaimit liked to have things his own way on the lead, and that wasn't a likely scenario due to the presence of several other speed-types, including Heavenwood, who, to recall, had not been easily discouraged in his most recent outing at today's level.

It was a Sunday and the Litfins were off to the mall for some last-minute shopping, so I wagered in advance at the neighborhood off-track betting parlor, expecting something along the lines of 6-1. It was with much consternation that I turned on the cable show that evening to see that Heavenwood had been sent off at only 3-1, and that he was involved in another dogfight on the front-end.

THIRD RACE **6 FURLONGS.** (Inner Dirt)(1.083) **CLAIMING.** Purse $20,000. 3-year-olds. Weight, 122 lbs. Non-winners of two races since November 15, allowed 3 lbs. Of a race since then, 5 lbs. Claiming price $35,000, for each $2,500 to $30,000, allowed 2 lbs. (Races when entered to be claimed for $25,000 or less not considered.)

Aqueduct
DECEMBER 18, 1994

Value of Race: $20,000 Winner $12,000; second $4,000; third $2,200; fourth $1,200; fifth $600. Mutuel Pool $195,886.00 Exacta Pool $441,893.00

Last Raced	Horse	M/Eqt.	A.	Wt	PP	St	¼	½	Str	Fin	Jockey	Cl'g Pr	Odds $1
4Dec94 9Aqu5	Heavenwood	b	3	113	9	3	3½	2hd	1hd	1hd	Santagata N	30000	3.35
2Dec94 6Aqu1	Level Land	b	3	112	8	2	21	1½	2hd	2nk	Perez R B5	35000	14.20
8Dec94 4Aqu2	Lightnin' Cat	b	3	113	6	4	4hd	31	31½	3½	Leon F	30000	6.20
21Jun94 7Bel5	Lord Sage	f	3	117	5	8	84	61	4hd	4nk	Lovato A J	35000	12.50
10Dec94 4Aqu4	Meadowcoaster		3	117	7	1	1hd	51	53	56½	Alvarado F T	35000	8.90
2Dec94 4Aqu3	Fleet Call	b	3	113	2	5	6½	72	63	65½	Pezua J M	30000	10.40
4Dec94 7Pha3	Dancing Lobo	b	3	113	4	9	9	83	73	73½	McCarthy M J	30000	14.60
7Dec94 6Aqu7	Clever Packets	b	3	115	1	6	5hd	9	8½	84½	Migliore R	32500	14.70
30Nov94 2Aqu1	Iclaimit	b	3	113	3	7	72	4hd	9	9	Chavez J F	30000	1.60

OFF AT 1:25 Start Good. Won driving. Time, :231, :471, :593, 1:121 Track fast.

$2 Mutuel Prices:			
9–HEAVENWOOD	8.70	6.10	4.00
8–LEVEL LAND		12.00	6.10
6–LIGHTNIN' CAT			4.90

$2 EXACTA 9–8 PAID $103.50

B. g, (May), by Baederwood–Failing Light, by Cyane. Trainer Ferraro James W. Bred by Manfuso Robert T & Voss Katherine M (Md).

HEAVENWOOD was prominent from the start, moved to near equal terms with LEVEL LAND in upper stretch, then proved best after a long drive. LEVEL LAND was with the pace from the start, edged clear on the turn, then battled gamely when challenged to drop a close decision after a long drive. LIGHTNIN' CAT finished willingly three wide for a share. LORD SAGE came in slightly at the break, then finished well outside but could not get up. MEADOWCOASTER raced in contention but lacked a solid closing response. FLEET CALL came in at the break, then failed to be a factor. DANCING LOBO took up at the start when in tight. ICLAIMIT took up at the start when pinched back, moved to a striking position four wide approaching the stretch, then flattened out. FLEET CALL and LIGHTNIN' CAT raced with mud caulks.

Thankfully, Heavenwood was just as game as he had been on November 29, and eked out a hard-fought win to pay $8.70. Had I known he would be that short a price, I might've used him as a key in exactas or in the Pick 3, or lowered the win bet. Sometimes, ignorance is bliss.

As happened to me with Heavenwood, you'll get lucky and cash a ticket now and then without access to all the latest information — in this particular case, the odds, which were lower than expected. In the long run, however, ignorance is not bliss. Late-breaking information provides alert players with a significant edge, a point that was driven home effectively by the seventh race of January 12:

7 **Aqueduct**

1 MILE 70 YARDS **(Inner Dirt). (1:393) ALLOWANCE. Purse $46,000. Fillies and mares, 4-year-olds and upward which have not won a race of $22,000 at one mile or over in 1994/95. Weight, 122 lbs. Non-winners of $20,000 at one mile or over in 1994/95, allowed 3 lbs. Of $20,000 since August 1, 5 lbs. Of $20,000 in 1994, 7 lbs. (Maiden, claiming, starter and restricted races not considered.)**

Coupled – Ensign Joanne and Avie's Daisy

Little Buckles
Own: Jay Cee Jay Stable & Wachtel Edward
NELSON D (46 9 3 3 .20)

Ch. f. 4
Sire: Buckley Boy (Alydar)
Dam: Petite Nina (Native Aid)
Br: Sheehan Farms Ltd (Ont-C)
Tr: Destefano John M Jr (8 0 2 2 .00)

115

Lifetime Record:	21 4 5 5	$157,581			
1994	13 3 3 3	$124,788	Turf	1 0 0 0	
1993	8 1 2 2	$32,793	Wet	5 1 0 0	$18,792
Aqu	7 2 2 2	$68,022	Dist	9 2 2 2	$90,228

16Dec94–8Aqu	fst	170	[•]	:231	:48	1:141	1:45	3↑	ⒻAlw 38000N4X	60	2	2	2hd	2hd	35½	49½	Luzzi M J		115 b	3.20	63–30	Miss Pocket Court1176 Footing1103 Dixie Luck115½	Tired	5
2Dec94–8Med	fst	1 1/16		:232	:461	1:103	1:42	3↑	ⒻPrncssRooney40k	76	4	1	1½	1hd	34	311¼	Luzzi M J	L	113 b	5.40	90–11	Why Be Normal1176 Naked Glory1135¼ Little Buckles113nk	Weakened	10
18Nov94–6Aqu	fst	6½f		:224	:454	1:094	1:16	3↑	ⒻAlw 42000N$Y	83	3	3	42½	32½	35	28	Davis R G		112 b	9.40	93–14	InsideInformtion1208 LittleBuckles112hd RechForClvr11710	Up for place	5
5Nov94–10Med	fst	170		:223	:453	1:111	1:42		ⒻCoopersFerry35k	46	2	6	67½	53¾	714	722¼	Luzzi M J		112 b	1.90	64–19	Perfect Night1142½ Just A Little Kiss1164 Family Effort1122	No factor	8
16Oct94–7Bel	fst	1		:233	:47	1:113	1:381	3↑	ⒻAlw 46000N$Y	90	4	3	31	1½	1hd	3¾	Luzzi M J		112 b	7.60	71–27	Incinerate122½ Imah115nk Little Buckles1124¼	Bid weakened	6
23Sep94–8Bel	my	7f		:23	:46	1:093	1:221	3↑	ⒻAlw 36000N4X	72	2	4	43	32½	45½	511½	Luzzi M J		113 b	3.40	81–14	Footing113nk Aly's Conquest1156 Big Rhonda1155	No factor	5
8May94–8Bel	my	1		:224	:452	1:093	1:341		ⒻAcorn-G1	51	5	4	21½	33½	510	523¾	Luzzi M J		121 b	7.20	68–17	InsideInformtion12111 CinnmonSugr1211½ SovereignKitty1213¾	Gave way	5
23Apr94–5Aqu	fst	1		:232	:463	1:104	1:362	3↑	ⒻAlw 33000N3X	92	6	1	1½	11	13½	11¼	Luzzi M J		111 b	2.60	86–25	Little Buckles1111¼ Wings Point1193½ Quinpool1191	Driving	6
2Apr94–9Spt	fst	1 1/16		:23	:473	1:121	1:45		ⒻNatJClubOaks150k	89	2	4	31	22	2hd	2½	Luzzi M J		115 b	*1.70	90–13	Forcing Bid117½ Little Buckles1153¾ Merry Colleen113nk	Willingly	10
6Mar94–8Aqu	fst	1 1/16	[•]	:242	:483	1:132	1:454		ⒻBusher BCH-G3	75	7	3	3½	3nk	2hd	32	Luzzi M J		114	1.30	74–24	Forcing Bid1122 Ask Shananie118hd Little Buckles114nk	Willingly	7

WORKOUTS: Jan 6 Bel tr.t 4f fst :484 H *4/32* Dec 31 Bel tr.t 5f fst 1:004 H *2/14* ●Oct 29 Bel tr.t 5f fst :59 H *1/10*

Endless Desire

Own: R Paradise Stable

PEREZ R B (153 27 26 20 .18)

B. m. 6
Sire: Manila (Lyphard)
Dam: Lepa (Fappiano)
Br: Tilly Foster Farms (NY)
Tr: Bailie Sally A (4 0 0 1 .00)

112⁵

Lifetime Record :	29 5 5 6	$168,770			
1994	10 1 1 4	$47,490	Turf	3 0 0 0	
1993	14 2 3 2	$84,520	Wet	2 0 0 0	$200
Aqu	7 1 2 1	$47,420	Dist	6 1 1 1	$44,180

22Dec94- 8Aqu fst 6f ▣ :23 :463 :59 1:114 3↑ⒻAlw 42000N$Y 81 3 5 43½ 44 44 33½ Perez R B5 110 3.55 80-22 Reach For Clever1153 Via Dei Portici115½ Endless Desire1103¾ Mild rally 7
8Dec94- 8Aqu fst 6f ▣ :224 :463 :59 1:114 3↑ⒻAlw 42000N$Y 78 1 8 42½ 52½ 51¾ 42¾ Velazquez J R 117 7.30 81-18 Marilyn's Magic114¾ Personal Girl114½ Via Dei Portici1141½ Broke slowly 9
23Nov94- 8Aqu fst 6f :223 :463 :59 1:114 3↑ⒻAlw 42000N$Y 77 1 5 41½ 42½ 44½ 36½ Velazquez J R 115 9.00 76-21 Lilly's Moment1193½ Marilyn's Magic1153 Endless Desire1151½ No late bid 5
4Jun94- 8Atl fst 5½f :213 :443 :564 1:031 3↑ⒻAlw 11000N2Y 80 2 5 54½ 44½ 37 37½ Molina V H L 119 3.60 93-12 Cool Number1192¾ Princess Sybil1154¾ Endless Desire1195½ Mild rally 5
25May94- 6GS sly 1 :24 :471 1:113 1:371 3↑ⒻAlw 20000N$mY 65 5 4 43 55½ 511 615½ Molina V H L 115 3.00 80-14 Secret Assembly1157¾ Rocky Marshua1153 Acting Proud119½ Tired 6
6May94- 8Pha fst 6f :214 :452 :582 1:113 3↑ⒻAlw 21000N$Y 70 6 6 64½ 54½ 45 32¾ Molina V H 116 6.90 80-20 Cool Number116nk Clever Mary1162½ Endless Desire1162 Finished well 7
16Apr94- 5Aqu sly 6f :213 :444 :571 1:102 ⒻHandicap50k 28 3 4 412 510 517 526½ Migliore R 114 7.40 63-09 Strategic Reward112nk Air Port Won115½ Deputy Miss1146¾ Outrun 5
20Mar94- 8Aqu fst 6f ▣ :223 :454 :582 1:111 3↑ⒻDistaff H-G2 73 5 5 65½ 86¾ 710 610¾ Migliore R 113 12.20 76-21 Classy Mirage1144½ Jill Miner1141¾ Air Port Won109½ No factor 8
15Feb94- 6Aqu fst 6f ▣ :222 :454 :583 1:112 ⒻHandicap40k 91 1 5 47 45½ 42 1no Migliore R 116 6.20 86-22 Endless Desire116no Deputy Miss1181½ Air Port Won1162½ Driving 7
27Jan94- 6Aqu fst 1⅛ ▣ :234 :481 1:142 1:48 ⒻAlw 34000N4X 81 3 2 2½ 21 22½ 24 Migliore R 117 2.60 61-35 Fleeting Ways1174 Endless Desire1174½ All Power11215 Second best 5

WORKOUTS: ●Jan 4 Bel tr.t 5f fst :593 H 1/27 Dec 31 Bel tr.t 5f fst 1:03 B 3/14 Dec 16 Bel tr.t 5f fst 1:03 B 12/29 Dec 1 Bel 3f fst :36 H 2/9 Nov 21 Bel 3f fst :37 B 7/16 Nov 11 Bel 5f fst 1:013 B 4/10

Shellster

Own: Willmott Stables

VELAZQUEZ J R (135 17 19 15 .13)

Dk. b or br f. 4
Sire: Seattle Slew (Bold Reasoning)
Dam: Weber City Miss (Berkley Prince)
Br: Allen Joseph & Seminole Syndicate (Ky)
Tr: Hushion Michael E (42 9 3 9 .21)

115

Lifetime Record :	9 3 2 2	$68,565			
1994	9 3 2 2	$68,565	Turf	0 0 0 0	
1993	0 M 0 0		Wet	3 0 1 1	$9,960
Aqu	0 0 0 0		Dist	4 1 1 1	$29,565

17Dec94- 9TP my 1⅛ :224 :454 1:103 1:431 3↑ⒻMy Charmer47k 70 3 7 78 77½ 79 913¾ Kutz D 114 8.40 77-20 Sadie'sDream1191 Laura'sPistolette1145 BlushingMggie117nk No factor 11
3Dec94- 9TP fst 1⅛ :232 :473 1:13 1:452 3↑ⒻAlw 28400N2X 79 1 2 21½ 21 21½ 12 Arguello F A Jr 114 *1.20 80-22 Shellster1142 Enchanted Acorn1116 Fred's Affair114nk Steady drive 8
22Nov94- 8CD fst 1⅛ :243 :492 1:152 1:47 3↑ⒻAlw 39900N2X 77 9 2 2hd 1hd 1hd 2¾ Woods C R Jr 118 4.90 78-21 Best Of Memories118¾ Shellster118½ Bunting111½ Dueled, good try 10
28Oct94- 7Kee fst 1⅛ :233 :474 1:132 1:454 3↑ⒻAlw 31250N2X 74 3 3 33 21 31½ 31 Woods C R Jr 111 *2.50 79-20 Blushing Maggie115hd Naughty Pam113¾ Shellster111nk No late response 11
15Sep94- 8TP fst 1 :233 :473 1:133 1:401 3↑ⒻAlw 23100N2L 80 5 3 32 1½ 11½ 13½ Woods C R Jr 118 *.50 71-30 Shellster1183½ Karaoke Kid1158 Glad For Emily1153½ Steady urging 7
20Aug94- 1Sar my 1⅛ :50 1:151 1:394 1:522 3↑ⒻAlw 30000N1X 70 1 2 2½ 2½ 1hd 2no Davis R G 112 *1.20 74-26 Sterling Pound112no Shellster1122½ Sapor1121 Lost bob 4
23Jly94- 8Sar sly 7f :22 :451 1:102 1:24 3↑ⒻAlw 28000N1X 68 1 6 57 66 46 39½ Davis R G 112 11.20 76-12 Clever Act116¾ Recognizable1138½ Shellster1123 No threat 7
10Jun94- 3CD fst 6f :214 :454 :583 1:112 3↑ⒻMd Sp Wt 74 11 6 72¾ 44½ 31½ 1nk Martinez J R Jr 112 6.30 89-09 Shellster112nk Clever Act110¾ Garden Paradise1193 Fully extended 12
20Apr94- 5OP fst 6f :214 :454 :582 1:112 ⒻMd Sp Wt 57 12 9 88½ 74¾ 65½ 55 Valenzuela P A 120 *1.20 79-16 ColorMyBby120hd SunLightTo1203 StylishLilChoice1201½ Lacked late bid 12

WORKOUTS: Jan 4 Bel tr.t 4f fst :50 B 30/50 Dec 30 Bel tr.t 4f fst :512 B 11/20 Nov 17 CD 5f my 1:023 B 2/27 Oct 17 CD 5f fst 1:013 B 2/32

Ensign Joanne (SCR)

Own: Paraneck Stable

RYDOWSKI S R (62 7 3 2 .11)

B. m. 5
Sire: Blue Ensign (Hoist the Flag)
Dam: Holy Question (Holy War)
Br: Ketring Brenda & Gary (Fla)
Tr: Aquilino Joseph (37 4 1 5 .11)

115

Lifetime Record :	42 4 16 8	$214,601			
1994	10 1 1 1	$38,500	Turf	2 0 0 0	
1993	20 1 8 6	$114,921	Wet	7 1 5 0	$51,945
Aqu	11 1 5 3	$91,711	Dist	5 0 2 2	$40,541

22Dec94- 8Aqu fst 6f ▣ :23 :463 :59 1:114 3↑ⒻAlw 42000N$Y 72 1 6 55 55½ 57 47½ Rydowski S R 122 b 15.50 77-22 Reach For Clever1153 Via Dei Portici115½ Endless Desire1103¾ Even trip 7
15Dec94- 8Aqu fst 6f ▣ :223 :462 :591 1:123 3↑ⒻHandicap45k 67 1 4 410 47½ 45 33½ Rydowski S R 113 b 16.20 76-16 Vivano121½ Lena's Angel1223 Ensign Joanne1138½ Bothered early 5
10Dec94- 5Aqu fst 1⅛ ▣ :243 :483 1:134 1:452 3↑ⒻAlw 36000N3X 50 5 4 46½ 510 519 522½ Migliore R 117 b 9.60 55-23 Miss Fix It1172 Safe At Home1151 Manila Lila11712 Done early 5
30Nov94- 8Aqu fst 7f :232 :471 1:124 1:254 3↑ⒻAlw 34000N3X 68 5 4 42½ 31½ 53½ 54½ Rydowski S R 119 b 11.50 70-21 Big Rhonda1151½ Safe At Home115no Shiner1173 Lacked rally 7
17Nov94- 2Aqu fst 6f :223 :464 :584 1:113 3↑ⒻAlw 32000N2X 76 1 4 44½ 42½ 21½ 1½ Rydowski S R 117 b 13.00 84-16 Ensign Joanne117½ The Bink1205½ The Faster You Get1152¾ Wide, driving 5
2Nov94- 6Aqu my 6f :221 :46 :581 1:104 3↑ⒻAlw 32000N2X 67 5 7 79 54½ 37½ 211½ Rydowski S R 117 b 24.25 75-22 Recognizable11511 EnsignJoanne117½ TheFsterYouGet1156½ Up for place 7
25Jun94- 6Bel fm 1 Ⓣ :221 :451 1:094 1:333 3↑ⒻAlw 32000N2X — 6 5 751 910 — — Cruguet J 119 b 37.00 — 11 Dayflower1199 JivingAround1193½ UnchrtedWters111nk Done early, eased 9
12Jun94- 2Bel fst 1 :231 :461 1:111 1:364 3↑ⒻAlw 32000N2X 50 4 3 42 42 56½ 515 Davis R G 119 b 7.40 62-14 Jade Flush1144¾ Fittin Purrfect1111 Dancer's Gate119nk Tired 5
30May94- 4Bel fst 6½f :221 :454 1:111 1:18 3↑ⒻAlw 30000N2X 65 3 5 66½ 64¾ 64½ 47¾ Davis R G 121 b 10.00 75-16 Pamzig1214 WaterResistant1212 OurDearDn121½ Checked, pinched brk 7
18May94- 9Bel wf 6f :214 :45 :58 1:111 3↑ⒻAlw 30000N2X 71 3 5 68 77 53½ 45½ McCauley W H 119 b 15.20 79-16 Saxuality114hd Firstflagtofly1114 Lady Hunter1101½ No threat 7

WORKOUTS: Nov 24 Aqu 4f fst :49 B 1/1 Nov 12 Aqu 4f fst :494 B 7/10 Oct 25 Aqu 4f fst :492 B 2/6 Oct 19 Aqu 5f fst 1:03 B 2/3 Oct 13 Aqu 5f fst 1:011 H 2/7

Avie's Daisy

Own: Paraneck Stable

RYDOWSKI S R (62 7 3 2 .11)

Ch. m. 7
Sire: Lord Avie (Lord Gaylord)
Dam: My Little Molly (Golden Eagle II)
Br: Jilerlane Stables (Md)
Tr: Aquilino Joseph (37 4 1 5 .11)

115

Lifetime Record :	82 11 14 11	$441,425			
1995	1 0 0 0		Turf	4 0 0 0	
1994	20 6 3 1	$59,385	Wet	17 4 3 2	$127,194
Aqu	29 7 8 2	$235,589	Dist	35 6 10 3	$237,632

7Jan95- 8Aqu my 170 ▣ :243 :492 1:152 1:46 3↑ⒻWoodhaven H55k 76 5 5 42 31½ 53½ 63½ Rydowski S R 110 b 11.25 65-35 Starry Val112no Footing1131 Sterling Pound114¾ Tired 7
23Dec94- 8Aqu fst 1⅛ ▣ :241 :484 1:15 1:48 3↑ⒻHandicap50k 72 7 7 75½ 42 32 52½ Rydowski S R 114 b 7.50 62-28 Miss Pocket Court116nk Starry Val1132 Incinerate122no No factor 7
17Dec94- 8Aqu wf 1¼ ▣ :49 1:134 1:401 2:063 3↑ⒻLadies H-G2 75 4 2 31 31 63½ 68½ Pezua J M 110 b 29.75 87-35 Tara Roma1143½ Beloved Bea113hd Dancer's Gate1121½ Tired 10
2Dec94- 8Med fst 1⅛ :232 :461 1:103 1:42 3↑ⒻPrncssRooney40k 70 9 8 710 78½ 810 614¾ Rydowski S R 113 b 41.20 86-11 Why Be Normal1176 Naked Glory1135½ Little Buckles113nk No factor 10
19Nov94- 7Aqu wf 1⅛ :47 1:12 1:38 1:511 3↑ⒻHandicap50k 62 4 4 43½ 55 59½ 517¾ Bravo J 112 b 11.40 62-20 Imah1186 Tara Roma1161½ Dahar's Best111¾ No factor 5
28Oct94- 8Aqu fst 1 :231 :46 1:103 1:37 3↑ⒻAlw 46000N$mY 69 6 6 52½ 45 67½ 612 Rodriguez O7 108 b 28.50 71-23 In Her Glory1101 Aztec Hill1154 Hooded Dancer1152 No menace 7
13Oct94- 4Bel fst 1⅛ :234 :473 1:121 1:44 3↑ⒻClm 75000 77 3 6 42½ 51¾ 24 25½ Rodriguez O7 110 b 8.40 76-16 Hooded Dancer1135½ Avie's Daisy1104 Alkris113no Second best 7
5Oct94- 8Bel fst 1⅛ :234 :473 1:121 1:432 3↑ⒻAlw 46000N$mY 77 5 5 53½ 53½ 55½ 511½ Chavez J F 122 b 17.20 74-21 Incinerate1154 Aquilegia119hd Elizabeth Bay1221½ No factor 5
20Sep94- 8Bel fst 1 :241 :473 1:114 1:364 3↑ⒻAlw 46000N$Y 81 3 6 62½ 63 64½ 55¾ Pezua J M 115 b 15.60 73-23 Elizabeth Bay1191½ Imah1153½ Belle Nuit115nk No factor 6
21Aug94- 6Sar sly 1⅛ :473 1:121 1:371 1:502 3↑ⒻJA Morris H-G1 78 4 7 78½ 65 610 618¾ Chavez J F 110 b 29.10 65-25 Link River1142¾ You'd Be Surprised1206½ Dispute119½ No factor 7

WORKOUTS: Nov 27 Aqu 4f fst :493 B 7/21 Nov 13 Aqu 5f fst 1:03 B 7/10 Nov 8 Aqu 5f fst 1:01 H 2/4

Evi Bee

Own: Donaldson Robert

ALVARADO F T (118 23 20 21 .19)

Ch. f. 4
Sire: Bounding Basque (Grey Dawn II)
Dam: Spectacular Belle (Crimson Satan)
Br: Robinson J Mack (Ky)
Tr: Ferriola Peter (18 2 5 4 .11)

115

Lifetime Record :	11 4 2 1	$37,298			
1994	11 4 2 1	$37,298	Turf	2 0 0 0	
1993	0 M 0 0		Wet	2 1 0 0	$8,700
Aqu	1 0 0 0	$1,680	Dist	3 1 0 0	$11,580

21Dec94- 4Aqu fst 170 ▣ :241 :481 1:131 1:441 3↑ⒻClm c-50000 41 6 7 710 711 515 424½ Caraballo J C 116 f 20.00 53-23 S. S. Sparkle110nk Bonnie Shopper10812 Lasting Shore11712 No factor 7
Claimed from Baylis Thomas H, Hall Aimee D Trainer
18Nov94- 9Med sly 1⅛ :232 :464 1:111 1:423 ⒻHoney Bee H-G3 73 5 4 511 57½ 66¾ 57½ Caraballo J C L 116 f 18.00 90-02 Sterling Pound114¾ Footing1135¾ Perfect Night115¾ No rally 6
5Nov94- 3Suf fst 170 :233 :48 1:134 1:453 3↑ⒻAlw 13720N3X 70 2 5 65 52¾ 2½ 11½ Caraballo J C LB 118 3.50 76-27 Evi Bee1181½ Dolly116nk Fatal Romance116½ 4 wide, driving 7
15Oct94-11Rkm fm 1 Ⓣ :222 :463 1:12 1:39 3↑ⒻAlw 12740N3X 57 5 5 613 1015 1014 1011 Caraballo J C LB 118 f 14.80 79-10 Perfect Night1141½ Catch A Flight1161 Reality Gal1202 Outrun 10
18Sep94-10Rkm my 140 :242 :493 1:154 1:45 3↑ⒻAlw 11760N3L 71 1 4 47½ 21½ 11 12½ Caraballo J C LB 118 f *2.40 75-27 Evi Bee1182½ Blue Blazer1161½ Born Under A Star1151½ 3 wide, driving 8
5Sep94-10Bel fm 1⅛ Ⓣ :231 :462 1:104 1:413 ⒻClm 50000 33 2 5 74 95½ 1115 1122 Smith M E 116 f 13.70 68-13 Shahra Bay111nk Caroline Of Kent1142½ Jupiter Assembly116¾ Faded 12
13Aug94- 9Rkm fst 6f :213 :45 :573 1:102 ⒻRockette20k 69 6 5 68 612 610 37¾ Vega H LB 117 f 13.40 85-12 Carmen Copy1225¾ Runaway Fling1172 Evi Bee1171 Late run 2 wide 8
11Jly94- 8Rkm fst 6f :221 :462 :592 1:122 3↑ⒻAlw 11760N3L 67 7 6 55½ 44 23 24 Vega H LB 112 f *1.30 79-24 Preening1164 Evi Bee1121½ She's More Daring1124½ 4 wide, flattened out 9
16Jun94-10Rkm fst 6f :22 :454 :59 1:124 3↑ⒻAlw 10780N2L 62 7 6 68½ 68 36½ 14½ Caraballo J C LB 117 f *.80 81-19 Evi Bee1174½ Malingerer1161½ Flexible Curves1161½ Caught wide, driving 7
28May94- 8Suf fst 6f :221 :454 :584 1:122 3↑ⒻMd Sp Wt 72 8 1 2½ 21 3½ 1hd Jellison J A B 114 *2.10 86-14 Evi Bee114hd Amazing Silence114hd Napeno11410 2 wide, driving 10

WORKOUTS: Jan 4 Aqu ▣ 4f fst :494 B 2/12 Dec 4 Suf 5f fst 1:032 B 2/7 Oct 28 Suf 6f fst 1:192 B 1/3

Belle Nuit
Own: Amherst Stable
PEZUA J M (91 10 13 11 .11)

Ch. m. 5
Sire: Dr Carter (Caro–Ir)
Dam: Belle Noel (Tom Rolfe)
Br: Amherst Stable (NY)
Tr: Johnson Philip G (22 1 5 3 .05)

115

Lifetime Record: 22 5 2 5 $159,632											
1994	10	0	0	3	$26,680	Turf	12	3	1	4	$109,122
1993	12	5	2	2	$132,952	Wet	2	0	1	0	$4,750
Aqu	1	0	0	0	$3,000	Dist	2	0	0	0	$7,500

23Dec94-8Aqu	fst	1 1/16 ⊡	:241	:484	1:15	1:48	3↑ ⓕHandicap50k	72	6	5	41½	31½	52¼	42¾	Pezua J M	114 f	28.50	63–28	Miss Pocket Court116nk Starry Val1132 Incinerate122no	No rally	7
4Dec94-8Aqu	fst	1⅛	:493	1:143	1:392	1:52	3↑ ⓕⓈMontauk H54k	71	1	5	56	63½	510	514½	Luzzi M J	113 f	6.20	61–34	Beloved Bea1136 Hey Baba Lulu116¾ Lottsa Talc1191½	Tired	7
10Nov94-7Aqu	sly	7f	:23	:461	1:113	1:241	3↑ ⓕAlw 42000N$Y	60	2	5	39	412	515	517	Leon F	115 f	13.90	66–19	Deputy Miss1155½ Tensie's Pro108½ Via Dei Portici1151	No factor	5
20Sep94-8Bel	fst	1	:241	:473	1:114	1:364	3↑ ⓕAlw 46000N$Y	83	5	5	52½	52	43½	35	Samyn J L	115 f	8.70	74–23	Elizabeth Bay1191½ Imah1153½ Belle Nuit115nk	Mild gain	6
17Aug94-9Sar	fm	1⅛ Ⓣ	:464	1:10	1:334	1:462	3↑ ⓕⓈYaddo H86k	77	3	8	78½	76½	59	512	Samyn J L	113 fb	5.50e	83–10	Irish Linnet1231 It's Personal1115 All Tango1105	No threat	10
7Aug94-10Rkm	fm	*1⅛ Ⓣ				1:473	3↑ ⓕSpicyLivngH-G3	89	2	11	108½	910	57½	35½	Hernandez R	LB 112 f	36.00	91–18	Suspect Terrain1113 Icy Warning1152½ Belle Nuit112½	Slow st, 2w, rallied	11
13Jly94-8Bel	fm	1 1/16 Ⓣ	:241	:48	1:113	1:404	3↑ ⓕⓈMt Vernon H55k	84	7	3	41¾	3nk	62½	64¼	Samyn J L	115 f	7.60	89–09	Irish Actress116¾ Great Triumph113no Tiffany's Taylor120nk	Tired	8
5Jun94-8Bel	fm	1⅜ Ⓣ	:47	1:11	1:351	2:113	3↑ ⓕShpshdBay H-G3	83	7	9	914	96¼	98	910½	Samyn J L	111 f	28.60	85–08	Market Booster114½ Irish Linnet1151 Fairy Garden120hd	Outrun	9
22May94-7Bel	gd	1 1/16 Ⓣ	:254	:501	1:133	1:441	3↑ ⓕHandicap48k	87	7	2	31½	41¼	41½	42	Santos J A	115 f	2.90e	73–24	Tiffany's Taylor116hd Star Guest1131 Garendare113¾	No late bid	8
6May94-8Bel	fm	1 1/16 Ⓣ	:244	:474	1:12	1:413	3↑ ⓕAlw 44000N$Y	82	3	7	76	62¾	42½	39¼	Samyn J L	115 f	4.10	80–15	Tiffany's Taylor1151½ Mckaymackenna1158 Belle Nuit1151½	Five wide	7

WORKOUTS: Jan 9 Bel tr.t 4f fst :484 B 5/46 Jan 3 Bel tr.t 4f fst :474 H 3/22 Dec 20 Bel tr.t 4f fst :48 H 3/39 Dec 14 Bel tr.t 4f fst :492 B 11/42 Nov 27 Bel tr.t 1⅛ fst 1:583 B 1/1 Nov 21 Bel tr.t 1 fst 1:411 B 1/1

Miss Fix It
Own: Larson Stables & Riccio Ellen
BECKNER D V (—)

Ch. m. 5
Sire: Bucksplasher (Buckpasser)
Dam: Z Boob (Ziad)
Br: Irish Acres Farm (Ill)
Tr: Parisella John (26 4 8 4 .15)

117⁵

Lifetime Record: 24 6 6 1 $143,188											
1994	12	3	1	1	$59,040	Turf	3	0	1	0	$10,900
1993	9	2	4	0	$47,080	Wet	3	0	1	1	$10,040
Aqu	2	1	0	0	$22,440	Dist	4	2	1	0	$39,560

21Dec94-4Aqu	fst	170 ⊡	:241	:481	1:131	1:441	3↑ ⓕClm 50000	39	1	2	2½	33½	412	525½	Luzzi M J	119 f	*.70	51–23	S. S. Sparkle110nk Bonnie Shopper10812 Lasting Shore11712		7
Bobbled start, tired																					
10Dec94-6Aqu	fst	1 1/16 ⊡	:243	:483	1:134	1:452	3↑ ⓕAlw 36000N3X	88	3	1	12	11	13	12	Luzzi M J	117 f	*1.50	78–23	Miss Fix It1172 Safe At Home1151 Manila Lila11712	Driving	5
29Nov94-8Aqu	wf	1⅛	:474	1:121	1:382	1:514	3↑ ⓕAlw 36000N3X	86	3	1	11½	11	1hd	31¼	Luzzi M J	117 f	*1.20	76–24	Dancer's Gate119no Manila Lila1171¼ Miss Fix It1175	Weakened	6
12Jly94-1Bel	fst	1 1/16	:234	:471	1:12	1:424	ⓕClm 30000	98	5	1	11	11½	18	114	Luzzi M J	117 f	*1.70	88–24	Miss Fix It11714 Miss Cover Girl1132 Ukrainian Gal1175	Handily	8
30May94-2Bel	fm	1 1/16 Ⓣ	:23	:461	1:103	1:413	ⓕClm 47500	68	6	1	1½	2hd	52¼	98½	Luzzi M J	115 f	3.60	80–12	Dark Star Line1141 Kris' Dear Deby1132½ Hurry Up Marya113½	Gave way	10
8May94-3Bel	sly	1 1/16 ⊗	:23	:461	1:113	1:442	ⓕClm 47500	76	1	1	1½	11	1½	2hd	Luzzi M J	115 f	*1.70	80–17	Rebecca Lauren113hd Miss Fix It1151¾ Interrupta1177½	Gamely	6
28Apr94-8Aqu	fst	6f	:223	:461	:583	1:112	3↑ ⓕAlw 31000N3X	78	5	4	11	1½	2½	51¾	Luzzi M J	117 f	*.80	83–19	Cala Star117no Smart Holly110nk DTuesday Edition1171½	Took up 1/8 pl	6
Placed 4th through disqualification.																					
22Apr94-4Aqu	fst	1⅛	:47	1:122	1:383	1:513	ⓕClm 25000	89	3	1	110	16	18	112½	Luzzi M J	117	6.60	78–27	Miss Fix It11712 Lahfeh117nk Jettaway Jus1176	Ridden out	8
14Mar94-5Spt	fst	6f	:222	:46	:583	1:114	ⓕⓈClm 25000	64	7	1	2hd	11	1hd	51½	Diaz J L	L 116 f	10.70	84–17	Super Deb114nk Yukon Connie121nk Miss Bethalto114hd	Faded	8
4Mar94-9Spt	fst	6f	:222	:462	:59	1:121	3↑ ⓕⓈAlw 27170N3X	59	5	2	31½	22	53	76½	Razo E Jr	L 116 f	3.60	77–20	Yukon Connie116nk Permanant Miss1161¼ Shezalong1164	Tired	8

WORKOUTS: Nov 9 Aqu 4f fst :494 B 7/12 Oct 15 Aqu 5f fst 1:03 B 2/3

Handicapping this $46,000 classified allowance route the night before, I was of the opinion that, assuming an honest racetrack, it set up nicely for a closer. This was due to the presence of Little Buckles and Miss Fix It, who figured to knock themselves out in a fight for the early lead. This was too bad, I thought, for Little Buckles' earlier races on the inner track were mostly hidden from the public's view, and they indicated she was quite at home:

Little Buckles
Own: Wachtel Edwin H
LUZZI M J (17 1 3 4 .06)

Ch. f. 3 (Jan)
Sire: Buckley Boy (Alydar)
Dam: Petite Nina (Native Aid)
Br: Sheehan Farms Ltd (Ont–C)
Tr: Destefano John M Jr (1 0 0 1 .00)

121

Lifetime Record: 14 4 4 3 $135,791											
1994	6	3	2	1	$102,998	Turf	1	0	0	0	
1993	8	1	2	2	$32,793	Wet	3	1	0	0	$18,792
Bel	0	0	0	0		Dist	1	1	0	0	$19,800

23Apr94-5Aqu	fst	1	:232	:463	1:104	1:362	3↑ ⓕAlw 33000N3X	92	6	1	1½	11	13½	11¼	Luzzi M J	111 b	2.60	86–25	Little Buckles1111¼ Wings Point1193½ Quinpool1191	Driving	6
2Apr94-9Spt	fst	1 1/16	:23	:473	1:121	1:45	ⓕNatJClubOaks150k	89	2	4	31	22	2hd	2½	Luzzi M J	115 b	*1.70	90–13	Forcing Bid117½ Little Buckles1153¾ Merry Colleen113nk	Willingly	10
6Mar94-8Aqu	fst	1 1/16 ⊡	:242	:483	1:132	1:454	ⓕBusher BCH-G3	75	7	3	3½	3nk	2hd	32	Luzzi M J	114	1.30	74–24	Forcing Bid1122 Ask Shananie118hd Little Buckles114nk	Willingly	7
22Feb94-6Aqu	fst	1 1/16 ⊡	:24	:491	1:144	1:472	ⓕAlw 30000N2X	91	5	1	11	11½	18	112	Luzzi M J	116	*1.00	68–28	Little Buckles11612 Polar Princess116½ Do It Fast1216	Mild drive	5
23Jan94-5Aqu	fst	170 ⊡	:24	:482	1:134	1:444	ⓕBusanda53k	81	2	5	53	41½	2hd	21	Luzzi M J	112	*.40e	73–31	Ask Shananie1121 Little Buckles1121¾ Penny's Reshoot1166½	Willingly	6
13Jan94-4Aqu	sly	170 ⊡	:241	:494	1:17	1:494	ⓕAlw 28000N1X	79	2	1	11	11	12	16¼	Luzzi M J	116	*1.90	49–58	Little Buckles1166¼ Bravada1164¼ Forcing Bid1111	Driving	10
20Dec93-8Aqu	fst	6f ⊡	:223	:46	:583	1:113	ⓕMeritus53k	74	4	5	57	45½	46	34¼	Luzzi M J	116	3.90e	81–22	Penny'sReshoot1162¾ PleasantDilemm1211½ LittleBuckles1161½	Mild rally	6
10Dec93-7Aqu	fst	6f ⊡	:223	:461	:591	1:122	ⓕAlw 28000N1X	71	3	5	74	52¼	21½	21½	Davis R G	116	*2.10	79–22	Truth And Beauty1181½ Little Buckles1165 Bravada118hd	Rallied wide	8
27Oct93-7Grd	fst	6½f	:231	:463	1:113	1:18	ⓕClm 50000	71	3	4	31	1hd	22	24¾	McAleney J S	115	*2.70	86–12	Lets Be Alert1194¾ Little Buckles1154 Rusty Brown114hd	Gave best inside	10
16Oct93-9WO	sly	1 1/16	:232	:471	1:123	1:454	ⓕPr Elzabth-G1C	51	3	2	25	44½	610	616½	McAleney J S	119	18.70	70–10	Term Limits1194 Alywow119no Blushing Blond1195½	Four wide, faded	6

WORKOUTS: Apr 16 Bel tr.t 3f fst :383 B 14/15 Mar 26 Bel tr.t 5f fst 1:02 B 6/18 Mar 20 Bel tr.t 4f fst :474 H 4/35 ●Feb 15 Bel tr.t 5f fst 1:02 H 1/16

Earlier pp's from Little Buckles' career showed four routes on the inner track the previous winter, and all had been good efforts: wins in the preliminary N1X and N2X allowance conditions, a placing in the Busanda, and a close-up third in the Grade 3 Busher. Another thing also became apparent about Little Buckles: she much preferred to control the early pace. Her inner track victories, both blowouts, had come when she was able to get clear early leads — a trend that continued on the main track in April when she won her N3X condition.

But Miss Fix It would make things miserable for Little Buckles on the front-end. The 5-year-old mare had been in front at the first call in all the routes showing in her pp's, with the exception of her most recent start, when she bobbled at the start.

Many serious horseplayers, contrary to popular belief, hold down day jobs, so they might scan through a card the night before, make note of their plays for the next day, and not really pay all that much attention to late scratches, especially if they're in races deemed unplayable. But from a pace point of view, this race became a lot more playable when Miss Fix It was scratched off the program.

Little Buckles had suddenly become the lone speed on the rail, and as the card unfolded, it became obvious that the rail was the only path that was producing winners. Several horses had gone wire to wire, and even the closers had won by slipping through on the fence.

Little Buckles most recent Beyer of 60 was among the lowest in the field, but that fading fourth place finish of December 16 was not the right race with which to gauge her potential:

EIGHTH RACE

Aqueduct

DECEMBER 16, 1994

1 MILE 70 YARDS. (Inner Dirt)(1.39³) ALLOWANCE. Purse $38,000. Fillies and mares, 3-year-olds and upward which have not won four races other than maiden, claiming or starter. Weights: 3-year-olds, 120 lbs. Older, 122 lbs. Non-winners of two races other than maiden or claiming at a mile or over since November 15, allowed 3 lbs. Of such a race since then, 5 lbs.

Value of Race: $38,000 Winner $22,800; second $7,600; third $4,180; fourth $2,280; fifth $1,140. Mutuel Pool $157,572.00 Exacta Pool $304,896.00

Last Raced	Horse	M/Eqt. A.Wt	PP	St	¼	½	¾	Str	Fin	Jockey	Odds $1
19Nov94 2Aqu⁶	Miss Pocket Court	bf 5 117	5	5	5	5	3¹½	1³½	1⁶	Migliore R	10.40
18Nov94 9Med²	Footing	3 110	1	2	1ʰᵈ	1ʰᵈ	1ʰᵈ	2²	2³	Perez R B⁵	*1.60
22Nov94 8Aqu³	Dixie Luck	3 115	3	3	3ʰᵈ	4³	4¹	4⁸	3¼	Leon F	1.60
2Dec94 8Med³	Little Buckles	b 3 115	2	1	2¹½	2¹½	2ʰᵈ	3¹	4¹⁷	Luzzi M J	3.20
30Nov94 8Aqu¹	Big Rhonda	f 3 115	4	4	4⁴	3ʰᵈ	5	5	5	Chavez J F	7.80

*—Actual Betting Favorite.

OFF AT 3:36 Start Good. Won driving. Time, :23¹, :48, 1:14¹, 1:40², 1:45 Track fast.

$2 Mutuel Prices:

7-MISS POCKET COURT	22.80	6.40	3.10
2-FOOTING		3.90	2.50
5-DIXIE LUCK			2.90

$2 EXACTA 7-2 PAID $70.50

B. m, by Court Trial–Pocket Power, by Full Pocket. Trainer Hushion Michael E. Bred by Mangurian Mr & Mrs H T Jr (Fla).

MISS POCKET COURT trailed the field early, eased out three wide on the far turn to launch her bid, drove clear into the lane, then held sway under mild encouragement. FOOTING was pressured on the front throughout by LITTLE BUCKLES, then held for the place. DIXIE LUCK outfinished the others. LITTLE BUCKLES was used pressing the pace and weakened late. BIG RHONDA raced four wide into the first turn and could not keep pace. DIXIE LUCK and MISS POCKET COURT raced with mud caulks.

Owners— 1, Hauman Eugene E & Schwartz Barry K; 2, Cherry Valley Farm; 3, Bohemia Stable; 4, Jay Cee Jay Stable & Wachtel Edward; 5, Flying Zee Stables

Trainers— 1, Hushion Michael E; 2, Mott William I; 3, Jerkens H Allen; 4, Destefano John M Jr; 5, Martin Jose

Scratched— Artful Pleasure (3Dec94 9LRL⁴), Acting Proud (19Nov94 2AQU¹)

Key race-devotees were aware that Miss Pocket Court had come back to score a repeat victory in a $50,000 overnight handicap on December 23. (Her name is circled, indicating she won her next start, and the upward-pointing arrow written in the margin indicates the win came for a bigger purse). Footing, the horse who had dueled with Little Buckles, had not won her next start, but she had been second by a nose in a minor stake when brought back on January 7.

The crucial late information, the scratch of Miss Fix It and the inside-speed bias, made Little Buckles a virtual cinch in this spot. But the crowd installed Endless Desire at odds-on, due, I would imagine, to her steady recent line of Beyers in the high-70s to low-80s, and the fact that most public handicappers had picked her as the likeliest to benefit from an anticipated speed duel. The crowd perceived Little Buckles as erratic, an "in-and-outer", although she had consistently shown the ability to win whenever allowed to dictate the pace. I thought she deserved a prime win bet.

SEVENTH RACE
Aqueduct
JANUARY 12, 1995

1 MILE 70 YARDS. (Inner Dirt)(1.39^{3}) ALLOWANCE. Purse $46,000. Fillies and mares, 4-year-olds and upward which have not won a race of $22,000 at one mile or over in 1994/95. Weight, 122 lbs. Non-winners of $20,000 at one mile or over in 1994/95, allowed 3 lbs. Of $20,000 since August 1, 5 lbs. Of $20,000 in 1994, 7 lbs. (Maiden, claiming, starter and restricted races not considered.)

Value of Race: $46,000 Winner $27,600; second $9,200; third $5,060; fourth $2,760; fifth $1,380. Mutuel Pool $140,074.00 Exacta Pool $302,707.00

Last Raced	Horse	M/Eqt.	A.	Wt	PP	St	¼	½	¾	Str	Fin	Jockey	Odds $1
16Dec94 ^{8}Aqu^{4}	Little Buckles	b	4	115	1	1	1^{1}	$1^{1\frac{1}{2}}$	1^{4}	1^{6}	1^{9}	Nelson D	3.10
22Dec94 ^{8}Aqu^{3}	Endless Desire	b	6	112	2	2	2^{3}	2^{5}	2^{2}	$2^{3\frac{1}{2}}$	2^{4}	Perez R B^{5}	0.90
7Jan95 ^{8}Aqu^{6}	Avie's Daisy	b	7	115	4	5	$4^{\frac{1}{2}}$	3^{1}	3^{8}	3^{8}	3^{7}	Rydowski S R	6.00
23Dec94 ^{8}Aqu^{4}	Belle Nuit	f	5	115	6	6	$5^{\frac{1}{2}}$	6	5^{1}	4^{2}	4^{1}	Pezua J M	9.10
21Dec94 ^{4}Aqu^{4}	Evi Bee	f	4	115	5	4	6	$5^{2\frac{1}{2}}$	6	$5^{\frac{1}{2}}$	5^{4}	Alvarado F T	22.40
17Dec94 ^{9}TP^{9}	Shellster	f	4	115	3	3	3^{2}	$4^{1\frac{1}{2}}$	4^{hd}	6	6	Velazquez J R	5.00

OFF AT 3:01 Start Good. Won driving. Time, :24, :48, 1:12, 1:37^{3}, 1:41^{4} Track fast.

$2 Mutuel Prices:			
2–LITTLE BUCKLES	8.20	3.70	2.40
3–ENDLESS DESIRE		3.30	2.30
1A–AVIE'S DAISY			2.50

$2 EXACTA 2–3 PAID $22.00

Ch. f, by Buckley Boy–Petite Nina, by Native Aid. Trainer Destefano John M Jr. Bred by Sheehan Farms Ltd (Ont-C).

LITTLE BUCKLES sprinted clear in the early stages, was rated on the front for five furlongs, opened a comfortable advantage on the turn, then steadily increased her margin under brisk left hand encouragement. ENDLESS DESIRE stalked the early pace outside the winner, couldn't stay with that one while under the whip on the turn but continued on willingly to clearly best the others. AVIE'S DAISY lodged a mild rally along the inside leaving the far turn but couldn't sustain her bid. BELLE NUIT never reached contention while saving ground. EVI BEE was never close while three wide. SHELLSTER was finished early. AVIE'S DAISY and SHELLSTER wore mud caulks.

Owners— 1, Jay Cee Jay Stable & Wachtel Edward; 2, R Paradise Stable; 3, Paraneck Stable; 4, Amherst Stable; 5, Donaldson Robert; 6, Willmott Stables

Trainers—1, Destefano John M Jr; 2, Bailie Sally A; 3, Aquilino Joseph; 4, Johnson Philip G; 5, Ferriola Peter; 6, Hushion Michael E

Scratched— Ensign Joanne (22Dec94 ^{8}AQU^{4}), Miss Fix It (21Dec94 ^{4}AQU^{5})

Allowed to click off a succession of :24 quarters while well in control, and running over a track that was carrying inside speed, Little Buckles had a four-length lead approaching the stretch and still hadn't been asked for any serious exertion. The final margin was nine lengths, and it was all thanks to a late scratch that dramatically altered the complexion of the race.

DURING THE DEAD OF WINTER in New York, you try not to get too fancy. Simple things like a conditioning edge mean a great deal, especially during prolonged stretches of inclement weather that wreak havoc with training schedules.

The fifth race on February 2 was for 3-year-old maiden fillies, and contained an absolute standout in terms of current condition. I've written in the post-time odds next to the names of all nine entrants. Make a case for or against, based primarily on who is likely to have the superior conditioning foundation:

5 **Aqueduct**

6 Furlongs **(Inner Dirt). (1:08^{3}) MAIDEN SPECIAL WEIGHT. Purse $28,000. Fillies, 3-year-olds. Weight, 121 lbs.**

Waiting For Love 5-1
Own: Magahn Ross
MARTIN G J (168 16 20 17 .10)

Dk. b or br f. 3 (Apr)
Sire: Hay Halo (Halo)
Dam: Sail to Papa (Sail On–Sail On)
Br: Thornmar Farm (Md)
Tr: Thompson J Willard (22 1 2 2 .05)

114^{7}

Lifetime Record :	4 M 1 0	$8,820			
1995	1 M 1 0	$6,000	Turf	0 0 0 0	
1994	3 M 0 0	$2,820	Wet	0 0 0 0	
Aqu [•]	2 0 1 0	$7,800	Dist	2 0 0 0	$1,020

4Jan95–6Aqu fst	1^{70} [•]	:24	:48^{2}	1:15	1:46^{3}	ⒻMd Sp Wt	24	**58**	2	3	3^{1}	$2^{2\frac{1}{2}}$	2^{6}	2^{8}	Martin G J^{7}	114	13.90	57–35	Ammy Hils121^{8} Waiting For Love114$^{8\frac{1}{2}}$ Your Approval116^{7}	Second best	7
16Dec94–3Aqu fst	1^{70} [•]	:23^{3}	:49	1:14^{4}	1:45^{3}	ⒻMd Sp Wt	24	**52**	6	6	$5^{4\frac{1}{2}}$	$5^{6\frac{1}{2}}$	$5^{7\frac{1}{2}}$	$4^{10\frac{3}{4}}$	Santagata N	117 f	5.40	59–30	Spire112^{3} Your Approval117^{3} Ammy Hils117$^{4\frac{3}{4}}$	No rally	7
25Nov94–4Med fst	6f	:22	:45^{1}	:58	1:11^{4}	ⒻMd Sp Wt	23	**46**	4	8	$9^{7\frac{3}{4}}$	$9^{7\frac{1}{4}}$	$6^{7\frac{1}{4}}$	$4^{3\frac{1}{2}}$	Santagata N	117	2.70e	78–11	Legalese117$^{\frac{3}{4}}$ Unreal Tears117$^{\frac{3}{4}}$ Wilson's Courage117^{2}	Some gain	10
30Sep94–4Med fst	6f	:22^{2}	:46	:58^{2}	1:12	ⒻMd Sp Wt	22	**51**	5	9	$9^{6\frac{3}{4}}$	$9^{6\frac{3}{4}}$	$7^{5\frac{1}{2}}$	5^{1}	Beckner D V^{5}	112	4.20e	80–10	Sweet Adell117$^{\frac{3}{4}}$ Slick N' Loyal117^{hd} Ring By Spring117^{no}	Tired	9

WORKOUTS: Jan 28 Aqu [•] 3f fst :36^{3} H *1/3* Jan 24 Aqu [•] 4f fst :50 B *7/12* Jan 18 Aqu [•] 6f fst 1:15^{3} B *1/1* Dec 28 Aqu [•] 5f fst 1:03 B *3/5* ●Dec 9 Med 5f fst 1:00^{2} H *1/8* Nov 21 Med 4f fst :51 B *12/15*

Irene's Fairytale 43-1
Own: Kassin Sam
ALVARADO F T (189 32 37 31 .17)

Dk. b or br f. 3 (Jan)
Sire: Red Ransom (Roberto)
Dam: No Fairytales (Dixieland Band)
Br: Sam Kassin (Ky)
Tr: Tesher Howard M (35 6 6 4 .17)

121

Lifetime Record :	2 M 0 0	$840			
1995	1 M 0 0	$840	Turf	0 0 0 0	
1994	1 M 0 0		Wet	0 -0 0 0	
Aqu [•]	2 0 0 0	$840	Dist	2 0 0 0	$840

11Jan95–6Aqu fst	6f	[•] :23^{3}	:48	1:01^{1}	1:15	ⒻMd Sp Wt	32	**18**	6	6	$6^{9\frac{3}{4}}$	5^{9}	5^{13}	$5^{12\frac{1}{4}}$	Luzzi M J	121	39.00	55–22	Select Account116$^{1\frac{1}{2}}$ Ray'sCraftyLady121^{1} RoseRhapsody121^{nk}	No threat	8

Mystic Mel 8-1
Own: Tucker Jeffrey
MIGLIORE R (196 41 35 36 .21)

Dk. b or br f. 3 (Feb)
Sire: Turkoman (Alydar)
Dam: Estate Carlton (Tom Rolfe)
Br: H. E. Pabst & T. J. Pabst (Ky)
Tr: O'Connell Richard (39 4 6 5 .10)
121

Lifetime Record :	2 M 0 1	$4,760			
1995	1 M 0 0	$1,680	Turf	0 0 0 0	
1994	1 M 0 1	$3,080	Wet	0 0 0 0	
Aqu ⊡	2 0 0 1	$4,760	Dist	2 0 0 1	$4,760

11Jan95-6Aqu fst 6f ⊡ :233 :48 1:011 1:15 ⒻMd Sp Wt 25+ 42 1 4 23½ 24½ 23 42½ Velazquez J R 121 2.55 65-22 Select Account1161¼ Ray's Crafty Lady1211 Rose Rhapsody121nk Tired 8
30Dec94-3Aqu fst 6f ⊡ :232 :474 1:004 1:142 ⒻMd Sp Wt 24 57 1 6 32 44½ 46½ 36¾ Velazquez J R 117 5.20 64-24 Impish Saga1172 Ravishing Raven1124¾ Mystic Mel1171¾ Finished evenly 9
WORKOUTS: Jan 29 Bel tr.t 4f fst :49 H 4/12 Jan 23 Bel tr.t 4f fst :50 B 13/31 Dec 27 Bel tr.t 4f fst :474 H 2/50 Dec 21 Bel tr.t 4f fst :48 H 4/28 Dec 14 Bel tr.t 5f fst 1:014 Hg4/27 Dec 9 Bel tr.t 5f fst 1:022 B 16/49

Red Falls 40-1
Own: Double T Stable
BECKNER D V (50 6 6 4 .12)

B. f. 3 (Feb)
Sire: Charging Falls (Taylor's Falls)
Dam: Ted the Terrible (Wonder Lark)
Br: Jocelyn McKathan (Fla)
Tr: Jayko John C (7 0 2 0 .00)
121

Lifetime Record :	2 M 0 0	$65		
1994	2 M 0 0	$65	Turf	0 0 0 0
1993	0 M 0 0		Wet	0 0 0 0
Aqu ⊡	0 0 0 0		Dist	1 0 0 0

28Aug94-5Sar fst 6f :221 :454 :582 1:114 ⒻMd Sp Wt 17 5 7 87½ 98½ 812 720½ Hernandez R 117 54.30 62-14 Moroccan Magic117¾ Lizzie Toon1173 Wonaria117¾ Pinched break 9
22Apr94-3Hia fst 3f :22 :34 ⒻMd 25000 — 9 10 98 66¾ Russ M L 116 7.70 85-14 Short Stroke116nk Sheri's Jetstream1162 Sugar BearShelby1162¾ Mild bid 11
WORKOUTS: Jan 31 Bel tr.t 3f fst :371 B 7/17 ●Jan 25 Bel tr.t 5f fst 1:014 H 1/12 Jan 19 Bel tr.t 4f fst :473 Hg2/28 Jan 6 Bel tr.t 4f fst :513 B 23/32 Dec 31 Bel tr.t 3f fst :382 B 13/19

Morning Date 27-1
Own: Chen Daniel J
VELAZQUEZ J R (197 26 31 24 .13)

Ro. f. 3 (Jan)
Sire: Swing Till Dawn (Grey Dawn II)
Dam: Viznaga (Balconaje)
Br: Hi Card Ranch (Cal)
Tr: Hertler John O (28 0 2 2 .00)
121

Lifetime Record :	0 M 0 0	$0	
1995	0 M 0 0	Turf	0 0 0 0
1994	0 M 0 0	Wet	0 0 0 0
Aqu ⊡	0 0 0 0	Dist	0 0 0 0

WORKOUTS: Jan 30 Bel tr.t 4f fst :491 B 5/20 Jan 25 Bel tr.t 4f fst :484 H 8/33 Jan 20 Bel tr.t 5f fst 1:024 H 8/16 Jan 11 Bel tr.t 4f fst :502 Bg16/34 Jan 5 Bel tr.t 5f fst 1:042 B 4/6 Dec 29 Bel tr.t 4f fst :491 Hg7/25 Dec 21 Bel tr.t 3f fst :364 Bg6/13

Lori's Jewels 17-1
Own: Dethomasi Carlo
VIVES L (—)

B. f. 3 (Mar)
Sire: Bold Josh (Tentam)
Dam: Heist the Jewels (Jason Jeffrey)
Br: Carlo De Thomasi (NJ)
Tr: Hamer William E (—)
1147

Lifetime Record :	1 M 0 1	$1,370			
1995	1 M 0 1	$1,370	Turf	0 0 0 0	
1994	0 M 0 0		Wet	1 0 0 1	$1,370
Aqu ⊡	0 0 0 0		Dist	0 0 0 0	

20Jan95-10GS sly 5½f :221 :47 1:002 1:072 ⒻⓈMd Sp Wt 31- 30 1 3 1hd 12½ 1hd 31½ Vives L5 114 f 13.20 77-17 Merry Mood119¾ Mynameaintmary119¾ Lori's Jewels1143¾ Weakened 11
WORKOUTS: Jan 30 GS 4f fst :49 B 4/8 ●Jan 18 GS 3f fst :353 H 1/12 Jan 11 GS 6f fst 1:15 Bg2/4 Nov 4 Del 5f fst 1:052 Bg5/5

Attractive Missile 4-1
Own: Brody Mr & Mrs Jerome
LUZZI M J (196 25 22 31 .13)

Gr. f. 3 (Feb)
Sire: Relaunch (In Reality)
Dam: Montage (Alydar)
Br: Gallagher's Stud (NY)
Tr: Corbellini William R (—)
121

Lifetime Record :	4 M 2 0	$14,000			
1994	4 M 2 0	$14,000	Turf	0 0 0 0	
1993	0 M 0 0		Wet	1 0 0 0	
Aqu ⊡	0 0 0 0		Dist	1 0 1 0	$6,160

22Nov94-5Aqu wf 7f :223 :461 1:122 1:253 ⒻMd Sp Wt 28+ 39 2 7 43 74½ 612 516¾ Luzzi M J 117 b 2.75 59-24 Thunderlake1174½ Hamba1121¼ Ammy Hils1175 No factor 7
23Oct94-3Aqu fst 6½f :223 :454 1:112 1:18 ⒻMd Sp Wt 18+ 61 8 7 53 52½ 45½ 46 Luzzi M J 117 b 2.15 85-11 Wonaria1101 Just For Fun1171 Some Sweet1174 Broke slowly 8
14Oct94-3Bel fst 7f :231 :47 1:12 1:252 ⒻMd Sp Wt 18¼ 69 5 8 76 41½ 32 24 Smith M E 117 b *.80 72-19 CndinHlo1174 AttrctivMissil117¾ JustForFun1172½ Checked break, wide 9
15Sep94-3Bel fst 6f :223 :454 :574 1:104 ⒻMd Sp Wt 20 72 5 8 54½ 53½ 33 22¾ Smith M E 117 2.50 84-12 American Star1122¾ Attractive Missile1173 Lizzie Toon117nk Second best 9
WORKOUTS: Jan 28 Bel tr.t 4f fst :474 Hg3/20 Jan 19 Bel tr.t 5f fst 1:021 B 5/14 Dec 29 Bel tr.t 4f fst :52 B 22/25 ●Nov 15 Bel 4f fst :471 Hg1/22 Nov 9 Bel 5f fst 1:011 H 9/22 Nov 4 Bel 5f fst 1:02 B 2/24

Ray's Crafty Lady 2-1
Own: Winbound Farms
NELSON D (94 18 7 6 .19)

Ro. f. 3 (May)
Sire: Crafty Prospector (Mr. Prospector)
Dam: Faultless Too (Tudor Grey)
Br: J. I. Racing, Inc. (Ky)
Tr: Contessa Gary C (37 2 2 2 .05)
121

Lifetime Record :	2 M 1 1	$8,600			
1995	1 M 1 0	$5,600	Turf	0 0 0 0	
1994	1 M 0 1	$3,000	Wet	0 0 0 0	
Aqu ⊡	1 0 1 0	$5,600	Dist	1 0 1 0	$5,600

11Jan95-6Aqu fst 6f ⊡ :233 :48 1:011 1:15 ⒻMd Sp Wt 25- 45 7 1 13½ 14½ 13 21¼ Alvarado F T 121 *2.25 67-22 SlctAccont1161¼ Ry'sCrftyLdy1211 RosRhpsody121nk Speed, couldn't last 8
17Jun94-5Bel fst 5½f :22 :46 :582 1:05 Md Sp Wt 46 1 2 13 11 23½ 312½ Luttrell M G5 107 7.70 77-15 ManeIngredient1159½ FortunateErrol1153 Ray'sCraftyLdy107nk Gave way 4
WORKOUTS: ●Jan 30 Bel tr.t 3f fst :351 H 1/8 Jan 24 Bel tr.t 4f fst :481 H 6/40 Jan 4 Bel tr.t 5f fst 1:014 H 4/27 Dec 30 Bel tr.t 6f fst 1:19 B 3/3 Dec 23 Bel tr.t 5f fst 1:02 B 4/26 Dec 17 Bel tr.t 4f fst :48 H 2/30

Enchancement 2-1
Own: Harbor View Farm
PEREZ R B (241 43 41 35 .18)

Ch. f. 3 (Feb)
Sire: It's Freezing (T. V. Commercial)
Dam: Alyaffirm (Alydar)
Br: Harbor View Farm (Ky)
Tr: Jerkens H Allen (36 4 8 8 .11)
1165

Lifetime Record :	0 M 0 0	$0	
1995	0 M 0 0	Turf	0 0 0 0
1994	0 M 0 0	Wet	0 0 0 0
Aqu ⊡	0 0 0 0	Dist	0 0 0 0

WORKOUTS: Jan 26 Bel tr.t 5f fst 1:03 B 10/11 ●Jan 13 Bel tr.t 4f fst :473 Hg1/17 ●Jan 6 Bel tr.t 6f fst 1:182 B 1/4 Dec 28 Bel tr.t 5f fst 1:04 B 15/23 Dec 18 Bel tr.t 4f fst :513 B 10/11

The co-favorites at 2-1 are Ray's Crafty Lady and the first time-starter from the relatively high-profile Harbor View Farm and Allen Jerkens, Enchancement.

Ray's Crafty Lady is the clear-cut pacesetter, but the signs are not encouraging. She earned a Beyer of 46 early in her 2-year-old season when she gave way after taking the lead; in her return race of January 11 she surrendered a three-length lead through a final furlong in a slow :13 4/5, earning a Beyer of 45. She was no faster now than she had been seven months earlier, but she was just as short-winded, and there was nothing especially positive to be taken from her blowout in :35 1/5 a few days ago: we *know* she has speed, she just hasn't been able to carry it far enough. This will be her second start back from a layoff following a taxing, all-out try in which she'd been bet to favoritism; a bounce was certainly within the realm of possibility.

Enchancement is the hot firster on the strength of her connections and the bullet gate work of :47 3/5, and she has to be respected. Should any other filly be deemed playable, we'd be sure to protect by using her underneath Enchancement in an exacta.

The third choice is Attractive Missile, and despite the fact that she boasts the three highest Beyers, she is an easy throwout on grounds of current condition. This has nothing to do with the fact that she hasn't been out in two and a half months, for many horses are playable in such situations; it has to do with the negative signs shown before and after the break. To begin with, Attractive Missile was a slow-breaking money burner in the fall, having beaten a total of three horses out of the gate in four starts, all of which she lost at odds of 5/2 or less. More ominously, her Beyers had declined each time out, from a 72 to a 69 to a 61 to a 39. This is in direct contrast to the line of healthy, developing young horses, which tend to improve in surges from month to month as they mature (for much more on this, consult the chapter on condition analysis in *Expert Handicapping*). After finishing up the track in her last start November 22, Attractive Missile had not worked out for more than five weeks, and after loping along through a slow :52 breeze on December 29, she had not worked again for another three weeks, finally getting back to the track for a five-furlong drill on January 19. The decline in Beyers, combined with the layoff and the infrequent, irregularly spaced workouts are glaring negatives, as is her habit of spotting the field a headstart.

Several others have had minimal activity lately: Red Falls showed little last April, showed even less in August, and is 40-1 for no-win connections. Morning Date is a firster being ignored on the board at 27-1, and she hails from a barn that's winless with 28 starters. Lori's Jewels has never been this far, and couldn't hold a clear lead in the slop at Garden State in her debut; she'll be hard-pressed to get clear from Ray's Crafty Lady in this match up.

Irene's Fairytale and Mystic Mel at least show a pair of recent sprints, but neither could get by Ray's Crafty Lady through that slow final fraction on January 11.

The filly with an edge in condition is Waiting For Love, who is cutting back to a sprint after two routes, the latest of which was a placing to Ammy Hils, who had returned to finish a close-up second in an allowance on January 27. Note that her Beyer of 58 from that race is exceeded only by Attractive Missile, whom we've already tossed, and that she was eight lengths clear of the third finisher after an improved show of early speed. In fact, Waiting For Love had been two and a half lengths from the lead after six furlongs in 1:15, which gave her a six-furlong split of roughly 1:15 3/5. She had come back on January 18 with a six-furlong workout on the inner track in 1:15 3/5, which was almost as fast as Ray's Crafty Lady had run in her return race.

So, here's a horse who gained ground through the final stages of her two previous starts at today's distance, who is emerging from a pair of stamina-building routes, and who was closer to the pace last time out than she'd ever been before. Since then she'd been given three workouts, including a six-furlong drill in time as fast as her rivals had been running in the afternoons, a half-mile breeze six days later, and a :36 3/5 blowout four days after that.

Ray's Crafty Lady is going to fend *this* filly off in the stretch? I don't think so. It was prime bet time.

FIFTH RACE

Aqueduct

FEBRUARY 2, 1995

6 FURLONGS. (Inner Dirt)(1.06³) MAIDEN SPECIAL WEIGHT. Purse $28,000. Fillies, 3-year-olds. Weight, 121 lbs.

Value of Race: $28,000 Winner $16,800; second $5,600; third $3,080; fourth $1,680; fifth $840. Mutuel Pool $140,576.00 Exacta Pool $228,504.00 Triple Pool $183,037.00

Last Raced	Horse	M/Eqt. A.Wt	PP	St	¼	½	Str	Fin	Jockey	Odds $1
4Jan95 6Aqu²	Waiting For Love	3 114	1	6	2½	1³	1⁷	16½	Martin G J⁷	5.20
11Jan95 6Aqu⁵	Irene's Fairytale	3 121	2	7	3½	3¹	2⁴	26½	Alvarado F T	43.00
22Nov94 5Aqu⁵	Attractive Missile	3 121	7	9	5³	5⁴	3¹	3nk	Luzzi M J	4.10
20Jan95 10GS³	Lori's Jewels	f 3 114	6	4	4½	4hd	42½	4½	Vives L⁷	17.90
	Enchancement	3 116	9	8	6¹	6¹	5²½	5⁶	Perez R B⁵	2.45
11Jan95 6Aqu⁴	Mystic Mel	3 121	3	3	8½	8hd	6¼	63½	Migliore R	8.90
	Morning Date	3 121	5	2	9	9	8²	75½	Velazquez J R	27.00
28Aug94 5Sar⁷	Red Falls	3 121	4	5	7½	7hd	9	8nk	Beckner D V	40.25
11Jan95 6Aqu²	Ray's Crafty Lady	3 121	8	1	12½	2½	71½	9	Nelson D	2.00

OFF AT 2:08 Start Good. Won driving. Time, :23¹, :48, 1:00⁴, 1:14¹ Track fast.

$2 Mutuel Prices:

1–WAITING FOR LOVE	12.40	5.60	3.40
2–IRENE'S FAIRYTALE		25.60	11.00
7–ATTRACTIVE MISSILE			4.70

$2 EXACTA 1–2 PAID $294.50 $2 TRIPLE 1–2–7 PAID $2,144.00

Dk. b. or br. f, (Apr), by Hay Halo–Sail to Papa, by Sail On–Sail On. Trainer Thompson J Willard. Bred by Thornmar Farm (Md).

WAITING FOR LOVE never far back, angled out while accelerating to the front on the turn, then drew off under intermittent right hand encouragement. IRENE'S FAIRYTALE raced in close contention slightly off the rail to the top of the stretch but was no match for the winner while clearly best of the others. ATTRACTIVE MISSILE was pinched at the start, after breaking a bit slowly, gradually gained while three wide on the turn then lacked a strong closing bid. LORI'S JEWELS settled just off the pace while saving ground, angled between horses while rallying mildly on turn and flattened out. ENCHANCEMENT never reached contention after breaking a bit slowly. MYSTIC MEL had no speed. MORNING DATE was never close after being bumped at the start. RED FALLS was never a factor. RAY'S CRAFTY LADY sprinted clear in the early stages, set the pace to the turn and gave way. ENCHANCEMENT and RAY'S CRAFTY LADY wore mud caulks.

Owners— 1, Magahn Ross; 2, Kassin Sam; 3, Brody Mr & Mrs Jerome; 4, Bethomasi Carlo; 5, Harbor View Farm; 6, Tucker Jeffrey; 7, Chen Daniel J; 8, Deer View Stable & Double T Stable; 9, Winbound Farms

Trainers—1, Thompson J Willard; 2, Tesher Howard M; 3, Corbellini William R; 4, Hamer William E; 5, Jerkens H Allen; 6, O'Connell Richard; 7, Hertler John O; 8, Jayko John C; 9, Contessa Gary C

Waiting For Love tracked Ray's Crafty Lady through the first quarter, ran by that filly as if she were tied to the five-sixteenths pole and quickly drew away. Attractive Missile was as slow from the gate as she had been in all four of her starts last fall, and was under a full-out drive to gain third money. Irene's Fairytale inherited second position when Ray's Crafty Lady stopped, and no one had the ability and/or the inclination to make a run at her in the stretch, including Enchancement, who also broke slowly.

HORSES IN GOOD CONDITION can go a long way up the class ladder in the winter, and in so doing make quite a lot of money for their connections, because this is the time of year when current form often supersedes class. Players with a dogmatic approach to traditional class factors such as purse values and claiming prices, along with those players who refuse to relax their standards regarding the desired profile of upwardly-mobile allowance horses, miss out on some high-percentage plays. Physically fit and well-meant horses who are suited to the prevailing conditions can, and regularly do, make a mockery of rigid class labels during the winter.

Let's take a look at the diverse backgrounds of a few winter wonders from 1995, starting with Crafty and Goodbye To You, a pair of 5-year-olds who found the Fountain of Youth over the Big A's frozen tundra:

Crafty
Own: Bligh Jay W & Kruse David R
MIGLIORE R (118 35 21 20 .30)

Ch. h. 5
Sire: Crafty Prospector (Mr. Prospector)
Dam: Tribal to Do (Restless Native)
Br: Longleaf Pine Farm (Fla)
Tr: Young Steven W (4 2 0 1 .50)

122

Lifetime Record:	22 6 4 5	$321,143			
1995	3 2 0 0	$49,948	Turf	1 0 0 0	
1994	10 2 2 3	$74,370	Wet	2 0 1 0	$8,800
Aqu	2 2 0 0	$44,400	Dist	0 0 0 0	

31Mar95-8Aqu	fst	7f		:23 :462 1:104 1:232	Alw 42000N$Y	97	7	1	1½	1½	12½	1½	Migliore R	122	*1.00	87-19	Crafty122½ Blum Gone1141½ Dibbs N' Dubbs1141¾	All out	8
18Feb95-8Aqu	fst	6f	⊡	:224 :453 :573 1:101 3↑	CoaltownBCH-G3	82	5	1	32	43	58	512½	Migliore R	113	3.00	79-18	Mining Burrah1172 Crafty Alfel1162 Boom Towner120½	Done early	5
19Jan95-8Aqu	fst	6f	⊡	:233 :463 :581 1:102	Alw 36000N4X	98	2	2	1½	11½	14	14	Migliore R	119	*.40	91-18	Crafty1194 Fighting Daddy1171¼ Tali Hai1174	Drew away	5
30Dec94-8Aqu	fst	6f	⊡	:233 :474 :594 1:122 3↑	Alw 34000N3X	100	3	1	1hd	1hd	12½	12½	Migliore R	119	*.85	81-24	Crafty1192½ Sonny's Bruno1151¼ Direct Satellite1177	Driving	7
4Dec94-9Aqu	fst	7f		:224 :46 1:103 1:232 3↑	Alw 32000N2X	103	6	1	2½	2½	14	13½	Migliore R	117	5.60	87-15	Crafty1173½ Our Emblem1151 Brett's Jet1152¾	Driving	9
13Oct94-8SA	fst	6f		:213 :442 :562 1:084 3↑	Alw 38000N2X	50	5	1	2hd	23½	67½	817¾	Flores D R	LB 116 f	23.80	75-13	Argolid1132½ Goldigger's Dream1163½ Paster's Caper1174½	Gave way	8
25Sep94-9Fpx	fst	6f		:213 :452 :58 1:103 3↑	Alw 35280N2X	71	4	1	2½	32	23	36	Flores D R	LB 120 f	*1.00	90-09	Touch The Moon1204½ Fittobetried1151½ Crafty120no	Just held 3rd	6
27Mar94-2SA	fm	1	Ⓣ	:234 :483 1:113 1:36	Alw 44000N2X	66	3	1	51¾	87	87½	812½	Delahoussaye E	LB 116 b	10.00	72-15	Tychonic1162¾ Tabac116no Shandon Lake116nk	Speed, tired	8
10Mar94-3SA	fst	7f		:222 :443 1:091 1:22	Alw 41000N3L	87	5	2	42¼	43¼	2½	21	Delahoussaye E	LB 116	*.80	91-10	Gavel Gate1161 Crafty1162½ I'm Checkin' Out1171¼	Led deep stretch	5
20Feb94-7SA	wf	1 1/16		:231 :471 1:112 1:421	Alw 44000N2X	94	5	1	2hd	1½	12½	21¼	Delahoussaye E	LB 116	1.70	83-13	Marfamatic1111¼ Crafty116¾ Issel The Missle115¾	Outfinished	5

WORKOUTS: Apr 19 Bel tr.t 3f fst :364 B *4/15* ●Apr 11 Bel 6f fst 1:12 H *1/6* Mar 25 Bel tr.t 5f fst 1:011 H *2/24* Mar 18 Bel tr.t 5f fst 1:002 H *2/18* Mar 12 Bel tr.t 4f fst :49 B *12/28* Feb 14 Bel tr.t 4f fst :481 B *2/19*

Crafty had won just twice from 17 career starts in southern California, and had been unable to advance through the non-winners of two other than (N2X) allowance condition. Freshened from mid-October to December and shipped east by trainer Steve Young, the horse zoomed through his conditions with three consecutive victories, all front-running blowouts. After finding graded stakes competition a bit much, he was able to post a hard-fought win in a classified allowance on March 31, even though he was conceding eight pounds to his closest pursuers. All in all, four wins from five starts is a pretty good winter's work!

1a Goodbye To You
PP-7
Own: Young Steven W
MIGLIORE R (293 67 51 49 .23)

Dk. b or br g. 5
Sire: Sunny Clime (In Reality)
Dam: Sweet Jen (Full Out)
Br: Young Steven W (Cal)
Tr: Young Steven W (8 4 0 1 .50)

117

Lifetime Record:	22 3 6 4	$100,975			
1995	3 1 0 1	$24,760	Turf	0 0 0 0	
1994	11 1 4 1	$49,565	Wet	3 1 1 0	$22,500
Aqu ⊡	4 2 0 1	$42,760	Dist	17 3 5 3	$85,400

5Feb95-8Aqu	fst	6f	⊡	:231 :472 1:003 1:14	Alw 34000N3X	74	6	4	2½	2hd	2hd	43¼	Migliore R	119 b	*.60	70-28	Baypark1173 Rachmanoff112no Jericho Blaise117nk	Lugged in stretch	6
21Jan95-7Aqu	my	6f	⊡	:223 :454 :574 1:103	Alw 31040N2X	96	3	1	11	12	15	13	Migliore R	119 b	*1.65	90-14	Goodbye To You1193 Ocean Splash1177½ Pro On Ice112nk	Ridden out	4
8Jan95-4Aqu	fst	6f	⊡	:231 :463 :591 1:121	Alw 32000N2X	87	5	2	31½	31	31½	33½	Migliore R	122 b	*1.10	78-27	Vallata Lane1191 Bold Spector1172½ Goodbye To You1221½	Even trip	5
18Dec94-5Aqu	fst	6f	⊡	:23 :471 :592 1:112 3↑	Alw 30000N1X	89	5	4	32	2hd	12½	16	Velazquez J R	117 b	*2.70	86-22	Goodbye To You1176 Francis Marion115nk Lulu's Little Boy1152½	Driving	10
15Oct94-9SA	fst	6½f		:22 :45 1:091 1:152 3↑	Clm 16000	66	10	4	3½	41	97¾	1111	Flores D R	LB 116 b	10.00	84-08	VlueTheVenue116no ShoDnGoff1111¾ H'sLikThWind1161	Wide, gave way	11
27Sep94-7Fpx	fst	6f		:221 :453 :581 1:102 3↑	Clm 20000	74	6	4	2½	31	45	47	Guerra W A	LB 116 b	14.20	90-08	Powerofthninetys1192 Video Alert116hd Holiday Point1165	Steadied 1/4	6
4Sep94-5Dmr	fst	6f		:213 :443 :563 1:092 3↑	Ⓢ Alw 41276N1X	68	11	10	119½	1110	109½	118	Valenzuela F H	LB 119 b	18.60	86-06	Swift Walker118nk Flight Of Majesty119nk Copelan's Eagle119½	Outrun	11
26May94-4Hol	fst	6f		:22 :45 :571 1:093	Ⓢ Alw 37000N1X	72	1	5	41¼	42½	53	79	Nakatani C S	LB 116 b	*2.20	83-13	MyPrvtPryrs1164 TochThMoon1192 Mr.ClPrspctr1161	Inside, gave way	7
6May94-8Hol	fst	6½f		:213 :442 1:084 1:153 3↑	Ⓢ Alw 37000N1X	76	2	1	31½	31	34½	44¾	Flores D R	LB 119 b	1.90	86-06	Bolger's Lead119¾ Me And Mr. T.115no Cuepredictive1144	Saved ground	5
24Mar94-7SA	fst	6f		:214 :441 :561 1:081	Ⓢ Alw 37000N1X	93	7	3	41¼	42	22½	23½	Nakatani C S	LB 118 b	*1.60	92-09	YearsOfDreming1213½ GoodbyeToYou1182 Queen'sPge118hd	Second best	7

WORKOUTS: Feb 26 Bel tr.t 3f fst :363 H *4/21* Feb 18 Bel tr.t 5f fst 1:013 B *7/19* ●Dec 28 Bel tr.t 5f fst 1:01 H *1/23* ●Dec 9 Bel tr.t 6f fst 1:14 H *1/10*

Goodbye To You shows the same basic m.o. for Young: going nowhere on the southern California circuit at one-for-18 lifetime, freshened up after stopping badly in a mid-October sprint at Santa Anita (for just a $16,000 claiming tag), and shipped to Aqueduct. Bang, zoom, the gelding wins a preliminary allowance by six widening lengths first time out of the box — even though he couldn't get a sniff against Cal-breds out west. Two starts later, on January 21, came an easy wire-to-wire score in the N2X condition; the gelding would go on to finish first (only to be disqualified) in a N3X allowance in March.

Horses hardly need to hail from a major circuit such as southern California to make hay at the Big A. Those from the weaker northern California circuit can do quite nicely, as Cocoa Lad showed:

Cocoa Lad
Own: Sanders Melissa I
CHAVEZ J F (161 31 17 23 .19) **$17,500**

Dk. b or br g. 6
Sire: Devil's Bag (Halo)
Dam: Ballena Ridge (Riva Ridge)
Br: Mabee Mr & Mrs John C (Ky)
Tr: Parisella John (65 16 11 8 .25)

117

Lifetime Record: 16 5 0 2 $51,700										
1995	1	0	0	0		Turf	1	0	0	0	
1994	6	1	0	2	$8,000	Wet	3	1	0	1	$6,200
Aqu ⊡	1	0	0	0		Dist	14	5	0	2	$50,950

21Jan95-3Aqu	my	6f	⊡ :222 :452 :573 1:102	Clm 25000	98 4 3 1½ 11½ 14 14¼	Chavez J F	117 f	2.35	91-14	Cocoa Lad1174¼ Pension Fraud119¾ Prioritizer1131	Ridden out	6
Disqualified from purse money												
17Nov94-6BM	my	6f	:222 :454 :58 1:103	3↑ Clm c-12500	66 2 7 63¼ 31½ 33 37	Baze R A	LB 117	*.90	81-16	Sailing North1173 Blaze Borealis1174 Cocoa Lad1172	Wide turn	8
Claimed from Golden Eagle Farm, Shoemaker Leonard Trainer												
6Nov94-4BM	sly	6f	:224 :454 :582 1:113	3↑ Clm 8000	95 2 1 1hd 12 13 16	Baze R A	LB 117	*1.60	83-24	Cocoa Lad1176 AssumeTheThrone1191½ LetsTellShane117hd	Steady drive	7
22Oct94-3BM	fst	6f	:222 :451 :573 1:101	3↑ Clm 10000	76 2 4 2hd 1hd 2hd 32¼	Baze R A	LB 117	3.30	88-12	Source Of Pleasure117nk Shofar To1172 Cocoa Lad1173	Weakened	6
8Oct94-2BM	fst	6f	:221 :443 :563 1:093	3↑ Clm 12500	66 1 2 2hd 21½ 46 57	Espinoza V	LB 117	2.90	86-09	Wanpum1191½ Silver Stan1172½ Sit Look And Hope1171	Gave way	6
16Feb94-6GG	fst	6f	:211 :43 :553 1:084	Clm 25000	66 8 1 3nk 32½ 68¾ 811½	Espinoza V5	LB 114 fb	7.20	83-11	Bobba Robba1171 Icy Kevin117hd Media Plan1171½	Stopped	8
12Jan94-8BM	fst	6f	:214 :441 :563 1:093	ClmStk40000	66 6 3 52½ 54½ 66¼ 611	Baze R A	LB 121	*1.40	82-16	QuiteExtrordinary1211½ ValidPleasure1211¼ ToughToCrack117¾	Wide t[illegible]	[illegible]
19Dec93-8BM	fm	4½f Ⓣ	:21 :452 :52	3↑ Handicap25k	70 6 3 34½ 77 77½	Espinoza V	LB 108	2.50	88 04	NaevusStar1061 ZephyrArt1151½ QuiteExtrordinary1151	Brushed stretch	[illegible]
5Dec93-6Hol	fst	6f	:213 :442 :563 1.09	3↑ Clm 25000	94 3 4 1hd 1½ 1½ 1¾	Antley C W	LB 117	*3.20	95-10	Cocoa Lad117¾ Auriga1172½ Lord Byron1173½	Driving	10
3Nov93-7SA	fst	6f	:213 :443 :57 1:092	3↑ Clm 50000	83 6 3 21 2hd 2hd 45¼	Desormeaux K J	LB 116	9.20	85-14	Outlawed118no Rathsallah1161¾ What A Spell1113½	Bid, weakened	7

WORKOUTS: Jan 11 Aqu ⊡ 5f fst 1:054 B *5/6* Jan 6 Aqu ⊡ 4f fst :51 B *4/7* Dec 31 Aqu ⊡ 4f fst :52 B *7/16*

Entered for as little as $8,000 at Bay Meadows, the gelding was claimed out of a third place finish for $12,500 in November, freshened up and sent to John Parisella in New York, and promptly smashed a field of $25,000 sprinters under a hand ride.

A Bimp in the Eye, whose past performances are shown below, was blanked at the Meadowlands in the fall of 1994, but became another success story for the "Club Med to Club Dead" Aqueduct angle during the early part of 1995:

A Bimp in the Bye
Own: Lamarca Stable
CHAVEZ J F (23 6 2 3 .26)

B. m. 5
Sire: Silent Screen (Prince John)
Dam: Stephie Brown Eyes (Explodent)
Br: Barge Marc (Ky)
Tr: Anderson William D (—)

117

Lifetime Record: 25 7 4 1 $87,775										
1995	5	3	1	0	$48,400	Turf	1	0	0	0	
1994	7	0	1	1	$4,590	Wet	3	0	1	1	$7,755
Aqu	3	0	2	0	$9,460	Dist	2	2	0	0	$17,400

4Mar95-6Aqu	fst	6f	⊡ :224 :464 1:001 1:132	ⒻAlw 32000N2X	69 5 2 52 43½ 31 1nk	Chavez J F	122	3.00	76-24	ABimpInTheBye122nk Hppenchnc1123½ PromisdRlic1174	Wide, hard drive	5
19Feb95-6Aqu	fst	6f	⊡ :224 :464 :593 1:124	ⒻAlw 30000N1X	84 3 2 2½ 31 31½ 1nk	Chavez J F	117	5.40	79-22	ABmpInThB117nk MssShplftr1173½ EphrcIntrld1176½	Altered course 1/2 pl	6
26Jan95-3Aqu	fst	6f	⊡ :232 :48 1:01 1:141	ⒻClm 17500	78 1 4 2½ 11½ 12 14½	Chavez J F	117	4.70	72-26	A Bimp In The Bye1174½ Bunny's Touch1153 Miss Smart1136	Drew away	6
12Jan95-3Aqu	fst	6f	⊡ :231 :472 1:002 1:132	ⒻClm 12000	73 7 4 73¾ 54 21 2nk	Migliore R	114	14.70	76-20	Green Reader119nk A BimpInTheBye1146½ PaperRain117no	Rallied six wide	9
7Jan95-6Pha	sly	6f	:221 :453 :58 1:11	ⒻClm 11000	37 5 12 109¾ 1010 1014 1013½	Colton R E	116 f	*2.90	73-17	PrettyForest1163½ Simulcspy1162¾ ChrlestonDnce116½	Off slow, very dull	12
10Dec94-1Med	sly	6f	:214 :45 :573 1:104	3↑ ⒻClm 12500	73 7 4 34 34 34 31½	Colton R E	116	9.80	85-17	Notice Taken1191¼ Copelan's Charm116nk A Bimp In TheBye1164½	Mild bid	9
30Nov94-5Med	fst	6f	:223 :46 :581 1:102	3↑ ⒻClm 12500	51 6 4 55 53½ 63 57½	McCauley W H	116	6.90	82-13	Claymore Gal1132¼ Missle Lock1162¾ Sharp Reef116hd	Even trip	7
11Nov94-3Med	fst	6f	:222 :454 :574 1:103	3↑ ⒻAlw 22000N1X	51 5 5 53½ 54 58½ 59¼	Santagata N	116	5.60	79-12	Greek Fiesta114¾ Sandye's Sensation1145½ Hidden Crest1141½	Even trip	7
19Oct94-4Aqu	fst	7f	:231 :463 1:114 1:25	ⒻClm 14000	46 3 4 63½ 52¾ 54½ 512½	Migliore R	117	4.00	66-20	All Power113¾ Grab The Glory112nk Fortune Wand1144	No factor	6
4Oct94-5Med	fst	6f	:223 :452 :58 1:104	3↑ ⒻClm 10000	73 3 6 53½ 53 53¼ 2hd	McCauley W H	116	4.20	87-15	Safe Shelter116hd A Bimp In The Bye116nk Manor North1163	Just missed	7

WORKOUTS: Dec 28 GS 5f fst 1:023 B *5/16*

After languishing in cheap claiming races, the mare found herself on the inner track, running four terrific races (from on and from off the early pace) and advancing through allowance conditions back-to-back.

Horses who've had a lot of racing aren't the textbook prototype of allowance winners, but the ranks are thin at this time of year, and it's not uncommon to see horses with past performances that look like this:

Grab The Glory
Own: My Paradise Farms
MIGLIORE R (75 21 14 14 .28) **$50,000**

B. m. 5
Sire: Alphabatim (Verbatim)
Dam: Hope of Glory (Mr Leader)
Br: McKellen Donald (Md)
Tr: Friedman Mitchell (23 7 4 4 .30)

116

Lifetime Record: 49 16 6 11 $185,247										
1995	7	3	1	0	$62,700	Turf	1	0	0	0	
1994	14	3	3	4	$51,850	Wet	5	1	0	1	$9,245
Aqu	5	1	1	2	$31,190	Dist	3	2	0	1	$43,500

18Mar95-3Aqu	fst	1⅛	:482 1:141 1:394 1:522	ⒻAlw 36000N3X	86 5 1 1½ 1½ 1hd 1nk	Migliore R	116	6.30	78-31	Grab The Glory116nk Forcing Bid11313 Shellster1135	Pressued, gamely	8
10Mar95-4Aqu	fst	170	⊡ :234 :483 1:14 1:444	ⒻClm 19000	82 3 3 41½ 31½ 1hd 14¼	Migliore R	116	3.35	74-33	GrbTheGlory1164¼ Biogio'sGirl112hd UpsttFlyr1091	Svd grnd, going away	6
2Mar95-8Aqu	fst	170	⊡ :24 :481 1:131 1:421	ⒻAlw 36000N3X	49 6 4 31 41½ 68 621½	Migliore R	117	3.25	65-14	Manor Queen117nk Forcing Bid1176½ Shellster1171¼	Wide, tired	6
16Feb95-8Aqu	fst	1 1/16	⊡ :232 :474 1:13 1:464	ⒻAlw 36000N3X	57 11 6 55½ 66½ 810 515½	Perez R B5	114	*2.45	55-30	Royal Cozzene1172½ Forcing Bid1171½ Said Privately1173½	Wide, tired	12
3Feb95-8Aqu	fst	1 1/16	⊡ :24 :483 1:14 1:48	ⒻAlw 36000N3X	83 5 3 21½ 21 21½ 2nk	Migliore R	119	*1.65	65-30	Tuscany Breeze110nk Grab The Glory1191¾ Manor Queen1174	Gradual gain	7
29Jan95-4Aqu	fst	1⅛	⊡ :481 1:141 1:412 1:544	ⒻAlw 34000N2X	88 5 3 33½ 22 11½ 14¾	Migliore R	117	3.55	62-35	Grab The Glory1174¾ Delta West117½ Cherry Glow1173	Good trip	7
13Jan95-7Aqu	fst	6f	⊡ :23 :463 :591 1:121	ⒻAlw 32000N2X	73 5 3 43½ 52¼ 41½ 42½	Migliore R	119	11.40	79-18	Allen's Cheer1121½ For Sport1171 Cleverly Intended122no	In traffic 1/4 pl	7
14Dec94-7Aqu	fst	1 1/16	⊡ :234 :492 1:144 1:471	3↑ ⒻAlw 34000N2X	77 4 2 31½ 41½ 33 42¾	Lantz J A5	117	4.50	66-27	Saratoga April117¾ Upstate Flyer112¾ Cherry Glow1151¼	Weakened	8
7Dec94-7Aqu	fst	1 1/16	⊡ :231 :472 1:124 1:451	3↑ ⒻAlw 32000N1X	76 4 4 62½ 31½ 11½ 1½	Lantz J A5	112	7.10	79-21	Grab The Glory112½ Blazing Clearance1157 Doc's Josephine112no	Driving	12
17Nov94-7Aqu	fst	7f	:231 :47 1:123 1:26	3↑ ⒻAlw 30000N1X	64 8 1 41¾ 31 31½ 31½	Migliore R	117	4.10	72-16	Grab115nk Silver Victory1081¼ Grab The Glory1172¼	Willingly	9

It took Grab the Glory 41 starts, but she finally got her first allowance victory during the first week of inner track racing, December 7. Able to retain good form throughout the winter, the mare subsequently won three of her next eight starts, chalking up two more allowance wins along the way.

As Grab The Glory shows, a horse needn't be a shipper to suddenly rise through the ranks. And when a horse is handled by a trainer such as Gasper Moschera, who is noted for developing horses that hold their form for extended periods of time, there's no limit to how far up the ladder it may go:

```
1x  Electrojet                          B. g. 6                                            Lifetime Record :  60 15 15  9   $343,670
    PP - 4                               Sire: Gate Dancer  (Sovereign Dancer)      1995   3 1 1 0     $40,000   Turf   2 0 0 1     $2,640
Own: Davis Barbara J                     Dam: Favorite Song  (Pia Star)            1994  23 11 5 4    $202,280   Wet   11 3 2 1    $54,720
MIGLIORE R (325 76 54 56 .23)            Br:  Merrill Kenneth F (Fla)         112  Aqu   19 5 5 3    $142,760   Dist   3 0 1 0    $11,080
                                         Tr:  Moschera.Gasper S (172 38 28 31 .22)

1Mar95-8Aqu gd  ⬚ :23   :47 1:111 1:422 3↑ Handicap50k   106 4 5 511 561 2hd 12   Migliore R   118 b  2.60  93-12 Electrojet1182 Major Pots11611 Iron Gavel11611      Wide 1/4, going away 6
8Feb95-8Aqu fst 11⁄8 ⬚ :48  1:124 1:392 1:521 3↑ Assault H-G3  95 1 8 891 761 661 6102 Velazquez J R 112 b 1.95e 64-40 More To Tell1141 Danzig's Dance1152 Jacksonport11213  No threat 9
6Jan95-7Aqu fst 11⁄4 ⬚ :491 1:134 1:39 2:042 3↑ Handicap50k   97 4 4 461 321 231 241  Migliore R   122 b  2.20 102-21 Major Pots1164 Electrojet12224 Jacksonport12154  Second best 6
31Dec94-7Aqu fst 11⁄8 ⬚ :24  :473 1:124 1:46 3↑ Handicap50k  102 5 4 49  433 1hd 11  Migliore R   114 b  2.15  75-34 Electrojet1141 Country Sky1104 Key Contender12031  Driving 5
8Dec94-7Aqu fst 11⁄8 ⬚ :232 :473 1:121 1:434 3↑ Alw 36000N3X  101 3 4 331 32  21 111  Perez R B5   114 b *1.55 86-21 Electrojet11411 Gallapiat's Moment11712 Private Plan11731  Driving 5
30Nov94-7Aqu fst 11⁄8 ⬚ :50  1:142 1:394 1:521 3↑ Alw 36000N2X  92 4 4 21  21 21 111  Migliore R   117 b *1.45 75-27 Electrojet11721 Five Star General1174 Fanchee1104      Driving 7
25Nov94-4Aqu fst 11⁄8 ⬚ :482 1:123 1:38 1:511 3↑ Clm 45000    95 7 3 32  211 11 11  Perez R B5   110 b  2.80e 80-13 Electrojet1102 Ambush Alley1131 Alpstein1144       Driving 7
19Nov94-6Aqu wf 1  :23  :462 1:114 1:361 3↑ Alw 34000N2X      92 6 4 55  21 21 221  Perez R B5   112 b  1.60e 84-20 Sky Hero11023 Electrojet1125 Brett's Jet11551      Rallied wide 7
4Nov94-2Aqu fst 1  :23  :46 1:111 1:371 3↑ Clm 25000         87 2 6 521 41  11 11  Alvarado F T 117 b *.95e 82-14 Electrojet1171 Sorabosia1172 Red Scamper1102    Stumbled turn, drv 7
13Oct94-1Bel fst 11⁄8 ⬚ :49 1:112 1:422 3↑ Clm 25000        93 3 7 661 42  331 231  Smith M E   117 b *1.50e 87-16 Lightning Runner11231 Electrojet11711 Akiko11741  Rallied wide 9
WORKOUTS:  Feb 23 Bel tr.t 3f fst :39 B 9/13   Feb 1 Bel tr.t 4f fst :49 B 11/26
```

Electrojet had been to the post no less than 50 times by the fall of 1994 and could most accurately be classified as a hard-knocking "career claimer" who paid his way. But under Moschera's tutelage, the veteran won five times from the end of November through March 1, rolling through allowances and on into the overnight handicap ranks.

More To Tell was less heavily-raced heading into the winter, but the pattern of advancement is similar with this Moschera-trained colt:

```
1a  More To Tell                        Dk. b or br c. 4                                   Lifetime Record :  28 10  4  7   $348,420
    PP - 3                               Sire: Moro  (Full Out)                      1995   4 3 0 0    $148,365   Turf   1 0 0 0
Own: Davis Barbara J                     Dam: Good Heaven's Girl  (Authenticity)    1994  22 6 3 7    $179,555   Wet   4 2 1 1    $69,749
ALVARADO F T (303 53 59 48 .17)          Br:  Davis Albert & Barbara J (NY)   121  Aqu   11 7 2 0    $244,220   Dist   0 0 0 0
                                         Tr:  Moschera Gasper S (172 38 28 31 .22)

20Feb95-8Aqu fst 11⁄8 ⬚ :473 1:121 1:382 1:513 3↑ Stymie H-G3   109 7 6 681 441 31 13  Alvarado F T 118 *.95 78-29 More ToTell1183 AztecEmpire1102 FederalFunds1091  Wide, going away 7
8Feb95-8Aqu fst 11⁄8 ⬚ :48 1:124 1:392 1:521 3↑ Assault H-G3  112 2 9 78  54  41 151  Alvarado F T 114 1.95e 75-40 More To Tell1145 Danzig's Dance1152 Jacksonport11212  Going away 9
22Jan95-8Aqu wf 1 ⬚ :234 :473 1:114 1:431 3↑ ⓢKingsPoint H55k 103 7 5 521 311 2hd 1no Alvarado F T 120 *1.60 89-23 MorToTll120no DoublClvdos1182 ExcllntTippr117hd Four wide, hard drive 7
16Jan95-8Aqu gd 11⁄8 ⬚ :231 :46 1:093 1:41 3↑ Aqueduct H-G3  87 5 5 514 512 512 6142 Alvarado F T 114 3.80 85-20 Danzig'sDnce1115 KeyContender1154 GoldenLrch1124  Lacked response 8
29Dec94-8Aqu fst 170 ⬚ :231 :47 1:132 1:43 3↑ Alw 46000N$Y   110 1 5 59  41 .16 115  Alvarado F T 120 2.65 83-35 More To Tell12015 Aztec Empire1226 Gulf Reckoning1208  Driving 7
23Dec94-7Aqu fst 11⁄8 ⬚ :462 1:114 1:442 3↑ Alw 38000N4X   110 3 6 571 44 3nk 1nk Alvarado F T 115 10.60 83-23 More To Tell115nk Golden Larch11273 Yeckley1177  Driving 7
22Nov94-7Aqu wf 6f   :222 :462 :583 1:11 3↑ Alw 34000N3X    96 8 7 851 721 21 11  Perez R B5   110 2.70e 87-24 More To Tell1101 Fighting Daddy11731 Blum Gone1191 Five wide, driving 8
9Nov94-5Aqu fst 7f   :224 :46 1:111 1:233 3↑ Alw 34000N3X    79 7 3 710 78 671 611  Beckner D V5  110 1.95e 75-14 ⒹGoldenLrch1101 AdvncedPlcmnt11721 FightingDddy1171 Took up turn 7
  Placed 5th through disqualification
18Oct94-7Aqu fst 7f   :231 :46 1:102 1:224 3↑ Alw 34000N3X    94 6 5 551 66 32 321  Smith M E   116 7.00 88-15 Mr. Tyler1142 Golden Larch111nk More To Tell1166  Rallied wide 9
29Sep94-7Bel fst 6f   :22  :45 :572 1:094 3↑ ⓢAlw 32000N2X  96 1 6 57  541 2hd 12  Perez R B5   109 4.80 92-15 MoreToTll1092 MmorisOfLind1143 Rj'sChrtr1133  Saved ground, driving 9
WORKOUTS:  Mar 6 Bel tr.t 5f fst 1:022 B 2/6   Jan 11 Bel tr.t 4f fst :481 H 4/34   Dec 19 Bel tr.t 4f fst :474 H 2/27
```

Most New York-breds find it tough sledding after winning their N2X condition, which is the last available state-bred allowance, and usually need a drop to the claiming ranks to compete effectively. But More To Tell became a dual Grade 3-winner on the inner track, winning five races on that surface in slightly under two months.

During the early part of the 1995 season Moschera also guided an Ogden Phipps/Shug McGaughey castoff named Iron Gavel, who had been competing in claiming races for as little as $17,500, through a multi-race winning streak that climaxed with a 23-1 upset score in the Grade 2 Excelsior Handicap.

Transition Time

SPRING DOESN'T OFFICIALLY begin for New York horseplayers — and for many of the high-profile "designer" barns such as Phipps & McGaughey, Team Lukas, and the Allen Paulson/Bill Mott juggernaut, until the scene shifts to Belmont Park in May. But there is a period of transition from winter to spring that begins sometime around mid-March, coinciding with the conclusion of Gulfstream Park's winter meeting.

Many of the stables that wintered in sunny Florida have an eye toward the rich purses offered by Kentucky in the spring, and move directly from Gulfstream to Keeneland, and on to Churchill Downs before circling back to Belmont Park in May. But Aqueduct also receives an influx of horses from southern Florida, and that, along with the shift to the main track, signals that the period of transition from winter to spring has begun.

Each and every year, right around mid-March, players will start to notice horses that do something like this:

Yourmissinthepoint
Own: Parezo Mark
MIGLIORE R (28 7 5 5 .25)

B. g. 4
Sire: Mugatea (Hold Your Peace)
Dam: Head Teller (Silent Screen)
Br: Serna Julian Jr (Fla)
Tr: Klesaris Robert P (5 3 2 0 .60)

119

Lifetime Record:	6	2	1	1	$27,360					
1995	4	1	1	0	$22,410	Turf	0	0	0	0
1994	2	1	0	1	$4,950	Wet	0	0	0	0
Aqu	0	0	0	0		Dist	0	0	0	0

11Mar95-6Aqu	fst	$1\frac{1}{16}$ ⊡	$:23^{4}$	$:48^{1}$	$1{:}13^{1}$	$1{:}45^{1}$	Alw 32000N1X	97	2	2	3^{2}	1^{hd}	1^{5}	1^{11}	Migliore R	114 fb	2.40	79–25	Yourmissinthepoint114^{11} King Protea$103^{1\frac{1}{2}}$ Get Behind Me$114^{\frac{1}{2}}$	Driving	6
4Feb95-5GP	fst	$1\frac{1}{16}$	:23	:47	1:13	$1{:}47^{3}$	Alw 26000N1X	66	11	11	$10^{9\frac{1}{2}}$	9^{11}	$7^{9\frac{1}{4}}$	$5^{8\frac{1}{4}}$	Boulanger G	119 f	6.10	62–26	Grey Chandon119^{2} Happy Fella$119^{3\frac{1}{2}}$ Grand Glimmer$119^{2\frac{1}{4}}$		12
Eight wide top str, belated bid																						
18Jan95-8GP	fst	7f	$:22^{3}$	$:45^{2}$	$1{:}10^{1}$	1:23	Alw 25000N1X	67	4	5	$7^{3\frac{3}{4}}$	$8^{6\frac{1}{2}}$	$7^{9\frac{3}{4}}$	$6^{11\frac{1}{2}}$	Castillo H Jr	119 f	9.70	77–18	April Christmas$119^{2\frac{3}{4}}$ Turkomatic119^{3} Island Dash$119^{1\frac{1}{2}}$	Failed to menace	9
1Jan95-8Crc	fst	7f	$:22^{4}$	$:46^{4}$	$1{:}12^{1}$	1:26	Alw 17000N1X	78	9	5	3^{2}	$4^{3\frac{1}{2}}$	$2^{1\frac{1}{2}}$	2^{hd}	Castillo H Jr	119 f	*1.90	82–19	JustARomn119^{hd} Yourmissnthpont119^{1} CruclTm119^{4}	Lugged in, gamely	9
13Dec94-10Crc	fst	7f	$:23^{1}$	$:46^{4}$	$1{:}12^{1}$	1:25	3↑ Alw 17000N1X	83	9	3	$3^{\frac{1}{2}}$	3^{2}	4^{4}	3^{3}	Mickens T J5	113 f	30.90	84–17	Propulsor118^{2} Heads Up Turk119^{1} Yourmissinthepoint$113^{4\frac{1}{2}}$	No excuse	10
1Dec94-2Crc	fst	6f	$:22^{2}$	$:46^{2}$	$:59^{4}$	$1{:}13^{1}$	3↑ Md 12500	70	9	4	$5^{5\frac{1}{2}}$	$4^{8\frac{1}{2}}$	3^{3}	$1^{1\frac{1}{4}}$	Boulanger G	121	*1.30	81–18	Yourmissinthepoint$121^{1\frac{1}{4}}$ Freewhlin'Frnk$121^{5\frac{1}{2}}$ Vlid'sGun$114^{4\frac{1}{4}}$	Going away	9

WORKOUTS: Mar 4 Bel tr.t 4f fst $:50^{4}$ B *34/44* Feb 27 Bel tr.t 4f fst $:50^{1}$ B *14/20* Jan 28 Crc 3f fst $:37^{3}$ B *14/36*

Yourmissinthepoint shipped north from Florida and exploded to an 11-length victory on March 11. His Beyer Speed Figure came in at 97, which was 14 points (several lengths) higher than anything he'd run previously. Horses running their eyeballs out first time out in New York is a fairly common phenomenon with these Florida shippers in March, so much so that it is commonly referred to by the New York regulars as the "Gulfstream Mystique."

Although Yourmissinthepoint was a 4-year-old at the time of his big win, he was a lightly-raced horse, and his record typifies what might otherwise be anticipated of 3-year-olds who make the trip from Florida to New York: for a combination of reasons, they have a significant edge on their winter-worn counterparts.

This was never brought to light more vividly than during the last weekend of March, with racing now being conducted on the main track once again.

This was a weekend during which ship-in 3-year-olds from Florida dominated, starting with a horse who ran second in Saturday's fifth:

Placid Fund
Own: Rosenthal Mrs Morton
MADRID A JR (35 0 7 5 .00)

Ch. c. 3 (Mar)
Sire: Dixieland Band (Northern Dancer)
Dam: Sunset Strait (Naskra)
Br: Morton Rosenthal (Ky)
Tr: Schosberg Richard (12 2 4 3 .17)

120

Lifetime Record:	4	M	2	0	$9,580						
1995	3	M	2	0	$9,580	Turf	0	0	0	0	
1994	1	M	0	0		Wet	1	0	1	0	$3,420
Aqu	1	0	1	0	$6,000	Dist	0	0	0	0	

25Mar95-5Aqu	fst	1	$:23^{4}$	$:47^{3}$	$1{:}13^{4}$	$1{:}39^{2}$	Md Sp Wt	78	10	1	2^{hd}	1^{hd}	$2^{\frac{1}{2}}$	$2^{\frac{3}{4}}$	Madrid A Jr	120 b	18.60	71–25	Treasure Cay$120^{\frac{3}{4}}$ Placid Fund$120^{4\frac{3}{4}}$ Classy Moment$120^{4\frac{1}{2}}$	Dueled, gamely	11
26Feb95-3GP	wf	7f	$:22^{2}$	$:45^{4}$	$1{:}11^{2}$	$1{:}24^{4}$	Md 57500	69	9	2	$5^{\frac{3}{4}}$	$4^{\frac{1}{2}}$	1^{hd}	$2^{\frac{3}{4}}$	Davis R G	118	10.60	78–18	Quick Study$120^{\frac{3}{4}}$ Placid Fund118^{3} Brave Warrior$120^{3\frac{1}{2}}$		10
Brushed leaving bkstr, second best																					
12Feb95-3GP	fst	7f	$:22^{4}$	$:46^{2}$	$1{:}11^{3}$	$1{:}25^{2}$	Md 50000	56	9	11	$10^{6\frac{1}{2}}$	$9^{9\frac{3}{4}}$	$7^{7\frac{1}{4}}$	$5^{7\frac{3}{4}}$	Davis R G	120	12.80	68–20	Dancing Lad120^{3} Traveling Jeff120^{1} Tonya's Dancer$120^{1\frac{1}{2}}$	Mild bid	11
11Aug94-3Sar	fst	5f	$:22^{4}$	$:46^{2}$		:59	Md Sp Wt	38	1	1	$7^{9\frac{1}{2}}$	$8^{6\frac{1}{2}}$	$7^{6\frac{1}{2}}$	$6^{11\frac{1}{4}}$	Luzzi M J	118	23.40	77–14	Magical Call118^{no} Mountain Of Laws118^{4} Hopkins Forest$118^{2\frac{3}{4}}$	No threat	8

WORKOUTS: Mar 17 GP 4f fst :49 H *6/33* Mar 11 GP 4f fst $:48^{3}$ H *3/39* Feb 8 GP 4f fst $:48^{4}$ H *6/41* Feb 3 GP 3f fst :37 B *8/34* Jan 28 GP 5f fst $1{:}02^{1}$ B *11/37* Jan 19 GP 5f fst 1:02 B *12/40*

Placid Fund leapt to a new high in terms of Beyer figures, posting a 78 after dueling the entire way and settling for the place behind another Gulfstream shipper, a 3-5 shot from Phipps & McGaughey named Treasure Cay.

Three races later, New York's first major stepping-stone to the Kentucky Derby, the one-mile Gotham Stakes, was chewed up and spit out by Talkin Man (who eventually went off the 4-1 second choice in Louisville):

Talkin Man
Own: Kinghaven Farms & Stollery Helen G
SELLERS S J (—)

Dk. b or br c. 3 (Feb)
Sire: With Approval (Caro)
Dam: Pookette (Miswaki)
Br: Kinghaven Farms Ltd & Angus Glen Farm Ltd (Ont-C)
Tr: Attfield Roger L (1 1 0 0 1.00)
123

Lifetime Record :	7	4	1	0	$377,967						
1995	1	1	0	0	$150,000	Turf	0	0	0	0	
1994	6	3	1	0	$227,967	Wet	0	0	0	0	
Aqu	1	1	0	0	$150,000	Dist	1	1	0	0	$102,372

25Mar95-8Aqu	fst	1	:232 :464 1:121 1:364	Gotham-G2	105	7	4	4¾	2hd	1½	17	Smith M E	122	7.20	85-25	Talkin Man1227 Da Hoss1172 DeviousCourse1175½	Four wide, going away 11
5Nov94-8CD	fst	1 1/16	:231 :47 1:123 1:442	B C Juv-G1	72	1	2	21	2hd	912	1016	Smith M E	122	11.10	76-07	Timber Country1222 Eltish1223 Tejano Run1221¼	Pressed, tired 13
23Oct94-6WO	fst	1⅛	:48 1:122 1:383 1:523	®CornatnFty-G1C	82	5	1	11	21	14	16½	Landry R C	122	*.20	83-19	Talkin Man1226½ All Firmed Up1223½ Regal Discovery1222½	Handily 7
9Oct94-8WO	fst	1 1/16	:231 :463 1:114 1:463	Grey-G3	81	3	2	1hd	1½	14	14¾	Landry R C	117	*1.00	83-21	Talkin Man1174¾ Raji1137¾ Celestial Star1134¼	10
Drifted turn, much the best																	
20Aug94-8WO	fst	6½f	:231 :454 1:101 1:163	Swynford-G3C	91	5	3	1hd	1½	12	15	Seymour D J	115	*.80	96-11	Talkin Man1155 All Firmed Up1175 Raji1152	Ridden out three path 6
23Jly94-9WO	fst	6f	:221 :45 :58 1:111	®Vandal-G3C	73	4	2	3½	2hd	2½	23½	Seymour D J	115	4.15	85-08	Tethra1223½ Talkin Man1156½ Big Red Rumm115hd	Second best 5
10Jly94-3WO	fst	5f	:214 :454 :592	Md Sp Wt	48	9	11	910	912	811	45	Seymour D J	115	6.30	88-08	Mysterious Vice1152¾ White Ensign1152 Rambling River115nk	12
Bumped start, five wide turn, finished well																	

WORKOUTS: Apr 9 Kee 6f gd 1:13 B 1/2 ●Apr 2 Kee 5f fst 1:004 B 1/9 Mar 19 Pay 6f my 1:201 B 3/7 ●Mar 6 Pay 5f fst 1:031 B 1/9 ●Feb 28 Pay 5f fst 1:041 B 1/7 Feb 21 Pay 4f my :503 B 1/2

Talkin Man hadn't run at Gulfstream, but he had trained in Florida at Payson Park over a deep and demanding surface, and improved 15 Beyer points over his previous best effort, earning a 105 for his seven-length romp at 7-1.

The ninth race was won by Can't Believe It:

Can't Believeit
Own: Gallagher James H
COOPER G J (49 4 4 10 .08)

B. g. 3 (Mar)
Sire: Unreal Zeal (Mr. Prospector)
Dam: Majestic Madonna (Majestic Light)
Br: Mrs. James H. Gallagher (Fla)
Tr: Gullo Gary P (15 5 2 1 .33)
114[7]

Lifetime Record :	14	4	2	3	$51,050						
1995	5	3	0	2	$41,500	Turf	2	0	0	0	$310
1994	9	1	2	1	$9,550	Wet	2	1	1	0	$7,860
Aqu	2	2	0	0	$31,800	Dist	2	2	0	0	$31,800

25Mar95-9Aqu	fst	1	:232 :472 1:133 1:41	Clm 40000	74	7	2	2½	12½	12	11¼	Chavez J F	119 fb	*1.75	64-25	Can't Believeit1191¼ Conduit Street116¾ Elk Basin1163¾	Fully extended 9
16Mar95-4Aqu	fst	1	:232 :47 1:12 1:38	Clm 45000	74	3	2	11	11½	11½	12	Chavez J F	112 fb	3.75	79-24	Can't Believeit1122 Back Ring Al109¾ Vega's Secret1155¼	Mild drive 6
6Feb95-3GP	fst	6f	:23 :464 :594 1:13	Clm 25000	68	5	5	52½	41½	1½	31½	Fires E	L 117 fb	*1.60	73-26	Quixote's Luck119½ The Great Manolo1171 Can't Believeit1172½	8
Bounced around start, between horses, weakened																	
23Jan95-4GP	fst	7f	:221 :451 1:111 1:243	Clm 20000	68	8	3	51¾	43	11	34¾	Fires E	L 117 fb	4.40	75-18	He Runs For Daddy1172 Lucky Bird1172¾ Can't Believeit1174	Weakened 11
7Jan95-11GP	sly	7f	:222 :452 1:104 1:244	Clm 16000	69	4	5	22½	21½	23	1no	Fires E	L 117 fb	2.50	79-12	Can't Believeit117no Tar Buggy11711 Bears The One1172	Wide, just up 8
20Dec94-8Crc	fm	*1 1/16 ⓣ	1:442	Alw 17500N1X	-0	10	3	32	1017	1026	1041½	Velez J A Jr	L 117 fb	38.10	41-15	Cuzzin Jeb1208 Bullet Trained117hd Dot's Silver B.120nk	Stopped badly 10
4Dec94-5Crc	fst	6f	:214 :46 :592 1:134	Clm 25000	62	7	2	54¼	41¾	11	2hd	Velasquez J	L 115 fb	10.10	78-20	HighNHoly115hd Can'tBelieveit115nk StandingPat117¾	4-wide bid, gamely 8
18Nov94-7Crc	fst	6f	:224 :463 :591 1:121	Clm 30000	54	2	3	2½	32	34½	47¼	Nunez E O	L 113 fb	18.90	79-11	Notebook P. C.1133½ Trusted Advisor1152½ Is It Possible1151¼	Gave way 5
6Nov94-4Crc	fst	6f	:224 :46 :584 1:12	Clm 30000	60	3	3	11	3nk	32½	46½	Douglas R R	L 114 fb	3.50	80-12	Tommy Toy1151 Is It Possible1151¾ Notebook P. C.1153¾	Faded 5
20Oct94-8Crc	fm	*1 1/16 ⓣ	1:462	Alw 19500N1X	48	6	1	1hd	53½	57½	58	Castaneda M	L 115 b	3.20	64-28	Val's Prince1153¾ Mighty Tomba1151 Hurri Up Defense115½	Tired 8

WORKOUTS: Mar 7 Crc 4f fst :522 B 20/23

All out to win by a nose for $16,000 at Gulfstream, the 3-year-old gelding was under only a "mild drive" to win for $45,000 at Aqueduct with a lifetime-best Beyer of 74 on March 16, and, though fully extended this time, repeated with another 74.

Sunday's opener brought another ship-in winner from Florida, the 3-year-old filly Seeking Account:

Seeking Account
Own: Austin Dale H

B. f. 3 (Apr)
Sire: Seeking the Gold (Mr. Prospector)
Dam: Personal Triumph (Private Account)
Br: Peter E. Blum (Ky)
Tr: Schosberg Richard (—)

Lifetime Record :	2	1	0	0	$18,290					
1995	2	1	0	0	$18,290	Turf	0	0	0	0
1994	0	M	0	0		Wet	0	0	0	0
CSC	0	0	0	0		Dist	0	0	0	0

26Mar95-1Aqu	fst	1	:233 :474 1:141 1:401 3	ⒻMd Sp Wt	60	7	2	2½	1hd	1½	12	Davis R G	120	2.35	68-30	SeekingAccount1202 Enchancement12010 CrftyLdy1205	Stalked, gamely 7
16Mar95-6GP	fst	6f	:223 :444 :572 1:104 3	ⒻMd Sp Wt	58	4	11	89½	810	58	511¼	Davis R G	120	9.60	75-14	I Scream Melissa1209 Mary Mcglinchy120½ Penetralia120½	Belated bid 12

WORKOUTS: Mar 12 GP 4f fst :484 H 5/33 Mar 6 GP 5f fst 1:023 B 21/31 Feb 28 GP 5f fst 1:013 B 12/33 Feb 22 GP 4f fst :483 Hg8/72 Feb 15 GP 5f fst 1:032 Bg35/51 Feb 8 GP 5f fst 1:062 B 48/49

Seeking Account exhibited one of my favorite result-chart angles, one that shows how misleading the raw running positions in the past performances can sometimes be. Examining the first race of the filly's life, it's impossible to get a true picture of how strongly she closed in the final quarter *relative to all but one of her rivals.*

Yes, her running line conveys an "even" effort, showing her nine and a half lengths behind the leader after a quarter, 10 lengths behind after half a mile, eight lengths behind at the stretch call, and slightly more than 11 lengths behind at the finish. But, who was she running *behind?*

SIXTH RACE 6 FURLONGS. (1.074) MAIDEN SPECIAL WEIGHT. Purse $29,000. Fillies, 3-year-olds. Weight, 120 lbs.

Gulfstream

MARCH 16, 1995

Value of Race: $29,000 Winner $17,400; second $5,220; third $2,900; fourth $1,160; fifth $290; sixth $290; seventh $290; eighth $290; ninth $290; tenth $290; eleventh $290; twelfth $290. Mutuel Pool $211,951.00 Perfecta Pool $248,540.00 Trifecta Pool $224,758.00

Last Raced	Horse	M/Eqt. A.Wt	PP	St	$\frac{1}{4}$	$\frac{1}{2}$	Str	Fin	Jockey	Odds $1
20Feb95 6GP6	I Scream Melissa	3 120	1	5	1^{hd}	1^{hd}	1^5	1^9	Bravo J	27.30
	Mary Mcglinchy	L 3 120	9	9	10^5	10^5	$8\frac{1}{2}$	$2\frac{1}{2}$	Krone J A	8.70
	Penetralia	3 120	5	10	9^4	7^{hd}	$6\frac{1}{2}$	$3\frac{1}{2}$	Santos J A	18.30
20Feb95 6GP3	Emma Loves Marie	3 120	7	4	6^1	4^3	$3\frac{1}{2}$	$4^{1\frac{1}{2}}$	Smith M E	4.60
	Seeking Account	3 120	4	11	8^{hd}	$8^{2\frac{1}{2}}$	$5^{2\frac{1}{2}}$	5no	Davis R G	9.60
	Easy To Cope	L 3 120	10	2	$2^{2\frac{1}{2}}$	$2^{3\frac{1}{2}}$	$2^{1\frac{1}{2}}$	6^4	Ramos W S	15.80
26Feb95 6GP5	Roadways	3 120	12	1	11^{hd}	$11^{2\frac{1}{2}}$	11^7	7^1	Martin C W	42.60
26Nov94 6CD7	Gray Niner	Lb 3 120	6	8	5^{hd}	$6\frac{1}{2}$	$9^{1\frac{1}{2}}$	8^1	Peck B D	18.70
	Ionlyhaveeyesforu	3 120	3	6	3^{hd}	$3^{1\frac{1}{2}}$	4^1	9^{nk}	Bailey J D	0.70
20Feb95 6GP7	Supreme Order	3 120	2	7	$4^{2\frac{1}{2}}$	5^2	$7^{1\frac{1}{2}}$	10^3	Barton D M	43.60
	U S Charmer	3 120	11	3	7^3	9^3	$10\frac{1}{2}$	$11^{10\frac{1}{2}}$	Turner T G	63.30
	Foolish Angel	L 3 113	8	12	12	12	12	12	Soodeen R7	71.20

OFF AT 3:17 Start Good. Won driving. Time, :22³, :44⁴, :57², 1:10⁴ Track fast.

$2 Mutuel Prices:

1–I SCREAM MELISSA	56.60	24.60	9.60
9–MARY MCGLINCHY		10.80	6.00
5–PENETRALIA			11.20

$2 PERFECTA 1 & 9 PAID $840.40 $2 TRIFECTA 1–9–5 PAID $6,445.80

Ch. f, (May), by Carson City–Diplomatic Trust, by Diplomatic. Trainer Fisher John R S. Bred by Offutt–Cole Farm (Ky).

I SCREAM MELISSA sprinted to a slim lead inside, set the pace while under pressure from EASY TO COPE, settled in the stretch with a clear advantage then, under strong handling, won very convincingly while drifting out. MARY MCGLINCHY unhurried early, rallied in the drive to take down the place. PENETRALIA unhurried early, then closed with a good late rally in the drive. EMMA LOVES MARIE reserved early, made a run leaving the turn seven wide to be a forward factor then weakened in the drive. SEEKING ACCOUNT reserved early, then closed with a belated bid. EASY TO COPE vied for the early lead from the beginning then weakened in the stretch. ROADWAYS void of early foot then made a mild late bid. GRAY NINER reserved early then faded. IONLYHAVEEYESFORU, a forward factor early, gave way. SUPREME ORDER, within striking distance early, faltered. U S CHARMER reserved early then stopped. FOOLISH ANGEL was no factor.

Owners— 1, Campbell Alex G Jr; 2, Dinwiddle Farm; 3, Marablue Farm; 4, Knight Landon; 5, Austin Sandra H & Heatherwood Farm; 6, Hooper Fred W; 7, Fisher Mary V; 8, Tafel James B; 9, Caronia Charles A; 10, Humphrey G Watts Jr; 11, Dirienzo O N & Torsilieri C J; 12, Stutzman Nancy

Trainers— 2, Arnold George R II; 3, Schulhofer Flint S; 4, Badgett William Jr; 5, Schosberg Richard; 6, Serpe Philip M; 7, Werstler Charles R; 8, Nafzger Carl A; 9, Hough Stanley M; 10, Arnold George R II; 11, Reid Robert E Jr; 12, Mastronardi Nick Jr

Scratched— Antelope Flats, Lizzie Toon (26Feb95 6GP3), Wood Pajamas (2Mar95 2GP7), No Punch Intended (3Mar95 6GP10).

The winner of the race was I Scream Melissa, who wired the field while expanding her margin rapidly through the final quarter. Remove I Scream Melissa from the race, however, and here's how Seeking Account's adjusted running line would look:

$$7^{9\ 1/4} \qquad 7^{9\ 3/4} \qquad 4^3 \qquad 4^{2\ 1/4}$$

Quite a different line, eh? That's because Seeking Account's move on the rest of the field was happening at the exact same point where the winner was opening up her lead.

To make sure I don't miss hidden moves such as these, I make it a point to circle in my charts any wire-to-wire victories accomplished in this manner. The horses running behind the winner who gain in position but not in overall beaten lengths have actually closed much more powerfully than is shown by the numbers in their subsequent past performance line.

THE FEATURE RACE on Sunday, March 26, was the $75,000-added Cicada Stakes for 3-year-old fillies. I have written in the post-time odds next to the names of the seven contestants. Considering the fact that Florida shippers have been running amok, do any of the prices seem somewhat out-of-whack?

8 Aqueduct

7 Furlongs. (1:201) 3rd Running of THE CICADA. Purse $75,000 Added. Fillies, 3-year-olds. By subscription of $75 each which should accompany the nomination, $350 to pass the entry box, $400 to start with $75,000 added. The added moeny and all fees to be divided 60% to the winner, 20% to second, 11% to third, 6% to fourth and 3% to fifth. Weight, 121 lbs. Non-winners of $50,000 since January 1 or $30,000 twice since then, allowed 3 lbs. $50,000 or $20,000 twice, 5 lbs. $20,000 or two races other than maiden or claiming, 7 lbs. A race other than maiden or claiming, 9 lbs. Starters to be named at the closing time of entries. Trophies will be presented to the winning owner, trainer and jockey. Closed Saturday, March 11 with 16 nominations.

Evil's Pic 5-1

Own: Shapiro Theodore W
LUZZI M J (40 12 5 1 .30)

Ch. f. 3 (Mar)
Sire: Piccolino (Fappiano)
Dam: Evil's Sister (Medieval Man)
Br: T. Shapiro (WV)
Tr: Tesher Howard M (3 2 0 0 .67)

121

Lifetime Record: 7 6 1 0 $138,153

1995	2	2	0	0	$64,800	Turf	0	0	0	0	
1994	5	4	1	0	$73,353	Wet	0	0	0	0	
Aqu	0	0	0	0		Dist	1	1	0	0	$19,313

12Feb95-7Aqu fst 6f	⊡ :231	:474	1:003	1:132	ⒻDrlyPrecious53k	84	2	5	53	3½	1hd	12	Luzzi M J	121	*.40	76-26	Evil's Pic1212 Ride The Wind118 6½ Foxy Scarlet114 1½	Boxed in, stead 3/8	5
8Jan95-8Aqu fst 6f	⊡ :222	:462	1:00	1:133	ⒻRuthless54k	77	4	8	86½	53¾	1hd	11	Luzzi M J	118	1.80	75-27	Evil's Pic1181 Surprise Girl112 4½ Crafty Josie114nk	Driving	8
26Dec94-5Aqu fst 6f	⊡ :224	:463	:591	1:12	ⒻAlw 46000NC	84	1	1	43½	44½	2hd	1nk	Luzzi M J	121	*1.55	83-21	Evil's Pic121nk Crafty Jam116 1½ Ride The Wind11111	Driving	5
22Oct94-6CT fst 7f	:234	:474	1:132	1:274	ⓇTri-StateFty29k	68	4	1	2½	2hd	13	15	Bourne L J	121	*.50	84-21	Evil's Pic1215 Ani's Ara1247 Which One's That114½	Ridden out	7
10Oct94-10Del fst 6f	:22	:462	:584	1:104	ⒻEverget29k	94	10	8	84¾	3nk	18	117	Luttrell M G	116	4.40f	93-21	Evil's Pic11617 Racing Starflight116½ Brush With Royalty116nk	Sharp	12
2Sep94-3Bel fst 6f	:223	:46	:581	1:111	ⒻMd 35000	65	8	12	118¾	106¾	54	1hd	Smith M E	117	*2.40	85-12	Evil'sPic117hd Ftnoflivingwaters115 2½ NtureStory117nk	Brk slow, wide, drv	12
23Aug94-6Del fst 6f	:23	:471	:594	1:12	ⒻMd Sp Wt	59	6	6	64¾	41½	22½	24½	Murphy C K	118	2.90	82-14	Brush With Royalty118 4½ Evil's Pic11812 Super Twin118hd	Green	12

WORKOUTS: Mar 22 Bel tr.t 4f fst :481 B 6/22 Mar 16 Aqu 6f fst 1:12 H 1/1 Mar 11 Bel tr.t 5f fst 1:03 B 13/28 Mar 3 Bel tr.t 4f fst :514 B 18/19 Feb 10 Bel tr.t 3f fst :364 B 6/16 Feb 2 Bel tr.t 5f fst 1:013 B 3/10

Distinctive Ruby 24-1

Own: Robsham Einar P
VELAZQUEZ J R (38 6 7 3 .16)

Dk. b or br f. 3 (Apr)
Sire: Distinctive Pro (Mr. Prospector)
Dam: Ruby Wax (Gallant Romeo)
Br: E. Paul Robsham (NY)
Tr: Lewis Lisa L (1 1 0 0 1.00)

116

Lifetime Record: 5 3 1 0 $67,500

1995	2	1	0	0	$16,200	Turf	0	0	0	0	
1994	3	2	1	0	$51,300	Wet	0	0	0	0	
Aqu	2	1	1	0	$34,500	Dist	1	1	0	0	$18,000

4Mar95-9GP fst 1 1/16	:224	:462	1:113	1:444	ⒻBonnie Miss-G2	42	2	1	12½	33½	818	928	Barton D M	112 f	15.10	56-22	Mia's Hope117 1¼ Minister Wife119 2¼ Incredible Blues117nk	Stopped	9
5Feb95-1GP fst 6½f	:231	:463	1:112	1:181	ⒻAlw 27000N2X	88	3	2	12	12½	15	14¾	Santos J A	121	*.50	84-16	DistinctiveRuby121 4¾ HipHipHurRhy1213 Coldhrtedprincss121 2½	Handily	6
3Dec94-7Aqu fst 7f	:224	:462	1:122	1:254	ⒻⓈAlw 30000N1X	83	1	5	1½	1½	12	13½	Luzzi M J	116 f	1.65	75-24	Distinctive Ruby116 3½ Foxy Scarlet1214 Infallible1167	Driving	6
13Nov94-7Aqu fst 6f	:224	:464	:59	1:114	ⒻⓇN Y Stallion75k	87	5	3	1½	2hd	2½	21	Smith M E	114	*.60	82-22	Rogues Walk1161 Distinctive Ruby114 5½ Foxy Scarlet112 5¾	Second best	8
15Oct94-1Bel fst 6f	:223	:461	:584	1:114	ⒻⓈMd Sp Wt	85	1	1	13	17	110	112	Smith M E	117	*2.10	82-18	Distinctive Ruby11712 Quality Control1172 Russian Ensign110 1½	Handily	14

WORKOUTS: Mar 22 Bel tr.t 4f fst :474 B 4/22 ●Feb 26 GP 5f fst 1:00 H 1/22 Feb 22 GP 4f fst :52 B 62/72 Jan 27 GP 5f fst 1:00 H 2/30 Jan 21 GP 5f fst 1:021 B 14/34 Jan 13 GP 4f fst :51 B 25/29

Lucky Lavender Gal 27-1

Own: Worswick Dolores
DAVIS R G (4 2 0 1 .50)

B. f. 3 (Feb)
Sire: Carson City (Mr. Prospector)
Dam: La Reine Rouge (King's Bishop)
Br: Ronald Worswick (Ky)
Tr: White William P (—)

114

Lifetime Record: 4 2 0 1 $23,025

1995	2	1	0	0	$16,425	Turf	0	0	0	0	
1994	2	1	0	1	$6,600	Wet	0	0	0	0	
Aqu	0	0	0	0		Dist	1	1	0	0	$15,000

27Feb95-1GP fst 6f	:222	:45	:571	1:101	ⒻAlw 28500N2X	79	1	4	45½	46½	46	47	Boulanger G	121	6.70	82-17	PhoneThDoctor118 2½ DixilndGold121 1¾ TwistALim118 2¾	Lacked response	6
29Jan95-7GP fst 7f	:223	:46	1:113	1:251	ⒻAlw 25000N1X	83	7	2	53½	31½	1hd	1hd	Boulanger G	118	16.40	77-21	Lucky Lavender Gal118hd Flagstone Ferdie11810 Because I'm Gold1181		7

Drifted in deep str, bumped, fully extended

30Dec94-8Crc fst 6f	:223	:464	1:001	1:133	ⒻAlw 17000N1X	61	4	6	62¾	54½	44½	43¾	Boulanger G	117	2.90	75-21	Coldhartedprincess117no ⒹElapsed Time110 2½ Shananie's Light120 1½		9

Steadied early, lacked rally Placed third through disqualification.

12Jun94-2Crc fst 5f	:221	:464		1:003	ⒻMd 25000	58	3	4	23	21½	12½	16	Boulanger G	117	*1.60	86-14	Lucky Lavender Gal1176 Wartoendallwars1172 Sechen117 2½	Ridden out	7

WORKOUTS: ●Mar 18 Crc 5f fst :593 H 1/42 Mar 11 Crc 5f fst 1:02 B 4/33 Feb 18 Crc 4f fst :484 B 2/53 Feb 11 Crc 5f fst 1:013 H 2/34 ●Jan 23 Crc 5f fst 1:012 H 1/34 Jan 16 Crc 5f fst 1:014 H 2/16

Wild Wings 5-1

Own: Martin Michael T & Quarter Keg Stb
PEREZ R B (34 5 6 5 .15)

Ro. f. 3 (Apr)
Sire: Scarlet Ibis (Cormorant)
Dam: Paula Sue (Restivo)
Br: William Garbarini & Michael T. Martin (NY)
Tr: Schosberg Richard (4 0 2 1 .00)

116

Lifetime Record: 8 3 3 0 $78,250

1995	3	2	1	0	$43,200	Turf	0	0	0	0	
1994	5	1	2	0	$35,050	Wet	2	1	0	0	$21,270
Aqu	3	1	1	0	$26,280	Dist	2	0	1	0	$8,280

8Mar95-6Aqu fst 6f	⊡ :223	:45	:573	1:11 3↑	ⒻⓈAlw 32000N2X	103	1	3	13	16	110	114	Perez R B	109	*.30	88-20	Wild Wings10914 Distinct Manner119 4¾ Winloc's Peggy1083	Handily	6
17Feb95-6Aqu fst 6f	⊡ :224	:46	:581	1:103	ⒻⓈAlw 30000N1X	103	2	2	1hd	11	16	115	Perez R B5	109	*.45	90-21	Wild Wings10915 GreenStrawberry114 2½ OurBlueDiamond1173	Ridden out	9
29Jan95-5Aqu fst 6f	⊡ :231	:473	1:01	1:151	ⒻⓈAlw 30000N1X	64	9	3	41½	31	33	2¾	Perez R B5	111	*.70	66-26	Winloc's Peggy114¾ Wild Wings1111 Lady By Design116¾		9

Broke inward, bumped 1/4 pl

11Dec94-8Aqu wf 1 1/16	⊡ :231	:46	1:12	1:454	ⒻⓈEast View54k	67	6	2	2hd	2½	36	410	Davis R G	114	4.30	66-22	Rogues Walk121 1½ Foxy Scarlet114 2¾ Friendly Beauty1216	Dueled tired	7
24Nov94-6Aqu fst 7f	:224	:464	1:131	1:264	ⒻⓈAlw 30000N1X	76	2	2	11	12½	11	2no	Smith M E	121	3.80	70-24	Blum Beauty116no Wild Wings1215 Katie's Flag11111	Lost bob	7
10Nov94-9Aqu my 1	:232	:47	1:14	1:40	ⒻⓈMd Sp Wt	69	9	1	2½	12	15	16¾	Smith M E	117	*1.55	68-32	Wild Wings117 6¾ Sammycat1124 Follow The Flag112¾	Handily	11
26Oct94-9Aqu fst 7f	:231	:47	1:123	1:26	ⒻⓈMd Sp Wt	61	6	6	31	31½	42½	43	Smith M E	117	3.05	71-19	Distinctly Patti117 1½ Foxy Scarlet112no Sammycat112 1½	No late bid	10
12Aug94-2Sar fst 6f	:222	:461	:59	1:124	ⒻⓈMd Sp Wt	59	7	5	31½	21	22	21½	Smith M E	117	5.30	76-15	Farewell Embrace117 1½ Wild Wings117 1½ Flannel Sheets117nk	Second best	13

WORKOUTS: Mar 20 Bel tr.t 5f fst 1:034 B 6/9 Mar 5 Bel tr.t 5f fst 1:012 B 2/9 Feb 11 Bel tr.t 5f fst 1:021 B 5/10 Jan 23 Bel tr.t 5f fst 1:011 H 3/16 ●Jan 16 Bel tr.t 3f fst :344 H 1/8 ●Dec 31 Bel tr.t 4f fst :482 H 1/32

Forested 16-1

Own: Perez Robert
CHAVEZ J F (41 11 6 5 .27)

B. f. 3 (Apr)
Sire: Country Pine (His Majesty)
Dam: Passolyn (Fast Passer)
Br: Larry Dellay & Curmar (NY)
Tr: Callejas Alfredo (2 0 1 0 .00)

114

Lifetime Record: 5 2 2 0 $9,838

1994	5	2	2	0	$9,838	Turf	0	0	0	0	
1993	0	M	0	0		Wet	1	0	1	0	$2,000
Aqu	0	0	0	0		Dist	1	0	1	0	$2,000

25Dec94♦ Remon(Pan)	gd *6f	LH 1:161	ⒻHandicap J J Vallarino Hcp 5000	1no	Aguirre E	118	–	Forested118no La Capannina1183 Lucha Villa1175	4th early,tracked leader,rallied to lead on line	6
Tr: Roberto Arango										
27Nov94♦ Remon(Pan)	my *7f	LH 1:294	ⒻCl Cuerpo Bomberos de Panama-G3 Stk 12000	21½	Aguirre E	115	–	La Capannina115 1½ Forested115 1½ Bon Bon Fli1201	Trailed, 4th after 2f,bid 1f out,second best	7
6Nov94♦ Remon(Pan)	fst *5½f	LH 1:082	ⒻAllowance Race Alw 5500	11½	Aguirre E	112	3.50	Forested112 1½ Liz Lorena1163 All Reality109 1½	Prassed pace in 2nd,led over 1f out,driving	6
23Oct94♦ Remon(Pan)	fst *6f	LH 1:15	ⒻMaiden Race Maiden 5000	49¼	Aguirre E	114	–	Amazing Return115 1¾ Recompensalo115 3½ Holly Memories1114	Never a factor	6
16Oct94♦ Remon(Pan)	fst *5½f	LH 1:08	ⒻMaiden Race Maiden 5000	23	Aguirre E	113	–	Liz Lorena1113 Forested1133 Holly Memories110 2½	Chased in 5th,late gain into 2nd	8

WORKOUTS: Mar 22 Bel tr.t 3f fst :361 H 3/7 ●Mar 16 Bel tr.t 4f fst :464 Hg1/22 Mar 8 Bel tr.t 7f fst 1:30 B 1/1 Feb 28 Bel tr.t 6f sly 1:144 H (d) 1/1 Feb 18 Bel tr.t 4f fst :48 H 8/39

Stormy Blues 4-5
Own: Finkelstein David & Harriet
SANTOS J A (2 0 0 0 .00)

B. f. 3 (May)
Sire: Cure the Blues (Stop the Music)
Dam: Gussie's Appeal (Valid Appeal)
Br: Clyde Rice (Fla)
Tr: Schulhofer Flint S (3 0 0 0 .00)
118

Lifetime Record:	6 4 0 2	$403,740			
1994	6 4 0 2	$403,740	Turf	0 0 0 0	
1993	0 M 0 0		Wet	0 0 0 0	
Aqu	0 0 0 0		Dist	1 0 0 1	$24,000

5Nov94-5CD fst 1 1/16 :23 :461 1:112 1:451 ⒻB C Juv Fil-G1 85 10 13 1314 813 56½ 34 Santos J A 119 8.40 84-07 Flanders119hd Serena's Song1194 Stormy Blues119½ Rallied 13
9Oct94-9Lrl fst 7½f :233 :464 1:112 1:301 ⒻSelima-G3 81 2 3 2½ 22 11 11¼ Santos J A 119 *.20 — — Stormy Blues1191¼ Special Broad1193¾ Upper Noosh1197¼ Driving 6
17Sep94-4Bel fst 1 :23 :462 1:11 1:35 ⒻMatron-G1 95 5 3 32½ 31 2½ 23¼ Santos J A 119 2.50 85-10 Flanders1193¼ Stormy Blues1194½ Pretty Discreet119½ No match 6
Awarded first purse money
29Aug94-8Sar fst 7f :214 :444 1:101 1:23 ⒻSpinaway-G1 85 1 6 21 31½ 22½ 35¼ Santos J A 119 *.70 85-13 Flanders1194¾ Sea Breezer119½ Stormy Blues119nk Checked turn 6
6Aug94-9Mth fst 6f :214 :451 :58 1:11 ⒻSorority-G3 89 9 2 52¼ 31 13 19 Krone J A 119 *.50 84-16 Stormy Blues1199 Cat Appeal119¾ A Real Eye Opener119no Easily 9
1Jly94-3Bel fst 5½f :221 :454 :58 1:042 ⒻMd Sp Wt 99 1 2 1½ 11 18 116 Santos J A 115 1.60 93-15 Stormy Blues11516 Wonaria115¾ Moroccan Magic1158 Kept to drive 5
WORKOUTS: ●Mar 21 Bel tr.t 4f fst :464 B 1/32 Mar 12 GP 4f fst :48 H 2/33 Mar 7 GP 5f fst 1:024 B 25/32 Mar 2 GP 4f fst :49 B 5/29 Feb 25 GP 5f fst 1:02 B 6/24 Feb 20 GP 5f fst 1:003 Hg 2/36

Dancin Renee 7-2
Own: Bacon Sanford
VELEZ J A JR (1 1 0 0 1.00)

B. f. 3 (Mar)
Sire: Distinctive Pro (Mr. Prospector)
Dam: Lolli Lucka Lolli (Sweet Candy)
Br: Bacon Sanford (NY)
Tr: Triola Robert (1 1 0 0 1.00)
116

Lifetime Record:	3 3 0 0	$59,400			
1995	3 3 0 0	$59,400	Turf	0 0 0 0	
1994	0 M 0 0		Wet	0 0 0 0	
Aqu	1 1 0 0	$27,600	Dist	2 2 0 0	$42,600

15Mar95-7Aqu fst 7f :222 :45 1:10 1:232 ⒻAlw 44620NC 92 2 4 1½ 1½ 11 14 Velez J A Jr 116 *.45 87-14 Dancin Renee1164 Varsity Gold1165½ Enhearten111nk Brk slw, mild drive 4
12Feb95-4GP fst 7f :221 :451 1:103 1:234 ⒻAlw 25000N1X 90 1 5 11 1½ 12½ 12½ Velez J A Jr 121 3.50 84-20 Dancin Renee1212½ Clear Mandate1182½ Sea Breezer1184 Driving 7
19Jan95-2Aqu fst 6f ⊡ :233 :47 :59 1:113 ⒻⓈMd Sp Wt 82 2 4 1½ 13½ 19 112 Rydowski S R 121 *1.00 85-18 Dancin Renee12112 Quaker Street1214½ Moni Woman121½ Handily 7
WORKOUTS: Feb 22 Crc 5f fst 1:023 B 2/22 Feb 9 Crc 4f fst :50 B 9/30 ●Jan 12 Aqu ⊡ 4f gd :481 H 1/4 Dec 31 Crc 5f fst 1:033 B 15/35

Odds-on for her first start as a 3-year-old was Stormy Blues, who had finished third in the Breeders' Cup Juvenile Fillies when last seen in November. It was hard to say just what kind of race Scotty Schulhofer's filly might put forth, for although she had won by 16 lengths first time out of the box as a 2-year-old while receiving a Beyer of 99, the race had been at five and a half furlongs and four of her five subsequent Beyers at longer distances had been in the 80s.

On the whole, and excepting the New York-bred Panamanian invader Forested, the field was very competitive. Evil's Pic had won her last six races; Wild Wings had won her last two by a combined margin of 29 lengths; and Dancin Renee was unbeaten and untested after three front-running routs from as many trips. Also in the field were a pair of Gulfstream shippers, Distinctive Ruby and Lucky Lavender Gal.

Horses grow and mature quite significantly from the fall of their 2-year-old year to the following spring, so it was hard to get excited about odds of 4-5 on a filly like Stormy Blues, especially with so many good fillies in the race.

The second thought I had about the race was that Wild Wings, after pairing up those Beyers of 103, was ready to come back to earth. Whenever a horse makes a big jump in figures to a new lifetime top and then pairs up that number next time out, the stress of that double-barreled exertion is guaranteed to knock out just about any horse, especially a filly. After a 27-point jump from a previous high of 76 to a 103, followed by another 103 last time out, Wild Wings figured to bounce badly.

This was a race where the prices dictated the play. Looking at the records of the Gulfstream shippers before the odds were known, it was hard to latch onto either of them as a "most likely winner." The best I could do was to mention Lucky Lavender Gal third in my pre-race *Form* analysis: "...ships up for connections who won last November's Meritus Stakes with Calder invader Bluff's Dividend at 5-1; belongs in exotics at nice price."

The filly's only previous seven-furlong start had produced her best Beyer, an 83, and she had won a prolonged drive while exchanging bumps with the runnerup, as the duo drew off from the rest of the field by 10 lengths. Although she'd come up flat when tried at the next allowance level, she had followed with a :59 3/5 workout on March 18 that was fastest of 42 at the distance. A check of the work-tab showed that the next-fastest time had been 1:01 flat, and that Lucky Lavender Gal had drawn this comment: "...finished well, out in 1:14." The best *six-furlong* workout that morning had gone in 1:16!

None of this by itself, the trainer's previous stakes-success with a Florida shipper, the good race at today's distance, the morning exploits, was enough to make a strong case for Lucky Lavender Gal, who was, after all, stepping up in class. But when all these little things were combined, and a check of the toteboard said she was 27-1, she certainly belonged in some exactas at such a "nice price." Also very attractive was the 24-1 being offered on the other Gulfstream shipper, Distinctive Ruby, who had won a more advanced N2X sprint in Florida just a few days after Lucky Lavender Gal's preliminary allowance win.

Given odds as generous as 24-1 and 27-1, this was no time to split hairs, and there was absolutely no need to. With two live longshots against an odds-on favorite who hadn't been out in nearly five months, I bet both Gulfstream shippers to win, boxed them in exactas, and put both of them in the second slot under Stormy Blues on the chance that she was ready to deliver a big race.

Turned out, Stormy Blues was ready, but Lucky Lavender Gal simply ran right out of her skin:

EIGHTH RACE
Aqueduct
MARCH 26, 1995

7 FURLONGS. (1.20^1) 3rd Running of THE CICADA. Purse $75,000 Added. Fillies, 3-year-olds. By subscription of $75 each which should accompany the nomination, $350 to pass the entry box, $400 to start with $75,000 added. The added moeny and all fees to be divided 60% to the winner, 20% to second, 11% to third, 6% to fourth and 3% to fifth. Weight, 121 lbs. Non-winners of $50,000 since January 1 or $30,000 twice since then, allowed 3 lbs. $50,000 or $20,000 twice, 5 lbs. $20,000 or two races other than maiden or claiming, 7 lbs. A race other than maiden or claiming, 9 lbs. Starters to be named at the closing time of entries. Trophies will be presented to the winning owner, trainer and jockey. Closed Saturday, March 11 with 16 nominations.

Value of Race: $81,450 Winner $48,870; second $16,290; third $8,960; fourth $4,887; fifth $2,443. Mutuel Pool $194,526.00 Exacta Pool $283,138.00 Triple Pool $245,340.00

Last Raced	Horse	M/Eqt.	A.	Wt	PP	St	¼	½	Str	Fin	Jockey	Odds $1
27Feb95 ^{1}GP^4	Lucky Lavender Gal		3	114	3	4	3^2	$3^{1/2}$	1^3	1^5	Davis R G	27.75
5Nov94 ^{5}CD^3	Stormy Blues		3	118	6	2	5^{hd}	$5^{1/2}$	$3^{2 1/2}$	$2^{3/4}$	Santos J A	0.80
15Mar95 ^{7}Aqu^1	Dancin Renee		3	116	7	1	$2^{1/2}$	$1^{1 1/2}$	2^1	$3^{1/2}$	Velez J A Jr	3.50
25Dec94 REM^1	Forested		3	114	5	5	7	7	$4^{1 1/2}$	4^4	Chavez J F	16.00
12Feb95 ^{7}Aqu^1	Evil's Pic		3	121	1	7	$6^{1/2}$	6^{hd}	5^2	5^3	Luzzi M J	5.90
4Mar95 ^{9}GP^9	Distinctive Ruby	f	3	116	2	6	4^1	$4^{1/2}$	6^{12}	6	Velazquez J R	24.75
8Mar95 ^{6}Aqu^1	Wild Wings		3	116	4	3	$1^{1/2}$	$2^{1/2}$	7	—	Perez R B	5.20

Wild Wings:Eased

OFF AT 4:06 Start Good. Won driving. Time, :23, :46^2, 1:10^3, 1:23^2 Track fast.

$2 Mutuel Prices:				
	3–LUCKY LAVENDER GAL	57.50	9.70	5.70
	6–STORMY BLUES		2.50	2.30
	7–DANCIN RENEE			2.90

$2 EXACTA 3–6 PAID $156.50 $2 TRIPLE 3–6–7 PAID $612.00

B. f, (Feb), by Carson City–La Reine Rouge, by King's Bishop. Trainer White William P. Bred by Ronald Worswick (Ky).

LUCKY LAVENDER GAL forced the early pace along the rail, eased back a bit leaving the five-eighths pole, angled out while rallying on the turn, came in slightly while accelerating to the front in upper stretch, drew off under left hand encouragement. STORMY BLUES reserved early, trailed on the far turn, closed the gap while rallying three wide on the turn, then outfinished DANCIN RENEE for the place. DANCIN RENEE forced the early pace from outside, opened a clear advantage on the turn, checked along the rail in upper stretch, weakened in the drive. FORESTED trailed early, checked between horses on the far turn, advanced four wide into the stretch, then rallied mildly in the middle of the track. EVIL'S PIC failed to threaten while saving ground. DISTINCTIVE RUBY lodged a mild rally between horses on the turn and flattened out. WILD WINGS was used up battling for the early lead. A claim of foul lodged by the rider of DANCIN RENEE against the winner for interference in upper stretch was disallowed.

Owners— 1, Worswick Dolores; 2, Finkelstein David & Harriet; 3, Bacon Sanford; 4, Perez Robert; 5, Shapiro Theodore W; 6, Robsham Einar P; 7, Martin Michael T & Quarter Keg Stb

Trainers—1, White William P; 2, Schulhofer Flint S; 3, Triola Robert; 4, Callejas Alfredo; 5, Tesher Howard M; 6, Lewis Lisa L; 7, Schosberg Richard

A couple of weeks after the dust had settled and Lucky Lavender Gal was being prepared for a run at the Grade 2 Comely Stakes, trainer Bill White was interviewed by the New York Racing Association's Mike Watchmaker, and offered these insights into the success of Florida shippers to New York during the transition time:

"Horses who train in Miami in the winter are double tough when they ship north for the first start or two. The level of competition they face is a big factor. The Gulfstream meet may only be second to Saratoga in terms of quality. Also, Florida horses usually

don't miss a day of training during the winter and when they go north, they face horses who have been forced to train in inclement weather. Shipping into colder temperature is another factor, no question. When that frost hits these horses, they feel good, their appetite picks up and they become more aggressive. When we got up there she was a tiger. (The exercise rider) had to be tied on when we took her out of her stall."

THE TREND CONTINUED in the days following Lucky Lavender Gal's upset of the Cicada:

Henbane's Girl
Own: G Lack Farms
PEREZ R B (98 11 15 12 .11)

B. f. 3 (Feb)
Sire: Henbane (Alydar)
Dam: Basic Beauty (Big Burn)
Br: Ralph C. Sessa (Fla)
Tr: Klesaris Robert P (21 7 5 0 .33)

1135

Lifetime Record:	2 1 1 0	$19,050			
1995	2 1 1 0	$19,050	Turf	0 0 0 0	
1994	0 M 0 0		Wet	0 0 0 0	
Aqu	1 1 0 0	$16,800	Dist	1 1 0 0	$16,800

30Mar95-4Aqu	fst	6f	:223	:461	:582	1:114	ⒻMd Sp Wt	73	2	4	1½	11	13½	13½	Migliore R	120 b	3.90	83–17	Henbane'sGirl1203½ ArcticPtience1201¾ LizzieToon120½ Speed, drew clear 6
1Mar95-3GP	fst	6½f	:221	:454	1:122	1:194	ⒻMd 32000	58	9	4	31½	2hd	13½	2½	Velez J A Jr	120 b	6.00	75–18	CrsonKitty120½ Henbne'sGirl120hd ArcticPtinc1203¼ Gave way grudgingly 11

WORKOUTS: Mar 27 Bel tr.t 3f fst :373 H *10/15* Mar 24 Bel tr.t 4f fst :503 B *20/24* ●Feb 22 Crc 6f fst 1:152 Hg *1/4* Feb 15 Crc 5f fst 1:022 Bg *12/34* Feb 8 Crc 4f fst :502 B *16/25* Jan 25 Crc 4f fst :52 B *29/32*

Henbane's Girl missed narrowly for a $32,000 claiming tag in her debut at Gulfstream, shipped to Aqueduct and drew well clear in a special-weight sprint, a "class move" maidens aren't supposed to make.

Vigan
Own: Paulson Allen E
LUZZI M J (92 20 17 5 .22) **$25,000**

B. c. 4
Sire: Blushing John (Blushing Groom)
Dam: Northern Aspen (Northern Dancer)
Br: Paulson Allen E (Ky)
Tr: Zito Nicholas P (3 1 0 0 .33)

116

Lifetime Record:	10 1 0 1	$11,040			
1995	3 1 0 0	$7,440	Turf	3 0 0 0	
1994	7 M 0 1	$3,600	Wet	2 0 0 1	$3,600
Aqu	1 1 0 0	$7,200	Dist	1 1 0 0	$7,200

30Mar95-3Aqu	fst	1	:23	:463	1:122	1:382	Md 25000	70	5	3	2½	2hd	14	113½	Luzzi M J	120 b	7.00	77–26	Vigan12013 According To Cole115nk Chocolate Wizard1206	Ridden out	8
24Feb95-6GP	fst	7f	:221	:453	1:113	1:25	Md 30000	38	7	10	97¾	97½	88¾	715	Samyn J L	L 118 b	15.70	63–17	SrtogSles1183 GoldZenith1185 Bethlehem'sPride1184	Failed to menace	11
27Jan95-3GP	fst	7f	:222	:46	1:114	1:252	Md 32000	37	12	1	73¾	73½	914	1016½	Samyn J L	120 b	11.70e	60–25	JourneysExpress1181½ StageCenter1203½ ProsperousBirdie120no	Gave way	12
9Oct94-5Bel	fm	1¼ Ⓣ	:473	1:123	1:382	2:033	3↑ Md Sp Wt	44	11	1	11	11	65½	916	Beckner D V5	114 b	58.40	56–21	Gone Dancing Again1191¼ Haagbah1193 Thunderbolted122nk	Used in pace	11
1Oct94-6Bel	my	1 1/16 ⊗	:232	:464	1:12	1:443	3↑ Md Sp Wt	35	1	1	1½	31½	312	325¼	Beckner D V5	114	23.30	54–19	Royce Joseph1192¼ Mt. Telemark11923 Vigan1142½	Tired	6
14Sep94-1Bel	fm	1 1/16 Ⓣ	:233	:464	1:12	1:433	3↑ Md Sp Wt	36	3	3	26	44½	78½	817¼	Cruz E F	118	50.10	61–14	Skipton1182¼ Gem Seeker118¾ Royce Joseph1181	Tired	10
26Aug94-1Sar	sly	1⅛ ⊗	:47	1:123	1:392	1:531	3↑ Md Sp Wt	34	2	5	55	48	511	520	Sellers S J	117	11.80	50–30	Silver Safari1171¼ Crafty Truce1172¾ Sup WithTheDevil11214	Broke slowly	6
19Jly94-5Bel	fst	7f	:224	:454	1:112	1:243	3↑ Md Sp Wt	26	8	3	53	86	915	925½	Beckner D V5	111	50.70	54–19	Crafty Mist1161¼ Level Land1165½ Fleet Stalker1163½	Done early	9
4Jly94-10Bel	fm	1 1/16 Ⓣ	:234	:471	1:104	1:411	3↑ Md Sp Wt	31	8	2	31	75½	815	924¾	Cruz E F	116	47.10	65–10	Dutchess First1164¼ Sophie's Friend1161¼ Thirty Good Ones1161¾	Tired	10
5Jun94-3Bel	fst	7f	:222	:453	1:101	1:222	3↑ Md Sp Wt	50	2	10	1012	108	1011	1019	Luzzi M J	114	53.40	72–11	PartyMnners1145 Convince1142 RoyceJoseph114hd	Broke slowly, outrun	10

WORKOUTS: Mar 12 GP 5f fst 1:031 B *21/29* Feb 18 GP 5f fst 1:013 B *11/40* Feb 13 GP 5f fst 1:06 B *31/35* Feb 4 GP 6f fst 1:153 B *5/17* Jan 21 GP 5f fst 1:014 B *8/34*

A race before Henbane's Girl won, Vigan, who had never been closer to the winner than 15 lengths in nine attempts, ran the race of his life first time up from Florida, and won by the length of the stretch.

Spring

THE FIRST SATURDAY in May means one thing to the casual racing fans of America — the Kentucky Derby. But for dyed-in-the-wool horseplayers it also signifies the true arrival of spring in New York, for it is the first Saturday of racing at Belmont Park's spring-summer meeting.

Not only is it the beginning of a new meeting, it is, for all intents and purposes, the beginning of the grass-racing season as well (although a handful of races may be run over Aqueduct's ramshackle turf course toward the end of April).

The idea of lightly-raced horses going to the grass for the first time should be an exciting prospect for players because, while pedigree and trainer histories are the most important factors in maiden and preliminary allowance grass races, the crowd, which is forever enamored of good last-race finish positions and close-up beaten lengths, does not always bet accordingly.

Many grass-oriented stables point for the opening of the Belmont meet. Walking through the backyard paddock area and up to the press box at Belmont for the first time in more than six months, I reminded myself that I was going to be looking for, and aggressively wagering on, lightly-raced horses switching to the grass with the requisite pedigrees, especially if they were from barns with a winning history at this sort of thing.

I didn't have to wait long. The first race on Saturday, May 6 was the essence of what Belmont is all about in the spring: a mile on the Widener (outer) turf course for 3-year-old maidens that drew an overflow field. Three of the four entrants with experience on grass, Colonel Bart, Ransom Me Daddy, and Romulo, were attracting most of the play, at odds of 2-1, 3-1 and 5-1, respectively. Of the eight horses trying grass for the first time, Identity was 9-1, the first time-starter Herneztt was 11-1, and everyone else was 13-1 or better:

1 Belmont Park

1 MILE. (Turf). (1:322) MAIDEN SPECIAL WEIGHT. Purse $32,000. 3-year-olds and upward. Weights: 3-year-olds, 113 lbs. Older, 122 lbs.

WIDENER TURF COURSE — 1 MILE — START — FINISH

Romulo

Own: Condren & Cornacchia & Paulson
LUZZI M J (5 0 1 2 .00)

B. c. 3 (Jan)
Sire: Strawberry Road (Whiskey Road)
Dam: Different Worlds (Cornish Prince)
Br: Paulson Allen E (Ky)
Tr: Zito Nicholas P (—)
113

Lifetime Record:	3 M 1 0	$4,780			
1995	3 M 1 0	$4,780	Turf	1 0 1 0	$4,320
1994	0 M 0 0		Wet	0 0 0 0	
Bel Ⓣ	0 0 0 0		Dist Ⓣ	0 0 0 0	

16Feb95-10GP fm *1 1/16 Ⓣ :232 :482 1:134 1:451+ Md Sp Wt 66 5 4 44½ 32 52 23½ Bravo J 120 10.20 78-13 Seminole Storm1203½ Romulo120nk Stolen Goods1202½ 10
Bumped hard start, gamely
29Jan95-6GP fst 7f :224 :461 1:121 1:253 Md Sp Wt 51 10 2 21½ 21½ 88¼ 813¼ Boulanger G 120 71.30 62-21 Joy Drive1202¼ Handsome Devil120¾ Valid Vengeance1201½ Gave way 10
4Jan95-1GP fst 7f :224 :462 1:12 1:251 Md Sp Wt 39 9 1 95½ 1010 815 818¼ Boulanger G 120 35.70 59-19 Ops Smile1202½ Broad Search1206¾ Berry Honest1201½ Outrun 10
WORKOUTS: Apr 30 Bel 5f fst 1:04 B 28/30 Apr 22 Kee 4f fst :51 B 53/61 Apr 14 Kee 5f fst 1:041 B 27/29 Apr 11 Kee 5f fst 1:022 B 7/18 Apr 6 Kee 5f fst 1:053 B 17/17 Mar 25 GP 5f fst 1:032 B 10/11

Kefalonians

Own: Amvrosiatos A & Vangelatos P
CHAVEZ J F (11 2 2 1 .18)

B. c. 3 (Mar)
Sire: Val de l'Orne (Fr) (Val de Loir)
Dam: Demean (Dewan)
Br: Rock Hill Farm (Ont-C)
Tr: Sciacca Gary (2 0 1 0 .00)
113

Lifetime Record:	2 M 0 0	$0			
1995	2 M 0 0		Turf	0 0 0 0	
1994	0 M 0 0		Wet	0 0 0 0	
Bel Ⓣ	0 0 0 0		Dist Ⓣ	0 0 0 0	

15Apr95-3Aqu fst 7f :221 :452 1:112 1:242 Md Sp Wt 31 9 2 87 911 914 924 Chavez J F 121 27.25 58-17 Twosie Stamp1211¼ Fidgetyfeet1213 Cat Be Nimble121hd No response 10
1Apr95-5Aqu fst 6½f :222 :452 1:111 1:18 Md Sp Wt 13 4 5 815 822 819 826¾ Smith M E 120 b 14.20 63-13 Davenport1204 Dazz1201½ Exemplar1201 Checked, pinched break 8
WORKOUTS: Apr 25 Bel 4f fst :484 B 7/28 Apr 11 Bel 4f fst :473 H 2/18 Mar 27 Bel tr.t 4f fst :484 B 2/19 Mar 21 Bel tr.t 4f fst :491 B 19/32 Mar 16 Bel tr.t 5f fst 1:05 Bg 2/5 Mar 10 Bel tr.t 7f fst 1:323 B 1/1

Then Some

Own: Russi Drin T
PERSAUD R (1 0 0 0 .00)

B. c. 3 (Apr)
Sire: Puntivo (Restivo)
Dam: Peace Garden (Menocal)
Br: Harriet C. Huebeck & Elmer Heubeck, Jr. (Fla)
Tr: Dupps Kristina (2 0 0 0 .00)
103 10

Lifetime Record:	0 M 0 0	$0			
1995	0 M 0 0		Turf	0 0 0 0	
1994	0 M 0 0		Wet	0 0 0 0	
Bel Ⓣ	0 0 0 0		Dist Ⓣ	0 0 0 0	

WORKOUTS: Apr 30 Bel 4f fst :48 Hg 7/41 Apr 24 Bel 6f fst 1:141 H 2/7 Apr 18 Bel 6f fst 1:132 H 3/6 Apr 8 Bel 3f fst :39 Bg 17/23 Apr 4 Bel tr.t 4f fst :494 B 6/17 Mar 15 Bel tr.t 4f fst :492 H 9/20 Feb 19 Bel tr.t 4f fst :51 B 22/28 Feb 11 Bel tr.t 3f fst :373 B 12/29 Feb 1 Bel tr.t 3f fst :374 B 11/19 Dec 9 Bel tr.t 3f fst :383 B 26/27

Ransom Me Daddy

Own: Teinowitz Phillip
SANTOS J A (7 1 2 0 .14)

B. c. 3 (Mar)
Sire: Red Ransom (Roberto)
Dam: Happy Sunshine (Secreto)
Br: Galbreath/ Phillips Racing (Ky)
Tr: Schulhofer Flint S (6 0 2 0 .00)
113

Lifetime Record:	7 M 1 2	$9,000			
1995	2 M 1 1	$5,400	Turf	3 0 1 1	$5,400
1994	5 M 0 1	$3,600	Wet	0 0 0 0	
Bel Ⓣ	0 0 0 0		Dist Ⓣ	0 0 0 0	

29Mar95-11Hia fm *1 1/16 Ⓣ 1:413 Md Sp Wt 65 7 6 43½ 42¾ 31½ 24½ Boulanger G 121 2.70 89-06 Storm Hawk1214½ Ransom Me Daddy1211½ Buck North121no Rallied 10
16Feb95-6GP fm *1 1/16 Ⓣ :231 :48 1:123 1:434+ Md Sp Wt 74 3 6 64 64½ 41½ 33½ Santos J A 120 11.80 85-13 SocialApproval1203½ OhSoFabulous120no RansomMeDddy1201¾ Late rally 9
30Nov94-3Aqu fst 1 :224 :461 1:122 1:382 Md Sp Wt 44 2 8 710 65½ 513 523 Migliore R 118 16.80 53-27 Blizzard1185½ Underhill118hd First Night1131½ No factor 8
8Nov94-3Aqu fm 1 1/16 Ⓣ :222 :464 1:111 1:444 Md Sp Wt 29 4 3 33½ 37½ 417 522 Santos J A 118 5.90 63-13 Debonair Dan1183 Crimson Guard1185 Crowning Halo11810 Tired 8
25Oct94-5Aqu fst 1 ⊗ :223 :451 1:104 1:372 Md Sp Wt 65 9 3 612 47½ 35 37½ Santos J A 118 23.70 74-21 Krabbie1181½ Skipper1135½ Ransom Me Daddy1185½ Mild rally 10
16Oct94-3Bel fst 7f :231 :472 1:123 1:252 Md Sp Wt 47 8 8 96 84½ 69¼ 814¼ Migliore R 118 47.00 61-18 Stauder113nk Devious Course1184¾ Slice Of Reality1134¼ No factor 11
4Oct94-3Bel fst 6f :224 :463 :583 1:11 Md Sp Wt 46 6 6 63½ 73¾ 69 614¼ Santos J A 118 25.30 72-14 Thunder Gulch118no Porphyry118½ Last Effort1181½ Checked 1/2 pl 9
WORKOUTS: May 4 Bel 4f fst :491 B 23/46 Apr 29 Bel 4f fst :504 B 30/50 Apr 17 Hia 4f fst :494 B 9/13 Apr 11 Hia 4f fst :494 B 5/15 Apr 6 Hia 4f fst :50 B 7/11 Mar 26 Hia 4f fst :483 B 5/12

Northern King

Own: Anderson Ralph R
PEREZ R B (5 0 1 0 .00)

Dk. b or br c. 3 (Jan)
Sire: Greinton (Green Dancer)
Dam: Hopebloomseternal (Lyphard)
Br: Mandysland Farm (Ky)
Tr: Dutrow Richard E (1 0 0 1 .00)
108 5

Lifetime Record:	4 M 0 1	$6,350			
1995	4 M 0 1	$6,350	Turf	2 0 0 1	$4,440
1994	0 M 0 0		Wet	0 0 0 0	
Bel Ⓣ	0 0 0 0		Dist Ⓣ	0 0 0 0	

28Apr95-5Aqu fm 1⅛ Ⓣ :48 1:122 1:381 1:504 3↑ Md Sp Wt 60 9 6 53 64 43½ 44¾ Krone J A 113 7.00 81-10 Inittowinit1141½ Cringe1131¾ King Of The City1131½ Wide, no rally 10
15Apr95-1Aqu fst 7f :23 :461 1:114 1:234 Md Sp Wt 56 7 3 63½ 53 34 415¼ Valdivia J7 114 37.25 70-17 FlyingChevron1215 LstEffort1219¾ SecondChildhood121¾ Steadied turn 10
2Feb95-10GP fm *1⅛ Ⓣ :48 1:131 1:373 1:503+ Md Sp Wt 68 3 9 99¼ 76½ 33½ 32¾ Nunez E O 120 f 17.40 89-01 Noble 'n Heart1201½ Baldy's Dream1201¼ Northern King1203½ Late rally 10
22Jan95-6GP fst 6f :222 :454 :581 1:11 Md Sp Wt 61 3 10 95 79¾ 715 713 Nunez E O 120 104.40 72-15 Gadzook1201½ Black Balled120hd Phidias Frieze1206 Mild bid 12
WORKOUTS: Apr 24 Aqu 5f fst 1:03 B 4/4 Apr 11 Aqu 5f fst 1:014 B 3/3 Apr 1 Crc 5f fst 1:063 B 42/43 Mar 26 Crc 4f fst :493 B 11/50 Mar 1 Crc 3f fst :363 H 3/15 Feb 23 Crc 4f fst :50 B 10/29

Herneztt

Own: Saba Raul
VALDIVIA J JR (6 0 2 1 .00)

B. c. 3 (Jan)
Sire: Alwuhush (Nureyev)
Dam: Tex Fina (Utopico)
Br: Raul Antonio Saba de Rivero (Fla)
Tr: Penna Angel Jr (—)
106 7

Lifetime Record:	0 M 0 0	$0			
1995	0 M 0 0		Turf	0 0 0 0	
1994	0 M 0 0		Wet	0 0 0 0	
Bel Ⓣ	0 0 0 0		Dist Ⓣ	0 0 0 0	

WORKOUTS: May 4 Bel 3f fst :372 B 13/25 Apr 30 Bel 5f fst 1:013 Hg 13/30 Apr 24 Bel 4f fst :491 B 16/32 Apr 3 GP 5f fst 1:033 B 12/16 ●Mar 28 GP 3f fst :36 Hg 1/8 Mar 23 GP 4f fst :503 B 9/15 Mar 17 GP 3f fst :37 Hg 6/17 Mar 12 GP 4f fst :484 H 5/33 Mar 2 GP 4f fst :50 B 11/29 Feb 25 GP 3f fst :38 B 19/26 Jan 30 GP 4f fst :512 B 36/43 Jan 24 GP 4f fst :52 B 22/31

Farranfore

Own: Meriwether John W
ALVARADO F T (8 1 0 1 .13)

Ch. g. 3 (Apr)
Sire: Dahar (Lyphard)
Dam: My Dear Frances (Caro)
Br: F.A. Genter Stables, Inc. (Ky)
Tr: Freeman Willard C (—)
113

Lifetime Record:	2 M 0 0	$230			
1995	2 M 0 0	$230	Turf	0 0 0 0	
1994	0 M 0 0		Wet	0 0 0 0	
Bel Ⓣ	0 0 0 0		Dist Ⓣ	0 0 0 0	

15Apr95-3Aqu fst 7f :221 :452 1:112 1:242 Md Sp Wt 47 4 10 109 1014 710 616½ Davis R G 121 50.75 66-17 Twosie Stamp1211¼ Fidgetyfeet1213 Cat Be Nimble121hd Broke slowly 10
18Feb95-4GP fst 6f :214 :45 :573 1:11 Md Sp Wt 41 5 11 915 914 715 818¼ Davis R G 120 59.50 67-16 Houston Hawk1202½ Treasure Cay1204 Speedy Trick120nk No threat 11
WORKOUTS: Apr 29 Bel 5f fst 1:054 B 18/18 Apr 11 Bel 5f fst 1:013 B 11/18 Apr 3 Aik 5f fst 1:032 B 1/1 Mar 19 Aik Ⓣ 4f fm :51 B (d) 1/1 Feb 11 GP 3f fst :382 Bg 11/30 Feb 8 GP 3f fst :383 Bg 15/19

Colonel Bart
Own: Chen Daniel J
MIGLIORE R (10 2 0 2 .20)

Dk. b or br g. 3 (Feb)
Sire: Blazing Bart (The Bart)
Dam: Verbatims Girl (Verbatim)
Br: David Burton & Sara Burton (Fla)
Tr: Parisella John (—)

113

Lifetime Record:	6 M 2 0	$16,200			
1995	1 M 1 0	$6,000	Turf	4 0 2 0	$16,200
1994	5 M 1 0	$10,200	Wet	0 0 0 0	
Bel Ⓣ	1 0 0 0	$1,800	Dist Ⓣ	0 0 0 0	

28Apr95-1Aqu fm 1⅛ Ⓣ :481 1:123 1:363 1:493 3↑ Md Sp Wt 72 3 5 56 3½ 22 24 Migliore R 113 3.10 88–10 Ago108[4] Colonel Bart113½ Menzies113[9] Rallied inside 9
27Nov94-3Aqu sf 1 1/16 Ⓣ :23 :484 1:153 1:482 Md Sp Wt 53 5 8 85½ 74½ 47 45½ Perez R B5 113 *1.10 61–29 Australasia118¼ Devon's Tune118²¾ Fidgetyfeet118½ Five wide 10
20Nov94-5Aqu fst 1 ⊗ :234 :472 1:123 1:374 Md Sp Wt 44 4 7 88½ 98½ 915 920¾ Perez R B5 113 15.00 58–25 Nostra113½ Storm Hawk118¾ Paragallo's Hope118½ No factor 10
22Oct94-5Aqu gd 1 1/16 Ⓣ :232 :484 1:141 1:454 Md Sp Wt 68 8 7 65½ 45 26 22 Smith M E 118 *1.05e 78–16 Pastures New113[2] Colonel Bart118[8] Mr Market118[no] Second best 10
12Oct94-3Bel fm 1 1/16 Ⓣ :234 :473 1:12 1:423 Md Sp Wt 71 3 10 86 83½ 54 44½ Perez R B5 113 38.80 80–18 Claudius118[nk] Nostra113[3] Noble 'n Heart118½ Rallied wide 10
29Sep94-9Bel fst 6f :224 :461 :584 1:113 Md 35000 39 3 9 89 96¾ 69 612½ Perez R B5 113 8.90 70–15 Candy Cone114[9] Suprise World118½ Firstontherun113½ Steadied 1/2 pl 10

WORKOUTS: ●Apr 21 Aqu 4f fst :484 H 1/7 Apr 12 Aqu 6f fst 1:172 B 3/3 Apr 8 Aqu 6f fst 1:162 B 1/3 Apr 3 Aqu 5f fst 1:03 H 2/2 Mar 29 Aqu 4f fst :51 B 8/8

Identity
Own: Avanzino Kenneth C
SAMYN J L (5 0 0 3 .00)

Dk. b or br c. 3 (Mar)
Sire: Personal Flag (Private Account)
Dam: Nasty Letters (Nasty and Bold)
Br: Free F William (NY)
Tr: Skiffington Thomas J (—)

113

Lifetime Record:	5 M 2 2	$21,060		
1995	2 M 1 1	$9,300	Turf	0 0 0 0
1994	3 M 1 1	$11,760	Wet	0 0 0 0
Bel Ⓣ	0 0 0 0		Dist Ⓣ	0 0 0 0

17Apr95-1Aqu fst 1⅛ :49 1:15 1:414 1:544 3↑ [S]Md Sp Wt 44 8 10 108½ 31½ 24 313 Smith M E 113 f *1.25 53–24 Winfield D. H.113[10] Irish Patriot106²½ Identity113½ Steadied early, wide 11
29Mar95-5Aqu fst 1 :234 :472 1:131 1:383 [S]Md Sp Wt 63 4 11 97½ 95¼ 33½ 24 Smith M E 120 f 3.20 72–19 Thepromonroe120[4] Identity120[5] Selected Sauce120[nk] Rallied five wide 13
1Dec94-9Aqu fst 1 :233 :473 1:134 1:394 [S]Md Sp Wt 40 3 10 117¾ 106¼ 611 417 Davis R G 118 f *1.95 52–29 Revolutionary Era118[1] Slew's Miner118[2] Smart Account118[14] Wide trip 14
9Nov94-9Aqu fst 1 :24 :482 1:142 1:412 [S]Md Sp Wt 54 8 4 53 2hd 1½ 2½ Smith M E 118 f *1.50 60–33 Dig Zig118½ Identity118³½ Irish Patriot118¾ Bid, weakened 10
25Oct94-9Aqu fst 7f :23 :461 1:121 1:244 [S]Md Sp Wt 56 7 5 95 63½ 34 37½ Smith M E 118 5.30 72–17 Blum's Legend118²½ Ormsby118[5] Identity118[2] Wide, flattened out 10

WORKOUTS: Apr 12 Bel 4f fst :48 H 4/27 Mar 25 GP 4f fst :49 H 6/17 Mar 20 GP Ⓣ 6f fm 1:184 B (d) 1/3 Mar 12 GP 5f fst 1:024 H 15/29 Mar 6 GP 5f fst 1:031 B 24/31 Feb 28 GP 5f fst 1:023 B 22/33

Raffie's Rullah
Own: Prieger Henry H
SANTAGATA N (8 0 2 0 .00)

Dk. b or br c. 3 (Mar)
Sire: Distinctive Pro (Mr. Prospector)
Dam: Raffinesse (Dschingis Khan)
Br: Henry H. Prieger (NY)
Tr: Diamond Stephan S (—)

113

Lifetime Record:	1 M 0 0	$0		
1995	1 M 0 0		Turf	0 0 0 0
1994	0 M 0 0		Wet	0 0 0 0
Bel Ⓣ	0 0 0 0		Dist Ⓣ	0 0 0 0

21Apr95-5Aqu fst 6f :223 :462 :583 1:112 3↑ [S]Md Sp Wt 29 10 7 1010 911 812 821 Dunkelberger T L5 109 f 14.50 64–15 No Secrets114[5] Mr. Decker118½ Victor V. C.114[2] No threat, wide trip 10

WORKOUTS: Apr 30 Bel 6f fst 1:142 H 6/11 Apr 17 Bel 6f fst 1:151 Hg5/9 Apr 11 Bel 5f fst 1:011 B 8/18 Apr 2 Bel tr.t 4f fst :50 B 10/16 Mar 26 Bel tr.t 4f fst :514 B 37/41 Mar 19 Bel tr.t 3f fst :40 B 14/14

Gooree King
Own: Cojuangco Eduardo M Jr
DUNKELBERGER T L (5 0 1 0 .00)

Dk. b or br c. 3 (May)
Sire: Manila (Lyphard)
Dam: Sandy's Pleasure (Dash o' Pleasure)
Br: Gooree Pastoral Company (Ky)
Tr: Jolley Leroy (—)

108[5]

Lifetime Record:	1 M 0 0	$0		
1995	1 M 0 0		Turf	0 0 0 0
1994	0 M 0 0		Wet	0 0 0 0
Bel Ⓣ	0 0 0 0		Dist Ⓣ	0 0 0 0

1Apr95-5Aqu fst 6½f :222 :452 1:111 1:18 Md Sp Wt 37 8 2 55 613 711 716¼ Santagata N 120 10.30 74–13 Davenport120[4] Dazz120½ Exemplar120[1] Finished early 8

WORKOUTS: Apr 26 Bel 7f fst 1:291 B 4/5 Apr 17 Bel 6f fst 1:133 H 3/9 Apr 9 Bel 3f fst :37 B 3/9 ●Mar 25 Bel tr.t 4f fst :463 Hg 1/37 Mar 17 Cam 4f fst :50 B 3/7 Mar 10 Cam 5f fst 1:03 Bg 1/2

Raised By Natives
Own: Pepperell Stable
CRUGUET J (1 0 0 0 .00)

B. g. 3 (May)
Sire: Fast Gold (Mr. Prospector)
Dam: Madam Q. (Raise a Cup)
Br: Larry McGinnis & Robert A. Lundy (Ky)
Tr: Cotter Mary M (1 0 0 0 .00)

113

Lifetime Record:	3 M 1 0	$4,240		
1995	1 M 0 0		Turf	0 0 0 0
1994	2 M 1 0	$4,240	Wet	0 0 0 0
Bel Ⓣ	0 0 0 0		Dist Ⓣ	0 0 0 0

4Jan95-9Aqu fst 170 [•] :241 :483 1:151 1:482 Md Sp Wt 16 6 3 68½ 610 715 823 Alvarado F T 122 b 12.30 33–35 Kan't Stop Kris122[hd] Screen Oscar122[3] Easy Does It122⁶½ Tired 9
17Dec94-1Aqu fst 1 1/16 [•] :241 :493 1:17 1:521 Md 45000 39 2 1 1hd 2hd 2hd 23 Cruguet J 114 b 11.90 41–35 I Do I Do114[3] Raised By Natives114[2] Detached113[4] Second best 6
8Dec94-5Aqu fst 6f [•] :23 :47 :591 1:12 Md Sp Wt 43 1 6 43 57 510 515½ Cruguet J 118 b 63.50 67–18 Trailblazer118[1] Hanging Road113[3] Classy Moment118[10] No threat 9

WORKOUTS: May 4 Bel 5f fst 1:002 H 7/33 Apr 26 Bel 1 fst 1:47 B 2/2 Apr 18 Bel 3f fst :39 B 12/13

The quartet with grass experience had all run fairly well, but hadn't exactly done anything to distinguish themselves in limited opportunities on turf. Romulo had run gamely for second, earning a Beyer of 66 when sent to the grass at Gulfstream; Ransom Me Daddy's two grass efforts in Florida had resulted in second and third place-finishes and corresponding Beyers of 65 and 74; Northern King brought home a check in two previous grass starts, with Beyers of 60 and 68; and Colonel Bart, making his first start in five months, had closed for the runnerup spot with a Beyer of 72 at Aqueduct a week earlier. There was little to separate them, and one was left with the notion that if another entrant responded favorably to the surface switch, the race was theirs for the taking.

I preferred Kefalonians, even though the son of Val de l'Orne had beaten a grand total of one horse in two dirt sprints at the Big A the previous month. His pedigree was heavily tilted toward turf, as *Maiden Stats* revealed:

	SIRE INFO								DAM INFO										SIBLING INFO	
Horse	# wnr/str	2yo wnr/str	% 1st	awd	Mud w%/sts	Turf w%/sts	% 1stT	Spl	prf	Dpl	# fls	# wnr/str	# sw	2yo wnr/str	awd	Mud w%/sts	Turf wnr/str	Dosage Index	Top Sibling	/Earn
EEPYOURPOWDERDRY	10/ 22	4/ 17	0	7.1	21/ 34	0/ 3	0	0.30	w	0.22	3	1/ 2	0	1/ 2	6.0	0/ 4	0/ 0	2.56	Head Brother	/$ 3.
EEZE IT	92/ 121	34/ 77	9	7.1	14/ 353	15/ 379	8	1.17	w	2.22	7	4/ 6	1	3/ 5	7.5	38/ 8	1/ 2	3.80	Justice Will Come	/$ 83
EFALONIANS	237/ 343	40/ 153	7	8.2	11/ 598	10/1059	16	1.71	w	1.51	10	5/ 7	0	2/ 3	7.6	25/ 32	2/ 2	1.29	+Kuri Kiata	/$ 8
EGLER	112/ 156	44/ 94	18	6.3	13/ 326	2/ 95	0	1.31	sw	2.63	5	1/ 3	0	0/ 1	6.0	0/ 1	0/ 2	3.40	Fibar	/$ 1
EIBER KEEBER	269/ 388	67/ 181	10	7.4	15/ 551	8/ 424	3	2.88	uc	0.60	7	2/ 3	0	1/ 2	7.4	0/ 10	1/ 2	1.33	Tributex	/$ 6
ELLCOURT MISS	274/ 379	64/ 180	12	7.6	14/ 647	10/ 794	5	3.55	sw	3.83	10	6/ 7	1	0/ 4	8.3	13/ 15	1/ 5	1.43	Rampart Road	/$31
ELLYBEAN	54/ 85	17/ 57	9	6.3	11/ 145	4/ 27	0	0.45	w	0.42	4	1/ 2	0	1/ 2	6.0	0/ 0	0/ 0	13.00	Jean's Heart	/$

Not only did the progeny of Val de l'Orne win at a 16 percent clip in their initial forays on the grass, but the dam had been a potent grass-producer too: both of her previous turf starters had won on the green. What's more, the dam's top earner to date was Kefalonians' full sister, Kuru Klata. And I knew who she was:

Kuru Klata — B. f. 3(Mar), by Val de l'Orne-Fr—Demean, by Dewan
CHAVEZ J F (136 25 15 11 .18) — Br.—Rock Hill Farm (Md)
Own.—Vangelatos Peter — Tr.—Sciacca Gary (54 16 5 7 .30) — **111**
Lifetime 11 2 0 2 $39,870 — 1993 10 2 0 1 $36,990 — 1992 1 M 0 1 $2,880 — Turf 5 2 0 1 $36,990 — Wet 1 0 0 0

5Jun93- 2Bel	fm	1 1/16 [T]	:464	1:102	1:403	(F)Tanya	72	5	7	66	52½	65½	79¾	Chavez J F		116	4.20	83-13	RssnBrd116½BrghtPnn1184McStrt-GB116	Broke slowly	9
5Jun93-Run in Divisions																					
21May93- 7Bel	fm	1 1/16 [T]	:47	1:112	1:43	3↑(F)Alw 28500	80	5	5	54	53	43½	11½	Chavez J F		115	5.50	81-20	KuruKlt1151½BluTss-Ir115hdSpctclr119	Sted alter cours	8
12May93- 5Bel	fm	1 1/16 [T]	:472	1:114	1:43	3↑(F)Md Sp Wt	76	8	3	42	3½	2½	1hd	Chavez J F		115	15.10	81-19	KrKlt115hdSymphonyLdy1151¾MrryMMrryM115	Driving	9
28Apr93- 5Aqu	gd	1 1/16 (T)	:484	1:133	1:461	(F)Md Sp Wt	65	6	2	11	32½	44	49¼	Chavez J F	b	122	4.80	71-20	BlngKd1224¾MgclQn-Ir1222½NAtllAtAll122	Speed, tired	7
19Apr93- 5Aqu	yl	1 1/16 (T)	:492	1:15	1:48	(F)Md Sp Wt	68	3	2	21½	21½	31½	34½	Chavez J F	b	122	16.40	66-26	Plsntvill122nkRigningLdy1224¼KuruKlt122	Lacked rally	8
26Mar93- 7Aqu	fst	1 1/16 [•]	:481	1:132	1:462	(F)Md Sp Wt	47	7	1	13½	2hd	34½	512	Chavez J F	b	121	13.60	61-23	ChrkTggy1216¾ThrnyRdg121nkNAccnt121	Used in pace	7
25Feb93- 5Aqu	fst	1 1/16 [•]	:491	1:15	1:48	(F)Md Sp Wt	40	2	1	12	21	48	616½	Chavez J F	b	121	16.80	48-20	Interrupta1214HelloHnne1215¼ThornyRidge121	Used up	8
14Feb93- 5Aqu	my	170 [•]	:471	1:13	1:444	(F)Md Sp Wt	52	5	1	11	22	25	56	Chavez J F	b	121	35.30	72-18	SplnddLnch1212½JnnfrSrB.116noFlgLk121	Used in pace	10
29Jan93- 3Aqu	fst	6f [•]	:231	:471	1:132	(F)Md Sp Wt	36	7	3	64¼	96½	911	1014¾	Chavez J F		121	42.60	61-24	PrincesseNiner1162CtCrcker1213¾NwAccount121	Faded	11
8Jan93- 6Aqu	fst	6f [•]	:231	:464	1:112	(F)Md Sp Wt	48	9	2	52¾	66½	710	612¾	Chavez J F		121	12.60	73-15	AndovrSqur1216NwAccount1212¾GorgLghts121	No rally	10

LATEST WORKOUTS Jun 2 Bel 4f fst :474 H

6/18 1¼ (T) Alw NW2 $6–

Kuru Klata had been handled by the same owner, breeder and trainer as Kefalonians when a 3-year-old of 1993, had also been ridden by Jorge Chavez, and she had accounted for three of Gary Sciacca's meet-leading total of 31 victories at Belmont's spring meeting that year. Her past performances show how she was unable to get out of her own way on the dirt, and that she improved big-time when switched to grass in the spring, breaking her maiden at 15-1 on May 12 and repeating in an allowance nine days later. The hand-written notation underneath the pp's you see here indicates that on June 18, she won a mile and a quarter, non-winners of two other than allowance on the turf, and paid a mutual of $6.

That was one of the lowest prices registered by a Sciacca-trained winner at the 1993 spring meet. His horses met with uncommon success on the grass, and their recent form gave little or no suggestion of the big effort that was to be forthcoming:

Turkolady — Ch. f. 4, by Turkoman—Pure Platinum, by Singh
CHAVEZ J F (142 25 16 12 .18) — Br.—Backer John W (Ky)
Own.—More-N-More Stable — Tr.—Sciacca Gary (55 16 5 7 .29) — **117**
Lifetime 27 4 3 5 $95,340 — 1993 3 2 0 0 $27,600 — 1992 21 2 3 4 $66,180 — Turf 12 4 1 1 $69,800 — Wet 2 0 0 1 $5,700

9Jun93- 4Bel	fm	1 1/16 (T)	:474	1:12	1:422	(F)Clm 50000	84	2	5	43	41¼	1½	11½	Pezua J M	b	117	12.00	84-15	Turkoldy1171½BeyondSlew1131½HuckstrRos113	Driving	11
21May93- 2Bel	fm	1¼ [T]	:484	1:373	2:022	(F)Clm 35000	84	9	5	53	1½	1½	11¾	Chavez J F	b	11[illegible]	12.70	78-20	Trkoldy1171¾Stphn'sJoy119hdMssPocktCort117	Driving	12
5May93- 5Bel	fm	1 1/16 (T)	:464	1:11	1:433	(F)Clm 45000	-0	4	6	75¾	1011	1027	1057½	Santos J A	b	114	19.50	— —	HomebyTn1133¼BridjtHony1132½Mxmount117	Gave way	10
28Dec92- 7Aqu	fst	1 1/16 [•]	:472	1:131	1:464	3↑(F)Alw 31000	58	7	5	58½	88¼	813	713	Bruin J E	b	115	25.70	61-24	Lizeality115noSablWy1123¾WitAminuteAngie115	Outrun	8
20Dec92- 9Aqu	gd	1 1/16 [•]	:473	1:123	1:454	(F)Clm 45000	51	2	4	4¾	42½	612	717	Bruin J E	b	114	12.80	62-20	BlushingMoon1074RbccLurn1111¼BuckSomBll116	Tired	8
22Nov92- 7Aqu	gd	1	:452	1:104	1:371	3↑(F)Alw 31000	42	1	6	77	88½	712	724¾	Bailey J D		115	14.30	51-20	She'sAcademic117¾LdyJennF.115¾Lizelity115	No factor	9
6Nov92- 5Aqu	my	1	:481	1:133	1:39	(F)Clm 75000	71	3	2	22½	21½	33½	34¾	Bailey J D		111	2.80	62-29	BckSomBll1114Tffny'sTylor111¾Trkldy111	Lacked rally	5
6Nov92-Originally scheduled on turf																					
29Oct92- 5Aqu	fm	1 1/16 (T)	:472	1:114	1:432	3↑(F)Alw 31000	77	10	9	94½	63¾	73½	75¼	Romero R P		114	14.90	89-19	RightWingHot117noPuzl-Ir1121½Sh'sAcdmic117	Outrun	10
9Oct92- 8Bel	fst	1 1/16	:46	1:11	1:434	3↑(F)Alw 31000	70	5	4	4¾	2hd	24	27	Bailey J D		114	3.30	76-17	Sunblaze1147 Turkolady1143½ Miner'sGame114	2nd best	5
28Sep92- 7Bel	my	1 1/16	:461	1:112	1:442	3↑(F)Alw 31000	75	5	1	2½	2½	42	43	Davis R G		113	7.20	77-22	A'sDs1101¼ThrtghtChrms1101½Strmng122	Dueled wknd	6

LATEST WORKOUTS Jun 2 Bel 4f fst :492 B — May 16 Bel 5f fst 1:002 H — May 1 Bel 5f fst 1:012 H — Apr 26 Bel 5f fst 1:014 H

Turkolady, shown above, was in abysmal form when shelved at the end of the 1992 season, returned on May 5 to be all but eased, but then proceeded to win back-to-back grass races at 12-1.

Majesty's Time — Ch. h. 6, by Majesty's Prince—Torelia, by Torsion
CHAVEZ J F (—) — Br.—Whitbred Howard T (NY)
Own.—Whitbred Howard T — Tr.—Sciacca Gary (—)
117

Lifetime							
20 5 2 3	1992	11	2	0	3	$69,819
$177,849	1991	5	0	2	0	$14,520
	Turf	9	1	2	1	$47,919
	Wet	5	2	0	2	$87,540

26Dec92- 8Aqu	fst	1$\frac{1}{16}$ [•]	:47^{3}	1:12^{1}	1:43^{4}	3↑[S]Alex MRobb	82	8	5	7^{6}	11^{9}	10$^{9\frac{3}{4}}$	9^{12}	Chavez J F	119	20.70	77-19	Bill Of Rights115^{nb}Curbex119^{4}ExcellentTipper126	Tired	12
23Nov92- 8Aqu	my	1$\frac{3}{8}$	:50^{3}	1:40^{2}	2:20^{3}	3↑Handicap	85	4	4	2^{hd}	2^{hd}	3$^{4\frac{1}{2}}$	5$^{9\frac{3}{4}}$	Chavez J F	116	*1.60	57-34	CaptiveTune112$^{4\frac{3}{4}}$Asserche117$^{\frac{3}{4}}$BoldBlazer116	Bid, tired	6
6Nov92- 8Aqu	my	1$\frac{3}{8}$	:48^{4}	1:39^{4}	2:17^{3}	3↑Handicap	96	2	3	3^{5}	3$^{2\frac{1}{2}}$	2^{hd}	3^{nk}	Chavez J F	112	2.00	82-29	Asserch112^{no}TwothTwist110^{nk}Mjsty'sTim112	Sharp try	6
6Nov92-Originally scheduled on turf																				
23Oct92- 8Aqu	fm	1$\frac{1}{8}$ Ⓣ	:48^{3}	1:12^{1}	1:49^{1}	3↑[S]A-T Cole H	95	6	3	3$^{1\frac{1}{2}}$	3^{2}	5^{4}	4$^{4\frac{1}{2}}$	Chavez J F	114	12.50	92-07	Forlbnd115$^{1\frac{3}{4}}$EbonyMgc114$^{1\frac{1}{2}}$Fourstrdv120	Lacked rally	8
27Sep92- 8Bel	sly	7f	:22^{3}	:46	1:24^{2}	3↑[S]Hudson H	86	2	7	2^{1}	4$^{1\frac{1}{2}}$	2$^{\frac{1}{2}}$	3^{nk}	Chavez J F	114	*1.70	82-14	ArgyleLk113^{nk}WhizAlong110^{no}Mjsty'sTim114	Sharp try	9
13Sep92- 7Bel	gd	1$\frac{1}{16}$ Ⓣ	:47^{4}	1:12	1:42	3↑Alw 37000	98	3	1	1^{1}	1$^{\frac{1}{2}}$	1^{2}	1^{1}	Chavez J F	117	9.50	86-23	Mjsty'sTm117^{1}WldCtrct119^{nk}HghIndDvoton117	Driving	7
19Aug92- 8Sar	gd	1$\frac{1}{8}$ Ⓣ	:46^{4}	1:10^{2}	1:47^{4}	3↑[S]West PointH	86	8	6	6$^{4\frac{1}{2}}$	5$^{3\frac{1}{2}}$	8$^{4\frac{1}{2}}$	9^{10}	McCauley W H	114	17.60	81-16	WildCtrct109$^{2\frac{3}{4}}$ExcellentTipper118^{nk}SocilRtir121	4 wide	14
31Jly92- 1Sar	sly	1	:47^{1}	1:11^{4}	1:36^{1}	3↑Alw 33000	101	1	1	1^{2}	1$^{1\frac{1}{2}}$	1^{2}	1$^{7\frac{1}{2}}$	Chavez J F	117	*.90	— —	Majesty's Time117$^{7\frac{1}{2}}$ Nucleus119^{nk}Prevailed117	Driving	4
31Jly92-Originally scheduled on turf																				
20Jly92- 7Bel	fm	1$\frac{1}{16}$ [T]	:47^{1}	1:10^{3}	1:41^{2}	3↑Alw 33000	90	6	5	4$^{3\frac{1}{2}}$	4$^{3\frac{1}{2}}$	4^{5}	5^{4}	Chavez J F	117	5.60	87-15	Punchpssr117$^{\frac{1}{2}}$MuchoPrcos117$^{\frac{3}{4}}$UpnFront117	Four wide	8

LATEST WORKOUTS ●Apr 30 Bel 5f fst :59^{4} H Apr 25 Bel tr.t 5f fst 1:02^{3} B Apr 18 Bel tr.t 5f fst 1:01^{3} B Apr 13 Bel tr.t 4f fst :47^{4} B

5/7 1 1/16 [T] $46K Alw $46^{00}

Majesty's Time had not been postward since the day after Christmas when he lit up the toteboard on May 7 for a $46 payoff in a classified allowance on the turf:

Zero To Sixty — B. c. 4, by Cougar II—Gorgeous Dee, by Dewan
CHAVEZ J F (142 25 16 12 .18) — Br.—Hancock Arthur B III (Ky)
Own.—More-N-More Stable — Tr.—Sciacca Gary (55 16 5 7 .29)
117

Lifetime						
10 1 2 0	1993	6	1	1	0	$22,120
$27,840	1992	4	M	1	0	$5,720
	Turf	7	1	2	0	$27,630

5Jun93- 5Bel	fm	1$\frac{1}{16}$ Ⓣ	:47	1:10^{3}	1:41^{2}	3↑Alw 28500	82	1	1	1$^{\frac{1}{2}}$	2$^{1\frac{1}{2}}$	3$^{1\frac{1}{2}}$	2^{5}	Chavez J F		117	*2.10	84-13	AmericanNavy117^{5}ZeroToSixty117^{1}Siempre117	Gamely	9
23May93- 5Bel	fm	1$\frac{3}{8}$ Ⓣ	:49^{4}	1:39^{2}	2:15^{1}	3↑Alw 30500	85	2	1	1^{1}	1^{hd}	3^{nk}	5$^{2\frac{1}{4}}$	Chavez J F		117	3.50	89-12	Hungrkill117$^{\frac{3}{4}}$AlKrnk-Ir117$^{\frac{3}{4}}$Thinkrnot117	Used in pace	8
30Apr93- 5Aqu	fm	1$\frac{1}{16}$ Ⓣ	:47^{1}	1:11^{2}	1:42^{3}	3↑Md Sp Wt	88	3	3	3$^{2\frac{1}{2}}$	2$^{\frac{1}{2}}$	2^{hd}	1$^{\frac{3}{4}}$	Chavez J F		124	7.60	98-08	ZroToSxty124$^{\frac{3}{4}}$AInSocology115^{2}JohnnysGlry115	Driving	10
21Apr93- 6Hia	fm	*1$\frac{1}{8}$ Ⓣ			1:47^{2}	Clm 40000	68	7	8	7$^{5\frac{1}{2}}$	6^{6}	8^{13}	8$^{17\frac{1}{2}}$	Ferrer J C	b	117	24.60	86 —	SquareCut117$^{5\frac{1}{2}}$BruceWhtKin113$^{4\frac{1}{4}}$Brnger115	No factor	10
21Feb93- 6GP	fm	*1$\frac{3}{8}$ Ⓣ			2:19^{4}	Alw 22000	67	1	1	1^{hd}	1^{hd}	4$^{6\frac{1}{2}}$	6$^{10\frac{1}{4}}$	Romero R P		113	3.00	65-17	Competition117$^{4\frac{1}{4}}$ [D]Sportin' Charles112$^{\frac{3}{4}}$ RiteBuck114		10
21Feb93-Checked sharply leaving final turn; Placed fifth through disqualification																					
7Feb93- 8GP	fst	1$\frac{1}{8}$	:49^{2}	1:14^{4}	1:53^{3}	Alw 21000	63	5	2	2^{hd}	2$^{\frac{1}{2}}$	6$^{7\frac{3}{4}}$	6$^{13\frac{1}{2}}$	Romero R P	L	113	41.40	55-26	RunwyRomeo113^{4}FreebiOn112^{1}CountryTown107	Faded	9
22Dec92- 1Aqu	fst	170 [•]	:48^{3}	1:13^{2}	1:42^{3}	3↑Md Sp Wt	56	6	4	4$^{5\frac{1}{2}}$	6$^{7\frac{3}{4}}$	7^{13}	7$^{18\frac{3}{4}}$	Chavez J F	b	120	9.60	73-09	PureRumor120^{8}FlyingColonel120$^{5\frac{1}{2}}$AllCndin120	No rally	8
16Dec92- 1Aqu	fst	1$\frac{1}{16}$ [•]	:49	1:13^{4}	1:46	3↑Md Sp Wt	54	4	1	1$^{\frac{1}{2}}$	1^{hd}	5$^{5\frac{1}{4}}$	5$^{12\frac{3}{4}}$	Romero R P		120	3.60	65-18	PaperHat120$^{4\frac{1}{4}}$AllCandin120$^{\frac{1}{2}}$FlyingColonel120	Steadied	5
12Nov92- 6Aqu	sf	1$\frac{3}{8}$ Ⓣ	:52	1:44^{4}	2:26^{2}	3↑Md Sp Wt	75	6	1	1^{1}	1$^{\frac{1}{2}}$	1^{2}	2^{nk}	Romero R P		120	12.10	51-37	Pedantical120^{nk}ZeroToSixty120$^{\frac{3}{4}}$OffTheCuff120	Gamely	11
25Oct92- 2Aqu	gd	1$\frac{1}{8}$ Ⓣ	:49	1:14	1:52^{1}	3↑Md Sp Wt	70	11	1	1$^{\frac{1}{2}}$	1^{1}	3$^{1\frac{1}{2}}$	6$^{7\frac{3}{4}}$	Romero R P		119	31.60	74-21	Cmpttn112$^{1\frac{1}{2}}$LnnrdSphn119^{hd}OffThCff119	Used in pace	12

LATEST WORKOUTS Jun 15 Bel tr.t 5f fst 1:02 B May 11 Bel 4f fst :49^{4} B

Zero To Sixty had not won early at the Belmont meet, but came close, winning toward the tail-end of the Big A session, April 30. Note the dramatic 20-point improvement in Beyer figures for the maiden win at better than 7-1.

Note that Chavez was riding these bombers for the most part.

To me, Kefalonians almost had to run a big race in this spot, based on the past history of Sciacca, the presence of Chavez in the saddle, and the fact that he was a full brother to Kuru Klata, who had improved markedly on the grass for the same connections.

When lightly-raced horses with suitable pedigrees and capable handlers go to the grass for the first time, they are well-meant no matter how horrible their dirt-form has been. The surface change means everything. It is a whole new ball game:

FIRST RACE **1 MILE. (Turf)(1.32^{2}) MAIDEN SPECIAL WEIGHT. Purse $32,000. 3–year–olds and upward. Weights: 3–year–olds, 113 lbs. Older, 122 lbs. (Day 4 of a 57 Day Meet. Clear. 60.)**

Belmont

MAY 6, 1995

Value of Race: $32,000 Winner $19,200; second $6,400; third $3,520; fourth $1,920; fifth $960. Mutuel Pool $258,591.00 Exacta Pool $493,869.00

Last Raced	Horse	M/Eqt.	A.	Wt	PP	St	¼	½	¾	Str	Fin	Jockey	Odds $1
15Apr95 ^{3}Aqu^{9}	Kefalonians		3	113	2	4	1½	2½	2^{1}	1½	$1^{1\frac{1}{2}}$	Chavez J F	17.00
28Apr95 ^{5}Aqu^{4}	Northern King		3	110	5	5	3^{hd}	4^{hd}	3½	$3^{2\frac{1}{2}}$	2^{1}	Perez R B^{5}	10.30
28Apr95 ^{1}Aqu^{2}	Colonel Bart	b	3	114	8	9	11^{1}	9^{hd}	8^{2}	$5^{1\frac{1}{2}}$	3^{1}	Migliore R	2.05
29Mar95 ^{11}Hia^{2}	Ransom Me Daddy		3	113	4	6	7^{hd}	8½	5½	4^{hd}	4½	Santos J A	3.20
	Then Some		3	103	3	12	2^{hd}	1½	1^{hd}	2^{hd}	$5^{2\frac{1}{4}}$	Persaud Randi^{10}	29.25
1Apr95 ^{5}Aqu^{7}	Goorce King	b	3	108	11	2	6½	5½	$4^{1\frac{1}{2}}$	6^{2}	$6^{1\frac{3}{4}}$	Dunkelberger T L^{5}	21.60
	Herneztt		3	106	6	8	9^{hd}	10^{1}	9½	$9^{3\frac{1}{2}}$	7½	Valdivia J Jr^{7}	11.80
17Apr95 ^{1}Aqu^{3}	Identity	f	3	113	9	10	10½	7½	6½	7^{1}	8^{2}	Samyn J L	9.50
16Feb95 ^{10}GP^{2}	Romulo		3	113	1	3	4½	6½	7½	8½	9^{6}	Luzzi M J	5.50
15Apr95 ^{3}Aqu^{6}	Farranfore		3	113	7	11	8½	3½	$10^{1\frac{1}{2}}$	$10^{2\frac{1}{2}}$	$10^{5\frac{1}{2}}$	Alvarado F T	13.20
21Apr95 ^{5}Aqu^{8}	Raffie's Rullah	f	3	114	10	7	12	12	11^{5}	11^{8}	11^{13}	Madrid A Jr	96.00
4Jan95 ^{9}Aqu^{8}	Raised By Natives	bf	3	113	12	1	5^{hd}	11^{1}	12	12	12	Cruguet J	62.00

OFF AT 1:02 Start Good. Won driving. Time, :24^{1}, :48^{2}, 1:13, 1:37^{4} Course good.

$2 Mutuel Prices:				
	3–KEFALONIANS	36.00	16.40	10.40
	6–NORTHERN KING		9.30	4.50
	9–COLONEL BART			2.80

$2 EXACTA 3–6 PAID $493.50

B. c, (Mar), by Val de l'Orne (Fr)–Demean, by Dewan. Trainer Sciacca Gary. Bred by Rock Hill Farm (Ont–C).

KEFALONIANS dueled outside THEN SOME into upper stretch, surged to the front in midstretch, then edged clear while drifting out. NORTHERN KING raced in close contention between horses for six furlongs, then held well for the place. COLONEL BART outrun for a half, advanced between horses on the turn, checked slightly in midstretch then closed late for a share. RANSOM ME DADDY rated in the middle of the pack for five furlongs, swerved out while gaining in midstretch then finished evenly. THEN SOME away slowly, rushed up along the inside, dueled inside the winner into upper stretch and weakened. GOOREE KING raced within striking distance while four wide for six furlongs then lacked a strong closing bid. HERNEZTT steadied along the inside at the half mile pole and failed to threaten thereafter. IDENTITY raced five wide throughout. ROMULO up close early while between horses, faded after going five furlongs. FARRANFORE rushed up along the inside, checked on the far turn then gave way. RAFFIE'S RULLAH never reached contention. RAISED BY NATIVES showed only brief speed while five wide.

Owners— 1, Amvrosiatos A & Vangelatos P; 2, Anderson Ralph R; 3, Chen Daniel J; 4, Teinowitz Phillip; 5, Russi Drin T; 6, Cojuangco Eduardo M Jr; 7, Saba Raul; 8, Avanzino Kenneth C; 9, Condren & Cornacchia & Paulson; 10, Meriwether John W; 11, Prieger Henry H; 12, Pepperell Stable

Trainers—1, Sciacca Gary; 2, Dutrow Richard E; 3, Parisella John; 4, Schulhofer Flint S; 5, Dupps Kristina; 6, Jolley Leroy; 7, Penna Angel Jr; 8, Skiffington Thomas J; 9, Zito Nicholas P; 10, Freeman Willard C; 11, Diamond Stephan S; 12, Cotter Mary M

Overweight: Northern King (2), Colonel Bart (1), Raffie's Rullah (1).

Scratched— Rafanel (10Feb95 ^{6}GP^{5}), Brave Warrior (14Mar95 ^{6}GP^{4}), Detached (19Apr95 ^{4}AQU^{4}), Prime Magic (28Apr95 ^{1}AQU^{6}), Evil Ways (22Apr95 ^{3}AQU^{5}), Lunatic Luke (23Dec94 ^{3}AQU^{7}), Whose On First (27Apr95 ^{9}AQU^{2}), Prospects Of Gold (19Apr95 ^{4}AQU^{8})

I had no opinion about the second half of the daily double, but that didn't mean this opportunity couldn't be taken advantage of aggressively. I divided my bet into two parts, 50 percent to win, and 50 percent for exactas: For every $4 ticket putting Kefalonians over the four equally-matched horses with grass experience (a $16 play), a $2 saver was purchased using him underneath those horses (an $8 play).

There's something to be said for keeping a trainer's winning past performances on hand, and having access to pertinent pedigree information.

THE SIMULCASTING EXPLOSION of recent years has taken the racing game by storm, and I've found that one of the most reliable and profitable spot-play methods involves simply researching pedigrees in maiden and preliminary allowance grass races and betting on the horses who offer an attractive combination of suitable bloodlines and price. It's fast and easy handicapping because it doesn't require poring over the past performances of unfamiliar horses, or maintaining comprehensive records about unfamiliar track surfaces and layouts. And the payoffs are at times truly mind-boggling.

Belmont was beaming in the signal from Arlington Park starting around mid-June, and each day I'd scan the entries in search of a pedigree-oriented play. Arlington Park is in the suburbs of Chicago, in the Central time zone, which is an hour earlier than New York. It was just after six o'clock, New York time. Belmont's live program had long since been completed for the day, and the press box had all but emptied out, with only me and two racing writers for the *New York Post*, Rick Lang and David Grening, still pecking away at our laptops (with one eye on the Arlington monitor). Some 1,500 miles away, a dozen maidens were about to go postward in a nine-furlong grass race, and there was a horse in it that I'd been waiting for all day long:

6 Arlington

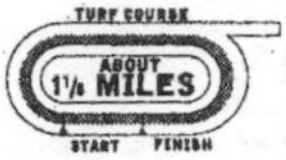

About 1⅛ MILES. **(Turf). (1:471) MAIDEN SPECIAL WEIGHT. Purse $19,000 (plus $6,840 IOA for ICF.) Fillies, 3 and 4-year-olds. Weights: 3-year-olds, 113 lbs. 4-year-olds, 122 lbs. (Preference to horses that have not started for less than $30,000.)**

1 Betsy Wolf

Own: Panic Stable
ALLEN K K (2 0 0 1 .00)

Gr. f. 3 (Mar)
Sire: Wolf Power (Flirting Around)
Dam: Betsy Mack (Mr. Redoy)
Br: Clark Sandra D & Tucker Jan (Ky)
Tr: Janks Christine K (6 0 1 1 .00)

L 113

Lifetime Record:	9 M 4 0	$15,145		
1995	6 M 4 0	$13,160	Turf	0 0 0 0
1994	3 M 0 0	$1,985	Wet	0 0 0 0
AP Ⓣ	0 0 0 0		Dist Ⓣ	0 0 0 0

16Jun95-3Spt	fst	6f	:223 :462 :583 1:112	3↑ ⒻMd Sp Wt	63 5 2 54 33 21½ 21¾	Meier R	L 113 b	3.20	85-13	Sonyarita1141¾ Betsy Wolf1134½ Pink Fizz1131¼	Loomed boldly 8
4Jun95-3Spt	fst	6f	:223 :464 :583 1:111	3↑ ⒻMd Sp Wt	64 5 3 45 43½ 24 25	Meier R	L 113 b	3.30e	83-18	La Nina De Orumila1135 Betsy Wolf1137 Rumble Seat1146½	Mild rally 8
27May95-5Spt	fst	1	:24 :482 1:142 1:411	3↑ ⒻMd Sp Wt	43 6 7 65¾ 46½ 511 517¼	Razo E Jr	L 114 b	7.50	57-26	Rascality1143½ Marla1137 Nifty Nicki121nk	Bore out turn 9
27Apr95-5Spt	gd	1	:243 :49 1:144 1:43	3↑ ⒻMd Sp Wt	56 4 6 32 21 21½ 24	Razo E Jr	L 114 b	3.30	61-32	Poison Petals1134 Betsy Wolf1144½ Precious Prodigy1143	Crowded start 8
8Apr95-4Spt	fst	1	:241 :483 1:144 1:413	3↑ ⒻMd Sp Wt	40 8 6 43 54 58 410½	Razo E Jr	114	*.70e	61-19	ChrissyB1131½ Shsjustlittlbit1131 Brittny'sPrtnr1148	Wide thruout, bled 8
19Mar95-5Spt	fst	6f	:22 :46 :582 1:122	3↑ ⒻMd Sp Wt	41 1 5 66½ 69½ 48½ 27½	Marquez C H Jr	113	4.90	74-15	Whirlpool1157½ Betsy Wolf113hd Houstous1132½	Late wide bid 9
18Aug94-3AP	fst	1	:23 :454 1:114 1:393	ⒻMd Sp Wt	24 3 7 52½ 34 315 416	Meier R	118	2.00	55-22	Southern Letters11811 Chronicler1183 Sizzlin Sunshine1181½	Tired 7
31Jly94-4AP	fst	5½f	:22 :46 :59 1:06	ⒻMd Sp Wt	45 6 9 106½ 109¾ 58 44¾	Fires E	118	5.90	78-18	ⒹJ.R.'sChoice1184 BlondMoment118½ LadyHotDnce118nk	Late wide bid 10
16Jly94-7AP	fst	5½f	:222 :462 :592 1:062	ⒻMd Sp Wt	32 1 11 1211 1016 810 510¼	Fires E	118	7.80	71-19	Just One Moment118nk Southern Letters1182 GlareIce1185½	Late wide bid 12

WORKOUTS: Jun 26 AP 5f fst 1:021 B *14/50* May 22 Spt 5f fst 1:044 B *20/31* May 12 Spt 4f fst :522 B *31/42* Apr 22 Spt 5f fst 1:04 B *25/37* Apr 17 Spt 4f fst :51 B *6/20* Apr 1 Spt 5f fst 1:034 B *26/45*

2 Sean's Woodman

Own: Devenport Roger J
ROMERO R P (7 1 1 0 .14)

Dk. b or br f. 3 (Feb)
Sire: Woodman (Mr. Prospector)
Dam: Midnight Pumpkin (Pretense)
Br: Hermitage Farm,Inc (Ky)
Tr: Kelly Larry (4 1 1 0 .25)

113

Lifetime Record:	4 M 0 0	$607		
1995	1 M 0 0		Turf	0 0 0 0
1994	3 M 0 0	$607	Wet	0 0 0 0
AP Ⓣ	0 0 0 0		Dist Ⓣ	0 0 0 0

3Feb95-7OP	fst	1	:231 :471 1:132 1:404	3↑ ⒻMd Sp Wt	26 8 10 914 1014 1117 1024½	Romero S P	114 f	56.30	50-23	Myabya122½ Lil's Memory114½ Lady Baiul1146	In tight 11
2Dec94-2RP	fst	170	:233 :474 1:133 1:463	ⒻAlw 8430N1X	43 6 9 910 98½ 510 46	Landeros B C	B 114	9.60	53-32	RelaunchPrincess1142 SleekNUnique1152 DixielandSafri1142	Mild rally 10
20Nov94-8RP	gd	7f	:222 :45 1:123 1:271	ⒻCimarron27k	31 6 7 710 714 614 613½	Landeros B C	B 114 f	60.60	57-27	Miss Abbott114½ War Thief1143½ Bayou Bird1141	Outrun 8
2Nov94-9RP	fst	7f	:221 :452 1:11 1:243	ⒻMd Sp Wt	32 9 10 108¼ 910 613 516½	Landeros B C	B 120 f	12.00	67-22	Bayou Bird1207½ Miss Abbott1201 Lady Baiul1205½	Showed little 10

WORKOUTS: May 6 Kee 3f fst :374 B *9/14* Apr 25 Kee 5f gd 1:052 B *15/17* Apr 18 Kee Ⓣ 4f fm :491 B (d) *1/2*

3 Plenty Charming

Own: Russell L Reineman Stable Inc
WALLS M K (7 0 1 0 .00)

Dk. b or br f. 3 (Jan)
Sire: Broad Brush (Ack Ack)
Dam: Charming Accent (Cassaleria)
Br: Nuckols Charles Jr & Sons (Ky)
Tr: Springer Frank R (1 0 0 1 .00)

113

Lifetime Record:	3 M 0 1	$4,800			
1995	3 M 0 1	$4,800	Turf	0 0 0 0	
1994	0 M 0 0		Wet	1 0 0 0	$1,600
AP Ⓣ	0 0 0 0		Dist Ⓣ	0 0 0 0	

12May95-5CD	fst	1	:224 :46 1:113 1:362	3↑ ⒻMd Sp Wt	34 2 6 74 912 919 825¾	Martinez W	111 b	8.30	69-09	Fluffkins1128 Zigana1131¼ Mayhew113½	No factor 12
21Apr95-2Kee	my	1⅛	:49 1:143 1:41 1:543	ⒻMd Sp Wt	46 12 5 53 45½ 511 413	Gryder A T	116 b	*2.20	48-33	Dramatrix1165½ Marla1162½ Pretend1165	Evenly 12
8Apr95-3Kee	fst	1 1/16	:232 :48 1:142 1:473	ⒻMd Sp Wt	59 9 11 1011 104½ 310 37	Gryder A T	117 b	8.10e	64-29	Robalana1175 Be In Style1172 Plenty Charming117¾	11

Fractious gate, in tight start

WORKOUTS: Jun 22 AP 4f fst :471 H *3/27* Jun 11 AP 4f fst :513 B *8/11* Apr 5 Kee 4f fst :52 B *23/25*

4 Jukebox Dance

Own: Swartz Vincent
MCMAHON C J (2 0 0 0 .00)

B. f. 3 (Feb)
Sire: Fred Astaire (Nijinsky II)
Dam: My Honeydew (Tilt Up)
Br: Vincent J. Swartz, Joseph Paglini, et al. (Ill)
Tr: Swartz Monique (—)

L 108⁵

Lifetime Record:	4 M 0 0	$668			
1995	3 M 0 0	$514	Turf	0 0 0 0	
1994	1 M 0 0	$154	Wet	1 0 0 0	$154
AP Ⓣ	0 0 0 0		Dist Ⓣ	0 0 0 0	

2Jun95-2Spt	fst	6f	:222 :463 :592 1:13	ⒻⓈMd Sp Wt	12 3 8 910 815 917 819¼	Lasala J	L 119 b	63.50	60-21	Trailing Edge1197 She'sjustmystyle1192 Quack A Doodle119½	No factor 10
12May95-5Spt	fst	6f	:221 :454 :59 1:132	ⒻⓈMd Sp Wt	19 4 5 47 411 68½ 710½	Silva C H	L 119 b	16.90	66-15	Just Dimples1192½ Billie Dee1193½ Set Your Limit119no	Faltered early 10
19Mar95-2Spt	fst	1	:25 :50 1:154 1:414	3↑ ⒻⓈMd Sp Wt	18 8 7 76½ 78 713 720½	Enriquez I D	114	26.80	50-22	ForceMajeure1134 PeninsulaPlayer1212 ClassicPssion1211½	Outrun, bled 8
8Dec94-2Haw	sly	6f	:224 :471 :593 1:124	ⒻⓈMd Sp Wt	8 5 5 43½ 58½ 1015 1120	Lasala J	119	11.80	60-18	Papa's Lisa1192¼ Up This Day1191¼ Delzzad1196	Brief speed 12

WORKOUTS: ●Jun 27 AP 4f fst :47 H *1/42* Jun 19 AP 6f fst 1:163 B *3/5* May 29 Spt 5f fst 1:061 B *20/22* May 7 Spt 4f fst :52 B *17/30* May 1 Spt 5f fst 1:013 Hg*2/32* Apr 24 Spt 4f fst :52 B *10/30*

5 Disco Doll

Own: Miles Steve
SIBILLE R (16 2 2 3 .13)

Dk. b or br f. 3 (May)
Sire: Diesis (Sharpen Up)
Dam: Disconiz (Northern Dancer)
Br: Albert G. Clay & Michael Ryan (Ky)
Tr: Nafzger Carl A (4 0 1 1 .00)

113

Lifetime Record:	1 M 0 1	$3,430			
1995	1 M 0 1	$3,430	Turf	1 0 0 1	$3,430
1994	0 M 0 0		Wet	0 0 0 0	
AP Ⓣ	0 0 0 0		Dist Ⓣ	0 0 0 0	

15Jun95-6CD	fm	1 Ⓣ	:232 :464 1:121 1:38	3↑ ⒻMd Sp Wt	57 6 4 2hd 1hd 3nk 42	Peck B D	110	5.30	80-10	ⒹIn The Library112no Shaa Wing110¾ Deer Jackie1211¼	10

Bid weakened late Placed third through disqualification.

WORKOUTS: Jun 26 AP 4f fst :49 B *11/47* Jun 11 CD 5f fst 1:022 B *13/24* Jun 6 CD 5f fst 1:013 B *2/20* Jun 3 CD 4f my :49 B *10/45* May 29 CD 5f fst 1:022 Bg*9/31* May 25 CD 5f sly 1:04 B *9/14*

6 All The Rage

Own: Pin Oak Stable
GUIDRY M (27 4 5 4 .15)

B. f. 3 (Feb)
Sire: Lyphard (Northern Dancer)
Dam: Laugh and Be Merry (Erins Isle)
Br: Pin Oak Stud Inc (Ky)
Tr: Mott William I (—)

113

Lifetime Record:	2 M 0 0	$2,880			
1995	2 M 0 0	$2,880	Turf	2 0 0 0	$2,880
1994	0 M 0 0		Wet	0 0 0 0	
AP Ⓣ	0 0 0 0		Dist Ⓣ	0 0 0 0	

17Jun95-2Bel	fm	1 1/16 🅃	:242 :474 1:12 1:431	3↑ ⒻMd Sp Wt	65 10 8 86¼ 85¼ 76 56½	Smith M E	113	3.90	73-12	Retained Earning113¾ Twilight Forest1134 Aesthete1131¾	No rally 10
4Jun95-10Bel	fm	1 1/16 Ⓣ	:23 :462 1:11 1:411	3↑ ⒻMd Sp Wt	63 8 9 106¾ 95¾ 67 410¾	Smith M E	113	6.50	81-08	FashionStr1125¾ RisingReson1124¾ Arunforyourmoney112nk	Broke slowly 10

WORKOUTS: May 31 Bel 5f fst 1:004 H *9/37* May 14 Bel 5f fst 1:034 B *42/59* Apr 24 Pay 5f fst 1:062 B *7/8* Apr 17 Pay 5f fst 1:081 B *5/6*

7 Ruby Ransom

Own: Stronach Frank H
ALBARADO R J (30 6 6 3 .20)

Dk. b or br f. 3 (Feb)
Sire: Red Ransom (Roberto)
Dam: Amelia Bearhart (Bold Hour)
Br: Richard D. Maynard (Ont-C)
Tr: Barber Kenneth (—)

113

Lifetime Record:	2 M 0 0	$1,707		
1995	1 M 0 0	$651	Turf	0 0 0 0
1994	1 M 0 0	$1,056	Wet	0 0 0 0
AP Ⓣ	0 0 0 0		Dist Ⓣ	0 0 0 0

2Apr95-1WO	fst	5f	:221 :452 :573	3↑ ⒻMd Sp Wt	44 3 5 65 68½ 612 516¼	Landry R C	114 b	*1.15	78-10	Scotzanna1148 Shebandowana1134½ Valid Style114¾	Saved ground 6
18Jun94-2WO	fst	5f	:221 :453 :582	ⒻMd Sp Wt	51 2 6 32 43½ 47 47½	Kabel T K	114 b	2.40	90-07	Regal Halo114¾ With Care1151 Pound Sterling1145¾	Well placed off rail 8

WORKOUTS: Jun 25 AP 5f fst 1:01 B *8/53* Jun 14 Kee 5f fst 1:02 B *4/10* Jun 6 Kee 6f sly 1:17 B *2/2* May 30 Kee 5f fst 1:034 B *12/13* May 27 Kee 5f fst 1:021 B *2/9* May 20 Kee 6f fst 1:162 B *3/3*

8 Shimmering Snow
Own: Appleton Arthur I
GRYDER A T (29 4 5 8 .14)
B. f. 3 (Jun)
Sire: Frosty the Snowman (His Majesty)
Dam: Lyphard's Dancer (Lyphard)
Br: Appleton Arthur I (Fla)
Tr: Goldfine Lou M (5 0 1 1 .00)
L 113
Lifetime Record : 2 M 0 0 $380
1995 2 M 0 0 $380 Turf 0 0 0 0
1994 0 M 0 0 Wet 0 0 0 0
AP Ⓣ 0 0 0 0 Dist Ⓣ 0 0 0 0
4Jun95-3Spt fst 6f :223 :464 :583 1:111 3↑ ⒻMd Sp Wt 16 6 2 22 32 512 524 Silva C H 113 2.60 64-18 La Nina De Orumila1135 Betsy Wolf1137 Rumble Seat1146½ Brief speed 8
25Jan95-6GP fst 6f :223 :462 1:00 1:132 ⒻMd Sp Wt 21 3 9 97½ 86¾ 913 919¾ Smith M E 120 2.50 53-25 Hair Cut1202¾ Hurricane Cat120nk Jovial Joust120nk Showed little 10
WORKOUTS: Jun 25 AP 6f fst 1:15 B 2/7 Jun 20 AP 5f fst 1:02 B 8/20 Jun 14 AP 4f fst :491 B 6/17 May 30 Spt 5f fst 1:032 B 18/33 May 18 Spt 4f fst :513 B 5/21 May 5 Spt 3f fst :39 B 9/12

9 Blend In
Own: Darjean Paul
DIAZ J L (15 0 2 1 .00)
Ch. f. 3 (Jan)
Sire: Sword Dance (Nijinsky II)
Dam: Blue Hen Blend (Artaius)
Br: Sidney L. Port Trust 72270 & Jackie W. Ramos (Ky)
Tr: Darjean Paul (3 0 0 0 .00)
L 113
Lifetime Record : 1 M 0 0 $150
1995 1 M 0 0 $150 Turf 0 0 0 0
1994 0 M 0 0 Wet 0 0 0 0
AP Ⓣ 0 0 0 0 Dist Ⓣ 0 0 0 0
16Jun95-3Spt fst 6f :223 :462 :583 1:112 3↑ ⒻMd Sp Wt 26 7 4 76½ 813 811 716¼ Sorrows A G Jr L 113 *2.70e 71-13 Sonyarita1141¾ Betsy Wolf1134½ Pink Fizz1131¼ No rally, wide 8
WORKOUTS: Jun 11 Spt 5f fst 1:03 B 12/24 Jun 1 Haw 3f fst :392 B 5/5 May 31 Haw 5f fst 1:044 B 3/5 May 26 Spt 4f fst :53 B 36/58 Apr 25 Haw 5f fst 1:02 B 2/2 Apr 19 Spt 5f fst 1:06 B 28/35

10 Quack A Doodle
Own: Rattray Lee
RIVERA H JR (8 1 1 1 .13)
Dk. b or br f. 3 (Apr)
Sire: Quack (T. V. Lark)
Dam: Junior Lynx (Assagai Jr.)
Br: John Wiseman & Candy Wiseman (Ill)
Tr: Gore Terrel (5 1 0 0 .20)
113
Lifetime Record : 2 M 0 2 $3,586
1995 2 M 0 2 $3,586 Turf 0 0 0 0
1994 0 M 0 0 Wet 0 0 0 0
AP Ⓣ 0 0 0 0 Dist Ⓣ 0 0 0 0
18Jun95-5Spt fst 1 :242 :491 1:151 1:411 3↑ Ⓕ[S]Md Sp Wt 45 2 4 43½ 53 56 36½ Rivera H Jr 114 b *1.30e 67-26 Loose Park1144 Shesjustalittlebit1132½ Quack A Doodle114½ Split rivals 9
2Jun95-2Spt fst 6f :222 :463 :592 1:13 Ⓕ[S]Md Sp Wt 37 4 7 45 511 49 39 Rivera H Jr 119 b 10.50 70-21 Trailing Edge1197 She'sjustmystyle1192 Quack A Doodle119½ Evenly 10
WORKOUTS: May 26 Spt 5f fst 1:012 Hg 2/60 May 20 Spt 4f fst :543 B 18/23 May 12 Spt 5f fst 1:022 Hg 9/39 May 7 Spt 4f fst :50 Bg 3/30 May 3 Spt 4f fst :532 B 16/21 Apr 24 Spt 4f fst :52 B 10/30

11 Lovely Sebeecha
Own: Awaytheygo Stable
SILVA C H (15 1 3 2 .07)
Dk. b or br f. 3 (Apr)
Sire: Tsunami Slew (Seattle Slew)
Dam: Precocious Lass (Distinctive)
Br: Eileen H. Hartis (Ky)
Tr: Cilio Gene A (11 2 3 3 .18)
L 113
Lifetime Record : 5 M 1 2 $7,880
1994 5 M 1 2 $7,880 Turf 0 0 0 0
1993 0 M 0 0 Wet 0 0 0 0
AP Ⓣ 0 0 0 0 Dist Ⓣ 0 0 0 0
25Nov94-1Med fst 6f :221 :444 :571 1:101 ⒻMd Sp Wt 71 5 4 43 37 45½ 32½ Martin C W L 117 18.10 87-11 Big City Bound1171¾ Keyser Ridge117¾ Lovely Sebeecha1174 Mild bid 7
28Oct94-4Med fst 6f :222 :452 :573 1:101 ⒻMd Sp Wt 48 6 4 73 89 713 615¼ Smith M E L 117 2.90e 75-13 Select Key1173½ Keyser Ridge1178 Keep The Record1171½ Outrun 10
5Oct94-5Bel fst 1 :232 :471 1:124 1:392 ⒻMd Sp Wt 42 1 1 2½ 64¼ 76¼ 712½ McCauley W H 117 9.10 53-21 Mistress S.112¾ Foxy Scarlet117nk Limit1122½ Gave way 7
20Sep94-6Med fst 6f :222 :46 :583 1:12 ⒻMd Sp Wt 52 5 4 32 44½ 44¾ 25 Wilson R 117 *1.50 76-17 RobinsGone1175 LovelySebeech1173 TemprncTwoStp1171¾ Second best 7
24Aug94-6Mth fst 6f :222 :461 :584 1:114 ⒻMd Sp Wt 48 4 8 41¼ 43½ 36 36¾ Bravo J 117 *1.10 73-19 Almamony1175½ Effervescence1171¼ LovelySebeech117¾ Finished evenly 8
WORKOUTS: Jun 8 AP 4f gd :51 B 7/9

12 Precious Prodigy
Own: McKellar Joseph P
LAVIOLETTE B S (15 1 2 1 .07)
B. f. 3 (May)
Sire: Mister Modesty (Nijinsky II)
Dam: Stuffing (Turkey Shoot)
Br: Mr. & Mrs. Prescott L. McCardell (Ky)
Tr: McKellar Joseph P (—)
L 113
Lifetime Record : 4 M 0 2 $4,085
1995 4 M 0 2 $4,085 Turf 0 0 0 0
1994 0 M 0 0 Wet 0 0 0 0
AP Ⓣ 0 0 0 0 Dist Ⓣ 0 0 0 0
15Jun95-7Spt fst 1 :241 :484 1:141 1:40 3↑ ⒻMd Sp Wt 55 1 5 76¾ 810 78¼ 46¾ Laviolette B S L 113 19.80 73-21 CoolCooCoo1132¾ NiftyNicki1213¼ YemayaAchab114¾ Late four wide bid 9
27May95-5Spt fst 1 :24 :482 1:142 1:411 3↑ ⒻMd Sp Wt 55 3 8 912 911 49 410¾ Laviolette B S 114 32.30 63-26 Rascality1143½ Marla1137 Nifty Nicki121nk Late wide bid, bled 9
27Apr95-5Spt gd 1 :243 :49 1:144 1:43 3↑ ⒻMd Sp Wt 48 1 7 77½ 710 36½ 38½ Guidry M 114 3.00 56-32 Poison Petals1134 Betsy Wolf1144½ Precious Prodigy1143 4 wide bid 8
13Apr95-3Spt gd 6f :23 :472 1:004 1:142 3↑ ⒻMd 20000 47 4 7 811 813 68 34¾ Guidry M 114 6.70 67-26 Bsquerville1143½ BimiLorri'sMgic1211¼ PreciousProdigy114½ Belated bid 9
WORKOUTS: Jun 9 Spt 4f fst :523 B 15/24 May 23 Haw 5f gd 1:014 H 4/14 May 12 Haw 5f fst 1:032 B 12/21 ●Apr 8 Spt 4f fst :482 Hg 1/37 Mar 31 Spt 5f fst 1:043 Hg 52/77

With the exception of the first two betting choices, All The Rage and Disco Doll, everyone in the field was trying turf for the first time. I had looked everyone up in my copy of *Maiden Stats* that morning and had found nothing exceptional. Except this:

	SIRE INFO								DAM INFO										SIBLING INFO		YRLG SALES INFO		
Horse	# wnr/str	2yo wnr/str	% 1st	awd	Mud w%/sts	Turf w%/sts	% 1stT	Spl	prf	Dpi	# fls	# wnr/str	# sw	2yo wnr/str	awd	Mud w%/sts	Turf wnr/str	Dosage Index	Top Sibling	/Earn$	Price/Sire avg	# Rnk/sld	Stud Fee
ELY INTENTIONS									sp		1							1.59			$ 12k/$ 10k	4/ 10	NA
ELY JOHANNA	4/ 14	2/ 7	0	5.8	18/ 11	0/ 1	0	0.21	up		2							1.18					
ELY PERSONALITY	244/ 340	58/ 174	6	7.6	10/ 673	12/1696	10	1.37	p	1.41	4	2/ 3	0	0/ 2	6.2	0/ 3	0/ 1	2.20	Timeless Elegance	/$ 50k			
ELY REBECCA	4/ 4	4/ 4	25	6.3	25/ 4	0/ 1	0	1.47	w		1							9.67			$ 1.2k/$ 1.8k	4/ 4	2.5k
ELY SEBEECHA	112/ 166	33/ 100	3	7.5	9/ 289	13/ 660	8	1.21	sp	1.37	10	5/ 7	0	1/ 5	8.1	6/ 16	4/ 5	7.00	Dawn O' The Dance	/$147k	$ 30k/$ 14k	3/ 23	25k
ELY SNOW	37/ 70	12/ 37	8	6.4	9/ 47	0/ 22	0	1.33	w		1							3.80					
E MY COLOR	2/ 8	1/ 2	0	6.4	13/ 8	0/ 6	0	0.10	w	0.13	7	1/ 5	0	0/ 1	6.0	0/ 3	0/ 0	3.00	Miss Slewsiana	/$ 2.2k			

Bingo. Lovely Sebeecha stood out like a beacon in the night. Her pedigree was route-oriented, as the average winning distances (awd) for her sire and dam were 7.5 furlongs and 8.1 furlongs, respectively. More importantly, Lovely Sebeecha's dam, Precocious Lass, had produced five previous turf starters — and four of them had won!

Even though they both had turf experience, I thought the two favorites were vulnerable. All The Rage was trained by Bill Mott, who was currently in the midst of what would turn out to be an Eclipse-winning season for himself and Cigar; the bay filly had disappointed twice with the main string at Belmont, and had been cast adrift to compete for the lesser purses in the midwest. Disco Doll had lost ground through a very ordinary final quarter in her debut two weeks earlier at Churchill Downs, and would be attempting an additional furlong.

Ruby Ransom was a daughter of Red Ransom, whose progeny win their fair share first time on turf, but there was nothing on the dam's side to suggest she would move up on grass. Moreover, judging from the money she'd attracted in two previous starts at Woodbine, those close to her had expected good races on dirt, but she had taken a pratfall on both occasions.

I bet Lovely Sebeecha to win for $50, along with $20 worth of exacta savers in this fashion: $4 exactas using her underneath the two favorites, along with a pair of $6 exactas using her underneath Betsy Wolf and Shimmering Snow.

Betsy Wolf and Shimmering Snow didn't show anything noteworthy in *Maiden Stats*, but they boasted other redeeming features. Betsy Wolf figured to get a ground-saving trip from her rail post, had been racing in improved form since adding Lasix, and had a decent enough turf pedigree.

Shimmering Snow was a homebred from Arthur Appleton, a true pillar of the turf who bred, owned and raced, among others, the sensational Jolie's Halo; the filly had flashed speed first time back from a layoff earlier in the month, was getting Lasix for the first time, and boasted an excellent score of 300 on Tomlinson ratings (more on that coming up shortly).

Grening and I hadn't discussed the race beforehand, having each been preoccupied with the details of our 9-to-5 jobs, but by the far turn it became apparent that his immediate financial solvency was intricately wrapped up in Shimmering Snow, who was out winging on a comfortable lead.

My enthusiasm for Lovely Sebeecha had been tempered somewhat, due to her outside post and the fact that she showed a sparse workout line for her first start since November (perhaps she had been training on a private farm?), and as the field came to midstretch I had already chalked this race up in the loss column. Shimmering Snow had opened up a six-length advantage, and Lovely Sebeecha, whom I had glimpsed only briefly at the back of the picture as the field approached the quarter pole, was nowhere in sight.

Then, in an instant, Lovely Sebeecha was a bolt out of the blue, moving like a brown flash from the left side of the television screen to the right. At first, I was ecstatic just to see her at all, and hoped she might somehow pass the half-dozen or so other horses in front of her to finish second behind Shimmering Snow. In the matter of a few strides she had done that, and then came barreling down on the leader in the final yards...only to fall a nose short:

SIXTH RACE
Arlington
JUNE 30, 1995

ABOUT 1⅛ MILES. (Turf)(1.47^1) MAIDEN SPECIAL WEIGHT. Purse $19,000 (plus $6,840 IOA for ICF.) Fillies, 3 and 4-year-olds. Weights: 3-year-olds, 113 lbs. 4-year-olds, 122 lbs. (Preference to horses that have not started for less than $30,000.)

Value of Race: $19,000 Winner $11,400; second $3,420; third $1,900; fourth $760; fifth $190; sixth $190; seventh $190; eighth $190; ninth $190; tenth $190; eleventh $190; twelfth $190. Mutuel Pool $148,833.00 Exacta Pool $125,181.00

Last Raced	Horse	M/Eqt.	A.	Wt	PP	St	¼	½	¾	Str	Fin	Jockey	Odds $1
4Jun95 ^{3}Spt^5	Shimmering Snow	L	3	113	8	5	1^2	$1^{1\frac{1}{2}}$	1^2	1^6	1no	Gryder A T	10.20
25Nov94 ^{1}Med^3	Lovely Sebeecha	L	3	113	11	9	6^{hd}	9^3	$8^{\frac{1}{2}}$	7^{hd}	$2^{4\frac{1}{2}}$	Silva C H	10.00
16Jun95 ^{3}Spt^2	Betsy Wolf	Lb	3	114	1	2	$7^{\frac{1}{2}}$	5^4	$2^{\frac{1}{2}}$	$2^{2\frac{1}{2}}$	3no	Razo E Jr	9.00
18Jun95 ^{5}Spt^3	Quack A Doodle	b	3	114	10	10	9^1	$7^{\frac{1}{2}}$	7^2	8^1	$4^{\frac{1}{2}}$	Rivera H Jr	22.60
3Feb95 ^{7}OP^{10}	Sean's Woodman	f	3	114	2	8	12	11^1	$9^{2\frac{1}{2}}$	9^5	$5^{3\frac{1}{4}}$	Romero R P	32.70
17Jun95 ^{2}Bel^5	All The Rage	b	3	114	6	6	$4^{\frac{1}{2}}$	4^{hd}	4^{hd}	4^{hd}	$6^{\frac{3}{4}}$	Guidry M	1.60
15Jun95 ^{7}Spt^4	Precious Prodigy	L	3	113	12	12	11^{hd}	12	11	11	$7^{\frac{1}{2}}$	Laviolette B S	39.30
2Apr95 ^{1}WO^5	Ruby Ransom	b	3	113	7	7	$2^{\frac{1}{2}}$	$2^{\frac{1}{2}}$	3^1	5^{hd}	8^{nk}	Albarado R J	15.40
15Jun95 ^{6}CD^4	Disco Doll		3	114	5	4	$3^{2\frac{1}{2}}$	3^1	5^3	$3^{\frac{1}{2}}$	9^{nk}	Sibille R	2.00
12May95 ^{5}CD^8	Plenty Charming	b	3	114	3	3	$10^{\frac{1}{2}}$	$10^{\frac{1}{2}}$	10^5	10^{hd}	$10^{\frac{3}{4}}$	Walls M K	24.80
2Jun95 ^{2}Spt^8	Jukebox Dance	L	3	108	4	1	8^3	6^5	6^6	$6^{\frac{1}{2}}$	11	McMahon C J^5	52.60
16Jun95 ^{3}Spt^7	Blend In	Lb	3	113	9	11	5^1	8^{hd}	—	—	—	Diaz J L	63.10

Blend In:Eased

OFF AT 5:09 Start Good. Won driving. Time, $:23^2$, :48, $1:12^3$, $1:39^2$, $1:53^3$ Course yielding.

$2 Mutuel Prices:

8–SHIMMERING SNOW	22.40	8.60	5.80
11–LOVELY SEBEECHA		10.00	7.00
1–BETSY WOLF			5.40

$2 EXACTA 8–11 PAID $190.40

B. f, (Jun), by Frosty the Snowman–Lyphard's Dancer, by Lyphard. Trainer Goldfine Lou M. Bred by Appleton Arthur I (Fla).

SHIMMERING SNOW sprinted clear, dropped inside early, drew out leaving top of stretch, shortened stride inside sixteenth pole, all out to narrowly last. LOVELY SEBEECHA lacked early speed, rallied wide leaving upper stretch, continued full of run to just miss. BETSY WOLF steadied while between horses midway backstretch, made a run at winner second turn, unable to sustain bid. QUACK A DOODLE rallied between horses leaving upper stretch, crowded inside sixteenth pole. SEAN'S WOODMAN, void of early speed, rallied belatedly. ALL THE RAGE, four wide into second turn, tired between horses. PRECIOUS PRODIGY rallied late while wide. RUBY RANSOM raced forwardly between horses to top of stretch, tired. DISCO DOLL was through early. PLENTY CHARMING steadied off JUKEBOX DANCE opening eighth. JUKEBOX DANCE saved ground to no avail. BLEND IN bore out first turn, stopped while wide backstretch, eased second turn. Race run on lane one.

Owners— 1, Appleton Arthur I; 2, AwayTheyGo Stable; 3, Panic Stable; 4, Rattray Lee; 5, Devenport Roger J; 6, Pin Oak Stable; 7, McKellar Joseph P; 8, Stronach Frank H; 9, Miles Steve; 10, Russell L Reineman Stable Inc; 11, Swartz Vincent; 12, Darjean Paul

Trainers—1, Goldfine Lou M; 2, Cilio Gene A; 3, Janks Christine K; 4, Gore Terrel; 5, Kelly Larry; 6, Mott William I; 7, McKellar Joseph P; 8, Barber Kenneth; 9, Nafzger Carl A; 10, Springer Frank R; 11, Swartz Monique; 12, Darjean Paul

Overweight: Betsy Wolf (1), Quack A Doodle (1), Sean's Woodman (1), All The Rage (1), Disco Doll (1), Plenty Charming (1).

I was happy enough. The betting pools between Belmont and Arlington were not commingled, so while the exacta came back $190.40 in Chicago, it was worth a bit more than $300 in New York: a lovely "saver." Grening's complexion, however, was ashen. He had keyed Shimmering Snow up-and-down in exactas and trifectas with everyone who had been on the TV screen a mere sixteenth of a mile from the wire, and he had appeared headed for the cashing windows until Lovely Sebeecha came from out of nowhere to spoil everything.

I understood how Dave came to light upon Shimmering Snow as his key horse, but he was into his dogeard copy of *Maiden Stats* as much as I was, if not more so, and for the life of me I couldn't fathom how he'd left Lovely Sebeecha out of his exotic bet-mix.

"You didn't use her?" I asked.

"Of course not, there was nothing in the book about *her*."

"Sure there was. She's a half-sister to four other grass winners."

"Whaaat?!?"

Dave opened his copy of *Maiden Stats* again, thumbed to the Ls, and ran his finger down the list. There was only one problem: he was looking under LOVLEY instead of LOVELY. "Uh, Dave, it's under L-O-V-E...", and before I could say the next letter his head fell into his hands, his jaw dropped open, and he uttered a truly mournful sigh. Then he hurled his copy of *Maiden Stats* farther than I ever would've believed one could be thrown.

THERE ARE MANY sources of excellent peripheral information for handicappers, so there is just no excuse for not being prepared about pedigrees. They provide overlays on a consistent basis. Besides *Maiden Stats*, two excellent sources include: Mike Helm's *Exploring Pedigree*, as well as his annual *Sire Ratings* (City Miner Books, Berkeley, Cal., 1994), and Lee Tomlinson's *Mudders & Turfers*.

Exploring Pedigree contains listings for more than 2,200 sires, with class ratings that project at what level a sire's progeny are likely to be competitive; a stamina index that projects how far a sire's progeny are likely to run; and ratings for grass, as well as for wet and tiring tracks. In the text itself, Helm illustrates how the ratings are integrated with non-pedigree factors such as speed and pace, trainer angles and toteboard action.

Mudders & Turfers is a booklet updated semi-annually, that lists 3,000 or so sires whose offspring are likely to be seen most often at U.S. tracks, and assigns them two separate numerical rankings, one for mud and one for turf, ranging from a low of 0 to a high of 300.

Tomlinson suggests factoring in the dam's sire as well, but since it is less important than the runner's sire, only half the assigned rating should be credited. For example, if a runner's sire received a 220, and the dam's sire received a 200, the final rating would be 320 (220 plus half of 200). In cases where the sire is not listed, Tomlinson recommends using the sire's sire, and reducing that one's rating by 20 percent to compensate for the unknown factor.

The ratings were first brought to the mainstream by Mark Cramer in his book, *Kinky Handicapping*, and I can also vouch for their veracity in the course of day-to-day play. It's beneficial to have access to these numbers, because unlike high-rated speed figure horses which often are badly overbet, high-rated pedigree horses are regularly overlooked by the crowd.

Fast-forward for a moment to mid-August, to see what I mean:

4 **Saratoga**

1 1/16 MILES. **(Inner Turf). (1:39^4) MAIDEN SPECIAL WEIGHT. Purse $32,000. Fillies, 2-year-olds. Weight, 117 lbs. (Preference to fillies that have not started for a claiming price).**

Thunderestimate
Own: Flying Zee Stables
DAVIS R G (92 9 12 20 .10)
Dk. b or br f. 2 (Jan)
Sire: Thunder Puddles (Speak John)
Dam: Golden Sweetheart (Strike Gold)
Br: Flying Zee Stables (NY)
Tr: O'Connell Richard (16 1 4 0 .06)
117
Lifetime Record: 0 M 0 0 $0
1995 0 M 0 0 | Turf 0 0 0 0
1994 0 M 0 0 | Wet 0 0 0 0
Sar Ⓣ 0 0 0 0 | Dist Ⓣ 0 0 0 0
WORKOUTS: Aug 9 Sar Ⓣ 6f fm 1:17^4 B (d) *1/2* Jly 28 Sar 5f fst 1:04^2 B *26/28* Jly 17 Bel 4f fst :50 B *36/62* Jly 9 Bel 4f fst :52 Bg *47/48* Jly 4 Bel 4f fst :50^3 B *57/71* Jun 28 Bel 4f fst :49^2 B *30/58*

Rosa
Own: Paulson Allen E
BECKNER D V (41 1 5 1 .02)
B. f. 2 (Feb)
Sire: Strawberry Road (Aus) (Whiskey Road)
Dam: Irish Slew (Seattle Slew)
Br: Paulson Allen E (Ky)
Tr: Zito Nicholas P (27 3 3 7 .11)
117
Lifetime Record: 1 M 0 0 $1,800
1995 1 M 0 0 $1,800 | Turf 1 0 0 0 $1,800
1994 0 M 0 0 | Wet 0 0 0 0
Sar Ⓣ 0 0 0 0 | Dist Ⓣ 0 0 0 0
30Jun95-2Bel fm 6f Ⓣ :22^2 :46^2 :58^2 1:10^4 ⒻMd Sp Wt 66 10 12 12^{9½} 8^{3¾} 4^{2½} 4^{1¾} Beckner D V 115 7.00 80-18 CsnovStorm115^{nk} Lizzy'sPlsur115½ IrishDisy110^1 Brk slowly, seven wide 12
WORKOUTS: Aug 3 Sar tr.t 5f fst 1:05^2 B *5/7* Jly 25 Sar tr.t 5f fst 1:04^2 B *6/7* Jly 15 Bel 4f fst :51 B *28/31* Jly 9 Bel 4f fst :49^4 B *29/48* Jun 23 Bel 5f gd 1:04 B *19/22* ●Jun 15 Bel 5f gd 1:01^3 Hg *1/14*

Criminaly Inclined
Own: Freed Jane M
VELAZQUEZ J R (75 12 9 5 .16)
B. f. 2 (Feb)
Sire: Criminal Type (Alydar)
Dam: Sahera (Al Nasr)
Br: Regency Stables (Ky)
Tr: Contessa Gary C (11 1 0 2 .09)
117
Lifetime Record: 2 M 1 0 $3,056
1995 2 M 1 0 $3,056 | Turf 1 0 0 0 $1,656
1994 0 M 0 0 | Wet 0 0 0 0
Sar Ⓣ 0 0 0 0 | Dist Ⓣ 0 0 0 0
3Jly95-6Mth fm 5f Ⓣ :21^3 :45^3 :58^2 ⒻHol Wildcat27k 37 1 5 5^8 5^{8½} 5^9 4^{9½} Santagata N 113 5.20 72-18 Forever Pals116$1¼$ Shanade116$1½$ Stormy Krissy110$6¾$ No bid 5
9Jun95-1Atl fst 5f :23 :46^4 :59^1 Md Sp Wt 34 4 5 2^2 2^2 2^7 2^{7¼} Taylor K T 115 3.50 81-16 HitTheTriple118$7¼$ CriminalyInclined115^3 SilverWinged116$¾$ Second best 6
WORKOUTS: Aug 5 Sar 6f fst 1:19 B *6/6* Jly 29 Sar tr.t 3f fst :37^2 B *3/15* Jly 20 Sar 5f fst 1:03 B *15/24* Jun 4 Fai 4f fst :53^2 Bg *6/6* Jun 1 Fai 4fw fst :52 B (W) *2/2*

Turkappeal
Own: Four Horseman's Ranch & Salzman E
CHAVEZ J F (100 18 15 5 .18)
B. f. 2 (Jan)
Sire: Turkoman (Alydar)
Dam: Chief Appeal (Valid Appeal)
Br: Four Horsemen's Ranch (Fla)
Tr: Salzman J Edwin Jr (—)
117
Lifetime Record: 2 M 2 0 $9,702
1995 2 M 2 0 $9,702 | Turf 0 0 0 0
1994 0 M 0 0 | Wet 0 0 0 0
Sar Ⓣ 0 0 0 0 | Dist Ⓣ 0 0 0 0
25Jly95-6Pim fst 5½f :22^1 :45^2 :57^2 1:03^3 ⒻMd Sp Wt 55 1 7 7^{10} 6^{8½} 5^{5½} 2^{8¾} Johnston M T 119 *1.30 94-04 Season's Flair119$8¾$ Turkappeal119$¾$ Kilmore Kerry119$3¼$ Passed faders 9
1Jly95-3Lrl fst 5f :22^3 :46^3 :59^3 ⒻMd Sp Wt 50 4 2 3^{6½} 3^7 2^{3½} 2^{¾} Hamilton S D 119 5.40 88-16 Mama G119$¾$ Turkappeal119$4½$ Kilmore Kerry119^5 Gamely 8
WORKOUTS: Jly 18 Lrl 5f fst 1:02^4 B *13/21* Jun 27 Lrl 5f gd 1:02^1 B *4/24* Jun 13 Lrl 4f fst :50 Bg *21/43* Jun 6 Lrl 5f fst 1:02 B *12/26* May 30 Lrl 4f gd :49 H *6/30* May 23 Lrl 3f fst :37 Bg *8/17*

Sue the Fox
Own: Due Process Stable
DECARLO C P (12 0 2 1 .00)

Ch. f. 2 (May)
Sire: Devil's Bag (Halo)
Dam: Toredo (El Gran Senor)
Br: Due Process Stable Inc (Ky)
Tr: Gleaves Philip A (2 0 0 0 .00)

117

Lifetime Record:	1 M 0 0	$0			
1995	1 M 0 0		Turf	0 0 0 0	
1994	0 M 0 0		Wet	0 0 0 0	
Sar Ⓣ	0 0 0 0		Dist Ⓣ	0 0 0 0	

21Jly95-6Sar fst 5½f :21^4 :45^2 :58 1:05 ⒻMd Sp Wt 7 2 9 9^{15} 9^{11} 9^{16} 9$^{26\frac{1}{2}}$ Santos J A 119 12.10 69-10 Crafty But Sweet119^{nk} Fast Busy119^6 Afirmada119^{hd} Broke slowly 9

WORKOUTS: Aug 7 Sar 5f fst 1:04 B *33/40* Aug 2 Sar 6f fst 1:19 B *7/8* Jly 28 Sar 4f fst :50^2 B *28/39* Jly 15 Sar 4f fst :49^3 B *2/3* ●Jly 10 Sar 5f fst 1:03^1 B *1/4* Jun 20 Sar tr.t 3f fst :38^1 Bg*3/9*

Money Clip
Own: Turf Stables Inc
KRONE J A (74 6 13 7 .08)

B. f. 2 (Apr)
Sire: Pirate Army (Roberto)
Dam: Green Sum (Green Forest)
Br: Charles T. Wilson Jr. (Ky)
Tr: Kessinger Burk Jr (11 1 1 1 .09)

117

Lifetime Record:	0 M 0 0	$0			
1995	0 M 0 0		Turf	0 0 0 0	
1994	0 M 0 0		Wet	0 0 0 0	
Sar Ⓣ	0 0 0 0		Dist Ⓣ	0 0 0 0	

WORKOUTS: ●Aug 9 Sar tr.t 4f fst :50 B *1/13* Aug 3 Sar 5f fst 1:04^4 Bg*24/27* Jly 26 Sar 5f fst 1:05 B *43/47* Jly 20 Sar tr.t 4f fst :52^1 B *22/28* Jun 28 CD 4f fst :50^1 B *18/32*

Peaceful Approval
Own: Live Oak Plantation
BAILEY J D (101 22 11 13 .22)

Gr/ro f. 2 (Jan)
Sire: With Approval (Caro)
Dam: Banner Bound (Linkage)
Br: Live Oak Stud (Fla)
Tr: Kelly Patrick J (18 2 2 2 .11)

117

Lifetime Record:	3 M 0 1	$4,200			
1995	3 M 0 1	$4,200	Turf	1 0 0 0	$900
1994	0 M 0 0		Wet	0 0 0 0	
Sar Ⓣ	0 0 0 0		Dist Ⓣ	0 0 0 0	

26Jly95-2Sar fst 6f :22^2 :46^2 :58^4 1:11^4 ⒻMd Sp Wt 40 5 6 6$^{3\frac{1}{4}}$ 7$^{5\frac{3}{4}}$ 7$^{7\frac{1}{2}}$ 7$^{14\frac{1}{2}}$ Bailey J D 118 9.90 67-14 Echo Echo Echo118^3 La Rosa118$^{9\frac{1}{2}}$ Lovington118$^{\frac{1}{2}}$ Shuffled back 1/2 pl 11
12Jly95-1Bel fst 6f ⊗ :22^1 :45^3 :58^1 1:11^4 ⒻMd Sp Wt 52 10 8 9$^{8\frac{1}{2}}$ 6$^{5\frac{1}{4}}$ 5^6 3$^{2\frac{3}{4}}$ Samyn J L 115 8.80e 79-14 Here'sLondon115$^{2\frac{1}{2}}$ RpidSelection115^{nk} PecfulApprovl115^{no} Rallied inside 10
30Jun95-2Bel fm 6f Ⓣ :22^2 :46^2 :58^2 1:10^4 ⒻMd Sp Wt 58 2 10 10$^{7\frac{1}{2}}$ 12$^{5\frac{1}{2}}$ 8$^{5\frac{1}{4}}$ 5$^{4\frac{3}{4}}$ Bailey J D 115 4.40 77-18 Casanova Storm115^{nk} Lizzy's Pleasure115$^{\frac{1}{2}}$ Irish Daisy110^1 Mild gain 12

WORKOUTS: Aug 7 Sar 4f fst :49^2 B *25/63* Aug 3 Sar 3f fst :36^4 H *4/11* Jly 21 Sar 3f fst :37 B *7/13* Jly 7 Bel 3f fst :38^2 B *28/30* Jun 24 Bel 4f fst :48^3 H *13/91* Jun 18 Bel 3f fst :38 Bg*14/19*

Roman Connection
Own: Porreco Louis J
MIGLIORE R (46 4 5 11 .09)

Dk. b or br f. 2 (May)
Sire: Danzig Connection (Danzig)
Dam: Lady Calpurnia (Proudest Roman)
Br: Stephens Lucille E (Ky)
Tr: Frommer Timothy G (—)

117

Lifetime Record:	1 M 0 0	$170			
1995	1 M 0 0	$170	Turf	0 0 0 0	
1994	0 M 0 0		Wet	0 0 0 0	
Sar Ⓣ	0 0 0 0		Dist Ⓣ	0 0 0 0	

30May95-3Mth gd 5f :22^2 :47^2 1:00^3 ⒻMd Sp Wt 20 4 5 6^{10} 7^{15} 7^{14} 7$^{15\frac{1}{4}}$ Lopez C C 117 37.20 66-27 Forever Pals117$^{1\frac{1}{4}}$ Midnight Train117^1 Lunar Antics117$^{\frac{1}{2}}$ Outrun 7

WORKOUTS: Aug 3 Fai Ⓣ 1 fm 1:46^2 B *1/1* Jly 28 Fai Ⓣ 1 fm 1:49 B (d) *1/1* Jly 5 Fai 5fw fst 1:03^3 B (W) *1/1* Jun 29 Fai Ⓣ 6f fm 1:16 B (d) *1/1* May 27 Fai 3f fst :38 B *1/1* May 20 Fai 4f fst :50 Bg *1/1*

Lucy's Niece
Own: Close Lucy H
MAPLE E (40 4 5 6 .10)

Dk. b or br f. 2 (Apr)
Sire: Cryptoclearance (Fappiano)
Dam: Leaping Lucy (Restless Native)
Br: Parrish Hill Farm & Phillip Teinowitz (Ky)
Tr: Duncan Susan A (2 0 0 1 .00)

117

Lifetime Record:	2 M 0 0	$900			
1995	2 M 0 0	$900	Turf	0 0 0 0	
1994	0 M 0 0		Wet	0 0 0 0	
Sar Ⓣ	0 0 0 0		Dist Ⓣ	0 0 0 0	

28Jly95-2Sar fst 6f :22^1 :46 :58^3 1:11^4 ⒻMd Sp Wt 30 1 6 8$^{7\frac{3}{4}}$ 8$^{7\frac{1}{2}}$ 6^{10} 5^{18} Maple E 118 19.20 64-15 CoxesFstest118^2 Thsky'sthlimit118$^{4\frac{1}{2}}$ ComCsul118$^{6\frac{1}{2}}$ Brk slowly, no threat 8
12Jly95-1Bel fst 6f ⊗ :22^1 :45^3 :58^1 1:11^4 ⒻMd Sp Wt 47 9 9 8^8 4$^{3\frac{1}{4}}$ 6$^{6\frac{1}{2}}$ 7^5 Maple E 115 23.30 77-14 Here'sLondon115$^{2\frac{1}{2}}$ RpidSelection115^{nk} PecfulApprovl115^{no} Drifted, tired 10

WORKOUTS: Jly 23 Sar tr.t 4f fst :51^1 B *15/27* Jly 5 Bel 5f fst 1:04^2 B *24/29* Jun 21 Bel 4f fst :50 Bg*51/71* Jun 15 Bel 4f gd :49 B *11/21* Jun 8 Bel 4f fst :50^3 Bg*36/44* Jun 2 Bel 4f fst :50^4 Bg*33/43*

Majestic Dream
Own: Darby Dan Farm
DAVIS R G (92 9 12 20 .10)

Ch. f. 2 (Feb)
Sire: Majestic Light (Majestic Prince)
Dam: Dream Creek (The Minstrel)
Br: Galbreath & Phillips Racing Partnership (Ky)
Tr: Toner James J (6 0 0 2 .00)

117

Lifetime Record:	0 M 0 0	$0			
1995	0 M 0 0		Turf	0 0 0 0	
1994	0 M 0 0		Wet	0 0 0 0	
Sar Ⓣ	0 0 0 0		Dist Ⓣ	0 0 0 0	

WORKOUTS: Aug 4 Sar 5f sly 1:03 B *3/5* Jly 29 Sar 4f fst :48^2 Hg*11/42* Jly 23 Sar tr.t 4f fst :51 B *12/27* Jly 15 Bel 3f fst :36^3 Bg*16/30*

Two-year-old fillies on Saratoga's inner turf course: a situation containing a high element of uncertainty. This particular field of 10 included three first time-starters; four others trying the grass for the first time; and three more who have *sprinted* on turf. No one has ever been beyond six furlongs, and no one has ever been on this turf course. A full field of green, headstrong 2-year-olds careening into that first hairpin turn often resembles a pile of runaway bumper cars more than anything else. With so many unknowns in a race like this, the cardinal rule is to never, never key on a horse who is a short price. Find longshots with solid credentials and go from there. In this particular race, a flip through *Maiden Stats* didn't reveal much to sink one's teeth into, but the Tomlinson turf ratings helped to shape a potential play:

	Rating	Odds
Thunderestimate	165	35-1
Rosa	260	Even
Criminally Inclined	195	21-1
Turkappeal	270	9-2
Sue the Fox	305	17-1
Money Clip	250	10-1
Peaceful Approval	185	7-2
Roman Connection	225	24-1
Lucy's Niece	150	27-1
Majestic Dream	295	23-1

THE CROWD WAS SEVERELY overbetting Rosa off her debut outing, in which she recorded the best Beyer (66) despite a slow break and a wide trip. How would she handle two turns? Was she an habitually slow breaker? At even-money she could be used as a small saver on top in exactas, perhaps, but nothing more.

Three fillies, Turkappeal (270), Sue the Fox (305), and Majestic Dream (295) had Tomlinson ratings superior to Rosa's 260, and the two last-mentioned runners were huge prices. In this situation, a conservative swing for the fences was in order: I boxed those three in exactas, boxed Sue the Fox and Majestic Dream again, and bet the two longest-priced fillies to win:

FOURTH RACE **Saratoga** **AUGUST 11, 1995**

1$\frac{1}{16}$ MILES. (Inner Turf)(1.39^4) MAIDEN SPECIAL WEIGHT. Purse $32,000. Fillies, 2-year-olds. Weight, 117 lbs. (Preference to fillies that have not started for a claiming price).

Value of Race: $32,000 Winner $19,200; second $6,400; third $3,520; fourth $1,920; fifth $960. Mutuel Pool $418,808.00 Exacta Pool $581,771.00 Quinella Pool $119,677.00

Last Raced	Horse	M/Eqt.	A.	Wt	PP	St	¼	½	¾	Str	Fin	Jockey	Odds $1
	Majestic Dream		2	117	10	9	6½	8^1	$7^{1\frac{1}{2}}$	2^{hd}	$1^{2\frac{1}{2}}$	Davis R G	23.20
26Jly95 ^{2}Sar^7	Peaceful Approval		2	117	7	6	7^1	5^{hd}	4^{hd}	3^1	$2^{2\frac{1}{2}}$	Bailey J D	3.60
25Jly95 ^{6}Pim^2	Turkappeal		2	117	4	3	2^1	2½	1½	1½	3^{nk}	Chavez J F	4.80
	Money Clip		2	117	6	10	10	10	10	4½	4½	Krone J A	10.30
30Jun95 ^{2}Bel^4	Rosa		2	117	2	2	3½	4½	5½	5^1	5^6	Beckner D V	1.15
28Jly95 ^{2}Sar^5	Lucy's Niece		2	117	9	8	5^2	6^1	6^1	9^1	6^{hd}	Maple E	27.50
30May95 ^{3}Mth^7	Roman Connection		2	117	8	7	4^1	3^1	3^1	10	7^{hd}	Migliore R	24.75
21Jly95 ^{6}Sar^9	Sue the Fox		2	117	5	4	8^{hd}	9^2	9^{hd}	7^{hd}	$8^{1\frac{1}{4}}$	Decarlo C P	17.80
	Thunderestimate		2	117	1	5	9^3	7½	8^2	8^1	9^2	Santos J A	35.25
3Jly95 ^{6}Mth^4	Criminaly Inclined		2	117	3	1	1^1	1½	2½	6^1	10	Velazquez J R	21.30

OFF AT 2:36 Start Good. Won driving. Time, :23^2, :48^2, 1:13^1, 1:38^2, 1:44^3 Course firm.

$2 Mutuel Prices:

10–MAJESTIC DREAM	48.40	17.00	11.40
7–PEACEFUL APPROVAL		5.40	3.60
4–TURKAPPEAL			5.00

$2 EXACTA 10–7 PAID $202.50 $2 QUINELLA 7–10 PAID $90.00

Ch. f, (Feb), by Majestic Light–Dream Creek, by The Minstrel. Trainer Toner James J. Bred by Galbreath & Phillips Racing Partnership (Ky).

MAJESTIC DREAM unhurried for six furlongs, launched a rally from outside leavin the turn, then unleashed a strong late run to win going away. PEACEFUL APPROVAL carried wide on the first turn, gradually worked her way forward on the far turn, made a run to threaten while bumping with ROSA in upper stretch, but couldn't match strides with the winner in the lane. TURKAPPEAL forced the early pace between horses, surged to the front on the turn, continued on the lead into midstretch, then weakened. MONEY CLIP trailed to the turn, rallied belatedly between horses. ROSA raced in good position while saving ground for six furlongs, angled out to threaten entering the stretch then lacked the needed response when called upon. LUCY'S NIECE reserved for five furlongs, bumped with ROMAN CONNECTION at the top of the stretch, then lacked a strong closing bid. LUCY'S NIECE raced in close contention while three wide to the turn, steadied while being bumped approaching the stretch and was never close thereafter. SUE THE FOX bore out on the first turn and failed to threaten thereafter. THUNDERESTIMATE never reached contention. CRIMINALY INCLINED was used up setting the early pace.

Owners— 1, Darby Dan Farm & Phillips Jodie; 2, Live Oak Plantation; 3, Four Horseman's Ranch & Salzman E; 4, Turf Stables Inc; 5, Paulson Allen E; 6, Close Lucy H; 7, Porreco Louis J; 8, Due Process Stable; 9, Flying Zee Stables; 10, Freed Jane M

Trainers— 1, Toner James J; 2, Kelly Patrick J; 3, Salzman J Edwin Jr; 4, Kessinger Burk Jr; 5, Zito Nicholas P; 6, Duncan Susan A; 7, Frommer Timothy G; 8, Gleaves Philip A; 9, O'Connell Richard; 10, Contessa Gary C

Scratched— Ethyl Mae, Kaleidoscope (2Aug95 ^{4}SAR^6), Assets On Ice, Silver Smile (1Aug95 ^{4}FL^3), Irish Daisy (16Jly95 ^{6}BEL^4), Stormy Emotions (16Jly95 ^{2}BEL^7), Illume (26Jly95 ^{2}SAR^8), Get Even, Lovington (26Jly95 ^{2}SAR^3), With Passion (12Jly95 ^{1}BEL^{10})

As so often happens in these baby races on Saratoga's inner turf, Sue the Fox bore out sharply into the clubhouse turn, and she took Peaceful Approval with her. Even without Sue the Fox, the exacta box looked like a touchdown coming to midstretch with Turkappeal and Majestic Dream running one-two, but somchow Peaceful Dream, who had been carried wide on that first turn and then had bumped with a fading Rosa in upper stretch, righted herself and overhauled Turkappeal for the place spot. Conventional wisdom holds that horses such as Majestic Dream should be avoided because of their extreme outside posts in races featuring a short run to the first turn; but it's impossible to predict which 2-year-olds are going to blow that turn, and which ones they're going to carry out to the parking lot. The only way to combat this swirling mass of uncertainty is by taking the best of the price. Majestic Dream ran to her solid grass pedigree, paying $48.40, and the daughter of Majestic Light went on to win stakes races later in the year.

JUMPING BACK in our time machine and journeying back to May, we should pause for a moment to consider the importance of the running surface in the outcome of races. This is not only true for turf races featuring lightly-raced horses, it is also true for the grizzled old geldings of the game in the muck and mire of wet dirt (in all its varying degrees). Some horses, such as Brett's Jet (shown below), are especially intriguing:

Brett's Jet
Own: Joques Farm
ALVARADO F T (89 10 11 9 .11)

Ch. g. 3 (Mar)
Sire: Little Missouri (Cox's Ridge)
Dam: Lodge Pole (Mehmet)
Br: Audette F J & Joan I (Fla)
Tr: Moschera Gasper S (54 9 7 17 .17)

115

Lifetime Record: 15 8 1 3 $76,175											
1994	14	8	1	3	$75,895	Turf	1	0	0	0	
1993	1	M	0	0	$280	Wet	1	1	0	0	$12,000
Aqu	1	1	0	0	$16,800	Dist	2	2	0	0	$23,415

12Nov94-5Aqu fst 1	:23 :454 1:104 1:363	Clm 45000	92	1 3 33 2½ 13 13½	Alvarado F T		114 b	*1.25	85-23	Brett's Jet1143½ Fleet Eagle1137½ Time In The City1175½	Driving	5
30Sep94-7Bel fst 1 1/16	:232 :471 1:124 1:444	Clm 35000	96	4 5 63½ 32 13 17	Alvarado F T		117 b	2.50	78-29	Brett's Jet1177 Mean Pancho11211 Heavenwood112nk	Wide, driving	7
15Aug94-4Sar yl 1 1/16 Ⓣ	:232 :464 1:111 1:424	Clm 70000	4	1 10 1024 1027 1032 1040½	Smith M E		113 b	7.30	39-21	Head Trip1172 Best Of Music1137 Natural Fact1171½	Outrun	10
29Jly94-4Sar my 1⅛ ⊗	:492 1:142 1:402 1:534	Clm c-35000	80	5 6 52 31 2hd 1nk	Luttrell M G5		112 b	*1.60	67-30	Brett's Jet112nk Bomb Free11710 Burn The Toast117hd	Lugged in, driving	6
Claimed from Alexander Bruce, Alexander Bruce Trainer												
10Jly94-8FL fst 1 3/16	:491 1:134 1:383 1:582 3↑	Alw 7500s	72	1 4 32½ 32 32½ 35	Hulet L		112 b	*.90	106-09	North Warning113hd Coby Escapade1134¾ Brett's Jet1124½	No closing bid	6
12Jun94-10Tdn fst 1	:24 :482 1:132 1:392 3↑	Alw 10500N1m	76	2 6 64 32 12 12¾	Rivera H Jr	B	119 b	*.30	90-13	Brett'sJet1192¾ ReflectiveLight1161½ BlzingProspector1165½	Hand ridden	6
27May94-7WO fst 1 1/16	:243 :494 1:142 1:453	Clm 37500	72	5 5 43½ 3½ 1½ 1½	Landry R C		115 b	2.50	88-13	Brett's Jet115½ Winter Renegade1182½ Mactaquac1153¼		5
Good move rail into slow pace, held gamely stretch												
14May94-4WO fst 1 1/16	:231 :473 1:131 1:47	Clm 30000	69	2 6 510 45 23 22	Landry R C		115 b	4.95	79-22	DanceTower1132 Brett'sJet1154½ DufferinStrek1151	Inside, finished well	6
31Mar94-9Tam fst 1 1/16	:24 :482 1:132 1:462	Alw 7000N1m	69	2 4 46½ 33½ 35 33½	Sanchez H A		122 b	2.60	86-16	Letters Of Truth1173½ Twopiece Dinner109no Brett'sJet1222	Hung stretch	7
18Mar94-8Tam fst 7f	:231 :471 1:132 1:271	Clm 12500	65	5 9 97¾ 53 1½ 11½	Sanchez H A		119 b	*.90	82-20	Brett's Jet1191½ Brett's Sunny1161 Jovial Bid1161½	Driving	10

WORKOUTS: Oct 30 Bel tr.t 4f fst :482 H *4/11* Oct 23 Bel tr.t 4f fst :492 B *7/20* Sep 22 Bel 4f fst :491 B *21/53* Sep 16 Bel tr.t 3f fst :393 B *6/6* Aug 23 Sar tr.t 4f fst :512 B *17/28*

This gelding doesn't care what kind of dirt he's on, just as long as it's dirt: his last six wins have come at Tampa Bay, Woodbine, Thistledowns, in the mud at Saratoga, at Belmont, and at Aqueduct. Simply wind Brett's Jet up, and he runs anywhere, sprinting or routing, around one turn or two. But just look at what happened when Gasper Moschera claimed the son of Little Missouri and tried him on the grass August 15: he simply could not pick up his feet. Placed back on dirt next time out, he resumed his winning ways.

Some horses, like Brett's Jet, are at home no matter what kind of dirt they run on. For that matter, Cigar was Horse of the Year after a 1995 campaign that saw him win all 10 of his starts, from Gulfstream Park, to Hollywood Park, to Suffolk Downs, to Oaklawn Park, to Pimlico, and finally to Belmont. He didn't care what kind of dirt it was, but this superhorse was nothing more than an ordinary, underachieving allowance horse languishing on grass until the tail-end of his 4-year-old season, when he was finally put back on dirt.

As I said, there are all kinds of ways to determine whether a horse will feel at home in today's footing. Sometimes, though, the only insights available are the ones you come up with on your own by rummaging through that pile of old, yellowing *Forms* that's taking up most of the space in your makeshift office at home. Sometimes, though, it's well worth the trouble:

3 Belmont Park

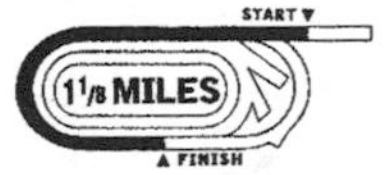

1⅛ MILES. (1:452) **CLAIMING. Purse $14,000. 4-year-olds and upward. Weight, 122 lbs. Non-winners of two races at a mile or over since April 5, allowed 2 lbs. Such a race since March 29, 4 lbs. Two such races since March 4, 6 lbs. Claiming price $14,000, for each $1,000 to $12,000, allowed 2 lbs. (Races where entered for $10,000 or less not considered.)**

Yaros
Own: Perroncino John S
AGOSTO R (9 0 0 1 .00) **$12,000**

B. h. 6
Sire: Rare Brick (Rare Performer)
Dam: Lightning Mountain (Cox's Ridge)
Br: Loblolly Stable (Ky)
Tr: Terracciano Neal (2 0 0 0 .00)

1075

Lifetime Record: 62 13 13 10 $289,294											
1995	8	1	1	1	$21,525	Turf	1	0	0	0	
1994	24	4	5	3	$75,590	Wet	10	3	3	2	$65,920
Bel	14	4	2	3	$75,560	Dist	11	3	3	2	$62,880

23Apr95-3Aqu fst 1	:24 :473 1:131 1:39	Clm 16000	56	1 4 1hd 2½ 64½ 610¼	Dunkelberger T L5	113 fb	4.80	64-19	Churkin1161¼ Cross Ice Pass1162½ Runaway Chris116¾	Dueled inside	9
30Mar95-6Aqu fst 1	:231 :454 1:102 1:361	Clm 25000	65	3 1 1hd 3½ 66 615¼	Nelson D	118 b	8.70	73-26	AdvncedPlcement1223 StudleyDoRight1123 LordBeer1143½	Used in pace	6
11Mar95-2Aqu fst 170 ⊡	:243 :483 1:132 1:432	Clm 20000	68	2 2 1hd 2hd 55½ 512½	Nelson D	118 fb	2.40	69-25	Advanced Placement1171½ Stately Wager116hd Jessup North1203¼	Tired	6
24Feb95-6Aqu fst 170 ⊡	:232 :47 1:12 1:413	Clm 35000	75	2 3 31½ 41½ 47½ 513	Nelson D	113 fb	*2.65	77-29	Birdie's Fly1161 Ambush Alley114hd Sparkling Sky1097	Gave way, wide	6
12Feb95-2Aqu fst 1 1/16 ⊡	:251 :501 1:15 1:474	Clm 30000	92	6 2 2½ 1hd 14 13½	Nelson D	113 fb	5.00	66-39	Yaros1133½ Heavenwood113no Private Plan1155	Drew off	6
1Feb95-3Aqu fst 170 ⊡	:24 :481 1:131 1:432	Clm 30000	94	1 1 1½ 11½ 11 21	Nelson D	113 fb	1.65	80-28	Private Plan1131 Yaros11310 Kristen's Baby117½	Couldn't last	6
20Jan95-2Aqu sly 1 1/16 ⊡	:224 :462 1:113 1:443	Clm 30000	81	4 2 2hd 11 2hd 32½	Nelson D	113 fb	6.50	79-16	A Call To Rise1172 Rocking Josh117½ Yaros1134	Dueled, weakened	5
4Jan95-1Aqu fst 1 1/16 ⊡	:234 :48 1:131 1:472	Clm c-22500	78	5 3 2½ 2½ 32½ 45½	Lantz J A5	110 b	8.20	62-35	Jason Dean1121¼ Devoted Glory115nk Stately Wager1154	Weakened	8
Claimed from Pizzo Joseph Jr, Galluscio Dominic G Trainer											
23Dec94-1Aqu fst 1 1/16 ⊡	:234 :492 1:15 1:471	Clm c-17500	91	1 1 1½ 1½ 11 1¾	Lantz J A5	114 b	*1.40	69-28	Yaros114¾ Stately Wager1173 Halo Habit1136	Driving	8
Claimed from Jewel-e Stables, Friedman Mitchell Trainer											
9Dec94-3Aqu fst 1⅛ ⊡	:481 1:131 1:394 1:53	Clm 17500	83	6 5 43½ 32½ 2hd 12	Migliore R	117 b	*1.55	71-25	Yaros1172 Pal's Memory112hd Possibilities1155	Driving	6

Sailing On Aprayer

Own: Pollard Damon

COOPER G J (7 0 2 0 .00) $13,000

Dk. b or br g. 6
Sire: Air Forbes Won (Bold Forbes)
Dam: I Believe (Believe It)
Br: O'Neill W R (Ky)
Tr: Pollard Damon (1 1 0 0 1.00)

107⁷

		Lifetime Record :	55 10 13 11	$202,256
1995	6 2 0 2	$19,080	Turf	0 0 0 0	
1994	17 2 4 4	$41,830	Wet	6 1 2 1	$19,730
Aqu	19 5 3 3	$61,200	Dist	10 3 2 1	$49,920

14Apr95–9Aqu fst 6f :223 :454 :573 1:10 Clm 10000 73 4 7 64½ 33 46½ Cooper G J⁷ 110 b 3.20 86–10 Publicized114⁶¼ Sulaco109ⁿᵒ Phantom Finn117ⁿᵒ Saved ground 9
8Mar95–2Aqu fst 1⁷⁰ :244 :49 1:141 1:453 Clm c–10000 69 3 2 3¹ 1ʰᵈ 3¹ 33½ Graell A 122 fb 2.20 66–34 DevotedGlory113⁴¼ MrSledge106⁵ SailingOnApryer122¹⁰ Led briefly turn 5
  Claimed from G Lack Farms, Klesaris Robert P Trainer
19Feb95–9Aqu fst 1⁷⁰ :223 :48 1:14 1:453 Clm 15500 69 4 6 65¾ 31 42½ 54 Graell A 113 fb 3.60 66–29 Jessup North117ⁿᵏ Wild Dante110½ Pal's Memory113³ Flattened out 10
2Feb95–1Aqu fst 1 :223 :49 1:143 1:481 Clm 15500 88 7 3 1½ 1ʰᵈ 1ʰᵈ 1ⁿᵒ Graell A 115 fb *1.65 64–42 Sailing On Aprayer115ⁿᵒ Dizzy Devil117⁶¼ Charming Buck117³ Long drive 8
22Jan95–1Aqu gd 1⅛ :473 1:114 1:373 1:573 Clm 12000 87 6 3 2½ 2½ 33½ 33½ Graell A 115 fb 1.70 82–23 DialedForRunning113ⁿᵒ McComas113³¼ SilingOnAprayer115¹¼ Forced pace 8
11Jan95–9Aqu fst 1⅛ :482 1:141 1:401 1:531 Clm 12000 91 4 2 2ʰᵈ 1¹½ 15 1½ Graell A 113 fb 5.40 70–38 SilingOnAprayer115½ McComas113¾ Rogersdividnds114³ Ridden out 10
27Nov94–4Aqu fst 1 :24 :473 1:131 1:392 Clm 17500 77 4 3 34 33 33½ 35 Migliore R 117 fb 4.90 78–17 DevotedGlory117½ CommnderEvndr117⁴½ SilingOnApryr117³¼ No late bid 6
15Nov94–9Aqu fst 7f :23 :461 1:11 1:234 Clm c–13000 83 7 2 67 64¾ 33 22½ Mojica R Jr 115 fb *2.20 83–17 Triodet115²½ Sailing On Aprayer115½ I'll Take A Stand117⁵ Rallied wide 8
  Claimed from Rottkamp John R, Odintz Jeff Trainer
25Oct94–2Aqu wf 1⅛ :451 1:104 1:234 1:50² Mojica R Jr 115 fb 4.20 85–17 Poughkeepsie Gypsy115ʰᵈ Sailing On Aprayer115² CincoRey117³¼ Gamely 8
9Oct94–2Bel fst 6½f :23 :462 1:11 1:174 Clm 13000 75 2 5 5² 31 2¹ 43 Graell A 117 b 4.50 81–11 I'll TakeAStand117¹ DoctorFish117¹½ Prioritizer117² Wide, flattened out 8

WORKOUTS: Apr 7 Bel tr.t 5f fst 1:01² H 2/5 Mar 18 Bel tr.t 5f fst 1:03 B 11/18 Feb 13 Aqu ⬤ 4f fst :52² B 5/6

Litigation Rex

Own: Cohen Max R

MARTIN G J (11 1 0 2 .09) $13,000

B. h. 5
Sire: Alydar (Raise a Native)
Dam: Princess Juliet (Gallant Romeo)
Br: Calumet Farm (Ky)
Tr: Meittinis Louis N (2 1 0 0 .50)

109⁵

		Lifetime Record :	28 2 2 4	$48,935
1995	9 1 0 2	$16,365	Turf	1 0 0 0	
1994	17 1 2 1	$30,510	Wet	3 0 0 0	
Bel	6 0 0 0		Dist	4 0 0 1	$5,565

23Apr95–3Aqu fst 1 :24 :473 1:131 1:39 Clm 16000 55 6 8 96¾ 99 77½ 710¾ Martin G J⁵ 111 21.80 63–19 Churkin116¹½ Cross Ice Pass116²½ Runaway Chris116¾ No threat 9
10Apr95–9Aqu fst 1⅛ :223 :45 1:094 1:36 Clm 16000 77 3 9 910 99½ 77¼ 35¾ Martin G J⁵ 109 22.50 83–18 Rogersdividends116⁴¾ Le Risky112¹ Litigation Rex109ⁿᵏ Belated rally 9
29Mar95–9Aqu fst 1⅛ :493 1:14 1:384 1:52 Clm 14000 71 7 8 76¾ 69 59¾ Mojica R Jr 114 12.10 70–19 Rogersdividends118³¾ Stately Wager115⁷ Eire Power114¾½ No threat 8
16Mar95–9Aqu fst 1⅛ :501 1:15 1:401 1:531 Clm 15000 78 6 8 85¾ 810 53½ 43½ Martin G J⁷ 109 21.50 71–24 Possibilities118ⁿᵒ RedScamper113ʰᵈ SttelyWger120³ Brk slow, wide 1/4 pl 8
4Mar95–9Aqu fst 1⅛ :23 :471 1:124 1:462 Clm 15500 65 2 8 810 610 411 410½ Mojica R Jr 115 9.30 62–21 Possibilities118⁶¾ Red Scamper113ʰᵈ PrsonlDirctor110ⁿᵏ Four wide, no threat 8
19Feb95–9Aqu fst 1⁷⁰ :223 :48 1:14 1:453 Clm 15500 70 10 10 10¹² 74½ 54 43¾ Mojica R Jr 115 17.80 65–29 Jessup North117ⁿᵏ Wild Dante110½ Pal's Memory113³ Five wide 10
5Feb95–1Aqu fst 1⅛ :24 :483 1:15 1:503 Clm 20000N2L 74 2 7 68½ 46 22 1½ Mojica R Jr 113 20.90 52–47 Litigation Rex113⁵ Varricchio113² Foolin Around117³½ Going away 8
28Jan95–1Aqu fst 1⅛ :484 1:152 1:42 1:552 Clm 20000N2L 51 7 4 79 79 511 417 Mojica R Jr 113 8.60 42–34 ConnecticutYnk115ⁿᵒ Dpndblnss115¹¹ MyOnlyHop113⁵½ Passed tired ones 9
14Jan95–4Aqu fst 6f :224 :454 :582 1:112 Clm 22500N2L 75 1 9 89¾ 87¼ 49 36½ Beckner D V⁵ 110 18.90 79–19 Mutuality113⁵½ Jelly Roll Blues117¹ Litigation Rex110²½ 9
  Checked break, 5 wide turn
30Dec94–4Aqu fst 1⅛ :23² :481 1:142 1:474 3+ Clm 30000N2L 61 8 11 11¹¹ 11¹³ 7¹³ 516½ Carr D 113 19.20e 50–39 Iron Mountain110¹² Royce Joseph108²½ Final Alliance113½ Some gain 11

Slews Gold

Own: Garren Murray M

RYDOWSKI S R (7 0 1 1 .00) $13,000

B. h. 5
Sire: Slew O' Gold (Seattle Slew)
Dam: Julie Prince (Majestic Prince)
Br: Fawn Leap Farm (Ky)
Tr: Garren Murray M (4 0 0 2 .00)

114

		Lifetime Record :	58 4 5 10	$158,592
1995	7 0 0 1	$990	Turf	3 0 0 0	$440
1994	23 0 0 2	$3,720	Wet	5 0 0 1	$3,840
Aqu	16 1 2 4	$42,040	Dist	6 0 0 2	$6,000

29Apr95–1Aqu fst 7f :224 :46 1:113 1:244 Clm 10000 61 7 8 107½ 99 55½ 37¾ Rydowski S R 114 b 32.50 72–18 Stolen Zeal119⁵ Mr Vincent107²¾ Slews Gold114¼ Belated rally 10
17Apr95–1Aqu fst 1⅛ :474 1:124 1:384 1:521 Clm 10000 35 3 4 48¼ 710 920 832½ Rydowski S R 113 b 12.30e 46–24 Halo Habit113¼½ Duel Zone108⁷ Bailadoro106³¼ Done early 9
10Apr95–9Aqu fst 1 :223 :45 1:094 1:36 Clm 16000 61 2 7 76¼ 88¾ 911 914½ Dunkelberger T L 107 b 23.40 74–18 Rogersdividends116⁴¾ Le Risky112¹ Litigation Rex109ⁿᵏ No threat 9
17Mar95–9Aqu fst 7f :23 :461 1:102 1:233 Clm 15500 60 9 6 72¾ 76 88½ 911 Graell A 112 fb 21.60e 75–17 Magic Ruckus116¹ Cross Ice Pass110ⁿᵏ Berseto107ʰᵈ Four wide 10
12Mar95–1Aqu fst 6f :224 :462 :59 1:122 Clm 11000 49 5 7 78½ 77½ 69 710½ Rodriguez E M 115 f 36.75 70–19 Phantom Finn116⅜ Callisto116⅜ Gold Candy Too116½ Bumped start 8
3Mar95–4Aqu fst 6f :223 :454 :583 1:114 Clm 13000 44 7 8 811 810 813 715½ Persaud R¹⁰ 105 fb 44.75 63–18 Cesar B.119¹½ Gold Candy Too133¾ Brush Full117³ Broke slowly 8
18Feb95–1Aqu fst 6f :223 :461 :591 1:13 Clm 13000 48 7 8 10¹¹ 11¹² 11¹²10¹¹ Martin G J⁷ 108 fb 38.75 67–19 Cesar B.117ⁿᵒ Sunshine Ed119ʰᵈ Groovy Attire117½ No threat 11
3Dec94–2Aqu fst 7f :222 :453 1:113 1:254 Clm 13000 56 5 3 55½ 610 69½ 513 Cayo D J 115 fb 15.60 62–24 Triodet115⁵ True Dutch109²½ Saratoga Ridge113¾ No factor 8
20Nov94–2Aqu fst 1 :23 :4 4 1:122 1:392 Clm 13000 48 6 2 5¼ 34 58 513½ Leon F 115 fb 12.30 58–25 Devoted Glory117² Jason Dean112⁵¾ Eire Power117² Faded 6
15Nov94–9Aqu fst 7f :23 :461 1:11 1:234 Clm 13000 58 8 4 77¼ 7½ 69 514 Pezua J M 115 fb 10.50 71–17 Triodet115²½ Sailing On Aprayer115½ I'll Take A Stand117⁵ No threat 8

WORKOUTS: May 8 Bel tr.t 5f fst 1:02 B 1/1 Apr 26 Bel tr.t 4f fst :49³ B 8/21 Apr 6 Bel tr.t 4f fst :47⁴ H 3/32 Mar 10 Bel tr.t 3f fst :37 H 3/8

Primo Maschio

Own: DeMarco Fiore J & Frank V

LEON F (8 1 0 1 .13) $12,000

B. g. 5
Sire: Val de l'Orne (Fr) (Val de Loir)
Dam: Our Sister Shel (Hold Your Peace)
Br: DeMarco Fiore & Frank (NY)
Tr: Myer Pat (—)

112

		Lifetime Record :	41 4 3 3	$100,448
1995	9 1 0 1	$23,605	Turf	9 0 1 1	$7,850
1994	11 1 1 0	$26,820	Wet	7 2 1 0	$37,265
Bel	10 1 1 0	$17,720	Dist	10 0 1 0	$8,760

30Apr95–2Aqu fst 1⅛ :49 1:143 1:404 1:542 Clm 10500 75 7 7 79 67 54 54½ Leon F 112 b 16.50 63–26 Red Scamper116ⁿᵏ Eire Power116²½ Brush Full114²½ No threat 7
17Apr95–9Aqu fst 1⅛ :474 1:124 1:364 1:521 Clm 10000 67 7 7 79 46½ 46½ 412½ Velazquez J R 116 b 5.70 67–24 Halo Habit113¼½ Duel Zone108⁷ Bailadoro106³½ Flattened out 9
8Apr95–3Aqu wf 1⅛ :48 1:123 1:38 1:51 Clm 10500 79 2 2 21 31 3⁵ 54½ Velazquez J R 116 b 26.50 81–22 Devoted Glory119⁷ Runaway Chris119⁴ Eire Power116½ Bid, tired 8
29Mar95–9Aqu fst 1⅛ :482 1:131 1:391 1:521 Clm 10500 68 8 10 66¼ 6½ 57 413 Velazquez J R 116 b 30.75 69–19 Rogersdividends118¹¼ Runaway Chris119⁴¼ Sulaco108¹¼ Wide, flattened out 9
18Mar95–1Aqu fst 1⅛ :481 1:132 1:392 1:524 Clm 10000 49 6 6 610 510 513 521 Nelson D 114 b 15.30 55–31 Rogersdividnds118¹ RunwyChris118¹½ BrushFull113¹⁰ Brk slow, no threat 6
2Mar95–4Aqu fst 1¼ :482 1:14 1:402 2:061 Clm 10000 73 6 3 45 41½ 31½ 33¾ Nelson D 117 b 8.60 93–14 Hugatag117¹½ Power Bolt117² Primo Maschio117ʰᵈ Wide, no late bid 6
25Feb95–4Aqu fst 6f :223 :48 1:131 1:264 Clm 10000 55 4 8 79¼ 812 719 732½ Nelson D 119 b 13.50 52–32 Mc Comas116²¾ The Mechanic113½ Shepskate119ⁿᵏ No threat 8
12Feb95–1Aqu fst 1⅛ :491 1:144 1:421 1:553 Clm 14000 33 8 4 79¾ 812 719 732½ Nelson D 119 b 13.20 45–32 CharmingBuck117³¼ HloHbit113² TwoTheTwist115⁴¼ Stead, drifted 3/4 pl 8
28Jan95–4Aqu fst 1⅛ :224 :472 1:132 1:481 ⓢAlw 34000N2X 80 2 3 33½ 33½ 22 12 Nelson D 117 b 37.75 64–34 Prlmo Maschio117² Vindicator117¹½ Addy Nashua117½ Good trip 8
18Dec94–4Aqu fst 1⁷⁰ :224 :461 1:141 1:44 3+ ⓢAlw 34000N2X 20 5 5 43½ 5⅛½ 516 536½ Nelson D 117 b 10.80 42–29 Flying Groom115¹¼ Limited War115⁶ Lake112¹⁶ Outrun 7

WORKOUTS: Mar 15 Bel tr.t 3f fst :38⁴ B 10/12

Duel Zone

Own: Rich Jill P

DUNKELBERGER T L (15 0 3 1 .00) $12,000

B. g. 7
Sire: Zoning (Hoist the Flag)
Dam: Hulas Doll (Exclusive Fleet)
Br: Rich D C (NY)
Tr: Corbellini William R (—)

107⁵

		Lifetime Record :	52 3 9 11	$120,887
1995	6 0 1 1	$4,075	Turf	18 0 2 4	$30,550
1994	14 2 2 3	$31,622	Wet	3 0 2 1	$10,240
Bel	4 1 0 0	$17,400	Dist	10 1 3 1	$38,730

30Apr95–2Aqu fst 1⅛ :49 1:143 1:404 1:542 Clm 10500 77 5 3 46½ 34 42½ 43½ Dunkelberger T L 107 b 5.40 65–26 Red Scamper116ⁿᵏ Eire Power116²½ Brush Full114²½ Steadied 13/16 pl 7
17Apr95–9Aqu fst 1⅛ :474 1:124 1:384 1:521 Clm 10000 84 6 5 58½ 34½ 21½ 21½ Dunkelberger T L 108 b 4.90 77–24 Halo Habit113¼½ Duel Zone108⁷ Bailadoro106³½ Rallied inside 9
5Apr95–4Aqu fst 1⅛ :47 1:121 1:251 1:52 Clm 10000 62 8 1 84½ 54 3¹ 31 Rydowski S R 116 b 3.30 69–19 Mr Sledge110⁵ Publicized116¾ Duel Zone116² Improved position 8
29Mar95–9Aqu fst 1⅛ :493 1:14 1:384 1:521 Clm 15000 70 5 7 79 55 57 710½ Rydowski S R 116 b 17.20 69–19 Rogersdividends118³¾ Stately Wager115⁷ Eire Power114¾½ Checked break 8
17Mar95–9Aqu fst 7f :23 :461 1:102 1:233 Clm 16500 72 6 9 95½ 98½ 66 65½ Rydowski S R 114 29.50 81–17 Magic Ruckus116¹ Cross Ice Pass110ⁿᵏ Berseto107ʰᵈ No threat 10
8Mar94–4Aqu fst 6f :222 :452 :581 1:12 Clm 19000 67 7 7 616 69 610 58½ Santagata N 114 17.40 75–20 Nicks Court116ⁿᵏ Concorde Cal116ⁿᵏ Sacre Bleu116⁴½ Bothered break 7
4Dec94–8FL fst 1 :24 :473 1:114 1:374 3+ Alw 7000N4L 66 3 5 53⅓ 41½ 3² 33½ Hiraldo J L 119 fb 6.50 94–05 Mt. Shannon116¹¼ Whose Jacques117² Duel Zone119¹½ Bid, hung 7
25Nov94–8FL fst 1 :24 :473 1:13 1:411 3+ Alw 7000N4L 50 8 5 51½ 55½ 56½ 33¼ Hiraldo J L 119 fb 3.75 92–05 Sanfran116⁵ Carrea119¼ Ichabod Rider117½ 7 wide 7/8 pole 8
7Nov94–10FL fst 1⁷⁰ :231 :461 1:131 1:442 3+ Alw 7000N3L 71 4 3 41½ 41½ 1½ 15 Hiraldo J L 116 fb 2.45 89–23 Duel Zone116⁵ Red Roses For Me114²½ Winning Plot116³ Drew off 7
30Oct94–7FL fst 1⁷⁰ :223 :47 1:131 1:373 3+ Alw 7000N3L 73 4 1 41⅓ 2⁶ 31⁰ 31⁰ Hiraldo J L 116 fb 2.85 89–10 Ichabod Rider112²¾ Winning Plot116ʰᵈ Duel Zone116¹ Finished well 6

WORKOUTS: ⬤Mar 3 Bel tr.t 4f fst :47² Hg 1/19 Feb 25 Bel tr.t 4f fst :51² B 33/39

The third race on Friday, May 12 was one of those bread-and-butter events that help fill out the cards at every track in the country: a claiming route for older horses on the lower end of the class spectrum. The field was reduced to seven after a couple of late scratches, and the race was to be contested over a drying out track labeled muddy.

Given the prevailing track conditions, Duel Zone was a high-percentage play and a wonderful opportunity at 4-1, despite a career record of 3-9-11 from 52 starts that suggested a gelding riddled with inconsistency. Far from it. Duel Zone actually was as reliable as the tides, and his dependability was shown only partially by his published record on wet tracks: 0-2-1 from three starts. Were that the whole story, the gelding would merit a long look in this spot by virtue of in-the-money finishes in each of three starts on wet tracks. But for whatever reason, the computer programmers at the *Form* chose to exclude "good" tracks from the wet-track records, even though some good tracks contain more moisture than those labeled "wet fast," which are considered "wet" in the career box.

Go figure.

It follows, naturally, that players aware of horses' hidden form on good tracks have a tremendous edge when such conditions are the order of the day.

It so happened that Duel Zone and I had been through a couple of real-life encounters over the years, so I was very much aware that the gelding had hidden, but quite demonstrable, prowess on tracks containing moisture. Why, three years earlier almost to the day, Duel Zone had broken his maiden in a route over a good track at Belmont:

FOURTH RACE
Belmont
MAY 18, 1992

1 ¹⁄₁₆ MILES. (1.402) MAIDEN SPECIAL WEIGHT. Purse $26,000. 3–year–olds and upward foaled in New York State and approved by the New York State–bred Registry. Weight: 3–year–olds 115 lbs., older 124 lbs.

Value of race $26,000; value to winner $15,600; second $5,720; third $3,120; fourth $1,560. Mutuel pool $191,181. Quinella Pool $111,453 Exacta Pool $380,548

Last Raced	Horse	M/Eqt.A.Wt	PP	St	¼	½	¾	Str	Fin	Jockey	Odds $1
20Apr92 9Aqu³	Duel Zone	b 4 124	2	7	8ʰᵈ	8ʰᵈ	7¹	1ʰᵈ	12¾	Migliore R	7.20
3May92 4Aqu³	Teddy C.	b 3 115	7	6	7²	6ʰᵈ	6ʰᵈ	4ʰᵈ	2¾	Krone J A	1.90
9May92 1Bel⁵	Look's Like Bob	b 3 115	1	5	4ʰᵈ	3ʰᵈ	3ʰᵈ	2ʰᵈ	3¾	Rojas R I	11.80
20Apr92 9Aqu¹¹	C. C. Sharpe	4 117	4	8	6½	7²	5ʰᵈ	3ʰᵈ	4ⁿᵒ	McMahon H I⁷	30.10
7May92 3Bel³	Sink the Ship	3 115	5	2	3ʰᵈ	4ʰᵈ	2ʰᵈ	5¹²	5⁷	Cruguet J	6.80
10Apr92 9Aqu⁴	Stock in Play	3 115	8	4	5¹	5½	8²	6³	6⁶	Maple E	5.40
1May92 3Pha²	Buckfinder's Ninja	3 115	3	3	1½	1½	1ʰᵈ	7⁵	7⁴	Verge M E	~2.80
16Apr92 5Aqu⁵	Rullah Judge	b 3 115	6	1	2½	2¹½	4½	8²	8½	Vasquez M O	79.20
10May92 10GS⁵	Cool Cop	3 115	9	9	9	9	9	9	9	Picon J	10.50

OFF AT 2:30 Start good, Won driving. Time, :23³, :47 , 1:11⁴, 1:37², 1:43⁴ Track good.

$2 Mutuel Prices:				
2-(B)-DUEL ZONE		16.40	5.40	4.00
7-(G)-TEDDY C.			3.80	3.20
1-(A)-LOOK'S LIKE BOB				5.80

$2 QUINELLA 2-7 PAID $22.80 $2 EXACTA 2-7 PAID $56.20

Duel Zone didn't win again until nearly two years later, but when he did break through, it was over another good track. I recalled the race vividly, for he had cost me a win bet on runnerup Athleague back on April 6, 1994:

Duel Zone
Own: Rich Jill P

HIRALDO J L (489 61 65 67 .12)

B. g. 6
Sire: Zoning (Hoist the Flag)
Dam: Hulas Doll (Exclusive Fleet)
Br: Rich D C (NY)
Tr: Lecesse Michael (72 14 7 6 .19)

116

Lifetime Record :	39	2	6	8	$107,852						
1994	7	1	0	1	$22,662	Turf	18	0	2	4	$30,550
1993	8	0	1	0	$13,710	Wet	2	0	1	1	$8,840
FL	1	0	0	0	$222	Dist	9	1	1	2	$31,280

29Aug94-7FL	fst	1		:223	:45	1:093	1:371	3↑ Alw 7400N4L	64	6	5	511	511	59	55	Hiraldo J L	116 fb	7.60	96 —	Only By Luck119½ Starkwell1161½ Poughkeepsie Gypsy1161¾	Even try 8
6Aug94-6Sar	yl	1⅛	[T]	:484	1:132	1:383	1:502	3↑ [S]Alw 32000N2X	49	9	4	42½	108¾	1013	920¼	Carr D	117 b	82.40	63-24	Johnny North1122 Royal Pelliknow1121½ Green Gaitor117nk	Wide trip 11
22Apr94-7Aqu	yl	1 1/16	Ⓣ	:241	:483	1:14	1:461	3↑ Alw 31000N2X	24	4	10	912	1014	1021	1030	Migliore R	124 b	21.10	48-22	VictoryCross1191 TunbridgeWlls1191½ GlIopingThundr119hd	Broke slowly 10
6Apr94-6Aqu	gd	1⅛		:472	1:113	1:372	1:504	[S]Alw 29000N1X	90	6	4	35	12	12½	13	Carr D	117 b	5.40	82-21	Duel Zone1173 Athleague1179½ C. C. Sharpe1175¼	Driving 7
20Mar94-1Aqu	fst	170	[•]	:241	:491	1:151	1:45	[S]Alw 28000N1X	50	1	5	43½	43½	39	316¼	Carr D	117 b	6.90	57-32	Bob H.1172¼ Tomahawk Man11714 Duel Zone1171½	Saved ground 5
6Mar94-1Aqu	fst	1 1/16	[•]	:24	:482	1:124	1:452	[S]Alw 28000N1X	63	2	8	811	88½	76	511¼	Carr D	117 b	23.00	67-24	Kc's Personal Flag1171¾ Vindicator1174½ Sturdy Dancer1221½	Broke slowly 8
27Jan94-7Aqu	fst	170	[•]	:241	:493	1:16	1:464	[S]Alw 28000N1X	57	3	8	79½	67½	56	411½	Vega H	117 b	34.50	52-35	Pago's Whim1174½ Tunbridge Wells1171½ Tomahawk Man1175½	No threat 10
18Dec93-4Aqu	fst	1 1/16	[•]	:234	:48	1:124	1:464	3↑ [S]Alw 30000N1X	59	1	8	811	89½	710	613	Maple E	117 b	9.10e	58-22	AdvncedPlcement115hd TunbridgeWells1156 Kc'sPersonlFlg1151½	Outrun 8
26Nov93-4Aqu	fst	1		:251	:494	1:152	1:403	3↑ [S]Alw 30000N1X	50	6	6	53	42	45	48½	Maple E	117 b	*3.00	52-38	Twice The Debt1153¾ Tunbridge Wells115nk Alpstein1154½	No threat 7
10Nov93-4Aqu	yl	1⅛	Ⓣ	:474	1:134	1:40	1:531	3↑ [S]Alw 30000N1X	62	10	9	87¼	74½	47	49¼	Maple E	117 b	9.30	68-24	Skimp1155 Doctor Disaster1173 Alpstein1151¼	Saved ground 12

WORKOUTS: Jly 8 Sar tr.t 3f fst :383 Bg4/8

Duel Zone's third (and most recent win) had been delivered at Finger Lakes the previous November. Though the track was listed fast for his five-length tally, a check of the result charts revealed the surface had been drying out, and had been listed as good through the first seven races before being upgraded to fast:

SEVENTH RACE
Finger Lakes
NOVEMBER 7, 1994

6 FURLONGS. (1.084) ALLOWANCE. Purse $7,400. Fillies and mares, 3-year-olds and upward which have never won four races. Weights: 3-year-olds, 120 lbs. Older, 122 lbs. Non-winners of two races since October 7, allowed 3 lbs; A race since then, 6 lbs. (Races where entered for a claiming price of $20,000 or less not considered in allowances).

Value of Race: $7,400 Winner $4,440; second $1,480; third $740; fourth $370; fifth $222; sixth $148. Mutuel Pool $26,290.00 Exacta Pool $73,735.00

Last Raced	Horse	M/Eqt.	A.	Wt	PP	St	¼	½	Str	Fin	Jockey	Odds $1
25Oct94 8FL4	Swings Well	bf	3	117	3	1	1hd	1hd	22	1¾	Davila J R Jr	2.90
21May94 9FL1	Patchesofsunshine	b	4	116	1	5	3hd	32	1hd	25¾	Nicol P A Jr	2.30
25Oct94 8FL3	Lady Chiller	bf	3	114	6	4	42	46	47	32	Dominguez C V	1.50
30Oct94 4FL1	Grey Hildy	b	4	116	4	2	23	2½	3hd	42	Messina R	5.90
28Oct94 9FL4	Peaceful Secret	f	6	110	2	6	6	6	6	52½	John K7	13.50
28Oct94 9FL5	Raspberry Fool	bf	4	119	5	3	56	56	53	6	Iorio S Jr	18.10

OFF AT 2:05 Start Good. Won driving. Time, :224, :461, :593, 1:121 Track good.

$2 Mutuel Prices:			
3-(C)-SWINGS WELL	7.80	3.50	2.30
1-(A)-PATCHESOFSUNSHINE		3.00	2.50
6-(F)-LADY CHILLER			2.40

$2.00 EXACTA 3-1 PAID $36.00

B. f, (Apr), by Ends Well-Late Night Disco, by Marshua's Dancer. Trainer Genecco Leo Jr. Bred by John Ellis & Mr. & Mrs.

TENTH RACE
Finger Lakes
NOVEMBER 7, 1994

1 MILE 70 YARDS. (1.401) ALLOWANCE. Purse $7,000. 3-year-olds and upward which have never won three races. Weights: 3-year-olds, 120 lbs. Older, 122 lbs. Non-winners of two races since October 7, allowed 3 lbs; A race since then, 6 lbs. (Races where entered for a claiming price of $20,000 or less not considered in allowances).

Value of Race: $7,000 Winner $4,200; second $1,400; third $700; fourth $350; fifth $210; sixth $140. Mutuel Pool $30,406.00 Exacta Pool $69,719.00

Last Raced	Horse	M/Eqt.	A.	Wt	PP	St	¼	½	¾	Str	Fin	Jockey	Odds $1
30Oct94 7FL3	Duel Zone	bf	6	116	4	4	52	41	4½	12½	15	Hiraldo J L	2.45
24Oct94 7FL3	Red Roses For Me	b	3	114	3	2	2½	22	21	21½	22¼	Saul D	4.20
30Oct94 7FL2	Winning Plot	b	6	116	6	5	7	7	67	44	33	Frates D	4.15
23Oct94 1FE7	Bette Talk	f	4	116	5	3	32½	31	1½	32	410¾	Iorio S Jr	20.50
22Oct94 6FL6	Rabun	bf	3	114	2	6	63½	63	52½	57	515½	Dominguez C V	1.65
25Oct94 7FL4	De Mitey Wan	b	3	114	1	1	1hd	1hd	3hd	614	67	Messina R	11.30
25Oct94 4FL1	Sir Speechless	b	3	114	7	7	4hd	5hd	7	7	7	Faine C	21.70

OFF AT 3:20 Start Good. Won driving. Time, :24, :473, 1:131, 1:40, 1:442 Track fast.

$2 Mutuel Prices:			
4-(D)-DUEL ZONE	6.90	4.10	2.70
3-(C)-RED ROSES FOR ME		4.70	2.60
6-(F)-WINNING PLOT			2.70

$2.00 EXACTA 4-3 PAID $39.60

B. g, by Zoning-Hulas Doll, by Exclusive Fleet. Trainer Lecesse Michael. Bred by Rich D C (NY).

Duel Zone's last two Beyers, both earned on fast tracks, totaled 161 — some 20 points faster than the last two of any rival. He figured to run at least as well, and probably would improve, over a surface he relished.

Yaros and Sailing On Aprayer, meanwhile, had been racing in much sharper form earlier in the year, but their most recent races suggested they were on a downward form-cycle trend. Despite that, they were installed as the first two betting choices at 9-5 and 5-2. They dueled down the backstretch, with Duel Zone tracking comfortably from outside. The mud lark rapidly splashed clear after inhaling the pacesetters midway on the turn, and expanded his lead to the wire:

THIRD RACE
Belmont
MAY 12, 1995

1⅛ MILES. (1.452) CLAIMING. Purse $14,000. 4–year–olds and upward. Weight, 122 lbs. Non–winners of two races at a mile or over since April 5, allowed 2 lbs. Such a race since March 29, 4 lbs. Two such races since March 4, 6 lbs. Claiming price $14,000, for each $1,000 to $12,000, allowed 2 lbs. (Races where entered for $10,000 or less not considered.)

Value of Race: $14,000 Winner $8,400; second $2,800; third $1,540; fourth $840; fifth $420. Mutuel Pool $203,742.00 Exacta Pool $431,532.00

Last Raced	Horse	M/Eqt.	A.	Wt	PP	St	¼	½	¾	Str	Fin	Jockey	Cl'g Pr	Odds $1
30Apr95 2Aqu4	Duel Zone	b	7	107	6	2	42	2hd	11	15	19	Dunkelberger T L5	12000	4.10
3May95 1Bel6	Graduate School	b	4	116	7	1	61	5hd	4½	21	24	Chavez J F	14000	4.60
30Apr95 2Aqu5	Primo Maschio	b	5	112	5	3	3½	42½	3½	31½	32	Leon F	12000	8.80
23Apr95 3Aqu7	Litigation Rex		5	109	3	7	7	7	7	51½	41	Martin G J5	13000	15.40
23Apr95 3Aqu6	Yaros	bf	6	107	1	5	1½	1hd	21½	41½	51¾	Agosto R5	12000	2.65
29Apr95 1Aqu3	Slews Gold	b	5	114	4	6	51	63	61	6½	61¼	Rydowski S R	13000	22.70
14Apr95 9Aqu4	Sailing On Aprayer	b	6	108	2	4	2hd	3½	52	7	7	Cooper G J7	13000	1.80

OFF AT 1:59 Start Good. Won driving. Time, :24, :471, 1:114, 1:371, 1:501 Track muddy.

$2 Mutuel Prices:

7–DUEL ZONE	10.20	4.50	3.00
8–GRADUATE SCHOOL		5.40	3.70
6–PRIMO MASCHIO			4.70

$2 EXACTA 7–8 PAID $45.40

B. g, by Zoning–Hulas Doll, by Exclusive Fleet. Trainer Corbellini William R. Bred by Rich D C (NY).

DUEL ZONE stalked early while three wide, took the lead on the far turn, repulsed a mild challenge from GRADUATE SCHOOL entering the stretch then drew away under left hand encouragement. GRADUATE SCHOOL reserved early, rallied four wide to threaten on the turn, but couldn't sustain his bid. PRIMO MASCHIO forced the pace between horses to the turn and tied. LITIGATION REX never reached contention after breaking slowly. YAROS dueled along the rail to the far turn and gradually tired thereafter. SLEWS GOLD was never a serious threat. SAILING ON APRAYER was used up battling for the early lead. All but SAILING ON APRAYER wore mud caulks.

Owners— 1, Rich Jill P; 2, Ackerley Bros Farm & Ackerley R G; 3, DeMarco Fiore J & Frank V; 4, Cohen Max R; 5, Perroncino John S; 6, Garren Murray M; 7, Pollard Damon

Trainers—1, Corbellini William R; 2, Lake Robert P; 3, Myer Pat; 4, Meittinis Louis N; 5, Terracciano Neal; 6, Garren Murray M; 7, Pollard Damon

Overweight: Sailing On Aprayer (1).

Scratched— Hot Slew (3May95 1BEL8), Sulaco (14Apr95 9AQU2)

What's shown in printed past performances is necessarily a capsulized portrait of horses' abilities and preferences. Anything you can add to the richness of the overall picture enables the development of solid opinions on horses that do not inspire the confidence of John Q. Punter.

BECAUSE TURF RACING gets into high gear in May and early June, handicappers will be confronted with a constant barrage of grass horses who are returning from layoffs. For this reason, it's important to keep in tune with the trainers who are capable of sending out "live" layoff runners.

Consider the eighth race, May 31, an allowance for 3-year-olds and up at a mile on the Widener course. The first six choices in the wagering were making either the first or second start in their current form cycle:

8 Belmont Park

1 MILE. **(Turf). (1:322) ALLOWANCE. Purse $36,000. 3–year–olds and upward which have never won three races. Weights: 3–year–olds, 114 lbs. Older, 124 lbs. Non–winners of $18,000 twice since April 27, allowed 2 lbs. $8,500 since May 3, 4 lbs. (Claiming races not considered in allowances.)**

Proceeded
Own: Harbor View Farm
BECKNER D V (46 3 5 3 .07)

B. g. 4
Sire: Affirmed (Exclusive Native)
Dam: Bowl of Honey (Lyphard)
Br: Clovelly Farms (Ky)
Tr: Jerkens H Allen (38 9 8 5 .24)

120

Lifetime Record:	4 2 1 0	$42,900			
1995	4 2 1 0	$42,900	Turf	1 1 0 0	$19,200
1994	0 M 0 0		Wet	1 1 0 0	$16,800
Bel Ⓣ	0 0 0 0		Dist Ⓣ	0 0 0 0	

30Apr95–5Aqu fm	1 1/16 Ⓣ	:224	:463	1:111	1:433	3↑ Alw 32000N2L	83	7	4	49	45	12	13½	Beckner D V	120 f	4.00	91–09	Proceeded1203½ Dial Trial1121¼ No Storm1201½	Four wide, going away 10		
15Mar95–4Aqu fst 6f		:224	:462	:583	1:111	Alw 30000N1X	81	7	3	31	2hd	1hd	2½	Beckner D V	114 f	*1.60	85–14	Ball's Bluff115½ Proceeded114½ Lulu's Little Boy1102	Gamely 7		
20Feb95–4Aqu fst 6f	⊡	:232	:471	1:00	1:123	Alw 30000N1X	70	2	4	1½	4½	3nk	54¾	Beckner D V	117 f	*.30e	75–25	Here's Noah114¾ Lulu's LittleBoy1092 FacetiousBuck114½	Dueled inside 7		
21Jan95–5Aqu my 6f	⊡	:224	:462	:583	1:113	Md Sp Wt	81	6	2	2hd	11	16	15½	Beckner D V	122 f	8.10	85–14	Proceeded1225½ M.d.'s Relampago122½ Danzigs Pride1226	Ridden out 7		

WORKOUTS: May 27 Bel 6f gd 1:161 B *1/2* ●Apr 28 Bel tr.t 4f fst :482 H *1/7* Apr 19 Bel tr.t 3f fst :38 B *9/15* Apr 8 Bel tr.t 5f fst 1:031 B *9/16* Mar 11 Bel tr.t 4f fst :493 B *16/39*

Dutchess First
Own: Haverhals Jacob
KRONE J A (77 19 13 15 .25)

B. g. 4
Sire: Diesis (Sharpen Up)
Dam: Dutchess Best (Blakeney)
Br: Saddle Home Farm (Ky)
Tr: Dickinson Michael W (3 1 1 0 .33)

120

Lifetime Record:	6 2 0 0	$35,325			
1994	6 2 0 0	$35,325	Turf	6 2 0 0	$35,325
1992	0 M 0 0		Wet	0 0 0 0	
Bel Ⓣ	2 2 0 0	$34,200	Dist Ⓣ	0 0 0 0	

14Oct94–10Med fm	1 1/16 Ⓣ	:23	:464	1:11	1:414	3↑ Alw 23000N2X	55	10	6	69¾	76¾	11101115¼		McCauley W H	L 113	*1.80	77–07	Jimlew1152½ Raise Your Blade116hd Water Skipper116nk	Tired 11		
3Sep94–10Mth fm	1⅛ Ⓣ	:472	1:113	1:35	1:48	+ Choice H-G3	78	7	3	31½	42	65	69	Colton R E	L 112	7.10	87–12	Pennine Ridge116nk Honorable Flight1174½ Myrmidon112¾	Tired 7		
31Jly94–7Mth sf	1 1/16 Ⓣ	:242	:483	1:133	1:461	Restoration40k	84	8	5	55	41½	43	66	Bravo J	L 117	*2.70	67–33	WkeUpAlrm1133¼ AtomicPower1151 AllegedImprssion122nk	No solid bid 10		
19Jly94–7Bel fm	1 1/16 Ⓣ	:234	:463	1:111	1:42	3↑ Alw 30000N1X	87	5	5	66½	52¼	22	1¾	Krone J A	116	4.10	88–11	DutchssFrst116¾ GrouchoGucho117nk GllntGst1116	Check early, driving 10		
4Jly94–10Bel fm	1 1/16 Ⓣ	:234	:471	1:104	1:411	3↑ Md Sp Wt	85	10	4	54	33	12	14¼	Krone J A	116	5.30	90–10	Dutchess First1164¼ Sophie's Friend1161¼ Thirty Good Ones1161¾	Drew off 10		
5Jun94–3Pim fm	1⅛ Ⓣ	:472	1:123	1:383	1:513	3↑ Md Sp Wt	69	6	4	34½	32½	44	56½	Hamilton S D	112	10.70	70–25	Vladivostok1163 Don't Cha Stop112½ Rugged Bugger1142½	Weakened 8		

WORKOUTS: May 25 Fai 5f fst 1:05 B *9/9* May 13 Fai 5f fst 1:042 B *6/6* May 4 Fai 5f fst 1:052 B *7/8* Apr 27 Fai 6f fst 1:18 B *1/1*

Arz

Own: Haley Terrence W & Wickman Joseph F
PEREZ R B (91 12 17 8 .13)

Dk. b or br c. 4
Sire: Known Fact (In Reality)
Dam: Last Request*Ir (Dancer's Image)
Br: Shadwell Farm Inc & Shadwell Estate Co Ltd (Ky)
Tr: Lake Robert P (17 1 3 2 .06)
1175

Lifetime Record :	20 2 5 4	$48,729			
1995	8 1 2 1	$32,180	Turf	14 1 3 3	$18,469
1994	6 0 1 2	$5,403	Wet	2 0 0 0	$1,920
Bel (T)	0 0 0 0		Dist (T)	9 1 1 3	$13,893

6May95-6Bel fst 1 1/8 :24 :47 1:112 1:433 3+ Alw 34000N2L 88 1 3 1hd 1½ 14 16½ Velazquez J R 120 b 20.60 81-15 Arz1206½ West Buoyant115hd Easy Miner120¾ Brk slowly, going away 7
30Apr95-5Aqu fm 1 1/16 (T) :224 :463 1:111 1:433 3+ Alw 32000N2L 69 8 8 711 55½ 42½ 46½ Velazquez J R 120 b 27.50 85-09 Proceeded1203½ Dial Trial1121½ No Storm1201½ Saved ground, weakened 10
22Apr95-9Aqu gd 1 1/16 :24 :48 1:124 1:442 Clm 50000 55 5 6 611 77 710 817¾ Santos J A 116 b 6.90 69-16 Bonus Award112nk Berseto1131½ Royal Ninja110½ No threat 9
7Apr95-2Aqu fst 6f :224 :472 :594 1:121 Clm 35000N2L 72 7 6 66½ 3½ 21 21½ Velazquez J R 116 b 2.00e 79-19 Kris' Rainbow1141½ Arz1163 Graduate School1161½ Rallied four wide 8
31Mar95-2Aqu fst 6f :223 :464 :59 1:113 Clm c-25000N2L 70 3 4 55 66 44 35 Lovato F Jr 116 fb 8.80 79-19 Dependableness114no Metroplex1145 Arz1161 Checked 7/16 pl 7
Claimed from Schwartz Barry K, Hushion Michael E Trainer
24Feb95-1Aqu wf 6f ⊡ :23 :461 :581 1:104 Clm 35000N2L 64 3 6 75½ 88 57 49 Migliore R 116 fb 3.65 80-16 Plutonius1123½ River Arly111½ Robber Baron1155 Steadied 5/16 pl 9
2Feb95-3Aqu fst 6f ⊡ :233 :48 1:003 1:133 Clm 30000N2L 69 2 7 65 65½ 34½ 24½ Migliore R 113 fb 6.30 70-26 Mine D'or1134½ Arz1132 Final Reality108no Checked 5/16 pl 9
7Jan95-3Aqu my 6f ⊡ :224 :47 1:001 1:132 Clm 35000N2L 65 1 6 56½ 45½ 44 44½ Migliore R 117 fb 5.00 72-28 Bay Dancer1103½ Lord Sage117no Nowsthetimetobrite1181 No factor 6
23Sep94♦ Haydock(GB) yl *140 (T)LH 1:454 3+ Dream Mile Handicap Hcp 15000 818¾ Carlisle N 135 7.00 Celestial Choir1353½ Harding122½ Master Beveled1191½ 11
Tr: Harry Thomson Jones
Chased in 4th to halfway,weakened
29Aug94♦ Ripon(GB) gd 1 (T)RH 1:382 3+ Ripon Rowels Handicap Hcp 17600 35 Price R 117 10.00 Hunters Of Brora1191½ Moving Arrow1243½ Arz1171½ 11
Rated at rear,outside bid 3f out,no late responseo

WORKOUTS: ●May 16 Bel tr.t 5f fst 1:02 B 1/6 Apr 16 Bel tr.t 5f fst 1:031 B 7/10 Mar 29 Bel tr.t 4f fst :50 B 16/31 Mar 22 Bel tr.t 4f fst :484 B 9/22

Moscow Magic

Own: Pen-Y-Bryn Farm
SANTOS J A (86 14 9 13 .16)

B. c. 4
Sire: Nijinsky's Secret (Nijinsky II)
Dam: Penny Flight (Damascus)
Br: Pen Y Bryn Farm (Ky)
Tr: Whiteley David A (—)
120

Lifetime Record :	12 2 1 3	$54,300			
1995	1 0 0 0	$280	Turf	7 2 1 2	$48,000
1994	9 2 1 2	$50,780	Wet	0 0 0 0	
Bel (T)	4 1 1 1	$28,640	Dist (T)	0 0 0 0	

25Jan95-7GP fm *1 1/8 (T) :47 1:121 1:364 1:492 + Alw 28000N2X 82 2 10 107¾ 96 66½ 65 Santos J A 119 f *2.60 93-02 Sole Bird119¾ Naked Way119nk Kassec1191¾ 10
Mild bid wide str
11Nov94-7Aqu fst 1 ⊗ :232 :464 1:121 1:364 3+ Alw 34000N2X 67 2 8 817 75 49 414 Bailey J D 115 f 4.20 70-21 Iron Gavel1172 Five Star General1176 Klondike Clem1156 No threat 8
19Oct94-6Aqu fm 1 1/16 (T) :233 :484 1:124 1:431 3+ Alw 34000N2X 88 5 7 74½ 73¾ 31½ 31½ Bailey J D 114 f *.90 92-08 Thrhrvrdvn117¾ GrochoGcho117½ MoscwMgc114no Brk slow, chckd turn 7
17Jly94-8Bel fm 1¼ (T) :47 1:104 1:343 1:593 Lexington-G3 92 6 9 910 96½ 73½ 52 Santos J A 114 f 3.50 90-09 Holy Mountain1121½ Islefaxyou112nk Check Ride117no Rallied wide 10
17Jun94-7Bel fm 1¼ (T) :481 1:113 1:354 1:594 3+ Alw 32000N2X 94 5 6 68½ 31 2½ 21½ Perret C 111 f 3.90 90-10 Noble Sheba1191½ Moscow Magic1112 Grateful Appeal111hd Second best 9
30May94-6Bel fm 1¼ (T) :491 1:13 1:371 2:013 3+ Alw 30000N2L 92 3 8 88½ 52 2½ 11 Perret C 112 f 3.10 82-12 Moscow Magic1121 Check Ride1123 Nice Try George1142 Driving 8
11May94-6Bel fm 1¼ (T) :49 1:123 1:37 2:013 3+ Alw 30000N1X 80 6 9 73½ 32 26 38½ Perret C 112 f 3.00 73-21 MtchlssDncr1198½ MsclStorm119nk MoscowMgc1124 Wide bid, weakened 9
27Feb94-11GP fm *1 1/8 (T) :472 1:13 1:384 1:53 + Md Sp Wt 76 3 8 86 62½ 1hd 14 Perret C 120 f 2.10 80-16 Moscow Magic1204 Joyful Dancing120¾ Matra1152 10
Seven wide top str, driving
20Jan94-6GP fst 1 1/16 :24 :483 1:13 1:45 Md Sp Wt 52 7 7 63½ 75½ 1010 913 Perret C 120 f 7.70 72-11 Signal Tap1203 Andover Road120nk In A Schocking Way1204 12
Steadied first turn, gave way
4Jan94-5GP fst 1 1/16 :24 :484 1:132 1:461 Md Sp Wt 67 5 9 96 44½ 36½ 49½ Penna D 120 15.50 69-21 Lahint1202½ Signal Tap1206½ Sangre De Toro120½ 12
Slow start, lacked late response

WORKOUTS: May 26 Bel 5f sly 1:021 B 2/4 May 24 Bel 4f fst :511 B 30/36 May 21 Bel 4f fst :482 B 18/112 May 16 Bel 3f fst :364 B 9/18 May 14 Bel 3f fst :364 B 2/28

Super Twenty Five

Own: Live Oak Plantation
SAMYN J L (34 0 3 8 .00)

B. g. 4
Sire: Valid Appeal (In Reality)
Dam: Miss Angel T. (Talc)
Br: Live Oak Stud (Fla)
Tr: Kelly Patrick J (27 1 7 3 .04)
120

Lifetime Record :	19 2 3 2	$54,090			
1995	6 1 1 0	$14,770	Turf	10 2 3 1	$50,660
1994	8 1 2 2	$37,700	Wet	2 0 0 0	$340
Bel (T)	2 1 1 0	$24,600	Dist (T)	0 0 0 0	

21Apr95-9Kee gd 1 1/16 (T) :223 :464 1:122 1:444 Alw 39000N2X 70 9 4 45½ 1½ 43½ 68 Fires E L 114 6.60 74-18 Secret Fan113nk Kumhwa1131 Seattle Rob1135 Inside bid, tired 10
23Mar95-7Hia fm *1 1/16 (T) 1:414 Alw 16000N2X 81 7 2 21½ 21½ 24 26 Fires E 114 3.80 87-05 Youthful Legs1146 Super Twenty Five1141 Super Tuned1141¾ Gamely 10
8Mar95-10GP sly 1 1/16 ⊗ :234 :474 1:121 1:45 Alw 34000N2X 43 4 3 54 57½ 612 624 Santos J A 119 6.80 59-22 Royal Judge11910 Mephistopheles119½ Maddy's Best119¾ Gave way 7
5Feb95-8GP fm 1 1/16 (T) :233 :472 1:11 1:414 + Alw 28000N2X 86 9 2 33 32 33 52½ Samyn J L 119 6.20 85-15 Gator Spirit119¾ Darby Stubbles1191 Malmo119½ Faded 12
22Jan95-7GP fst 6f :221 :45 :573 1:102 Alw 28300N2X 37 3 7 77 910 914 925½ Samyn J L 122 30.20 62-15 Turf Star1222½ Pro Brite1192 Lake Ali1195 No factor 9
1Jan95-11Crc fm 5f (T) :221 :46 :574 Alw 17000N1X 85 7 5 32 42½ 2hd 13 Samyn J L 119 *1.20 95-05 Super Twenty Five1193 Nortech1191 Assorted Donuts119nk 4-wide bid 9
27Nov94-5Aqu sf 1 1/8 (T) :482 1:141 1:404 1:53 3+ Alw 32000N1X 72 6 2 1hd 2hd 41 56½ Leon F 115 3.75 68-29 Mr Hydro117no Gold Guardian115½ Price Rise1155 Dueled, tired 11
22Oct94-7Aqu gd 1 1/16 (T) :241 :481 1:123 1:443 3+ Alw 32000N1X 81 3 1 11 1½ 11 2¾ Leon F 119 7.00 85-16 Skipton114¾ Super Twenty Five119hd Beware The Quest1142 Gamely 10
6Oct94-5Bel fm 1 1/16 (T) :233 :471 1:113 1:434 3+ Md Sp Wt 83 4 1 1hd 1hd 12 11¾ Leon F 119 2.60 77-20 Super Twenty Five1191¾ Majestic Tax117hd Strauss119nk Driving 8
14Sep94-3Bel fm 1 1/16 (T) :233 :472 1:12 1:423 3+ Md Sp Wt 79 3 1 12½ 11½ 2hd 22 Leon F 118 17.90 81-14 Yokohama1182 Super Twenty Five1181¾ Hawkeye Bay1183 Gamely 10

WORKOUTS: May 24 Bel 3f fst :364 H 2/14 May 13 Bel tr.t 4f fst :493 B 12/33 May 5 Bel 4f fst :484 H 7/24 Apr 14 Kee 4f fst :494 B 19/38 Apr 8 Kee 4f fst :493 B 31/43 Mar 18 Hia 4f fst :472 H 4/34

Kerfoot Corner

Own: Rokeby Stables
BAILEY J D (67 18 9 6 .27)

Dk. b or br g. 4
Sire: Danzig (Northern Dancer)
Dam: Rokeby Rose (Tom Rolfe)
Br: Mellon Paul (Va)
Tr: Miller MacKenzie (9 1 2 1 .11)
120

Lifetime Record :	8 2 3 1	$58,690			
1995	1 0 1 0	$6,800	Turf	1 0 1 0	$6,600
1994	6 2 2 1	$51,890	Wet	2 0 1 0	$8,480
Bel (T)	1 0 1 0	$6,600	Dist (T)	0 0 0 0	

10May95-6Bel wf 6f :221 :452 :572 1:094 3+ Alw 34000N2X 86 2 5 42½ 2hd 21 24 Bailey J D 119 b 3.15 88-14 Churka1104 Kerfoot Corner119½ Lake Ali1168 Broke slowly, wide 5
4Nov94-6CD fst 6½f :223 :453 1:11 1:174 3+ Alw 37460N2X 87 1 12 83¾ 87½ 66 33 Bailey J D L 114 b 4.20 87-11 Skyphone1141 Sierra Cat1132 Kerfoot Corner114hd Mild gain 12
2Sep94-6Bel fst 1 1/16 :232 :464 1:11 1:422 3+ Alw 32000N1X 89 5 4 42 3½ 1hd 12½ Bailey J D 113 b *.70 90-10 Kerfoot Corner1132½ Absent Minded113nk Per Pop1174¾ Wide, driving 9
23Jly94-7Sar sly 7f :221 :451 1:091 1:214 3+ Alw 28000N1X 63 1 5 44 32 49 421¼ Bailey J D 111 b 2.30 75-12 Prenup1117¾ Skyphone1115 A Track Attack1118½ Lacked rally 6
30Jun94-6Bel fm 1 1/16 (T) :222 :451 1:101 1:414 3+ Alw 30000N2L 85 6 4 44½ 2hd 2½ 2½ Bailey J D 111 *.60 89-16 BermudCedr111nk KerfootCornr111½ CommodorAdmirl1136 Wide, hung 8
24May94-6Bel fst 1 :224 :461 1:11 1:362 3+ Alw 30000N1X 91 4 3 42 2½ 2hd 2nk Bailey J D 112 1.90 81-24 Possibilities112nk Kerfoot Corner1127 Final Clearance113hd Second best 6
13May94-1Bel fst 6f :231 :461 :581 1:101 3+ Md Sp Wt 84 1 2 41 4¾ 31 1¾ Bailey J D 115 6.60 90-14 Kerfoot Corner115¾ Count On Broadway115no Plutonius1151½ Driving 8
30Sep93-5Bel fst 6f :222 :46 :582 1:112 Md Sp Wt 52 3 4 65½ 64½ 67 613¾ Bailey J D 118 *1.40 69-22 Bermuda Cedar1186 Prank Call118nk Plutonius1181¾ No factor 9

WORKOUTS: May 28 Bel 5f fst :59 H 2/56 May 22 Bel 4f fst :482 B 7/39 May 16 Bel 4f fst :48 B 3/21 ●May 6 Bel 6f fst 1:13 B 1/5 ●May 1 Bel 3f sly :363 B (d) 1/8

Gallant Guest

Own: N Y Chezam Stable
SMITH M E (68 19 11 10 .28)

B. g. 4
Sire: Cutlass (Damascus)
Dam: Early Invitation (Be My Guest)
Br: Somers Ed (Fla)
Tr: Martin Jose (18 1 1 4 .06)
120

Lifetime Record :	24 2 6 3	$64,375			
1995	6 1 1 0	$18,260	Turf	13 0 4 3	$32,290
1994	17 1 5 3	$45,765	Wet	3 0 1 0	$2,330
Bel (T)	7 0 2 2	$22,880	Dist (T)	1 0 1 0	$7,040

19Apr95-5Aqu fst 1 1/8 :48 1:124 1:392 1:524 3+ Alw 32000N1X 75 7 2 2hd 11½ 32½ 46½ Valdivia J7 113 fb 10.50 70-20 ScreenOscar1124 SaveTheWhle1102 DeceptiveStroke112nk Dueled, tired 8
14Apr95-3Aqu fst 1 :232 :461 1:113 1:374 Clm 30000N2L 71 4 1 11½ 13 13 14 Valdivia J7 111 fb 2.10 80-13 GallantGuest1114 FinalReality108¾ GrduteSchool1184½ Drifted, held well 7
31Mar95-9Hia fm *1 1/16 (T) 1:431 Alw 15000N1X 59 1 1 1½ 2hd 43 513 Valdivia J Jr L 114 b 3.30 73-15 Gem Seeker1145 Proof Time1194½ Assorted Donuts1143 9
Drifted out first turn, faded
15Mar95-9GP fst 1 1/16 ⊗ :232 :47 1:112 1:454 Alw 26000N2L 71 4 1 12½ 3½ 21½ 24 Fires E L 119 b 12.60 75-23 Steady Kid1194 Gallant Guest1194 King Kalea119nk Second best 7
19Feb95-4GP fm *1 1/16 (T) :471 1:122 1:371 1:491 + Alw 26000N1X 35 3 2 1hd 2hd 67¾ 923½ Sellers S J L 119 fb 4.00 76-03 Splashing Believer1192 King Kalea119½ Roto11911 Faltered 10
28Jan95-4GP fst 6f :213 :44 :57 1:104 Alw 25000N1X 40 1 10 63¾ 812 1020 1021½ Santos J A L 119 b 9.00 65-16 Island Dash1192½ Turn West1223½ Count Joseph1191½ Stopped 11
11Oct94-4Bel fm 1 1/16 (T) :234 :464 1:11 1:414 Clm 50000 75 3 1 1½ 1hd 21½ 67 Chavez J F 117 b *2.30 82-17 Wavering Man1132¾ O' Lucky Star115no Francis Marion1132½ Dueled inside 10
17Sep94-2Bel fm 1 (T) :22 :45 1:092 1:343 3+ Alw 32000N1X 81 4 2 1hd 11 14 21 Chavez J F 113 b *2.80e 88-10 Reason Prevails1131 Gallant Guest1131 Dissertation1082 Couldn't last 12
4Sep94-7Bel fm 1 1/16 (T) :244 :474 1:11 1:411 3+ Alw 32000N2L 78 8 2 33½ 34 34 35½ Chavez J F 113 b 20.30 85-10 InsideTheBeltway1132 HolyMountain1133½ GallantGuest1131½ No late bid 9
15Aug94-4Sar yl 1 1/16 (T) :232 :464 1:111 1:424 Clm 70000 43 9 4 34 33½ 69 723 Velazquez J R 113 11.10 57-21 Head Trip1172 Best Of Music1137 Natural Fact1171½ Gave way 10

WORKOUTS: May 19 Bel tr.t 3f sly :384 B 3/3 ●May 16 Bel tr.t 3f fst :37 B 1/7 ●Apr 30 Bel tr.t 4f fst :48 H 1/17 ●Apr 11 Bel tr.t 3f fst :353 H 1/14 Mar 26 Hia 4f fst :473 H 2/12 Mar 11 Hia 5f fst 1:022 B 22/34

Gallant Guest
Own: N Y Chezam Stable
SMITH M E (68 19 11 10 .28)

B. g. 4
Sire: Cutlass (Damascus)
Dam: Early Invitation (Be My Guest)
Br: Somers Ed (Fla)
Tr: Martin Jose (18 1 1 4 .06)

120

Lifetime Record: 24 2 6 3 $64,375											
1995	6	1	1	0	$18,260	Turf	13	0	4	3	$32,290
1994	17	1	5	3	$45,765	Wet	3	0	1	0	$2,330
Bel Ⓣ	7	0	2	2	$22,880	Dist Ⓣ	1	0	1	0	$7,040

19Apr95- 5Aqu fst 1⅛ :48 1:124 1:392 1:524 3↑ Alw 32000N1X 75 7 2 2hd 1½ 3½ 4¾ Valdivia J7 113 fb 10.50 70-20 ScreenOscar1124 SaveTheWhle1102 DeceptiveStroke112nk Dueled, tired 8
14Apr95- 3Aqu fst 1 :232 :461 1:113 1:374 Clm 30000N2L 71 4 1 1½ 13 13 14 Valdivia J7 111 fb 2.10 80-13 GallantGuest1114 FinalReality108¾ GrduteSchool1184½ Drifted, held well 7
31Mar95- 9Hia fm *1 1/16 Ⓣ 1:431 Alw 15000N1X 59 1 1 1½ 2hd 43 513 Valdivia J Jr L 114 b 3.30 73-15 Gem Seeker1145 Proof Time1194½ Assorted Donuts1143 9
Drifted out first turn, faded
15Mar95- 9GP fst 1 1/16 ⊗ :232 :47 1:112 1:454 Alw 32000N2L 71 4 1 12½ 3½ 21½ 24 Fires E L 119 b 12.60 75-23 Steady Kid1194 Gallant Guest1194 King Kalea119nk Second best 7
19Feb95- 4GP fm *1⅛ Ⓣ :471 1:122 1:371 1:491+ Alw 26000N1X 35 3 2 1hd 2hd 67¾ 923¼ Sellers S J L 119 fb 4.00 76-03 Splashing Believer1192 King Kalea119½ Roto11911 Faltered 10
28Jan95- 4GP fst 6f :213 :44 :57 1:104 Alw 25000N1X 40 1 10 63¾ 812 1020 1021¼ Santos J A L 119 b 9.00 65-16 Island Dash1192½ Turn West1223½ Count Joseph1191½ Stopped 11
11Oct94- 4Bel fm 1 1/16 Ⓣ :234 :464 1:11 1:414 Clm 50000 75 3 1 1½ 1hd 21½ 67 Chavez J F 117 b *2.30 82-17 Wavering Man1132¾ O' Lucky Star115no Francis Marion1132½ Dueled inside 10
17Sep94- 2Bel fm 1 Ⓣ :22 :45 1:092 1:343 3↑ Alw 32000N1X 81 4 2 1hd 11 14 21 Chavez J F 113 b *2.80e 88-10 Reason Prevails1131 Gallant Guest1131 Dissertation1082 Couldn't last 12
4Sep94- 7Bel fm 1 1/16 [T] :244 :474 1:11 1:411 3↑ Alw 32000N2L 78 8 2 33½ 34 34 35¼ Chavez J F 113 b 20.30 85-10 InsideTheBeltway1132 HolyMountain1133¼ GallantGuest1131¼ No late bid 9
15Aug94- 4Sar yl 1 1/16 Ⓣ :232 :464 1:111 1:424 Clm 70000 43 9 4 34 33½ 69 723 Velazquez J R 113 11.10 57-21 Head Trip1172 Best Of Music1137 Natural Fact1171½ Gave way 10
WORKOUTS: May 19 Bel tr.t 3f sly :384 B 3/3 ●May 16 Bel tr.t 3f fst :37 B 1/7 ●Apr 30 Bel tr.t 4f fst :48 H 1/17 ●Apr 11 Bel tr.t 3f fst :353 H 1/14 Mar 26 Hia 4f fst :473 H 2/12 Mar 11 Hia 5f fst 1:022 B 22/34

Viva Sabona
Own: Garren Murray M
CHAVEZ J F (111 19 14 15 .17)

B. g. 3 (Mar)
Sire: Sabona (Exclusive Native)
Dam: Fabulous Vee (Somethingfabulous)
Br: Mattison Coleman (Ky)
Tr: Garren Murray M (21 1 1 2 .05)

110

Lifetime Record: 12 2 2 0 $33,830											
1995	9	2	2	0	$31,865	Turf	2	0	0	0	$465
1994	3	M	0	0	$1,965	Wet	3	1	1	0	$15,400
Bel Ⓣ	0	0	0	0		Dist Ⓣ	0	0	0	0	

21May95- 7Bel fst 6f :222 :461 :583 1:114 3↑ Alw 32000N1X 59 9 6 63¾ 73¾ 118½ 1110½ Davis R G 112 b 5.90 71-22 Jump The Shadow1121½ Frisco Gold1211½ Jo Ran Express114¾ Wide, tired 12
11May95- 8Bel my 7f :221 :443 1:093 1:214 3↑ Alw 32000N1X 86 1 1 31 2hd 21 24 Chavez J F 110 b 8.00 88-11 Flying Chevron1124 Viva Sabona1104 Placid Fund112¾ Dueled, held well 8
4May95- 4Bel fst 1 1/16 :231 :462 1:113 1:443 Clm c-35000 74 5 1 1hd 1hd 11½ 23 Davis R G 116 b 3.30 73-18 Kan't Stop Kris1123 Viva Sabona1162½ Deep Sun1062½ Pressed, drifted 9
Claimed from Ellis Robert C Jr, Hills Timothy A Trainer
22Apr95- 2Aqu fst 7f :221 :451 1:11 1:241 Clm 25000 84 5 5 66½ 55 2½ 11¾ Davis R G 118 b 3.85 83-17 VivSbon1181¾ HnbnsJourny1184½ VlidMotion1142 Checked brk, four wide 6
31Mar95- 6Hia fst 7f :232 :461 1:11 1:24 Clm 40000 58 8 2 3nk 2hd 33½ 58 Bravo J L 119 b 6.10 81-19 Fiery Temper1161¾ Sunny Rican1166 Leap With Joy116no Weakened 9
10Mar95- 8GP gd *1 1/16 Ⓣ :234 :474 1:124 1:431+ Alw 32000N1X 53 10 4 45½ 56½ 1018 1018 Boulanger G 119 b 58.00 74-14 Claramount Hill1191½ Indomable1192½ Count De Monnaie119nk Stopped 10
26Feb95- 2GP wf 7f :221 :453 1:113 1:251 Md 30000 67 2 7 1hd 12 12½ 16½ Bravo J 118 b 5.60 77-18 Viva Sabona1186½ Sky Searcher1181 Classic Arts1189 Driving 12
4Feb95- 6GP fst 1 1/16 :232 :471 1:131 1:47 Md Sp Wt 50 7 3 41 45½ 614 721½ Davis R G 120 b 52.10 51-26 Da Bull1205½ Crimson Guard1203 Crimson12010 Faded 11
14Jan95- 5GP sly 1⅛ ⊗ :473 1:13 1:40 1:533 Md Sp Wt 53 6 1 1½ 2hd 49½ 415½ Davis R G 120 b 9.60 53-25 Native Tribe1203 Jimboombob1203½ Cayman Slough1209 9
Raced well off rail, weakened
28Dec94- 9Crc fm *1⅛ Ⓣ 1:541 Md Sp Wt 46 3 5 58½ 108½ 711 79½ Santos J A 119 4.70 38-49 Gold Facts1193¼ Val D're Val D'la1191½ Ricky's Shadow119nk 10
Bumped hard start, bumped backstretch
WORKOUTS: May 29 Bel tr.t 3f sly :362 B 1/3 Apr 17 Bel 5f fst :592 H 3/22 ●Mar 26 Hia 5f fst :594 H 1/11

Check Ride
Own: Royal Lines Stable & Whelan David
KRONE J A (77 19 13 15 .25)

Gr. c. 4
Sire: Tsunami Slew (Seattle Slew)
Dam: Bid Me Adieu (Spectacular Bid)
Br: Whelan Dawn E (Ky)
Tr: Hough Stanley M (28 4 8 2 .14)

120

Lifetime Record: 15 2 5 1 $93,983											
1995	1	0	0	0	$2,160	Turf	14	2	5	1	$93,983
1994	10	1	3	1	$65,283	Wet	0	0	0	0	
Bel Ⓣ	8	1	4	1	$65,573	Dist Ⓣ	3	1	1	0	$21,370

17May95- 6Bel fm 1 1/16 [T] :233 :462 1:101 1:413 3↑ Alw 36000N2X 87 7 3 32½ 31½ 32 42¾ Krone J A 118 *2.45 85-12 Arduous1181 Wavering Man118¾ Gem Seeker1181 Lacked rally 10
8Aug94- 8Sar fm 1⅛ Ⓣ :472 1:113 1:362 1:483 HallOfFame-G2 86 2 6 74½ 74½ 41½ 85¾ Samyn J L 117 15.60 78-11 Islefaxyou1132 Jaggery John1221½ [DH]Lahint115 13
Steadied early, in traffic turn
17Jly94- 8Bel fm 1¼ [T] :47 1:104 1:343 1:593 Lexington-G3 92 10 3 32½ 31 31 31¾ Samyn J L 117 6.70 90-09 Holy Mountain1121½ Islefaxyou112nk Check Ride117no Willingly 10
25Jun94- 8Bel fm 1 1/16 Ⓣ :224 :452 1:083 1:394 Hill Prince-G3 94 8 2 31½ 31 22 22½ Smith M E 119 10.30 96-11 Pennine Ridge1122½ Check Ride1192½ Add The Gold1141½ Second best 9
12Jun94- 8Mth fm 1 1/16 Ⓣ :224 :461 1:094 1:41 + JohnMcSorley35k 90 1 3 33 32½ 1hd 11½ Bravo J 113 *1.70 93-07 Check Ride1131½ Mr. Impatience1171½ Red Tazz1157 6
Balked gate, lugged in stretch, drvg
30May94- 6Bel fm 1¼ [T] :491 1:13 1:371 2:013 3↑ Alw 30000N2L 90 7 1 2½ 1½ 1½ 21 Samyn J L 112 *2.90 81-12 Moscow Magic1121 Check Ride1123 Nice Try George1142 Good effort 8
15May94- 4Bel fm 1 1/16 Ⓣ :231 :46 1:10 1:404 3↑ Alw 30000N2L 89 6 1 12 11 11 2no Samyn J L 111 4.30 94-12 Prayer Warrior119no Check Ride1112¾ Redenham119no Gamely 10
3May94- 7Bel gd 1 Ⓣ :232 :462 1:103 1:352 3↑ Alw 30000N1X 81 8 2 2½ 2hd 1hd 52 Samyn J L 110 *2.30 83-15 Gone For Real114½ Prayer Warrior119no The Plainsman1121 Dueled, tired 12
1Apr94- 6Hia fm *1⅛ Ⓣ 1:503 Alw 16500N1X 74 4 4 74½ 85¾ 63½ 44 Ramos W S 116 *1.50 75-16 DangerRanger1161¼ GallantGuest1162¾ MightyQuill119no Belated bid, wide 10
19Mar94-11Hia fm *1 1/16 Ⓣ 1:412 Citation40k 72 7 2 22½ 42½ 53½ 55½ Maple E 112 4.90 89-07 Youthful Legs112nk Beware The Quest1123 Theater Of War1132¼ Faded 7
WORKOUTS: May 25 Bel 5f fst 1:03 B 7/7 May 16 Bel 3f fst :361 B 4/18 May 7 Bel 5f fst :593 H 4/23 May 2 Bel 4f gd :50 B 16/22 Apr 23 Bel 4f fst :482 H 10/28

Gem Seeker
Own: DeSeroux Laura & Port Sidney L
SAMYN J L (34 0 3 8 .00)

Ch. c. 4
Sire: Jade Hunter (Mr. Prospector)
Dam: Vaguely Essence (Vaguely Noble)
Br: San Gabriel Investments (Ky)
Tr: Clement Christophe (15 3 0 5 .20)

120

Lifetime Record: 8 2 3 1 $49,560											
1995	3	2	0	1	$27,360	Turf	5	2	2	1	$40,560
1994	4	M	3	0	$22,200	Wet	1	0	1	0	$6,600
Bel Ⓣ	2	0	1	1	$10,560	Dist Ⓣ	0	0	0	0	

17May95- 6Bel fm 1 1/16 [T] :233 :462 1:101 1:413 3↑ Alw 36000N2X 89 1 5 42½ 42½ 21 31¾ Samyn J L 118 3.90 86-12 Arduous1181 Wavering Man118¾ Gem Seeker1181 Rail bid, weakened 10
31Mar95- 9Hia fm *1 1/16 Ⓣ 1:431 Alw 15000N1X 88 2 6 67½ 53 11½ 15 Douglas R R 114 *.90 86-15 Gem Seeker1145 Proof Time1194¼ Assorted Donuts1143 9
Crowded, pinched back start, driving
20Jan95- 2GP fm *1⅛ Ⓣ :474 1:131 1:382 1:514+ Md Sp Wt 82 3 3 43 32 22 12¼ Samyn J L 120 *.60 86-13 Gem Seeker1202¼ Thirty Good Ones1201¾ Dixieland King120nk 10
Six wide top str, driving
15Nov94- 3Aqu gd 1 1/16 Ⓣ :224 :48 1:123 1:453 3↑ Md Sp Wt 77 9 8 713 55 2½ 2no Samyn J L 120 4.20 81-19 John's Call120no Gem Seeker1208¾ Exclusive Casino1201 Sharp try 9
1Oct94- 4Bel my 1 1/16 ⊗ :23 :462 1:12 1:452 3↑ Md Sp Wt 72 3 1 12 16 13 23 Samyn J L 119 *1.10 72-19 Ace The Test1173 Gem Seeker11917 Thunderbolted12210 Weakened 7
14Sep94- 1Bel fm 1 1/16 [T] :233 :464 1:12 1:433 3↑ Md Sp Wt 69 5 5 47½ 23 13 22¼ Smith M E 118 *2.80 76-14 Skipton1182¼ Gem Seeker118¾ Royce Joseph1181 Bid, weakened 10
15Jly94- 3Hol fst 7f :214 :443 1:101 1:23 3↑ Md Sp Wt 68 8 4 11½ 13 1½ 47¼ Black C A B 117 4.20 82-12 Dancing Torch117no Western Trip1172¼ Colonial Reel1175 Weakened 8
28Dec93- 6SA fst 6f :214 :441 :562 1:083 Md Sp Wt 43 5 7 51¾ 66¼ 813 919 Black C A B 118 8.00 75-05 Isitingood1183¼ Commanche Trail1182 White Statuary118¾ Gave way 9
WORKOUTS: Apr 26 Bel 3f fst :362 H 3/16 Mar 16 GP 4f fst :514 B 38/40 Mar 2 GP 4f fst :52 B 25/29

The 2-1 favorite was Kerfoot Corner, who had been a troubled-trip second in his 4-year-old debut three weeks earlier. Proceeded and Check Ride were co-second choices at 3-1; Proceeded was a lightly-raced gelding who had won his grass debut directly off a freshening of slightly more than six weeks; Check Ride had raced evenly, finishing a close-up fourth when favored in his 4-year-old bow two weeks ago. Gem Seeker had been a length in front of Check Ride first time back from a 46-day freshening, and was the fourth choice at 7-1. Neither Dutchess First, at 10-1, nor Moscow Magic, at 13-1, had been out in months.

With the exception of Moscow Magic, a deep closer who was probably ironing out the kinks with an eye toward a future try at his optimum distance of a mile and a quarter, precious little separated the remaining quintet — each of whom had proven capable of Beyering in the mid-to-upper 80s.

This was one of those races where the initial stages of the handicapping process had not pointed out a clear course of action; it would be necessary to consult the toteboard and observe the post parade and pre-race warmups before a final decision could be reached.

As it happened, Dutchess First, at 10-1, was the best price among the five contenders, which was due to the fact that he hadn't been out since mid-October, when he had finished last as the 9-5 favorite in an allowance at the Meadowlands. There had still been several weeks of grass racing remaining in the Northeast that fall, so the fact that the well-regarded Dutchess First had not raced again after running so poorly suggested he'd sustained some sort of season-ending injury; this is why I tend to give horses the benefit of the doubt when they show an ugly-looking line just prior to being shelved. The trick here was gauging whether Dutchess First was ready to fire first time back.

I thought 10-1 odds on that proposition represented good value. Dutchess First made an exceptionally good appearance going to the post (players desiring to learn more about evaluating horses physicality are urged to read *Postures, Profiles and Performance*, written by Joe Takach, who has also produced two videos on the subject: *Beat the Beam*, and *Spotting the Ready-to-win Racehorse*). Plus, he had won both of his starts on Belmont grass at the 1994 spring-summer meeting; although those wins had come after a prep at Pimlico, it was conceivable that trainer Michael Dickinson had simply brought the horse to Belmont when he believed him to be ready. And if that were the case, then Dickinson must have felt Dutchess First did not need a prep race this time.

Indeed, trainer-handicappers were aware that Dickinson had been bombarding the Northeast (and points as far west as Sportsman's Park) with fit-and-ready returnees from his base of operations in Fair Hill, Maryland:

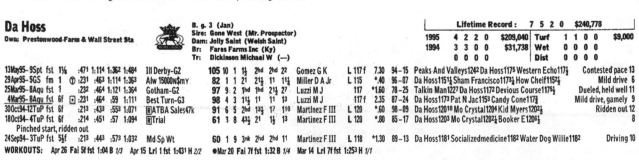

Da Hoss had been acquired by Prestonwood Farm and sent to winter with Dickinson after running the fastest six furlongs ever by a 2-year-old: 1:07 1/5 over a sun-baked highway at Turf Paradise. Making his first start in over four months, the gelding had won Aqueduct's Grade 3 Best Turn Stakes under mild urging. Far from bouncing off that effort, he had subsequently sandwiched a pair of runnerup finishes in Grade 2 stakes routes around an allowance win on grass, an indication that he had been given a particularly stout conditioning foundation in preparation for the rigors that lay ahead.

It's Personal
Own: Prestonwood Farm
LUZZI M J (104 12 20 15 .12)

Dk. b or br m. 5
Sire: Personal Flag (Private Account)
Dam: Dance Hall Girl (Guerrero)
Br: Nielsen Gerald A (NY)
Tr: Dickinson Michael W (5 2 1 1 .40)

113

Lifetime Record:	17 6 4 1	$215,406			
1995	2 2 0 0	$69,000	Turf	9 4 1 0	$113,474
1994	10 3 2 0	$110,634	Wet	2 1 1 0	$20,340
Bel Ⓣ	5 2 0 0	$40,554	Dist Ⓣ	0 0 0 0	

19May95-9Pim gd	1 1/16 ⊗	:234 :474 1:122 1:433	3↑ ⒻGalloretteH-G3	96	4	2	21½	11	14	14	Krone J A	L 112 f	5.10	90-14	It's Personal1124 Churchbell Chimes112hd Open Toe1139½	Ridden out 6
4May95-6GS yl	170 Ⓣ	:231 :474 1:12 1:411	3↑ ⒻAlw 15000N$mY	87	6	1	11½	11	11½	1¾	Elliott S	L 114	2.60	93-09	It's Personal114¾ Kira's Dancer1131¼ Churchbell Chimes114¾	Driving 7
12Nov94-8Aqu gd	1½ Ⓣ	:51 1:153 2:071 2:314	3↑ ⒻLongIslandH-G2	37	9	4	1½	32	1024	12361½	Velazquez J R	111	7.80e	60-03	Market Booster1158½ Tiffany's Taylor114no Lady Affirmed113¾	Gave way 12
15Oct94-7Bel fm	1 1/16 [T]	:25 :483 1:112 1:403	3↑ Ⓕ[S]TiconderogaH75k	74	6	2	21	21	34	711½	Samyn J L	115	3.00	81-05	Putthepowdertoit1155 Great Triumph1121½ Irish Linnet1261	Tired 11
7Oct94-9Med fm	1 1/16 Ⓣ	:234 :481 1:114 1:423	3↑ ⒻViolet H-G3	97	6	1	1hd	12	13½	11½	Velazquez J R	111	6.80	88-13	It's Personal1111½ Carezza115½ Artful Pleasure109no	Driving 11
10Sep94-8Bel fm	1 1/16 [T]	:233 :462 1:102 1:392	3↑ ⒻNobleDamsIH-G3	34	9	1	11½	2hd	1022	1033¾	Krone J A	109 b	7.40	65-11	Irish Linnet1176½ Statuette1131 Cox Orange117¾	Used up 10
17Aug94-9Sar fm	1⅛ Ⓣ	:464 1:10 1:334 1:462	3↑ Ⓕ[S]Yaddo H86k	102	8	2	2½	11	12	21	Krone J A	111 b	6.60	94-10	Irish Linnet1231 It's Personal1115 All Tango1105	Gamely 10
13Jly94-8Bel fm	1 1/16 Ⓣ	:241 :48 1:113 1:404	3↑ Ⓕ[S]Mt Vernon H55k	93	5	1	2hd	2hd	2hd	41	Davis R G	112 b	3.20	93-09	IrishActress116¾ GrtTriumph113no Tiffny'sTylor120nk	Weakened slightly 8
2Jly94-6Bel fm	1 1/16 Ⓣ	:233 :46 1:10 1:412	3↑ Ⓕ[S]Alw 32000N2X	97	3	2	31½	31	1½	16½	Davis R G	119	3.20	91-15	It's Personal1196½ Tensie's Pro1063¾ Dana's Wedding1171½	Ridden out 10
12Jun94-5Bel fm	1 1/16 [T]	:231 :464 1:11 1:413	3↑ Ⓕ[S]Alw 30000N1X	84	6	1	11½	11½	12	11	Davis R G	119 b	6.60	88-08	It's Personal1191 Royal Pelliknow1146 Royal Cozzene1142¾	Driving 8

WORKOUTS: Apr 30 Fai 4f fst :51 B 1/1

It's Personal had evidently been hampered by some sort of breathing/bleeding problem toward the tail-end of her 1994 campaign, but had come back on Lasix for two starts on turf and dirt earlier this month (May), and had won them both.

Counterthreat
Own: Dickinson Michael W
KRONE J A (83 20 15 15 .24) $30,000

Dk. b or br g. 3 (May)
Sire: Proud Birdie (Proud Clarion)
Dam: Count 'n Time (Jig Time)
Br: Carl Hughes (Fla)
Tr: Dickinson Michael W (3 1 1 0 .33)

109

Lifetime Record:	3 M 1 0	$3,200		
1995	1 M 1 0	$3,200	Turf	0 0 0 0
1994	2 M 0 0		Wet	0 0 0 0
Bel	1 0 1 0	$3,200	Dist	0 0 0 0

17May95-1Bel fst	1 1/16	:24 :481 1:144 1:482	3↑ Md 30000	65	10	5	42½	2hd	1½	2nk	Krone J A	110 f	19.30	57-32	Furious Folly113nk Counterthreat110hd Brave Warrior1081½	Wide, gamely 13
8Nov94-1Pha fst	170	:234 :483 1:143 1:46	Md Sp Wt	15	4	1	2½	67	618	624¼	Ryan K	L 121 f	13.60	46-33	Spanish Charge12110 Sir Alexander121¾ Golden Lord1212½	Stopped 7
16Oct94-6Pha fst	170	:221 :461 1:131 1:451	Md Sp Wt	20	7	5	512	610	712	718½	Ryan K	120 f	16.00	55-22	Devil's Brew1202¾ Arcentales1201½ Wild Point1208	No factor 9

WORKOUTS: May 13 Fai 3f fst :372 B 1/2 May 4 Fai 4f fst :531 B 5/6 Apr 26 Fai 3f fst :38 B 1/1

Counterthreat, like Da Hoss and It's Personal, had been away since the previous autumn. He didn't win his maiden-claiming route on May 17 but he certainly had been well meant, fighting gamely through a bitter stretch drive to miss by a scant neck at nearly 20-1. (Trainer-handicapping not only provided a strong clue that any Dickinson-trained returnees were live right now, it also indicated that front bandages were not the negative with Dickinson that they often are with other horsemen: note that Da Hoss, It's Personal and Counterthreat all ran well in front wraps.)

With such overwhelming evidence on the readiness of Dickinson's layoff runners, handicappers were obliged to support them at 10-1:

EIGHTH RACE
Belmont
MAY 31, 1995

1 MILE. (Turf)(1.322) ALLOWANCE. Purse $36,000. 3-year-olds and upward which have never won three races. Weights: 3-year-olds, 114 lbs. Older, 124 lbs. Non-winners of $18,000 twice since April 27, allowed 2 lbs. $8,500 since May 3, 4 lbs. (Claiming races not considered in allowances.)

Value of Race: $36,000 Winner $21,600; second $7,200; third $3,960; fourth $2,160; fifth $1,080. Mutuel Pool $237,272.00 Exacta Pool $317,325.00 Triple Pool $271,924.00

Last Raced	Horse	M/Eqt.	A.	Wt	PP	St	¼	½	¾	Str	Fin	Jockey	Odds $1
14Oct94 10Med11	Dutchess First		4	120	2	7	84	6½	8½	3½	13	Luzzi M J	10.40
10May95 6Bel2	Kerfoot Corner	b	4	120	6	5	51	5½	5½	1½	23	Bailey J D	2.00
25Jan95 7GP6	Moscow Magic	f	4	120	4	10	10	9½	6½	4½	31½	Santos J A	13.60
17May95 6Bel3	Gem Seeker		4	120	10	9	7hd	82	7½	51½	4hd	Samyn J L	7.00
17May95 6Bel4	Check Ride		4	120	9	6	6hd	7½	2hd	21	51	Krone J A	3.25
30Apr95 5Aqu1	Proceeded	f	4	120	1	4	3½	41	4½	61	65½	Beckner D V	3.40
19Apr95 5Aqu4	Gallant Guest	bf	4	120	7	1	1hd	11	11	82	7nk	Smith M E	23.80
21Apr95 9Kee6	Super Twenty Five		4	120	5	3	41½	3hd	3hd	7½	82½	Leon F	30.00
6May95 6Bel1	Arz	b	4	117	3	8	9½	10	10	92½	95½	Perez R B5	25.50
21May95 7Bel11	Viva Sabona	b	3	110	8	2	26	22½	9hd	10	10	Chavez J F	39.25

OFF AT 4:30 Start Good. Won driving. Time, :22, :452, 1:104, 1:354 Course firm.

$2 Mutuel Prices:			
2-DUTCHESS FIRST	22.80	10.40	6.70
7-KERFOOT CORNER		3.60	3.40
5-MOSCOW MAGIC			6.30

$2 EXACTA 2-7 PAID $100.00 $2 TRIPLE 2-7-5 PAID $753.00

B. g, by Diesis–Dutchess Best, by Blakeney. Trainer Dickinson Michael W. Bred by Saddle Home Farm (Ky).

DUTCHESS FIRST reserved early while saving ground, steadied while lacking room on the turn, angled out in upper stretch, then unleashed a strong late run to win going away. KERFOOT CORNER settled in the middle of the pack for five furlongs, circled five wide into the stretch, accelerated to the front, opening a clear lead in midstretch, but couldn't withstand the winner's late charge. MOSCOW MAGIC trailed for a half after breaking slowly, circled six wide to reach contention at the top of the stretch, then lacked a strong closing bid. GEM SEEKER unhurried for six furlongs while between horses, failed to threaten while improving his position. CHECK RIDE settled just off the early pace, rallied three wide to threaten on the turn, battled between horses into midstretch and tired. PROCEEDED raced up close to the turn then tired in the drive. GALLANT GUEST set the pace under pressure to the top of the stretch and tired. SUPER TWENTY FIVE well placed early, rallied between horses while four wide on the turn, then flattened out. ARZ never reached contention. VIVA SABONA was used up forcing the early pace.

Owners— 1, Haverhals Jacob; 2, Rokeby Stables; 3, Pen-Y-Bryn Farm; 4, DeSeroux Laura & Port Sidney L; 5, Royal Lines Stable & Whelan David; 6, Harbor View Farm; 7, N Y Chezam Stable; 8, Live Oak Plantation; 9, Haley Terrence W & Wickman Joseph F; 10, Garren Murray M

Trainers—1, Dickinson Michael W; 2, Miller MacKenzie; 3, Whiteley David A; 4, Clement Christophe; 5, Hough Stanley M; 6, Jerkens H Allen; 7, Martin Jose; 8, Kelly Patrick J; 9, Lake Robert P; 10, Garren Murray M

Scratched— Holy Mountain (19Nov94 8AQU12), Indian Sun (3May95 6CD4), Kan't Stop Kris (20May95 2BEL7), Erumpent O'rolli (24May95 5BEL9)

EIGHT DAYS LATER, a short-term trainer trend similar to Dickinson's spotlighted another well-meant returnee on the grass, the Leo O'Brien-trained Tiffany's Taylor. What's more, this 5-year-old had won first time back from a layoff in each of the three previous years, which qualified her among the finalists for *Bet of the Meet.*

8 Belmont Park

1 1/16 MILES. **(Inner Turf). (1:391) ALLOWANCE. Purse $48,000. Fillies and mares, 4-year-olds and upward which have not won a sweepstake of $25,000 in 1994–95. Weight, 122 lbs. Non-winners of $20,000 twice at a mile or over since October 1, allowed 3 lbs. $25,000 on the turf in 1995 or $20,000 twice on the turf since August 1, 6 lbs. $20,000 at a mile or over since October 1, or $15,000 twice on the turf in 1995, 9 lbs. (Maiden and claiming races not considered in allowances). (High weights preferred.)**

INNER TURF COURSE — 1 1/16 MILES — START — FINISH

Lotta Dancing

Own: Doubleday Heidi

DAVIS R G (110 13 21 13 .12)

B. f. 4
Sire: Alydar (Raise a Native)
Dam: Lotka (Danzig)
Br: Kennelot Stables Ltd (Ky)
Tr: McGaughey Claude III (22 3 4 3 .14)

119

Lifetime Record:	9 5 3 0	$139,415			
1995	4 2 2 0	$64,422	Turf	2 1 1 0	$38,822
1994	5 3 1 0	$74,993	Wet	2 0 2 0	$29,960
Bel (T)	0 0 0 0		Dist (T)	1 1 0 0	$29,422

28Apr95-9Kee fm 1⅛ (T) :484 1:133 1:374 1:492 ⒻAlw 45590C 91 2 4 46 43½ 34 22 Sellers S J 113 *1.10 88-06 Polish Treaty1132 Lotta Dancing113nk Heavenliness1123½ Gained place 6

14Apr95-9Kee fm 1 1/16 (T) :233 :474 1:123 1:431 ⒻAlw 44180NC 94 4 6 65½ 55 33 11½ Smith M E 113 2.80 90-13 LottDncing1131½ Onceinbluemmoon1122½ RomnHeiress1122 Steady drive 8

13Mar95-7GP sly 1 1/16 ⊗ :24 :484 1:131 1:451 ⒻAlw 40590N4X 74 4 3 31 31 46½ 27½ Sellers S J 116 *.40 74-19 Hadee Mae1187½ Lotta Dancing1162¾ Cut The Pot116nk 4

Nine wide top str, rallied

23Feb95-9GP fst 7f :224 :461 1:11 1:233 ⒻAlw 29000N3X 89 8 1 61¾ 52¼ 32 1¾ Sellers S J 116 *.90 85-20 Lotta Dancing116¾ Very Sentimental118¾ Kudos For Sweets1164¼ 8

Seven wide top str, ridden out

20May94-9Pim fst 1⅛ :47 1:114 1:374 1:51 ⒻBlackEydSsn-G2 63 6 10 1112 1314 1120 819¾ Sellers S J 114 5.70 70-24 Calipha1142¼ Bunting1147 Golden Braids1141 Wide 13

4May94-7CD fst 1 1/16 :234 :473 1:131 1:454 ⒻAlw 34020N2X 80 5 6 67½ 43 32½ 1nk Sellers S J 121 *.80 85-16 Lotta Dancing121nk Joan Noble1211½ Show Special1211½ Hard drive 9

10Apr94-8Kee my *7f :223 :453 1:114 1:282 ⒻBeaumont-G2 76 1 1 43 42¾ 32½ 24 Sellers S J 113 *1.60 83-15 Her Temper1124 Lotta Dancing1131 Term Limits1214½ 6

In tight, checked 3/16s, altered course, 2nd best

1Mar94-8GP fst 7f :221 :444 1:102 1:24 ⒻAlw 28000N2L 70 5 4 63¾ 54¼ 72¾ 1¾ Sellers S J 121 *1.20 83-12 Lotta Dancing121¾ Lady Tori118¾ Dazzle Me Darling1181½ 9

Seven wide top str, driving

6Feb94-6GP fst 7f :223 :452 1:104 1:233 ⒻMd Sp Wt 76 3 6 3nk 1hd 12 13½ Sellers S J 121 *1.10 85-11 Lotta Dancing1213½ Code Of Old1214¼ Blushing Maggie1211¼ Handily 10

WORKOUTS: Jun 5 Bel 4f fst :49 B *19/36* May 29 Bel 4f my :494 B (d) *2/11* May 22 Bel 5f fst 1:012 H *10/43* May 13 Bel 5f fst 1:003 H *4/33* Apr 26 Kee 4f fst :472 H *2/25* Apr 13 Kee 3f fst :364 B *6/15*

Knocknock

Own: Schwartz Herbert

SAMYN J L (47 0 6 9 .00)

Dk. b or br f. 4
Sire: Dynaformer (Roberto)
Dam: Bonnie Empress (Young Emperor)
Br: Schwartz Herbert T (Ky)
Tr: Schwartz Scott M (17 0 3 2 .00)

116

Lifetime Record:	19 4 2 4	$125,756			
1995	2 0 0 0		Turf	16 4 2 3	$124,076
1994	13 3 2 3	$107,876	Wet	0 0 0 0	
Bel (T)	8 1 2 1	$41,754	Dist (T)	8 2 0 2	$67,436

28May95-8Bel fm 1 1/16 (T) :23 :461 1:10 1:404 ⒻAlw 48000N$mY 82 7 4 54 53 76½ 77¾ Luzzi M J 115 32.25 86-14 Grafin1184 Coronation Cup118½ Statuette121no Bumped 1/4 pl 8

18May95-8Bel fm 1 (T) :232 :463 1:104 1:352 ⒻAlw 40000N4X 72 5 5 87¼ 85¾ 74½ 79¼ Luzzi M J 113 18.80 77-14 Great Lady Mary1131¾ Vice On Ice1131¾ Great Triumph114nk No threat 8

13Nov94-3Aqu gd 1⅛ (T) :47 1:12 1:382 1:511 3↑ ⒻAlw 36000N3X 92 2 2 28 25 2½ 12¼ Luzzi M J 115 5.20 84-16 Knocknock1152¼ Manila Lila117nk Waquoit's Tune1123 Driving 10

26Oct94-7Aqu gd 1⅛ (T) :482 1:132 1:381 1:504 3↑ ⒻAlw 36000N3X 79 9 3 31½ 31 85¾ 65¼ Santos J A 114 4.60 80-15 Caress119nk Manila Lila1171¾ Petiteness116nk Tired 10

14Oct94-3Med fm 1 1/16 (T) :223 :461 1:103 1:413 ⒻJersey Blues40k 83 7 3 44 42 42 43¾ Santos J A 116 *1.50 89-07 Accountinquestion1162¼ Casa Eire1161 New Wave121½ No solid rally 7

1Oct94-8Bel sf 1 1/16 [T] :243 :49 1:141 1:463 ⒻRarePerfumH-G2 85 7 3 31 32 45 47¼ Santagata N 114 9.00 56-37 Jade Flush1116½ Lady Affirmed117¾ Saxuality117no No late bid 8

5Sep94-9Med fm 1 1/16 (T) :23 :471 1:111 1:412 ⒻBoilnSprngH-G3 89 1 5 64¼ 42½ 34 34¼ Santagata N 115 6.40 90-12 Avie's Fancy1193 Teasing Charm1131¼ Knocknock1151¾ Mild bid 7

24Aug94-6Sar gd 1 1/16 (T) :242 :481 1:123 1:433 3↑ ⒻAlw 32000N2X 91 7 4 43 31½ 2hd 1¾ Day P 112 *1.60 76-22 Knocknock112¾ Uncharted Waters1123½ Kris's Kiss117½ Driving 9

3Aug94-9Sar yl 1 1/16 (T) :231 :48 1:123 1:434 ⒻNijana-G3 94 5 3 33 85 51½ 33½ Day P 114 22.60 71-25 Alywow1213½ Irish Forever121no Knocknock1142 Willingly 9

Run in divisions

7Jly94-7Bel fm 1¼ [T] :501 1:142 1:381 2:014 3↑ ⒻAlw 32000N2X 86 3 4 42½ 52½ 54½ 33¼ Smith M E 116 6.00 78-16 Teasing Charm114nk Jiving Around1173 Knocknock1161½ Mild rally 7

WORKOUTS: May 9 Aqu 5f fst 1:052 B *6/6* May 4 Aqu 5f fst 1:043 B *4/4* Apr 27 Aqu 5f fst 1:04 B *6/9* Apr 22 Aqu 5f fst 1:033 B *4/6* Apr 17 Aqu 5f fst 1:031 B *1/3* Apr 12 Aqu 4f fst :52 B *8/11*

Island Of Silver

Own: Godolphin Racing Inc

SANTOS J A (123 24 11 18 .20)

Ch. f. 4
Sire: Forty Niner (Mr. Prospector)
Dam: Embellished (Seattle Slew)
Br: Eaton Farms Inc, Red Bull Stable et al (Ky)
Tr: McLaughlin Kiaran P (17 2 3 2 .12)

116

Lifetime Record:	14 6 2 3	$89,710			
1995	3 1 0 0	$30,240	Turf	9 4 2 2	$50,212
1994	9 5 2 2	$56,743	Wet	2 1 0 0	$30,240
Bel (T)	0 0 0 0		Dist (T)	0 0 0 0	

26May95-8Bel my 1 1/16 :233 :463 1:11 1:414 ⒻAlw 48000N$mY 40 5 1 1½ 24 518 535 Velazquez J R 116 *1.10 55-20 Vinista12210 Starry Val1228 Dancer's Gate11112 Used up 5

12May95-8Bel my 1 1/16 ⊗ :23 :453 1:102 1:431 ⒻAlw 48000N$YmT 92 3 2 1hd 1½ 11½ 1nk Smith M E 114 9.30 83-23 Island Of Silver114nk Starry Val1178 Dancer's Gate1124 Fully extended 6

19Feb95♦ NadAlSheba(UAE) fst *1¼ LH 2:072 3↑ Handicap (Class 2) Hcp 13600 625¾ Carroll J 130 – Karoo Lark1134¾ Highland Dress1225 Lost Soldier1311½ 7

Tr: Hilal Ibrahim

Led after 2f,headed 4f out,weakened 3f out.No betting

15Dec94♦ NadAlSheba(UAE) fst *1¼ LH 2:093 3↑ Handicap (Class 1) Hcp 16300 316½ Carroll J 126 – Cayumanque1321½ Azhar13215 Island Of Silver126 3

Tracked leader,bid 3f out,weakened 2f out.No betting

1Dec94♦ NadAlSheba(UAE) fst *1¼ LH 2:072 3↑ Handicap (Class 2) Hcp 13600 16 Carroll J 127 – Island Of Silver1276 Iftakhaar12314 Esbooain132 3

Led throughout,unchallenged.No betting

29Aug94♦ Newcastle(GB) fm *1¼ (T) LH 2:072 3↑ ⒻVirginia Rated Hcp (Listed) Stk 24100 21¼ Dettori L 133 *2.50 Monaassabaat1271¼ Island Of Silver1332½ Sue's Artiste1181¼ 7

Tr: John Gosden

Tracked leader,led 2-1/2f out,headed 100y out

9Aug94♦ Bath(GB) gd *1¼ (T) LH 2:081 3↑ ⒻUpavon Stakes (Listed) Stk 25800 11 Dettori L 117 *.80 Island Of Silver1171 Noble Rose1173½ Dance To The Top1173 8

Led throughout,roused over 1f out,ridden out

27Jly94♦ Goodwood(GB) gd 1⅛ (T) RH 1:552 3↑ ⒻDrayton Handicap Hcp 18800 12 Dettori L 135 *1.25 Island Of Silver1352 Lady Williams1133½ Bird Of Time1231¼ 11

Chased leader in hand,led over 2f out,pushed clear 1f out

15Jly94♦ Newbury(GB) gd *1¼ (T) LH 2:08 ⒻWhite Horse Handicap Hcp 10000 13½ Dettori L 133 *4.00 Island Of Silver1333½ Tandia124no Regal Pursuit1192 11

Soon led,drew clear over 2f out,won under wraps

Tango Charlie
Own: Team Canonie Inc
KRONE J A (114 25 17 25 .22)

Ch. m. 6
Sire: Cure The Blues (Stop the Music)
Dam: La Vie (Le Fabuleux)
Br: Mill Ridge Farm Ltd (Ky)
Tr: Hough Stanley M (31 4 8 2 .13)

113

Lifetime Record: 31 6 2 9 $235,127
1995 5 0 0 0 $8,400 Turf 21 3 1 4 $187,047
1994 4 1 1 1 $40,880 Wet 2 1 0 1 $16,645
Bel ⓣ 2 0 0 0 $2,760 Dist ⓣ 11 1 0 2 $69,167

28May95-8Bel fm 1 1/16 ⓣ :23 :461 1:10 1:404 ⒻAlw 48000N$mY 84 5 3 32 31 23 66¾ Perez R B5 111 b 8.90 87-14 Grafin1184 Coronation Cup118½ Statuette121no Bid, tired 8
2Apr95-11Hia fm 1 1/8 ⓣ 1:39 3↑ ⒻHia Bud BCH107k 73 11 5 55½ 67½ 1010 1011¼ McCauley W H L 113 b 16.30 92 — Cox Orange120nk Apolda1121¼ P J Floral114nk 11
Bumped first turn, faltered
11Mar95-7GP fm 1 1/16 ⓣ :233 :484 1:132 1:432+ 3↑ ⒻBuckramOakH-G3 94 8 6 31½ 41½ 1hd 41½ Krone J A L 112 b 16.20 77-18 Cox Orange1181¼ Weekend Madness118nk Ma Guerre113hd Weakened 11
24Feb95-4GP fm *1 1/16 ⓣ :234 :484 1:124 1:423+ ⒻAlw 40000N$mY 93 7 2 2hd 1hd 1hd 4½ Suckie M C L 114 b 7.00 95 — La Turka114no Shir Dar116hd Icy Warning114nk 9
Six wide top str, weakened
23Jan95-8GP fm 1 1/16 ⓣ :24 :473 1:12 1:422+ ⒻAlw 40000N$mY 80 8 3 1½ 1½ 21½ 58½ Suckie M C L 115 b 11.80 75-16 Cox Orange1154¼ Track Gossip1151½ P J Floral1151½ Weakened 9
2Apr94-11Hia fm 1 1/8 ⓣ 1:421 3↑ ⒻHia Bud BCH108k 81 2 2 2½ 1hd 2½ 107¼ Ramos W S L 114 b 4.90 85-10 Winnetka1132¼ Topsa114no La Piaf113no Faltered 11
12Mar94-4GP fm 1 1/16 ⓣ :231 :461 1:10 1:392+ 3↑ ⒻBuckrmOak H-G3 95 7 7 617 516 62¾ 35¼ McCarron C J L 115 b 19.20 94-02 Marshu'sRiver1155¼ Sheil'sRevenge117no TngoChrlie115nk Rallied outside 7
10Feb94-8GP fm *1 ⓣ :232 :464 1:11 1:374 ⒻAlw 42000N$Y 93 8 7 62¾ 41½ 1hd 11¾ Smith M E L 114 b 4.90 91-10 Tango Charlie1141¾ Terre Haute116½ Herat O' Mine114nk 10
Split horses upper str, driving
17Jan94-7GP fm *1 1/8 ⓣ :492 1:133 1:384 1:53 +ⒻClm c-90000 90 3 5 57 34 22½ 22 Bailey J D L 118 b 4.60 78-15 P J Floral1132 Tango Charlie118no French Steal1221¾ Rallied 10
Claimed from Canonie Tony Jr, Hough Stanley M Trainer
4Jly93-11Rkm fm 1 1/16 ⓣ :231 :473 1:114 1:43 3↑ ⒻRkm BC H104k 89 4 3 33 21½ 22½ 56½ Rojas R I LB 113 b 32.20 91-10 Via Borghese1152¾ Navarra1132 Miss Otis1101 Weakened 9
WORKOUTS: Jun 4 Bel 5f fst 1:011 B 3/11 May 21 Bel 5f fst 1:001 H 3/53 May 13 Bel 5f fst 1:003 H 4/33 May 4 Bel 3f fst :362 B 5/25 Mar 30 GP 4f fst :511 B 8/8 Mar 24 GP ⓣ 4f fm :50 B (d) 8/20

Statuette
Own: Blum Peter E
SMITH M E (97 25 15 14 .26)

B. m. 5
Sire: Pancho Villa (Secretariat)
Dam: Mine Only (Mr. Prospector)
Br: Blum Peter E (Ky)
Tr: Clement Christophe (23 4 1 6 .17)

119

Lifetime Record: 22 6 5 7 $316,620
1995 4 1 0 3 $49,269 Turf 19 5 4 6 $283,356
1994 8 1 2 2 $75,417 Wet 0 0 0 0
Bel ⓣ 11 3 4 3 $167,008 Dist ⓣ 12 3 3 5 $212,561

28May95-8Bel fm 1 1/16 ⓣ :23 :461 1:10 1:404 ⒻAlw 48000N$mY 89 1 8 88 84½ 44 34½ Smith M E 121 *1.00 89-14 Grafin1184 Coronation Cup118½ Statuette121no Bumped 1/4 pl 8
30Apr95-8Aqu fm 1 1/16 ⓣ :222 :454 1:103 1:42 3↑ ⒻBeaugay H-G3 91 5 8 717 87 54½ 33¼ Smith M E 116 *1.35 95-09 Caress1132¾ Shir Dar113¾ Statuette1161¼ Wide, belated rally 8
17Apr95-7Aqu fm 1 ⓣ :233 :481 1:124 1:372 3↑ ⒻHandicap50k 96 7 6 65½ 53 3½ 12 Smith M E 118 *.90 93-10 Statuette1182 Teasing Charm117no Tee Kay1152½ Wide, going away 7
5Mar95-10GP fm *1 1/16 ⓣ :233 :47 1:104 1:404+ ⒻAlw 44000N$mY 97 5 7 65 55 2hd 3nk Smith M E 114 2.90 104 — Irving's Girl114no Romy114nk Statuette1142¼ 10
Lacked response, inside
18Oct94-8Aqu fm 1 1/8 ⓣ :481 1:121 1:364 1:483 3↑ ⒻAthenia H-G3 87 3 9 96½ 104 73 55 Smith M E 112 *1.90e 92-03 Lady Affirmed1111¾ Irving's Girl1101¼ Cox Orange116no 11
Blocked 1/4 pl, steadied late
7Oct94-9Med fm 1 1/16 ⓣ :234 :481 1:114 1:423 3↑ ⒻViolet H-G3 92 1 10 85¼ 75¼ 44½ 42 Smith M E 114 *2.40 86-13 It's Personal1111½ Carezza115½ Artful Pleasure109no Finished well 11
10Sep94-8Bel fm 1 1/16 Ⓣ :233 :462 1:102 1:392 3↑ ⒻNobleDamslH-G3 94 5 10 1010 83½ 45½ 26½ Smith M E 113 *1.20e 92-11 Irish Linnet1176½ Statuette1131 Cox Orange117¾ Rallied inside 10
7Aug94-10Rkm fm *1 1/8 ⓣ 1:473 3↑ ⒻSpicyLivngH-G3 84 7 8 75½ 78 47 67½ McCauley W H B 115 3.70 88-18 SuspectTerrain1113 IcyWrning1152½ BelleNuit112½ Inside, flattened out 11
3Jly94-7Bel fm 7f ⓣ :231 :46 1:091 1:212 3↑ ⒻDrumtop55k 95 2 5 42½ 2½ 2hd 21 Smith M E 119 2.80 94-09 Lady Affirmed1081 Statuette119nk Sh Bang1141½ Gamely 6
15Jun94-8Bel fm 1 ⓣ :231 :46 1:09 1:324 3↑ ⒻJustAGame II55k 95 3 3 32½ 2½ 23 36¼ Samyn J L 119 3.60 92-09 Elizabeth Bay1146 Tiffany's Taylor117nk Statuette1198 Bid, weakened 5
WORKOUTS: Jun 5 Bel 3f fst :36 B 2/20 May 27 Bel 3f gd :363 B 5/9 May 21 Bel 4f fst :484 B 34/112 May 13 Bel 3f fst :38 B 16/25 Apr 27 Bel 3f fst :372 B 4/11 Apr 11 Bel 4f fst :49 B 9/18

Tiffany's Taylor
Own: Maher Theresa
VELAZQUEZ J R (108 20 7 12 .19)

B. m. 6
Sire: Titanic (Alydar)
Dam: Tiffany Dream (Blue Ensign)
Br: Giardina Jay A (NY)
Tr: O'Brien Leo (44 12 8 4 .27)

113

Lifetime Record: 42 9 10 3 $316,517
1994 12 2 4 1 $132,477 Turf 22 5 7 1 $215,183
1993 12 3 2 1 $86,660 Wet 11 1 3 1 $49,239
Bel ⓣ 10 2 2 1 $83,078 Dist ⓣ 12 4 2 1 $114,748

4Dec94-8Aqu fst 1 1/8 :493 1:143 1:392 1:52 3↑ ⒻⓈMontauk H54k 81 3 7 66½ 53 46 48 Migliore R 119 b 1.80e 68-34 Beloved Bea1136 Hey Baba Lulu116¾ Lottsa Talc1191¼ No threat 7
12Nov94-8Aqu gd 1½ ⓣ :51 1:153 2:071 2:314 3↑ ⒻLongIslandH-G2 88 7 9 94¾ 53½ 27 28½ Migliore R 114 b 14.90 88-03 MarketBooster1158½ Tiffany'sTaylor114no LdyAffirmed113¾ Up for place 12
18Oct94-8Aqu fm 1 1/8 ⓣ :481 1:121 1:364 1:483 3↑ ⒻAthenia H-G3 84 8 10 106¾ 94 104¾ 66½ Cruguet J 113 b 12.30 90-03 Lady Affirmed1111¾ Irving's Girl1101¼ Cox Orange116no No threat 11
15Oct94-7Bel fm 1 1/16 Ⓣ :25 :483 1:112 1:403 3↑ ⒻⓈTiconderogaH75k 78 11 9 87½ 88 77 59½ Migliore R 118 b *.60e 83-05 Putthepowdertoit1155 Great Triumph1121½ Irish Linnet1261 Late gain 11
27Sep94-8Bel sly 1 ⊗ :222 :444 1:093 1:363 3↑ ⓈAshlyTCole H56k 81 1 5 55¾ 44½ 43½ 46½ Velazquez J R 114 b 3.30 74-23 Terrorist1084 Corma Ray1152 My Mogul112nk Saved ground 7
29Aug94-7Sar fm 1⅜ Ⓣ :501 1:153 1:403 2:164 3↑ ⒻWaya55k 95 6 2 45 43 2hd 2nk Velazquez J R 113 b 2.30e 82-18 SaratogaSource113nk Tiffny'sTylor113½ MrketBooster122½ Rallied inside 7
21Aug94-7Sar sly 1 1/8 ⊗ :472 1:124 1:394 1:534 3↑ ⒻClm 100000 78 2 2 2½ 2hd 1½ 2no Velazquez J R 122 b 2.80 67-25 SchwayBabySwy114no Tiffny'sTylor1222 EenieMeenieMiney1147½ Gamely 5
7Aug94-10Rkm fm *1 1/8 ⓣ 1:473 3↑ ⒻSpicyLivngH-G3 79 10 9 119 1010 913 810 Mojica R Jr B 114 4.80 86-18 Suspect Terrain1113 Icy Warning1152½ Belle Nuit112½ Inside, no factor 11
13Jly94-8Bel fm 1 1/16 ⓣ :241 :48 1:113 1:404 3↑ ⒻⓈMt Vernon H55k 93 3 5 51¾ 62 52½ 3¾ Velazquez J R 120 *.80e 93-09 Irish Actress116¾ Great Triumph113no Tiffany's Taylor120nk Finished well 8
15Jun94-8Bel fm 1 ⓣ :231 :46 1:09 1:324 3↑ ⒻJustAGame II55k 96 1 4 43½ 43 35 26 Velazquez J R 117 3.50 92-09 Elizabeth Bay1146 Tiffany's Taylor117nk Statuette1198 Up for place 5
WORKOUTS: Jun 1 Bel Ⓣ 7f fm 1:31 B (d) 2/2 May 21 Bel 6f fst 1:14 H 3/22 May 14 Bel 6f fst 1:16 B 5/12 May 5 Bel 6f fst 1:152 B 4/12 Apr 21 HF 4f fst :504 B 2/2

Irving's Girl
Own: Anstu Stable
BAILEY J D (94 23 17 9 .24)

B. m. 5
Sire: Badger Land (Codex)
Dam: Card Table (Bold Bidder)
Br: Spring Farm (Ont-C)
Tr: Schulhofer Flint S (35 2 3 6 .06)

119

Lifetime Record: 29 6 6 3 $217,831
1995 5 1 1 0 $44,800 Turf 25 5 5 2 $193,641
1994 10 1 4 1 $78,756 Wet 0 0 0 0
Bel ⓣ 10 2 2 1 $67,290 Dist ⓣ 18 5 3 2 $141,113

19May95-8GS yl 1 1/8 ⓣ :471 1:12 1:374 1:482 3↑ ⒻVineland H-G3 89 8 8 88 83½ 44 45 Samyn J L 115 3.00 102-03 Northern Emerald1152¾ Kris's Kiss1092¼ Kira's Dancer113hd Some gain 8
15Apr95-9Hia fm 1 1/8 ⓣ 1:483 3↑ ⒻBlackHelenH-G3 73 6 6 62¾ 61¾ 710 713¼ Madrid S O 115 9.50 76-12 Alice Springs1203¼ Apolda1132¼ Cox Orange121nk No factor 7
5Mar95-10GP fm *1 1/16 ⓣ :233 :47 1:104 1:404+ ⒻAlw 44000N$mY 98 2 6 33½ 33½ 31½ 1no Bailey J D 114 *2.20 104 — Irving's Girl114no Romy114nk Statuette1142¼ 10
Steadied midstr, altered course, fully extended
8Feb95-9GP fm 1 1/8 ⓣ :482 1:113 1:353 1:472+ 3↑ ⒻSuwaneeRvrH-G3 95 6 4 43 45½ 43½ 23¾ Smith M E 113 13.90 91-09 Cox Orange1163¾ Irving's Girl1131 Alice Springs1202 Rallied 7
22Jan95-3GP fm 1 1/16 ⓣ :234 :48 1:12 1:424+ ⒻAlw 40000NC 87 5 5 55½ 63 66½ 56½ Santos J A 114 5.90 75-21 Elizabeth Bay116¾ Olden Lek1161 Caress1162¾ No threat 7
3Dec94-9Crc gd 1 1/8 ⓣ :49 1:131 1:38 1:503 3↑ ⒻMy Charmer H100k 96 1 6 53½ 42½ 44½ 42½ Santos J A 114 4.80 — — Caress114no Putthepowdertoit1142 Cox Orange116nk Late gain inside 12
18Oct94-8Aqu fm 1 1/8 ⓣ :481 1:121 1:364 1:483 3↑ ⒻAthenia H-G3 94 2 4 41½ 41½ 2½ 21¾ Krone J A 110 7.40e 95-03 Lady Affirmed1111¾ Irving's Girl1101¼ Cox Orange116no Rallied inside 11
7Oct94-9Med fm 1 1/16 ⓣ :234 :481 1:114 1:423 3↑ ⒻViolet H-G3 87 5 7 74½ 54½ 66¾ 64½ Krone J A 114 2.90 84-13 It's Personal1111½ Carezza115½ Artful Pleasure109no Even trip 11
3Sep94-6Bel fm 1 1/16 Ⓣ :25 :48 1:111 1:404 3↑ ⒻAlw 38000N4X 102 5 4 32 2½ 2½ 1nk Krone J A 117 2.60 92-14 Irving's Girl117nk Dahlia's Dreamer11710 La Turka117¾ Driving 5
21Aug94-8Mth gd 1 1/16 ⓣ :241 :48 1:122 1:443+ 3↑ ⒻEatontown40k 86 5 6 66½ 31½ 35 22½ Perret C 114 *2.30 72-27 Verbal Volley1192½ Irving's Girl114hd Uptown Show1132 Up for place 8
WORKOUTS: Jun 1 Bel Ⓣ 5f fm 1:022 B (d) 6/12 May 27 Bel tr.t 4f gd :493 B 3/7 May 14 Bel 5f fst 1:012 H 12/59 May 7 Bel 4f fst :484 B 11/35 Apr 23 Hia 4f fst :50 B 7/8 Apr 11 Hia ⓣ 5f fm 1:031 B (d) 2/3

Leo N' Me
Own: Smith Ralph E
MARTIN G J (65 6 6 10 .09)

Dk. b or br m. 5
Sire: Stacked Pack (Majestic Light)
Dam: More Berries (Ballymore)
Br: Rusty Mac Stables (NY)
Tr: O'Brien Leo (44 12 8 4 .27)

111⁵

Lifetime Record: 36 4 2 3 $87,350
1995 2 1 0 0 $21,600 Turf 16 2 2 2 $52,460
1994 14 0 1 2 $17,130 Wet 8 0 0 0 $3,540
Bel ⓣ 14 2 2 2 $52,460 Dist ⓣ 11 2 2 1 $48,380

14May95-10Bel fm 1 1/16 Ⓣ :244 :481 1:121 1:431 3↑ ⒻⓈAlw 36000N2X 84 5 10 84½ 72¾ 51½ 11¾ Martin G J5 115 11.70 80-12 Leo N' Me1151¾ Bien Sucre1103 Very True112½ Brk slow, checked 1/4 10
10May95-1Bel wf 6f :22 :451 :574 1:112 ⒻClm 14000 49 7 3 43 65 97 99¼ Velazquez J R 116 11.10 74-14 Personaltestimony1122¾ Chalynn109nk Palm Beach Dewey116hd Gave way 10
10Dec94-2Aqu fst 6f ⊡ :232 :473 1:001 1:13 ⒻClm 12000 39 2 4 54½ 44 59 49¼ Velazquez J R 113 6.40 68-20 Somthingscandalous1124 Music Tower1171½ Pet Carr1144 No threat 7
30Nov94-6Aqu fst 1 :233 :471 1:124 1:393 3↑ ⒻⓈAlw 34000N2X 41 1 5 36½ 48 514 518¼ Martin G J10 108 8.60 52-27 Et Vous1156 Shiani1171½ Toe Tappen1103 No threat 6
1Nov94-5Aqu sly 6f :223 :46 :583 1:112 3↑ ⒻⓈAlw 32000N2X 55 4 4 53¾ 63½ 46½ 411¼ Frost G C 117 14.10 74-18 Muddle1101 Sam'sInControl11510 Alexa'sLuckyStar115nk No threat, wide 6
29Oct94-9Aqu fm 1 1/8 ⓣ :483 1:13 1:374 1:503 3↑ ⒻClm 45000 66 9 6 712 810 710 911½ Frost G C 113 16.40 76-13 Spectaculaire1132¼ Louisville Lu1171 Miss Pocket Court1131 Outrun 10
14Oct94-6Bel fm 1¼ Ⓣ :483 1:13 1:38 2:021 3↑ ⒻClm 35000 66 9 9 812 84½ 76½ 66¾ Velazquez J R 117 5.20 72-14 SlewTheDuchess1171¼ Dan'sWedding117no FrenchStel117¾ Checked early 9
12Oct94-4Bel fm 1 1/16 Ⓣ :251 :483 1:122 1:423 3↑ ⒻClm 45000 51 4 8 86½ 910 914 917¼ Velazquez J R 113 8.70 66-18 Joy Of Life110½ Miss Pocket Court113¾ Hurry Up Marya1132½ 9
Took up early, steadied 9/16 pl, wide
22Sep94-4Bel fm 1 1/16 Ⓣ :251 :483 1:123 1:442 3↑ ⒻClm 35000 81 3 3 52½ 42½ 54½ 2¾ Velazquez J R 117 3.50 73-18 Turkolady117¾ Leo N' Me117nk Crandall117½ Steadied 1/2 pl 8
4Sep94-6Bel fm 1 ⓣ :224 :46 1:101 1:344 3↑ ⒻⓈAlw 34000N2X 79 10 4 53 41½ 32 31¾ Velazquez J R 117 11.40 86-10 Dinner Diamond117¾ HighTalent1171 LeoN'Me117nk Checked early, wide 12
WORKOUTS: May 7 Bel 5f fst 1:031 B 19/23

Tiffany's Taylor doesn't show any layoff wins in her past performances, but players should have no trouble deducing that she won her first two starts of the 1994 season, since she was 2-for-12 with neither victory appearing in her last 10 races. That fact, however, hardly scratched the surface of what Tiffany's Taylor was all about:

Tiffany's Taylor					B. m. 5															Lifetime Record :		31 8 6 2	$210,440	
Own: Maher Teresa M					Sire: Titanic (Alydar)															1994	1 1 0 0	$26,400	Turf	14 4 4 0 $123,24
					Dam: Tiffany Dream (Blue Ensign)															1993	12 3 2 1	$86,660	Wet	9 1 2 1 $38,36
					Br: Giardina Jay A (NY)														116	Bel ⑦	6 1 1 0	$35,360	Dist ⑦	9 3 2 0 $79,24
VELAZQUEZ J R (69 9 10 12 .13)					Tr: O'Brien Leo (26 7 2 2 .27)																			
6May94- 8Bel fm 1⅛ ⑦ :244 :474 1:12 1:41³ 3↑ ⑤Alw 44000N$Y					102 1 6 6⁵ 7³¾ 1½ 11½		Velazquez J R		115	10.50	90 - 15	Tiffany's Taylor115½ Mckaymackenna115⁵⁸ Belle Nuit115¼											Driving
25Nov93- 7Aqu gd 1⅛ :484 1:14 1:381 1:50² 3↑ ⑤Alw 44000Nc					87 2 9 86 74½ 2⁴ 1⁵		Cruguet J		122	4.10	86 - 09	Gainzer117⁵ Tiffany's Taylor122¼ Chipaya122ⁿᵏ											Rallied wide
18Nov93- 8Aqu yl 1⅛ :484 1:142 1:401 1:52³ 3↑ ⑤Alw 44000N$mY					91 1 8 74½ 63½ 1½ 1²		Cruguet J		119	8.10	80 - 20	Tiffany's Taylor119² French Steal117¼ Park Dream117ʰᵈ											Driving
17Oct93- 7Bel sf 1⅛ ⑦ :243 :481 1:13¼ 1:46¼ 3↑ ⑤Alw 36000N4X					81 6 5 55¼ 52½ 54½ 54¼		Cruguet J		117	6.80	60 - 35	Sheila's Revenge114¼¾ Park Dream114¾ Winnetka117ʰᵈ											Lacked rally
11Oct93- 8Bel fm 1⅛ ⑦ :24 :463 1:10 1:40¼ 3↑ ⑤Ashly Cole H73k					81 2 7 76 76¼ 53½ 59½		Cruguet J		110	10.70e	85 - 12	Preporant117⁴ Scott The Great117³ Forlibend113⁴											No threat
20ct93- 9Med yl 1⅛ ⑦ :234 :482 1:131 1:44¼ 3↑ ⑤Montclair35k					71 10 7 64½ 73¾ 75 98		Migliore R		117	2.60	69 - 26	Belle Of Amherst117¼¾ Whimscial Melody113½ Topsa117ⁿᵏ											Outrun
27Aug93- 6Sar fm 1⅛ ⑦ :233 :464 1:10⁴ 1:41² 3↑ ⑤Alw 32500N3X					91 2 5 5⁴ 41½ 1½ 1²		Migliore R		117	3.10	87 - 12	Tiffany's Taylor117² Dahlia's Dreamer117½ Life Is Delicious114²½											Driving
15Aug93- 5Sar fm 1⅛ ⑦ :231 :462 1:101 1:40¼ 3↑ ⑤Clm 85000					91 6 5 54½ 41½ 2ʰᵈ 2½		Migliore R		116	3.30	93 - 13	Belle Of Amherst114ʰᵈ Tiffany's Taylor116½ Spectaculaire112³											Gamely
2Aug93- 4Sar fm 1⅛ ⑦ :231 :471 1:10³ 1:41³ 3↑ ⑤Clm 75000					88 1 4 43½ 4³ 2½ 1³		Migliore R		117	21.70	86 - 11	Tiffany's Taylor117³ Cazzy B.117¼ Spectaculaire115¼											Driving
5Apr93- 8Aqu fst 1 :23 :46 1:10³ 1:36³ 3↑ ⑤Alw 32500N3X					55 5 7 76¾ 77¼ 78¼ 718¼		Velazquez J R		117	14.70	63 - 24	Reach For Clever117ⁿᵒ Cadillac Women117ⁿᵏ Starry Val117¾											Outrun
WORKOUTS: May 3 Bel 4f fst :47¼ H 2/47 Apr 23 Bel 4f fst :48³ H 10/39 ● Apr 16 Bel tr.t 5f my :59⁴ H 1/30 Apr 9 Bel tr.t 3f fst :37³ B 16/39																								

These pp's from earlier in her career reveal Tiffany's Taylor won her seasonal bow at Belmont on May 6, 1994, paying a $23 mutual in a classified allowance; the Beyer of 102 indicates she had been at her absolute peak that day. The bottom of the pp's shows that she returned from a layoff of almost four months on August 2, 1993, and smashed a field of high-priced claimers to the tune of a $45.40 payoff.

THIRD RACE
Aqueduct
MARCH 14, 1992

6 FURLONGS. (1.08) CLAIMING. Purse $22,000. Fillies, 3-year-olds. Weights, 121 lbs. Non-winners of two races since February 15 allowed 3 lbs. Of a race since then 5 lbs. Claiming Price $50,000; for each $2,500 to $45,000 2 lbs. (Races when entered to be claimed for $40,000 or less not considered.)

Value of race $22,000; value to winner $13,200; second $4,840; third $2,640; fourth $1,320. Mutuel pool $238,470. Exacta Pool $545,451.

Last Raced	Horse	M/Eqt.A.Wt	PP St	¼	½	Str	Fin	Jockey	Cl'g Pr	Odds $1
4Sep91 8Bel⁵	Tiffany's Taylor	3 116	5 4	2ʰᵈ	3¹	1²	15¼	Santiago A	50000	7.70
7Feb92 2Aqu²	Kate's College	3 116	4 1	4½	2¼	2¹½	2¼	Migliore R	50000	1.30
28Feb92 5Aqu⁶	Kersey	b 3 116	6 5	3¹	2¹	32½	34¾	Smith M E	50000	3.40
7Mar92 1Aqu¹	Angel Top	b 3 116	4 3	41½	5½	4ʰᵈ	41½	McCuley WH	50000	2.50
27Feb92 7Aqu⁹	Bear Beauty	3 113	1 2	5ʰᵈ	6	5¹	59½	Gryder A T	45000	27.10
28Feb92 7Aqu⁷	Hex Appeal	3 112	2 1	1¹	1ʰᵈ	6	6	Madrid A Jr	45000	6.70

OFF AT 1:57 Start good. Won driving. Time, :23¼, :47, :59³, 1:12¹ Track fast.

$2 Mutuel Prices:

5-(F)-TIFFANY'S TAYLOR	17.40	5.40	3.40
3-(D)-KATE'S COLLEGE		3.00	2.40
6-(G)-KERSEY			3.20

$2 EXACTA 5-3 PAID $53.20

B. f, (Feb), by Titanic—Tiffany Dream, by Blue Ensign. Trainer O'Brien Leo. Bred by Giardinia Jay A (NY).

TIFFANY'S TAYLOR, never far back, swung three wide to launch her bid on the turn then drew off under brisk urging. KATE'S COLLEGE bobbled at the start, was unhurried early, rapidly moved into contention while

The result chart shown above is from March 14, 1992, and shows that the winner, Tiffany's Taylor, had last raced on September 4 of the previous year.

What we have here is a mare with a three-year history of winning first time back from a layoff. Not only that, trainer handicappers know that O'Brien is in the midst of a torrid hot streak with returnees:

Fourstars Allstar					B. h. 7															Lifetime Record :		52 13 11 8	$1,448,069	
Own: Bomze Richard & Dileo Philip F					Sire: Compliance (Northern Dancer)															1995	2 2 0 0	$79,050	Turf	45 12 10 6 $1,392,528
					Dam: Broadway Joan (Bold Arian)															1994	11 1 3 2	$219,665	Wet	3 1 0 1 $17,280
					Br: Bomze Richard M (NY)														118	Atl ⑦	1 0 1 0	$95,000	Dist ⑦	5 0 2 0 $121,092
SANTOS J A (—)					Tr: O'Brien Leo (—)																			
29May95- 8Bel fm 1 ⑦ :233 :464 1:10¼ 1:34² Alw 48000N$Y					106 1 2 2½ 2½ 2¼ 1ⁿᵏ		Santos J A		123 b	2.40	91 - 14	Fourstars Allstar123ⁿᵏ Bonus Award113½ Kiri's Clown123⁶½											Fully extended 7
29Apr95- 8Aqu fm 1⅛ ⑦ :223 :462 1:10 1:41³ 3↑ Ft Marcy H-G3					105 5 6 6⁵ 54 11 14		Santos J A		118 b	6.10	101 - 05	Fourstars Allstar118⁴ Chief Master112¾ A In Sociology118¹											Going away 8
15Oct94- 8Bel fm 1⅛ :233 :461 1:09¼ 1:40¼ 3↑ ⑤Mohawk H75k					95 6 2 2¹½ 2¹ 2³ 5²½		Migliore R		122 b	4.10	94 - 05	My Mogul112¼ Head Trip112¼ A In Sociology123ⁿᵏ											Forced pace 7
9Oct94- 8Kee gd 1 ⑦ :232 :462 1:11³ 1:38³ 3↑ KeenelandBC-G3					77 9 5 44½ 68 811 812¼		Migliore R		126 b	5.40	64 - 25	Weekend Madness123¼ Words Of War123¼ Pennine Ridge123ⁿᵏ											Tired 10
17Sep94- 7Bel fm 1⅜ ⑦ :48 1:12¼ 1:36 2:11³ 3↑ Man O'War-G1					96 8 5 53 52¼ 64½ 77¾		Santos J A		126 b	7.60	88 - 14	Royal Mountain Inn126½ Flag Down126½ Fraise126½											Flattened out 9
3Sep94- 8Bel fm 1⅛ ⑦ :241 :471 1:10² 1:40 3↑ Bel Bud BCH-G3					103 6 6 6⁴ 74¾ 52¼ 2²		Santos J A		119 b	3.60	96 - 14	AInSociology116² FourstrsAllstr119ⁿᵏ HomeOfThe Fre114ⁿᵒ											Rallied inside 10
25Aug94- 9Sar sf 1⅛ ⑦ :483 1:141 1:40⁴ 1:54¼ 3↑ ⑤West Point H84k					72 1 6 52¾ 43½ 46¼ 416¼		Santos J A		124 b	*1.10	39 - 25	ExcellentTipper115⁵ MyMogul112¼¾ PridOfSummr116⁶½											Lacked response 8
25Jly94- 8Sar fm 1⅛ ⑦ :232 :464 1:10⁴ 1:41¼ 3↑ Daryl'sJoyH-G3					102 2 8 74 73½ 33¼ 32¼		Santos J A		120 b	*1.00	86 - 15	A In Sociology115ⁿᵏ Namaqualand113² Fourstars Allstar120ⁿᵏ											9
Lacked room, blocked 1/4 pl																								
26Jun94- 7Atl fm 1⅛ ⑦ :473 1:10² 1:34¼ 1:52³ 3↑ CaesrsIntlH-G1					107 4 4 43½ 41¾ 1¹ 2ⁿᵒ		Bravo J		117 b	6.20	98 - 06	Lure123ⁿᵒ Fourstars Allstar117¾ Star Of Cozzene121¼											Game try 5
19Jun94- 9Rkm fm *1⅛ ⑦ 1:46³ 3↑ NH Sweeps H-G3					103 8 6 54½ 5⁷ 2³ 3½		Santos J A		B 120 b	*.90	100 - 09	Kiri'sClown113½ RiverMjesty115ʰᵈ FourstrsAllstr120³											2 wide, not enough 8
WORKOUTS: Jun 20 Bel 5f fst 1:01² B 5/17 Jun 12 Bel 3f sly :37⁴ B 5/9 May 21 Bel 6f fst 1:14 H 3/22 May 14 Bel 4f fst :49¹ B 32/85 Apr 24 Bel 5f fst 1:01³ B 10/23 Apr 18 Bel tr.t 5f fst 1:01¹ B 2/11																								

Fourstars Allstar had returned in top form to kick off his 7-year-old campaign, winning back-to-back grass routes, including the Fort Marcy Handicap.

Runaway Brian
Own: Coppola Albert P
MIGLIORE R (49 5 7 6 .10)

Ch. c. 4
Sire: Runaway Groom (Blushing Groom)
Dam: Raja Dora (Raja Baba)
Br: Albert P. Coppola (Va)
Tr: O'Brien Leo (22 6 3 2 .27)

122

Lifetime Record :	6 1 1 0	$23,500			
1995	1 1 0 0	$18,000	Turf	0 0 0 0	
1994	5 M 1 0	$5,500	Wet	2 0 1 0	$5,500
Bel [T]	0 0 0 0		Dist [T]	0 0 0 0	

7May95-5Bel	fst	6f	:22^2	:45^2	:57^3	1:10^1 3↑ Md Sp Wt	79	1	1	2½	2½	2½	1^{nk}	Velazquez J R	122	29.00	90-11	Runaway Brian122^{nk} Scenturion113^3 Real Silk113$^{1\frac14}$	Hard drive 12		
12Nov94-11Lrl	fst	6f	:22^1	:46	:58^2	1:10^4 3↑ Md Sp Wt	-0	4	6	7^{10}	7^{12}	10^{21}	10$^{35\frac12}$	Reynolds L C	120	22.00	50-12	South West Hostage120½ Mighty Red122¾ Clever Am I120^4	Outrun 10		
29Aug94-9Sar	fst	7f	:22	:45^1	1:11	1:24^1 3↑ Md Sp Wt	44	6	7	8^7	10$^{9\frac34}$	8$^{5\frac12}$	8^{18}	Leon F	117	17.50	66-13	Silver Fox117^{nk} Andover Road117^{11} Iron Mountain117^5	No factor 11		
21Aug94-1Sar	sly	6½f	:22^2	:46	1:12	1:18^2 3↑ Md Sp Wt	56	5	1	2½	1½	2^1	2$^{9\frac12}$	Leon F	117	13.10	73-20	Spanos117$^{9\frac12}$ Runaway Brian117^4 Charlie Cush117^{hd}	Held place 8		
29Jly94-2Sar	my	6f	:22^2	:45^3	:57^4	1:10^3 3↑ Md Sp Wt	54	5	2	3^1	5$^{5\frac12}$	7^{10}	6$^{21\frac14}$	Leon F	116	24.50	67-19	Scherbo116$^{5\frac12}$ Timeless Dream116^6 April Christmas116$^{1\frac34}$	Tired 7		
18Jun94-3Lrl	fst	7f	:23^4	:47^3	1:12^1	1:25 3↑ Md Sp Wt	4	9	3	6^4	10^{18}	10^{22}	10$^{33\frac34}$	Lozano W Jr	113	41.70	50-13	Young Jones114¾ Sandman Sims113$^{2\frac14}$ Bold Private115$^{1\frac34}$	Faltered 10		

WORKOUTS: Apr 30 Bel 5f fst 1:02 H *19/30* Apr 24 Bel 7f fst 1:28^2 B *1/2* Apr 19 Bel 4f fst :49^1 B *8/17* Apr 12 Bel 5f fst 1:00^4 H *5/19* Apr 6 Bel tr.t 5f fst 1:03^1 B *9/23* Mar 31 Bel tr.t 5f fst 1:01^3 H *10/24*

A bit more than a week after Fourstars Allstar won the Fort Marcy, Runaway Brian made his first start as a 4-year-old and improved leaps and bounds over his most recent running lines, upsetting maidens at $60 on May 7 after dealing with race-long pace pressure.

7 Fourstar Brother
PP - 8
Own: Bomze Richard & Dileo Philip F
VELAZQUEZ J R (117 21 10 13 .18)

B. g. 3 (Mar)
Sire: Compliance (Northern Dancer)
Dam: Broadway Joan (Bold Arian)
Br: Richard Bomze (NY)
Tr: O'Brien Leo (50 13 10 4 .26)

112

Lifetime Record :	3 1 0 0	$19,200			
1995	1 1 0 0	$19,200	Turf	1 1 0 0	$19,200
1994	2 M 0 0		Wet	0 0 0 0	
Bel [T]	1 1 0 0	$19,200	Dist [T]	1 1 0 0	$19,200

7Jun95-1Bel	gd	1$\frac{1}{16}$ [T]	:23^4	:47^2	1:12	1:44^1 3↑ [S]Md Sp Wt	80	10	2	2½	1^1	1^8	1^{10}	Migliore R	113	2.45e	77-22	FourstrBrother113^{10} Strivr113^6 NwYorkLights113$^{2\frac12}$	Brk slow, ridden out 10
20Oct94-2Aqu	fst	6f	:22^1	:46^3	1:00	1:13 [S]Md Sp Wt	20	6	6	7^{11}	7^7	7^{11}	7$^{16\frac34}$	Smith M E	118	2.35e	60-18	Ave's Flag118^3 Gold Toes118^1 Slew's Miner118^2	Outrun 7
5Oct94-3Bel	fst	7f	:23	:46^4	1:12^1	1:25^4 [S]Md Sp Wt	40	4	9	9$^{6\frac14}$	6$^{6\frac34}$	5^7	6^{13}	Migliore R	118	3.90e	61-27	Count J. R.118$^{1\frac14}$ Slew's Miner118½ Maltbie118^7	Pinched break 11

WORKOUTS: May 14 Bel 4f fst :49^1 B *32/85* May 6 Bel tr.t 3f fst :36^3 H *3/8* Apr 24 Bel 5f fst 1:01^3 H *10/23*

Barely 24 hours earlier, Fourstar Brother had been hand-ridden to a 10-length victory while making his first start since October.

Tiffany's Taylor had won off layoffs with machine-like consistency all through her career, and O'Brien currently was winning with seemingly every returnee he saddled. That kind of double-barreled pattern combination is mighty hard to beat:

EIGHTH RACE
Belmont
JUNE 8, 1995

1$\frac{1}{16}$ MILES. (Inner Turf)(1.39^1) ALLOWANCE. Purse $48,000. Fillies and mares, 4-year-olds and upward which have not won a sweepstake of $25,000 in 1994–95. Weight, 122 lbs. Non-winners of $20,000 twice at a mile or over since October 1, allowed 3 lbs. $25,000 on the turf in 1995 or $20,000 twice on the turf since August 1, 6 lbs. $20,000 at a mile or over since October 1, or $15,000 twice on the turf in 1995, 9 lbs. (Maiden and claiming races not considered in allowances). (High weights preferred.)

Value of Race: $48,000 Winner $28,800; second $9,600; third $5,280; fourth $2,880; fifth $1,440. Mutuel Pool $265,169.00 Exacta Pool $330,630.00 Triple Pool $285,656.00

Last Raced	Horse	M/Eqt.	A.	Wt	PP	St	¼	½	¾	Str	Fin	Jockey	Odds $1
4Dec94 ^{8}Aqu^4	Tiffany's Taylor	bf	6	113	6	6	3$^{1\frac12}$	3^1	2½	1½	1^4	Velazquez J R	5.00
28May95 ^{8}Bel^3	Statuette		5	119	5	5	6^2	5^{hd}	4^{hd}	3½	2^{hd}	Smith M E	1.90
19May95 ^{8}GS^4	Irving's Girl		5	119	7	7	4^{hd}	6$^{1\frac12}$	5$^{1\frac12}$	4^1	3$^{1\frac34}$	Bailey J D	3.75
28Apr95 ^{9}Kee^2	Lotta Dancing		4	119	1	1	7½	7½	7^{hd}	5^3	4^{hd}	Davis R G	4.10
28May95 ^{8}Bel^6	Tango Charlie	b	6	113	4	4	2½	2^1	1^{hd}	2$^{1\frac12}$	5^5	Krone J A	13.90
14May95 ^{10}Bel^1	Leo N' Me		5	111	8	8	8	8	8	6½	6^3	Martin G J^5	26.25
28May95 ^{8}Bel^7	Knocknock		4	116	2	2	5^1	4½	6½	7$^{1\frac12}$	7^4	Samyn J L	36.25
26May95 ^{8}Bel^5	Island Of Silver		4	116	3	3	1$^{1\frac12}$	1½	3^1	8	8	Santos J A	5.10

OFF AT 4:31 Start Good. Won driving. Time, :24^2, :48^1, 1:12, 1:35^2, 1:41^2 Course firm.

$2 Mutuel Prices:				
	6–TIFFANY'S TAYLOR	12.00	5.30	3.30
	5–STATUETTE		3.30	2.70
	7–IRVING'S GIRL			3.10

$2 EXACTA 6–5 PAID $50.00 $2 TRIPLE 6–5–7 PAID $150.00

B. m, by Titanic–Tiffany Dream, by Blue Ensign. Trainer O'Brien Leo. Bred by Giardina Jay A (NY).

TIFFANY'S TAYLOR stalked three wide for five furlongs, took the lead entering the stretch, then drew off under pressure. STATUETTE rated between horses to the turn, outfinished IRVING'S GIRL for the place. The later raced within striking distance while four wide to the turn and finished willingly for a share. LOTTA DANCING reserved for six furlongs, while between horses, failed to threaten with a mild late rally. TANGO CHARLIE forced the early pace between horses, gained a slim lead on the turn then tired in the final eighth. LEO N' ME raced wide after breaking slowly. KNOCKNOCK saved ground and tired. ISLAND OF SILVER was used up setting the early pace.

Tiffany's Taylor stalked the leaders under a firm hold for the first six furlongs, took charge approaching midstretch and drew off with authority for a very predictable four-length win, paying $12.

Three days later, as if to show that his run wasn't finished, O'Brien struck yet again with a romping returnee. Like Fourstar Brother, Basin Lane was also stretching out and moving to the turf:

Basin Lane
Own: Bomze Richard & Connaughton Bernard
MIGLIORE R (86 8 18 7 .09)

Dk. b or br c. 3 (Apr)
Sire: Private Terms (Private Account)
Dam: Luxury (Jaipur)
Br: Estate of Mrs. Joseph Walker, Jr. (Pa)
Tr: O'Brien Leo (62 15 11 6 .24)

112

Lifetime Record:	2 1 1 0	$24,700			
1995	1 1 0 0	$19,200	Turf	1 1 0 0	$19,200
1994	1 M 1 0	$5,500	Wet	1 0 1 0	$5,500
Bel Ⓣ	1 1 0 0	$19,200	Dist Ⓣ	0 0 0 0	

11Jun95-5Bel fm 1 1/16 Ⓣ :23^4 :47 1:11^1 1:41 3↑ Md Sp Wt 92 6 1 1^1 1½ 1^5 1^{11} Migliore R 114 *2.10 93-08 Basin Lane114^{11} Dynamic Propulsion113½ Cringe113^2 Ridden out 12
30Jly94-5Sar my 6f :22^2 :46^3 :59^2 1:12^1 Md Sp Wt 79 4 8 5^3 4^1 2^1 2^{nk} Velazquez J R 118 4.70 80-20 Fey Tru118^{nk} Basin Lane118^{8¾} Milwaki118^{3½} Brk slow, wide, bump 8
WORKOUTS: Jun 7 Bel 4f fst :49^2 Bg *15/46* May 24 Bel 4f fst :51^4 B *32/36* May 14 Bel tr.t 4f fst :50^3 B *29/41* May 6 Bel tr.t 3f fst :39 B *7/8*

A BASIC WORK HABIT of successful horseplay is to find out things about races that other people miss, so handicappers need to commit some time to record keeping. Of course, this entails maintaining a file of result charts — from your main circuit *at least*, and preferably a set from a feed-in track (for example, in the winter, New York players need to keep close tabs on Gulfstream in anticipation of the winter-to-spring transition).

When going over a day's charts with your fine-tooth comb, make notations concerning pertinent conditions likely to be forgotten at a later date: wind direction and velocity, noting when the track surface changes from harrowed to floated (and vice versa) when thunderstorms hit during mid-card, or when the track is drying out; anything that puts the day's events in sharper focus.

After I get my key race listings up to date (if you don't know what a key race is please consult Steve Davidowitz' *Betting Thoroughbreds)*, I like to do a quick scan of comparative fractional times, searching for races that deviated from the norm in either a positive or negative sense. I don't get involved with numerical pace ratings for a number of reasons (discussed at some length in *Expert Handicapping*): beaten-lengths margins at all calls except the finish are the estimations of the chart-caller and vary from track to track, as do the run-ups from the gate to where the timing of races actually begins, and so on. However, I do believe in the power of instant variants (as we saw in some earlier example races); races that were above average for their class deserve to be highlighted for future reference.

For instance, by comparing the sixth and eighth races from March 31, players can infer that the sixth was above average in terms of fractional and final times. The sixth was a $30,000 claimer carrying a purse of $19,000, and looked like this:

SIXTH RACE
Aqueduct
MARCH 31, 1995

6 FURLONGS. (1.08) CLAIMING. Purse $19,000. 3-year-olds and upward. Weight, 122 lbs. Non-winners of two races since January 25, allowed 2 lbs. A race since February 15, 4 lbs. A race since January 11, 6 lbs. Claiming price $30,000, for each $2,500 to $25,000, allowed 2 lbs. (Races where entered for $22,500 or less not considered.)

Value of Race: $19,000 Winner $11,400; second $3,800; third $2,090; fourth $1,140; fifth $570. Mutuel Pool $169,918.00 Exacta Pool $306,463.00

Last Raced	Horse	M/Eqt.	A.	Wt	PP	St	¼	½	Str	Fin	Jockey	Cl'g Pr	Odds $1
15Oct94 ^{5}Bel^4	Moby Jak	b	6	116	5	5	5½	5^1	3^{hd}	1^{nk}	Nelson D	30000	6.10
18Feb95 ^{6}Aqu^6	Bold Spector	f	4	116	4	1	2½	2^{hd}	1^{hd}	2^2	Luzzi M J	30000	2.70
8Mar95 ^{4}Aqu^1	Nicks Court	b	4	116	6	3	4^{1½}	3^{1½}	2½	3^{1¾}	Velazquez J R	30000	3.10
17Mar95 ^{9}Aqu^1	Magic Ruckus	bf	7	114	1	4	3½	4^{1½}	5^{2½}	4^1	Martinez J R Jr	27500	5.60
26Mar95 ^{4}Aqu^5	Fog Storm		4	118	3	2	1½	1^{hd}	4^1	5^5	Davis R G	30000	3.25
11Mar95 ^{4}Aqu^2	Judge Hewes	b	4	112	2	6	6	6	6	6	Chavez J F	25000	4.70

OFF AT 3:10 Start Good. Won driving. Time :23, :46^2, :58^3, 1:11 Track fast.

$2 Mutuel Prices:			
5-MOBY JAK	14.20	5.90	3.10
4-BOLD SPECTOR		4.20	2.60
6-NICKS COURT			2.60

$2 EXACTA 5-4 PAID $78.50

Dk. b. or br. g, by Cojak–Closing Charger, by Native Charger. Trainer Lenzini John J Jr. Bred by Cohen A & Randy (NY).

MOBY JAK reserved for a half, advanced four wide into the stretch, then wore down BOLD SPECTOR in the final seventy yards. BOLD SPECTOR forced the pace between horses for a half, surged to the front in midstretch, continued on the lead into deep stretch, and yielded grudgingly. NICKS COURT never far back, made a run three wide to challenge at the quarter pole, battled heads apart into midstretch then weakened. MAGIC RUCKUS steadied behind the leaders on the far turn, angled four

EIGHTH RACE
Aqueduct
MARCH 31, 1995

7 FURLONGS. (1.201) ALLOWANCE. Purse $42,000. 4-year-olds and upward which have not won $25,000 in 1994–95, other than maiden, claiming, starter or restricted. Weight, 122 lbs. Non–winners of $20,000 twice since October 1, allowed 3 lbs. $22,000 in 1995, 5 lbs. $9,600 three times since August 1, 8 lbs. (Races where entered for $60,000 or less not considered in allowances.)

Value of Race: $42,000 Winner $25,200; second $8,400; third $4,620; fourth $2,520; fifth $1,260. Mutuel Pool $210,224.00 Exacta Pool $255,924.00 Triple Pool $226,850.00

Last Raced	Horse	M/Eqt.	A.	Wt	PP	St	¼	½	Str	Fin	Jockey	Odds $1
18Feb95 8Aqu5	Crafty		5	122	7	1	1½	1½	12½	1½	Migliore R	1.00
18Mar95 4Aqu2	Blum Gone	bf	5	114	2	5	54	4hd	2hd	21½	Luzzi M J	11.50
14Mar95 5GP1	Dibbs N' Dubbs	bf	7	114	8	2	3½	31	31½	31¾	Samyn J L	3.85
18Mar95 7Aqu3	Golden Cloud	b	7	110	4	4	4hd	51½	5½	4no	Perez R B5	6.00
18Mar95 7Aqu4	Popol's Gold		4	114	3	6	8	61	61	53	Chavez J F	6.70
5Mar95 8Aqu5	Preporant	b	6	114	6	3	2½	2½	4½	61	Davis R G	10.80
7Sep94 8Bel4	Classi Envoy	b	5	114	1	8	6½	71½	71	76	Velazquez J R	43.75
11Feb95 6Aqu7	Kyoko		5	114	5	7	7½	8	8	8	Santos J A	20.60

OFF AT 4:05 Start Good For All But CLASSI ENVOY. Won driving. Time :23, :462, 1:104, 1:232 Track fast.

$2 Mutuel Prices:			
9–CRAFTY	4.00	4.00	3.60
3–BLUM GONE		6.10	5.20
10–DIBBS N' DUBBS			4.40

$2 EXACTA 9–3 PAID $42.40 $2 TRIPLE 9–3–10 PAID $112.50

Ch. h, by Crafty Prospector–Tribal to Do, by Restless Native. Trainer Young Steven W. Bred by Longleaf Pine Farm (Fla).

CRAFTY outsprinted rivals for the early advantage, extended his lead in upper stretch then was all out to hold off BLUM GONE in the final strides. BLUM GONE settled in good position while saving ground for six furlongs, closed steadily but could

The eighth was a classified allowance carrying a $42,000 purse, more than twice as much the claiming race, yet the quarter and half-mile splits are identical, and the final time of the claimer is just a tick slower than the six-furlong split of the allowance.

Now that the sixth compares so favorably with the higher-class race, we want to scrutinize the running lines closely to see what was going on. An important thing to look for is horses who "won the battle but lost the war." That is, horses who won a pace duel, but lost the race. Bold Spector, who finished second in the $30,000 claimer we're looking at now, is a perfect illustration: note how he pressed Fog Storm's pace for a quarter, continued to battle between horses (position-wise, the toughest place to be) as Nicks Court ranged up outside, and how he continued on to finish second, beaten just a neck, while Fog Storm and Nicks Court succumbed from the pressure and faded out of the picture at the finish. Bold Spector lost the race (to a stretch runner who benefited from the pace development), but he "won" the inner battle, and was worth following if and when he was put into an easier match up. That opportunity came 36 days later:

5 **Belmont Park**

6 Furlongs. **(1:074) CLAIMING. Purse $20,000. 4–year–olds and upward. Weight, 122 lbs. Non–winners of two races since March 23, allowed 2 lbs. A race since March 29, 4 lbs. Two races since March 10, 6 lbs. Claiming price $25,000, for each $2,500 to $20,000, allowed 2 lbs. (Races where entered for $18,000 or less not considered.)**

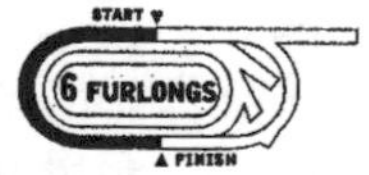

Coupled – Imaging and Cross Ice Pass

Medical Pro
Own: Perroncino John S
AGOSTO R (2 0 0 1 .00) **$25,000**

Ch. c. 4
Sire: Prosper Fager (Mr. Prospector)
Dam: Sandy Lake (L'Heureux)
Br: Lake Don (Fla)
Tr: Terracciano Neal (1 0 0 0 .00)

1097

Lifetime Record: 36 9 5 3 $145,820											
1995	5	0	0	1	$4,090	Turf	1	0	0	0	$350
1994	21	8	3	1	$130,330	Wet	8	4	1	1	$56,470
Bel	4	0	2	0	$12,760	Dist	22	5	4	0	$83,390

26Apr95–7Aqu fst	7f		:22	:444	1:102	1:232	Alw 36000N4X	50	5	1	2hd	2½	610	623	Pezua J M	114 fb	15.20	64–19	Hold My Tongue1142 Able Buck114½ Blum Gone1147	Dueled, tired	7
14Apr95–6Aqu fst	6f		:22	:452	:572	1:092	Clm 45000	77	3	3	1½	1½	32½	48¼	Nelson D	112 fb	3.90	87–10	One Big Hug1163 Carsey's Pal1165 Fabersham111nk	Used in pace	6
6Apr95–6Aqu fst	6½f		:222	:452	1:10	1:162	Clm 40000	87	3	2	11½	11	31	34½	Nelson D	116 fb	2.75	93–08	Fabersham1111½ Gallpit'sMoment1123 MediclPro1164	Dueled, weakened	6
14Jan95–8Aqu fst	6f	⊡	:221	:444	:57	1:101	3↑ Paumonok H55k	60	4	1	3½	33	611	618¾	Alvarado F T	114 fb	5.70	73–19	Crafty Alfel1155¼ Yeckley1091½ Fabersham1144	Gave way	6
4Jan95–7Aqu fst	6f	⊡	:221	:461	:584	1:113	3↑ Handicap46k	64	7	1	2hd	1½	34½	713½	Lumpkins J	116 fb	3.70	71–22	Crafty Alfel1171½ Blare Of Trumpets1178 Fabersham122¾	Faded	7
15Dec94–7Aqu fst	6f	⊡	:23	:461	:581	1:104	3↑ Alw 42000N$Y	101	2	3	11½	11½	12½	12¼	Lumpkins J	111 fb	11.40	89–16	Medical Pro1112¼ Golden Tent119½ Chanels Titanic1131½	Driving	7
7Dec94–8Aqu fst	6f	⊡	:223	:454	:58	1:102	3↑ Alw 34000N3X	84	4	2	11	1½	1½	62¼	Agosto R7	108 fb	6.50	89–12	Fighting Daddy112no MemoriesOfLinda115nk BlumGone119½	Used in pace	7
9Nov94–5Aqu fst	7f		:224	:46	1:111	1:233	3↑ Alw 34000N3X	—	2	4	1½	1½	—	—	Agosto R7	113 fb	2.95	— 14	[D]Golden Larch1101 Advanced Placement1172½ Fighting Daddy1171¾		7
Bumped, clipped heels, lost rider Placed 6th through disqualification.																					
1Nov94–8Aqu sly	6f		:22	:45	:572	1:103	3↑ Alw 32000N2X	95	1	3	12	12½	13	11½	Agosto R7	113 fb	*2.25	89–18	Medical Pro1131½ Catchin Air1152½ Bermuda Cedar1152½	Driving	6
23Oct94–6Aqu wf	7f		:224	:453	1:101	1:231	3↑ Alw 30000N1X	91	3	3	16	13½	13	1¾	Agosto R7	107 fb	3.05	88–11	Medical Pro107¾ Code Home114¾ Bold Spector1142¼	Driving	7

WORKOUTS: ●Mar 29 Aqu 5f fst 1:003 H *1/4* Mar 22 Aqu 4f fst :461 H *1/2* Mar 15 Aqu 3f fst :37 B *4/5* Feb 22 Aqu ⊡ 4f fst :474 H *2/5* ●Feb 17 Aqu ⊡ 4f fst :492 B *1/4* ●Feb 10 Aqu ⊡ 3f fst :361 H *1/4*

Bold Spector

Own: Austin Dale H & Heatherwood

SANTOS J A (7 1 2 0 .14) $25,000

B. g. 4
Sire: Afleet (Mr. Prospector)
Dam: Bold Lady Anne (Bold Josh)
Br: Conner Edward C (Ky)
Tr: Schosberg Richard (4 1 1 0 .25)

116

Lifetime Record: 13 3 3 2 $70,940									
1995	4	0	2	0	$11,220	Turf	0 0 0 0		
1994	9	3	1	2	$59,720	Wet	2 0 0 1	$3,600	
Bel	4	0	1	1	$8,120	Dist	10 3 3 1	$67,340	

31Mar95-6Aqu fst 6f	:23 :462 :583 1:11	Clm 30000	91 4 1 2½ 2hd 1hd 2nk	Luzzi M J	116 f	*2.70	87-19	Moby Jak116nk Bold Spector1162 Nicks Court1161¾	Gamely	6
18Feb95-6Aqu fst 6f ⊡	:224 :461 :59 1:12	Alw 34000N3X	66 5 2 21 53½ 65¾ 69	Madrid A Jr	117 f	3.90	74-18	Jericho Blaise1173½ Thru 'n Thru117nk Cocoa Lad1173	Gave way turn	6
25Jan95-7Aqu fst 6f ⊡	:223 :462 :591 1:124	Alw 34000N3X	50 1 5 33 58 513 515	Luzzi M J	117 f	3.05	64-24	Top End1195 Vallata Lane1196½ Daunting Era1172	Fractious gate	6
8Jan95-4Aqu fst 6f ⊡	:231 :463 :591 1:121	Alw 32000N2X	93 3 1 1hd 1hd 1hd 21	Luzzi M J	117 f	3.35	81-27	Vallata Lane1191 Bold Spector1172¼ Goodbye To You1221¼	Second best	5
4Dec94-5Aqu fst 6f	:224 :462 :582 1:111	Clm 45000	94 4 1 1½ 1hd 12½ 14½	Luzzi M J	115 f	2.00	86-15	Bold Spector1154½ Francis Marion113¾ Homah Halo1173	Driving	5
23Nov94-6Aqu fst 6f	:221 :461 :582 1:104 3↑	Alw 32000N2X	84 4 4 52 51¾ 55½ 59	Luzzi M J	120 f	5.30	79-21	Thru 'n Thru115½ Catchin Air1157 Bull IntheHeather1171	Bumped break	7
3Nov94-7Aqu fst 6f	:221 :454 :58 1:103 3↑	Alw 30000N1X	86 5 3 22½ 1hd 11½ 11½	Luzzi M J	115 f	*1.25	89-15	Bold Spector1151½ Goldstar Road1154 Flying Cherub117nk	Driving	6
23Oct94-6Aqu wf 7f	:224 :453 1:101 1:231 3↑	Alw 30000N1X	88 5 1 26 33½ 33 31½	Luzzi M J	114 f	3.55	86-11	Medical Pro107½ Code Home114¾ Bold Spector1142½	No late bid	7
7Oct94-2Bel fst 6f	:231 :463 :582 1:102	Clm 45000	87 1 2 31½ 51½ 21½ 23	Luzzi M J	113	6.20	88-16	Heroic Pursuit113¾ Bold Spector1135 Lightnin' Cat114nk	Up for place	6
13Sep94-2Bel fst 6f	:224 :46 :574 1:103	Clm 35000	79 7 1 1½ 2hd 23 32	Davis R G	117	12.70	86-20	Catchin Air1131¾ Raja's Charter117hd Bold Spector117¾	Bid, weakened	10

WORKOUTS: Apr 29 Bel tr.t 4f fst :501 B 12/25 ●Apr 16 Bel tr.t 3f fst :361 H 1/11 Mar 29 Bel tr.t 4f fst :511 B 26/31 Mar 23 Bel tr.t 3f fst :363 H 8/17 Feb 11 Bel tr.t 4f fst :484 H 6/40

Baypark

Own: Sommer Viola

LUZZI M J (5 0 1 2 .00) $25,000

Dk. b or br g. 6
Sire: Time To Explode (Explodent)
Dam: Here Come Some (Star Spangled)
Br: Anderson Farms (Ont-C)
Tr: Martin Frank (2 1 0 0 .50)

116

Lifetime Record: 59 8 5 11 $174,087									
1995	9	2	1	3	$54,000	Turf	3 0 0 0	$1,401	
1994	21	3	1	4	$50,963	Wet	9 3 1 1	$47,509	
Bel	4	0	0	2	$4,680	Dist	20 3 3 2	$76,574	

12Apr95-3Aqu fst 7f	:222 :451 1:101 1:23	Clm 25000	87 6 5 44½ 42½ 32 32	Luzzi M J	120	6.60	87-14	Regal Mike116hd Fabian1182 Baypark1201	Three wide, even late	9
30Mar95-5Aqu fst 6f	:222 :453 :58 1:102	Clm c-20000	85 6 4 53 31½ 31½ 23	Alvarado F T	120	2.15	87-17	Pension Fraud1133 Baypark1201¾ Groovy Attire118no	Up for place	7
Claimed from Joques Farm, Moschera Gasper S Trainer										
23Mar95-5Aqu fst 7f	:222 :462 1:121 1:243	Clm 20000	81 4 6 26 23 1½ 31¾	Alvarado F T	116	*1.50	79-17	Wild Dante114¾ Prioritizer1161 Baypark1163½	Weakened	8
18Mar95-7Aqu fst 6½f	:223 :461 1:102 1:163	Alw 42000N$Y	68 3 6 54½ 76 67 613	Dunkelberger T L5	117	17.80	84-15	Mr. Tyler1172½ Able Buck1141¾ Golden Cloud1106½	Saved ground	7
9Mar95-7Aqu wf 6f ⊡	:231 :463 :583 1:103	Clm 50000	84 3 2 2½ 2hd 22 42	Migliore R	118	*1.35e	88-18	Golden Cloud112hd Imaging1131½ Fabersham117nk	Forced pace, tired	7
11Feb95-6Aqu fst 6f ⊡	:24 :473 1:001 1:133	Alw 36000N4X	92 7 2 41½ 41½ 22 1no	Alvarado F T	119	7.70	75-33	Baypark119no Yeckley117¾ Fighting Daddy117nk	Four wide trip	7
5Feb95-8Aqu fst 6f ⊡	:231 :472 1:003 1:14	Alw 34000N3X	83 4 2 53½ 41½ 1hd 13	Alvarado F T	117	3.65	73-28	Baypark1173 Rachmanoff112no Jericho Blaise117nk	Going away	6
21Jan95-3Aqu my 6f ⊡	:222 :452 :573 1:102	Clm c-25000	80 5 1 2½ 21½ 66 67	Luzzi M J	117	2.70	84-14	Cocoa Lad1174¼ Pension Fraud119¾ Prioritizer1131	Stead 3/16 pl, tired	6
Claimed from Meadow Val Stable, Dutrow Richard E Trainer										
11Jan95-3Aqu fst 6f ⊡	:231 :463 :59 1:121	Clm 25000	84 4 7 43 53½ 31½ 3nk	Luzzi M J	117	9.90	82-22	Raja'sCharter110nk MagicRuckus117no Baypark1172½	Bump, blocked 1/8 pl	10
30Dec94-1Aqu fst 6f ⊡	:233 :48 1:01 1:134 3↑	Clm 22500	73 1 5 2½ 2½ 3nk 33½	Luzzi M J	115	6.20	71-24	Pension Fraud1171¼ Fighting Daddy1222 Baypark1152¾	Weakened	7

WORKOUTS: ●Apr 23 Bel tr.t 4f fst :461 H 1/18 Mar 4 Bel tr.t 4f fst :48 H 8/44

Publicized

Own: Tam Ping W

VELAZQUEZ J R (7 2 0 1 .29) $22,500

B. g. 4
Sire: Afleet (Mr. Prospector)
Dam: Miss Cream Puff (Creme dela Creme)
Br: Kinsman Stud Farm (Fla)
Tr: Lake Robert P (1 0 0 0 .00)

114

Lifetime Record: 17 3 6 0 $53,025									
1995	9	1	4	0	$17,175	Turf	0 0 0 0		
1994	8	2	2	0	$35,850	Wet	3 1 0 0	$19,200	
Bel	0	0	0	0		Dist	10 2 4 0	$28,890	

22Apr95-1Aqu fst 6f	:22 :454 :583 1:114	Clm 20000	83 5 4 64½ 51¾ 31½ 2½	Santos J A	116	9.00	82-17	Groovy Attire118½ Publicized1162 Pension Fraud115hd	Finished well	7
14Apr95-9Aqu fst 6f	:223 :454 :573 1:10	Clm 10000	89 3 3 2hd 1hd 13 16½	Davis R G	114	4.90	92-10	Publicized1146½ Sulaco109no Phantom Finn117no	Going away	7
5Apr95-4Aqu fst 7f	:231 :47 1:121 1:251	Clm 10000	77 2 5 11 11 2hd 22½	Davis R G	116	*1.55	76-21	Mr Sledge1162½ Publicized1167 Duel Zone1162	Dueled, held well	8
29Mar95-2Aqu fst 1⅛	:482 1:133 1:391 1:521	Clm 10000	67 9 1 12 1½ 35 513½	Davis R G	113	7.20	65-19	Devoted Glory1197 Runaway Chris1194½ Sulaco1081½	Used in pace	10
17Mar95-9Aqu fst 7f	:224 :453 1:102 1:233	Clm 17500	62 2 10 41½ 65 76 710½	Alvarado F T	116	5.10	76-17	Magic Ruckus1161 Cross IcePass110nk Berseto107hd	Broke slowly, rushed	10
8Mar95-4Aqu fst 6f ⊡	:222 :452 :581 1:12	Clm 17500	75 4 4 43½ 44 45 45½	Martin G J7	109	*2.00	78-20	NicksCourt116nk ConcordeCal116nk ScreBleu1164¾	Sved ground, willingly	7
24Feb95-3Aqu fst 6f ⊡	:224 :462 :582 1:104	Clm 17500	79 4 6 32½ 21 22½ 23½	Martin G J7	110	3.65	86-16	Groovy Attire1173½ Publicized1101 Prioritizer1177¾	Broke in air	6
11Feb95-9Aqu fst 6f ⊡	:23 :47 1:001 1:14	Clm 17500	76 7 5 33 32½ 33½ 64½	Velazquez J R	117	10.00	68-33	Raja's Charter112½ Ken's Landing117¾ Sacre Bleu1172	Tired	11
5Feb95-9Aqu fst 6f ⊡	:231 :472 1:002 1:14	Clm 14000	83 6 1 21½ 21½ 2½ 2hd	Velazquez J R	117	8.50	73-28	Callisto113hd Publicized1172 Cesar B.1171½	Couldn't last	9
29Nov94-4Aqu wf 1	:223 :453 1:112 1:372	Clm 35000	— 4 1 31½ 85¾ 910 —	Maple E	119	11.80	— 24	Churkin1173 Geret's Jewel117nk Rogersdividends119nk	Gave way, eased	9

WORKOUTS: Apr 30 Bel tr.t 4f fst :481 H 2/17 Feb 19 Bel tr.t 6f fst 1:151 B 1/3

Pension Fraud

Own: Oakridge Stable

SANTAGATA N (8 0 2 0 .00) $25,000

Dk. b or br g. 7
Sire: Temperence Hill (Stop the Music)
Dam: Peggy's Fling (Delta Judge)
Br: Olsson Sture G (Md)
Tr: Dunham Bob G (—)

120

Lifetime Record: 96 12 22 20 $397,435									
1995	9	2	1	2	$32,085	Turf	11 0 1 3	$17,260	
1994	28	3	5	3	$71,200	Wet	20 3 9 3	$99,200	
Bel	17	2	2	3	$53,720	Dist	36 6 8 8	$165,325	

22Apr95-1Aqu fst 6f	:22 :454 :583 1:114	Clm c-20000	78 1 7 77½ 74½ 63½ 32½	Perez R B5	115	*2.05	80-17	GroovyAttire118½ Publicized1162 PnsionFrud115hd	Broke slowly, rallied	7
Claimed from October Moon Stable, Galluscio Dominic G Trainer										
12Apr95-3Aqu fst 7f	:222 :451 1:101 1:23	Clm 22500	85 2 8 55 53 42 53½	Perez R B5	111	4.10	86-14	Regal Mike116hd Fabian1182 Baypark1201	Split horses, no rally	9
30Mar95-5Aqu fst 6f	:222 :453 :58 1:102	Clm 20000	93 3 5 43 54½ 11 13	Perez R B5	113	3.55	90-17	PensionFraud1133 Bayprk1201¾ GroovyAttire118no	Four wide, going away	7
23Mar95-5Aqu fst 7f	:222 :462 1:121 1:243	Clm 25000	74 3 5 68½ 45 52 45	Santagata N	120	4.10	76-17	Wild Dante114¾ Prioritizer1161 Baypark1163½	No late bid	8
11Mar95-4Aqu fst 6f ⊡	:223 :46 :583 1:111	Clm 30000	83 6 5 52¾ 62¾ 53½ 34	Santagata N	116	2.75	83-16	Love Jazz120¾ Judge Hewes1123½ Pension Fraud116hd	Mild rally	8
18Feb95-3Aqu fst 6f ⊡	:23 :463 :591 1:12	Clm 32500	88 2 4 63½ 52½ 3nk 2nk	Santagata N	115	10.50	83-18	Love Jazz114nk Pension Fraud1152 Nymphist1192	Rallied inside	7
1Feb95-3Aqu fst 170 ⊡	:24 :481 1:131 1:432	Clm 32500	76 2 2 2½ 32 35 411½	Luzzi M J	115	5.20	69-28	Private Plan1131 Yaros11310 Kristen's Baby117½	Forced pace, tired	6
21Jan95-3Aqu my 6f ⊡	:222 :452 :573 1:102	Clm c-25000	87 2 4 55 55 45½ 24¼	Rydowski S R	119	*1.40e	87-14	Cocoa Lad1174¼ Pension Fraud119¾ Prioritizer1131	Late gain	6
Awarded first purse money Claimed from Perroncino John S, Terracciano Neal Trainer										
12Jan95-4Aqu fst 6f ⊡	:231 :464 :59 1:114	Clm 32500	79 7 2 56 55 86¾ 56½	Rydowski S R	115	7.10	77-20	Nymphist1172¾ Current Impact119nk Nowhere Man1171½	Wide trip	7
30Dec94-1Aqu fst 6f ⊡	:233 :48 1:01 1:134 3↑	Clm 25000	81 5 3 65 43 1hd 11¼	Rydowski S R	117	4.10	74-24	Pension Fraud1171¼ Fighting Daddy1222 Baypark1152¾	Driving	7

Cross Ice Pass

Own: My Paradise Farms

ALVARADO F T (8 1 0 1 .13) $20,000

Ch. g. 4
Sire: Pass the Line (Pas Seul)
Dam: Hold Your Kiss (Hold Your Peace)
Br: Stanley Ersoff (Fla)
Tr: Friedman Mitchell (—)

112

Lifetime Record: 24 3 3 3 $59,890									
1995	5	0	2	0	$7,150	Turf	4 1 0 0	$14,100	
1994	15	2	1	2	$36,660	Wet	3 2 0 0	$25,500	
Bel	9	1	0	2	$23,580	Dist	8 2 0 2	$31,890	

23Apr95-3Aqu fst 1	:24 :473 1:131 1:39	Clm c-16000	73 7 2 31½ 31½ 1hd 21¼	Velazquez J R	116	6.20	73-19	Churkin1161¼ Cross Ice Pass1162½ Runaway Chris116¾	Couldn't last	9
Claimed from Friendship Stable, Barbara Robert Trainer										
8Apr95-5Aqu fst 6f	:22 :45 :574 1:11	Clm 16000	78 6 6 67½ 66 53½ 42	Perez R B5	111	2.75	85-10	Nowhere Man116hd Unreal Mot116½ Appealing Tracy1131½	Mild gain	7
23Mar95-5Aqu fst 7f	:222 :462 1:121 1:243	Clm 25000	72 5 4 58 55½ 64 56	Perez R B5	111	3.80	75-17	Wild Dante114¾ Prioritizer1161 Baypark1163½	Evenly, four wide	8
17Mar95-9Aqu fst 7f	:224 :453 1:102 1:233	Clm 15500	82 7 5 62¾ 55 53 21	Perez R B5	110	*3.10	85-17	Magic Ruckus1161 Cross Ice Pass110nk Berseto107hd	Rallied four wide	10
1Feb95-9Aqu fst 6f ⊡	:223 :46 :584 1:121	Clm 17500	62 7 9 96¾ 87¾ 88½ 79½	Perez R B5	112	5.20	73-21	Dernier's Lass117¾ MagicRuckus117½ Vaal'sGorgeous117no	Broke slowly	10
31Dec94-2Aqu fst 11⁄16 ⊡	:243 :483 1:141 1:473	Clm 35000	64 5 3 35 44½ 67 614	Perez R B5	112	4.70	53-34	Brett's Jet117¾ Free Agent1171¼ Tea In My Eye1158	Tired	8
24Dec94-7Aqu my 11⁄16 ⊡	:244 :46 1:114 1:442 3↑	Alw 34000N2X	53 7 6 614 613 620 630¼	Maple E	115	5.60	52-32	Sir Wollaston11510 Bull Inthe Heather117hd Geret's Jewel11512	Outrun	7
10Dec94-4Aqu fst 170 ⊡	:241 :491 1:141 1:433	Clm 30000	82 4 3 31½ 41½ 41 2hd	Maple E	113	10.80	80-23	Geret'sJewel117hd CrossIcePass113nk MeanPncho115¾	Lacked room 3/16	7
19Nov94-1Aqu gd 7f	:23 :462 1:12 1:25	Clm 25000	77 4 5 61¾ 54½ 41 3nk	Maple E	117	2.70	79-21	Ken's Landing112no Mean Pancho112hd Cross Ice Pass1174½	Rallied inside	7
6Nov94-9Aqu wf 6f	:221 :454 :581 1:11	Clm 17500	77 8 5 45 44 32 1¾	Maple E	117	4.10	87-17	Cross Ice Pass117¾ Brush Full1121¾ Spirited Player1131¾	Driving	11

WORKOUTS: Mar 11 Bel tr.t 5f fst 1:013 H 5/28 Mar 6 Bel tr.t 4f fst :492 B 4/14 Feb 25 Bel tr.t 4f fst :492 H 19/39

Groovy Attire
Own: Borosh Shirley & Vita Joseph S
MIGLIORE R (10 2 0 2 .20) **$25,000**

B. g. 6
Sire: Groovy (Norcliffe)
Dam: High Style (King Pellinore)
Br: Evans Mrs D W (Ky)
Tr: Borosh Allen (—)

120

Lifetime Record: 21 6 5 5 $82,182										
1995	7	3	0	2	$29,040	Turf	1	0	0	0	$650
1994	6	3	0	1	$24,050	Wet	5	1	0	2	$18,072
Bel	2	0	1	1	$8,160	Dist	18	6	4	5	$77,982

22Apr95-1Aqu fst 6f	:22	:454	:583	1:114	Clm 20000	84	3	6	41½	2hd	11	1½	Migliore R	118 fb	3.80	83-17	GroovyAttire118½ Publicizd1162 PnsionFrud115hd	Bumped break, all out	7
30Mar95-5Aqu fst 6f	:222	:453	:58	1:102	Clm 20000	81	2	7	1½	2hd	21	34¾	Migliore R	118 f	*1.80	85-17	Pension Fraud1133 Baypark1201¾ GroovyAttire118no	Broke slowly, rushed	7
24Feb95-3Aqu fst 6f ⊡	:224	:462	:582	1:104	Clm 17500	87	3	2	11	1½	12½	13¼	Migliore R	117 f	*1.30	89-16	GroovyAttire1173¼ Publicized1101 Prioritizer1177¾	Challenged, drew clear	6
18Feb95-1Aqu fst 6f ⊡	:223	:46	:591	1:13	Clm 14000	75	8	10	56¾	34½	23	3nk	Migliore R	117 f	5.00	78-18	Cesar B.117no Sunshine Ed119hd Groovy Attire117½	Rallied wide	11
27Jan95-8Suf fst 6f	:222	:463	1:00	1:132	Clm 20000	49	1	3	24	511	511	617¼	Hampshire J F JrLB	116 f	*1.10	61-35	Armed At Dark1164½ Ambraco1161½ Armagh County116½	Stopped inside	6
16Jan95-9Suf sly 6f	:221	:461	:594	1:141	PrivateTerms25k	89	1	4	1½	11	2hd	41½	Hampshire J F JrLB	114 f	12.00	76-34	Twinkle A Little113no Alyten115no Prolanzier1161¼	Off rail, weakened	9
8Jan95-9Suf sly 6f	:224	:473	1:011	1:153	Clm 16000	79	5	5	1½	1½	11	11½	Baez R LB	119 f	3.20	70-40	Groovy Attire1191½ Sunshine Ivory116no Ben Co Co116nk	Inside, driving	8
14Dec94-9Suf fst 6f	:222	:463	:592	1:122 3↑ Alw 12740N3L		78	5	5	1hd	12½	15	12½	Hampshire J F JrLB	122	*.90	86-25	GroovyAttire1222½ BrassyLoopie1183 RndomPlesure1151	Inside, driving	9
30Nov94-8Suf fst 6f	:224	:463	:591	1:121 3↑ Alw 11760N2L		82	1	4	11½	11½	14	11½	Hampshire J F JrLB	119 f	1.80	87-20	Groovy Attire1191½ Romancing Susan1141½ All Man11610	Inside, driving	9
20Nov94-8Suf fst 6f	:223	:463	1:001	1:141 3↑ Alw 11760N2L		67	6	3	2½	1½	1½	41¾	Hampshire J F JrLB	119 f	2.40	75-28	What A Ham1181 Romancing Susan114nk MajorMover117½	3w turn, tired	9

WORKOUTS: ●Apr 14 Suf 4f fst :484 Hg 1/8 Mar 29 Suf 3f fst :373 B 8/22

Fabian
Own: G Lack Farms
CHAVEZ J F (11 2 2 1 .18) **$25,000**

B. c. 4
Sire: Carr de Naskra (Star de Naskra)
Dam: La Cavatina (Green Dancer)
Br: Grimm Dean & Kelly Thomas J (NY)
Tr: Klesaris Robert P (2 1 0 0 .50)

116

Lifetime Record: 18 4 4 5 $105,000										
1995	8	2	1	4	$57,360	Turf	1	0	0	0	
1994	10	2	3	1	$47,640	Wet	4	0	2	0	$13,400
Bel	3	0	0	0	$1,080	Dist	6	2	1	2	$46,600

12Apr95-3Aqu fst 7f	:222	:451	1:101	1:23	Clm 25000	92	9	1	79½	65	11½	2hd	Chavez J F	118 b	*.90e	89-14	Regal Mike116hd Fabian1182 Baypark1201	Wide, couldn't last	9
30Mar95-7Aqu fst 6f	:223	:462	:582	1:11	Alw 34000N3X	78	2	5	45½	52¾	31½	42¾	Martin G J7	112 b	13.40	84-17	Expressed1191½ Bay Dancer117½ Justfortherecord1141	Late gain	5
15Mar95-8Aqu fst 6½f	:221	:452	1:111	1:18	ⓈAlw 32000N2X	78	1	8	32½	31½	11	12	Migliore R	117 b	*2.65	90-14	Fabian1172 Crafty Harold110¾ Michael Chris107nk	Going away	11
20Feb95-9Aqu fst 1 1/16 ⊡	:234	:483	1:143	1:471	ⓈAlw 34000N2X	77	4	4	43½	3½	21	35½	Alvarado F T	117 b	5.00	63-29	Track Topper1171½ Crooked Heels1104 Fabian1172	Chased, weakened	10
12Feb95-6Aqu fst 6f ⊡	:233	:48	1:003	1:133	ⓈAlw 32000N2X	71	6	3	63¾	55	46½	33½	Rydowski S R	116 b	2.80	71-26	Gravel King1113 Crafty Harold119½ Fabian1161	Steadied turn	6
1Feb95-6Aqu fst 6f ⊡	:222	:454	:583	1:121	ⓈAlw 32000N2X	80	1	8	56½	57	45½	32	Martin G J7	110 b	5.70	80-21	Congoline1172 Fini Cassette117hd Fabian110nk	Late gain	10
16Jan95-7Aqu gd 1 1/16 ⊡	:232	:474	1:123	1:442	ⓈAlw 34000N2X	70	3	2	21	2½	27	39½	Rodriquez E M	117 b	1.60e	73-20	Come On Talc1178½ Klondike Clem1171 Fabian1175½	Forced pace, tired	6
1Jan95-2Aqu gd 6f ⊡	:232	:472	1:002	1:134	ⓈAlw 30000N1X	66	5	1	52¾	41¾	31½	1nk	Rodriquez E M	117 b	1.95	74-20	Fabian117nk Accordion110hd Mat's Era112hd	Driving	5
2Nov94-7Aqu my 6½f	:223	:471	1:122	1:19 3↑ ⓈAlw 30000N1X		83	8	5	54	41½	2½	23	Pezua J M	115 b	4.50	83-22	Pro On Ice1173 Fabian1151¾ Crafty Harold115no	Rallied wide	9
18Oct94-9Aqu fst 7f	:223	:452	1:104	1:24	Clm 22500	83	8	4	53	21	1hd	13	Pezua J M	115 b	7.90	84-15	Fabian1153 Colonel Slade110nk Iclaimit1171	Driving	9

A cursory pace analysis suggests that the race sets up for a closer, due to the presence of several horses with early speed: Medical Pro, Bold Spector, Publicized (sometimes), and Groovy Attire. That is one of the main reasons that Fabian was favored at 2-1.

But does the race really set up that way? Medical Pro's condition is suspect judging from his three races since returned from a layoff, and his record indicates a horse who caves in unless able to dominate the first fraction. Groovy Attire often breaks tardily, and last time out he was life-and-death to defeat Publicized — a gelding whose only victory in at least the past five months came for a $10,000 claiming tag.

Bold Spector is an early pace horse, *but he does not require the early lead to put forth his best effort.* Note the allowance win of November 3. Also, Bold Spector handles prolonged pace pressure, as evidenced by his win of December 4, and by his pace duel victory last time out. Chances are, Bold Spector will break Medical Pro's will without too much trouble and inherit the lead at some point on the turn:

FIFTH RACE
Belmont
MAY 6, 1995

6 FURLONGS. (1.074) CLAIMING. Purse $20,000. 4-year-olds and upward. Weight, 122 lbs. Non-winners of two races since March 23, allowed 2 lbs. A race since March 29, 4 lbs. Two races since March 10, 6 lbs. Claiming price $25,000, for each $2,500 to $20,000, allowed 2 lbs. (Races where entered for $18,000 or less not considered.)

Value of Race: $20,000 Winner $12,000; second $4,000; third $2,200; fourth $1,200; fifth $600. Mutuel Pool $343,143.00 Exacta Pool $474,288.00 Triple Pool $324,971.00

Last Raced	Horse	M/Eqt.	A.	Wt	PP	St	¼	½	Str	Fin	Jockey	Cl'g Pr	Odds $1
31Mar95 6Aqu2	Bold Spector	f	4	116	2	1	32½	32	1hd	11½	Santos J A	25000	4.10
22Apr95 1Aqu1	Groovy Attire	bf	6	120	7	8	2½	1½	2½	22½	Migliore R	25000	9.30
22Apr95 1Aqu2	Publicized		4	114	4	3	4hd	4½	31	3½	Velazquez J R	22500	21.30
12Apr95 3Aqu3	Baypark		6	116	3	4	51½	5½	4hd	4no	Luzzi M J	25000	4.40
23Apr95 3Aqu2	Cross Ice Pass		4	112	6	6	72	61½	51	52	Alvarado F T	20000	7.60
12Apr95 3Aqu2	Fabian	b	4	116	8	7	8	7½	6hd	6no	Chavez J F	25000	2.35
22Apr95 1Aqu3	Pension Fraud		7	120	5	5	6½	8	8	74½	Santagata N	25000	14.90
26Apr95 7Aqu6	Medical Pro	bf	4	109	1	2	11	21	7½	8	Agosto R7	25000	3.75

OFF AT 2:55 Start Good. Won driving. Time, :222, :45, :57, 1:092 Track fast.

$2 Mutuel Prices:			
3–BOLD SPECTOR	10.20	6.10	4.80
8–GROOVY ATTIRE		8.60	5.70
5–PUBLICIZED			9.40

$2 EXACTA 3–8 PAID $93.50 $2 TRIPLE 3–8–5 PAID $679.00

B. g, by Afleet–Bold Lady Anne, by Bold Josh. Trainer Schosberg Richard. Bred by Conner Edward C (Ky).

BOLD SPECTOR settled just off the early pace, angled three wide while rallying on the turn, surged to the front in midstretch, then edged clear under pressure. GROOVY ATTIRE away a bit slowly, rushed up from outside to contest the early pace, took the lead on the turn, dueled heads apart leaving the furlong marker then held well for the place. PUBLICIZED steadied sharply inside GROOVY ATTIRE nearing the half mile pole, advanced four wide into the stretch, then finished willingly for a share. BAYPARK went evenly while saving ground. CROSS ICE PASS was never a serious threat. FABIAN checked while breaking inward at the start, was never close thereafter. PENSION FRAUD never reached contention while saving ground. MEDICAL PRO was used up setting the early pace.

Owners— 1, Austin Dale H & Heatherwood; 2, Borosh Shirley & Vita Joseph S; 3, Tam Ping W; 4, Sommer Viola; 5, My Paradise Farms; 6, G Lack Farms; 7, Oakridge Stable; 8, Perroncino John S

Trainers—1, Schosberg Richard; 2, Borosh Allen; 3, Lake Robert P; 4, Martin Frank; 5, Friedman Mitchell; 6, Klesaris Robert P; 7, Dunham Bob G; 8, Terracciano Neal

Fabian was claimed by Popolo Nicholas A; trainer, Galluscio Dominic G.

Scratched— Imaging (6Apr95 6AQU8), Devoted Glory (23Apr95 3AQU9)

As expected, Medical Pro cracked when unable to open up a big lead, and Bold Spector outdueled Groovy Attire to edge clear in the final furlong at a generous $10.20 mutual. Had Groovy Attire not compromised his chances with another poor break, the margin might've been closer.

THE SHOWPIECE EVENT of Belmont's spring-summer meeting is, of course, the Belmont Stakes for 3-year-olds. But the most prestigious race for older males is the Metropolitan Handicap, better known simply as the Met Mile. A flat mile around a single turn is an extremely demanding test, the human equivalent of which would be the 440-yard dash; it is neither a sprint nor a route, but requires of its participants the ability to run full tilt virtually from start to finish, combining the speed of a sprinter with the staying power of a router.

Since the prize is a Grade 1 title and a winner's share of $300,000, it's safe to say that the Met Mile should be on anyone's Top Ten list of the most demanding horse races in the world.

Strangely enough, the angle that led to finding Bold Spector in a $30,000 claiming race also played a pivotal role in determining a 6-1 overlay in the Grade 1 Met:

9

Belmont Park

1 MILE. **(1:32^3) 102nd Running of THE METROPOLITAN HANDICAP. Purse $500,000 Guaranteed. Grade I. 3-year-olds and upward. By subscription of $500 each which should accompany the nomination; $2,500 to pass the entry box, $2,500 to start. The purse to be divided 60% to the winner, 20% to second, 11% to third, 6% to fourth and 3% to fifth. Weights Wednesday, May 24. Starters to be named at the closing time of entries. Trophies will be oresented to the winning owner, trainer and jockey. Closed Saturday, May 3, with 31 nominations.**

Lite The Fuse
Own: Dutrow Richard E
KRONE J A (72 18 12 14 .25)

B. c. 4
Sire: Buckaroo (Buckpasser)
Dam: Annie's Dream (Droll Role)
Br: Dutrow Richard E (Fla)
Tr: Dutrow Richard E (4 1 1 1 .25)

113

Lifetime Record :	6 4 1 1	$186,925			
1995	2 1 1 0	$111,520	Turf	0 0 0 0	
1994	4 3 0 1	$75,405	Wet	2 2 0 0	$33,600
Bel	3 2 0 1	$131,805	Dist	0 0 0 0	

6May95-8Bel	fst	7f	:22^2	:45	1:09	1:21^2	3↑ Carter H-G1	108	4	5	4^2	5^3	4^1	1no	Perez R B	111	4.70	94-06	Lite The Fuse111^{no} Our Emblem113^2 You And I113^1		9
Bobbled break, steadied 7/16 pole, split horses str, driving																					
17Apr95-8Aqu	fst	6f	:21^4	:44^1	:56^1	1:08^4	3↑ BoldRuler H-G3	109	2	4	1^2	1^1	1$^{\frac{1}{2}}$	2$^{1\frac{1}{4}}$	Krone J A	111	3.65	97-08	Rizzi112$^{1\frac{1}{4}}$ Lite The Fuse111^1 Evil Bear116^{nk}	Drifted, held place	6
9Oct94-8Bel	fst	6f	:22	:44^4	:56^3	1:09	3↑ Boojum H-G2	101	3	7	3$^{1\frac{1}{2}}$	2^1	3$^{2\frac{1}{2}}$	3$^{5\frac{1}{2}}$	Krone J A	110	*2.20	90-11	Meritocrat113^1 Birdonthewire117$^{4\frac{1}{2}}$ Lite The Fuse110^1	No late bid	8
25Sep94-7Bel	gd	6f	:21^3	:44^1	:56^1	1:08^3	3↑ Alw 42000N$Y	105	4	4	3$^{5\frac{1}{2}}$	3^4	2$^{\frac{1}{2}}$	1$^{1\frac{3}{4}}$	Krone J A	111	*.40	98-12	LiteTheFuse111$^{1\frac{3}{4}}$ MiningBurrh115^{hd} UnrelMot122$^{\frac{3}{4}}$	Checked turn, driving	4
26Aug94-7Sar	my	6f	:21^4	:45^1	:57^2	1:09^4	3↑ Alw 28000N2L	104	5	3	2^{hd}	1^3	1$^{3\frac{1}{2}}$	1$^{7\frac{1}{2}}$	Krone J A	114	*.20	92-17	Lite The Fuse114$^{7\frac{1}{2}}$ Pauliano112^{no} Judge Vonsteubon113^{10}	Mild drive	6
3Aug94-10Sar	wf	6f	:22	:44^4	:56^4	1:09^2	3↑ Alw 28000N2L	103	5	2	1^{hd}	1^1	1$^{2\frac{1}{2}}$	1^6	Krone J A	112	1.70	94-13	Lite The Fuse112^6 Concoctor112$^{\frac{3}{4}}$ Pauliano112^3	Ridden out	9

WORKOUTS: May 24 Aqu 5f fst :59^1 H *1/3* May 17 Aqu 5f fst :58^1 H *1/2* ●Apr 27 Aqu 5f fst :58^1 H *1/9* Apr 15 Aqu 3f fst :35^3 B *2/8* ●Apr 8 Aqu 5f fst :58 H *1/7* ●Mar 27 Aqu 4f fst :48 B *1/6*

Our Emblem
Own: Phipps Ogden
SANTOS J A (80 13 9 13 .16)

Dk. b or br c. 4
Sire: Mr. Prospector (Raise a Native)
Dam: Personal Ensign (Private Account)
Br: Phipps Ogden (Ky)
Tr: McGaughey Claude III (18 2 4 2 .11)

113

Lifetime Record :	12 3 3 1	$137,846			
1995	4 1 2 1	$66,716	Turf	0 0 0 0	
1994	5 1 1 0	$54,720	Wet	2 0 0 0	$30,000
Bel	3 1 1 0	$45,000	Dist	2 1 0 1	$29,456

6May95-8Bel	fst	7f	:22^2	:45	1:09	1:21^2	3↑ Carter H-G1	108	3	9	8$^{8\frac{1}{4}}$	7^7	3^1	2no	Santos J A	113	3.95	94-06	Lite The Fuse111^{no} OurEmblem113^2 YouAndI113^1	Bumped brk, five wide	9
1Apr95-8Aqu	fst	1	:23^2	:46	1:09^4	1:34^3	3↑ Westchstr H-G3	102	6	3	3^2	2^1	2^2	3$^{2\frac{3}{4}}$	Smith M E	110	*1.80	93-17	Mr. Shawklit112$^{1\frac{1}{2}}$ DevilHisDue124$^{1\frac{1}{4}}$ OurEmblem110^2	Wide bid, weakened	6
10Mar95-10GP	fst	7f	:22^2	:45^1	1:09	1:21^4	Alw 33000N2X	112	3	5	4$^{5\frac{1}{2}}$	3^5	2$^{2\frac{1}{2}}$	1$^{1\frac{3}{4}}$	Smith M E	119	*.80	94-15	Our Emblem119$^{1\frac{3}{4}}$ Imtoocool119$^{1\frac{3}{4}}$ Turkomatic122^9		7
Six wide top str, angled out ten wide, driving																					
10Feb95-9GP	fst	7f	:22^1	:45	1:09^3	1:23	Alw 27000N2X	107	8	7	5^4	3^{nk}	2^{hd}	2no	Smith M E	119	2.50	88-20	April Christmas122^{no} Our Emblem119$^{5\frac{1}{2}}$ Bull Inthe Heather119^5		9
Seven wide leaving bkstr, eight wide top str, just missed																					
4Dec94-9Aqu	fst	7f	:22^4	:46	1:10^3	1:23^2	3↑ Alw 32000N2X	95	3	7	4^2	3^2	2^4	2$^{3\frac{1}{2}}$	Davis R G	115	2.60	83-15	Crafty117$^{3\frac{1}{2}}$ Our Emblem115^1 Brett's Jet115$^{2\frac{3}{4}}$	In traffic	9
13May94-4Bel	fst	1$\frac{1}{16}$	:24	:47^3	1:12	1:43^1	3↑ Alw 32000N2X	90	5	7	6$^{2\frac{1}{2}}$	3^2	2$^{\frac{1}{2}}$	5$^{2\frac{3}{4}}$	Bailey J D	112	*1.00	83-17	Signal Tap114$^{\frac{3}{4}}$ Peace Baby119^1 Kc's Personal Flag119^{no}	Flattened out	7
16Apr94-9Aqu	my	1$\frac{1}{8}$	:47^2	1:11^2	1:36^2	1:49	Wood Mem-G1	81	8	8	5$^{2\frac{1}{2}}$	4^2	4$^{7\frac{1}{2}}$	4$^{16\frac{3}{4}}$	Davis R G	123	14.90	74-19	Irgun123$^{1\frac{1}{2}}$ Go For Gin123$^{8\frac{3}{4}}$ Shiprock123$^{6\frac{1}{2}}$	Flattened out	9
5Apr94-7Aqu	fst	1	:22^4	:45^3	1:10^1	1:35^3	Alw 29000N1X	94	8	7	7^6	4$^{4\frac{1}{2}}$	1^{hd}	1^6	Bailey J D	117	4.20	90-13	Our Emblem117^6 Doctrinaire117^1 Stoner Creek119$^{1\frac{1}{2}}$	Drew off	9
12Mar94-2GP	fst	7f	:22	:44^4	1:09^4	1:22^4	Alw 31600N1X	19	9	5	4$^{\frac{1}{2}}$	11^{10}	12^{23}	12$^{33\frac{1}{2}}$	Bailey J D	119	7.50	55-10	Superlative Code119$^{3\frac{1}{2}}$ A Firm Mister122$^{2\frac{3}{4}}$ Add The Gold122^{hd}	Stopped	12
20Oct93-8Aqu	sly	7f	:22^2	:45^2	1:09^4	1:22^3	Cowdin-G2	56	2	6	5$^{2\frac{1}{2}}$	4$^{2\frac{1}{2}}$	4^{10}	6^{20}	Bailey J D	122	4.10	71-13	You And I122^5 Bermuda Cedar122^{11} Gulliviegold122^{hd}	No threat	7

WORKOUTS: May 27 Bel 4f gd :48 B *2/18* May 22 Bel 5f fst :59^4 H *3/43* May 17 Bel 4f fst :54 B *37/38* ●May 4 Bel 4f fst :46^3 H *1/49* Apr 28 Bel 5f fst 1:01^1 B *4/16* Apr 19 Bel 4f fst :48^2 H *3/17*

Not Surprising

Own: Van Worp Robert Jr

Ch. g. 5
Sire: Medieval Man (Noholme II)
Dam: Tenderly Calling (Always Gallant)
Br: Raven Brook Farm Inc (Fla)
Tr: Van Worp Judson (—)

DAVIS R G (73 8 18 10 .11)

113

Lifetime Record:	32 14 3 3	$439,953			
1995	6 4 0 1	$129,018	Turf	3 1 1 0	$34,000
1994	10 3 3 0	$158,165	Wet	4 3 0 0	$102,900
Bel	0 0 0 0		Dist	0 0 0 0	

29Apr95-11Hia sly 1⅛ :464 1:104 1:35 1:481 3↑ Seminole H50k 105 1 6 2½ 1½ 12 12½ Castillo H Jr L 117 2.10 101-09 Not Surprising1172½ Pride Of Burkaan1171 Beyton1148 Ridden out 9
1Apr95-8Hia fst 7f :23 :46 1:093 1:221 3↑ HiaSprntChpH50k 105 2 6 41½ 31½ 2hd 12 Davis R G L 114 12.30 98-11 Not Surprising1142 Evil Bear118¾ Turf Star1121 Driving, inside 10
11Mar95-9GP gd 1 1/16 Ⓣ :224 :464 1:104 1:41 + 3↑ Ft Laudrl H-G3 93 5 5 73½ 96¾ 64½ 98½ Henry W T L 114 28.00 83-18 The Vid1203 Flying American113nk D J's Rainbow1141½ Gave way 12
18Feb95-11Tam fst 1 1/16 :233 :464 1:111 1:442 3↑ Tam Bud BC77k 99 4 3 32 3½ 16 1hd Henry W T L 114 3.20 100 — Not Surprising114hd Mighty Avanti1135 Boisterous1131½ All out 12
28Jan95-10Tam fst 7f :224 :452 1:101 1:231 3↑ B C Super45k 96 8 8 74½ 21 3nk 32½ Henry W T L 122 *.20 99-11 Boisterous1102½ Mr. Tooth116no Not Surprising1227½ Bid, hung 9
7Jan95-9Tam gd 6f :223 :461 :581 1:104 3↑ Pelican28k 105 9 2 56½ 41½ 16 111½ Henry W T L 113 *.90 98-16 Not Surprising11311 Honor Colony116no Reigning Glory122no Strong race 12
25Jly94-8Crc sly 1 1/16 ⊗ :243 :491 1:133 1:454 3↑ Handicap22k 85 4 6 62½ 53½ 45 58½ Ramos W S L 117 *.60 82-10 Silent Lake1121½ Departing Cloud1132¾ Jack's Hope1124 Showed little 6
16Jly94-11Crc fst 1⅛ :471 1:122 1:384 1:523 3↑ SpendABuckH100k 100 5 4 42 62½ 35 54½ Valles E S L 115 12.30 86-14 Daniel's Boy111¾ It'sali'lknownfact1103 Aggressive Chief115nk Faded 8
25Jun94-11Crc fst 7f :232 :462 1:103 1:232 3↑ Emrld DunesH100k 98 6 3 52½ 42½ 53 52½ Henry W T L 116 2.90 92-12 Swedaus111nk DH Score A Birdie113 DH Daniel's Boy111¾ 7
Seven wide top str, lacked response
4Jun94-9Crc yl 5f Ⓣ :221 :46 :574 3↑ Largo Mar H100k 100 1 8 93½ 83½ 32½ 22 Henry W T L 116 6.60 93-05 Cool Air1182 Not Surprising1161½ Absent Russian112nk Rallied 12

WORKOUTS: ●May 17 Hia 5f fst :592 H 1/4 ●Apr 24 Tam 5f fst 1:004 H 1/4 ●Apr 15 Tam 5f fst 1:002 H 1/17 ●Mar 25 Tam 3f fst :354 H 1/15 Mar 3 Tam 5f fst 1:014 H 2/13

Cleante (Arg)

Own: Whitham Janis R

Dk. b or br h. 6
Sire: Kleiglight (Majestic Light)
Dam: Orientadora (Pepenador)
Br: Haras El Malacate (Arg)
Tr: McAnally Ronald (—)

BAILEY J D (60 18 7 6 .30)

111

Lifetime Record:	23 10 2 2	$411,958			
1995	4 1 0 1	$40,425	Turf	15 5 2 1	$264,681
1994	4 0 0 1	$14,004	Wet	1 0 0 1	$11,250
Bel	0 0 0 0		Dist	4 3 0 1	$103,898

23Apr95-7SA fst 1 :222 :454 1:10 1:344 Ⓡ Bates Motel65k 110 4 4 33½ 32 33 15↓ McCarron C J LB 114 13.60 95-10 DH Tossofthecoin114 DH Cleante1145 Hill Pass114nk Closed gamely 6
11Mar95-8GG sly 1 :23 :461 1:094 1:35 3↑ Berkeley H83k 97 5 7 712 89½ 87½ 33 Chapman T M LB 115 16.80 92-15 Double Jab1152½ Corslew116½ Cleante115nk Wide late bid 8
10Feb95-3SA fm 1¼ Ⓣ :473 1:122 1:363 2:021 Alw 60000N$mY 76 5 2 21½ 35 610 610½ McCarron C J LB 116 9.30 68-21 Memento Mori1162 Serrant1162¾ L'express1161 Stalked, gave way 6
20Jan95-5SA gd 1 Ⓣ :23 :463 1:114 1:374 Alw 60000N$mY 91 7 6 610 55½ 57 47¼ McCarron C J LB 116 13.60 70-23 Caesour1163½ City Nights110nk Square Cut1163½ No late bid 8
7Oct94-8SA fm 1⅛ Ⓣ :464 1:103 1:351 1:472 3↑ Alw 60000N$mY 81 3 5 67 64½ 66½ 69¾ Delahoussaye E LB 116 3.90 72-18 Newton's Law114nk Daros1161½ Sneakin Jake1184 Pinched start 6
2Sep94-8Dmr fm 1 1/16 Ⓣ :252 :493 1:133 1:431 3↑ Ⓡ How Now H66k 93 1 3 44½ 53½ 54½ 53½ Pincay L Jr LB 117 5.60 87-09 Blaze O'brien116no Rapan Boy1202 Inner City119no No late bid 5
20Jly94-8Hol fm 1 1/16 Ⓣ :234 :473 1:111 1:412 + 3↑ Alw 55000N$mY 96 5 5 58 63½ 65½ 33½ Pincay L Jr LB 117 2.70 86-17 Rapan Boy115½ Brilliant Blue1162¾ Cleante117½ Up for 3rd 7
29Jun94-8Hol fm 1 1/16 Ⓣ :232 :47 1:111 1:404 + Alw 55000N$mY 85 1 5 53½ 74½ 64½ 47 Pincay L Jr B 117 *2.00 85-08 Inner City1171 Brilliant Blue1141 Earl Of Barking1215 No rally 7
11Dec93♦ San Isidro(Arg) fm *1 Ⓣ LH 1:323 3↑ Grn Prm Joaquin S de Anchorena-G1 1nk Herrera J 130 *.55 Cleante130nk Calouro119½ Soft Wear132nk 10
Tr: Vilmar Sanguinetti Stk 119000 *Towards rear,6th halfway,rallied 1f out,led final 16th,driving*
16Oct93♦ San Isidro(Arg) gd *1 Ⓣ LH 1:352 3↑ Gran Premio San Isidro-G1 16 Herrera J 131 *.50 Cleante1316 Correntino Bid1172½ Royal Martial132hd 6
Stk 77000 *Tracked leader, led 1f out, quickly clear*

WORKOUTS: May 27 Bel 4f gd :491 B 9/18 ●May 21 Hol 7f fst 1:244 H 1/7 May 14 Hol 6f fst 1:141 H 14/24 May 8 Hol 5f fst 1:004 H 12/37 May 2 Hol 4f fst :493 H 21/39 Apr 20 SA 5f fst 1:003 H 12/47

Key Contender

Own: Flying Zee Stables

Ch. h. 7
Sire: Fit to Fight (Chieftain)
Dam: Key Witness (Key to the Mint)
Br: Mellon Paul (Va)
Tr: Martin Jose (15 1 1 4 .07)

VELAZQUEZ J R (76 16 5 11 .21)

110

Lifetime Record:	51 14 16 6	$564,260			
1995	6 1 1 1	$56,930	Turf	1 0 0 0	
1994	10 4 2 2	$158,726	Wet	5 3 1 0	$82,166
Bel	23 6 9 5	$243,100	Dist	8 4 2 0	$116,620

4May95-8Bel fst 1 1/16 :223 :452 1:10 1:42 Alw 48000N$mY 103 3 2 21 31½ 31½ 3½ Velazquez J R 118 b 4.40 88-18 Slick Horn113nk As Indicated113nk Key Contender1181¾ Saved ground 5
15Apr95-8Aqu fst 1 :224 :452 1:10 1:352 Alw 46000N$Y 105 4 3 2hd 1hd 2hd 1hd Valdivia J7 112 b 19.10 92-10 KeyContendr112hd SlickHorn1166 Frmonthfrwy116nk Lost whip 1/4, game 8
25Mar95-11Hia fst 1⅛ :453 1:093 1:342 1:471 3↑ Widener H-G3 87 12 5 45 85½ 1413 1412½ Davis R G L 114 b 9.10 94-05 Party Manners1131½ Dusty Screen1151½ Pride Of Burkaan1161 Stopped 14
20Feb95-10Lrl fst 7f :222 :45 1:092 1:22 3↑ GenGeorge H-G2 96 4 6 56 66½ 74¾ 56½ Prado E S 115 b 11.40 92-15 Who Wouldn't119no Storm Tower1163½ Powis Castle1182½ Outrun 8
8Feb95-7Aqu fst 6f ⊡ :234 :47 :593 1:123 3↑ Handicap46k 86 3 5 54½ 56 57 55¾ Perez R B 118 fb 4.70 74-27 Boom Towner122¾ Mr. Shawklit1132 Prank Call111no Four wide 6
16Jan95-8Aqu gd 1 1/16 ⊡ :231 :46 1:093 1:41 3↑ Aqueduct H-G3 103 6 2 2½ 21 23 25 Luzzi M J 115 b 5.00 95-20 Danzig's Dance1115 Key Contender1154 Golden Larch1124 Forced pace 8
31Dec94-7Aqu fst 1 1/16 ⊡ :24 :473 1:124 1:46 3↑ Handicap50k 94 3 2 2hd 1hd 2hd 34½ Luzzi M J 120 b 3.40 70-34 Electrojet114½ Country Sky1104 Key Contender1203½ Weakened 5
10Dec94-8Aqu wf 1 3/16 ⊡ :472 1:121 1:372 1:562 3↑ QueensCntyH-G3 96 7 2 2½ 2½ 42½ 43½ McCauley W H 117 b *2.40 89-23 FdrlFunds112nk Jcksonport1101¾ ContrctCourt1161½ Bobbled break, wknd 8
26Nov94-8Aqu fst 1 :223 :454 1:111 1:36 3↑ NYRA Mile H-G1 91 1 6 53 54 611 612¾ Luzzi M J 115 b 13.10 75-28 Cigar1117 Devil His Due1242½ Punch Line1121 Broke slowly, tired 12
15Oct94-8Kee fst 1⅛ :473 1:12 1:372 1:50 3↑ Fayette109k 109 4 2 21½ 22½ 21½ 21½ Bruin J E 117 b *.90e 83-20 SunnySunrise1201½ KeyContender1172 PowerfulPunch117no Second best 7

WORKOUTS: ●May 25 Bel 4f fst :464 H 1/35 May 19 Bel 5f sly 1:003 H 1/1 May 12 Bel tr.t 4f my :492 B 1/2 Apr 26 Bel tr.t 4f fst :49 B 5/21 ●Apr 10 Bel tr.t 4f fst :48 B 1/7 ●Mar 19 Hia 5f fst :593 H 1/8

Silver Goblin

Own: Horton Al J

Gr. g. 4
Sire: Silver Ghost (Mr. Prospector)
Dam: Molly O'Horton (Zonic)
Br: Horton Al J (Okla)
Tr: Smith Kenny P (—)

CORDOVA D W (—)

120

Lifetime Record:	19 14 2 2	$1,025,395			
1995	4 3 1 0	$325,950	Turf	0 0 0 0	
1994	11 8 0 2	$518,000	Wet	1 1 0 0	$60,000
Bel	0 0 0 0		Dist	1 1 0 0	$22,800

15Apr95-9OP fst 1⅛ :462 1:104 1:352 1:471 Oaklawn H-G1 116 6 3 33½ 2hd 2hd 22½ Cordova D W L 119 f 4.60 100-13 Cigar1202½ Silver Goblin1194 Concern1221 7
Bumped, 4 wide early, led 3/4's, no match
25Mar95-9OP fst 1 1/16 :23 :461 1:111 1:423 Razorback H-G2 112 3 2 23 21½ 13½ 15½ Cordova D W L 124 f *.50 94-19 Silver Goblin1245½ Joseph's Robe111no Wooden Ticket1151½ Ridden out 6
25Feb95-9OP fst 1 1/16 :231 :46 1:101 1:42 Essex H-G3 109 2 2 21½ 21 1hd 17 Cordova D W L 122 f *.40 97-15 Silver Goblin1227 Prince Of The Mt.1131 Golden Gear1137 Ridden out 7
3Feb95-8OP fst 1 :224 :464 1:12 1:363 Alw 38000N$mY 112 3 2 2hd 12 15 18 Cordova D W L 121 f *.40 96-23 Silver Goblin1218 Dakota Danzig118hd Foxtrail1154 Ridden out 7
15Oct94-7RP my 1⅛ :464 1:111 1:361 1:491 RedEarthDby100k 106 2 2 22 31 11 13 Cordova D W LB 122 f *.40 97-12 Silver Goblin1223 Fly Cry1222 Joseph's Robe1186 Driving 6
13Sep94-9FP fst 1 1/16 :231 :464 1:112 1:442 FairmontDby-G3 105 5 2 2hd 1hd 1hd 12 Cordova D W L 124 f *.50 96-21 SilverGoblin1242 ShrpDrums1196½ RoylMinister113hd Early speed, driving 7
6Aug94-10Aks fst 1⅛ :481 1:131 1:373 1:494 OmahaGoldCp-G3 105 3 2 25 2½ 1hd 11½ Cordova D W LB 122 f *.50 90-17 SilverGoblin1221½ SharpDrums11361½ RonyPony1152½ Reserved, rallied well 7
10Jly94-8ArP fst 1 1/16 :222 :451 1:10 1:442 Colo Derby100k 97 5 3 21 16 110 117½ Cordova D W LB 124 f *.30 93-15 Silver Goblin12417 C'villes Quest124½ Sir Conway1248 Ridden out 8
19Jun94-8Hou fst 7f :22 :443 1:09 1:22 Tex Heritage60k 106 4 4 22 21 15 18½ Cordova D W L 122 f *.50 — — Silver Goblin1228½ Gate King113nk Andean Chasqui1171½ Ridden out 8
21May94-10Pim fst 1 3/16 :472 1:114 1:37 1:562 Preakness-G1 93 4 3 31½ 41½ 67½ 812 Cordova D W L 126 f 9.90 68-18 Tabasco Cat126¾ Go For Gin1266 Concern126½ 10
Hit gate start, nothing left

WORKOUTS: May 25 Bel 4f fst :493 B 18/35 May 17 Bel 6f fst 1:172 B 3/3 May 11 Bel 4f sly :503 B 6/6 Apr 12 OP 4f gd :512 B 12/17 Apr 5 OP 5f fst 1:03 B 10/21 Mar 21 OP 4f fst :491 B 6/26

You And I

Own: Gann Edmund A

Dk. b or br c. 4
Sire: Kris S. (Roberto)
Dam: La Chaposa (Ups)
Br: Fabry W A & Johnson Jeffrey E (Fla)
Tr: Frankel Robert (1 0 0 1 .00)

CHAVEZ J F (105 19 11 15 .18)

112

Lifetime Record:	11 4 0 2	$208,110			
1995	1 0 0 1	$16,500	Turf	2 0 0 0	$7,500
1994	8 2 0 1	$107,130	Wet	2 2 0 0	$86,280
Bel	3 2 0 1	$98,580	Dist	0 0 0 0	

6May95-8Bel fst 7f :222 :45 1:09 1:212 3↑ Carter H-G1 103 5 3 2hd 2½ 1½ 32 Alvarado F T 113 *3.20 92-06 Lite The Fuse111no Our Emblem1132 You And I1131 Dueled, weakened 9
5Sep94-8Dmr fm 1⅛ Ⓣ :474 1:114 1:362 1:483 Dmr Dby Inv-G2 82 9 3 33½ 53¾ 96¾ 108¼ Valenzuela P A B 122 10.40 85-08 Ocean Crest122½ Unfinished Symph122½ D Eagle Eyed1221½ Weakened 10
14Aug94-8Dmr fm 1 1/16 Ⓣ :234 :48 1:12 1:421 La Jolla H-G3 96 1 6 65 41¾ 42½ 4½ McCarron C J B 117 4.40 95-07 Marvin's Faith114no UnfinishedSymph120hd OceanCrest114nk Bumped late 7
16Jly94-9Lrl fst 6f :214 :444 :563 1:084 3↑ DeFrancsMem-G2 90 5 7 78 88½ 99 89 Davis R G 112 4.40 87-12 Cherokee Run1142½ Boom Towner119½ Fu Man Slew107½ No factor 11
11Jun94-6Bel fst 7f :22 :441 1:08 1:201 Riva Ridge-G3 108 4 3 21½ 2½ 11½ 12¾ McCarron C J 122 *2.80 102-03 You And I1222¾ End Sweep1143¾ Slew Gin Fizz1221½ Driving 9
16Apr94-5SA fst 6½f :213 :442 1:094 1:161 San Pedro110k 86 1 4 3nk 42 43 43 Almeida G F B 119 3.20 88-15 King's Blade117½ Al Renee1151½ Halloween Treat1171¼ Inside bid 9
19Mar94-8FG fst 1 1/16 :223 :454 1:103 1:424 La Derby-G3 85 4 4 86½ 52¾ 62¾ 77¼ Sellers S J 122 3.90 94 — Kandaly1181½ Game Coin118hd Argolid118no 10
Wide drive, little impact
30Jan94-9GP fst 7f :213 :44 1:081 1:211 Hutcheson-G2 100 2 3 21½ 31½ 33 33¾ Sellers S J 119 4.80 93-11 Holy Bull122¾ Patton1133 You And I1193 Lacked response 5
11Jan94-6GP sly 7f :223 :46 1:104 1:233 Alw 26400N2X 95 5 1 2hd 2½ 2hd 1nk Bailey J D 117 *.40 85-20 You And I117nk Pren De Ville11013 Crary1172 Fully extended 6
20Oct93-8Aqu sly 7f :222 :452 1:094 1:223 Cowdin-G2 99 3 3 1½ 2hd 11½ 15 Perret C 122 *1.80 91-13 You And I1225 Bermuda Cedar12211 Gulliviegold122hd Drew off 7

WORKOUTS: May 25 Hol 5f fst 1:001 H 8/43 May 18 Hol 6f fst 1:124 H 7/23 ●May 2 Hol 5f fst :59 H 1/32 Apr 26 Hol 7f fst 1:261 H 1/1 ●Apr 20 Hol 7f fst 1:263 H 1/11 Apr 14 Hol 6f fst 1:14 H 2/14

```
Mr. Shawklit                              Ch. c. 4                                          Lifetime Record :  17 6 4 0   $250,150
Own: Anchel Edward & Judith               Sire: Afleet (Mr. Prospector)                     1995  6 2 1 0  $102,857 | Turf  0 0 0 0
                                          Dam: Shawklit (Groshawk)                          1994  8 2 2 0   $94,453 | Wet   2 1 1 0  $50,355
LUZZI M J (80 7 16 13 .09)                Br:  Treasure Hill Farm Inc (Ky)            113   Bel   5 1 0 0   $19,920 | Dist  3 1 0 0  $65,760
                                          Tr:  Laboccetta Frank (3 0 0 0 .00)

6May95-8Bel fst 7f      :222 :45 1:09 1:212 3↑ Carter H-G1         96 8 1 52¼ 3½ 62¾ 65½ Luzzi M J    115   3.75 88-06 Lite The Fuse111no Our Emblem1132 You And I1131         Four wide, tired 9
1Apr95-8Aqu fst 1       :232 :46 1:094 1:343 3↑ Westchstr H-G3     107 5 1 1½ 11 12 11½   Luzzi M J    112   5.40 96-17 Mr. Shawklit1121½ Devil His Due1241¼ Our Emblem1102    Speed, drew clear 6
18Mar95-4Aqu fst 6f     :231 :462 :58 1:093 Alw 36000N4X           108 1 3 21 11 15 111½  Luzzi M J    114   *.60 94-15 Mr. Shawklit11411 Blum Gone117nk Prank Call114½          Ridden out 5
18Feb95-8Aqu fst 6f [•] :224 :453 :573 1:101 3↑ CoaltownBCH-G3     102 2 4 43 21 33 44½   Luzzi M J    110   9.00 87-18 Mining Burrah1172 Crafty Alfel1162 Boom Towner120½     Bid, tired 5
8Feb95-7Aqu fst 6f [•]  :234 :47 :593 1:123 3↑ Handicap46k          98 5 1 1½ 11½ 1½ 2¾   Luzzi M J    113   7.80 79-27 Boom Towner122¾ Mr. Shawklit1132 Prank Call111no     Brushed late 6
29Jan95-7Aqu fst 6f [•] :223 :454 :58 1:104 3↑ SprtngPlateH82k      92 4 5 56 54 57½ 68¼   Luzzi M J    111   4.60e 81-26 Mining Burrah1151¼ Boom Towner1194 Crafty Alfel118¾     Tired 7
28Jly94-9Sar sly 6f     :22 :452 :573 1:104 Screen King54k         91 3 2 23 3nk 2½ 1½    McCauley W H 115   5.30 87-17 Mr. Shawklit115½ Scarlet Rage1152 Groovy Jett1175     Wide, driving 5
   Run in divisions
7Jly94-8Bel fst 6f      :222 :453 :572 1:094 3↑ Alw 32000N3X        78 4 4 43½ 42½ 45 49½ Santagata N  113   5.20 82-12 Slew Gin Fizz1143 Scarlet Rage112nk Digging In1176¼      No threat 6
18Jun94-5Bel fst 6f     :214 :442 :564 1:093 3↑ Alw 30000N2X        93 7 4 54½ 31 2hd 11¼ Santagata N  112   5.20 93-10 Mr. Shawklit1121¼ Unreal Mot1191¼ Cross Ice Pass111no    Driving 7
28May94-7Bel fst 6f     :222 :453 :58 1:11 3↑ Alw 30000N2X          64 6 2 31 31½ 43½ 59   Bailey J D   112 b *1.00 77-14 Gulpha Gorge1212¼ Unreal Mot1212¼ Super Nip1212½       Gave way 6
WORKOUTS: ●May 21 Aqu 5f fst :59 H 1/12  May 1 Aqu 4f sly :47 H 1/1  Apr 26 Aqu 5f fst 1:004 B 1/2  ●Apr 20 Aqu 5f fst 1:003 B 1/4  Apr 12 Aqu 4f fst :472 B 2/11  Mar 29 Aqu 3f fst :374 B 8/9

Romarin (Brz)                             B. h. 5                                           Lifetime Record :  17 9 2 2   $434,255
Own: De Paula Machado Lin..o Eduardo      Sire: Itajara (Felicio)                           1995  5 2 1 1  $274,985 | Turf 11 6 1 1 $385,933
                                          Dam: Salluca (Sallust)                            1994  4 3 0 1  $141,158 | Wet   2 0 1 0  $20,000
SMITH M E (61 18 10 8 .30)                Br:  Haras Sao Jose E Expedictus (Brz)      116   Bel   0 0 0 0           | Dist  2 1 1 0  $21,306
                                          Tr:  Mandella Richard (—)

6May95-7CD fm 1⅛ Ⓣ :464 1:103 1:343 1:464 3↑ ET Classic-G2        107 9 1 11 11 11½ 11¼ Nakatani C S     L 118  6.80 97-02 Romarin1181¼ Blues Traveller1201¼ Hasten To Add120hd            12
   Drifted out start, ridden out
1Apr95-8SA fm 1 Ⓣ :223 :454 1:093 1:343 El Rincon H-G2             107 2 1 11 11 11 3½   Delahoussaye E  LB 120  3.20 92-07 Savinio116hd River Flyer121½ Romarin1204½             Rail, gamely 7
5Mar95-8SA sly 1 ⊗ :222 :462 1:123 1:403 Arcadia H-G2               99 2 1 11 12 14½ 2hd Nakatani C S    LB 120  *.80 66-42 College Town117hd Romarin12012 Finder's Fortune1143    Caught on wire 5
21Jan95-8SA gd 1¼ Ⓣ :47 1:131 1:383 2:053 SanMarcos H-G2            44 7 2 11½ 32 715 730 Nakatani C S     B 121 *1.40 32-38 River Flyer1181 Silver Wizard117nk Savinio1162      Tired, not abused 7
2Jan95-8SA fm 1⅛ Ⓣ :47 1:12 1:364 1:491 S Gabriel H-G2            104 6 1 11½ 11½ 12½ 11¼ Nakatani C S   B 119 *1.10 73-27 Romarin1191¼ Inner City1161 Ianomami1161           Rated, ridden out 6
27Nov94-9Hol gd 1 Ⓣ :232 :471 1:104 1:352 3↑ Hol Mile H150k       103 6 1 11 11½ 11½ 1½  Nakatani C S     B 117 *1.90 87-17 Romarin117½ Slew Of Damascus122¾ Inner City115no     Held on gamely 6
19Oct94-8SA fm 1 Ⓣ :224 :45 1:083 1:333 3↑ Alw 60000N$mY           106 3 1 11 11 12 11¼   Nakatani C S     B 115  4.20 97-03 Romarin1151¼ Savinio1154½ Recommendation115½        Strong hand ride 6
13Mar94♦ La Plata(Arg) fst *1 5/16 LH 2:111 3↑ Grn Prmio Asoc Latinoamericana-G1   32½ Pacheco E     123  17.55      Much Better132½ Enfatico1232 Romarin1236                 14
                                        Stk 272000                                                                         Led, dueled 1f out, headed final 16th
16Jan94♦ Cdad Jardim(Brz) fst *1¼ 2:032 3↑ Grande Premio Piratininga-G2   1                   118    -        Further Information unavailable                         10
23Dec93♦ Cdad Jardim(Brz) fm *1⅛ Ⓣ 1:504 Prova Especial Natal           1                   124    -        Further Information unavailable                          8
WORKOUTS: ●May 24 CD 5f fst :593 H 1/22  May 2 CD 5f my 1:013 B 2/25  Apr 26 CD 1 fst 1:402 B 1/1  Apr 20 CD 5f sly 1:03 B 4/7  Apr 14 SA 4f fst :503 H 31/35  Mar 25 SA 5f fst 1:031 H 74/85
```

Overnight rain rendered the main track muddy during the morning hours of Memorial Day, hastening the scratch of morning-line favorite Devil His Due, who was battling some nagging injuries. The track was muddy — and floated by the maintenance crew — through the early portion of the program, but had dried out sufficiently to be harrowed and upgraded to good as post time neared for the Met.

The favorite at 7-5 was Silver Goblin, an exceptionally fast and consistent gray gelding whose only out-of-the-money finish from 19 career starts had come as a 3-year-old in the Preakness, when he slammed into the side of the gate at the break. Silver Goblin had excellent tactical speed, and projected to get a good trip just off an early pace contested between Romarin and You And I.

Romarin had won four races since being imported to the U.S., all on grass when able to get clear through the early going. Romarin's three dirt wins had come in South America much earlier in his career against opposition of questionable quality, and his only dirt race in this country had seen him blow a clear lead at odds-on in an off-the-turf mile around two turns.

You And I, meanwhile, would be quite at home over Belmont's main track, where as a 3-year-old he had lowered the seven-furlong record to 1:20 1/5 in the Riva Ridge Stakes. He was two-for-two on wet tracks, so the moisture in the surface was certainly not a problem. But what were handicappers to make of his fading third place finish as the favorite in the Carter Handicap (which, ironically enough, had been run just a few races after Bold Spector's $25,000 claimer)?

A check of the Carter chart shows that You And I's two-length defeat was much better than it looked at first glance:

EIGHTH RACE

Belmont

MAY 6, 1995

7 FURLONGS. (1.20¹) 95th Running of THE CARTER HANDICAP. Purse $150,000 Guaranteed. Grade I. 3-year-olds and upward. By subscription of $150 each which should accompany the nomination, $750 to pass the entry box, $750 to start. The purse to be divided 60% to the winner, 20% to second, 11% to third, 6% to fourth and 3% to fifth. Weights Tuesday, May 2. Starters to be named at the closing time of entries. Trophies will be presented to the winning owner, trainer and jockey. Closed Saturday, April 22, with 27 nominations.

Value of Race: $150,000 Winner $90,000; second $30,000; third $16,500; fourth $9,000; fifth $4,500. Mutuel Pool $421,752.00 Exacta Pool $491,517.00 Triple Pool $378,844.00

Last Raced	Horse	M/Eqt. A.Wt	PP	St	¼	½	Str	Fin	Jockey	Odds $1
17Apr95 8Aqu²	Lite The Fuse	4 111	4	5	4hd	5³	4hd	1no	Perez R B	4.70
1Apr95 8Aqu³	Our Emblem	4 113	3	9	8½	7²	3hd	2²	Santos J A	3.95
5Sep94 8Dmr¹⁰	You And I	4 113	5	3	2½	2hd	1½	3¹	Alvarado F T	3.20
21Apr95 7Aqu¹	Crafty Alfel	f	7 113	2	6	6²	6¹	5¹½	4¹	Pezua J M	29.00
17Apr95 8Aqu³	Evil Bear	5 115	6	2	3½	1½	2½	5¹½	Migliore R	13.60
1Apr95 8Aqu¹	Mr. Shawklit	4 115	8	1	5²½	3¹½	6³	6⁶	Luzzi M J	3.75
24Apr95 10Hia⁵	Meadow Flight	4 116	7	7	7¹½	9	7½	7½	Lopez C C	31.75
6Apr95 NAS¹	Lost Soldier	5 111	9	8	9	8hd	8³½	8⁷	Velazquez J R	22.00
7Apr95 7Kee¹	Prenup	4 116	1	4	1hd	4¹	9	9	Chavez J F	3.75

OFF AT 4:23 Start Good. Won driving. Time, :22², :45, 1:09, 1:21² Track fast.

$2 Mutuel Prices:

4–LITE THE FUSE	11.40	5.10	4.10
3–OUR EMBLEM		5.30	3.20
7–YOU AND I			3.30

$2 EXACTA 4–3 PAID $63.50 $2 TRIPLE 4–3–7 PAID $304.50

B. c, by Buckaroo–Annie's Dream, by Droll Role. Trainer Dutrow Richard E. Bred by Dutrow Richard E (Fla).

LITE THE FUSE bobbled a bit then was in tight at the start, steadied behind the leaders nearing the far turn, raced just off the pace to the top of the stretch, split horses in upper stretch, battled inside OUR EMBLEM through the lane and prevailed in a long drive. OUR EMBLEM bumped at the start, was reserved for a half while three wide, swung five wide to launch his bid entering the stretch, made a strong run to challenge leaving the furlong marker, battled gamely into deep stretch and just missed. YOU AND I dueled between horses into midstretch and weakened from his early efforts. CRAFTY ALFEL bumped at the start, was unhurried early, gained between horses on the turn, made a run along the inside to reach contention in upper stretch, but couldn't sustain his bid. EVIL BEAR never far back, moved up between horses while three wide to gain a slim lead midway on the turn, continued on the front into upper stretch then tired. MR. SHAWKLIT settled just off the early pace, made a run four wide to threaten on the turn then tired in the drive. MEADOW FLIGHT was never a serious threat. LOST SOLDIER never reached contention. PRENUP dueled for the early lead along the rail then gave way on the turn. MR. SHAWKLIT wore mud caulks.

The footnote mentions that You And I dueled between horses. Note that he ran Prenup into the ground soon after going a quarter, and then withstood prolonged challenges from Evil Bear and Mr. Shawklit to reclaim the lead in midstretch, only to fall prey to a pair of off-the-pace runners in the final furlong. You And I had repelled three separate challenges and had been beaten just two lengths in the Carter — while making his first start in eight months. Not only did he figure to be tighter for his second excursion to Belmont, he might have an easier time of things on the front-end, since the grass horse Romarin was the only confirmed front runner in the race.

Where was Evil Bear, you might ask? Two days prior to the Met, he had won the Roseben Handicap:

NINTH RACE

Belmont

MAY 27, 1995

6 FURLONGS. (1.07⁴) 51st Running of THE ROSEBEN HANDICAP. Purse $75,000 added. Grade III. 3-year-olds and upward. By subscription of $75 each, which should accompany the nomination, $350 to pass the entry box, $400 to start with $75,000 added. The added money and all fees to be divided 60% to the winner, 20% to second, 11% to third, 6% to fourth and 3% to fifth. Weights Tuesday, May 23. Starters to be named at the closing time of entries. Trophies will be presented to the winning owner, trainer and jockey. Closed Saturday, May 13, with 18 nominations.

Value of Race: $80,449 Winner $48,270; second $16,090; third $8,849; fourth $4,827; fifth $2,413. Mutuel Pool $301,082.00 Exacta Pool $452,841.00 Minus Show Pool $694.25

Last Raced	Horse	M/Eqt. A.Wt	PP	St	¼	½	Str	Fin	Jockey	Odds $1
6May95 8Bel⁵	Evil Bear	5 116	1	3	3½	3½	1¹	1²	Santos J A	3.85
17Apr95 8Aqu¹	Rizzi	b	4 117	3	2	1½	1½	2hd	2½	Beckner D V	0.65
14May95 7Bel²	Vallata Lane	b	4 109	5	1	2²	2½	3²	3²½	Krone J A	11.90
6May95 5CD⁵	Waldoboro	4 115	4	5	5	5	4½	4²½	Smith M E	2.50
17May95 7Bel⁵	Farmonthefreeway	bf 5 110	2	4	4²½	4¹	5	5	Chavez J F	20.40

OFF AT 5:05 Start Good. Won driving. Time, :22, :44⁴, :57, 1:09³ Track fast.

$2 Mutuel Prices:

1–EVIL BEAR	9.70	2.90	2.10
4–RIZZI		2.40	2.10
6–VALLATA LANE			2.10

$2 EXACTA 1–4 PAID $21.40

Ch. h, by Medieval Man–Bearer of Tidings, by Mongo. Trainer Reid Robert E Jr. Bred by Debhil Thoroughbred Farm (Fla).

EVIL BEAR settled just off the early pace, launched a rally between horses while three wide at the quarter pole, accelerated to the front opening a clear advantage in midstretch, then drew away under right hand encouragement. RIZZI outsprinted rivals for the early advantage, set the pace under pressure while saving ground into upper stretch, then held well for the place. VALLATA LANE forced the pace outside RIZZI into upper stretch and weakened. WALDOBORO reserved for a half while saving ground, split horses in upper stretch then lacked a strong closing bid. FARMONTHEFREEWAY raced within striking distance while four wide for a half and tired. RIZZI and VALLATA LANE wore mud caulks.

Owners— 1, Sabini Joseph C; 2, Hobeau Farm; 3, Reynolds David P; 4, Hamilton Emory A; 5, R Kay Stable

Trainers— 1, Reid Robert E Jr; 2, Jerkens H Allen; 3, Kelly Timothy D; 4, McGaughey Claude III; 5, Araya Rene A

Scratched— Fly'n J. Bryan (10May95 6BEL⁵)

Evil Bear's mild upset of the Roseben underscored his fine recent form, and flattered You And I's effort in the Carter further still. Whenever a horse wins a pace duel and the horses he beat comes back to win, award the pace duel-winner an extra gold star.

I made Silver Goblin the most likely winner of the Met, but odds of 7-5 were unacceptably low in such a contentious event. I thought You And I would be able to fight his way to the lead through the opening six furlongs, and if he improved even slightly off his gritty in-fighting performance in the Carter he was a threat to be in the picture all the way down the stretch. At 6-1 he was an attractive proposition, and worth a win bet along with a saver exacta using Silver Goblin on top:

NINTH RACE

Belmont
MAY 29, 1995

1 MILE. (1.32³) 102nd Running of THE METROPOLITAN HANDICAP. Purse $500,000 Guaranteed. Grade I. 3-year-olds and upward. By subscription of $500 each which should accompany the nomination; $2,500 to pass the entry box, $2,500 to start. The purse to be divided 60% to the winner, 20% to second, 11% to third, 6% to fourth and 3% to fifth. Weights Wednesday, May 24. Starters to be named at the closing time of entries. Trophies will be presented to the winning owner, trainer and jockey. Closed Saturday, May 3, with 31 nominations.

Value of Race: $500,000 Winner $300,000; second $100,000; third $55,000; fourth $30,000; fifth $15,000. Mutuel Pool $545,148.00 Exacta Pool $538,585.00 Triple Pool $463,356.00

Last Raced	Horse	M/Eql. A.Wt	PP	St	¼	½	¾	Str	Fin	Jockey	Odds $1
6May95 8Bel³	You And I	4 112	7	2	2¹	1hd	1hd	1½	1¹	Chavez J F	6.70
6May95 8Bel¹	Lite The Fuse	4 113	1	7	5½	3¹	3¹	2²	2²½	Krone J A	5.50
6May95 8Bel²	Our Emblem	4 114	2	9	9	9	8½	4¹	3¹½	Santos J A	6.20
29Apr95 11Hia¹	Not Surprising	5 113	3	6	7⁷	6¹	4¹	3hd	4¹½	Davis R G	20.80
4May95 8Bel³	Key Contender	b 7 110	5	5	3hd	5²	5¹½	6²	5³	Velazquez J R	32.75
6May95 7CD¹	Romarin-BR	5 116	9	1	1½	2²	2²	5hd	6hd	Smith M E	4.50
23Apr95 7SA²	Cleante-AR	6 112	4	8	8³½	8²	9	8⁴	7¹½	Bailey J D	11.80
6May95 8Bel⁶	Mr. Shawklit	4 113	8	3	6hd	7⁶	7¹	7½	8¹²	Luzzi M J	26.00
15Apr95 9OP²	Silver Goblin	f 4 120	6	4	4¹½	4hd	6hd	9	9	Cordova D W	1.40

OFF AT 5:06 Start Good. Won driving. Time, :22¹, :44¹, 1:08³, 1:34³ Track good.

$2 Mutuel Prices:

8–YOU AND I	15.40	7.30	6.40
1–LITE THE FUSE		5.40	3.30
2–OUR EMBLEM			4.60

$2 EXACTA 8–1 PAID $94.00 $2 TRIPLE 8–1–2 PAID $375.50

Dk. b. or br. c, by Kris S.–La Chaposa, by Ups. Trainer Frankel Robert. Bred by Fabry W A & Johnson Jeffrey E (Fla).

YOU AND I alternated for the lead through brisk fractions while saving ground to the top of the stretch, shook off ROMARIN to get clear in midstretch then turned back LITE THE FUSE under steady right hand encouragement. LITE THE FUSE settled just behind the dueling leaders while saving ground, angled out on the turn, made a run to threaten in midstretch but could not overtake the winner. OUR EMBLEM trailed for five furlongs after breaking slowly, rapidly gained between horses on the turn, angled to the inside in upper stretch, then finished willingly along the rail to gain a share. NOT SURPRISING reserved for a half, closed the gap while saving ground to reach contention approaching the quarter pole but couldn't sustain his rally. KEY CONTENDER raced within striking distance while three wide for six furlongs and weakened in the drive. ROMARIN dueled outside the winner into upper stretch and tired from his early efforts. CLEANTE away a bit slowly, never reached contention. MR. SHAWKLIT was never a serious threat. SILVER GOBLIN raced just off the pace while five wide for five furlongs then gave way leaving the turn. NOT SURPRISING, KEY CONTENDER and MR. SHAWKLIT wore mud caulks.

Owners— 1, Gann Edmund A; 2, Dutrow Richard E; 3, Phipps Ogden; 4, Van Worp Robert Jr; 5, Flying Zee Stables; 6, De Paula Machado Linneo Eduardo; 7, Whitham Janis R; 8, Anchel Edward & Judith; 9, Horton Al J.

Trainers—1, Frankel Robert; 2, Dutrow Richard E; 3, McGaughey Claude III; 4, Van Worp Judson; 5, Martin Jose; 6, Mandella Richard; 7, McAnally Ronald; 8, Laboccetta Frank; 9, Smith Kenny P

Overweight: Our Emblem (1), Cleante-AR (1).
Scratched— Devil His Due (13May95 10PIM2)

You And I had a tougher time with Romarin than I had anticipated, but finally shook that rival off to get clear approaching the eighth pole. An expected challenge from Silver Goblin never came (subsequent X-rays revealed he suffered a career-threatening injury during the running), and You And I was able to turn the tables on Lite The Fuse and Our Emblem, who had swept by him in the final yards of the Carter.

BELMONT STAKES WEEK is a time when public handicappers and racing writers in the New York area like to be at their sharpest. With the Triple Crown in full swing, interest in the sport is naturally heightened and the press box is crawling with out-of-town press and electronic media from all over the world.

That's why it was a bit embarrassing for me to completely overlook a standout pace play in my *Form* analysis for the third race on Friday, June 9. The story did have a profitable ending, however: although I totally missed the attributes of You'renotlistening before my Wednesday evening deadline, I did get a flash of insight on the filly as I scanned the past performances the night before the race, which in turn triggered a closer inspection of her record. Like that old shampoo commercial with the jingle, "The closer you get, the better she looks," You'renotlistening looked better and better from every conceivable angle.

To begin with, examine the pace match up for the seven-furlong sprint, and try to form a mental image of the leaders at the first call:

3 Belmont Park

7 Furlongs. **(1:20¹) CLAIMING. Purse $25,000. Fillies and mares, 4–year–olds and upward. Weight, 122 lbs. Non–winners of two races since April 27, allowed 2 lbs. A race since May 4, 4 lbs. A race since April 20, 6 lbs. Claiming price $40,000, for each $2,500 to $35,000, allowed 2 lbs. (Races where entered for $30,000 or less not considered.)**

```
Runaway Fling                                  B. f. 4                                          Lifetime Record :  38  9 11  4   $158,490
Own: Hagedorn Charles C & Rottkamp John        Sire: Imperial Fling (Northern Dancer)           1995   9  1  3  1   $46,820 | Turf  5 0 1 0   $4,400
                                               Dam:  Run Cola Run (Run the Gantlet)             1994  24  7  8  1  $105,995 | Wet   1 0 0 1     $650
CHAVEZ J F (149 28 17 24 .19)       $35,000    Br:   Bar–Lyn Farm (Fla)                      112  Bel    3  0  3  0   $13,600 | Dist  2 1 1 0  $17,670
                                               Tr:   Odintz Jeff (9 0 1 0 .00)
28May95-2Bel fst 6f      :222 :46  :582 1:11      ⒻClm 35000        75 2 1 1hd 2hd 22 25        Chavez J F  116  4.00 81-15 ViaDeiPortici1165 RunawayFling1161 FortuneWnd1164     Dueled, held 2nd 5
21May95-4Bel fm 1   Ⓣ :223 :451 1:101 1:353     ⒻClm 45000        65 8 1 2½ 2hd 64¼ 89        Perez R B5  111 19.10 76-15 Ski At Dawn108hd Turkolady1143½ Royal Pelliknow1121¼  Used in pace 11
28Apr95-2Aqu fst 6f      :22  :462 :584 1:114     ⒻClm 35000        65 5 2 2½ 42 41½ 35         Chavez J F  116  3.35 78-18 Reach ForClever112no FortuneWand1165 RunawayFling1162½  Drifted turn 7
8Apr95-4Aqu fst 6f       :222 :46  :581 1:104     ⒻClm 50000        65 4 3 21 3½ 43½ 48¼        Davis R G   116  8.40 80-10 PersonalGirl1161¾ ViaDeiPortici115½ Lena'sAngel1166  Forced pace, tired 4
8Mar95-8Aqu fst 6f  ⊡ :224 :46  :582 1:113     ⒻAlw 42000N$Y     39 1 1 1½ 33 516 521½       Cooper G J7 115  9.70 63-20 Beckys Shirt1175 Via Dei Portici1152 Endless Desire1155  Drifted, tired 5
25Feb95-8Aqu fst 6f ⊡ :224 :46  :582 1:11   3↑ⒻCorrection H83k  81 2 1 1½ 2½ 21 76          Chavez J F  112 22.30 82-14 Lottsa Talc120nk Lilly's Moment1191¾ The Bink1122  Dueled, tired 9
12Feb95-8Aqu fst 6f ⊡ :234 :482 1:01  1:14   3↑ⒻHandicap46k     77 4 5 11½ 11 2½ 22¼        Chavez J F  117 *2.65 71-26 Tensie's Pro1172¼ Runaway Fling117nk Lena's Angel122hd  Held place 6
26Jan95-7Aqu fst 6f ⊡ :232 :474 1:003 1:134     ⒻAlw 36000N4X     82 1 2 11½ 11 12 11½        Chavez J F  117  4.40 74-26 Runaway Fling1171½ Tensie's Pro1173 Dixie Luck112¾  Strong urging 5
16Jan95-4Aqu gd 6f  ⊡ :223 :46  :583 1:112     ⒻClm 70000        66 4 3 2hd 12 2hd 22¼       Pezua J M   113 17.60 84-14 PersonlGirl1132¼ RunwyFling1133 King'sSweetst1132  Dueled, weakened 6
23Dec94-4Aqu fst 6f ⊡ :233 :481 1:004 1:133     ⒻClm 35000        73 2 4 11 11½ 12½ 13½       Chavez J F  118  *.75 75-26 Runaway Fling1183½ Allen's Cheer118¾ Pappa's Jen1165½  Mild drive 6

Alkris                                         B. m. 5                                          Lifetime Record :  35  7  3  4   $152,380
Own: Greenhouse Gary L. & Rubinstein Ron       Sire: Koluctoo Bay (Creme dela Creme)            1995   3  1  0  0   $16,980 | Turf  2 0 0 0
                                               Dam:  Jill the Queen (Clem Pac)                  1994  10  2  0  1   $44,040 | Wet   5 3 0 0  $46,320
SANTOS J A (127 24 11 19 .19)       $40,000    Br:   Williams Edward A (NY)                  120  Bel   10  5  1  1   $88,860 | Dist  4 1 1 0  $19,270
                                               Tr:   Sciacca Gary (58 13 8 9 .22)
  Entered 8Jun95- 8 BEL
11May95-4Bel my 1 1/16   :224 :454 1:103 1:431     ⒻClm 37500       78 6 3 43 2½ 11 12          Chavez J F  114 fb 7.20 83-22 Alkris1142 Unlawful Behavior1158 Bonnie Shopper1142  6
  Wide, challenged, clear
28Apr95-2Aqu fst 6f      :22  :462 :584 1:114      ⒻClm 35000       57 3 5 78 66½ 65 58¼        Santos J A  116 fb 24.75 75-18 Reach For Clever112no Fortune Wand1165 Runaway Fling1162½  No threat 7
10Feb95-3Aqu fst 6f ⊡ :232 :472 1:003 1:14       ⒻClm 45000       58 5 5 69 67½ 67¾ 511       Perez R B5  109 b 28.00 62-30 Creed'sLass1155 Marilyn'sMagic1135½ King'sSweetest114hd  Showed little 6
21Dec94-4Aqu fst 170 ⊡ :241 :481 1:131 1:441 3↑ⒻClm 50000       36 4 5 68½ 611 616 627¼     Chavez J F  117 b 18.30 50-23 S. S. Sparkle110nk Bonnie Shopper10812 Lasting Shore11712  Outrun 7
4Dec94-8Aqu fst 1⅛       :493 1:143 1:392 1:52 3↑ⒻⓈMontauk H54k  46 5 4 46 75½ 715 730      Chavez J F  110 b 13.80 46-34 Beloved Bea1136 Hey Baba Lulu116¾ Lottsa Talc1191¼  Tired 7
16Nov94-8Aqu fst 1       :24  :471 1:121 1:374 3↑ⒻAlw 36000N3X   54 3 3 49½ 47½ 410 417½    Santos J A  119 b 3.40 61-24 Recognizable1151½ Safe At Home1158 Big Rhonda1158  No factor 4
20Oct94-7Aqu gd 1        :233 :47  1:124 1:391 3↑ⒻⓈAlw 34000N2X  75 8 5 44½ 42 11½ 14       Chavez J F  117 b 2.40e 73-27 Alkris1174 New York Flag117hd Shiani1173  Wide, driving 8
13Oct94-4Bel fst 1 1/16  :234 :473 1:121 1:44  3↑ⒻClm 70000       71 5 2 22 31½ 35 39½       Chavez J F  113 b 10.40 72-16 Hooded Dancer1135½ Avie's Daisy1104 Alkris113no  Lacked rally 7
25Sep94-4Bel gd 1 1/16   :24  :472 1:12  1:434 3↑ⒻⓈAlw 34000N2X  57 1 1 2hd 3nk 75½ 89      Chavez J F  117 b 4.50 74-15 Lois' Flag1091½ ⒹNew York Flag112¾ Willspynow113nk  Used in pace 8
4Sep94-6Bel fm 1    Ⓣ :224 :46  1:101 1:344 3↑ⒻⓈAlw 34000N2X  -0 3 8 129¾ 1210 1230 1243¼ Chavez J F  117 b 20.20 45-10 Dinner Diamond117¾ High Talent1171 Leo N' Me117nk  Outrun 12
WORKOUTS:  ●Jun 1 Bel 3f fst :364 H 1/15   Apr 21 Bel tr.t 4f fst :484 B 2/8   Apr 15 Bel tr.t 4f fst :484 B 10/38

Dixie Brat                                     Ch. f. 4                                         Lifetime Record :  23  2 10  5   $124,398
Own: Vermeire Albert                           Sire: Dixieland Brass (Dixieland Band)           1995   3  0  0  0      $560 | Turf  0 0 0 0
                                               Dam:  Laughing Empress (Shecky Greene)           1994  15  1  8  3   $84,436 | Wet   6 0 2 3  $23,654
LUZZI M J (117 14 22 15 .12)        $35,000    Br:   Paul J. Roche (Ky)                      112  Bel    3  0  2  1   $17,040 | Dist  6 0 5 0  $29,640
                                               Tr:   Serpe Philip M (18 3 3 4 .17)
13Apr95-5Aqu fst 1       :231 :453 1:111 1:364     ⒻClm 35000       61 1 3 31½ 21 54½ 68        Luzzi M J     116  8.60 77-24 UnlwfulBhvior1112 Gn'sGryGirl118½ BonnShoppr1073½  Bid, flattened out 8
30Jan95-1GP sly 1 1/16   :23  :471 1:134 1:474     ⒻAlw 28000N2X    51 7 5 44½ 72¾ 612 617¼     Bravo J     L 121  7.40 52-34 High Mio Royal121¾ Bunting121½ Seeking The Circle1182½  Tired 7
12Jan95-7GP fst 1 1/16   :231 :472 1:124 1:463     ⒻAlw 28000N2X    73 2 7 78½ 53¾ 36 53½       Bailey J D    122 *1.30 74-26 My Lady T. J.119½ Licorice Taffeta1122¾ High Mio Royal122hd  Belated bid 10
26Dec94-7Aqu fst 1 1/16 ⊡ :232 :47 1:13 1:472 3↑ⒻAlw 34000N2X  77 4 4 33 3nk 2hd 3nk       Luzzi M J     120  6.50 68-25 Manor Queen115no ⒹCherry Glow115nk Dixie Brat12012  7
  Bumped late stretch, held well Placed second through disqualification.
18Dec94-6Aqu fst 1 1/16 ⊡ :242 :501 1:153 1:482 3↑ⒻAlw 32000N1X  65 1 1 1½ 2hd 11 12        Luzzi M J     115  *.70 63-29 Dixie Brat1152 Fawn's Angel115no Hidden Crest1152¼  Driving 7
29Nov94-7Aqu wf 6f       :223 :461 :584 1:112 3↑ⒻAlw 30000N1X   81 7 6 63 63½ 22½ 22        Luzzi M J     115  2.40 83-21 Jupiter Assembly1152 Dixie Brat1152 Bow Creek1101  Rallied wide 8
17Nov94-6Aqu fst 7f      :231 :464 1:114 1:243 3↑ⒻAlw 30000N1X  82 4 3 43½ 41½ 21½ 21       Smith M E     115 b 1.85 80-16 Turner's Bid1151 Dixie Brat1159 Doc's Josephine1178¼  Rallied wide 6
6Nov94-7CD fst 6½f       :223 :46  1:12  1:184 3↑ⒻAlw 29460N1X  71 8 6 75¾ 56½ 68 42½       Sellers S J L 113 b 3.60 82-12 Fast An Sexy112½ My Fling1191½ Lena Lingard113½  12
  Bore in, bumped start, no late gain
4Oct94-7Bel fst 7f       :231 :464 1:11  1:233 3↑ⒻAlw 30000N1X  74 2 3 32½ 31½ 25 25        Smith M E     114 b 1.70 80-14 Triumph At Dawn1175 Dixie Brat1147½ Tapteragramtod112¾  Second best 6
24Sep94-7Bel my 1        :231 :461 1:112 1:37  3↑ⒻAlw 32000N1X  69 3 2 22 21 1½ 31         Chavez J F    113 b *1.90 77-20 OneAccount117¾ IndianPardise114nk DixieBrt1139½  Bumped break, wknd 8
WORKOUTS:  Jun 3 Bel 5f fst 1:012 B 9/32   May 28 Bel tr.t 4f fst :521 B 34/37   Apr 4 Bel tr.t 4f fst :501 B 9/17   Mar 17 GP 4f fst :50 B 14/33   Mar 10 GP 4f fst :513 B 54/66
```

You'renotlistening

Own: Davis Barbara J

PEREZ R B (118 17 20 11 .14) $40,000

Ch. f. 4
Sire: Kennedy Road (Victoria Park)
Dam: Madeleine Gallay (L'Natural)
Br: Nahem Edward (Cal)
Tr: Moschera Gasper S (48 8 5 5 .17)

1115

Lifetime Record:	20 4 7 2	$135,073			
1995	7 1 2 1	$34,710	Turf	1 0 0 0	
1994	10 3 2 1	$83,163	Wet	2 0 1 0	$7,650
Bel	3 0 0 0	$3,210	Dist	1 0 0 0	$2,160

31May95-4Bel fst 6½f :23 :462 1:113 1:181 ⒻClm 50000 61 5 3 52½ 41½ 43½ 69¼ Alvarado F T 114 4.70 74-16 DHUnrelCupcke111 DHStrtegicRewrd1143½ EviBee1181 Four wide, tired 7
19May95-6Bel sly 6f :221 :451 :57 1:094 ⒻClm 75000 61 1 7 67½ 44½ 56 511½ Perez R B5 111 *1.45e 81-17 Manor Queen1126 Skip One112nk Our Shopping Spree1163 Broke slowly 7
5May95-6Bel fst 7f :223 :454 1:103 1:234 ⒻAlw 36000N3X 76 4 1 32 21 31 43½ Alvarado F T 114 *1.05 79-17 ExquisiteStar114no EnsignJoanne1092½ NastyCure114¾ Forced pace, tired 6
31Mar95-9SA fst 1 :23 :462 1:111 1:362 ⒻClm c-40000 86 5 2 26 21½ 1hd 21 Desormeaux K J LB 117 2.40 86-19 IddyBddyDollr1171 Yo'rnotlstnng117¾ ScorngRd1141 Caught near wire 9
Claimed from Charles Ronald L, Shulman Sanford Trainer
5Mar95-8GG my 6f :212 :44 :562 1:092 ⒻAlw 33000N3X 86 2 4 43 22 22 22 Warren R J Jr LB 115 2.50 90-12 MissBushett1182 You'renotlistening1151 TruceInBlnc1183 Second best 7
3Feb95-3SA fst 6f :213 :443 :563 1:092 ⒻClm c-32000 87 4 2 3nk 42 42½ 3¾ Desormeaux K J LB 118 *.90 89-12 FastRewrd117no SilentLord117¾ You'renotlistening118no Hung in stretch 5
Claimed from Shapiro Barry, Mitchell Mike Trainer
22Jan95-9SA fst 6½f :22 :444 1:09 1:151 ⒻClm c-20000 99 6 3 2hd 1hd 16 111 Desormeaux K J LB 117 *1.80 96-09 You'renotlistening11711 Icy Luck115½ Popcorn Magic1153½ Ridden out 12
Claimed from Mevorach Samuel, Lewis Craig A Trainer
7Dec94-7Hol fst 6f :222 :454 :572 1:094 ⒻClm c-32000 — 3 3 87¼ — — — McCarron C J LB 119 2.10 — 11 DSham Pain118hd Choobloo1172 Icy Luck117no 8
Pulled up, vanned off Claimed from Nahem Edward, Shirreffs John Trainer
16Nov94-5Hol fm 1 1/16 Ⓣ :223 :47 1:12 1:44 Clm 55000 38 1 4 44 85¾ 912 1024 Vitek J J5 LB 105 14.70 52-24 Gary's Lucky One1191 Attleboro1162½ Uronurown1162½ Rail, gave way 12
21Oct94-5SA fst 6f :214 :444 :563 1:091 ⒻClm 35000 92 1 4 1hd 11 12½ 16½ McCarron C J LB 114 *2.10 91-13 You'renotlistening1146½ Whatawoman116no CnyonWinds116nk Ridden out 9

WORKOUTS: May 15 Bel 4f gd :493 B 11/24 ●Apr 25 Bel tr.t 4f fst :48 H 1/9 ●Mar 25 SA 7f fst 1:262 H 1/7

Grab The Glory

Own: My Paradise Farms

MIGLIORE R (62 6 12 7 .10) $35,000

B. m. 5
Sire: Alphabatim (Verbatim)
Dam: Hope of Glory (Mr. Leader)
Br: McKellen Donald (Md)
Tr: Friedman Mitchell (23 2 4 2 .09)

112

Lifetime Record:	50 17 6 11	$202,647			
1995	8 4 1 0	$80,100	Turf	1 0 0 0	
1994	14 3 3 4	$51,850	Wet	5 1 0 1	$9,245
Bel	2 1 1 0	$10,500	Dist	3 0 1 2	$9,590

6Apr95-4Aqu fst 1⅛ :484 1:13 1:391 1:521 ⒻClm 50000 88 4 2 21 2½ 1½ 1nk Migliore R 116 *1.75 79-26 Grab The Glory116nk Miss Gold Peace1145½ Gene's Gray Girl107½ All out 4
18Mar95-3Aqu fst 1⅛ :482 1:141 1:394 1:522 ⒻAlw 36000N3X 86 5 1 1½ 1½ 1hd 1nk Migliore R 116 6.30 78-31 Grab The Glory116nk Forcing Bid11313 Shellster1135 Pressued, gamely 8
10Mar95-4Aqu fst 170 ⊡ :234 :483 1:14 1:444 ⒻClm 19000 82 3 3 41½ 31½ 1hd 14¼ Migliore R 116 3.35 74-33 GrbTheGlory1164¼ Biogio'sGirl112hd UpsttFlyr1091 Svd grnd, going away 6
2Mar95-8Aqu fst 170 ⊡ :24 :481 1:131 1:421 ⒻAlw 36000N3X 49 6 4 31 41½ 68 621½ Migliore R 117 3.25 65-14 Manor Queen117nk Forcing Bid1176½ Shellster1171½ Wide, tired 6
16Feb95-8Aqu fst 1 1/16 ⊡ :232 :474 1:13 1:464 ⒻAlw 36000N3X 57 11 6 55½ 66½ 810 515½ Perez R B5 114 *2.45 55-30 Royal Cozzene1172½ Forcing Bid1171½ Said Privately1173½ Wide, tired 12
3Feb95-8Aqu fst 1 1/16 ⊡ :24 :483 1:14 1:48 ⒻAlw 36000N3X 83 5 3 21½ 21 21½ 2nk Migliore R 119 *1.65 65-30 Tuscany Breeze110nk Grab The Glory1191¾ Manor Queen1174 Gradual gain 7
29Jan95-4Aqu fst 1⅛ ⊡ :481 1:141 1:412 1:544 ⒻAlw 34000N2X 88 5 3 33½ 22 11½ 14¾ Migliore R 117 3.55 62-35 Grab The Glory1174¾ Delta West117½ Cherry Glow1173 Good trip 7
13Jan95-7Aqu fst 6f ⊡ :23 :463 :591 1:121 ⒻAlw 32000N2X 73 5 3 43½ 52½ 41½ 42½ Migliore R 119 11.40 79-18 Allen's Cheer1121½ For Sport1171 Cleverly Intended122no In traffic 1/4 pl 7
14Dec94-7Aqu fst 1 1/16 ⊡ :234 :492 1:144 1:471 3↑ ⒻAlw 34000N2X 77 4 2 31½ 41½ 33 42¾ Lantz J A5 117 4.50 66-27 Saratoga April117¾ Upstate Flyer112¾ Cherry Glow1151½ Weakened 8
7Dec94-7Aqu fst 1 1/16 ⊡ :231 :472 1:124 1:451 3↑ ⒻAlw 32000N1X 76 4 4 62½ 31½ 11½ 1½ Lantz J A5 112 7.10 79-21 Grab The Glory112½ Blazing Clearance1157 Doc's Josephine112no Driving 12

WORKOUTS: Jun 1 Bel 4f fst :493 B 15/39 May 17 Bel tr.t 4f fst :494 B 4/14 Apr 26 Bel tr.t 3f fst :38 B 4/7

Needles Last

Own: DeMatteis Frederick

BECKNER D V (57 4 6 3 .07) $40,000

Dk. b or br f. 4
Sire: Romantic Lead (Silent Screen)
Dam: Artly Needles (Needles)
Br: Samantha Farms Inc (NY)
Tr: Priolo Philip (5 0 0 0 .00)

116

Lifetime Record:	26 3 3 2	$86,040			
1995	9 2 0 0	$40,980	Turf	0 0 0 0	
1994	16 1 3 2	$45,060	Wet	2 0 0 0	$1,920
Bel	5 1 0 1	$20,040	Dist	2 1 0 0	$20,580

19May95-9Bel sly 1 1/16 ⊗ :231 :462 1:113 1:433 ⒻClm 40000 40 4 9 65 64 811 821½ Dunkelberger T L5 111 b 35.75 59-21 Georgia Anna1135½ Sunshine Lindajane1124½ Lois' Flag1081 No threat 9
19Apr95-8Aqu fst 1 :231 :454 1:10 1:361 3↑ ⒻⓈBroadway H54k 49 6 7 77½ 810 816 825½ Dunkelberger T L 111 f 34.75 62-20 Lottsa Talc122nk Lilly's Moment1221¾ Our Springwater1126 No response 8
31Mar95-9Aqu fst 7f :224 :463 1:123 1:26 ⒻⓈAlw 32000N2X 67 9 2 76¾ 73 32 1hd Dunkelberger T L5 114 f 21.90 74-19 NeedlesLst114hd Bitt'sChrm119no DistinctMnnr1145½ Stead, blocked 1/4 pl 9
19Mar95-5Aqu fst 6f :223 :46 :583 1:114 ⒻⓈAlw 32000N2X 56 6 6 713 77½ 68½ 69½ Leon F 119 f 17.30 74-19 Accipiter's Star1143½ Distinct Manner1142 Fit To Flirt114hd No threat 7
8Mar95-9Aqu fst 1 1/16 ⊡ :241 :484 1:143 1:48 ⒻⓈAlw 34000N2X 60 2 — — 53½ 66 79¼ Leon F 113 f 8.00 56-34 Carr Star1084 New York Flag109no Critical Crew113nk Fog, faded 9
23Feb95-6Aqu fst 6f ⊡ :231 :464 :591 1:114 ⒻⓈAlw 32000N2X 64 6 3 611 54½ 54¾ 55¾ Leon F 118 f 25.00 78-17 Chow1101½ Distinct Manner1132 Accipiter's Star1142 Drifted, late gain 7
11Feb95-5Aqu fst 6f ⊡ :232 :483 1:023 1:16 ⒻⓈAlw 30000N1X 60 7 9 914 78 31 13½ Leon F 117 f 9.50 63-33 Needles Last1173½ Bitta'sCharm117no Jazzpacked1173½ Broke slowly, wide 9
22Jan95-9Aqu wf 1 1/16 ⊡ :241 :484 1:141 1:463 ⒻⓈAlw 32000N1X 51 1 10 76½ 64 47½ 410¼ Graell A 117 f 21.70 61-23 Now I Hope1176 BlarneystoneLass1122¾ HillisLee1171½ Improved position 11
14Jan95-9Aqu fst 6f ⊡ :231 :47 :592 1:124 ⒻⓈAlw 30000N1X 52 7 4 74¾ 64 66½ 58¼ Leon F 117 f 11.20e 71-19 Love That Jennie1172¾ Now I Hope1173 Sara Paul1171¾ Wide trip 7
16Dec94-7Aqu fst 1 1/16 ⊡ :24 :493 1:151 1:482 3↑ ⒻⓈAlw 32000N1X 52 6 8 92¾ 31½ 45½ 58¾ Chavez J F 115 5.00e 54-30 Lihue1173½ Tara's Tempest1084 Hillis Lee117½ Flattened out 10

WORKOUTS: Jun 1 Aqu Ⓣ 5f fm 1:054 B (d) 4/4

Saratoga April

Own: Giorgi Vincent Jr & Saccone Joseph

MARTIN G J (70 7 6 10 .10) $40,000

B. m. 7
Sire: Full Out (Never Bend)
Dam: Valid Design (Valid Appeal)
Br: GMV Bloodstock (Ky)
Tr: Ortiz Paulino O (11 2 0 2 .18)

1115

Lifetime Record:	87 12 18 18	$221,280			
1995	8 0 2 1	$16,900	Turf	5 0 0 1	$3,420
1994	26 3 8 8	$90,980	Wet	19 3 7 2	$63,255
Bel	17 2 5 4	$41,640	Dist	10 0 4 2	$18,305

7May95-2Bel fm 1 1/16 Ⓣ :244 :483 1:133 1:442 ⒻClm 40000 72 1 7 66 64¾ 33½ 35¼ Martin G J5 111 b 15.60 68-18 Joy Of Life116¾ Ski At Dawn1084¾ Saratoga April1112¼ Mild gain 10
29Apr95-2Aqu fst 7f :232 :471 1:121 1:251 ⒻClm 25000 71 2 5 42 43 32½ 21 Martin G J5 111 b 8.20 77-18 Somthingscandalous1141 SartogApril1114 GeorgiAnn1167 Finished well 6
31Mar95-7Aqu fst 1 :242 :474 1:122 1:374 ⒻAlw 36000N3X 72 4 3 2hd 54½ 55½ 56¾ Martin G J7 108 b 24.25 73-24 Creed'sLass1131½ Bravada1142 SeekingTheCircle116½ Middle move, tired 5
18Mar95-3Aqu fst 1⅛ :482 1:141 1:394 1:522 ⒻAlw 36000N3X 34 6 5 45½ 65 814 832¼ Cruguet J 113 b 14.00 45-31 Grab The Glory116nk Forcing Bid11313 Shellster1135 Drifted, wide, tired 8
2Mar95-8Aqu fst 170 ⊡ :24 :481 1:131 1:421 ⒻAlw 36000N3X 73 3 6 63½ 63½ 56 48 Cruguet J 117 b 16.50 79-14 Manor Queen117nk Forcing Bid1176½ Shellster1171½ Checked break 6
16Feb95-8Aqu fst 1 1/16 ⊡ :232 :474 1:13 1:464 ⒻAlw 36000N3X 53 3 3 34 44½ 610 817¾ Cruguet J 117 b 6.80 53-30 Royal Cozzene1172½ Forcing Bid1171½ Said Privately1173½ Tired 12
3Feb95-8Aqu fst 1 1/16 ⊡ :24 :483 1:14 1:48 ⒻAlw 36000N3X 68 7 5 54½ 65 67½ 69 Cruguet J 117 b 7.50 56-30 TuscnyBreeze110nk GrbTheGlory1191¾ MnorQun1174 Wide, flattened out 7
20Jan95-7Aqu sly 1 1/16 ⊡ :234 :482 1:124 1:451 ⒻAlw 36000N3X 73 2 3 3nk 2½ 23½ 23½ Cruguet J 117 b 3.30 75-16 Willspynow1173½ Saratoga April117½ Cheery Sun112½ Bid, weakened 6
31Dec94-6Aqu fst 1 1/16 ⊡ :242 :484 1:141 1:481 3↑ ⒻClm 35000 63 2 5 55 56½ 47 410½ Cruguet J 119 b 2.85 53-34 Gene'sGrayGirl1139½ BelieveInDoris1151 PalmBechDewey119no Even trip 8
14Dec94-7Aqu fst 1 1/16 ⊡ :234 :492 1:144 1:471 3↑ ⒻAlw 34000N2X 82 1 3 21½ 21 2hd 1¾ Cruguet J 117 b 9.70 69-27 Saratoga April117¾ Upstate Flyer112¾ Cherry Glow1151½ Driving 8

For most players, the headline in terms of a pace story-line is that Runaway Fling shakes out as the lone speed. The filly has been in front at the first call in six of her last nine sprints, second all other times. In this race, five of her six rivals — Alkris, Dixie Brat, Grab The Glory, Needles Last, and Saratoga April — are emerging from longer (and for the most part slower-paced) races in which they did not contest the lead.

Besides Runaway Fling, the only other true-blue sprinter is You'renotlistening. Runaway Fling is commonly perceived to enjoy a tactical advantage in this race as the lone speed, and thus flashes at 6-5 on the toteboard. In a much subtler way, You'renotlistening also projects to get a beneficial trip — as the *lone stalker*. She is co-second choice at 3-1.

Draw a line through Alkris' most recent race (over a muddy track she relished), scan through the early fractions and running positions of this field, and it becomes clear that You'renotlistening is the only filly in the race capable of keeping Runaway Fling within her sights. In fact, the recently-arrived filly cut some pretty flashy splits on the west coast, winning a pair of Santa Anita sprints (with the best Beyers in this field) on the lead in :21 4/5, :44 4/5, and in :22, :44 4/5. In the mud at Golden Gate, she was within three lengths of the lead after a quarter in :21 2/5, and within two lengths of a half in :44.

This filly has some gas.

More importantly, if she is outrun for the lead by Runaway Fling in the opening quarter and relegated to the role of pace-presser, as seems likely, she has an edge in turn times that indicates she can overhaul her target in the second fraction. Compare their turn times from 1995 sprints (adjusted for beaten lengths):

Runaway Fling	You'renotlistening
May 28 - :24 4/5	May 31- :23 1/5 (four wide)
Apr 28 - :24 4/5	May 19 - :22 2/5
Apr 8 - :23 2/5	May 5 - :23
Mar 8 - :23 4/5	Mar 5 - :22 2/5
Feb 25 - :23 2/5	Feb 3 - :23 2/5
Feb 12 - :24 3/5	Jan 22 - :22 4/5
Jan 26 - :24 2/5	
Jan 16 - :23 2/5	

I realize that in some cases we may be comparing apples and oranges, because these extrapolated second fraction-times are all taken "raw," directly out of the past performances with no regard for track variants, or adjustments of any kind. But, the overall picture is pretty clear: the fastest turn time Runaway Fling runs is :23 2/5, while You'renotlistening has only run a turn time as slow as :23 2/5 once!

Moreover, Runaway Fling seems like a need-to-lead type, doesn't she? Both wins in her current record came when able to open up early and maintain a clear advantage to the second call (after very slow half-miles in :47 4/5 and :48 1/5); whenever challenged in the second fraction, she fades. On the other hand, You'renotlistening won on January 22 after going head-and-head through the opening half mile; in a two-turn mile March 31, she overcame an early six-length deficit to get a short lead in midstretch, only to be run down near the wire.

Off her California form You'renotlistening looks good, so good that she was even-money first time out at Belmont on May 5. But after shipping east her form appears to have gone south, three local starts producing three out-of-the-money finishes by an aggregate 24 1/4 lengths. Has her form really dulled that much? Unlikely, since she was red-tagged out of her last four claiming-starts in California, even though she had pulled up and been vanned off the track in her final 1994 appearance.

You'renotlistening had been a victim of circumstances in her three starts over the track last month. In a N3X allowance on May 5 she had forced a half of :45 4/5 against Exquisite

Star — and because I've been keeping up to date with key races ever since reading Steve Davidowitz' *Betting Thoroughbreds* some two decades ago, I knew that Exquisite Star had returned to do this:

SEVENTH RACE
Belmont
JUNE 2, 1995

7 FURLONGS. (1.20^1) ALLOWANCE. Purse $38,000. Fillies and mares, 4-year-olds and upward which have not won four races other than maiden, claiming or starter. Weight, 122 lbs. Non-winners of $19,000 twice since April 26, allowed 2 lbs. $20,000 since May 3, 4 lbs. $9,000 since April 18, 6 lbs. (Races where entered for $60,000 or less not considered in allowances).

Value of Race: $38,000 Winner $22,800; second $7,600; third $4,180; fourth $2,280; fifth $1,140. Mutuel Pool $211,611.00 Exacta Pool $375,491.00

Last Raced	Horse	M/Eqt.	A.Wt	PP	St	¼	½	Str	Fin	Jockey	Odds $1
25May95 ^{8}Bel^4	Exquisite Star		4 120	2	1	1^1	1^2	1^6	1$^{10\frac{1}{2}}$	Santos J A	1.90
31Mar95 ^{7}Aqu^3	Seeking The Circle		4 116	4	4	3$^{\frac{1}{2}}$	2^{hd}	2$^{1\frac{1}{2}}$	2^{nk}	Bailey J D	1.45
27Aug94 ^{7}FL^2	She Rides Tonite	b	4 116	5	2	4$^{3\frac{1}{2}}$	4^2	3$^{\frac{1}{2}}$	3$^{1\frac{1}{2}}$	Chavez J F	3.05
13May95 ^{7}Bel^5	Willspynow		4 116	3	3	5	5	4$^{3\frac{1}{2}}$	4^{12}	Luzzi M J	19.10
16May95 ^{10}Hia^3	Future Answer	b	4 116	1	5	2^{hd}	3^1	5	5	Davis R G	5.00

OFF AT 3:59 Start Good. Won driving. Time, :22^4, :46^1, 1:11^2, 1:25 Track fast.

$2 Mutuel Prices:				
	2–EXQUISITE STAR	5.80	3.00	2.30
	4–SEEKING THE CIRCLE		2.90	2.20
	5–SHE RIDES TONITE			2.30

• $2 EXACTA 2–4 PAID $16.60

B. f, by Star de Naskra–El Hamo, by Search for Gold. Trainer Schosberg Richard. Bred by Poole Investments (Ky).

EXQUISITE STAR sprinted clear in the early stages, extended her lead in upper stretch, then drew away while being kept to the task. SEEKING THE CIRCLE chased the winner to the top of the stretch but was no match for that one while holding for the place. SHE RIDES TONITE raced just off the pace from outside to the turn then lacked a strong closing bid. WILLSPYNOW was never a serious threat. FUTURE ANSWER rushed up inside after breaking slowly, raced up close to the turn and gave way.

Owners— 1, Austin Dale H & Heatherwood Farm; 2, Kimmel Caesar P & Solondz Philip; 3, Winbound Farms; 4, Dor Sal Stable & Vigliotti Vincent; 5, Hooper Fred W

Trainers—1, Schosberg Richard; 2, Kimmel John C; 3, Sciacca Gary; 4, Bradley John M; 5, Picou James E

Exquisite Star was currently in raging form, having won by the length of the stretch when advanced to the N4X allowance level June 2.

I was willing to forgive You'renotlistening's May 19 debacle, when she had uncharacteristically come out of the gate behind the field, and had found herself considerably farther from the early lead than she was accustomed while getting a faceful of slop kicked back at her; nevertheless, she had picked up two positions and three lengths around the turn, and had continued on evenly against runaway winner Manor Queen. Thanks to Davidowitz and his concept of key races, I was aware of Manor Queen's latest exploits:

Manor Queen
Own: Behringer Edward C
SMITH M E (126 29 20 17 .23)

Dk. b or br f. 4
Sire: Wavering Monarch (Majestic Light)
Dam: Woodland Manor (Marine Patrol)
Br: Purdey William A (NJ)
Tr: O'Connell Richard (37 5 2 4 ,14)

118

Lifetime Record:	27	8	4	1	$168,045						
1995	10	3	1	1	$70,160	Turf	0	0	0	0	
1994	14	3	3	0	$72,685	Wet	6	2	0	0	$36,170
Bel	2	1	0	0	$21,000	Dist	3	0	2	0	$11,540

3Jun95–8Mth fst	6f	:22^3	:46^2	:59^1	1:11^4 3↑	Ⓕ[S]Handicap30k	80	1	4	2^2	2^2	2^{hd}	1$^{3\frac{1}{4}}$	Smith M E	L 119 f	*.90	80–21	Manor Queen119$^{3\frac{1}{4}}$ Donna Doo116$^{3\frac{1}{4}}$ Merri Tales120^4	Drew clear	8
19May95–6Bel sly	6f	:22^1	:45^1	:57	1:09^4	ⒻClm 65000	90	6	1	2$^{1\frac{1}{2}}$	1$^{\frac{1}{2}}$	1$^{3\frac{1}{2}}$	1^8	Chavez J F	112 f	5.50	92–17	MnorQueen112^8 SkipOne112^{nk} OurShoppingSpree116^3	Wide, ridden out	7
7May95–8Bel fst	1	:23^1	:46^1	1:11^1	1:37	ⒻAlw 40000N4X	66	8	4	5^4	4$^{2\frac{1}{2}}$	8^7	8$^{16\frac{1}{2}}$	Velazquez J R	116 f	17.20	61–23	FuturePretense113$^{3\frac{1}{4}}$ RegalSolution113$^{\frac{1}{2}}$ ChattCode114$^{\frac{3}{4}}$	Four wide, tired	8
21Apr95–4Aqu fst	7f	:23^3	:46^3	1:11^1	1:24^1	ⒻClm 55000	84	5	1	1^1	1$^{\frac{1}{2}}$	1$^{2\frac{1}{2}}$	2$^{\frac{1}{2}}$	Velazquez J R	116 f	*2.30	82–15	Evi Bee112$^{\frac{1}{2}}$ Manor Queen116$^{3\frac{3}{4}}$ Personal Girl116^{nk}	Couldn't last	6
1Apr95–7Aqu fst	6½f	:23^4	:46	1:10^3	1:16^3	ⒻAlw 42000N$Y	77	3	2	3$^{\frac{1}{2}}$	3^2	5$^{3\frac{1}{2}}$	6$^{6\frac{3}{4}}$	Velazquez J R	119 f	18.80	90–13	Incinerate117$^{2\frac{1}{4}}$ Unreal Cupcake119$^{1\frac{3}{4}}$ Via Dei Portici114$^{1\frac{1}{4}}$	Steadied 7/16 pl	7
19Mar95–8Aqu fst	7f	:23	:46	1:10	1:22^4 3↑	ⒻDistaff H-G2	85	7	1	6$^{3\frac{1}{2}}$	4$^{1\frac{1}{2}}$	7^5	8$^{7\frac{3}{4}}$	Chavez J F	110 f	62.75	82–19	Recognizable120^2 Beckys Shirt113$^{\frac{1}{2}}$ Kurofune Mystery116$^{2\frac{1}{2}}$	Wide, tired	8
2Mar95–8Aqu fst	170 [•]	:24	:48^1	1:13^1	1:42^1	ⒻAlw 36000N3X	87	2	1	2$^{\frac{1}{2}}$	1$^{\frac{1}{2}}$	1^1	1^{nk}	Chavez J F	117 f	9.50	87–14	Manor Queen117^{nk} Forcing Bid117$^{6\frac{1}{2}}$ Shellster117$^{1\frac{1}{4}}$	Hard drive	6
16Feb95–8Aqu fst	1$\frac{1}{16}$ [•]	:23^2	:47^4	1:13	1:46^4	ⒻAlw 36000N3X	45	8	4	6^6	9^{10}	9^{13}	10$^{22\frac{1}{4}}$	Nelson D	117 f	13.30	49–30	Royal Cozzene117$^{2\frac{1}{2}}$ Forcing Bid117$^{1\frac{1}{2}}$ Said Privately117$^{3\frac{1}{2}}$	Steadied 3/4 pl	12
3Feb95–8Aqu fst	1$\frac{1}{16}$ [•]	:24	:48^3	1:14	1:48	ⒻAlw 36000N3X	80	4	2	3$^{1\frac{1}{2}}$	3^3	3$^{3\frac{1}{2}}$	3^2	Nelson D	117 f	7.80	63–30	Tuscany Breeze110^{nk} Grab The Glory119$^{1\frac{3}{4}}$ Manor Queen117^4	Willingly	7
20Jan95–7Aqu sly	1$\frac{1}{16}$ [•]	:23^4	:48^2	1:12^4	1:45^1	ⒻAlw 36000N3X	69	4	4	4$^{2\frac{1}{4}}$	6$^{4\frac{1}{2}}$	6$^{5\frac{3}{4}}$	6$^{5\frac{1}{4}}$	Nelson D	119	3.40	73–16	Willspynow117$^{3\frac{1}{2}}$ Saratoga April117$^{\frac{1}{2}}$ CheerySun112$^{\frac{1}{2}}$	Wide, shuffled back	6

WORKOUTS: May 4 Bel tr.t 4f fst :51^3 B *37/44* Apr 18 Bel tr.t 4f fst :50^1 B *12/16* ●Mar 16 Bel tr.t 3f fst :36 H *1/19*

After winning in the slop by eight lengths, she had posted another big win in an overnight handicap at Monmouth.

As if You'renotlistening needed any more corroborating evidence, there was the matter of the class drop, which was larger-than-looked: Gasper Moschera was dropping her $10,000 in price, from $50,000 down to $40,000, but the drop might have been as much as $25,000.

You'renotlistening was exiting a race with the following conditions:

FOURTH RACE
Belmont
MAY 31, 1995

6½ FURLONGS. (1.14³) CLAIMING. Purse $32,000. Fillies and mares, 4-year-olds and upward. Weight, 122 lbs. Non-winners of two races since May 4, allowed 2 lbs. A race since April 20, 4 lbs. Two races since April 7, 6 lbs. Claiming price $60,000, for each $5,000 to $50,000, allowed 2 lbs. (Races where entered for $45,000 or less not considered.)

Value of Race: $32,000 Winners $12,800 each; third $3,520; fourth $1,920; fifth $960. Mutuel Pool $225,359.00 Exacta Pool $426,198.00 Quinella Pool $73,578.00

Last Raced	Horse	M/Eqt.	A.	Wt	PP	St	¼	½	Str	Fin	Jockey	Cl'g Pr	Odds $1
1Apr95 7Aqu2	DH Unreal Cupcake	b	5	111	2	4	3½	2hd	22½	1	Perez R B5	60000	1.05
19May95 6Bel4	DH Strategic Reward	b	6	114	6	1	12	11	1½	13½	Santos J A	50000	6.80
7May95 8Bel7	Evi Bee	bf	4	118	1	6	2hd	3½	3½	31	Davis R G	55000	6.30
30Apr95 9CD5	Pastel Parade		4	111	3	2	68	52	51½	43	Martin G J5	60000	24.00
2Feb95 7Aqu4	Roses For Regina		4	114	7	5	7	7	66	52	Krone J A	55000	8.70
19May95 6Bel5	You'renotlistening		4	114	5	3	52	43	4½	610	Alvarado F T	50000	4.70
19May95 6Bel2	Skip One	b	4	116	4	7	4hd	61½	7	7	Bailey J D	60000	6.10

DH—Dead Heat.

OFF AT 2:29 Start Good. Won driving. Time, :23, 1:11³, 1:18¹ Track fast.

$2 Mutuel Prices:

2–DH UNREAL CUPCAKE	2.80	2.70	2.30
6–DH STRATEGIC REWARD	5.00	6.00	3.40
1–EVI BEE			2.90

$2 EXACTA 2–6 PAID $14.00 $2 EXACTA 6–2 PAID $26.60 $2 QUINELLA 2–6 PAID $18.60

Unreal Cupcake—Ch. m, by Unreal Zeal–Crackers, by Singular. Trainer Levine Bruce N. Bred by Siegel Jan & Mace & Samantha (Fla).

Strategic Reward—Ch. m, by Bold Revenue–Ten Guineas, by Strategic Command. Trainer Schosberg Richard. Bred by Sabiston James T (Ont-C).

UNREAL CUPCAKE broke inward at the start, forced the pace from outside for a half then closed steadily to get up in the final strides. STRATEGIC REWARD sprinted clear in the early stages, led into deep stretch then was all out to dead heat for the win. EVI BEE raced in close contention between horses into upper stretch and held for a share. PASTEL PARADE was shuffled back while between horses at the five-eighths pole, and failed to seriously threaten thereafter. ROSES FOR REGINA never reached contention. YOU'RENOTLISTENING stalked four wide for a half, tired. SKIP ONE up close early between horses, gave way on the turn. UNREAL CUPCAKE and PASTEL PARADE wore mud caulks.

The maximum claiming price had been $60,000, but she had been in for the $50,000 minimum. Today, she was entered for the maximum price of $40,000, in a race with a minimum of $35,000. Theoretically, the drop could've been $60,000 down to $35,000. Note the purse on May 31 race was $32,000, compared to today's $25,000 — a significant drop.

For what it's worth, Runaway Fling was actually taking a slight step up, even though her $35,000 tag was identical to what she'd raced for last time out. Today, she was in for the minimum amount, but on May 28, she had been entered for the maximum in a $35,000 down to $30,000 race:

SECOND RACE
Belmont
MAY 28, 1995

6 FURLONGS. (1.07⁴) CLAIMING. Purse $24,000. Fillies and mares, 4-year-olds and upward. Weight, 122 lbs. Non-winners of two races since April 27, allowed 2 lbs. A race since April 20, 4 lbs. Two races since March 25, 6 lbs. Claiming price $35,000, for each $2,500 to $30,000, allowed 2 lbs. (Races where entered for $25,000 or less not considered.)

Value of Race: $24,000 Winner $14,400; second $4,800; third $2,640; fourth $1,440; fifth $720. Mutuel Pool $169,379.00 Exacta Pool $302,920.00 Quinella Pool $55,802.00

Last Raced	Horse	M/Eqt.	A.	Wt	PP	St	¼	½	Str	Fin	Jockey	Cl'g Pr	Odds $1
5May95 4Bel2	Via Dei Portici	bf	6	116	1	2	21	1hd	12	15	Luzzi M J	35000	1.25
21May95 4Bel8	Runaway Fling		4	116	2	1	1hd	22	22	21	Chavez J F	35000	4.00
5May95 4Bel3	Fortune Wand	f	6	116	5	5	43	41½	42½	34	Martinez J R Jr	35000	1.55
23Apr95 4Aqu1	Come On Joy	b	4	120	4	3	5	5	5	4no	Alvarado F T	35000	14.80
28Apr95 2Aqu4	Sam's In Control	b	4	112	3	4	31	31	3½	5	Davis R G	30000	7.20

OFF AT 1:29 Start Good. Won driving. Time, :22², :46, :58², 1:11 Track fast.

$2 Mutuel Prices:

1–VIA DEI PORTICI	4.50	2.60	2.10
2–RUNAWAY FLING		3.60	2.10
7–FORTUNE WAND			2.10

$2 EXACTA 1–2 PAID $19.60 $2 QUINELLA 1–2 PAID $12.40

No matter how I looked at the race Thursday night and again on Friday morning, I could envision no other scenario except this: Runaway Fling on the lead down the backstretch with You'renotlistening laying in easy striking range, and a big gap back to the others. Into the turn, You'renotlistening overhauls Runaway Fling, opens up on the field, and coasts home.

Steve Davidowitz happened to be in town covering the Belmont Stakes, and I was happy to fill him in about the key race-aspects of the situation. One good turn deserves another:

THIRD RACE
Belmont
JUNE 9, 1995

7 FURLONGS. (1.20^{1}) CLAIMING. Purse $25,000. Fillies and mares, 4-year-olds and upward. Weight, 122 lbs. Non-winners of two races since April 27, allowed 2 lbs. A race since May 4, 4 lbs. A race since April 20, 6 lbs. Claiming price $40,000, for each $2,500 to $35,000, allowed 2 lbs. (Races where entered for $30,000 or less not considered.)

Value of Race: $25,000 Winner $15,000; second $5,000; third $2,750; fourth $1,500; fifth $750. Mutuel Pool $252,045.00 Exacta Pool $453,897.00

Last Raced	Horse	M/Eqt.	A.	Wt	PP	St	¼	½	Str	Fin	Jockey	Cl'g Pr	Odds $1
31May95 ^{4}Bel^{6}	You'renotlistening		4	111	4	3	2^{3}	2^{1}	$1^{1\frac{1}{2}}$	$1^{\frac{3}{4}}$	Perez R B^{5}	40000	3.35
6Apr95 ^{4}Aqu^{1}	Grab The Glory		5	112	5	1	3^{1}	3^{1}	$2^{1\frac{1}{2}}$	$2^{3\frac{1}{2}}$	Migliore R	35000	3.55
13Apr95 ^{5}Aqu^{6}	Dixie Brat		4	112	3	4	4^{hd}	5^{1}	$4^{1\frac{1}{2}}$	$3^{1\frac{1}{2}}$	Luzzi M J	35000	9.60
11May95 ^{4}Bel^{1}	Alkris	bf	5	120	2	5	6^{5}	6^{3}	5^{hd}	4no	Santos J A	40000	8.20
28May95 ^{2}Bel^{2}	Runaway Fling		4	112	1	2	1^{1}	1^{1}	3^{1}	5^{nk}	Chavez J F	35000	1.25
7May95 ^{2}Bel^{3}	Saratoga April	b	7	111	7	6	$5^{1\frac{1}{2}}$	4^{1}	6^{4}	6^{9}	Martin G J^{5}	40000	8.50
19May95 ^{9}Bel^{8}	Needles Last	f	4	116	6	7	7	7	7	7	Beckner D V	40000	55.75

OFF AT 2:00 Start Good. Won driving. Time, :23^{1}, :46^{4}, 1:12, 1:25^{1} Track fast.

$2 Mutuel Prices:			
4–YOU'RENOTLISTENING	8.70	5.60	4.00
5–GRAB THE GLORY		4.50	3.20
3–DIXIE BRAT			4.70

$2 EXACTA 4–5 PAID $43.40

Ch. f, by Kennedy Road–Madeleine Gallay, by L'Natural. Trainer Moschera Gasper S. Bred by Nahem Edward (Cal).

YOU'RENOTLISTENING stalked the pace outside RUNAWAY FLING for a half, took charge in upper stretch, then turned back GRAB THE GLORY under brisk urging. GRAB THE GLORY raced in good position while three wide to the top of the stretch, then closed steadily but could not get up. DIXIE BRAT settled just off the pace while saving ground to the turn then finished evenly. ALKRIS checked slightly leaving the gate and failed to threaten thereafter. RUNAWAY FLING set the pace along the inside into upper stretch and tired. SARATOGA APRIL lodged a mild rally four wide on the turn, flattened out with the rider losing the whip inside the sixteenth pole. NEEDLES LAST trailed after breaking a bit slowly.

Owners— 1, Davis Barbara J; 2, My Paradise Farms; 3, Vermeire Albert; 4, Greenhouse Gary L & Rubinstein Ron; 5, Hagedorn Charles C & Rottkamp John; 6, Giorgi Vincent Jr & Saccone Joseph; 7, DeMatteis Frederick

Trainers—1, Moschera Gasper S; 2, Friedman Mitchell; 3, Serpe Philip M; 4, Sciacca Gary; 5, Odintz Jeff; 6, Ortiz Paulino O; 7, Priolo Philip

Runaway Fling was claimed by Pomerantz Lawrence J; trainer, Barbara Robert.

Scratched— Roses For Regina (31May95 ^{4}BEL^{5})

The race unfolded exactly as planned, at least through the first half mile. Runaway Fling cleared the field from her inside post and maintained a length-lead on You'renotlistening, who was three lengths ahead of the others after a quarter. You'renotlistening wrestled command from Runaway Fling and opened daylight coming to upper stretch, but suddenly Grab The Glory materialized on the outside, and looked as if she was going to spoil everything with a big late run in the final furlong. Thankfully, You'renotlistening had enough gas left in the tank to fight off the challenge.

HANDICAPPERS COULD EASILY be lulled into thinking there's little difference between racing on grass as opposed to dirt. The races take place on surfaces right next to each other and the horses look the same, one might reason, so how much difference could there be?

Though the grass course(s) are right alongside the dirt track, they might as well be on another planet, for that's how different the two genres really are. We've seen some examples of this phenomenon in maiden and preliminary allowance events, where grass-oriented pedigrees take precedence over all else. But in dealing with mature, well-seasoned grass runners, the most telling attributes are class and late speed.

That being the case, finding the most likely winner of a grass route usually has little to do with who has the best final-time speed figures, or who shakes out as the best early speed (exceptions occur when grass courses are abnormally hard or soft). Most, if not all of the pace situations we've covered so far are a potent source of live prospects in dirt races, but these same methods have little use on the grass. As a practical matter, players can forget about making realistic comparisons in terms of the early fractions of grass races, as James Quinn advised in *Figure Handicapping:*

"The courses are different. Horses exit on straightaways or out of chutes. The rails are up, the rails are down. The grass is long, the grass is cut short. The turns are sharper, the stretch run is shorter.

"The pace is different...tiring horses rarely survive on the grass, as they regularly do on dirt."

Figure Handicapping, by the way, is an extremely underrated book as far as I'm concerned, if for no other reason than its Appendix, which presents charts of late-speed turf figures for more than two dozen major and medium-sized tracks.

Turf racing is all about class, late speed, and trips. Because the turns are much sharper, saving ground is vital: one hardly ever sees a turf winner caught wide the entire way. But the price for a hedge-skimming position is often extracted as a lack of running room when tightly-bunched fields approach the decisive stretch-run.

If class and late speed are the most predictive factors in races for seasoned grass horses, then you should have little trouble finding a strong, yet somewhat overlooked contender in the 37th running of the Sheepshead Bay Handicap, which was the featured attraction on Sunday, June 4:

9 Belmont Park

1⅜ MILES. **(Outer Turf). (2:152) 37th Running of THE SHEEPSHEAD BAY HANDICAP. Purse $100,000 Added. Grade II. Fillies and mares, 3-year-olds and upward. By subscription of $100 each which should accompany the nomination; $500 to pass the entry box, $500 to start with $100,000 added. The added money and all fees to be divided 60% to the winner, 20% to second, 11% to third, 6% to fourth and 3% to fifth. Weights: Wednesday, May 31. Starters to be named at the closing time of entries. Trophies will be presented to the winning owner, trainer and jockey. The New York Racing Association Inc. reserves the right to transfer this race to the Main Track. Closed Saturday, May 20, with 20 nominations.**

Vice On Ice

Own: Burgundy Stable
SANTOS J A (108 20 10 16 .19)

Ch. f. 4
Sire: Vice Regent (Northern Dancer)
Dam: Wewarrenju (Damascus)
Br: Golden Richard L (Md)
Tr: Domino Carl J (14 5 3 1 .36)

111

Lifetime Record:	11	4	2	1	$89,510						
1995	2	1	1	0	$18,200	Turf	9	4	2	1	$88,100
1994	6	2	1	1	$54,600	Wet	0	0	0	0	
Bel Ⓣ	4	1	1	1	$23,900	Dist Ⓣ	0	0	0	0	

18May95-8Bel	fm	1	Ⓣ	:232 :463 1:104 1:352	ⒻAlw 40000N4X	88	6	7	56	52½	21	21¾	Davis R G	113 f	4.80	84-14	GreatLadyMry1131¾ ViceOnIce1131¾ GretTriumph114nk	Broke slowly, wide	8
1Apr95-9Hia	fm	*1 1/16	Ⓣ	1:404	ⒻAlw 17000N3X	85	6	8	85¾	85¾	74¼	1hd	Davis R G	114	4.60	98-02	Vice On Ice114hd Wadaz1141 Fappitass1142¼		12
Eight wide top str, driving																			
15Sep94-7Bel	fm	1	Ⓣ	:232 :461 1:092 1:331	3↑ ⒻAlw 36000N3X	70	10	5	41½	2½	63½	912¾	Velazquez J R	113 b	6.00	83-13	Lady Affirmed1134 Jiving Around117no ManilaLila1172¼	Bid, flattened out	10
3Aug94-7Sar	yl	1 1/16	Ⓣ	:233 :474 1:122 1:434	ⒻNijana-G3	78	4	4	53½	42	54½	511	Velazquez J R	118	4.30	64-25	CoronationCup1145 StretchDrive1144 GoldenTajniak1181	Flattened out	7
Run in divisions																			
3Jly94-9Lrl	fm	1⅛	Ⓣ	:484 1:142 1:402 1:53	ⒻPearlNcklace60k	82	4	8	812	712	32½	1¾	Johnston M T	114	*.70	65-34	Vice On Ice114¾ Sherunsfornanny1144½ Up An Eighth1144	Wide, driving	8
23Jun94-7Bel	fm	1	Ⓣ	:224 :452 1:093 1:34	3↑ ⒻAlw 30000N2L	88	6	5	63½	51¼	2½	14	Velazquez J R	111	4.10	92-10	[DH]Last Blood119 [DH]Vice On Ice1114 Aucilla1115	Wide, driving	12
8Jun94-7Bel	fm	1 1/16	Ⓣ	:232 :463 1:111 1:412	3↑ ⒻAlw 30000N1X	75	9	9	78	82¾	43	35¾	Velazquez J R	111	9.80	85-09	Coronation Cup1144¾ Staldancer1191 Vice On Ice111nk	Belated rally	12
15May94-8Hia	fm	1 1/16	Ⓣ	1:423	ⒻAlw 16500N1X	79	1	9	86	3nk	11	22	Castillo H Jr	113	7.10	88-09	Too Oh Five1132 Vice On Ice113no Spectacular April1143	Gamely	10
30Aug93-2Sar	fm	1	[T]	:234 :474 1:131 1:383	ⒻMd Sp Wt	62	1	4	42½	4¾	1½	12	Davis R G	117	6.50	84-15	Vice On Ice1172 [D]Vested Myth117½ Blazingcrypto1171	Driving	9
1Aug93-3Sar	fst	6f		:221 :454 :581 1:112	ⒻMd Sp Wt	33	5	7	41½	31½	47	515½	Chavez J F	117 f	7.50	69-11	Princess Tru1173½ Eastern Cracker1172 Polar Princess1179¾	Broke slowly	7

WORKOUTS: May 12 Bel 5f gd 1:06 B *9/10* May 4 Bel 6f fst 1:142 B *8/11* ●Apr 25 Bel 5f fst 1:001 H *1/26* ●Apr 11 GP 4f fst :493 B *1/6* Mar 28 GP Ⓣ 4f hd :49 B *9/24* Mar 22 GP 5f fst 1:014 H *9/21*

It's Personal

Own: Prestonwood Farm
LUZZI M J (104 12 20 15 .12)

Dk. b or br m. 5
Sire: Personal Flag (Private Account)
Dam: Dance Hall Girl (Guerrero)
Br: Nielsen Gerald A (NY)
Tr: Dickinson Michael W (5 2 1 1 .40)

113

Lifetime Record:	17	6	4	1	$215,406						
1995	2	2	0	0	$69,000	Turf	9	4	1	0	$113,474
1994	10	3	2	0	$110,634	Wet	2	1	1	0	$20,340
Bel Ⓣ	5	2	0	0	$40,554	Dist Ⓣ	0	0	0	0	

19May95-9Pim	gd	1 1/16	⊗	:234 :474 1:122 1:433	3↑ ⒻGalloretteH-G3	96	4	2	21½	11	14	14	Krone J A	L 112 f	5.10	90-14	It's Personal1124 Churchbell Chimes112hd Open Toe1139½	Ridden out	6
4May95-6GS	yl	170	Ⓣ	:231 :474 1:12 1:411	3↑ ⒻAlw 15000N$mY	87	6	1	11½	11	11½	1¾	Elliott S	L 114	2.60	93-09	It's Personal114¾ Kira's Dancer1131¼ Churchbell Chimes114¾	Driving	7
12Nov94-8Aqu	gd	1½	Ⓣ	:51 1:153 2:071 2:314	3↑ ⒻLongIslandH-G2	37	9	4	1½	32	1024	1236½	Velazquez J R	111	7.80e	60-03	Market Booster1158½ Tiffany's Taylor114no Lady Affirmed113¾	Gave way	12
15Oct94-7Bel	fm	1 1/16	[T]	:25 :483 1:112 1:403	3↑ Ⓕ[S]TiconderogaH75k	74	6	2	21	21	34	711½	Samyn J L	115	3.00	81-05	Putthepowdertoit1155 Great Triumph1121½ Irish Linnet1261	Tired	11
7Oct94-9Med	fm	1 1/16	Ⓣ	:234 :481 1:114 1:423	3↑ ⒻViolet H-G3	97	6	1	1hd	12	13½	11½	Velazquez J R	111	6.80	88-13	It's Personal1111½ Carezza115½ Artful Pleasure109no	Driving	11
10Sep94-8Bel	fm	1 1/16	[T]	:233 :462 1:102 1:392	3↑ ⒻNobleDamslH-G3	34	9	1	11½	2hd	1022	1033¾	Krone J A	109 b	7.40	65-11	Irish Linnet1176½ Statuette1131 Cox Orange117¾	Used up	10
17Aug94-9Sar	fm	1⅛	Ⓣ	:464 1:10 1:334 1:462	3↑ Ⓕ[S]Yaddo H86k	102	8	2	2½	11	12	21	Krone J A	111 b	6.60	94-10	Irish Linnet1231 It's Personal1115 All Tango1105	Gamely	10
13Jly94-8Bel	fm	1 1/16	Ⓣ	:241 :48 1:113 1:404	3↑ Ⓕ[S]Mt Vernon H55k	93	5	1	2hd	2hd	2hd	41	Davis R G	112 b	3.20	93-09	IrishActress116¾ GrtTriumph113no Tiffny'sTylor120nk	Weakened slightly	8
2Jly94-6Bel	fm	1 1/16	Ⓣ	:233 :46 1:10 1:412	3↑ Ⓕ[S]Alw 32000N2X	97	3	2	31½	31	1½	16½	Davis R G	119	3.20	91-15	It's Personal1196½ Tensie's Pro1063¾ Dana's Wedding1171¼	Ridden out	10
12Jun94-5Bel	fm	1 1/16	[T]	:231 :464 1:11 1:413	3↑ Ⓕ[S]Alw 30000N1X	84	6	1	11½	11½	12	11	Davis R G	119 b	6.60	88-08	It's Personal1191 Royal Pelliknow1146 Royal Cozzene1142¾	Driving	8

WORKOUTS: Apr 30 Fai 4f fst :51 B *1/1*

Market Booster

Own: Moyglare Stud
DAY P (7 1 2 0 .14)

B. m. 6
Sire: Green Dancer (Nijinsky II)
Dam: Final Figure (Super Concorde)
Br: Moyglare Stud Farm Ltd (Ky)
Tr: Lukas D Wayne (10 5 1 0 .50)

121

Lifetime Record:	32	9	5	4	$742,704						
1995	3	1	1	0	$93,731	Turf	28	9	5	3	$733,704
1994	12	3	0	3	$213,859	Wet	2	0	0	0	
Bel Ⓣ	3	1	0	0	$66,960	Dist Ⓣ	3	1	0	1	$76,584

27Apr95-8Kee	fm	1½	Ⓣ	:491 1:134 2:04 2:291	ⒻBewitch-G3	101	4	2	21	2hd	1hd	1½	Day P	L 119 b	*1.20	99-08	Market Booster119½ Memories1131¼ Abigailthewife1144	Hand urging	7
12Mar95-10GP	sf	1½	Ⓣ	:502 1:15 2:051 2:29	3↑ ⒻOrchid H-G2	101	4	3	43½	52¼	33	2½	Day P	L 116 b	7.30	74-25	Exchange120½ Market Booster116hd Northern Emerald115½	Rallied	10
19Feb95-9GP	fm	1⅜	Ⓣ	:493 1:14 1:381 2:142	3↑ ⒻVery One H50k	96	6	2	1½	1hd	1hd	42½	Bailey J D	L 117 b	2.20	92-03	P J Floral1131½ Trampoli118¾ Memories113hd	Faded	6
17Dec94-10Crc	gd	1½	Ⓣ	:484 1:132 2:034 2:284	3↑ ⒻLaPrevoyntH-G2	93	2	5	35	42	33½	35	Day P	L 118 b	*.90	81-14	Abigailthewife1144¾ Trampoli118nk MrketBooster1182	Bid between, hung	14
12Nov94-8Aqu	gd	1½	Ⓣ	:51 1:153 2:071 2:314	3↑ ⒻLongIslandH-G2	103	2	6	31	12	17	18½	Luzzi M J	115 b	7.70	97-03	Market Booster1158½ Tiffany's Taylor114no Lady Affirmed113¾	Mild drive	12
28Oct94-8Kee	fm	1½	Ⓣ	:48 1:123 2:05 2:311	3↑ ⒻDowager46k	89	4	3	2hd	2hd	1hd	11¼	Day P	L 123 b	2.90	89-14	MarketBooster1231¼ MyMandy114¾ FairyGrden115nk	Well ridden, driving	10
24Sep94-9Bel	sf	1¼	[T]	:49 1:141 1:401 2:052	3↑ ⒻFlowerBowlH-G1	57	10	6	31½	76¼	917	925¼	Santagata N	115 b	46.70	38-37	Dahlia's Dreamer11213 Alywow114nk Danish113nk	Tired	12
29Aug94-7Sar	fm	1⅜	[T]	:501 1:153 1:403 2:164	3↑ ⒻWaya55k	94	2	1	2½	11	3nk	3¾	Santos J A	122 b	3.40	81-18	Saratoga Source113nk Tiffany's Taylor113½ Market Booster122½	Gamely	7
10Jly94-8Bel	fm	1¼	[T]	:484 1:122 1:361 1:593	3↑ ⒻNew York H-G2	71	2	2	21	42½	67½	613¾	Santos J A	116 b	5.70	78-14	You'd Be Surprised118nk Dahlia's Dreamer1124½ Aquilegia1153	Tired	6
5Jun94-8Bel	fm	1⅜	[T]	:47 1:11 1:351 2:113	3↑ ⒻShpshdBay H-G3	103	9	3	36½	33½	21½	1½	Santos J A	114 b	21.00	96-08	Market Booster114½ Irish Linnet1151 Fairy Garden120hd	Driving	9

WORKOUTS: May 31 Bel 4f fst :502 B *57/70* May 25 Bel [T] 5f fm 1:001 H (d)*3/12* May 17 Bel 5f fst 1:02 B *8/20* May 9 Bel 4f fst :492 B *14/46* Apr 22 Kee 5f fst 1:012 B *3/19* Apr 13 Kee Ⓣ 5f fm 1:012 B (d)*2/5*

Northern Emerald

Own: Polk Hiram & Richardson David
B. m. 5
Sire: Green Dancer (Nijinsky II)
Dam: Tromphe de Naskra (Naskra)
Br: Oakbrook Farm (Ky)
Tr: Mott William I (29 12 5 6 .41)
PEREZ R B (104 15 19 10 .14)
116

Lifetime Record: 19 6 2 5 $213,502
1995 5 2 0 2 $83,721 | Turf 19 6 2 5 $213,502
1994 5 1 0 1 $43,061 | Wet 0 0 0 0
Bel Ⓣ 2 1 0 1 $32,952 | Dist Ⓣ 1 1 0 0 $24,000

19May95- 8GS yl 1⅛ Ⓣ :471 1:12 1:374 1:482 3↑ Ⓕ Vineland H-G3 100 4 6 76 62¾ 31 12¾ Perez R B L 115 *2.20 107-03 Northern Emerald1152¾ Kris's Kiss1092¼ Kira's Dancer113hd Mild drive 8
27Apr95- 8Kee fm 1½ Ⓣ :491 1:134 2:04 2:291 Ⓕ Bewitch-G3 91 5 4 43 43½ 45½ 45¾ Perret C L 114 5.40 93-08 Market Booster119¾ Memories1131¼ Abigailthewife1144 No rally 7
12Mar95- 10GP sf 1½ Ⓣ :502 1:15 2:051 2:29 3↑ Ⓕ Orchid H-G2 101 10 2 32 1hd 21½ 3½ Perret C L 115 27.50 74-25 Exchnge120½ MrketBoostr116hd NorthrnEmrld115½ Gave way grudgingly 10
29Jan95- 3GP fm 1⅜ Ⓣ :494 1:142 1:382 2:144 Ⓕ Handicap40k 92 2 3 34 31½ 11½ 11½ Perret C L 115 *1.30 92-06 Northern Emerald1151½ Petiteness1131½ La Turka1141½ 7
Six wide top str, driving
20Jan95- 9GP fm *1⅛ Ⓣ :223 :464 1:121 1:444 + Ⓕ Alw 33000N4X 87 3 6 57 31 1½ 32¼ Perret C L 117 3.80 82-13 Afaladja1171½ Ma Guerre1191 Northern Emerald1173½ Weakened 10
26Nov94- 7CD gd 1⅛ Ⓣ :224 :474 1:132 1:464 3↑ Ⓕ Alw 40260C 69 7 9 912 910 75½ 68 Perret C 116 *2.20 64-27 Nice Mistake1162½ Fleeting Ways116½ Nasdoria1162 No factor 10
5Jun94- 8AP fm 1⅛ Ⓣ :483 1:122 1:373 1:56 3↑ Ⓕ Modesty H-G3 89 4 5 75½ 96¾ 84¾ 84¾ Guidry M 114 4.40 82-13 D Aube Indienne114¾ Assert Oneself1151½ One Dreamer1171¾ 6 wide bid 9
28Apr94- 8Kee fm 1⅛ Ⓣ :473 1:121 1:38 1:501 Ⓕ Bewitch-G3 89 6 6 43 52½ 52½ 52½ Perret C 114 2.40 84-17 Freewheel1142 Key Chance114hd Amal Hayati119no Saved ground 6
16Mar94- 8GP fm 1½ Ⓣ :474 1:122 2:01 2:252 3↑ Ⓕ Orchid H-G2 99 5 2 2hd 1hd 2½ 32 Perret C 112 6.20 91-08 Trampoli1211½ GoodMorningSmile110¾ NorthernEmerld1121½ Weakened 7
25Feb94- 7GP fm *1⅛ Ⓣ :472 1:114 1:37 1:523 + Ⓕ Alw 31000N3X 94 4 9 811 73¾ 21½ 1nk Smith M E 116 *1.80 82-20 Northern Emerald116nk Ginny Dare116¾ Passing Vice1161½ Driving 10

WORKOUTS: May 31 Bel 4f fst :49 B 34/70 May 14 Bel 6f fst 1:183 B 10/12 Apr 15 CD 5f fst 1:043 B 22/26 Apr 8 CD 5f fst 1:05 B 22/23 Mar 31 GP 5f fst 1:04 B 2/3 Mar 23 GP Ⓣ 4f fm :504 B 16/18

Duda

Own: Paulson Madeleine A
Dk. b or br f. 4
Sire: Theatrical (Ire) (Nureyev)
Dam: Noble Times (Drums of Time)
Br: Paulson Allen E (Ky)
Tr: Mott William I (29 12 5 6 .41)
BAILEY J D (89 21 16 9 .24)
112

Lifetime Record: 11 4 2 2 $104,726
1995 3 1 0 1 $32,390 | Turf 9 3 2 2 $86,496
1994 8 3 2 1 $72,336 | Wet 1 1 0 0 $18,000
Bel Ⓣ 0 0 0 0 | Dist Ⓣ 0 0 0 0

19Apr95- 9Kee fm 1½ Ⓣ :501 1:15 2:053 2:292 Ⓕ Alw 46000N3X 95 1 6 73¾ 53¼ 1hd 13 Bailey J D L 114 *.70e 98 — Duda1143 Sudana1112½ Pam Slaughter113hd Ridden out 9
22Feb95- 8GP fm *1⅛ Ⓣ :471 1:12 1:364 1:483 + Ⓕ Alw 30000N3X 91 5 7 79½ 74½ 61½ 31 Botti E L 119 11.20 101 — Joy Of Ireland1181 Park Valley116no Duda1191½ 10
Six wide top str, late rally
22Jan95- 5GP fm 1⅛ Ⓣ :484 1:124 1:362 1:493 + Ⓕ Alw 30000N3X 80 1 10 98¼ 910 910 77 Smith M E L 117 2.20 77-21 Teasing Charm117¾ Waquoit's Tune1172½ Dahar's Best117hd No threat 12
23Nov94- 6CD fm 1⅛ Ⓣ :482 1:124 1:38 1:503 3↑ Ⓕ Alw 44100N$Y 82 7 6 74¾ 41 54 45¾ Day P L 118 4.10 72-17 Olden Lek114nk D Heavenliness1143 Valeta1212½ No rally 10
Placed third through disqualification.
12Oct94- 9Kee fm 1⅛ Ⓣ :474 1:131 1:38 1:50 3↑ Ⓕ Alw 30000N2X 85 7 8 62¾ 63¾ 3½ 1½ Day P L 117 *2.60 87-15 Duda117½ Offside Bar1111 Time To Dance113hd Hard drive 10
24Aug94- 6Sar gd 1⅛ Ⓣ :242 :481 1:123 1:433 3↑ Ⓕ Alw 32000N2X 81 2 5 65¾ 64 62½ 44¾ Smith M E 117 5.80 71-22 Knocknock112¾ Uncharted Waters1123½ Kris's Kiss117½ Mild gain 9
5Aug94- 7Sar my 1⅛ ⊗ :493 1:151 1:403 1:533 3↑ Ⓕ Alw 30000N1X 80 5 3 2½ 11 1hd 12½ Smith M E 114 5.50 68-28 Duda1142½ Joy Of Ireland1174 Bobbycom117 Driving 5
3Jly94- 5CD fm 1⅛ Ⓣ :471 1:12 1:381 1:51 3↑ Ⓕ Md Sp Wt 77 6 6 69 66 3nk 1½ Gomez G K L 112 *.90 76-15 Duda112½ Krasivi1121½ Cherokee Crossing1122 5 wide, lasted 10
25May94- 7CD fm 1⅛ Ⓣ :232 :464 1:12 1:44 3↑ Ⓕ Md Sp Wt 68 3 4 54½ 31½ 2½ 21½ Gomez G K 112 *.80 84-14 Gotta Wear Shades1111½ Duda112½ First Alliance1122½ 10
Leaned in, brushed 3/16, second best
26Feb94- 11GP fm *1⅛ Ⓣ :482 1:14 1:391 1:533 + Ⓕ Md Sp Wt 70 6 3 41¾ 21½ 1hd 2no Smith M E 120 *2.60 77-11 My Affection120no Duda1201½ Great Impulse1201¼ 10
Six wide top stretch, gave way grudgingly

WORKOUTS: Jun 1 Bel 5f fst 1:042 B 8/13 May 20 CD 6f fst 1:172 B 9/9 May 13 CD 6f fst 1:193 B 6/7 Apr 29 CD 4f fst :51 B 30/40 Apr 8 CD 5f fst 1:05 B 22/23 Mar 29 Pay 7f fst 1:352 B 1/1

Chelsey Flower

Own: Blasland Warren V Jr
B. f. 4
Sire: His Majesty (Ribot)
Dam: Chelsey Dancer (Affirmed)
Br: Hilary Boone Jr (Ky)
Tr: Margotta Anthony Jr (17 1 2 3 .06)
DECARLO C P (22 2 0 2 .09)
109

Lifetime Record: 15 3 2 1 $124,990
1995 3 1 1 0 $24,760 | Turf 13 3 2 1 $124,990
1994 7 0 1 1 $11,610 | Wet 0 0 0 0
Bel Ⓣ 4 2 1 1 $107,440 | Dist Ⓣ 0 0 0 0

21May95- 8Bel fm 1¼ Ⓣ :472 1:113 1:364 2:01 3↑ Ⓕ Alw 36000N2X 90 9 3 35 31 11½ 12¼ Decarlo C P 119 9.60 83-15 Chelsey Flower1192¼ Sudana1193 Assertive Dancer1191 Checked turn 10
15Apr95- 6Hia fm 1⅛ Ⓣ 1:481 Ⓕ Alw 17600N2X 87 5 3 2½ 1hd 2hd 21¼ Alligood M A L 114 6.80 91-12 LstBlood1121¼ ChelsyFlowr11410 GoodonyAmy1141¼ Gave way grudgingly 10
3Feb95- 8GP fm *1⅛ Ⓣ :232 :47 1:11 1:414 + Ⓕ Alw 28000N2X 76 7 2 22 66 69¾ 69¾ Samyn J L L 118 8.10 90 — Red Soul1183¾ Stretch Drive118nk Wood Of Binn1183 Faded 10
26Nov94- 5Aqu sf 1⅛ Ⓣ :482 1:141 1:402 1:53 3↑ Ⓕ Alw 34000N2X 56 5 2 21½ 67 913 817½ Samyn J L 115 7.00 58-29 Apolda1155½ Spectaculaire1174 Ali Glory1085 Forced pace 10
28Oct94- 7Aqu fm 1⅛ Ⓣ :474 1:12 1:372 1:504 3↑ Ⓕ Alw 34000N2X 77 8 2 46 55½ 87¼ 85¼ Chavez J F 114 *2.15 81-18 Aucilla1161 Great Lady Mary1143 Bold Rosa Lined1171 Done early 9
8Oct94- 4Bel fm 1⅛ Ⓣ :242 :472 1:112 1:422 3↑ Ⓕ Alw 34000N2X 84 2 3 35 33½ 22 22¾ Chavez J F 114 3.30 81-15 Caress1192¾ Chelsey Flower1142¾ Staldancer1172½ Willingly 10
3Aug94- 9Sar yl 1⅛ Ⓣ :231 :48 1:123 1:434 Ⓕ Nijana-G3 51 4 1 11 63½ 99½ 923 Sellers S J 118 fb 14.70 52-25 Alywow1213½ Irish Forever121no Knocknock1142 Used up 9
Run in divisions
17Jly94- 6Bel fm 1⅛ Ⓣ :232 :471 1:102 1:404 3↑ Ⓕ Alw 32000N2X 86 6 1 12½ 11 2hd 31¼ Chavez J F 111 fb 12.70 91-09 Jiving Around117½ Arctic Aaria117¾ Chelsey Flower111nk Weakened 8
15Mar94- 8GP fm 1⅛ Ⓣ :472 1:11 1:35 1:471 + Ⓕ Sweetst Chnt50k 31 13 1 2hd 911 1224 1226¼ Fires E 121 21.30 70-05 Malli Star1141½ Red Soul1135 Petiteness112no Faltered 13
23Feb94- 8GP gd *1⅛ Ⓣ :24 :481 1:122 1:472 + Ⓕ Alw 31500N2X 59 5 2 22 31½ 96 99 Bailey J D 118 *2.30 71-29 Malli Star118¾ Long Gone Blues118hd Leah Jolean118nk Stopped 10

WORKOUTS: May 14 Bel tr.t 4f fst :513 B 36/41 Mar 28 GP Ⓣ 4f hd :50 H 15/24 Mar 17 GP Ⓣ 4f fm :491 H 2/15 Mar 12 GP 4f fst :53 B 33/33

Danish (Ire)

Own: McCalmont Harry
B. f. 4
Sire: Danehill (Danzig)
Dam: Tea House (Sassafras)
Br: McCalmont Major V (Ire)
Tr: Clement Christophe (20 4 0 6 .20)
KRONE J A (97 22 16 19 .23)
116

Lifetime Record: 13 4 1 3 $205,854
1995 2 0 0 0 $3,780 | Turf 12 4 1 3 $204,474
1994 6 3 0 3 $187,839 | Wet 0 0 0 0
Bel Ⓣ 2 0 0 1 $26,400 | Dist Ⓣ 0 0 0 0

18May95- 8Bel fm 1 Ⓣ :232 :463 1:104 1:352 Ⓕ Alw 40000N4X 84 4 8 76¾ 62¾ 52¼ 43¾ Krone J A 113 *.65 82-14 Great Lady Mary1131¾ Vice On Ice1131¾ Great Triumph114nk 8
Blocked 1/4 pl, lacked room stretch
14Apr95- 7Aqu fst 1⅛ :463 1:103 1:361 1:492 Ⓕ Alw 46000N$mY 79 3 2 25 33½ 46½ 511¼ Krone J A 119 3.80 81-13 Little Buckles1172¼ Sovereign Kitty1195¾ Forcing Bid114hd Gave way 7
29Oct94- 8Kee fm 1⅛ Ⓣ :471 1:113 1:362 1:484 Ⓕ QnElizbthII-G1 107 5 7 63 62½ 21½ 12½ Krone J A 121 11.80 93-13 Danish1212½ Eternal Reve121nk Avie's Fancy121¾ 10
Leaned in bumped start, driving, clear
24Sep94- 9Bel sf 1¼ Ⓣ :49 1:141 1:401 2:052 3↑ Ⓕ FlowerBowlH-G1 84 2 2 2½ 23 28 313½ Krone J A 113 29.50 50-37 Dahlia's Dreamer11213 Alywow114nk Danish113nk Weakened 12
28Aug94 ♦ Deauville(Fr) yl *1¼ Ⓣ RH 2:144 Ⓕ Prix de la Nonette-G3 31 Dubroeucq G 128 25.00 Grafin128½ Maidment128½ Danish1281½ 7
Tr: John Hammond Stk 62900 *Led to 150y out, no answer to first two*
27Jly94 ♦ La Teste(Fr) fm *1 Ⓣ RH Ⓕ Prix La Sorellina (Listed) 1hd Dubroeucq G 119 3.50 Danish119hd Fire and Sword1191½ Amy Ride119½ 9
Stk 31500 *Led after 1f, held gamely. Time not taken*
21Jun94 ♦ Saint-Cloud(Fr) gd *1 Ⓣ LH 1:414 Prix Bosalino 11½ Marcus B 120 4.80 Danish1201½ White Girl120½ Most Beautiful117nk 9
Alw 26900 *Wire to wire, driving*
23May94 ♦ Wissembourg(Fr) gd *7½f Ⓣ LH Prix Martine Lutz 34½ Gruhn D 123 - Sigismond1384 Son Brondo136½ Danish123½ 11
Alw 7100 *Time not taken*
28Aug93 ♦ Curragh(Ire) gd 1 Ⓣ Str 1:412 EBF Futurity Stakes-G3 78 Hughes R 119 10.00 Cois Na Tine122¾ Ballykett Nancy1192 City Nights1222½ 7
Tr: Michael Kauntze Stk 34800 *Trailed throughout*
14Aug93 ♦ Curragh(Ire) yl 7f Ⓣ Str 1:312 EBF Tyros Stakes (Listed) 43½ Gilson P V 123 8.00 Majestic Role120¾ Gothic Dream1232 Via Condotti123¾ 11
Stk 20700 *Tracked leader, bid 2f out, dueled 1f out, faded late*

WORKOUTS: Jun 2 Bel 4f fst :49 B 14/41 May 27 Bel 4f gd :49 B 7/18 May 16 Bel 4f fst :491 B 10/21 May 9 Bel 3f fst :36 B 2/24 May 2 Bel 3f gd :354 B 2/18 Apr 25 Bel 4f fst :503 B 24/28

Were this a dirt race at a shorter distance, It's Personal would deserve serious consideration as the controlling speed. But in a Grade 2 stake at 11 furlongs on the grass, that circumstance is of little consequence: It's Personal has garnered all her victories at distances of a mile and a sixteenth or less; she will almost certainly be overwhelmed during the crucial final furlongs of this marathon, easy lead or not.

The favorite, hovering around even-money, was Market Booster, who won the Sheepshead Bay's 1994 renewal at 21-1. Market Booster has amassed turf earnings of $733,704, almost as much as her six rivals combined, and she gave Northern Emerald five pounds and a comprehensive beating in the Grade 3 Bewitch at a mile and a half scarcely five weeks ago; meeting that mare at the same weight-spread here, she appears a legitimate favorite to defend her title — especially since 3-1 second choice Danish (remember her from the Flower Bowl?) has thus far done her best racing at nine furlongs or less.

Four fillies in the race — Danish, Market Booster, Northern Emerald, and It's Personal — have recorded triple-digit Beyers, but the standout on "numbers" isn't among them. If Market Booster is the measuring stick in this race, and that mare required :25 1/5 seconds to finish her final quarter mile in Keeneland's 12-furlong Bewitch, what are fair odds on Duda, who covered the same territory roughly 10 lengths faster enroute to her N3X allowance win under a hand ride April 19?

Compare the Keeneland mile-and-a-half races turned in by Market Booster and Duda once again: Market Booster, head-and-head for the lead a quarter mile out, covers the last segment in: 25 1/5. Duda wipes out a deficit of 3 1/4 lengths through a :23 4/5 final fraction, giving her a scintillating adjusted come-home time of :23 1/5.

Clearly, Duda is developing into a formidable filly, and because she is from top-shelf connections the late bloomer has been afforded all the time she needed to get her act together. Duda's 3-year-old season was productive enough, as she made her way through the N2X allowance ranks in her penultimate start; but her two most recent outings strongly suggest she is on the verge of breaking through at the age of 4, which is not surprising in light of her pedigree, which is strongly oriented toward distance racing on grass. Duda's earnings on grass are the lowest in the Sheepshead Bay field, true enough, but does that necessarily mean she's outclassed? Were she from an ordinary background, barn, and bloodlines this might be construed as biting off more than she could chew, but Bill Mott never asks his horses to do anything they haven't been well prepared for, and Allen Paulson is an extremely well-heeled and patient owner.

Considering the fact that Duda has shown a steady pattern of improvement with her races well-spaced, the fact that Mott has picked out the Sheepshead Bay as her first assignment since mid-April is an unmistakable indication of confidence. Duda has been handled very patiently to this point in her career; her prodigious finishing kick first time beyond a mile and an eighth was the tip-off that she was ready to break through to the next level:

NINTH RACE
Belmont
JUNE 4, 1995

1⅜ MILES. (Inner Turf)(2.10^{1}) 37th Running of THE SHEEPSHEAD BAY HANDICAP. Purse $100,000 Added. Grade II. Fillies and mares, 3–year–olds and upward. By subscription of $100 each which should accompany the nomination; $500 to pass the entry box, $500 to start with $100,000 added. The added money and all fees to be divided 60% to the winner, 20% to second, 11% to third, 6% to fourth and 3% to fifth. Weights: Wednesday, May 31. Starters to be named at the closing time of entries. Trophies will be presented to the winning owner, trainer and jockey. The New York Racing Association Inc. reserves the right to transfer this race to the Main Track. Closed Saturday, May 20, with 20 nominations.

Value of Race: $109,500 Winner $65,700; second $21,900; third $12,045; fourth $6,570; fifth $3,285. Mutuel Pool $313,036.00 Exacta Pool $369,981.00 Triple Pool $331,965.00

Last Raced	Horse	M/Eqt.	A.	Wt	PP	¼	½	¾	1	Str	Fin	Jockey	Odds $1
19Apr95 ^{9}Kee^{1}	Duda		4	112	5	7	7	4^{1}	3^{hd}	1½	1^{1¼}	Bailey J D	5.90
18May95 ^{8}Bel^{4}	Danish-IR		4	116	7	6^{1}	6^{1}	7	6½	5^{3½}	2½	Krone J A	3.20
21May95 ^{8}Bel^{1}	Chelsey Flower		4	112	6	4^{2}	4^{1}	5^{1}	5½	4^{hd}	3^{nk}	Decarlo C P	12.70
19May95 ^{8}GS^{1}	ⒹNorthern Emerald		5	116	4	1½	2^{1}	2^{1}	2^{1}	2^{1}	4^{2¼}	Perez R B	6.40
27Apr95 ^{8}Kee^{1}	Market Booster	b	6	121	3	3½	3½	3^{hd}	4^{1}	3^{1}	5^{6}	Smith M E	1.10
18May95 ^{8}Bel^{2}	Vice On Ice		4	114	1	5½	5½	6½	7	7	6^{12½}	Santos J A	19.70
19May95 ^{9}Pim^{1}	It's Personal		5	113	2	2^{1}	1½	1½	1½	6^{hd}	7	Luzzi M J	8.70

Ⓓ–Northern Emerald disqualified and placed 5th.

OFF AT 5:05 Start Good. Won driving. Time, :23^{2}, :48^{2}, 1:13^{2}, 1:38^{1}, 2:02^{1}, 2:13^{3} Course firm.

$2 Mutuel Prices:				
	6–DUDA	13.80	6.80	5.70
	8–DANISH–IR		5.30	4.70
	7–CHELSEY FLOWER			7.10

$2 EXACTA 6–8 PAID $70.50 $2 TRIPLE 6–8–7 PAID $674.00

Dk. b. or br. f, by Theatrical (Ire)–Noble Times, by Drums of Time. Trainer Mott William I. Bred by Paulson Allen E (Ky).

DUDA trailed for a half, moved up steadily from outside along the backstretch, raced just outside MARKET BOOSTER leaving the far turn, launched a rally three wide entering the stretch, surged to the front in midstretch then was all out to hold off DANISH in the late stages. DANISH unhurried for seven furlongs, while three wide, closed the gap a bit in upper stretch then finished with good energy in the middle of the track but could not get up. CHELSEY FLOWER settled in the middle of the pack, steadied in traffic on the turn, closed late between horses to gain a share. NORTHERN EMERALD set or forced the pace from outside to the top of the stretch, drifted in while battling heads apart inside the furlong marker then weakened in the final sixteenth. MARKET BOOSTER settled just off the pace while saving ground, was boxed in along the rail through the turn, slipped through along the rail to challenge briefly in midstretch, then took up sharply while lacking room inside the furlong marker, failed to threaten thereafter. A claim of foul against the winner lodged by the rider of MARKET BOOSTER for interference in the stretch was disallowed. However, the stewards subsequently disqualified NORTHERN EMERALD from fourth and placed her fifth for interfering with MARKET BOOSTER in midstretch. VICE ON ICE reserved early, raced in traffic while saving ground on the turn, lacked a strong closing bid. IT'S PERSONAL set the pace along the inside to the top of the stretch and tired.

Owners— 1, Paulson Madeleine A; 2, McCalmont Harry; 3, Blasland W V Jr & Bouck W; 4, Polk Hiram & Richardson David; 5, Moyglare Stud; 6, Burgundy Stable; 7, Prestonwood Farm

Trainers—1, Mott William I; 2, Clement Christophe; 3, Margotta Anthony Jr; 4, Mott William I; 5, Lukas D Wayne; 6, Domino Carl J; 7, Dickinson Michael W

Overweight: Chelsey Flower (3), Vice On Ice (3).

Scratched— Abigailthewife (27Apr95 ^{8}KEE^{3})

Sent away at nearly 6-1, Duda was a prime bet. I bet her to win, and boxed her in exactas with Market Booster and Danish (the only Grade 1 winner in the field).

As so often happens in grass routes, the deciding factors were class, late speed and racing luck. Duda had plenty of class and late speed, and Market Booster had no racing luck. The prohibitive chalk was boxed in while saving ground through the final turn, and took up sharply along the inside when Northern Emerald drifted inward in deep stretch, finishing off the board. Duda was allowed to settle into stride through the opening half-mile, sacrificed a loss of ground on the final bend for a clear outside run straightening into the stretch, and swept by the field on the far outside coming to midstretch.

Duda was something of a disappointment after the Sheepshead Bay, losing her next four starts while sent postward as the favorite in three of them.

But after a lackluster fourth place finish over an extremely soft course at Belmont on the closing day of the fall meeting, Duda was flown to Hollywood Park for the prestigious Grade 1 Matriarch and caught a firm course for the first time in three months:

SIXTH RACE
Hollywood
NOVEMBER 26, 1995

1¼ MILES. (Turf)(1.57^{3}) 15th Running of THE MATRIARCH. Purse $700,000. Grade I. 3-year-olds and upward. By subscription of $1,000 each on or before Wednesday, July 19, which should accompany the nomination. To remain eligible the following payment must be made, $2,500 on or before Wednesday, October 4. Late nominations, for horses not previously nominated or not remaining eligible, may be made on or before Wednesday, November 15, by payment of $30,000 each, which should accompany the nomination, of which $26,500 is refundable if the nominee is entered and does not draw into the body of the race or if the nominee is not entered and a veterinarian certificate is produced indicating the horse is unfit to run. All nominees to pay $5,000 to enter and an additional $5,000 to start. Gross purse $700,000 of which $385,000 to be paid to the winner, $140,000 to second, $105,000 to third, $52,500 to fourth and $17,500 to fifth. Weights: 3-year-olds, 120 lbs. Older, 123 lbs. Starters to be named through the entry box by the closing time of entries. This race will not be divided. If the number of entries exceed fourteen (14), first preference will be given to graded or group stakes winners in 1995. Second preference will be given to those horses with the highest total earnings in 1995. Entry fees will be refunded to all horses which fail to draw into this race. Trophies will be presented to the winning owner, trainer and jockey. Closed Wednesday, July 19, with 70 nominations. 38 remained eligible Wednesday, October 4. Late nominations closed, Wednesday, November 15, $30,000 each, with two: Bold Ruritana and Windsharp.

Value of Race: $700,000 Winner $385,000; second $140,000; third $105,000; fourth $35,000 each. Mutuel Pool $570,429.20 Exacta Pool $387,263.00 Trifecta Pool $393,796.00 Quinella Pool $68,011.00

Last Raced	Horse	M/Eqt.	A.	Wt	PP	¼	½	¾	1	Str	Fin	Jockey	Odds $1
29Oct95 ^{9}Bel^{4}	Duda	LB	4	123	5	$1^{1\frac{1}{2}}$	10^{hd}	9^{hd}	9^{1}	5^{1}	1^{1}	Bailey J D	30.70
12Nov95 ^{8}SA^{2}	Angel In My Heart-FR	L	3	120	8	4^{1}	5^{1}	5^{2}	4^{hd}	4^{1}	2^{nk}	Asmussen C B	5.90
12Nov95 ^{8}SA^{6}	Wandesta-GB	L	4	123	10	6^{hd}	$8^{\frac{1}{2}}$	10^{hd}	10^{hd}	10^{2}	3no	Nakatani C S	a-6.50
29Oct95 ^{9}Bel^{2}	DH Windsharp	LB	4	123	12	$5^{\frac{1}{2}}$	3^{hd}	3^{1}	$3^{\frac{1}{2}}$	$3^{1\frac{1}{2}}$	4	Almeida G F	15.80
1Oct95 Lch^{3}	DH Balanka-IR	f	3	120	6	$9^{1\frac{1}{2}}$	7^{hd}	7^{hd}	6^{hd}	9^{hd}	4^{hd}	Black C A	f-25.30
21Oct95 ^{8}Kee^{4}	Sleep Easy	L	3	120	9	1^{1}	$1^{\frac{1}{2}}$	1^{hd}	1^{hd}	1^{hd}	6^{nk}	Desormeaux K J	a-6.50
12Nov95 ^{8}SA^{1}	Alpride-IR	L	4	123	11	2^{hd}	2^{1}	2^{1}	2^{hd}	2^{hd}	$7^{1\frac{1}{4}}$	McCarron C J	2.10
12Nov95 ^{8}SA^{3}	Bold Ruritana	LB	5	123	2	$3^{1\frac{1}{2}}$	$4^{\frac{1}{2}}$	4^{hd}	$5^{1\frac{1}{2}}$	6^{hd}	8^{hd}	Kabel T K	17.10
15Oct95 ^{4}WO^{2}	Matiara	B	3	120	7	10^{hd}	$11^{1\frac{1}{2}}$	$11^{1\frac{1}{2}}$	14	$11^{\frac{1}{2}}$	9no	Head F	4.20
21Oct95 ^{8}Kee^{7}	Bail Out Becky	LB	3	120	3	14	$13^{\frac{1}{2}}$	12^{hd}	11^{hd}	8^{hd}	$10^{\frac{3}{4}}$	Sellers S J	40.40
15Oct95 ^{4}WO^{6}	Morgana	LB	4	123	14	$12^{\frac{1}{2}}$	14	14	13^{1}	$13^{1\frac{1}{2}}$	11^{1}	Stevens G L	16.80
12Nov95 ^{8}Aqu^{1}	Caress		4	123	1	7^{hd}	$9^{1\frac{1}{2}}$	$8^{1\frac{1}{2}}$	$8^{\frac{1}{2}}$	7^{hd}	$12^{\frac{1}{2}}$	Davis R G	21.80
12Nov95 ^{8}SA^{4}	Flagbird	LB	4	123	13	$8^{\frac{1}{2}}$	6^{1}	$6^{\frac{1}{2}}$	7^{1}	12^{hd}	13^{1}	Delahoussaye E	10.50
4Nov95 ^{8}BM^{1}	Jo Knows	LB	5	123	4	13^{hd}	12^{hd}	13^{hd}	12^{1}	14	14	Solis A	f-25.30

DH—Dead Heat.
a-Coupled: Wandesta-GB and Sleep Easy.
f-Mutuel Field: Balanka-IR and Jo Knows.

OFF AT 3:14 Start Good. Won driving. Time, :24^{4}, :49^{3}, 1:13^{2}, 1:36^{3}, 2:00^{1} Course firm.

$2 Mutuel Prices:

5-DUDA	63.40	28.60	17.60
7-ANGEL IN MY HEART-FR		7.20	5.00
1A-WANDESTA-GB (a-entry)			5.40

$2 EXACTA 5-7 PAID $616.20 $2 TRIFECTA 5-7-1 PAID $3,929.00 $2 QUINELLA 5-7 PAID $219.60

Dk. b. or br. f, by Theatrical (Ire)-Noble Times, by Drums of Time. Trainer Mott William I. Bred by Paulson Allen E (Ky).

DUDA angled in early and saved ground to the second turn, went outside CARESS on that bend, swung five wide into the stretch and closed gamely under urging to gain the lead late and proved best. ANGEL IN MY HEART, was in a bit tight between foes on the first turn, remained between rivals on the backstretch and outside BOLD RURITANA on the second turn, angled out into the stretch and closed gamely between foes. WANDESTA, between rivals early and outside foes on the backstretch, moved

As Damon Runyon might've said: In grass races at classic distances the race isn't always to the strongest and swiftest finisher...but that's the way to bet.

Summer

SARATOGA IS NOT just a racetrack, it is an experience. Nestled in the foothills of the Adirondack mountains, the historic "Graveyard of Favorites" has been rhapsodized about in print by far more talented and illustrious racing writers than yours truly, so to go on and on about its charms would serve no great purpose. Suffice to say, if you've never been there, if you've become a bit jaded by a racing experience that often resembles nothing more than an electronic video game, you owe it to yourself to spend a weekend in Saratoga Springs, New York, where they have been racing thoroughbreds since the days of the Civil War.

The town is a throwback to a bygone era. For six weeks every summer it is inhabited by a higher concentration of horseplayers than any other place in the known universe. At Belmont Park and Aqueduct, when the racing is over, horseplayers go home; at the fabled Spa, they go out (so it's a good thing the area also boasts more bars per square mile than any other place in the universe). When you stay in Saratoga, you don't just play the horses, you eat, sleep and breathe them. It's sort of like summer camp for handicappers.

For nearly 130 years, from 1863 up until the beginning of the 1990s, the Saratoga meeting lasted four weeks, and the New York Racing Association ran ads proclaiming the track as "The August Place To Be." In recent years, however, the bottom line being what it is, the meet has been expanded an additional fortnight; in 1996 the session was scheduled to run through Labor Day, prompting many racetrack employees with school-age children to come up with unofficial slogans of their own, most of which contained language unsuitable for an advertising campaign.

Because the meet has been lengthened horses now have more of a chance to become acclimated to their summer surroundings, but the "horse for course" influence is still considerable: horses that have run well at Saratoga in years past tend to run back to that form, sometimes remarkably so: the legendary Fourstardave, retired at age 10 after three unsuccessful tries at the 1995 meet, won a race at the Spa each and every summer for eight years, beginning as a 2-year-old in 1987 and culminating in 1994, when, at the age of nine, he smoked a classified allowance field by five lengths on opening weekend. Fittingly, the venerable chestnut had a street near the track renamed in his honor during retirement ceremonies at the end of the '95 meet.

That Fourstardave won on the opening Sunday in 1994 brings up a point, one seldom mentioned about horses for courses at Saratoga: their edge is most potent at the beginning of the meet, before their rivals have had a chance to settle into their new digs, and before they've had a race over the course. Though I don't have any hard statistical evidence to back it up, I believe it's also true that turf horses tend to repeat from year to year at Saratoga more often than their counterparts on dirt — an important exception occurring with those horses who handle wet dirt. Slop and mud at Saratoga are different from other wet racing surfaces in the country, and success on other wet tracks is not an especially reliable barometer of success in Spa slop, just as horses who have not run well on other wet tracks may take to a wet Saratoga strip — sometimes quite unpredictably. The most reliable horses when the rains come are those that have run well on wet Saratoga tracks *before*. The *Form's* expanded career boxes have reduced the wager-value of this information to some extent, but opportunities still abound, as we shall see.

July 26

STEEPLECHASE RACING is part of the Saratoga mystique, though most of the hardened scribes in the press box hold it in about as much esteem as roller derby or pro wrestling. Many bettors shun these races too, particularly Pick 6 bettors. After several odds-on favorites went crashing through the pylons a few seasons ago, wiping out some big Pick 6 tickets, the steeplechasers were banished to the first race on the program. This seems to have worked out well for everyone: players who'd rather not get involved with the jumpers can sleep in, and still get some daily double action on races two and three.

Until the summer of '95 I was among the majority of hard-core players who would sooner bet on greyhounds than a steeplechaser. But all that changed after the first race on Wednesday, July 26, when a 6-year-old gelding named Mr. Skylark provided an unexpected windfall at 18-1:

1 **Saratoga**

2 1/16 MILES. **(Hurdles). (3:39^2) ALLOWANCE. Purse $30,000. 3-year-olds and upward which have not won a race other than maiden, claiming or starter. Weights: 3-year-olds, 140 lbs. 4-year-olds, 150 lbs. Older, 156 lbs. Non-winners in 1995, allowed 4 lbs. In 1994–95, 8 lbs. (Claiming and starter races not considered.)**

Coupled – Battleship Grey and Just You Dare(Ire); Brooknononsense, Logroller and Seminole Spirt; Sea Spruce and Mario(Ire)

Mr. Skylark
Own: Richardson Frank E

CLANCY S (—)

Dk. b or br g. 6
Sire: Imperial Falcon (Northern Dancer)
Dam: Fromdawntilldusk (Hoist the Flag)
Br: Watters Sidney Jr (Md)
Tr: Smithwick D Michael (—)

156

Lifetime Record :	**37**	**4**	**5**	**4**	**$81,559**	
Jumps 1992–95 :	**3**	**1**	**1**	**0**	**$11,114**	
1995	**2 1 1 0**	**$11,114**	**Turf**	**15 2 0 1**	**$32,920**	
1994	**3 0 0 0**	**$60**	**Wet**	**1 0 0 0**	**$1,740**	

20May95-1Mal	gd	*2¼	Hurdles				4:31^2	3↑ Md Sp Wt	—	4	3	3^{9¾}	2^2	1^½	1^2	Durkee B	154	-	— —	Mr. Skylark154^2 Lenape Sachem144^{20} Just You Dare154^{20}	Ridden out	5
14May95-3Wil	yl	*2½	Hurdles				4:56^1	3↑ Md Sp Wt	—	7	3	3^{4½}	4^{2½}	2^½	2^2	Durkee B	154	-	— —	Explosive Light142^2 Mr. Skylark154^3 Reverend R. D.135^2	Second best	6
30Oct94-7Fai	fm	*1¼ Ⓣ					2:12^3	3↑ Alw 1000NC	—	1	6	7^5	5^5	4^{15}	4^{15½}	Hobson S	L 155	2.10	86–03	Bartman152^{10} Doting145^{3¾} Halo For Silky138^{1¾}	Evenly	9
1Oct94-4Mid	fm	*2⅛	Hurdles				4:00^4	Md Sp Wt	—	5	9	4^¾	5^{4½}	6^{14}	7^{16¾}	Hobson S	156	-	— —	Donna's Pick156^{hd} Alight152^{1½} Roman Impulse152^{hd}	No threat	9
25Sep94-2Fx	fm	*2 Ⓣ					3:36	3↑ Alw 1000NC	—	8	2	1^1	2^{hd}	5^¾	7^{7½}	Hobson S	150	-	— —	Bryan Station150^3 Acallade's Capp133^{hd} Declare Your Wish150^½	Tired	7
24Nov93-8Lrl	fst	1$\frac{1}{16}$		:24^1	:48	1:12^2	1:44^3	3↑ Alw 22600N3X	67	2	8	7^{10}	8^{13}	8^{12}	8^{11½}	Skinner K	L 117	44.30	75–23	QulityRuler114^{2½} HveYouTestified117^½ WellInformed117^¾	Pinched back	8
9Nov93-9Lrl	fst	1$\frac{1}{16}$		:24	:47^2	1:12^2	1:44^1	3↑ Alw 22900N3X	66	3	9	9^{11}	8^{9¾}	7^{10}	7^{13¼}	Skinner K	L 119	33.10	76–20	Discernment117^4 Federal League112^{¾} Tidal Surge114^3	Wide	9
28Oct93-7Lrl	gd	1½ Ⓣ		:55^1	1:23^1	2:15^2	2:41^2	3↑ Alw 21200N2X	67	2	6	5^{2½}	3^{2½}	3^1	1^¾	Turner T G	L 117	12.90	43–58	Mr. Skylark117^¾ Bold Print117^½ My Man Pedro118^{nk}	Driving	10
17Oct93-8Lrl	fst	1⅛		:48^1	1:12^4	1:38	1:50^2	3↑ Alw 20600N2X	79	2	8	8^{15}	8^{13}	7^{10}	5^9	Saumell L	L 117	19.80	77–20	Sensational Eager117^{1½} Riskey Red118^4 Auntienan'sbrother117^{1¼}	Outrun	8
5Oct93-7Lrl	yl	1¼ Ⓣ		:51^1	1:16^2	1:42^4	2:08	3↑ Alw 21200N2X	62	4	10	8^{7½}	7^{6½}	8^{6¼}	8^{10½}	Saumell L	L 117	20.80	55–34	Legal Choice117^1 Third Eye117^½ Wine Prince115^{2½}	Wide	10

Don't feel too badly if the past performances seem like Greek. I'm the first one to admit I don't even know where most of these hunt meetings take place, let alone anything about how to handicap these races.

I didn't know anything about "Mid," or "Wil," or even "Mal," the places where Mr. Skylark had run his first three jump races. But I did remember cashing a bet on him on the grass at Saratoga before he was a jumper, when he was trained by Sid Watters Jr.:

NINTH RACE Saratoga AUGUST 22, 1992 — **1 ⅜ MILES.(InnerTurf). (2.13^{3}) MAIDEN SPECIAL WEIGHT. Purse $26,000. 3-years-old and upward. Weight: 3-year-olds, 117 lbs.; older, 122 lbs.**

Value of race $26,000; value to winner $15,600; second $5,720; third $3,120; fourth $1,560. Mutuel pool $398,832. Exacta Pool $479,046 Triple Pool $698,748

Last Raced	Horse	M/Eqt.	A.Wt	PP	¼	½	¾	1	Str	Fin	Jockey	Odds $1
12Aug92 1Sar2	Mr. Skylark		3 117	9	9	9	9	9	3½	13	Smith M E	2.20
10Aug92 6Sar2	Muy Mogambo	b	3 117	1	5	41	3hd	1hd	21½	2½	Perret C	1.50
3Aug92 6Sar4	Scout Setter	b	4 122	7	11½	11	21	21½	1hd	32¼	Day P	4.40
3Aug92 4WO2	All Canadian	b	3 117	2	32½	3½	41	31½	47	48½	Migliore R	7.20
14Aug92 2Sar8	One Bid Only	b	3 117	8	71	74	6hd	41	51	53½	Carr D	51.40
12Jly92 5Lrl14	Latinist		3 117	4	82½	82½	8½	8½	61½	63½	Brocklebank G V	59.90
29Jly92 6Sar6	Born a King		3 117	6	4hd	5hd	73	5½	73	73¼	Madrid A Jr	16.50
19Jly92 2Bel5	Sportin' Charles	b	3 117	5	61½	6½	5½	7hd	8½	81¾	Rojas R I	11.10
3Aug92 6Sar11	Colonial Freedom	b	3 117	3	2½	21½	1hd	61	9	9	Cruguet J	40.80

OFF AT 6:25 Start good. Won driving. Time, :24^{2}, :47^{3}, 1:13^{1}, 1:38^{3}, 2:03^{4}, 2:16^{1}, Course firm.

$2 Mutuel Prices:			
10-(J)-MR. SKYLARK	6.40	3.40	2.60
1-(A)-MUY MOGAMBO		2.80	2.40
8-(H)-SCOUT SETTER			3.00

$2 EXACTA 10-1 PAID $19.20 $2 TRIPLE 10-1-8 PAID $51.00

Dk. b. or br. c, (May), by Imperial Falcon—Fromdawntilldusk, by Hoist the Flag. Trainer Watters Sidney J Jr. Bred by Watters Sidney Jr (Md).

MR SKYLARK trailed for a mile, rapidly gained from outside on the turn then unleashed a powerful late run to win going away. MUY MOGAMBO, steadied along the inside on the first turn, angled to the outside after going a quarter of a mile, raced in close contention along the backstretch, drew alongside SCOUT SETTER to setter for the place. The latter battled along the inside the entire way and yielded grudgingly. ALL CANADIAN raced in close contention slightly off the rail to the turn and lacked a strong closing repsonse. ONE BID ONLY reserved early made

Going a mile and three-eighths on the inner turf (the course they run steeplechases on), Mr. Skylark had closed like a freight train in the ninth race on August 22, 1992, coming from last position midway on the final turn to win by three widening lengths. I remembered the race clearly because it had been the second half of the late double along with Travers-winner Thunder Rumble.

A lot of water had gone under the bridge since then, of course, and Mr. Skylark had been transformed into a jumper nearly a year ago, when he returned from a 10-month layoff at "Fx" (wherever that is) and tired to seventh after setting the early pace. The gelding's form in two October races was even worse, but some further R&R had served him quite well by May, and he ran two bang-up races within six days, placing at 2 1/2 miles and breaking his jump-maiden at 2 1/4 miles.

By now, all traces of Mr. Skylark's winning exploits at Saratoga had vanished from his past performances. Having not seen much in the way of betting opportunities during the first four days of the meet, I was on the muscle and ready for action.

"What the heck," I thought to myself. "I'll bet him, but I won't tell anyone":

FIRST RACE
Saratoga
JULY 26, 1995

2 1/16 MILES. (Hurdles)(3.39²) ALLOWANCE. Purse $30,000. 3-year-olds and upward which have not won a race other than maiden, claiming or starter. Weights: 3-year-olds, 140 lbs. 4-year-olds, 150 lbs. Older, 156 lbs. Non-winners in 1995, allowed 4 lbs. In 1994–95, 8 lbs. (Claiming and starter races not considered.)(Day 5 of a 34 Day Meet. Cloudy. 87.)

Value of Race: $30,000 Winner $18,000; second $6,000; third $3,300; fourth $1,800; fifth $900. Mutuel Pool $121,128.00 Exacta Pool $204,126.00

Last Raced	Horse	M/Eqt.	A.	Wt	PP	1	5	7	10	Str	Fin	Jockey	Odds $1
20May95 1Mal1	Mr. Skylark		6	156	4	1½	5½	7½	51	1½	12½	Durkee B	18.00
29May95 3Fai1	Stop and Listen		5	156	9	62	41	41½	3½	2hd	27	Delozier J W III	7.50
13May95 6PW1	Smart Jaune		6	156	12	12	12	5½	72½	34	32½	Neilson S	26.25
22Jun95 2Lrl3	Amending	b	5	148	2	101	32	1hd	4½	42	46	Miller B	6.00
29Jun95 1Atl1	Overnight Hero	f	10	148	7	4½	11½	23½	11	52	53¾	Walsh P B	12.20
29Jun95 1Atl2	Broad Branch		5	152	3	3½	6½	92½	84	68	69	Swartwout E	12.90
21May95 5Mor3	Brooknononsense		4	150	1	7½	9hd	10	10	8	75	Marzullo V	a-1.45
13Jun93 1Lrl2	Karetto-FR		6	148	5	21	2hd	31	6hd	7½	8	Osborne J A	27.75
23Jun95 2Lrl1	Sea Spruce		5	152	6	5hd	72	6hd	2hd	—	—	Thornton C	4.60
21May94 1Mgo1	Logroller		5	152	11	11hd	101	8½	92	—	—	Hobson S	a-1.45
21May95 1Lex1	Dashing Prince		5	156	8	81	11½	—	—	—	—	Teter J	47.50
14May95 3Wil1	Explosive Light	f	4	150	10	9½	81	—	—	—	—	Miller C	19.90

Sea Spruce:Fell; Logroller:Left course; Dashing Prince:Fell; Explosive Light:Fell
a-Coupled: Brooknononsense and Logroller.

OFF AT 1:01 Start Good from Flag. Won driving. Time, 3:41⁴ Course firm.
(Hand Timed)

$2 Mutuel Prices:				
	6–MR. SKYLARK	38.00	16.60	12.60
	10–STOP AND LISTEN		10.20	7.90
	12–SMART JAUNE			13.80

$2 EXACTA 6–10 PAID $366.50

Dk. b. or br. g, by Imperial Falcon–Fromdawntilldusk, by Hoist the Flag. Trainer Smithwick D Michael. Bred by Watters Sidney Jr (Md).

MR. SKYLARK gained a brief lead leaving the first jump, eased back a bit along the backstretch, settled behind horses to the final turn, launched a rally between horses entering the stretch, closed rapidly from outside to take the lead inside the final jump then drew clear under right hand encouragement. STOP AND LISTEN stalked the pace from outside a good portion of the way, checked slightly between horses on the far turn, made a run to challenge in midstretch, but couldn't stay with the winner through the final eighth. SMART JAUNE trailed early after getting away a bit slowly, moved into contention approaching the seventh jump, dropped back on the far turn, then failed to threaten while rallying mildly to gain a share. AMENDING steadily worked his way forward to gain a slim lead on the clubhouse turn the second time, remained a factor the far turn, then gradually tired thereafter. OVERNIGHT HERO alternated for the lead along the inside for a good part of the way, steadied along the inside when SEA SPRUCE drifting in causing crowding on the far turn, faded in the lane. BROAD BRANCH raced in the middle of the pack between horses to the turn and lacked a strong closing bid. BROOKNONONSENSE never reached contention. KARETTO was used up forcing the early pace. SEA SPRUCE drifted in causing crowding while taking the lead on the far turn, battled heads apart into midstretch then fell leaving the final jump. LOGROLLER was never close after breaking a bit slowly, then left the course in the stretch. DASHING PRINCE fell over the sixth jump. EXPLOSIVE LIGHT stumbled and fell over DASHING PRINCE. A claim of foul lodged by the rider of OVERNIGHT HERO against STOP AND LISTEN for interference on the far turn was disallowed.

Owners— 1, Richardson Frank E; 2, Bentley Gregory S; 3, Augustin Stables; 4, Sheppard Jonathan E; 5, Twyman Noel W; 6, Griggs John K; 7, Dempsey Warren R; 8, High Hedges Farm; 9, Lickle William C; 10, Payson Virginia Kraft; 11, Snasone Joseph C; 12, Peace John H

Trainers—1, Smithwick D Michael; 2, Carrier Russell N Jr; 3, Neilson Sanna; 4, Sheppard Jonathan E; 5, Twyman Noel W; 6, Griggs John K; 7, Voss Thomas H; 8, Oxley Gerald; 9, Hendriks Richard J; 10, Voss Thomas H; 11, Pinfield Timothy; 12, Miller F Bruce

Scratched— Battleship Grey (16Jly95 2SAR1), Water Skipper (22Jun95 2LRL4), Just You Dare (22Jun95 1LRL2), Mario (6Jly95 9DEL1), Seminole Spirt (20May95 5MGO5)

Mr. Skylark led over the first jump, but was eased back to the middle of the pack by the seventh fence and didn't seem much interested in the proceedings. But just as he had done on the inner course four years earlier, he unleashed a strong rally commencing on the far turn to win going away. All around him, horses were falling, stumbling, drifting out, or simply leaving the course; a dozen horses went to the post and only eight completed the race, which is not unusual when a full field must negotiate 10 jumps in close quarters.

Counting my lucky stars while collecting a $38 mutual, I was sure it would be a long time before the "hidden Spa form" angle presented itself again in the form of a jumper.

Strangely enough, only two weeks later, I happened upon a 9-year-old whose past performances you see below:

Green Highlander
Own: Lickle William C

TETER J (4 1 0 0 .25)

Ch. g. 9
Sire: Green Dancer (Nijinsky II)
Dam: Out Ruled (Court Ruling)
Br: Ledyard Lewis C (Pa)
Tr: Elliot Janet E (6 1 0 0 .17)

158

Lifetime Record :	49	10	10	7	$196,183
Jumps 1992-95 :	14	4	3	3	$89,964

1995	6	3	1	0	$35,814	Turf	16	2	6	3	$51,825
1994	4	0	1	2	$12,200	Wet	7	1	0	1	$20,514

10Aug95- 1Sar fm 2 1/16	Hurdles	3:38²	Hcp 25000s	—	7	2	2½	2hd	14	16½	Teter J	154	5.10	—	—	GrenHighlndr154 6½ EskimoCov152 4½ LonMountin144 3½	Stalked, drew clear	8
3Aug95- 9Del fm *1 1/16 Ⓣ	:24⁴ :48⁴ 1:13³ 1:44¹	3↑	Alw 13700N2X	54	8	8	89	911	98½	911	Hershbell A5	111	8.80	79 – 10		Owen Carrow116 1½ Moycullen117hd Petit Parisien109 4½	Showed nothing	9
20May95- 5Mal gd *2¼	Hurdles	4:29	Clm 20000	—	3	1	12	1¾	12	14	Teter J	156	-	—	—	Green Highlander156 4 King's Testamony143 5 Saudi Sea152 7	Handily	4
6May95- 5Bro fm *2¼	Hurdles	4:02	Ⓡ CapitalCupH20k	—	1	2	210	27	2hd	3½	Teter J	150	-	—	—	EskimoCove146nk Ⓓ CircuitBar154nk GreenHighlnder150 18	Gamely, missed	6
Placed second through disqualification.																		
8Apr95- 5AtH hd *2½	Hurdles	4:46⁴	Clm 20000	—	3	2	2½	13	16	115	Teter J	148	-	—	—	GreenHighlander148 15 King'sTestmony147 50 DoubleDter130	Ridden out	4
25Mar95- 6Aik hd *2¼	Hurdles	4:23	Palmetto Cup25k	—	5	2	46½	46½	611	617¾	Teter J	150	-	—	—	WoodyBoyWould148 4½ PyjamaPrde146 2 King'sTestmony144 1	No threat	6
15May94- 6Wil fm *2¼	Hurdles	4:12²	Alw 20000	—	3	2	26	22	36	311	Teter J	146	-	—	—	WoodyBoyWould141 1 Castleworth146 10 GreenHighlander146 7	Gave way	5
16Apr94- 4SoP fm *2¼	Hurdles	4:15¹	SandhllsCupH20k	—	2	2	45	21	23	26	Teter J	150	-	—	—	Cheering News154 6 Green Highlander150 7 SummerIsland144 5	Bid, tired	6
9Apr94- 3AtH fm *2⅛	Hurdles	3:55⁴	RobHumphryCH100k	—	8	1	11½	11½	1½	48½	Teter J	143	-	—	—	Warm Spell164½ Rolling Cart142 2 Castleworth144 6	Tired	7
2Apr94- 6Cam fm *1⅜ Ⓣ	2:21	3↑	Alw 1000NC	—	4	2	22½	34½	36	36¼	Teter J	154	-	—	—	Lonesome Glory154nk Message Pad151 6 Green Highlander154 4	Tired	6

WORKOUTS: Aug 1 Fai 4f (W) fst :50³ B *2/4*

Do you believe in speed figures for jumpers? What about instant variants? Take a look at Green Highlander's time for the win at "Mal" on May 20 going 2 1/4 miles, 4:29. Now, harken back to Mr. Skylark's past performances and note he broke his maiden at Mal that same day...in 4:31 2/5. More compelling, I believe, was that Green Highlander knew his way around Saratoga, a nugget of information that was concealed from the crowd:

SEVENTH RACE
Saratoga
JULY 31, 1991

1 ⅝ MILES.(Turf). (2.37) ALLOWANCE. Purse $29,000. 3-year-olds and upward, which have never won a race other than Maiden, Claiming or Starter. Weight: 3-year-olds 116 lbs. Older 122 lbs. Non-winners of a race other than claiming over a mile since July 1, allowed 3 lbs. Of such a race since June 15, 5 lbs.

Value of race $29,000; value to winner $17,400; second $6,380; third $3,480; fourth $1,740. Mutuel pool $258,212. Exacta Pool $484,027

Last Raced	Horse	M/Eqt.A.Wt	PP	¼	½	1	1⅜	Str	Fin	Jockey	Odds $1
6Jly91 7EIP¹	Torbay	4 117	8	7⁸	6hd	52½	3⁴	12½	12½	Smith M E	5.10
13Jly91 6Bel⁶	Green Highlander	5 117	3	1½	2³	1hd	1½	2⁶	2³	Samyn J L	2.10
13Jly91 6Bel⁸	Game Stopper	4 117	4	8	8	8	3²	3⁸½	Madrid A Jr	6.70
13Jly91 6Bel⁸	Rivar	b 4 117	7	4¹	7⁶	6½	5½	5hd	4²½	Migliore R	25.50
16Jly91 6Mth⁷	Charmin Cliff	6 117	2	3¹	1½	2⁴	42½	4½	5²	McCauley W H	14.80
17Jly91 7Bel¹	Acero	5 116	5	2½	3½	3hd	2hd	6⁴	6³	Chavez J F	4.30
21Jly91 3Sar⁴	Only Seventy	b 5 117	1	61½	4¹	4½	6hd	72½	7⁵	Velazquez J R	21.10
18Jun91 6Pha¹	Awrence	3 113	6	5hd	5½	7⁸	72½	8	8	Santos J A	2.80

OFF AT 4:10 Start good, Won driving. Time, :26¹, :50⁴, 1:15 , 1:39⁴, 2:04¹, 2:43 , Course firm.

$2 Mutuel Prices:

8-(I)-TORBAY	12.20	5.40	3.60
1-(C)-GREEN HIGHLANDER		3.40	2.60
4-(D)-GAME STOPPER			4.00

$2 EXACTA 8-1 PAID $51.00

Ch. g, by Secretariat—Devon Diva, by Minstrel. Trainer Bell Michael H. Bred by Juddmonte Farms (Ky).

TORBAY, reserved early while saving ground, angled to the outside along he backstretch, steadily gained to threaten on the turn accelerated to the front gaining a clear advantage in upper stretch and held sway under steady pressure. GREEN HIGHLANDER alternated for the lead along the inside to the turn, yielded to the winner in upper stretch and continued on well to best the others. GAME STOPPER, far back to th...

Going a mile and five-eighths as a spry 5-year-old, Green Highlander hadn't won, but he had finished a respectable second in an allowance on the main turf course. What's more, the Janet Elliot-trained gelding had come back 15 days later to deliver this performance in the mud:

SEVENTH RACE
Saratoga
AUGUST 15, 1991

1 ⅝ MILES. (2.45³) ALLOWANCE. Purse $31,000. 3-year-olds and upward which have never won two races other than Maiden, Claiming or Starter. Weights, 3-year-olds, 117 lbs. Older, 122 lbs. Non-winners of a race other than Maiden or Claiming over a mile since July 15 allowed, 3 lbs. Of such a race since July 1, 5 lbs. (ORIGINALLY SCHEDULED TO BE RUN AT 1 5/8 MILES TURF COURSE.)

Value of race $31,000; value to winner $18,600; second $6,820; third $3,720; fourth $1,860. Mutuel pool $299,292. Exacta Pool $456,842

Last Raced	Horse	M/Eqt.A.Wt	PP	¼	½	1	1⅜	Str	Fin	Jockey	Odds $1
31Jly91 7Sar²	Green Highlander	5 117	3	2¹	2²	1¹	1²	1³	12½	Samyn J L	7.00
2Aug91 7Sar³	Incredible	3 114	4	6	6	6	3²	33½	2nk	Antley C W	1.80
24Jly91 6Sar⁶	Chick Sails	b 4 117	2	3¹½	3¹	2²	2⁶	2¹	37½	Santos J A	8.30
2Aug91 7Sar²	Best Offer	b 4 112	5	4½	4hd	4½	512	4⁶	416	Mojica R Jr⁵	1.40
25Jun91 8Pim⁵	Plusser	3 112	1	1½	1½	32½	4hd	5	5	Krone J A	18.20
2Aug91 7Sar⁴	Marco Aurelio	4 117	6	5¹½	5⁴	510	6	—	—	Cordero A Jr	5.00

Marco Aurelio, Eased.

OFF AT 4:31 Start good. Won driving. Time, :49¹, 1:39⁴, 2:04², 2:30 , 2:43² Track muddy.

New track record

$2 Mutuel Prices:

3-(C)-GREEN HIGHLANDER	16.00	6.00	4.20
4-(D)-INCREDIBLE		3.20	3.00
2-(B)-CHICK SAILS			5.00

$2 EXACTA 3-4 PAID $53.40

Ch. g, by Green Dancer—Out Ruled, by Court Ruling. Trainer Elliot Janet. Bred by Ledyard Lewis C (Pa).

GREEN HIGHLANDER stalked the pace, outside PLUSSER for six furlongs, accelerated to the front entering the backstretch, increasing his margin opened a comfortable lead on the far turn, then held sway under good handling. INCREDIBLE outrun for a mile while saving ground, worked his way forward along the inside on the turn, angled out in upper stretch then outfinished CHICK SAILS for the place. CHICK SAILS raced in close contention while three wide to the top of the stretch and lacked a strong closing bid. BEST OFFER was never a serious threat. PLUSSER rushed up along the rail to gain the early advantage, set the pace along the inside for seven furlongs then gradually tired thereafter. MARCO AURELIO wide early, dropped out of contention after going a mile and was eased in the stretch.

They don't run too many 1 5/8-mile races on dirt, but a track record is a track record. Green Highlander had a history of running well on turf and on dirt at Saratoga, and paid $12.20 after prepping on the flat under an apprentice rider at Delaware Park a week earlier.

Now that I've conveyed everything I know about steeplechase racing, let's hope similar opportunities become an annual bonus for dedicated chart researchers.

Along those same lines, Mr. Skylark set the tone for a horse-for-course parade that began two days later.

Older But Smarter
Own: Drecchio Vincent
BAILEY J D (101 22 11 13 .22)
B. g. 6
Sire: Smarten (Cyane)
Dam: More Golden Times (Our Native)
Br: Garst Allen M (Md)
Tr: Tagg Barclay (10 2 0 1 .20)
123

Lifetime Record :	32 6 4 5	$218,663			
1995	5 1 1 0	$32,400	Turf	28 6 3 5	$213,753
1994	4 1 1 1	$40,809	Wet	0 0 0 0	
Sar (T)	2 2 0 0	$44,400	Dist (T)	13 3 1 2	$105,310

28Jly95–6Sar fm 1 1/16 (T) :23 :461 1:102 1:403 3↑ Alw 38000C 98 5 5 41½ 31½ 2½ 1nk Bailey J D 112 *2.65 96–07 OlderButSmrter112nk HedTrip115nk LostSoldier1133½ Took up sharply 7/16 7
8Jly95–6Bel fm 1 1/16 (T) :23 :454 1:092 1:391 3↑ Alw 48000N$mY 86 7 3 31½ 31½ 76½ 77¼ Stevens G L 115 3.00 95–11 Solenzano1152 Signal Tap121½ Scott The Great110¾ Stalked, tired 7
21Jun95–7Bel fm 1 (T) :232 :47 1:091 1:34 Alw 48000C 102 6 5 51¾ 2½ 2½ 2hd Perez R B5 109 20.30 93–18 Chief Master114hd OlderButSmarter109½ Solenzano1141 Bid, outfinished 8
27May95–7Bel fm 1 1/16 (T) :232 :461 1:10 1:402 Alw 48000C 68 6 3 31½ 3nk 54¾ 613¼ Krone J A 116 6.00 83–10 Correntino1131½ Lower Egypt1132 King's Theatre1192 No late bid 7
26Mar95–11Hia fm 1 1/16 (T) 1:40 3↑ RoyalPalm H-G3 93 3 5 57½ 33 31½ 64 Douglas R R L 114 9.40 94–01 DH DJ'sRinbow114 DH GoneForRel113¾ DngrRngr1121¾ Lacked response 13
17Sep94–9Pim fm 1 (T) :234 :462 1:093 1:344 3↑ Damascus H113k 93 2 3 43½ 44 32½ 44 Johnston M T 114 *1.40 90–09 Redcall1103½ Gilded Youth114nk Maryland Moon113hd Drifted out 8
8Aug94–6Sar fm 1 1/16 (T) :23 :462 1:101 1:412 3↑ Alw 36000N4X 105 1 2 21½ 1½ 13 14 Krone J A 117 4.70 87–11 Older But Smarter1174 Bonus Award119no Palashall117hd Drifted, driving 10
10Jly94–9Lrl fm 6f (T) :23 :464 :584 1:103 3↑ Mister Diz50k 96 5 1 43 34½ 34 2no Johnston M T L 115 2.60 88–12 Higher Strata115no Older But Smarter1152 Maryland Moon115½ Closed 7
26Jun94–7Lrl fm 6f (T) :222 :452 :571 1:091 3↑ Alw 22000N4X 91 10 3 31 32 2hd 3½ Johnston M T L 117 6.10 95–05 Lazy Luke117nk No Delay117hd Older But Smarter1172 Hung 11
13Aug93–6Pim fm 1 (T) :241 :474 1:114 1:374 3↑ Alw 25300N4X 80 7 3 32½ 32 41 55 Luzzi M J L 117 5.20 74–23 Up In Front117½ Straight Forward117¾ Punch Line1121 Gave way 7
WORKOUTS: Aug 8 Sar 4f fst :491 B *15/32* Jly 21 Sar 4f fst :503 B *39/50* Jly 6 Bel 3f fst :364 B *7/19* Jly 1 Bel 4f fst :52 B *48/52* Jun 15 Bel (T) 4f fm :474 H (d) *3/22* Jun 1 Bel (T) 5f fm 1:012 B (d) *2/12*

Older But Smarter leapt to new Beyer Speed Figure heights early at the 1994 Saratoga meet, winning by four lengths with a fig of 105 on August 8. The Barclay Tagg-trained gelding didn't win again for 355 days, getting up to win a classified allowance on July 28, despite taking up sharply into the far turn. He came back to win again at 4-1 on August 11.

The next turf race on the July 28 card was the Saratoga Budweiser Breeders' Cup Handicap, won by Weekend Madness:

Weekend Madness (Ire)
Own: New Phoenix Stable
SELLERS S J (18 5 1 1 .28)
B. m. 5
Sire: Dance of Life (Nijinsky II)
Dam: Spring Break (Cure the Blues)
Br: Hand Y Bloodstock Company (Ire)
Tr: Kessinger Burk Jr (2 0 0 0 .00)
120

Lifetime Record :	25 10 5 0	$651,344			
1995	6 2 2 0	$156,135	Turf	24 10 5 0	$651,344
1994	10 3 2 0	$330,417	Wet	1 0 0 0	
Bel (T)	0 0 0 0		Dist (T)	9 5 2 0	$352,490

28Jly95–8Sar fm 1 1/16 (T) :232 :47 1:11 1:401 3↑ (F)Sar Bud BCH-G3 104 5 4 42 41½ 1hd 11¾ Sellers S J 117 4.80 98–07 Weekend Madness1171¾ Irish Linnet1202 Allez Les Trois115hd Rail trip 7
7Jun95–9CD fm 1 (T) :23 :453 1:093 1:341 3↑ Alw 51500N$mY 86 5 8 813 76¼ 47½ 45¾ Sellers S J 118 *1.30 95–03 Rare Reason123nk Manilaman1182½ Night Silence1203 No late response 9
6May95–4CD fm 1 (T) :232 :471 1:111 1:343 3↑ (F)ProvidinMile86k 85 6 8 64 74½ 75 77¼ Sellers S J 123 *2.00 92–02 Bold Ruritana1233 Icy Warning1161½ Rapunzel Runz114no 4-wide 1/4 10
13Apr95–8Kee fm 1 1/16 (T) :233 :473 1:114 1:431 (F)Jenny Wiley-G3 100 9 7 54 31½ 3½ 2hd Sellers S J 121 *1.10 90–18 Romy118hd Weekend Madness121nk Bold Ruritana121½ 9
6-wide, backstretch, missed on wire
11Mar95–7GP fm 1 1/16 (T) :233 :484 1:132 1:432+ 3↑ (F)BuckramOakH-G3 95 3 4 73½ 73¼ 41¼ 21¼ Sellers S J 118 *1.40 78–18 Cox Orange1181¼ Weekend Madness118nk Ma Guerre113hd 11
Seven wide top str, rallied
12Feb95–8GP fm *1 1/16 (T) :231 :46 1:10 1:401+ Alw 40000N$mY 100 2 6 64¼ 52¼ 22½ 1nk Sellers S J 113 *1.60 107 — Weekend Madness113nk Solenzano1151½ Dominant Prospect115½ 10
Six wide top str, driving
5Nov94–3CD fm 1⅛ (T) :48 1:12 1:362 1:481 3↑ (F)Cardinal H117k 92 8 7 86 84¾ 32 43¼ Sellers S J 119 *2.40 87 — Bold Ruritana116¾ Eternal Reve1172 Monaassabaat113½ 11
6-wide 1/4 pole, no late response
9Oct94–8Kee gd 1 (T) :232 :462 1:113 1:383 3↑ KeenelandBC-G3 105 4 8 811 78 43 11½ Sellers S J 123 4.00 77–25 WeekendMdness1231½ WordsOfWr1231¼ PennineRidge123nk Driving, clear 10
24Sep94–3Due gd *1 (T) 1:371 3↑ (F)Rach Jackson150k 98 5 5 57 33½ 23 21 Sellers S J 119 2.60 88–11 WordsOfWr1191 WeekendMdness1192½ OneDrmr1222½ Easily second best 7
27Aug94–6AP fm 1 3/16 (T) :473 1:113 1:364 1:552 3↑ (F)Beverly D-G1 87 7 3 44½ 54½ 64 67¾ Sellers S J L 123 15.50 82–09 Hatoof123½ Flawlessly123½ Potridee123½ Brief speed 8
WORKOUTS: Sep 6 Sar (T) 3f fm :40 B (d) *3/3* ●Aug 30 Sar (T) 4f fm :46 H *1/7* ●Aug 25 Sar tr.t(T) 4f fm :471 H (d) *1/8* Aug 16 Sar tr.t(T) 3f fm :383 B *6/6* Aug 10 Sar (T) 4f fm :471 H (d) *1/1* Jly 22 Sar (T) 6f fm 1:13 H (d) *1/*

On the shelf after throat surgery to correct a breathing problem, the hard-hitting mare slipped through along the inside to win going away, and earned a Beyer of 104. She paid $11.60, even though she had shipped in and won the same race a year ago (with an identical 104 Beyer):

Weekend Madness (Ire)
Own: New Phoenix Stable
SELLERS S J (22 2 6 1 .09)
B. m. 5
Sire: Dance of Life (Nijinsky II)
Dam: Spring Break (Cure the Blues)
Br: Hand Y Bloodstock Company (Ire)
Tr: Kessinger Burk Jr (1 1 0 0 1.00)
123

Lifetime Record :	22 9 5 0	$556,039			
1995	3 1 2 0	$60,830	Turf	21 9 5 0	$556,039
1994	10 3 2 0	$330,417	Wet	1 0 0 0	
CD (T)	5 2 1 0	$163,252	Dist (T)	6 4 2 0	$274,507

13Apr95–8Kee fm 1 1/16 (T) :233 :473 1:114 1:431 (F)Jenny Wiley-G3 100 9 7 54 31½ 3½ 2hd Sellers S J 121 *1.10 90–18 Romy118hd Weekend Madness121nk Bold Ruritana121½ 9
6-wide, backstretch, missed on wire
11Mar95–7GP fm 1 1/16 (T) :233 :484 1:132 1:432+ 3↑ (F)BuckramOakH-G3 95 3 4 73½ 73¼ 41¼ 21¼ Sellers S J 118 *1.40 78–18 Cox Orange1181¼ Weekend Madness118nk Ma Guerre113hd 11
Seven wide top str, rallied
12Feb95–8GP fm *1 1/16 (T) :231 :46 1:10 1:401+ Alw 40000N$mY 100 2 6 64¼ 52¼ 22½ 1nk Sellers S J 113 *1.60 107 — Weekend Madness113nk Solenzano1151½ Dominant Prospect115½ 10
Six wide top str, driving
5Nov94–3CD fm 1⅛ (T) :48 1:12 1:362 1:481 3↑ (F)Cardinal H117k 92 8 7 86 84¾ 32 43¼ Sellers S J 119 *2.40 87 — Bold Ruritana116¾ Eternal Reve1172 Monaassabaat113½ 11
6-wide 1/4 pole, no late response
9Oct94–8Kee gd 1 (T) :232 :462 1:113 1:383 3↑ KeenelandBC-G3 105 4 8 811 78 43 11½ Sellers S J 123 4.00 77–25 WeekendMdness1231½ WordsOfWr1231¼ PennineRidge123nk Driving, clear 10
24Sep94–3Due gd *1 (T) 1:371 3↑ (F)Rach Jackson150k 98 5 5 57 33½ 23 21 Sellers S J 119 2.60 88–11 WordsOfWr1191 WeekendMdness1192½ OneDrmr1222½ Easily second best 7
27Aug94–6AP fm 1 3/16 (T) :473 1:113 1:364 1:552 3↑ (F)Beverly D-G1 87 7 3 44½ 54½ 64 67¾ Sellers S J L 123 15.50 82–09 Hatoof123½ Flawlessly123½ Potridee123½ Brief speed 8
27Jly94–9Sar yl 1 1/16 (T) :233 :473 1:122 1:433 3↑ (F)Sar Bud BCH155k 104 4 5 63½ 72½ 51¼ 1¾ Sellers S J 115 6.70 76–24 WeekendMdness115¾ You'dBeSurprised120nk Heed1103 Blocked, driving 8
4Jly94–9CD gd 1 (T) :234 :473 1:113 1:351 3↑ FirecrackerH113k 99 8 5 56 54¼ 41¼ 2½ Day P 111 4.40 96–07 First And Only118½ Weekend Madness1111½ Avid Affection112½ 8
Slow start, 5 wide, sharp
21May94–9CD fm 1 1/16 (T) :232 :464 1:11 1:404 (F)Mint Julep H85k 89 5 3 35½ 31 44 42¾ Woods C R Jr 121 *1.70 99–01 Words Of War117nk Freewheel1161¼ Eurostorm1121¼ Flattened out 10
WORKOUTS: May 3 CD 3f fst :353 H *5/35* Apr 27 CD (T) 4f fm :493 B (d) *1/2* Apr 10 CD 3f fst :362 B *2/9* Apr 4 CD 4f fst :484 B *3/10* Mar 28 CD 5f fst 1:014 B *4/5* Mar 8 GP 3f sly :38 B (d) *12/25*

The feature on the following afternoon, Saturday, July 29, was the Grade 1 Sword Dancer Handicap, a three-turn marathon at a mile and a half. Kiri's Clown had nearly wired the Sword Dancer's 1994 renewal at 15-1, and had been the final example in *Expert Handicapping:*

Kiri's Clown
Own: Cobble View & Sullimar Stable
DAVIS R G (63 9 11 11 .14)

Dk. b or br h. 6
Sire: Foolish Pleasure (What a Pleasure)
Dam: Kiri*GB (Kris)
Br: Landon & Sullivan Mary A (Fla)
Tr: Johnson Philip G (8 1 0 2 .13)

120

Lifetime Record : 37 12 4 3 $532,720										
1994	12	3	1	0	$289,564	Turf	35	12	4	3 $532,720
1993	7	2	1	2	$80,332	Wet	0	0	0	0
Aqu ⓣ	5	3	1	0	$118,197	Dist ⓣ	16	5	1	2 $158,755

19Nov94-8Aqu	sf	1⅜	ⓣ	:47⁴	1:13²	1:40³	2:20²	3↑ Red Smith H-G2	90	4	1	1½	1¹	2hd	6⁴	Luzzi M J	116	3.05e	78-18	Franchise Player109no Red Bishop1192¼ Same Old Wish112nk	Speed, tired	14
29Oct94-8Aqu	fm	1⅛	ⓣ	:49³	1:13²	1:37²	1:49¹	3↑ KnickerbkrH-G3	105	2	1	1¹	1¹	1²	1²	Luzzi M J	114	*1.65e	94-13	Kiri's Clown114² River Majesty1171¼ Red Earth111nk	Driving	12
8Oct94-7Bel	fm	1½	ⓣ	:47⁴	1:12	2:01	2:25⁴	3↑ TurfClassic-G1	81	1	1	12½	2½	47½	517¾	Luzzi M J	126	6.40	75-15	Tikkanen121nk Vaudeville121⁹ Yenda118⁷	Used in pace	6
17Sep94-7Bel	fm	1⅜	[T]	:48	1:12¹	1:36	2:11³	3↑ Man O'War-G1	105	6	1	1¹	1¹	2hd	42¾	Luzzi M J	126	9.60	93-10	Royal Mountain Inn126½ Flag Down1261¾ Fraise126½	Weakened	9
3Sep94-8Bel	fm	1 1/16	ⓣ	:24¹	:47¹	1:10²	1:40	3↑ Bel Bud BCH-G3	102	4	2	2½	2hd	1½	42¼	Luzzi M J	113	4.60e	96-14	AInSociology116² FourstrsAllstr119nk HomeOfTheFr114no	Bid, weakened	10
30Jly94-9Sar	gd	1½	[T]	:46²	1:11⁴	2:02³	2:28³	3↑ SwordDancrH-G1	107	1	1	1½	1½	1½	2¾	Luzzi M J	112	15.30	85-19	Alex The Great118¾ Kiri's Clown112² L'hermine112hd	Gamely	10
25Jly94-8Sar	fm	1 1/16	ⓣ	:23²	:46⁴	1:10⁴	1:41¹	3↑ Daryl'sJoyH-G3	95	9	4	42½	3²	5⁴	55½	Luzzi M J	114	4.70e	82-15	A In Sociology115nk Namaqualand113² Fourstars Allstar120nk	Tired	9
14Jly94-8Bel	fm	1¼	[T]	:46³	1:10⁴	1:34²	1:58³	3↑ Handicap48k	89	2	2	2²	2²	23½	54½	Luzzi M J	121	*2.20	92-05	Pescagani1163½ Heavy Rain113¾ Bisbalense114nk	Tired	7
19Jun94-9Rkm	fm	*1⅛	ⓣ				1:46³	3↑ NH Sweeps H-G3	104	1	1	1hd	1½	1³	1½	Luzzi M J	LB 113	8.70	101-09	Kiri's Clown113½ RiverMajesty115hd FourstarsAllstar120³	Inside, driving	8
10Jun94-6Bel	fm	7f	ⓣ	:22²	:44²	1:07⁴	1:20	3↑ Jaipur-G3	74	7	1	4²	31½	75½	7¹⁶	Luzzi M J	114	4.30	86 —	Nijinsky'sGold114nk DominntProspect1144½ HomeOfTheFr122²	Gave way	7

Run in divisions

WORKOUTS: Apr 12 Bel tr.t 3f fst :36¹ B *3/13* Apr 7 Bel tr.t 7f fst 1:29³ B *1/2* Apr 4 Bel tr.t 3f fst :36⁴ B *6/19* Mar 31 Bel tr.t 6f fst 1:15⁴ B *3/6* Mar 26 Bel tr.t 4f fst :49⁴ B *24/41*

While his entrymate A In Sociology had gone wire-to-wire in the Daryl's Joy on July 25, Kiri's Clown had meandered about, making sure not to badger his mate for the lead. Wheeled back five days later, he had almost held off Alex The Great after a gritty performance on the front-end.

After a hard duel in this year's Daryl's Joy, Kiri's Clown came back for another try in the Sword Dancer, this time prevailing by a neck over Awad (who came back to win the Arlington Million):

5 Kiri's Clown
Own: Cobble View & Sullimar Stable
LUZZI M J (—)

Dk. b or br h. 6
Sire: Foolish Pleasure (What a Pleasure)
Dam: Kiri*GB (Kris)
Br: Landon & Sullivan Mary A (Fla)
Tr: Johnson Philip G (—)

L 126

Lifetime Record : 45 15 4 5 $860,000										
1995	8	3	0	2	$327,280	Turf	43	15	4	5 $860,000
1994	12	3	1	0	$289,564	Wet	0	0	0	0
AP ⓣ	0	0	0	0		Dist ⓣ	3	0	0	1 $22,000

29Jly95-8Sar	fm	1½	[T]	:47¹	1:13	2:00⁴	2:25²	3↑ SwordDancrH-G1	109	9	1	1¹	1¹	1½	1nk	Luzzi M J	114	14.20	102-08	Kiri's Clown114nk Awad1211½ King's Theatre113²	Fully extended	13
24Jly95-8Sar	fm	1 1/16	ⓣ	:22³	:45⁴	1:10	1:40⁴	3↑ Daryl's Joy-G3	82	4	1	1½	1hd	2½	712¼	Luzzi M J	120	7.70	83-12	PrideOfSummer115hd FourstarsAllstr120⁵ JggeryJohn120¾	Dueled, tired	8
4Jly95-11Lrl	yl	1¼	ⓣ	:49⁴	1:15³	1:42¹	2:07⁴	3↑ FortMcHenryH115k	76	7	2	21½	2²	5¹⁰	811½	Luzzi M J	L 117	2.30	43-41	Warning Glance116½ Glenbarra114½ Lassigny116²	Gave way	11
18Jun95-10Rkm	fm	*1⅛	ⓣ				1:45³	3↑ NH Sweeps H-G3	112	6	2	1½	1½	13½	1⁴	Luzzi M J	LB 116	2.70	105-09	Kiri'sClown116⁴ PennineRidg1181¼ TorchRoug114⁴	Rated ins, ridden out	12
10Jun95-8Bel	fm	1¼	[T]	:46⁴	1:10²	1:34¹	1:58²	3↑ ETManhattan-G1	106	2	1	1¹	11½	1²	3¹	Luzzi M J	115	14.70	95-06	Awad121no Blues Traveller119¹ Kiri's Clown115nk	Speed, game	12
29May95-8Bel	fm	1	ⓣ	:23³	:46⁴	1:10¹	1:34²	Alw 48000N$Y	104	3	1	1½	1½	1½	3¾	Luzzi M J	123	*1.20	90-14	ForstrsAllstr123nk BonsAwrd113½ Kr'sClown1236½	Pressured throughout	7
6May95-7CD	fm	1⅛	ⓣ	:46⁴	1:10³	1:34³	1:46⁴	3↑ ET Classic-G2	98	1	4	41½	4²	52½	6⁴	Davis R G	L 118	11.10	93-02	Romarin1181¼ Blues Traveller1201¼ Hasten To Add120hd		12

Bobbled start, saved ground

15Apr95-6Aqu	gd	1 1/16	ⓣ	:22¹	:46⁴	1:12¹	1:45¹	3↑ Handicap50k	106	6	3	31½	31½	2hd	1nk	Davis R G	120	*2.20	83-17	Kiri's Clown120nk Inside The Beltway1145¾ Signe Divin118no	Rated, gamely	7
19Nov94-8Aqu	sf	1⅜	ⓣ	:47⁴	1:13²	1:40³	2:20²	3↑ Red Smith H-G2	98	4	1	1½	1¹	2hd	6⁴	Luzzi M J	116	3.05e	78-18	Franchise Player109no Red Bishop1192¼ Same Old Wish112nk	Speed, tired	14
29Oct94-8Aqu	fm	1⅛	ⓣ	:49³	1:13²	1:37²	1:49¹	3↑ KnickerbkrH-G3	105	2	1	1¹	1¹	1²	1²	Luzzi M J	114	*1.65e	94-13	Kiri's Clown114² River Majesty1171¼ Red Earth111nk	Driving	12

WORKOUTS: Aug 21 Sar tr.t 1 fst 1:46¹ B *1/1* Aug 16 Sar tr.t 6f fst 1:17 B *1/1* Aug 11 Sar tr.t 6f fst 1:17⁴ B *1/1* ●Aug 6 Sar tr.t 4f fst :49 B *1/24* Jly 20 Sar tr.t 4f fst :49³ B *4/28* Jly 13 Bel [T] 4f fm :51 B (d) *16/18*

Noteworthy too, are Kiri's Clown's wins in back-to-back runnings of the New Hampshire Sweeps Handicap over the quirky turf course at Rockingham Park. These repeated top-notch performances speak volumes for seasonal aspects of horses' form cycles and footing preferences, and how knowledgeable trainers orchestrate their recurrence.

Less than 24 hours later, another horse for course got the money on Saratoga grass, as Doctor Disaster, a 9-2 shot, wired his field at a mile and three-eighths while scattering a gaggle of surprised geese first time past the stands:

Doctor Disaster
Own: Olson James F

CHAVEZ J F (160 22 21 15 .14)

Dk. b or br g. 6
Sire: Palace Panther (Crystal Palace)
Dam: Victania (Ruritania)
Br: Walden Farm Breeding Assoc I (NY)
Tr: Brida Dennis J (29 2 3 5 .07)

110

Lifetime Record: 42 7 3 5 $159,945											
1995	9	3	0	0	$57,110	Turf	29	7	2	4	$154,205
1994	13	3	1	4	$75,040	Wet	1	0	0	0	
Sar Ⓣ	5	3	0	0	$52,800	Dist Ⓣ	1	1	0	0	$22,800

Entered 24Aug95- 9 SAR

9Aug95-7Sar	fm	1⅝	Ⓣ	:472	1:114	1:372	2:394	3↑	Alw 38000N3X	96	4	1	1½	11	11½	12	Chavez J F	114	3.45	93-09	DoctorDsstr1142 BstOfMsc117nk MoscwMgc1148	Challenged, drew clear 8
29Jly95-5Sar	fm	1⅜	[T]	:463	1:121	1:372	2:152	3↑	Clm 50000	92	4	1	13½	12½	11	1¾	Chavez J F	116	4.70e	89-08	DoctorDisster116¾ HvyRin1162 FwltyTowrs116no	Check, scattered geese 10
14Jly95-4Mth	fm	*1⅛	Ⓣ	:47	1:112	1:363	1:49	3↑	Clm 40000	91	8	1	14	11½	2hd	41	Pezua J M	111	8.60	95-09	Little Denny Mc115no Atomic Power117no Polesti1131	Good try 8
2Jly95-8Bel	sf	1	Ⓣ	:23	:471	1:123	1:391	3↑	Alw 38000N3X	73	2	1	2½	32	69	611¾	Alvarado F T	120	17.50	55-38	HolyMountain120½ WaveringMn1221½ TheWildIrishmn1152½	Used in pace 11
31May95-9Bel	fm	1¼	[T]	:461	1:11	1:372	2:021		Clm 45000	89	10	2	1½	1½	31½	62½	Chavez J F	112	6.80	75-21	Summer Senate114hd Fawlty Towers116¾ Royal Ninja112¾	Used in pace 12
29Apr95-6Aqu	fm	1⅛	Ⓣ	:48	1:122	1:371	1:492		Alw 36000N3X	87	4	1	11½	11½	2hd	62½	Chavez J F	113	8.90	91-05	GrndCntnntl114no SmOldWsh110hd ThWldIrshmn1191¼	Checked late, tired 9
17Apr95-4Aqu	fm	1⅛	Ⓣ	:481	1:123	1:374	1:503	3↑	Alw 36000N3X	80	3	1	11½	11	31½	44¼	Samyn J L	120	4.00	83-10	Trevelyan1201¼ Threeharvardvenue120no Jodi'sTheBest1203	Used in pace 8
11Mar95-12GP	gd	1½	Ⓣ	:472	1:122	2:031	2:272	3↑	Hcp 50000s	75	5	1	1hd	21	69	713½	Samyn J L	114	6.60	69-11	Heavy Rain1152¾ Berry Parkway1162 Skate On Thin Ice1141½	Faded 10
5Mar95-11GP	fm	*1½	Ⓣ	:481	1:123	2:024	2:261		Clm 40000	92	2	1	11	1½	1hd	1hd	Samyn J L	117	6.80	110 —	DoctorDisstr117hd LningrdSymphony1171½ WdColony117½	Fully extended 10
19Nov94-8Aqu	sf	1⅜	Ⓣ	:474	1:132	1:403	2:202	3↑	Red Smith H-G2	43	14	2	2½	1415	1430	1434¼	Lumpkins J	108	14.50f	48-18	Franchise Player109no Red Bishop1192¼ Same Old Wish112nk	Gave way 14

WORKOUTS: Jun 30 Bel 3f fst :364 H *15/44* Jun 16 Bel 3f fst :39 B *35/38* Jun 8 Bel [T] 6f fm 1:122 H (d) *1/3*

As his past performances show, Doctor Disaster came back to win another marathon on August 9, giving him three straight victories in three-turn races on Saratoga grass dating back to the previous meet:

Doctor Disaster
Own: Olson James F

SAMYN J L (21 5 5 3 .24)

Dk. b or br g. 6
Sire: Palace Panther (Crystal Palace)
Dam: Victania (Ruritania)
Br: Walden Farm Breeding Assoc I (NY)
Tr: Brida Dennis J (18 1 3 1 .06)

120

Lifetime Record: 35 5 3 5 $115,785											
1995	2	1	0	0	$12,950	Turf	22	5	2	4	$110,045
1994	13	3	1	4	$75,040	Wet	1	0	0	0	
Aqu Ⓣ	5	0	1	1	$10,920	Dist Ⓣ	5	0	1	1	$10,920

11Mar95-12GP	gd	1½	Ⓣ	:472	1:122	2:031	2:272	3↑	Hcp 50000s	75	5	1	1hd	21	69	713½	Samyn J L	114	6.60	69-11	Heavy Rain1152¾ Berry Parkway1162 Skate On Thin Ice1141½	Faded 10
5Mar95-11GP	fm	*1½	Ⓣ	:481	1:123	2:024	2:261		Clm 40000	92	2	1	11	1½	1hd	1hd	Samyn J L	117	6.80	110 —	DoctorDisstr117hd LningrdSymphony1171½ WdColony117½	Fully extended 10
19Nov94-8Aqu	sf	1⅜	Ⓣ	:474	1:132	1:403	2:202	3↑	Red Smith H-G2	35	14	2	2½	1415	1430	1434¼	Lumpkins J	108	14.50f	48-18	Franchise Player109no Red Bishop1192¼ Same Old Wish112nk	Gave way 14
5Nov94-1Aqu	yl	1$\frac{1}{16}$	Ⓣ	:241	:482	1:134	1:464	3↑	Alw 36000N3X	66	5	1	2½	62½	99	813½	Samyn J L	119	6.80	62-25	GoneForRel1171½ Threehrvrdvenue114¾ GrndContinntl1174¾	Dueled, tired 10
25Oct94-8Aqu	yl	1⅛	Ⓣ	:482	1:131	1:384	1:512	3↑	Alw 36000N3X	90	2	1	1½	11	11	31	Velazquez J R	119	7.50	82-17	Little Fran111nk Presently116¾ Doctor Disaster119½	Weakened 8
12Oct94-8Bel	fm	1¼	[T]	:473	1:12	1:37	2:022	3↑	Alw 34000N2X	89	2	1	1½	1hd	1hd	1nk	Samyn J L	117	2.60	78-18	Doctor Disaster117nk Best Of Music116nk Arduous1172¼	Driving 6
4Oct94-4Bel	yl	1$\frac{1}{16}$	Ⓣ	:231	:472	1:122	1:43	3↑	Alw 34000N2X	90	1	1	13½	1½	2hd	31½	Velazquez J R	117	8.10	82-23	Presently114hd Myrmidon1141¼ Doctor Disaster1174	Gamely 8
10Sep94-6Bel	fm	1¼	[T]	:472	1:113	1:36	2:001	3↑	Alw 34000N2X	87	3	1	12½	1½	1½	22½	Krone J A	117	5.20	86-11	Same Old Wish1172½ Doctor Disaster1171¼ Trevelyan1152½	Held place 9
27Aug94-2Sar	gd	1⅜	[T]	:472	1:131	1:39	2:173	3↑	Clm 35000	88	9	1	11	11½	1½	1nk	Samyn J L	117	6.80	78-29	Doctor Disaster117nk Two Wise1122 Power Bolt117nk	Driving 10
24Jly94-5Sar	fst	1⅛	⊗	:481	1:122	1:371	1:51		Clm 35000	—	3	2	21½	511	519	—	Samyn J L	119	4.80	— 19	Alpstein1171½ Border Cat1174½ Telegrapher1171	Gave way, eased 5

WORKOUTS: Apr 8 Bel 4f fst :521 B *30/32* Mar 1 GP 3f fst :371 B *8/16* ●Feb 18 HuF 3f fst :362 B *1/5* ●Feb 8 HuF 3f fst :353 H *1/6* ●Jan 30 HuF 3f fst :372 B *1/6* Jan 18 HuF 5f fst 1:053 B *1/1*

A few days later, another runner trained by Barclay Tagg reaffirmed her affinity for Saratoga grass:

La Turka
Own: De Hechavarria Luis

SANTOS J A (161 19 21 24 .12)

Dk. b or br m. 5
Sire: Turkoman (Alydar)
Dam: Aneka (Believe It)
Br: Jayeff B Stables (Ky)
Tr: Tagg Barclay (16 4 0 1 .25)

114

Lifetime Record: 32 9 4 8 $212,237											
1995	7	3	1	1	$83,101	Turf	27	7	3	7	$178,472
1994	14	3	1	5	$73,186	Wet	0	0	0	0	
Sar Ⓣ	2	2	0	0	$44,400	Dist Ⓣ	1	0	0	1	$5,200

6Aug95-7Sar	gd	1$\frac{3}{16}$	Ⓣ	:474	1:122	1:383	1:574	3↑	ⒻAlw 44000N$mY	97	1	2	31	1hd	11½	11½	Bailey J D	114 b	3.05	76-21	La Turka1141½ Symphony Lady1141 Chelsey Flower1221¼	Edged clear 6
9Jly95-3Lrl	fst	1$\frac{1}{16}$	⊗	:243	:49	1:133	1:444	3↑	ⒻAlw 30400NC	82	4	2	21	21	2½	1no	Reynolds L C	L 119 b	1.90	86-23	La Turka119no Mz. Zill Bear1172½ Nellie Custis11911	Driving 4
11Jun95-9Pim	fm	1½	Ⓣ	:49	1:134	2:024	2:292	3↑	ⒻApril Run34k	75	10	6	56½	57	55½	48	Johnston M T	L 119 b	*1.70	85-11	Nellie Custis1173 Joy Of Ireland1192 Open Toe1173	No menace 11
2Apr95-11Hia	fm	1$\frac{1}{16}$	Ⓣ				1:39	3↑	ⒻHia Bud BCH107k	79	2	6	77¾	78	88½	88¾	Ramos W S	L 114 b	30.60	94 —	Cox Orange120nk Apolda1121¼ P J Floral114nk	Faded 11
24Feb95-4GP	fm	*1$\frac{1}{16}$	Ⓣ	:234	:484	1:124	1:423	+	ⒻAlw 40000N$mY	94	9	7	41½	3½	3½	1no	Smith M E	L 114 b	7.90	95 —	La Turka114no Shir Dar116hd Icy Warning114nk	9
Seven wide top str, driving																						
29Jan95-3GP	fm	1⅜	Ⓣ	:494	1:142	1:382	2:144		ⒻHandicap40k	87	4	1	1½	1hd	21½	33	Smith M E	L 114 b	2.80	89-06	Northern Emerald1151½ Petiteness1131½ La Turka1141½	Weakened 7
13Jan95-4GP	fm	*1½	Ⓣ	:504	1:172	2:084	2:331		ⒻHandicap40k	93	1	1	12	2½	2½	23	Smith M E	L 113 b	7.40	72-16	Abigailthewife1183 La Turka1131¼ Petiteness1121	Gamely 9
27Dec94-10Crc	fm	1$\frac{1}{16}$	Ⓣ	:24	:491	1:133	1:442	3↑	ⒻAlw 21000NC	87	2	5	73½	74	41½	32¼	Smith M E	L 115 b	*1.40	76-21	Urus1151½ Track Gossip115¾ La Turka115nk	Bid, hung 9
29Oct94-9Lrl	fm	1$\frac{1}{16}$	Ⓣ	:233	:473	1:132	1:444	3↑	ⒻAlw 23000N4X	89	9	3	34	3nk	11½	3¾	Prado E S	L 117 b	2.30	77-27	Night Fax115¾ Promiseville114no La Turka1172¼	Hung 9
7Oct94-7Med	fm	170	Ⓣ	:222	:461	1:11	1:403	3↑	ⒻAlw 35000N$mY	88	5	11	105	62½	2½	2hd	Krone J A	L 115 b	*1.20	88-13	My Marchesa115hd La Turka1153½ Kira's Dancer119½	Caught, final strides 12

WORKOUTS: Aug 25 Sar tr.tⓉ 5f fm 1:021 B (d) *2/4* Aug 18 Sar tr.tⓉ 4f fm :502 B (d) *10/15* ●Aug 1 Lrl Ⓣ 4f fm :484 H (d) *1/10* Jly 25 Lrl Ⓣ 4f fm :503 B (d) *3/3* ●Jly 3 Lrl 5f fst :59 H *1/18* ●Jun 28 Lrl 5f gd 1:01 H *1/*

La Turka paid $8.10 after edging clear on August 6. These were her past performances when she came back to win the Waya Stakes, at a mutual of $11.80, on closing day, August 28.

Getting back to Doctor Disaster for a moment, alert readers might have noticed the half-mile split of :46 3/5 for his July 29 win and said, "Hmmm, how in the world was he able to hang on at a mile and three-eighths after setting such a demanding pace?"

If :46 3/5 sounds fishy, how about a first quarter in :21 3/5?

FIFTH RACE
Saratoga
JULY 29, 1995

1⅜ MILES. (Inner Turf)(2.13^{1}) CLAIMING. Purse $30,000. 3–year–olds and upward. Weights: 3–year–olds, 117 lbs. Older, 124 lbs. Non–winners of three races over a mile since May 3, allowed 3 lbs. Of two races over nine furlongs since June 7, 5 lbs. Of a race over a mile since then, 8 lbs. Claiming price $50,000. (Races where entered for $40,000 or less not considered.)

Value of Race: $30,000 Winner $18,000; second $6,000; third $3,300; fourth $1,800; fifth $900. Mutuel Pool $502,077.00 Exacta Pool $603,602.00 Triple Pool $525,868.00

Last Raced	Horse	M/Eqt.	A.	Wt	PP	¼	½	¾	1	Str	Fin	Jockey	Cl'g Pr	Odds $1
14Jly95 ^{4}Mth^{4}	Doctor Disaster		6	116	4	1^{5}	$1^{3\frac{1}{2}}$	1^{hd}	$1^{2\frac{1}{2}}$	1^{1}	$1^{\frac{3}{4}}$	Chavez J F	50000	a-4.70
12Jly95 ^{9}Bel^{1}	Heavy Rain		7	116	1	$2^{\frac{1}{2}}$	$3^{\frac{1}{2}}$	$4^{\frac{1}{2}}$	4^{hd}	$2^{\frac{1}{2}}$	2^{2}	Bailey J D	50000	1.85
21Jly95 ^{5}Sar^{7}	Fawlty Towers-IR		4	116	2	3^{3}	2^{1}	$3^{\frac{1}{2}}$	2^{hd}	$3^{\frac{1}{2}}$	3no	Migliore R	50000	5.40
4Jly95 ^{5}Bel^{8}	Rover Boy		5	116	9	10	10	10	10	7^{hd}	4no	Velasquez J	50000	66.25
31May95 ^{9}Bel^{7}	Frozen Reef	b	6	116	8	9^{4}	$9^{2\frac{1}{2}}$	$8^{\frac{1}{2}}$	9^{2}	8^{1}	5no	Velazquez J R	50000	11.80
4Jly95 ^{7}Lrl^{1}	Ascoflame	b	4	121	10	$7^{\frac{1}{2}}$	$8^{1\frac{1}{2}}$	$7^{1\frac{1}{2}}$	6^{1}	5^{1}	6^{nk}	Luzzi M J	50000	14.70
8Jly95 ^{10}Bel^{1}	Watrals Sea Trip		4	119	7	8^{hd}	7^{hd}	$9^{3\frac{1}{2}}$	8^{hd}	6^{1}	7^{1}	Alvarado F T	50000	a-4.70
30Jun95 ^{6}Bel^{3}	Summer Senate	b	9	116	6	$5^{1\frac{1}{2}}$	5^{hd}	$5^{1\frac{1}{2}}$	5^{1}	4^{hd}	8^{2}	Sellers S J	50000	3.05
12Jly95 ^{9}Bel^{5}	Palace Line		6	116	5	4^{hd}	6^{3}	6^{1}	$7^{\frac{1}{2}}$	9^{16}	9	Santos J A	50000	13.10
17Jly95 ^{8}Bel^{3}	Dynamite Laugh	b	4	116	3	6^{hd}	$4^{\frac{1}{2}}$	2^{1}	$3^{1\frac{1}{2}}$	10	—	Maple E	50000	34.00

Dynamite Laugh:Eased
a–Coupled: Doctor Disaster and Watrals Sea Trip.

OFF AT 3:08 Start Good. Won driving. Time, :21^{3}, :46^{3}, 1:12^{1}, 1:37^{2}, 2:02^{2}, 2:15^{2} Course firm.

$2 Mutuel Prices:

1–DOCTOR DISASTER (a–entry)	11.40	5.20	3.70
2–HEAVY RAIN		3.40	2.70
3–FAWLTY TOWERS–IR			3.90

$2 EXACTA 1–2 PAID $41.80 $2 TRIPLE 1–2–3 PAID $159.00

Dk. b. or br. g, by Palace Panther–Victania, by Ruritania. Trainer Brida Dennis J. Bred by Walden Farm Breeding Assoc I (NY).

DOCTOR DISASTER opened a long lead in the early stages, checked nearing the wire the first time while scattering a flock of geese, maintained a clear lead into the backstretch, shook off a mild challenge from DYNAMITE LAUGH at the five-eighths pole, regained a clear lead on the turn, continued on the front into the stretch, then turned back HEAVY RAIN under brisk urging. HEAVY RAIN checked slightly when behind the winner when the geese scattered in the early stages, settled in good position while saving ground into the stretch, then finished willingly but could not get up. FAWLTY TOWERS raced just behind the winner while between horses for most of the trip and lacked a strong closing bid. ROVER BOY trailed to the turn then rallied belatedly in the middle of the track. FROZEN REEF outrun for a mile, failed to threaten with a mild late rally. ASCOFLAME outrun early, lodged a mild rally four wide on the turn, then flattened out. WATRALS SEA TRIP failed to seriously threaten with a mild late run along the inside. SUMMER SENATE settled in the middle of the pack for a mile, made a run to threaten between horses into upper stretch, then gave way in the final eighth. PALACE LINE checked along the inside on the first turn, faded after going seven furlongs. DYNAMITE LAUGH checked early, rushed up to contest the pace after angling to the outside on the backstretch then gave way on the turn.

Well, don't buy that :46 3/5 half, or that :21 3/5 quarter, or any other fractional times from Saratoga's inner turf course, for that matter, at least when the temporary rails are in place. When that is the case, the races are not timed electronically, but rather by hand with a stopwatch, and badly, so that ordinary allowance horses such as Doctor Disaster are credited with absurdly fast fractions. This is not an isolated case, nor is it restricted to races at a mile and three-eighths. Two days after Doctor Disaster's race, a nine-furlong route received the following official time-line:

FIFTH RACE
Saratoga
JULY 31, 1995

1⅛ MILES. (Inner Turf)(1.47) MAIDEN SPECIAL WEIGHT. Purse $32,000. 3–year–olds and upward, foaled in New York State and approved by the New York State–Bred Registery. Weights: 3–year–olds, 117 lbs. Older, 122 lbs.

Value of Race: $32,000 Winner $19,200; second $6,400; third $3,520; fourth $1,920; fifth $960. Mutuel Pool $285,997.00 Exacta Pool $378,260.00 Triple Pool $369,104.00

Last Raced	Horse	M/Eqt.	A.	Wt	PP	St	¼	½	¾	Str	Fin	Jockey	Odds $1
7Jun95 ^{1}Bel^{2}	Striver	b	3	117	7	8	$7^{1\frac{1}{2}}$	$6^{1\frac{1}{2}}$	5^{1}	1^{hd}	$1^{2\frac{1}{2}}$	Velazquez J R	a-0.85
15Jly95 ^{2}Bel^{11}	Ruffed Grouse		4	122	1	1	$1^{\frac{1}{2}}$	1^{hd}	1^{hd}	$2^{\frac{1}{2}}$	2no	Nelson D	33.25
23Jly95 ^{3}Sar^{8}	Make No Mistake		6	122	6	5	2^{2}	2^{1}	$2^{1\frac{1}{2}}$	3^{1}	3no	Rydowski S R	10.70
14Jun95 ^{6}Bel^{6}	Mean Feat		3	112	5	4	6^{hd}	7^{1}	$7^{1\frac{1}{2}}$	$4^{\frac{1}{2}}$	$4^{1\frac{1}{4}}$	Leon F	54.75
12Jly95 ^{5}Bel^{3}	Worldly Slew		3	112	11	11	$8^{\frac{1}{2}}$	8^{1}	$8^{\frac{1}{2}}$	$8^{\frac{1}{2}}$	$5^{\frac{1}{2}}$	Belmonte L A^{5}	42.00
23Jly95 ^{3}Sar^{6}	No Sir	b	3	117	10	9	$3^{\frac{1}{2}}$	4^{3}	4^{3}	6^{1}	6^{hd}	Cruguet J	28.00
3Jly95 ^{5}Bel^{7}	Fast Ace	b	3	117	4	6	11	$9^{\frac{1}{2}}$	11	10^{5}	7^{hd}	Luzzi M J	20.50
21Jun95 ^{9}Bel^{4}	Storm Wave		3	117	3	2	10^{1}	11	9^{hd}	$5^{\frac{1}{2}}$	$8^{1\frac{1}{4}}$	Sellers S J	5.60
12Jly95 ^{5}Bel^{2}	Irish Patriot	[illegible]	[illegible]	[illegible]	[illegible]	3	9^{hd}	$10^{1\frac{1}{2}}$	$10^{1\frac{1}{2}}$	7^{hd}	$9^{2\frac{1}{2}}$	Day P	a-0.85
21Jun95 ^{9}Bel^{2}	Mad River Glenn	b	3	117	9	10	$5^{\frac{1}{2}}$	3^{1}	3^{hd}	9^{1}	10^{7}	Santos J A	3.90
15Jly95 ^{2}Bel^{7}	Sweetly Risen	f	3	117	8	7	4^{hd}	$5^{\frac{1}{2}}$	6^{1}	11	11	Bailey J D	19.60

a–Coupled: Striver and Irish Patriot.

OFF AT 3:07 Start Good. Won driving. Time, :21^{3}, :46^{1}, 1:11^{1}, 1:37^{1}, 1:49^{3} Course firm.

$2 Mutuel Prices:

1A–STRIVER (a–entry)	3.70	2.70	2.30
2–RUFFED GROUSE		16.80	8.60
6–MAKE NO MISTAKE			5.20

$2 EXACTA 1–2 PAID $103.50 $2 TRIPLE 1–2–6 PAID $771.00

Ch. g, (Feb), by Compliance–Mervat, by Vaguely Noble. Trainer O'Brien Leo. Bred by Gallagher's Stud (NY).

STRIVER reserved early, worked his way forward on the turn, accelerated to the front in midstretch, then drew clear under intermittent urging. RUFFED GROUSE set the pace under pressure into midstretch and outfinished MAKE NO MISTAKE for the place. MAKE NO MISTAKE forced the pace between horses the entire way and held for a share. MEAN FEAT in tight on the first

Another :21 3/5 quarter. Handicappers are asked to believe that Ruffed Grouse and the *6-year-old maiden* (ironically named) Make No Mistake dueled through a quarter in :21 3/5, a half in :46 1/5, and held to finish second and third.

I don't think so.

"When the meeting was extended they needed an extra lane to accommodate a greater number of races," explained Mark Berner, field operator for American Teletime in New York. "This happened after electronic timers had already been installed, and the New York Racing Association never installed electric eyes for the additional lanes."

This kind of inattention to detail would drive any self-respecting New York railbird into a rage were it taking place at Aqueduct in the dead of winter. But it's hard to get mad — or at least stay mad — at anything once you've settled in for the duration at the Spa. "No electronic turf times when the rails are up? Scandalous! Where should we eat dinner tonight?"

Don't be discouraged if you can't make sense of inner turf course fractions. The game's best minds have been wrestling with these esoteric problems for a long time. Len Ragozin, founder of *The Sheets*, has earned a well-deserved reputation for his meticulous attention to detail; nothing that might affect the accuracy of his graphed performance figures escapes his attention:

"Well...I defy anybody (chuckling noticeably) to take the times of Saratoga grass races, with any kind of chart they've got...and make any sense of what's going on up there," he once observed. "The fact of the matter is, there's quite a few races there, where they say it's being run at such-and-such a distance — and it isn't. It's kind of a casual meeting."

You can say that again.

August 4

HEAVY OVERNIGHT RAIN into the morning hours meant there would be no turf racing — but that didn't mean the horse-for-course angle was on the back burner, only that the venue had changed. Off-the-turf races present potentially value-rich situations because the *Form's* career totals list Saratoga grass races instead of past starts, if any, on Saratoga's main track. The players who dig the deepest have the edge.

The eighth race was an allowance for non winners of three races other than maiden, claiming or starter. Scheduled for the main turf, it had been switched to a main track that was labeled muddy by late afternoon. The field was reduced to six after late scratches:

8 **Saratoga**

1⅛ MILES. **(Turf). (1:452) ALLOWANCE. Purse $38,000. Fillies and mares, 3-year-olds and upward which have not won three races other than maiden, claiming or starter. Weights: 3-year-olds, 116 lbs. Older, 121 lbs. Non-winners of $21,000 twice on the turf since December 7, allowed 3 lbs. $19,200 twice at a mile or over since October 28, 6 lbs. $18,000 twice in 1994-95, 9 lbs. (Races where entered for $62,500 or less not considered in allowances.) (Preference by condition eligibility.)**

Uncharted Waters
Own: Steinberg Philip J
KRONE J A (51 4 11 2 .08)

B. f. 4
Sire: Blushing John (Blushing Groom)
Dam: Forever Waving (Hoist the Flag)
Br: Foxfield (Ky)
Tr: Jerkens H Allen (17 2 2 2 .12)

112

Lifetime Record:	**15**	**3**	**2**	**2**	**$79,275**						
1995	4	1	1	0	$31,360	Turf	11	1	2	2	$40,095
1994	8	0	1	2	$14,730	Wet	0	0	0	0	
Sar [T]	2	0	1	0	$7,040	Dist [T]	1	0	0	0	

3Jly95-7Bel	yl	1	[T]	:23	:463	1:111	1:362	3↑	ⒻAlw 38000N3X	93	7	2	22	1½	1hd	21¼	Krone J A	119	6.40	80-26	LadyReiko1211¼ UnchartedWaters1192¼ DinnerDimond1192¼	Bid, held well	8
18Jun95-6Bel	fm	1 1/16	[T]	:234	:464	1:102	1:413	3↑	ⒻAlw 38000N3X	79	2	5	67½	55	46½	47½	Krone J A	119	14.70	81-10	Firm Friend119hd Shocking Pleasure1123¾ Upper Noosh1123½	Evenly	8
24May95-6Bel	fst	6f		:23	:464	:584	1:111	3↑	ⒻAlw 36000N3X	25	3	2	44	56	517	529¾	Ramos W S	121	10.60	55-19	IncredibleBlues1124 MissGoldenCircle110¾ EnsignJonn11911	Done early	5
10May95-7Bel	gd	6½f		:224	:46	1:11	1:174	3↑	ⒻAlw 34000N2X	80	5	3	11	11	1½	11½	Ramos W S	119	7.40	86-14	Uncharted Waters1191½ CraftyJam1102 ChristmasCactus110no	Drew clear	6
28Oct94-7Aqu	fm	1⅛	[T]	:474	1:12	1:372	1:504	3↑	ⒻAlw 34000N2X	48	6	3	79½	99½	915	918½	Krone J A	114	6.20	68-18	Aucilla1161 Great Lady Mary1143 Bold Rosa Lined1171	Steadied early	9
1Oct94-8Bel	sf	1 1/16	[T]	:243	:49	1:141	1:463		ⒻRarePerfumH-G2	44	6	6	84¼	85	817	826	Samyn J L	110	23.90	37-37	Jade Flush1116½ Lady Affirmed117¾ Saxuality117no	No factor	8
7Sep94-7Bel	fm	1 1/16	[T]	:243	:48	1:114	1:413	3↑	ⒻAlw 34000N2X	76	7	3	52	51¾	62¾	67¼	Santos J A	113	4.10	83-15	Arctic Aaria117¾ Running On E1174 Aucilla1131¾	Faded	9
24Aug94-6Sar	gd	1 1/16	[T]	:242	:481	1:123	1:433	3↑	ⒻAlw 32000N2X	89	6	6	55½	53	3½	2¾	Krone J A	112	12.70	75-22	Knocknock112¾ UnchrtedWtrs1123½ Kris'sKiss117½	Wide, drifted stretch	9
3Aug94-9Sar	yl	1 1/16	[T]	:231	:48	1:123	1:434		ⒻNijana-G3	80	3	7	65	95¼	74½	710	Santos J A	114	25.30	65-25	Alywow1213½ Irish Forever121no Knocknock1142	No factor	9
Run in divisions																							
25Jun94-6Bel	fm	1	[T]	:221	:451	1:094	1:333	3↑	ⒻAlw 32000N2X	75	9	6	43	41½	36½	312½	Santos J A	111	5.20	81-11	Dayflower1199 Jiving Around1193½ UnchartedWaters1112	Bid, weakened	9

WORKOUTS: Aug 2 Sar 6f fst 1:16 B *2/8* Jly 29 Sar 4f fst :484 B *14/42* Jly 23 Sar 5f fst 1:00 H *2/30* Jly 19 Sar 7f fst 1:284 H *2/3* Jly 12 Bel tr.t 4f fst :491 B *10/31* May 20 Bel 4f my :491 B *2/6*

Said Privately

Own: Peters Betty M

NELSON D (10 0 1 1 .00)

B. m. 5
Sire: Private Account (Damascus)
Dam: Dire (Roberto)
Br: Beitz & Kaskel (Ky)
Tr: Johnstone Bruce (7 0 0 1 .00)

112

Lifetime Record :	34 3 1 4	$93,640			
1995	9 0 0 1	$14,220	Turf	16 1 1 1	$39,340
1994	10 0 0 1	$10,320	Wet	4 1 0 1	$23,160
Sar Ⓣ	4 1 0 0	$19,140	Dist Ⓣ	5 0 0 0	$2,160

4Jun95-6Bel fm 1 1/16 Ⓣ :233 :47 1:104 1:404 3↑ ⒻAlw 38000N3X 85 2 3 32½ 42½ 43 44 Nelson D 119 36.25 90-08 Aucilla119½ Joy Of Life1142½ Shocking Pleasure111½ Saved ground 6
24May95-7Bel fm 1 1/16 Ⓣ :231 :462 1:10 1:391 3↑ ⒻAlw 38000N3X 77 6 9 96½ 84½ 97½ 711¾ Madrid A Jr 119 b 31.50 90-07 Perfect Arc1095 Joy Of Life1191½ Aucilla1192 Saved ground 10
28Apr95-8Aqu fm 1 1/16 Ⓣ :233 :474 1:121 1:431 ⒻAlw 36000N3X 78 4 5 34½ 21½ 21½ 43½ Madrid A Jr 113 b 18.90 89-10 Stretch Drive116½ Manila Lila1131½ FirmFriend1131¾ Checked break, tired 6
18Mar95-3Aqu fst 1⅛ :482 1:141 1:394 1:522 ⒻAlw 36000N3X 57 7 8 88½ 76½ 510 418½ Madrid A Jr 113 b 26.00 60-31 Grab The Glory116nk Forcing Bid11313 Shellster1135 Improved position 8
2Mar95-7Aqu fst 1 1/16 ⊡ :241 :48 1:124 1:434 3↑ ⒻHandicap50k 67 5 2 31½ 43 59 516½ Madrid A Jr 110 b 18.90 70-14 ⒹCherokee Wonder1163½ Sterling Pound1223½ S. S. Sparkle116½ Used up 5
16Feb95-8Aqu fst 1 1/16 ⊡ :232 :474 1:13 1:464 ⒻAlw 36000N3X 76 1 10 89 55 23½ 34 Madrid A Jr 117 b 38.75 67-30 Royal Cozzene1172½ Forcing Bid1171½ Said Privately1173½ Saved ground 12
3Feb95-8Aqu fst 1 1/16 ⊡ :24 :483 1:14 1:48 ⒻAlw 36000N3X 71 3 6 65½ 55 45½ 57 Madrid A Jr 117 b 36.00 58-30 Tuscany Breeze110nk GrabTheGlory1191¾ ManorQueen1174 Saved ground 7
20Jan95-7Aqu sly 1 1/16 ⊡ :234 :482 1:124 1:451 ⒻAlw 36000N3X 70 1 6 53½ 54½ 55½ 55½ Madrid A Jr 117 b 12.70 73-16 Willspynow1173½ Saratoga April117½ Cheery Sun112½ No threat 6
5Jan95-8Aqu fst 170 ⊡ :234 :48 1:131 1:432 ⒻAlw 36000N3X 55 6 5 55 65 68½ 618½ Nelson D 117 30.50 63-14 Sea Ditty1176¾ Willspynow1171 Joan Noble1194½ Outrun 6
29Nov94-8Aqu wf 1⅛ :474 1:121 1:382 1:514 3↑ ⒻAlw 36000N3X — 2 4 414 513 621 — Velazquez J R 117 30.50 — 24 Dancer's Gate119no Manila Lila1171½ Miss Fix It1175 Outrun, eased 6

WORKOUTS: Jly 28 Sar tr.t 5f fst 1:04 B 4/14 Jly 15 Bel Ⓣ 4f fm :461 H (d) 1/3 Jly 7 Bel 5f fst 1:03 B 18/30 May 14 Bel 6f fst 1:153 H 4/12

Sapor

Own: Ryver Meadow Farms

VELAZQUEZ J R (50 8 6 3 .16)

B. f. 4
Sire: Caveat (Cannonade)
Dam: First Quad (Quadratic)
Br: Ryver Meadow Farms (Md)
Tr: Badgett William Jr (9 1 0 0 .11)

118

Lifetime Record :	20 3 7 4	$116,075			
1995	8 1 4 1	$58,330	Turf	1 0 0 0	
1994	11 2 3 2	$54,745	Wet	5 2 1 1	$41,600
Sar Ⓣ	0 0 0 0		Dist Ⓣ	0 0 0 0	

12Jly95-7Bel fst 7f :223 :452 1:10 1:23 3↑ ⒻAlw 36000N3X 74 8 2 63 43½ 45½ 58½ Velazquez J R 119 *2.65 78-14 FntsticWomn1158 LostPriri119no DstnctvRuby114nk Four wide, flattened 9
23Jun95-3Bel wf 1 1/16 :231 :46 1:102 1:422 ⒻClm 100000 84 3 2 2½ 2hd 22½ 25¾ Velazquez J R 117 4.80 81-23 Schway Baby Sway1135¾ Sapor1173½ Evi Bee1122½ Forced pace, weakened 5
18May95-7Bel gd 1 :233 :463 1:111 1:371 3↑ ⒻAlw 38000N3X 17 5 4 53 68½ 622 636¼ Velazquez J R 122 f *1.50 41-23 Nppelon1124 JupiterAssmbly122nk ChngForDollr1103 Four wide, no rally 6
29Apr95-7Aqu fst 1⅛ :48 1:124 1:391 1:523 ⒻAlw 50000NC 82 4 2 22½ 2½ 21 23¼ Velazquez J R 113 1.70 74-19 Incinerate1193¼ Sapor1132½ Unlawful Behavior1101¾ No match 5
12Apr95-8Aqu fst 1⅛ :48 1:124 1:384 1:513 ⒻAlw 34000N2X 89 6 3 27 25 1½ 13¼ Velazquez J R 113 *.95 82-19 Sapor1133¼ Tainted Angel1135 Doc's Josephine1161 Going away 6
11Mar95-3GP fst 1⅛ :474 1:122 1:373 1:501 3↑ ⒻDispute50k 95 6 2 2½ 2½ 2hd 2no Smith M E 116 3.30 86-11 Teewinot114no Sapor1165¾ Floramera1166 6
Seven wide top str, just missed, best of others
17Feb95-8GP fst 1 1/16 :231 :471 1:121 1:45 ⒻAlw 28000N2X 83 2 4 41¾ 42 41 32¾ Douglas R R 118 4.70 80-24 Seeking The Circle1181½ Norfolk Lavender1181½ Sapor1181½ 7
Steadied leaving final turn, angled outward str, late rally
11Jan95-10GP fst 7f :224 :454 1:104 1:234 ⒻAlw 27000N2X 84 4 6 51¾ 52 31 2nk Krone J A 119 7.70 84-16 Investalot122nk Sapor119nk Yougotabe Joking1224½ 7
Steadied leaving bkstr, rallied just missing
23Nov94-7Aqu fst 1⅛ ⊗ :492 1:144 1:411 1:542 3↑ ⒻAlw 34000N2X 60 5 5 31½ 31½ 28 213½ Smith M E 117 f *1.30 50-35 One Account11213 Sapor117½ Romancing Missy1173 Up for place 6
12Nov94-1Aqu fst 7f :234 :471 1:12 1:25 ⒻClm 50000 71 1 7 75 74½ 42 21½ Smith M E 119 6.10 77-19 Runaway Fling1121½ Sapor119¾ Skip One1161 Rallied wide 7

WORKOUTS: Jly 31 Sar 5f fst 1:01 H 3/34 Jly 25 Sar 4f fst :501 B 33/43 ●Jly 8 Bel 5f fst :594 H 1/27 Jly 1 Bel 4f fst :48 H 3/52 Jun 17 Bel 3f fst :36 H 4/27 Jun 11 Bel 4f fst :49 B 13/59

Blushing Maggie

Own: Lauer Michael E

BAILEY J D (66 16 5 11 .24)

Dk. b or br f. 4
Sire: Dynaformer (Roberto)
Dam: Quick Blush (Blushing Groom (Fr))
Br: O'Donnell Mrs Lee (Ky)
Tr: Lauer Michael E (4 0 0 1 .00)

115

Lifetime Record :	27 5 3 8	$140,528			
1995	8 0 2 1	$23,940	Turf	7 0 2 0	$20,760
1994	17 5 1 6	$114,046	Wet	6 1 0 3	$35,628
Sar Ⓣ	0 0 0 0		Dist Ⓣ	2 0 1 0	$9,200

6Jly95-9EIP fm 1 1/16 Ⓣ :234 :464 1:10 1:404 3↑ ⒻAlw 18055N$Y 82 2 1 1½ 2½ 31½ 43½ Bartram B E L 115 3.00 95-02 ⒹWicked Mama1122 Storm In Sight114hd PamSlaughter1181½ Pace, tired 6
1Jly95-8CD fm 1 Ⓣ :233 :473 1:121 1:351 3↑ ⒻAlw 41300N$mY 79 5 3 53 62½ 64 57¾ Fires E L 123 11.70 88-04 Icy Warning1162½ Mari's Key1233½ Shadow Miss116nk Tired 7
14Jun95-9CD fst 1 1/16 :241 :482 1:132 1:442 3↑ ⒻAlw 38580N$Y 79 8 7 76½ 65 45½ 310 Day P L 118 8.20 82-16 Catnip1189 Dancing With Deb1201 Blushing Maggie1183 9
Bumped start, improved position
26May95-9CD fst 1 1/16 :24 :48 1:131 1:453 3↑ ⒻAlw 44260N$Y 79 5 6 51¾ 63¾ 54½ 56½ Day P L 120 11.10 79-17 Private Status1183 Briar Road1181½ Free Ransom118nk No rally 7
5May95-7CD fst 1 1/16 :233 :464 1:114 1:432 3↑ ⒻLousvlBdBCH-G2 81 2 6 55½ 87¾ 810 810¼ Barton D M L 107 38.90 87-07 Fit To Lead1161½ Jade Flush1151½ Teewinot109¾ Inside, tired 9
22Apr95-9Kee fm 1⅛ Ⓣ :471 1:121 1:38 1:51 ⒻAlw 39100N3X 87 5 2 21½ 3½ 1hd 2hd Bailey J D L 114 7.00 82-15 Adaiyka117hd Blushing Maggie114nk Lady Lodger1112 Gamely 10
6Apr95-9TP fst 1⅛ :482 1:131 1:38 1:503 ⒻAlw 43900N1Y 86 1 3 31½ 21½ 25 28 Sellers S J L 118 1.90 82-25 Red Star1158 Blushing Maggie11815 Lao's Star1141 Second best 8
25Mar95-8TP fst 1 :231 :471 1:123 1:40 ⒻAlw 37500N3X 56 4 7 67½ 58 510 616½ Bartram B E L 115 *1.80 53-31 Defer West1133 Princess Nana1138 Taylor's Fireworks118½ Outrun 7
17Dec94-9TP my 1 1/16 :224 :454 1:103 1:431 3↑ ⒻMy Charmer47k 86 2 5 56 43½ 33½ 36 Bartram B E L 117 8.00 85-20 Sdie'sDrem1191 Lur'sPistolett1145 BlushingMggi117nk No late response 11
27Nov94-7Haw sly 170 :232 :461 1:104 1:401 3↑ ⒻQuickRewrdBC65k 78 7 7 79 611 48 310½ Guidry M 114 3.80 89 — MerryColleen1126½ NorthernRltion1094 BlushingMggi114½ Late wide bid 9

Dancing With Deb

Own: Lewis Debbie & Lee

DAVIS R G (61 7 7 12 .11)

Dk. b or br f. 4
Sire: Cox's Ridge (Best Turn)
Dam: Crystal Cream (Secretariat)
Br: G M Breeding Farms Inc (Ky)
Tr: Hennig Mark (15 1 3 3 .07)

115

Lifetime Record :	8 3 2 1	$89,514			
1995	4 1 1 0	$38,414	Turf	0 0 0 0	
1994	4 2 1 1	$51,100	Wet	2 2 0 0	$43,114
Sar Ⓣ	0 0 0 0		Dist Ⓣ	0 0 0 0	

30Jun95-9CD fst 1 1/16 :232 :471 1:122 1:441 3↑ ⒻAlw 45620N$Y 82 9 6 64½ 52½ 43½ 46 Sellers S J L 120 6.50 87-13 Briar Road1161½ Kathy O120no Jackpot Jenny1204½ 4 wide 2nd turn 8
14Jun95-9CD fst 1 1/16 :241 :482 1:132 1:442 3↑ ⒻAlw 38580N$Y 80 2 3 33½ 41½ 34 29 Woods C R Jr L 120 2.70 83-16 Catnip1189 Dancing With Deb1201 Blushing Maggie1183 Fully extended 9
26May95-9CD fst 1 1/16 :24 :48 1:131 1:453 3↑ ⒻAlw 44260N$Y 82 4 3 2hd 3nk 33 44¼ Sellers S J L 123 2.70 81-17 Private Status1183 Briar Road1181½ Free Ransom118nk Dueled, tired 7
23Apr95-4Kee wf 1 1/16 :234 :482 1:133 1:464 ⒻAlw 39000N2X 80 2 1 1hd 2hd 11½ 13 Bailey J D L 115 *.50 75-23 DncingWithDeb1153 AltrGuild1122 LittlePinkie1126 Well rated, driving 6
26Dec94-7SA fst 1 :232 :472 1:113 1:36 3↑ ⒻAlw 50000N2X 92 7 4 42½ 32½ 33½ 24 Delahoussaye E LB 119 1.50 85-13 CrissyAya1144 DancingWithDeb119hd EurekaLass1173 4 wide to 2nd turn 8
10Nov94-7Hol my 1 1/16 :231 :461 1:103 1:421 3↑ ⒻAlw 34000N1X 91 5 3 32½ 41¾ 11½ 17½ Delahoussaye E LB 119 6.10 90-13 Dancing With Deb1197½ Real Connection1161¾ Locate117½ Clear, driving 6
15Oct94-3SA fst 1 :222 :463 1:12 1:37 3↑ ⒻMd Sp Wt 79 8 2 31 1hd 11½ 1hd Stevens G L B 118 *2.10 84-13 Dancing With Deb118hd GiftToTheWorld1181 DixieDuo1184 Cleared, held 10
6Feb94-6SA fst 6½f :213 :442 1:084 1:15 ⒻMd Sp Wt 76 5 7 811 77½ 47 39 Stevens G L B 117 10.80 88-05 EmerldExpress1175½ Espdrille1173½ DncingWithDb1172¾ Passed tired ones 8

WORKOUTS: Jly 31 Sar 4f fst :491 H 25/54 Jly 18 Sar 4f fst :493 B 6/10 Jly 11 CD 4f fst :494 B 15/31 Jun 7 CD 5f fst 1:023 B 12/22 May 22 CD 4f fst :49 B 2/23 May 16 CD 5f fst 1:022 B 11/35

Safe At Home

Own: Minassian Harry

NO RIDER (—)

Dk. b or br f. 4
Sire: Homebuilder (Mr. Prospector)
Dam: Dazzled (Majestic Light)
Br: Stilz Brothers & Pin Oak Stable Inc (Ky)
Tr: Serpe Philip M (13 1 0 0 .08)

115

Lifetime Record :	24 4 8 7	$133,400			
1995	3 0 0 0	$300	Turf	2 0 0 1	$3,600
1994	18 4 7 6	$128,950	Wet	1 0 0 0	$1,920
Sar Ⓣ	0 0 0 0		Dist Ⓣ	0 0 0 0	

12Jly95-7Bel fst 7f :223 :452 1:10 1:23 3↑ ⒻAlw 36000N3X 68 1 8 85½ 76½ 67½ 611 Bailey J D 119 7.00 75-14 FantsticWomen1158 LostPririe119no DistinctiveRuby114nk Steadied 1/2 pl 9
3Jly95-7Bel yl 1 Ⓣ :23 :463 1:111 1:362 3↑ ⒻAlw 38000N3X 61 1 7 87½ 85¾ 78½ 816 Bailey J D 119 9.30 65-26 Lady Reiko1211½ Uncharted Waters1192½ Dinner Diamond1192½ No factor 8
16Jan95-8GP fst 1 1/16 :234 :481 1:122 1:452 ⒻAlw 30000N3X 81 9 7 86½ 66½ 63½ 53½ Bailey J D 117 2.80 79-23 Floramera1171½ Miss Nance117nk Me And The Boys119nk Belated bid 10
10Dec94-5Aqu fst 1 1/16 ⊡ :243 :483 1:134 1:452 3↑ ⒻAlw 36000N3X 85 1 3 36 35 33½ 22 Alvarado F T 115 2.40 76-23 Miss Fix It1172 Safe At Home1151 Manila Lila11712 Late gain 5
30Nov94-8Aqu fst 7f :232 :471 1:124 1:254 3↑ ⒻAlw 34000N3X 75 2 6 65½ 52½ 32 21½ Luzzi M J 115 *2.05 74-21 Big Rhonda1151½ Safe At Home115no Shiner1173 Up for place 7
16Nov94-8Aqu fst 1 :24 :471 1:121 1:374 3↑ ⒻAlw 36000N3X 83 1 4 36½ 33½ 21½ 21½ Bailey J D 115 2.70 77-24 Recognizable1151½ Safe At Home1158 Big Rhonda1158 No match 4
3Nov94-6Aqu fst 1 :24 :472 1:114 1:361 3↑ ⒻAlw 36000N3X 80 2 4 43 31½ 34 24¾ Luzzi M J 115 4.70 82-13 TriumphAtDawn1174¾ SafeAtHome115no SterlingPound1155 Up for place 4
18Oct94-5Aqu fst 1 :244 :48 1:114 1:36 3↑ ⒻAlw 36000N3X 77 4 3 43½ 32½ 37 310 Bailey J D 116 3.65 78-21 Aly's Conquest1147½ Nasty Cure1142¾ Safe At Home1166½ Lacked rally 4
16Sep94-6Bel fst 1 :23 :464 1:104 1:362 3↑ ⒻAlw 34000N2X 81 11 9 810 63½ 2½ 14 Bailey J D 113 7.60 81-19 Safe At Home1134 Regal Solution117½ Georgia Anna1171½ Driving 11
21Aug94-8Sar sly 1⅛ :473 1:13 1:393 1:53 3↑ ⒻAlw 32000N2X 68 1 3 38 32½ 34 411½ Sellers S J 112 6.30 60-25 Tara Roma1198 Helen Brann1123 Mrs. Marcos117nk Flattened out 5

WORKOUTS: Jly 29 Sar 5f fst 1:003 H 4/37 Jly 24 Sar 3f gd :374 B 9/14 Jun 24 Bel 4f fst :494 B 53/91 Jun 16 Bel 5f fst 1:021 B 14/48 Jun 15 Bel Ⓣ 5f fm 1:032 B (d) 4/11 Jun 9 Bel 7f fst 1:314 B 2/3

Favored at 3-2 was Dancing With Deb. Along with Safe At Home, she had been entered for the main track only. Dancing With Deb showed a wet track-record of two wins from as many starts including a lengthy score in the mud at Hollywood Park, and she was dropping in class out of tougher classified allowance conditions in which she'd been fairly competitive at Churchill Downs. Most recently, she had finished a respectable fourth after a wide trip.

There were two knocks on Dancing With Deb. To begin with, in four starts as a 4-year-old, the filly had recorded Beyers of 80, 82, 80, and 82 — consistent, but consistently several lengths slower than the level she had twice attained toward the end of her 3-year-old campaign. That she had been unable to run back to her best 3-year-old figures this far into her 4-year-old season was a negative sign of development.

Secondly, then crowd was overbetting her off the big mud win nearly nine months ago. Mud had not been the sole catalyst of her improvement to a Beyer of 91, because she had come right back with a 92 on a fast track at Santa Anita.

There was another filly in the field with a big wet track victory in 1994, but the race had long since been dropped from her past performances, and thus she was overlooked as the fourth choice at 5-1.

In order for players to come up with Blushing Maggie, they had to have good memories, a file of back charts from Saratoga, or a set of either Len Ragozin's *The Sheets* or Jerry Brown's *Thoro-graph* performance figures:

BLUSHING MAGGIE — '91 dk b/ f Dynaformer - Quick Blush

Month	2-YEAR-OLD	3-YEAR-OLD	4-YEAR-OLD
DEC		TP 11^1my	
NOV	CD 21^5gd	HAW 10^2sy CD 10^2	
NOV	CD 27^2gd	KEE 13^3	
OCT		KEE -17^1	
SEP		TP● 11^2	
SEP		RD -12^1	
AUG		⟨SAR 10sy SAR● 14^2⟩	
JUL			ELP / CD -14^2 -12
JUN		CD 19^3sy	CD 10
MAY		CD 16	CD 13^2
MAY		CD -19^2	
APR		CD 17^2sy	CD 14^3 KEE -10 TP 10^2
MAR		GP -19^1	TP 22
MAR		GP 13	
FEB		GP 20	
JAN		GP 18^1sy	

Sheet-style figures are a bit pricey unless you're a big bettor, selling at anywhere from $25 to $35 per day. But one important feature they provide is complete lifetime records at a glance. On sheets, horses receive figures that are modified by such factors as wind (velocity and direction), weight carried, and ground loss on turns — the theory being that these things affect final time, and they are quantifiable. The lower the number, the faster the race.

We won't delve into pattern theory here, since that was one of the main thrusts of *Expert Handicapping*, but in looking over Blushing Maggie's career, we notice that 16 races back she recorded what was then a lifetime-best figure of 10, and that the race had taken place in the slop at Saratoga. Scurrying back to our charts from the previous summer, we found Blushing Maggie indeed boasted hidden mud form at the Spa:

FOURTH RACE
Saratoga
AUGUST 18, 1994

1¹⁄₈ MILES. (1.47) CLAIMING. Purse $30,000. Fillies, 3-year-olds. Weight, 121 lbs. Non-winners of two races at a mile or over Since July 15, 1994, allowed 3 lbs. Of such a race since June 15, 5 lbs. Claiming price $75,000, for each $2,500 to $70,000, allowed 2 lbs. (Races when entered to be claimed for $65,000 or less not considered.)(ORIGINALLY SCHEDULED FOR TURF AT ONE MILE AND AN EIGHTH.)

Value of Race: $30,000 Winner $18,000; second $6,600; third $3,600; fourth $1,800. Mutuel Pool $255,029.00 Exacta Pool $362,911.00 Quinella Pool $67,591.00

Last Raced	Horse	M/Eqt. A.Wt	PP	St	¼	½	¾	Str	Fin	Jockey	Cl'g Pr	Odds $1
12Aug94 4Sar³	Blushing Maggie	3 112	4	2	1³	1⁵	1²	1hd	13½	Day P	70000	2.00
19Jly94 6Bel⁶	Jupiter Assembly	3 112	1	1	3½	2½	2³	2⁸	21³½	Perret C	70000	3.30
4Aug94 7Sar²	Glorious Purple	3 112	3	4	2½	32½	3¹	31½	3⁶	Davis R G	70000	2.40
4Aug94 7Sar⁴	Sun Attack	3 112	5	5	4hd	4⁹	41⁶	42¹	Velazquez J R	70000	2.80
4Aug94 7Sar⁵	Elan De Tammy	3 112	2	3	4½	5	5	5	5	Luzzi M J	70000	8.70

OFF AT 2:30 Start Good. Won driving. Time, :24, :48, 1:12⁴, 1:38, 1:50² Track sloppy.

$2 Mutuel Prices:	11-(L)-BLUSHING MAGGIE	6.00	3.40	2.40
	1A-(F)-JUPITER ASSEMBLY		4.20	2.80
	9-(J)-GLORIOUS PURPLE			2.40

$2 EXACTA 11-1 PAID $27.00 $2 QUINELLA 1-11 PAID $13.40

B. f, (Mar), by Dynaformer–Quick Blush, by Blushing Groom. Trainer Lauer Michael E. Bred by O'Donnell Mrs Lee (Ky).

BLUSHING MAGGIE opened a wide gap along the backstretch, raced uncontested on the lead for six furlongs, dug in when challenged in upper stretch then turned back JUPITER ASSEMBLY under brisk urging. JUPITER ASSEMBLY reserved for a half, closed the gap on the turn, drew on nearly even terms with the winner in midstretch but couldn't stay with that one in the final eighth. GLORIOUS PURPLE stumbled at the start, raced within striking distance to the turn and tired. SUN ATTACK was never a factor. ELAN DE TAMMY was outrun after being pinched at the start.

Owners— 1, Lauer Michael E; 2, Murphy Robert L Sr; 3, Reynolds David P; 4, My Jo Lee Stable; 5, Kirk David P
Trainers— 1, Lauer Michael E; 2, Reid Mark J; 3, Alexander Frank A; 4, O'Brien Leo; 5, Johnson Philip G
Scratched— Skaterish (23Jly94 10SAR⁵), Flyway Drive (5Aug94 7SAR⁴), Too Oh Five (3Aug94 7SAR⁶), Caroline Of Kent (2Jly94 4BEL³), Via Wood (1Jly94 7BEL⁹), Viva La Dance (25Jly94 7SAR⁷), Shahra Bay (12Jly94 6BEL⁷), Cut The Pot (4Aug94 7SAR¹)

Not only had the opportunistic filly won an off-the-turf route at today's nine-furlong distance, she had won convincingly.

Blushing Maggie had finished only a length behind Dancing With Deb after being bumped at the start of her most recent dirt race at Churchill Downs, and her winning experience in this unique footing constituted a significant advantage. For in-the-know bettors, so did the price:

EIGHTH RACE
Saratoga
AUGUST 4, 1995

1¹⁄₈ MILES. (1.47) ALLOWANCE. Purse $38,000. Fillies and mares, 3-year-olds and upward which have not won three races other than maiden, claiming or starter. Weights: 3-year-olds, 116 lbs. Older, 121 lbs. Non-winners of $21,000 twice on the turf since December 7, allowed 3 lbs. $19,200 twice at a mile or over since October 28, 6 lbs. $18,000 twice in 1994-95, 9 lbs. (Races where entered for $62,500 or less not considered in allowances.) (Preference by condition eligibility.)(ORIGINALLY SCHEDULED FOR TURF.)

Value of Race: $38,000 Winner $22,800; second $7,600; third $4,180; fourth $2,280; fifth $1,140. Mutuel Pool $346,695.00 Exacta Pool $365,431.00 Triple Pool $258,916.00

Last Raced	Horse	M/Eqt. A.Wt	PP	St	¼	½	¾	Str	Fin	Jockey	Odds $1
6Jly95 9ElP⁴	Blushing Maggie	4 115	4	4	3½	3½	3½	11½	1⁶	Bailey J D	5.60
12Jly95 7Bel⁵	Sapor	4 118	3	6	2½	2¹	1½	21½	21½	Velazquez J R	3.00
30Jun95 9CD⁴	Dancing With Deb	4 115	5	5	6	52½	51⁰	4¹	3no	Davis R G	1.55
3Jly95 7Bel²	Uncharted Waters	4 112	1	1	1¹	1hd	2²	3²	44½	Krone J A	2.75
12Jly95 7Bel⁶	Safe At Home	4 115	6	3	5½	41½	41½	5	5	Sellers S J	12.40
4Jun95 6Bel⁴	Said Privately	5 113	2	2	4½	6	6	—	—	Nelson D	19.60

Said Privately:Eased

OFF AT 4:45 Start Good. Won driving. Time, :24, :48, 1:12³, 1:39², 1:53 Track muddy.

$2 Mutuel Prices:	6-BLUSHING MAGGIE	13.20	5.70	2.50
	4-SAPOR		4.20	2.60
	9-DANCING WITH DEB			2.40

$2 EXACTA 6-4 PAID $42.60 $2 TRIPLE 6-4-9 PAID $110.50

Dk. b. or br. f, by Dynaformer–Quick Blush, by Blushing Groom (Fr). Trainer Lauer Michael E. Bred by O'Donnell Mrs Lee (Ky).

BLUSHING MAGGIE settled just off the early pace while between horses, angled in on the turn, rallied smartly along the rail to gain a clear lead in upper stretch, then drew off under brisk urging. SAPOR forced the early pace from outside, gained a slim lead on the turn, but couldn't stay with the winner through the lane. DANCING WITH DEB in traffic early, was unhurried for six furlongs while saving ground, angled out on the turn, then lacked a strong closing response. UNCHARTED WATERS set the pace under pressure to the turn, and gradually tired thereafter. SAFE AT HOME raced within striking distance from outside for seven furlongs and faded. SAID PRIVATELY checked on the first turn, was finished after going a half and was eased in the stretch. UNCHARTED WATERS and SAID PRIVATELY wore mud caulks.

Owners— 1, Lauer Michael E; 2, Ryver Meadow Farms; 3, Lewis Debbie & Lee; 4, Steinberg Philip J; 5, Minassian Harry; 6, Peters Betty M & Beitz Gail P
Trainers— 1, Lauer Michael E; 2, Badgett William Jr; 3, Hennig Mark; 4, Jerkens H Allen; 5, Serpe Philip M; 6, Johnstone Bruce
Overweight: Said Privately (1).
Scratched— Manila Lila (3Jly95 7BEL⁴), Chelsey Flower (23Jly95 7SAR²), Garza (2Jly95 10BEL⁸), Change Fora Dollar (8Jly95 9BEL³)

Under Jerry Bailey, who already had opened up a wide gap for the lead in the jockey standings at the meet, Blushing Maggie cut the corner while rallying near the quarter pole and drew off once straightened away into the lane, winning her off-the-turf allowance by open lengths for the second straight year.

This scenario plays itself out several times each summer. As part of their annual preparations for Saratoga, players are urged to research the past few meets so as not to be caught unaware when these terrific plays present themselves.

August 7

THREE DAYS AFTER Blushing Maggie splashed to victory, the courses had dried sufficiently to permit the resumption of grass racing. The domination of experienced Saratoga grass horses and/or those with the strongest finishing kick resumed as well.

In the morning, Jerry Bailey, who was in the midst of a career-defining, Eclipse Award-winning season as the regular rider of Cigar, had been officially inducted into racing's Hall of Fame, which is located right across the street from the track's main gate on Union Avenue. A few hours later, Bailey was aboard the favorite in the featured $125,000-added National Museum of Racing Hall of Fame Stakes.

The race was a Grade 2 route at nine furlongs, for 3-year-olds on the Mellon (outer) turf course, and appeared very contentious on paper. The race figured to be decided, as so many turf races are, by a combination of class, late speed, and racing luck. Examine the first four betting choices:

8 Saratoga

1⅛ MILES. **(Turf). (1:452) 10th Running of THE NATIONAL MUSEUM OF RACING HALL OF FAME. Purse $125,000 Added. Grade II. 3-year-olds. By subscription of $125 each, which should accompany the nomination. $625 to pass the entry box. $625 to start, with $125,000 added. The added money and all fees to be divided 60% to the winner, 20% to second, 11% to third, 6% to fourth and 3% to fifth. Weight, 123 lbs. Non-winners of $50,000 twice on the turf in 1995, allowed 3 lbs. A graded stakes on the turf, 5 lbs. $50,000 twice at a mile or over, 8 lbs. $30,000 twice over a mile, 11 lbs. Starters to be named at the closing time of entries. Trophies will be presented to the winning owner, trainer and jockey. The New York Racing Association reserves the right to transfer this race to the main track. Closed Saturday, July 22, with 31 nominations.**

Flitch
Own: Loblolly Stable
SMITH M E (84 14 10 17 .17)

Dk. b or br c. 3 (May)
Sire: Demons Begone (Elocutionist)
Dam: Whiffling (Wavering Monarch)
Br: Loblolly Stable (Ky)
Tr: Badgett William Jr (12 1 2 1 .08)

112

Lifetime Record:	13	3	2	3	$236,016						
1995	8	1	1	3	$178,056	Turf	2	0	0	2	$16,456
1994	5	2	1	0	$57,960	Wet	0	0	0	0	
Sar ⓣ	0	0	0	0		Dist ⓣ	0	0	0	0	

16Jly95-9Bel	fm	1¼ [T]	:494 1:141 1:381 2:013	Lexington-G3	91	3	8	86	41½	43	32	Velazquez J R	112 b	7.20	78-13	Green Means Go1191 Nostra1121 Flitch1121	In traffic 3/8 pl	9
10Jun95-10Bel	fm	1 1/16 ⓣ	:24 :472 1:112 1:411 3↑	Alw 38000N3X	89	3	7	74¼	63	42	31¾	Smith M E	113 b	7.30	90-06	Bit Of Puddin120nk Head Trip1201½ Flitch1131	Late gain	10
28May95-9Bel	fst	1⅛	:453 1:094 1:36 1:50	Peter Pan-G2	83	10	4	75	98½	77	79¾	Sellers S J	115 b	6.40	72-22	Citadeed112½ Pat N Jac113nk Treasurer1152½	Wide, no rally	10
22Apr95-9OP	fst	1⅛	:461 1:104 1:373 1:503	Ark Derby-G2	93	4	7	77	66½	22	21¼	Sellers S J	118 b	9.00e	85-17	Dazzling Falls1221¼ Flitch1182¼ On Target122½	4 wide 1/4	8
1Apr95-10Hia	fst	1⅛	:463 1:104 1:353 1:48	Flamingo-G3	92	7	8	67½	67	42½	46	Sellers S J	118	*1.20	96-08	Pyramid Peak118¾ Royal Mitch1225 Bullet Trained118nk	Belated bid	8
11Mar95-10GP	fst	1⅛	:471 1:113 1:362 1:493	Fla Derby-G1	89	1	7	73¾	810	58	47	Day P	122	7.70	82-11	Thunder Gulch122no Suave Prospect1225 Mecke1222	Belated bid, inside	10
15Feb95-7GP	fst	1 1/16	:231 :47 1:113 1:443	Alw 28000N2X	92	4	3	32½	2hd	11½	14¾	Smith M E	119	*.90	85-25	Flitch1194¾ Casperoo119no Royal Mitch122nk	Crowded start, driving	8
3Feb95-9GP	fst	1 1/16	:232 :471 1:113 1:45	Alw 40000NC	90	8	8	88	54	43	35½	Sellers S J	115	7.60	77-25	[D]Jambalaya Jazz1194 Star Standard1151½ Flitch115nk	Wide final turn, wide str, late rally	8
8Oct94-8Bel	fst	1 1/16	:232 :461 1:111 1:44	Champagne-G1	77	6	11	1112	94½	76	713½	Smith M E	122	9.60	69-17	Timber Country122½ Sierra Diablo1226½ On Target122nk	Checked break	11
22Sep94-7Bel	fst	1 1/16	:232 :472 1:113 1:433	Alw 32000N1X	83	5	5	52½	41	2½	1¾	Smith M E	117	*1.60	84-27	Flitch117¾ Reality Road1172 Tony Riccio1171¼	Driving	5

WORKOUTS: Jly 28 Sar [T] 5f fm 1:00 H (d) *1/3* Jly 13 Bel [T] 4f fm :492 B (d) *12/18* Jly 8 Bel 5f fst 1:004 B *6/27* Jly 2 Bel 4f sly :511 B *4/5* Jun 24 Bel 5f fst 1:013 H *20/64* Jun 17 Bel 4f fst :493 B *29/63*

Diplomatic Jet
Own: Hooper Fred W
VELAZQUEZ J R (62 11 8 4 .18)

Ch. c. 3 (Mar)
Sire: Roman Diplomat (Roberto)
Dam: Precious Jet (Tri Jet)
Br: Hooper Fred W (Fla)
Tr: Picou James E (10 3 1 0 .30)

120

Lifetime Record:	13	4	1	2	$124,982						
1995	3	1	0	0	$26,200	Turf	9	4	1	1	$118,982
1994	10	3	1	2	$98,782	Wet	0	0	0	0	
Sar ⓣ	1	1	0	0	$22,800	Dist ⓣ	1	0	0	0	$3,000

21Jly95-5Sar	fm	1 1/16 ⓣ	:223 :454 1:094 1:403 3↑	Alw 38000N$Y	99	4	7	75¾	53½	22	11¾	Velazquez J R	110	29.25	96-04	DiplomticJt1101¾ SrWollston1133½ LowrEgypt1142	Five wide, going away	10
1Feb95-4GP	fm	*1 ⓣ	:241 :471 1:101 1:352	Alw 40000NC	78	1	6	63½	53½	54¼	56	Bailey J D	L 117	2.70	97-03	Marcie's Ensign115hd Dan's Bet1151 NativeRegent1221¼	Failed to menace	7
2Jan95-[illegible]Crc	fm	1⅛ ⓣ	:49 1:131 1:382 1:5[illegible]	Trop Pk Dby-G3	7[illegible]	11	[illegible]	93½	74¼	42	54	Bailey J D	L 119	4.20	81 —	Mecke117¾ Val's Prince1121¼ Claudius119½	[illegible] bid between	14
27Nov94-10Crc	fm	1 1/16 ⓣ	:231 :474 1:113 1:44	City of Miam39k	83	9	5	54	54	55	52¼	Boulanger G	120	*1.30	78-29	Dan's Bet115hd Dixie Dynasty1151¾ Val's Prince115nk	Rallied	11
5Nov94-3Crc	fm	1 1/16 ⓣ	:224 :47 1:103 1:412	Alw 24500NC	84	1	4	44½	42¾	33	32¾	Boulanger G	120	*.60	90-07	Mecke1131¾ Val's Prince1151 Diplomatic Jet1203¼	Lacked response	9
8Oct94-8Bel	fst	1 1/16	:232 :461 1:111 1:44	Champagne-G1	73	7	7	83	82½	98½	916	Perret C	122	11.40	66-17	Timber Country122½ Sierra Diablo1226½ On Target122nk	Faded	11
25Sep94-6Bel	sf	1 1/16 [T]	:251 :491 1:141 1:463	Pilgrim-G3	99	4	2	21	2hd	15	112	Bailey J D	117	*.90	63-37	Diplomatic Jet11712 Houston Connection1156 Islamabad1153½	Ridden out	5
10Sep94-2Bel	fm	1 ⓣ	:23 :46 1:101 1:343	Alw 32000N1X	88	6	3	2½	2½	13	16¾	Bailey J D	117	2.60	89-11	Diplomatic Jet1176¾ Manila Thriller1175 Reality Road1172¼	Mild drive	7
28Aug94-11Mth	gd	1 ⓣ	:23 :472 1:124 1:384	ContntalMile30k	60	6	4	4½	2½	31½	26¾	Santagata N	119	2.90	65-25	My Sweet Lord1136¾ Diplomatic Jet119hd Culinary Delight11910	Held place	11
4Jly94-3Bel	fm	6f ⓣ	:221 :46 :574 1:094	Md Sp Wt	79	6	1	2hd	2hd	1hd	1nk	Bailey J D	115	7.80	87-13	Diplomatic Jet115nk Blues Fan1152 Banquet1153	Driving	11

WORKOUTS: Aug 5 Sar 3f fst :37 B *9/16* Jly 28 Sar [T] 6f fm 1:15 B (d) *2/2* Jly 17 Bel 1 fst 1:414 H *1/1* Jly 15 Bel 3f fst :353 H *5/30* Jly 10 Bel 1 fst 1:43 B *1/1* Jly 4 Bel 5f fst 1:013 B *10/30*

Nostra
Own: Condren & Cornacchia & Paulson
KRONE J A (62 6 12 4 .10)

B. c. 3 (Mar)
Sire: Greinton (GB) (Green Dancer)
Dam: Index's (Storm Bird)
Br: Paulson Allen E (Ky)
Tr: Zito Nicholas P (22 2 3 4 .09)

112

Lifetime Record: 11 2 7 2 $129,896

1995	7	1	5	1	$95,536	Turf	5 0 4 1	$66,536
1994	4	1	2	1	$34,360	Wet	3 1 2 0	$31,760
Sar Ⓣ	0	0	0	0		Dist Ⓣ	0 0 0 0	

16Jly95–9Bel fm 1¼ 🅃 :494 1:141 1:381 2:013 Lexington-G3 93 6 3 43 1hd 1½ 21 Krone J A 112 4.30 79–13 Green Means Go1191 Nostra1121 Flitch1121 Held well 9
11Jun95–6Bel fm 1¼ 🅃 :474 1:12 1:36 2:00 3↑ Alw 36000N2X 92 9 4 54½ 52½ 3½ 2¾ Krone J A 110 3.25 87–08 Proceeded120¾ Nostra110no Moscow Magic120nk Bid, held place 9
5May95–8CD fm 1 1/16 Ⓣ :231 :462 1:103 1:42 AmericanTurf118k 96 4 5 45 3nk 1hd 21½ Krone J A L 116 *3.10e 92–06 UnanimousVote1201½ Nostra1162 NtiveRegent123hd Bid, led, second best 12
9Apr95–8Kee fm 1 1/16 Ⓣ :223 :462 1:112 1:44 Transylvania68k 87 5 2 2½ 2hd 2½ 53 Bailey J D 118 3.20 83–12 🄳Ops Smile113nk Crimson Guard118hd 🄳Hawk Attack1132½ Bid, weakened 9
Placed third through disqualification.
14Mar95–9GP fst 1⅛ ⊗ :484 1:123 1:372 1:51 Palm Beach-G3 92 3 1 1½ 1½ 21½ 21 Bailey J D 114 *.20e 81–24 Admiralty1141 Nostra11415 Smells And Bells11418 4
Steadied midstr, best of others
20Feb95–9GP sly 1 1/16 ⊗ :23 :471 1:122 1:45 Lord Avie50k 92 6 3 1hd 2hd 2hd 2nk Bailey J D 112 *1.50 83–20 Marcie's Ensign114nk Nostra112nk Mecke12212 10
Broke inward start, gave way grudgingly
30Jan95–6GP sly 1 1/16 ⊗ :232 :48 1:132 1:462 Alw 26000N2L 88 7 3 33 22½ 2½ 1½ Bailey J D 120 *1.60 76–34 Nostra120½ Claramount Hill1176½ Otto's Brother120nk Fully extended 11
20Nov94–5Aqu fst 1 ⊗ :234 :472 1:123 1:374 Md Sp Wt 82 3 3 21½ 2½ 1½ 11¾ Beckner D V5 113 *1.80 79–25 Nostra1131¾ Storm Hawk118¾ Paragallo's Hope1188½ Driving 10
28Oct94–5Aqu fst 1 :224 :462 1:113 1:373 Md Sp Wt 70 8 3 31½ 32½ 35 38 Beckner D V5 113 *1.05 72–23 Principality1132 Slice Of Reality1186 Nostra1134¼ No late bid 8
12Oct94–3Bel fm 1 1/16 Ⓣ :234 :473 1:12 1:423 Md Sp Wt 80 2 3 32½ 41½ 2½ 2nk Beckner D V5 113 4.60e 85–18 Claudius118nk Nostra1133 Noble 'n Heart1181¼ Gamely 10

WORKOUTS: Jly 31 Sar tr.t 5f fst 1:041 B 7/12 Jly 24 Sar tr.t 4f fst :52 B 23/29 Jly 12 Bel 4f fst :50 B 47/60 ●Jly 6 Bel 5f fst 1:004 H 1/16 Jun 28 Bel 5f fst 1:012 B 17/42 Jun 21 Bel 5f fst 1:024 B 18/23

Claudius
Own: Al Maktoum Mohammed
BAILEY J D (84 19 8 12 .23)

Ch. c. 3 (Mar)
Sire: Majestic Light (Majestic Prince)
Dam: Classy Ellie (Irish River (Fr))
Br: Sturgill Richard & William (Ky)
Tr: Mott William I (22 8 4 3 .36)

120

Lifetime Record: 9 4 2 2 $202,560

1995	5	2	1	1	$106,680	Turf	9 4 2 2	$202,560
1994	4	2	1	1	$95,880	Wet	0 0 0 0	
Sar Ⓣ	0	0	0	0		Dist Ⓣ	1 0 0 1	$11,000

1Jly95–9Mth fm 1 1/16 Ⓣ :223 :451 1:09 1:41 + LamplightrH-G3 95 10 10 1014 95¾ 51½ 11 McCauley W H L 119 *1.40 93–07 Claudius1191 Smells And Bells116nk Why Stop Now113¾ 6 wide, driving 10
27May95–9GS fm 1 1/16 Ⓣ :24 :472 1:113 1:43 JerseyDerby-G2 94 2 9 911 35½ 33 2½ Bailey J D L 119 3.80 96–09 Da Hoss119½ Claudius1191¼ Crimson Guard123no 10
Traffic, stretch
22Apr95–5Aqu gd 1 1/16 Ⓣ :241 :484 1:141 1:453 3↑ Alw 34000N2X 90 6 6 611 65½ 1hd 13 Smith M E 113 b *.85 81–16 Claudius1133 Wavering Man120½ Geret's Jewel1202¾ 6
Awaited room 3/8, altered course 3/16 pl
29Jan95–5GP fm 1 1/16 ⊗ :243 :493 1:133 1:43 + Alw 28000N2X 62 4 8 52½ 68¼ 69¼ 510 Smith M E L 117 *.40 71–06 Cuzzin Jeb120¾ Andiamo1203 Highest Yield1172¼ No threat 8
2Jan95–[illegible]Crc fm 1⅛ Ⓣ :49 1:131 1:382 1:51 Trop Pk Dby-G3 84 1 14 148½ 138¾ 86½ 32 Smith M E L 119 *1.40 83 – Mecke117¾ Val's Prince1121¼ Claudius119½ 14
8-wide stretch, gained
26Nov94–5Hol gd 1 Ⓣ :23 :47 1:111 1:37 Generous-G3 88 1 8 44 43 43½ 31½ Desormeaux K J LB 121 *2.20 77–21 Native Regent1211 Dangerous Scenario116½ Claudius1211¾ Late bid 9
27Oct94–8Kee fm 1 1/16 Ⓣ :234 :49 1:142 1:452 Hopemont53k 82 5 8 94½ 52½ 41½ 11¼ Velazquez J R 115 *1.80 79–18 Claudius1151¼ Hawk Attack115no Dixie Dynasty1151½ 10
Bumped start, driving rail
12Oct94–3Bel fm 1 1/16 Ⓣ :234 :473 1:12 1:423 Md Sp Wt 81 5 6 64 51¾ 31 1nk Velazquez J R 118 *.70 85–18 Claudius118nk Nostra1133 Noble 'n Heart1181¼ Wide, driving 10
8Sep94–9Bel fm 1 Ⓣ :233 :464 1:113 1:353 Md Sp Wt 87 7 9 86¾ 63½ 41 2no Velazquez J R 118 15.00 84–13 Islamabad118no Claudius1184¾ Noble 'n Heart1183 Brk slow, rallied 11

WORKOUTS: Aug 2 Sar Ⓣ 5f fm 1:062 B (d) 1/1 Jly 25 Bel 7f fst 1:311 B 1/1 Jly 19 Bel 5f fst 1:02 B 14/21 Jly 13 Bel 🅃 5f fm 1:06 B (d) 9/9 Jun 24 Bel 6f fst 1:164 B 14/17 Jun 15 Bel 🅃 7f fm 1:292 B (d) 2/2

According to the recent Beyer Speed Figures of the quartet, the race was a toss-up among Diplomatic Jet, who had earned a 99 in defeating older classified allowance rivals over the same course on opening day, July 21; Nostra, who had been second best in his last three turf races with figures of 96, 92, and 93; and Claudius, with figures of 95 and 94 in his two most recent starts, both graded stakes on the New Jersey circuit. Flitch, according to his final-time figures of 91 and 89 in his first two starts on grass, was rated several lengths slower than the top trio.

But as we touched on with Duda in Belmont's Sheepshead Bay back in June, grass racing is much different than dirt racing, and in most situations class and closing fractions are the most predictive factors. I carry Xeroxed copies of the "Turf Figure Charts" from Quinn's afore-mentioned *Figure Handicapping* with me whenever I'm at the track. This is how the Hall of Fame contenders shaped up in terms of recent finishing ability — adjusted for lengths lost or gained in their respective final fractions:

Flitch	106, 116
Diplomatic Jet	100
Nostra	106, 106
Claudius	104, 106

Flitch's final quarter of :23 3/5 had earned a finishing figure of 106 in the Lexington, a closing response as potent as anyone else in this field, and he earned it despite encountering traffic at the 3/8's pole while rallying into a slow-paced mile and a quarter; the presence of one-dimensional speedballs Debonair Dan and No Secrets in this shorter route ensured a demanding pace.

The eye-catching figure, though, was the 116 Flitch earned in a N3X allowance against older horses when placed on grass for the first time — ironically enough, on the Belmont

Stakes undercard June 10. Flitch's half-brother, the ill-fated Preakness-winner and 3-year-old champion Prairie Bayou, had broken down on the backstretch as the favorite in the Belmont Stakes a year earlier. Mike Smith, an Eclipse-winning jockey the past two years, had ridden Prairie Bayou on that tragic afternoon, and he had been aboard Flitch when the Loblolly-owned colt roared home his final five-sixteenths of a mile in :29 3/5 seconds on June 10. John Velazquez had ridden Flitch in the Lexington but had also ridden Diplomatic Jet in his most recent race; he opted to stay with Diplomatic Jet in the Hall of Fame, enabling Smith to regain the mount on Flitch.

That figure of 116 begged attention, as it was faster by several lengths than anything his main rivals had accomplished. Moreover, Flitch had gained considerable seasoning in graded stakes on dirt before his connections decided that his late-running style was better suited to grass, and he was in receipt of an eight-pound pull in the weights from Claudius and Diplomatic Jet; under the Hall of Fame's allowance conditions, Flitch carried the same weight as Nostra — a colt still eligible for a N2X allowance.

Claudius was a legitimate contender in the race but 7-5 was an underlay, considering that his two best races had come at a shorter distance while on Lasix. Claudius would have to race without Lasix in the Hall of Fame, because the medication was not scheduled to be legalized in New York until Belmont's fall meet began on September 1.

Flitch was an inviting 5-1. With $80 to invest in the race, I bet $50 to win, and keyed him in the first and second positions of $2 trifectas (still called triples at the time) with the other three ($24). In the event that he ran into traffic and only managed to finish third, I keyed him in the that position underneath the others in $1 trifectas, which cost another $6:

EIGHTH RACE
Saratoga
AUGUST 7, 1995

1⅛ MILES. (Turf)(1.45²) 10th Running of THE NATIONAL MUSEUM OF RACING HALL OF FAME. Purse $125,000 Added. Grade II. 3-year-olds. By subscription of $125 each, which should accompany the nomination. $625 to pass the entry box. $625 to start, with $125,000 added. The added money and all fees to be divided 60% to the winner, 20% to second, 11% to third, 6% to fourth and 3% to fifth. Weight, 123 lbs. Non-winners of $50,000 twice on the turf in 1995, allowed 3 lbs. A graded stakes on the turf, 5 lbs. $50,000 twice at a mile or over, 8 lbs. $30,000 twice over a mile, 11 lbs. Starters to be named at the closing time of entries. Trophies will be presented to the winning owner, trainer and jockey. The New York Racing Association reserves the right to transfer this race to the main track. Closed Saturday, July 22, with 31 nominations.

Value of Race: $139,500 Winner $83,700; second $27,900; third $15,345; fourth $8,370; fifth $4,185. Mutuel Pool $437,061.00 Exacta Pool $429,583.00 Triple Pool $371,395.00

Last Raced	Horse	M/Eqt. A.Wt	PP	St	¼	½	¾	Str	Fin	Jockey	Odds $1
16Jly95 9Bel³	Flitch	b 3 113	1	2	6²	6½	5ʰᵈ	3ʰᵈ	1ⁿᵏ	Smith M E	5.50
21Jly95 5Sar¹	Diplomatic Jet	3 120	2	1	3ʰᵈ	3ʰᵈ	4²	1½	2³½	Velazquez J R	4.40
16Jly95 9Bel²	Nostra	3 112	5	5	4¹½	4¹½	3ʰᵈ	4²	3ⁿᵒ	Krone J A	7.10
1Jly95 9Mth¹	Claudius	3 120	6	8	8	8	8	5¹½	4³½	Bailey J D	1.40
16Jly95 9Bel⁴	Smells And Bells	b 3 112	7	6	7⁴	7¹½	7¹½	6²	5ⁿᵒ	Davis R G	8.20
27Jly95 7Sar²	No Secrets	3 113	3	3	2²	2¹½	2¹½	2ʰᵈ	6⁷	Migliore R	14.20
2Jly95 9AP²	Sikkim	b 3 113	8	7	5ʰᵈ	5¹	6½	7⁷	7¹²	Santos J A	13.70
28Jly95 4Sar¹	Debonair Dan	b 3 120	4	4	1¹½	1½	1ʰᵈ	8	8	Chavez J F	14.70

OFF AT 4:45 Start Good. Won driving. Time, :22⁴, :47², 1:11², 1:36¹, 1:48 Course good.

$2 Mutuel Prices:

1-FLITCH		13.00	6.70	4.90
2-DIPLOMATIC JET			5.90	5.20
5-NOSTRA				5.30

$2 EXACTA 1-2 PAID $92.00 $2 TRIPLE 1-2-5 PAID $401.50

Dk. b. or br. c, (May), by Demons Begone–Whiffling, by Wavering Monarch. Trainer Badgett William Jr. Bred by Loblolly Stable (Ky).

FLITCH settled in good position while saving ground along the backstretch, angled out to launch his bid on the turn, rallied four wide into the stretch, then finished determindly to wear down DIPLOMATIC JET in the final twenty yards. DIPLOMATIC JET was rated in good position just behind the dueling leaders while saving ground, checked a bit while waiting patiently for room nearing the quarter pole, slipped through along the rail to gain the lead in midstretch, continued on the front into deep stretch, but couldn't hold the winner safe. NOSTRA raced just outside DIPLOMATIC JET for five furlongs, edged closer while three wide on the turn, bumped with the winner while drifting out briefly in upper stretch, battled heads apart inside FLITCH into midstretch, then weakened in the final eighth. CLAUDIUS unhurried early, trailed to the top of the turn, angled out in upper stretch, failed to threaten with a mild late rally. SMELLS AND BELLS reserved for six furlongs, lodged a mild rally from outside on the turn, then flattened out. NO SECRETS angled outside DEBONAIR DAN entering the backstretch, forced the pace from outside for six furlongs, gained a slim lead on the turn, continued on the front into upper stretch then tired in the final eighth. SIKKIM raced within striking distance to the turn and lacked a further response. DEBONAIR DAN set the pace under pressure while saving ground to the far turn then gave way.

Owners— 1. Loblolly Stable; 2, Hooper Fred W; 3, Condren & Cornacchia & Paulson; 4, Al Maktoum Mohammed; 5, Downey Walter; 6, Gehl & G Lack Farm & Lazer II Stble; 7, Hudson River Farms; 8, Pokoik Lee

Trainers— 1, Badgett William Jr; 2, Picou James C; 3, Zito Nicholas P; 4, Mott William I; 5, Edwards Oliver; 6, Klesaris Robert P; 7, Kelly Larry; 8, Sciacca Gary

Overweight: Flitch (1), No Secrets (1), Sikkim (1).

Scratched— Claramount Hill (29Jly95 7SAR⁴)

$2 Pick-3 (3-4-1) Paid $193.00; Pick-3 Pool $186,526. $2 Pick-6
(8-6-8-3-4-1) 5 Correct 5 Tickets Paid $2,950.00; Pick-6 Pool
$78,683; Carryover Pool $44,259.

Flitch angled to the outside on the far turn while Diplomatic Jet saved ground waiting for an opening. It looked as though Diplomatic Jet wouldn't get through, but he forged to the lead when a hole opened in midstretch and seemed enroute to victory. But Flitch had by now gathered a full head of steam on the outside, and closed relentlessly to nail Diplomatic Jet in the final strides. Had no trifecta wagering been offered, the astronomical $92 exacta linking the third and second betting choices would've been quite all right with me.

THE HALL OF FAME STAKES completed a late Pick 3 (races 6, 7, & 8) worth $193. The first leg was also a nine-furlong grass race (this one on the inner course), and the winner looked like this:

Golden Explosive
Own: Joques Farm
SANTOS J A (75 5 11 11 .07) **$35,000**

Dk. b or br h. 7
Sire: Explosive Bid (Explodent)
Dam: Lady Flash (Charles Elliott)
Br: Stanton Patricia Anne (Fla)
Tr: Moschera Gasper S (24 3 4 3 .13)

114

Lifetime Record:	46	10	5	8	$188,556						
1995	3	1	0	2	$24,160	Turf	33	9	2	6	$168,580
1994	7	0	0	1	$4,920	Wet	0	0	0	0	
Sar (T)	5	2	0	1	$34,080	Dist (T)	7	2	1	0	$37,450

30Jun95-6Bel	fm	$1\frac{1}{16}$ [T]	$:24^3$	:48	$1:11^3$	$1:41^4$	Clm 40000	**97**	2	1	1^1	1^1	1^2	1^4	Santos J A	114	4.70	87–14	Golden Explosive114^4 Silver Safari118^{nk} Summer Senate111^1	Drew away	9
16Jun95-9Bel	fm	1 (T)	:22	:44	$1:09^2$	$1:33^4$	Clm 40000	**90**	7	2	2^9	2^1	1^1	$3^{2\frac{1}{2}}$	Smith M E	113	13.30	91–12	Fanchee$112^{\frac{3}{4}}$ Zee Buck112^{nk} Golden Explosive113^{nk}	Bid, weakened	12
29May95-2Bel	fm	$1\frac{1}{16}$ [T]	$:23^4$	$:46^3$	1:11	$1:41^4$	Clm 30000	**73**	6	1	1^{hd}	1^{hd}	$3^{3\frac{1}{2}}$	3^8	Smith M E	113	7.20	79–14	Zee Buck$114^{2\frac{1}{2}}$ Alpstein$112^{5\frac{1}{2}}$ Golden Explosive113^{nk}	Dueled, weakened	10
27Oct94-4Aqu	fm	$1\frac{1}{8}$ (T)	$:46^3$	$1:11^4$	$1:37^1$	1:50	3↑ Clm 35000	**71**	2	1	1^7	$1^{1\frac{1}{2}}$	$7^{2\frac{3}{4}}$	$7^{8\frac{1}{4}}$	Perez R B5	112	11.50	82–14	Wave Your Flag117^{nk} Alpine Choice117^{no} Border Cat$119^{1\frac{3}{4}}$	Used in pace	12
5Oct94-2Bel	gd	$1\frac{1}{16}$ (T)	$:23^3$	$:47^3$	1:12	$1:42^2$	3↑ Clm 35000	**64**	4	1	1^1	2^{hd}	5^4	$7^{10\frac{1}{2}}$	Perez R B5	112	4.30	75–21	Border Cat$117^{1\frac{1}{2}}$ Threeharvardavenue$117^{1\frac{1}{2}}$ Ijtihaad117^{nk}	Used in pace	10
11Sep94-9Bel	fm	$1\frac{1}{16}$ (T)	$:23^1$	$:46^1$	$1:10^1$	$1:40^3$	3↑ Clm 35000	**81**	1	1	1^1	$1^{\frac{1}{2}}$	$2^{\frac{1}{2}}$	$3^{4\frac{1}{4}}$	Smith M E	117	10.10	91–09	Clover City$117^{2\frac{1}{4}}$ Known Ranger117^2 Golden Explosive$117^{2\frac{3}{4}}$	Speed, tired	12
12Aug94-9Sar	fm	$1\frac{3}{16}$ (T)	$:46^1$	$1:10^2$	1:35	$1:53^3$	3↑ Clm 35000	**39**	4	1	1^1	2^{hd}	10^{14}	$11^{22\frac{3}{4}}$	Smith M E	117	5.20	74–10	Alpstein119^{hd} No Fumar117^2 Turtle Beach117^{nk}	Dueled inside	11
28Jun94-1Bel	fm	$1\frac{1}{16}$ (T)	$:23^2$	:46	1:10	$1:41^1$	Clm 35000	**84**	6	1	1^1	$1^{\frac{1}{2}}$	$2^{\frac{1}{2}}$	$4^{5\frac{1}{4}}$	Smith M E	117	4.50	87–12	Cranshw'sCorner117^2 SoSterling117^1 NorthernWitness$117^{2\frac{1}{4}}$	Weakened	10
21Jun94-4Bel	fm	$1\frac{1}{16}$ [T]	$:24^3$	$:48^1$	$1:12^2$	1:43	Clm 35000	**84**	6	1	1^2	1^1	2^2	$4^{4\frac{3}{4}}$	Smith M E	117	3.80	76–23	Southern Slew117^{nk} Bonus Award$119^{\frac{1}{2}}$ Bye Union Ave.117^4	Weakened	10
2Jun94-1Bel	fm	$1\frac{1}{16}$ (T)	$:23^2$	$:47^1$	$1:11^3$	$1:41^2$	Clm 35000	**87**	6	1	1^1	$1^{1\frac{1}{2}}$	1^{hd}	$5^{3\frac{1}{2}}$	Smith M E	117	3.00	87–13	Zee Buck$119^{2\frac{1}{2}}$ Turning For Home117^{hd} Glen Echo$117^{\frac{3}{4}}$	Used in pace	10

WORKOUTS: Aug 2 Sar tr.t 3f fst :38 B *7/14* Jly 26 Sar tr.t 4f fst $:49^2$ H *2/27* Jly 20 Sar tr.t 3f fst $:37^3$ B *5/16* Jly 17 Bel 4f fst $:48^4$ B *21/62*

Golden Explosive was the field's only two-time winner at the distance, and had won twice from five previous starts on Saratoga grass; indeed he was the only horse in the race with a Spa grass win.

SIXTH RACE **Saratoga** **AUGUST 7, 1995**

1⅛ MILES. (Inner Turf)(1.47) CLAIMING. Purse $26,000. 3-year-olds and upward. Weights: 3-year-olds, 116 lbs. Older, 122 lbs. Non-winners of three races at a mile or over since March 15, allowed 2 lbs. Of two races over a mile since April 10, 4 lbs. Of a race over nine furlongs since June 1, 6 lbs. Claiming price $40,000; if for $35,000 allowed 2 lbs.

Value of Race: $26,000 Winner $15,600; second $5,200; third $2,860; fourth $1,560; fifth $780. Mutuel Pool $404,228.00 Exacta Pool $596,677.00

Last Raced	Horse	M/Eqt.	A.	Wt	PP	St	¼	½	¾	Str	Fin	Jockey	Cl'g Pr	Odds $1
30Jun95 6Bel1	Golden Explosive		7	114	3	2	1^3	1^2	$1^{\frac{1}{2}}$	$1^{1\frac{1}{2}}$	$1^{3\frac{1}{2}}$	Santos J A	35000	2.15
12Jly95 9Bel3	Jessup North		5	118	7	5	$2^{\frac{1}{2}}$	3^{hd}	$2^{1\frac{1}{2}}$	$2^{\frac{1}{2}}$	2^{nk}	Velasquez J	35000	29.50
21Jly95 5Sar6	Secret Fan	b	5	116	5	6	$7^{1\frac{1}{2}}$	$5^{\frac{1}{2}}$	$4^{1\frac{1}{2}}$	$3^{1\frac{1}{2}}$	$3^{1\frac{1}{4}}$	Sellers S J	40000	6.80
1Jly95 6Mth3	Royal Ninja		9	114	10	1	9^1	9^3	8^1	8^1	$4^{\frac{1}{2}}$	Perez R B	35000	13.30
14Jly95 4Mth7	Bewray	b	7	114	9	10	$8^{1\frac{1}{2}}$	7^2	7^2	$7^{\frac{1}{2}}$	5no	Bailey J D	35000	30.75
30Jun95 6Bel8	Dr. Alfoos	b	5	114	8	7	$5^{\frac{1}{2}}$	$2^{\frac{1}{2}}$	3^{hd}	6^{hd}	6no	Krone J A	35000	13.60
4Jly95 5Bel2	Tamara R.	b	4	114	1	3	$3^{\frac{1}{2}}$	4^1	5^{hd}	$5^{\frac{1}{2}}$	7^{nk}	Day P	35000	7.50
30Jun95 6Bel5	Zee Buck	f	7	114	6	9	10	10	9^{10}	9^{24}	8^{hd}	Chavez J F	35000	3.70
29Jly95 5Sar10	Dynamite Laugh	b	4	116	2	8	$6^{\frac{1}{2}}$	$6^{\frac{1}{2}}$	$6^{\frac{1}{2}}$	$4^{\frac{1}{2}}$	9	Maple E	40000	33.25
4Jly95 10Bel1	Bonus Award		5	114	4	4	4^{hd}	8^3	10	10	—	Alvarado F T	35000	4.60

Bonus Award:Eased

OFF AT 3:39 Start Good. Won driving. Time, $:22^4$, $:48^1$, $1:12^3$, 1:37, $1:49^1$ Course good.

$2 Mutuel Prices:				
	3–GOLDEN EXPLOSIVE	6.30	4.70	3.40
	7–JESSUP NORTH		21.60	10.40
	5–SECRET FAN			4.60

$2 EXACTA 3–7 PAID $157.50

Dk. b. or br. h, by Explosive Bid–Lady Flash, by Charles Elliott. Trainer Moschera Gasper S. Bred by Stanton Patricia Anne (Fla).

GOLDEN EXPLOSIVE sprinted clear in the early stages, set the pace slightly off the rail to the turn, shook off JESSUP NORTH in upper stretch, then drew away under good handling. JESSUP NORTH never far back, made a run along the rail to

Golden Explosive went wire-to-wire, something of a rarity on the turf but possible when a sharp horse comfortable with the footing attains an easy lead. He returned $6.30 as the public choice. Brilliant Patriot won the seventh race, run on the main track, as the $6.60 second choice, and Flitch capped the $193 Pick 3. A straight $2 win parlay on the trio was worth a mere $135, so players received an extremely good value in the Pick 3, which is hardly an unusual state of affairs.

PLAYERS WHO NEEDED further proof of the dynamics of late speed as opposed to final-time figures on turf didn't have to wait long. Exactly one week later, an open allowance at nine furlongs on the outer turf carried a $50,000 purse, and brought together several 3-year-old fillies who had contested divisions of the Grade 3 Nijana Stakes twelve days earlier. Scan the records of the two favorites:

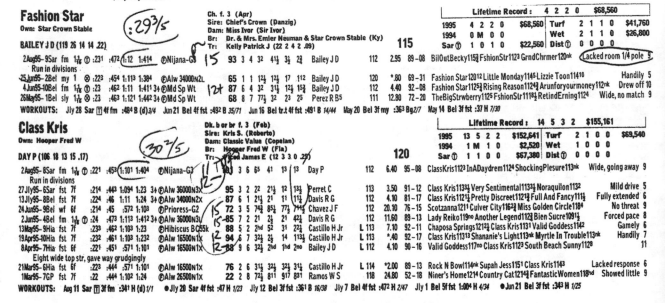

Class Kris had won her division of the Nijana by three convincing lengths in 1:40 4/5, earning a Beyer of 101. In the second division, Fashion Star had finished a close second, but the race had gone a full second slower than Class Kris' heat, and Fashion Star earned a 93, which meant Class Kris had run roughly six lengths faster.

Class Kris' Beyer advantage notwithstanding, Fashion Star had superior late speed and was very likely to win their head-to-head confrontation decisively. And because their races had been run on the same course on the same day, players did not need charts of any kind to see the considerable spread between the two.

Class Kris had been a length behind after six furlongs and had led to the wire August 2, giving her an adjusted final five-sixteenths in :30 2/5 seconds. Fashion Star had also gained roughly a length, but she was running into a much faster late pace, and her adjusted final fraction was :29 3/5 — four lengths faster than Class Kris. Noteworthy is that Fashion Star had delivered the faster final fraction despite a trouble line that said, "Lacked room 1/4 pole."

The result chart tells the tale:

EIGHTH RACE
Saratoga
AUGUST 14, 1995

1⅛ MILES. (Turf)(1.452) ALLOWANCE. Purse $50,000. Fillies, 3-year-olds. Weight, 123 lbs. Non-winners of $35,000 twice on the turf in 1995, allowed 3 lbs. $35,000 at a mile or over, 5 lbs. $21,000 twice on the turf, 8 lbs. $21,000, 11 lbs.

Value of Race: $50,000 Winner $30,000; second $10,000; third $5,500; fourth $3,000; fifth $1,500. Mutuel Pools Not Available

Last Raced	Horse	M/Eqt.	A.	Wt	PP	St	¼	½	¾	Str	Fin	Jockey	Odds $1
2Aug95 9Sar2	Fashion Star		3	115	5	7	41	3½	22	1hd	12½	Bailey J D	2.25
2Aug95 8Sar1	Class Kris		3	120	6	6	11½	11	1½	22	2½	Day P	1.95
2Aug95 9Sar6	Hawaiian Brave		3	112	3	3	62	61	5½	3½	31¾	Krone J A	2.75
2Aug95 8Sar4	Another Legend		3	118	1	1	31	41½	31	45	46½	Luzzi M J	9.30
18Jly95 7Lrl1	Short Time	b	3	112	4	4	7	7	7	58	520	Smith M E	17.20
5Aug95 7Sar3	Nappelon	b	3	120	2	2	52	52	63	7	6nk	Santos J A	23.70
30Jly95 3Sar1	Fantastic Women		3	115	7	5	21	2½	43	6½	7	Chavez J F	11.70

OFF AT 4:48 Start Good. Won driving. Time, :224, :463, 1:104, 1:36, 1:483 Course yielding.

$2 Mutuel Prices:			
6–FASHION STAR	6.50	3.20	2.40
7–CLASS KRIS		2.90	2.10
4–HAWAIIAN BRAVE			2.40

$2 EXACTA 6–7 PAID $14.00 $2 TRIPLE 6–7–4 PAID $32.20

Ch. f, (Apr), by Chief's Crown–Miss Ivor, by Sir Ivor. Trainer Kelly Patrick J. Bred by Dr. & Mrs. Emler Neuman & Star Crown Stable (Ky).

FASHION STAR settled just off the early pace, took up chase after CLASS KRIS on the turn, battled heads apart with that one into midstretch, then edged away under brisk urging. CLASS KRIS raced uncontested on the lead for five furlongs, dug in when challenged leaving the turn, battled heads apart into midstretch, but couldn't stay with the winner through the final eighth.

Class Kris secured an uncontested lead soon after the start and remained clear through the opening half — which would've been a telling tactical edge had the race been on dirt. On turf, it's a different ballgame. Fashion Star was allowed to settle into stride early, went after the pacesetter in earnest on the far turn, and edged clear to a daylight victory after gaining command in midstretch. The faster horse in terms of final time speed figures had been defeated by the faster late-pace horse.

It happens all the time.

August 10

SARATOGA OFFERS some of the classiest and competitive racing in the country, but not every race is an artistic success. That's okay, because some high-percentage plays are to be found in fields filled with marginal talent. Take the second race on August 10, for instance, a maiden sprint for New York-breds at six and a half furlongs:

2 **Saratoga**

6½ Furlongs **(1:142) MAIDEN SPECIAL WEIGHT. Purse $30,000. 3-year-olds and upward, foaled in New York State and approved by the New York State Bred Registry. Weights: 3-year-olds, 117 lbs. Older, 121 lbs. (Preference to horses that have not started for $40,000 or less in their last three starts.)**

Dapper Dutchman
Own: Bailie Sally A
RYDOWSKI S R (13 1 1 1 .08)

B. c. 3 (Apr)
Sire: Carr de Naskra (Star de Naskra)
Dam: Isle of Pines (Wajima)
Br: Sally Ann Bailie (NY)
Tr: Bailie Sally A (—)

117

Lifetime Record:	1 M 0 0		$0
1995	1 M 0 0	Turf	0 0 0 0
1994	0 M 0 0	Wet	0 0 0 0
Sar	0 0 0 0	Dist	0 0 0 0

15Jly95–2Bel fst 6f :224 :462 :584 1:113 3↑ [S]Md Sp Wt 30– **42** 5 5 62½ 52¾ 57 612½ Rydowski S R 113 41.25 70–11 Matthew W.1143 Scanner Pro1132½ Programable1143 Saved ground 12

WORKOUTS: ●Aug 8 Bel tr.t 3f fst :362 H *1/17* Jly 30 Bel 4f fst :473 H *9/45* Jly 22 Bel 4f fst :473 H *2/15* Jun 30 Bel 5f fst 1:014 H *14/35* Jun 23 Bel 5f gd 1:014 H *13/22* Jun 5 Bel tr.t 4f fst :521 B *4/4*

Plattkin
Own: Martino Phyllis
LOVATO F JR (7 1 2 0 .14)

B. g. 4
Sire: Late Act (Stage Door Johnny)
Dam: Glut's Kin (Water Prince)
Br: Galloping Acres Farm (NY)
Tr: Martino Phyllis (—)

121

Lifetime Record:	9 M 0 0		$720
1995	9 M 0 0 $720	Turf	0 0 0 0
1994	0 M 0 0	Wet	0 0 0 0
Sar	0 0 0 0	Dist	2 0 0 0

13Apr95–4Aqu fst 1 :232 :462 1:114 1:371 Md Sp Wt — 4 6 62¾ 65½ 617 — Santagata N 121 b 65.50 — 24 ErumpentO'rolli1144½ Bluffy1162¾ DiggersWell1211¾ Checked break, eased 6
26Mar95–5Aqu fst 6f :23 :471 :594 1:13 Md Sp Wt **21** 3 7 78¼ 56 512 617½ Rodriquez E M 122 b 55.75 59–17 Fort Edward122¾ Frisco Gold1223¾ Lovubaby12213 Broke slowly 8
22Mar95–1Aqu fst 6½f :23 :474 1:141 1:21 Md 25000 **15** 4 8 42 53 55½ 715 Cruguet J 120 20.70 60–20 LonlyGmblr120½ ChocltWzrd120no SpWthThDvl1203 Saved ground, tired 9
15Mar95–5Aqu fst 6½f :234 :461 1:124 1:193 Md Sp Wt 28+ **40** 1 7 54 67½ 76½ 77½ Rodriquez E M 120 74.00 75–14 Abtwil1201½ Whose On First120hd Erumpent O'rolli113no Saved ground 8
5Mar95–6Aqu fst 170 [•] :233 :474 1:142 1:462 Md Sp Wt — 1 4 58 58½ 716 — Rodriquez E M 122 39.75 — 33 It'sJohn'sTim122nk PrsonlAffir1155 PoltclProspct122hd Done early, eased 7
20Feb95–5Aqu fst 1⅛ [•] :493 1:151 1:414 1:551 Md Sp Wt **25** 1 9 915 822 827 832¾ Madrid A Jr 122 18.40 27–29 ClerSense1222¼ PoliticlProspct1224¾ It'sJohn'sTim1225¼ Lacked response 9
16Feb95–1Aqu fst 6f [•] :233 :473 1:003 1:134 Md Sp Wt **41** 4 6 716 710 78¾ 67¼ Rodriquez E M 122 30.00 67–21 DnzigsPride122½ LevThFlg1223½ ChocoltWizrd122nk Stead, pinched break 7
1Feb95–2Aqu fst 6f [•] :224 :464 :594 1:134 Md 35000 **38** 2 8 713 613 513 410¼ Rodriquez E M 122 56.00 64–21 John Karavas1186½ Instant Grudge1223¾ The Boz'n115no Broke slowly 9
28Jan95–5Aqu fst 6f [•] :24 :482 1:011 1:143 Md 35000 **11** 10 8 1011 914 917 921¾ Rodriquez E M 122 95.50 48–29 Szczepnkowski1222¾ AccordingToCole1222½ ChngingRhy1183¼ Never close 11

WORKOUTS: Jly 20 Sar 4f fst :50 B *17/23* Jly 5 Sar tr.t 3f fst :392 B *4/5* May 31 Sar Ⓣ 4f fm :52 B (d)*3/7* ●May 10 Sar Ⓣ 4f fm :494 B (d) *1/4*

Decimal Place

Own: Old Brookside Farm

VELAZQUEZ J R (74 12 9 5 .16)

B. g. 3 (May)
Sire: Amber Pass (Pass Catcher)
Dam: Rah Decimal (Decimator)
Br: Sunnyview Farm (NY)
Tr: Contessa Gary C (11 1 0 2 .09)

117

Lifetime Record:	6 M 0 0	$1,800		
1995	6 M 0 0	$1,800	Turf	1 0 0 0
1994	0 M 0 0		Wet	1 0 0 0
Sar	1 0 0 0	$1,800	Dist	0 0 0 0

26Jly95-4Sar fst 7f :222 :46 1:12 1:253 3↑[S]Md Sp Wt 47 7 9 118 1010 58 49½ Davis R G 117 40.75 68-14 Scanner Pro1171½ Carr Pool1175½ Raffie's Rullah1172½ Improved position 13
12Jly95-5Bel fst 1 :23 :463 1:114 1:383 3↑[S]Md Sp Wt 52 2 6 64 86 66 67½ Davis R G 113 b 14.60 63-23 Raising Peas1152 Irish Patriot1133 Worldly Slew108hd Checked turn 9
1Jly95-1Bel sly 6f :224 :464 :584 1:112 3↑[S]Md Sp Wt 6 1 4 43 45 512 726½ Davis R G 114 b 7.80 57-14 NewYorkLights11412 TriMyPtienc1145½ Aspinwll1142½ Saved ground, tired 9
21Jun95-9Bel fm 1 1/16 [T] :252 :481 1:124 1:44 3↑[S]Md Sp Wt 42 2 3 1½ 3nk 65½ 712 Davis R G 113 10.30 64-18 Hello Sunshine1133½ Mad River Glenn114nk Il Grappa113hd Dueled, tired 9
3Mar95-1Aqu fst 6f [•] :234 :482 1:004 1:133 [S]Md Sp Wt 43 4 7 41½ 52½ 54½ 66 Velazquez J R 122 8.20 69-18 Hopehecomplies1222½ Winloc's Zachary1221½ Ace In The Hole122no Tired 9
16Feb95-9Aqu fst 6f [•] :232 :472 1:00 1:13 [S]Md Sp Wt 27 1 10 1012 1011 912 917½ Velazquez J R 122 3.20 61-21 Game Card122hd Brandy For Melanie1178 Victor V. C.1224½ Poor break 10

WORKOUTS: Aug 7 Sar tr.t 3f fst :374 B 3/10 Jun 29 Bel 4f fst :491 B 17/49 Jun 14 Bel tr.t 4f gd :493 B 9/18 Jun 9 Bel 7f fst 1:31 B 1/3 May 31 Bel 4f fst :50 B 55/73

Fouldre

Own: Nuesch Felix J

BELMONTE L A (39 3 4 1 .08)

Dk. b or br g. 6
Sire: Thunder Puddles (Speak John)
Dam: Air Space (Five Star Flight)
Br: Nuesch Felix J (NY)
Tr: Destasio Richard A (6 0 0 1 .00)

116^5

Lifetime Record:	13 M 1 3	$24,410		
1995	5 M 0 1	$6,800	Turf	1 0 0 0
1994	6 M 1 2	$16,200	Wet	1 0 0 0
Sar	0 0 0 0		Dist	0 0 0 0

29Jun95-5Bel fst 7f :23 :471 1:13 1:26 3↑[S]Md Sp Wt 36 10 1 43 41½ 57 618 Alvarado F T 123 fb 30.00 53-22 Sunny Ghost1145½ Programable1149 Freeze The Raise116½ Tired 11
7Jun95-5Bel gd 1 1/16 [T] :231 :462 1:112 1:431 3↑[S]Md Sp Wt 42 10 7 67 65¾ 69½ 723½ Belmonte L A7 116 fb 30.75 58-22 Identity113nk Irish Patriot11320 Uncle Twist111nk No threat 10
25May95-3Bel fst 1 1/16 :234 :472 1:123 1:452 3↑[S]Md Sp Wt 53 3 3 21½ 32 45½ 410½ Cooper G J7 116 fb 13.40 61-29 Duchess's Secret114no Irish Patriot1138 Il Grappa1132½ Tired 9
7May95-3Bel fst 6f :224 :464 :584 1:111 3↑[S]Md Sp Wt 44 4 5 64½ 62¾ 44½ 48½ Valdivia J7 115 fb 14.80 76-11 ToughJake113nk SelectedSauce113¾ Winloc'sDr.Pete1137½ Bumped break 10
21Apr95-3Aqu fst 6f :223 :461 :584 1:12 3↑[S]Md Sp Wt 53 2 5 43½ 35 36 38½ Cooper G J7 116 fb 17.30 73-15 Lovubaby1236 Selected Sauce1142½ Fouldre116nk Saved ground 8
29Dec94-5Aqu fst 1 1/16 [•] :241 :491 1:153 1:50 3↑[S]Md Sp Wt 45 6 4 41½ 35 47½ 413¾ Santagata N 122 fb 1.50e 41-35 Firestar1201½ Abtwil12010 Iain's Storm1132 Even trip 7
22Dec94-3Aqu fst 6f [•] :234 :48 1:004 1:133 3↑[S]Md Sp Wt 48 7 1 31 21½ 33½ 37 Santagata N 122 fb 6.40 68-22 Carr De Napolis1201 Star Med1156 Fouldre1223 No late bid 8
29Nov94-9Aqu wf 7f :224 :463 1:122 1:254 3↑[S]Md Sp Wt 46 5 2 53¾ 77½ 69 711½ Lantz J A5 117 fb 9.40 63-21 Dearly Dunce1223 Temperence Reel120nk Instant Grudge1203½ Done early 8
16Nov94-1Aqu fst 1 :24 :48 1:14 1:392 3↑[S]Md Sp Wt 51 2 4 43½ 41¾ 46½ 410½ Beckner D V5 117 f 2.20e 60-24 VivLFlg115nk Sixfeetunder12010 TemperenceRel120nk Saved ground, tired 8
27Oct94-1Aqu fst 7f :224 :472 1:141 1:282 3↑[S]Md Sp Wt 55 2 5 67 52½ 32 31½ Beckner D V5 117 f *1.45 61-27 Stinky Dinky114¾ Raja's Image122½ Fouldre1171¾ Mild rally 7

WORKOUTS: Aug 7 Sar tr.t 3f fst :383 B 5/10 Jly 9 Bel tr.t 3f fst :38 B 9/10 Jun 18 Bel tr.t 3f fst :372 B 3/11 May 15 Bel tr.t 4f fst :491 B 8/21

Reputable Son

Own: Krakower Lawrence J

CHAVEZ J F (96 17 15 5 .18)

B. c. 3 (Jun)
Sire: Son of Repute (Northern Dancer)
Dam: Doctor Linda G. (Kirby Lane)
Br: Lawrence J. Krakower (NY)
Tr: Taylor Ronald J (1 0 0 0 .00)

117

Lifetime Record:	2 M 0 0	$215		
1995	2 M 0 0	$215	Turf	0 0 0 0
1994	0 M 0 0		Wet	0 0 0 0
Sar	0 0 0 0		Dist	0 0 0 0

1Apr95-4Hia fst 6f :23 :46 :591 1:123 Md 35000 23 11 1 74½ 610 812 814¾ Duys D C 122 6.70 63-11 Kilmer1223 Bronx Bill118½ Dockerty1222¼ Faded 11
19Mar95-12Hia fst 6f :224 :452 :572 1:102 Md Sp Wt 31 11 6 85 88½ 812 718½ Lopez C 121 5.80 70-09 Mollys Pot Shot1214 Flying Padre1214 To The Cross1211 No threat 12

WORKOUTS: Jly 26 Mth 5f fst 1:024 Bg13/16 Jly 9 Mth 5f fst 1:032 Bg15/20 Jly 1 Mth 5f fst 1:011 Hg2/25 Jun 26 Mth 3f gd :383 B 22/22 Jun 17 Mth 5f fst 1:022 Bg14/41 Jun 11 Mth 4f fst :482 Bg3/24

Raja Mania

Own: Anchel Edward

BECKNER D V (40 1 5 1 .03)

B. c. 3 (Apr)
Sire: Raja's Revenge (Raja Baba)
Dam: Taradiddle (Damascus)
Br: Anchel Mr & Mrs Michael (NY)
Tr: Laboccetta Frank (3 0 0 1 .00)

117

Lifetime Record:	2 M 0 0	$0		
1995	2 M 0 0		Turf	0 0 0 0
1994	0 M 0 0		Wet	0 0 0 0
Sar	0 0 0 0		Dist	0 0 0 0

17Jun95-1Bel fst 6f :223 :462 :584 1:113 3↑[S]Md Sp Wt 35 9 6 77 85¾ 910 1118½ Belmonte L A7 108 f 54.50 65-19 Tintinnabular1223¾ All For You1121 Matthew W.1136½ Tired 12
7Jun95-4Bel gd 6f :222 :454 :581 1:11 3↑Md 50000 13 4 7 810 710 713 826¼ Luzzi M J 114 34.00 60-09 Tenochtitlan1206 FatLady'sEncore110½ BelieveItSeventy1231½ No speed 8

WORKOUTS: Aug 5 Sar tr.t 4f fst :513 B 9/18 Jly 28 Sar tr.t 3f fst :37 H 5/17 Jly 21 Sar 5f fst 1:022 B 12/22 Jly 9 Aqu 3f fst :373 B 1/3 Jun 15 Aqu 3f fst :372 B 4/7 May 21 Aqu 5f fst 1:011 H 6/12

Demanding Terms

Own: Boto Stable

ALVARADO F T (31 3 4 1 .10)

Ro. c. 3 (Feb)
Sire: Private Terms (Private Account)
Dam: Demand Attention (Al Hattab)
Br: Boto Thoroughbreds Inc (NY)
Tr: Kelly Timothy D (7 0 1 0 .00)

117

Lifetime Record:	2 M 0 0	$960			
1995	2 M 0 0	$960	Turf	1 0 0 0	
1994	0 M 0 0		Wet	1 0 0 0	$960
Sar	0 0 0 0		Dist	0 0 0 0	

3Jly95-5Bel yl 1¼ [T] :481 1:133 1:39 2:051 3↑[S]Md Sp Wt 48 10 10 98½ 53½ 66 89¾ Alvarado F T 114 b 17.20e 52-26 Il Grappa113½ Segrenti1141½ Billy King122nk Flattened out 12
25Jun95-3Bel my 1 1/16 :232 :47 1:121 1:44 3↑Md Sp Wt 52 2 4 31 56¼ 511 518¾ Alvarado F T 114 b 21.00 60-31 ClernceCod1135¾ ThnSom1132 ScondChildhood1141 Saved ground, tired 7

WORKOUTS: Aug 2 Sar 5f fst 1:013 H 3/33 Jly 30 Sar 3f fst :372 H 9/19 Jly 23 Sar 4f fst :491 B 31/54 ●Jly 15 Bel 3f fst :35 H 1/30 Jun 15 Bel 5f gd 1:021 Bg6/14 Jun 10 Bel 4f fst :51 Bg26/33

Broadway Joey

Own: Campo John P & Nastasi Frank

DECARLO C P (12 0 2 1 .00)

B. c. 3 (Feb)
Sire: Chromite (Mr. Prospector)
Dam: Game Performance (Stage Door Johnny)
Br: Pinebourne Farm & John P. Campo (NY)
Tr: Campo John P (3 0 0 0 .00)

117

Lifetime Record:	2 M 0 0	$0		
1995	2 M 0 0		Turf	1 0 0 0
1994	0 M 0 0		Wet	0 0 0 0
Sar	0 0 0 0		Dist	0 0 0 0

14Jly95-9Bel fm 1 [T] :223 :454 1:101 1:35 3↑[S]Md Sp Wt -0 9 10 1017 1017 1024 1037 Decarlo C P 113 23.80 51-12 Top Tapper1223 Lunatic Luke1135 Church St. Dancer115hd No speed 10
21May95-5Bel fst 6f :224 :471 1:00 1:134 3↑[S]Md Sp Wt 24 12 14 1312 1312 1411 1314 Keim P M10 105 73.00 58-22 Mr. Decker117nk Freeze TheRaise1221¾ Winloc'sDr.Pete113hd Broke slowly 14

WORKOUTS: Aug 2 Sar tr.t 3f fst :37 H 5/14 Jly 26 Sar tr.t 4f fst :52 B 18/27 Jly 23 Sar tr.t 4f fst :512 B 16/27 Jun 15 Bel [T] 3f fm :384 B (d)3/3 May 17 Bel tr.t 4f fst :493 B 3/14

Hyperflite

Own: Lenzini John J Jr

NELSON D (13 0 1 1 .00)

Dk. b or br g. 3 (Apr)
Sire: Dominated (Exclusive Native)
Dam: Meg's Journal (Tumiga)
Br: Karutz Wallace S (NY)
Tr: Lenzini John J (—)

117

Lifetime Record:	3 M 0 0	$840		
1995	3 M 0 0	$840	Turf	0 0 0 0
1994	0 M 0 0		Wet	0 0 0 0
Sar	0 0 0 0		Dist	0 0 0 0

3Mar95-5Aqu fst 6f [•] :231 :471 1:001 1:131 [S]Md Sp Wt 45 2 7 88 76½ 68 57½ Nelson D 122 b 20.60 69-18 Brandy For Melanie122nk Mascarrade1176 Victor V.C.122nk Bumped 1/4 pl 10
8Feb95-3Aqu fst 6f [•] :232 :483 1:013 1:142 [S]Md Sp Wt 30 5 7 911 910 810 815½ Nelson D 122 33.25 55-27 Mr. Harry1222 Mascarrade1228 Tsunami Sammy1171½ No threat 11
26Jan95-9Aqu fst 6f [•] :233 :481 1:01 1:141 [S]Md Sp Wt 40 4 9 1010 911 912 815 Nelson D 122 32.75 57-26 LnnsWldAgn1176 BrndFrMln1222¾ NStrInHn1222½ Broke slowly, checked 10

WORKOUTS: Aug 5 Sar 3f fst :361 H 4/16 Jly 28 Sar tr.t 5f fst 1:052 B 9/14 Jly 5 Aqu 4f fst :502 B 5/8 Jun 30 Aqu 5f fst 1:014 H 2/4 Jun 24 Aqu 5f fst 1:032 B 6/6 Jun 1 Aqu [T] 4f fm :53 B (d)6/7

Search My Soul

Own: O'Bryant Jim & Snyder Ella

DAVIS R G (88 9 12 18 .10)

Dk. b or br g. 3 (May)
Sire: Selous Scout (Effervescing)
Dam: Soul Secret (Solford)
Br: Milfer Farm Inc (NY)
Tr: Peitz Daniel C (5 1 1 0 .20)

117

Lifetime Record:	1 M 0 0	$900		
1995	1 M 0 0	$900	Turf	0 0 0 0
1994	0 M 0 0		Wet	0 0 0 0
Sar	0 0 0 0		Dist	0 0 0 0

15Jly95-2Bel fst 6f :224 :462 :584 1:113 3↑[S]Md Sp Wt 44 12 11 83¾ 64½ 79 511½ Davis R G 113 5.70 71-11 Matthew W.1143 Scanner Pro1132½ Programable1143 Five wide 12

WORKOUTS: Aug 8 Sar 3f fst :374 B 14/16 Jly 31 Sar 5f fst 1:012 H 4/34 Jly 25 Sar tr.t 4f fst :524 B 27/28 Jly 12 Bel 3f fst :363 H 20/38 Jly 7 Bel 3f fst :364 Hg9/30 Jun 26 Bel tr.t 4f gd :52 B 12/13

Biggie Munn
Own: Russo August F

PEREZ R B (42 2 2 5 .05)

Dk. b or br g. 4
Sire: Great Neck (Tentam)
Dam: Glance At the Hour (Marshua's Dancer)
Br: Koerner John H (NY)
Tr: Hebert William (5 0 0 0 .00)

121

Lifetime Record:	5 M 0 0	$1,860			
1995	4 M 0 0	$1,860	Turf	3 0 0 0	$960
1994	1 M 0 0		Wet	1 0 0 0	
Sar	1 0 0 0	$900	Dist	0 0 0 0	

26Jly95-4Sar	fst	7f		:22^2	:46	1:12	1:25^3	3↑ [S]Md Sp Wt	29"	42	8	3	1½	1½	3^{3½}	5^{12}	Velazquez J R	122	27.50	66–14	Scanner Pro117^{1½} Carr Pool117^{5½} Raffie's Rullah117^{2½}	Dueled, tired 13
14Jly95-9Bel	fm	1	ⓣ	:22^3	:45^4	1:10^1	1:35	3↑ [S]Md Sp Wt	24–	47	3	4	2^2	2^2	4^{5½}	5^{13}	Perez R B	122	22.70	75–12	Top Tapper122^3 Lunatic Luke113^5 Church St. Dancer115^{hd}	Chased, tired 10
7Jun95-5Bel	gd	1$\frac{1}{16}$	ⓣ	:23^1	:46^2	1:11^2	1:43^1	3↑ [S]Md Sp Wt	30–	41	8	3	1½	1^{hd}	4^8	8^{24}	Martin G J^5	118	12.60	58–22	Identity113^{nk} Irish Patriot113^{20} Uncle Twist111^{nk}	Dueled, tired 10
19May95-2Bel	sly	1	⊗	:23	:46^4	1:12^2	1:39	3↑ [S]Md Sp Wt	22	27	12	5	5^4	5^3	7^8	8^{17½}	Cooper G J^5	118	65.50	51–21	Whose On First123^7 Uncle Twist111^{¾} The Boz'n118^4	Four wide, tired 12
26Nov94-2Aqu	sf	1⅛	ⓣ	:49^4	1:15^2	1:41^3	1:54^4	3↑ Md Sp Wt	27''	27	8	3	3^4	5^{3½}	10^{15}	10^{22¾}	Lantz J A^5	115	17.30	43–29	Sir Bert120^2 Poulet Chasseur120^{4½} Right Forward120^{1½}	Gave way 10

WORKOUTS: ●Jun 28 Sar ⓣ 4f fm :48 H (d) 1/5 Jun 21 Sar ⓣ 5f fm 1:02 H (d) 1/3 May 31 Sar ⓣ 4f fm :49 H (d) 2/7 May 17 Sar ⓣ 3f fm :36 H (d) 1/3 May 10 Sar ⓣ 5f fm 1:02 B (d) 2/8

Excluding Fouldre, six years old and still a non-winner, the 10 others in the lineup had gone postward a combined 33 times and had managed nary a single in-the-money finish! The closest anyone had been to the winner in their last start was seven and a half lengths, a dubious distinction belonging to Hyperflite, who had been working out irregularly and unremarkably for his first start since March.

Notwithstanding the fact that Biggie Munn had never been better than fifth, nor closer than a dozen lengths to the winner, the gelding stood out here by virtue of his early pace superiority. In his first-ever sprint attempt July 26, also his first start on a fast dirt track, Biggie Munn set a pressured pace of :22 2/5 and :46. He had tired steadily thereafter but was still within 3 1/2 lengths of the lead after six furlongs in 1:12. Nobody in the field came close to these kind of splits, and Biggie Munn's performance was made all the more impressive by a look back at the July 26 result chart:

FOURTH RACE
Saratoga
JULY 26, 1995

7 FURLONGS. (1.20^2) MAIDEN SPECIAL WEIGHT. Purse $30,000. 3-year-olds and upward, foaled in New York State and approved by the New York State-Bred Registry. Weights: 3-year-olds, 117 lbs. Older, 122 lbs. (Preference to horses that have not started for $40,000 or less in their last three starts

Value of Race: $30,000 Winner $18,000; second $6,000; third $3,300; fourth $1,800; fifth $900. Mutuel Pool $295,626.00 Exacta Pool $436,592.00 Quinella Pool $88,095.00

Last Raced	Horse	M/Eqt.	A.	Wt	PP	St	¼	½	Str	Fin	Jockey	Odds $1
15Jly95 ^{2}Bel^2	Scanner Pro	b	3	117	12	2	2^1	2^{2½}	1^2	1^{1½}	Bailey J D	0.65
3Jly95 ^{5}Bel^{12}	Carr Pool	b	3	117	10	7	3^{hd}	3½	2^{1½}	2^{5½}	Rydowski S R	9.00
5Jly95 ^{6}Del^2	Raffie's Rullah	f	3	117	2	5	9^{1½}	8^{1½}	4^2	3^{2½}	Nelson D	f-18.50
12Jly95 ^{5}Bel^6	Decimal Place		3	117	7	9	11^{½}	10^1	5½	4^{2½}	Davis R G	40.75
14Jly95 ^{9}Bel^5	Biggie Munn		4	122	8	3	1½	1½	3^{2½}	5^{hd}	Velazquez J R	27.50
14Jly95 ^{2}FL^2	Affirmed To Fight		3	117	11	10	13	9½	6^1	6^{6½}	Cruguet J	29.50
	Sacket's Six		3	117	4	12	8^{2½}	6^3	8^{hd}	7no	Maple E	13.30
1Jly95 ^{1}Bel^2	Tri My Patience	b	3	117	9	6	5½	4^{1½}	7^{1½}	8^5	Velasquez J	8.80
12Jly95 ^{5}Bel^7	Golden Marsh		3	117	1	4	6^{hd}	7^{hd}	10^{1½}	9¾	Perez R B	f-18.50
12Jly95 ^{5}Bel^8	Master Gregory		3	112	5	11	10^{hd}	11^{1½}	9^{1½}	10^3	Belmonte L A†5	63.75
	Spa City Slew		3	117	6	13	12^{hd}	13	11½	11no	Chavez J F	16.00
	Rainbow Russ	b	3	117	3	8	7^{hd}	12^1	13	12^{1½}	Migliore R	8.90
14Jly95 ^{9}Bel^9	Generous Slice	b	3	117	13	1	4^{1½}	5^{hd}	12½	13	Beckner D V	f-18.50

f-Mutuel Field: Raffie's Rullah and Golden Marsh and Generous Slice.

OFF AT 2:35 Start Good. Won driving. Time, :22^2, :46, 1:12, 1:25^3 Track fast.

$2 Mutuel Prices:			
11–SCANNER PRO	3.30	2.70	2.40
9–CARR POOL		6.10	4.80
13–RAFFIE'S RULLAH (f-field)			4.90

$2 EXACTA 11–9 PAID $18.20 $2 QUINELLA 9–11 PAID $14.20

B. c, (Mar), by Distinctive Pro–By all Logic, by Stevward. Trainer Towne Steve. Bred by Louis J. Felice (NY).

SCANNER PRO forced the pace from outside for a half, took charge in upper stretch, opened a clear lead in midstretch, then turned back CARR POOL under brisk urging. CARR POOL settled just behind the early leaders, angled out while rallying on the turn, made a run to threaten in upper stretch but couldn't overtake the winner while clearly second best. RAFFIE'S RULLAH outrun for a half while between horses, rallied mildly to gain a share. DECIMAL PLACE far back for a half, failed to threaten while improving his position. BIGGIE MUNN set the pace under pressure to the top of the stretch and tired from his early efforts. AFFIRMED TO FIGHT outrun early, failed to threaten while improving his position. SACKET'S SIX checked at the start, gradually gained on the turn, then lacked a strong closing bid. TRI MY PATIENCE saved ground and tired. GOLDEN MARSH faded after going a half. MASTER GREGORY never reached contention. SPA CITY SLEW checked while racing greenly in the early stages, and was never close thereafter. RAINBOW RUSS raced wide and tired. GENEROUS SLICE showed speed for a half then gave way. BIGGIE MUNN wore mud caulks.

This is one of my favorite pace angles: horse gets fried in a duel with a well-regarded rival, and comes back in a field where it figures to have a much easier time on the lead. Scanner Pro had been 3-5 and everyone's best bet when he pressed Biggie Munn through a quick half and emerged victorious July 26.

Today, there was no one with Scanner Pro's ability to take the starch out of Biggie Munn in the opening half mile; horses that can win two of a sprint's three fractions have an excellent chance to win — particularly when their opponents are of questionable quality. The favorite at a seriously overbet 8-5 was Search My Soul, a wide fifth, beaten almost a dozen lengths first time out. Biggie Munn was third choice at 5-1, a nifty overlay:

SECOND RACE **Saratoga** **AUGUST 10, 1995**

6½ FURLONGS. (1.14^{2}) MAIDEN SPECIAL WEIGHT. Purse $30,000. 3-year-olds and upward, foaled in New York State and approved by the New York State Bred Registry. Weights: 3-year-olds, 117 lbs. Older, 121 lbs. (Preference to horses that have not started for $40,000 or less in their last three starts.)

Value of Race: $30,000 Winner $18,000; second $6,000; third $3,300; fourth $1,800; fifth $900. Mutuel Pool $272,078.00 Exacta Pool $378,255.00 Quinella Pool $91,016.00

Last Raced	Horse	M/Eqt.	A.	Wt	PP	St	¼	½	Str	Fin	Jockey	Odds $1
26Jly95 4Sar^{5}	Biggie Munn		4	121	11	2	1½	1½	1^{3}	1^{2½}	Perez R B	5.70
26Jly95 4Sar^{4}	Decimal Place		3	117	3	7	8^{1½}	7^{3}	3½	2no	Velazquez J R	12.30
15Jly95 2Bel^{6}	Dapper Dutchman		3	117	1	3	2^{1}	2^{1½}	2^{1½}	3¾	Rydowski S R	8.10
3Jly95 5Bel^{8}	Demanding Terms		3	117	7	11	6½	4^{1½}	5^{hd}	4^{hd}	Alvarado F T	3.65
15Jly95 2Bel^{5}	Search My Soul	b	3	117	10	6	3^{1½}	3^{1}	4^{1}	5^{4}	Davis R G	1.60
29Jun95 5Bel^{6}	Fouldre	bf	6	116	4	4	4^{1}	5^{1½}	6^{2½}	6^{1}	Belmonte L A^{5}	14.20
3Mar95 5Aqu^{5}	Hyperflite		3	117	9	1	7½	6½	7^{1}	7^{2}	Nelson D	20.00
13Apr95 4Aqu^{6}	Plattkin	b	4	121	2	8	10^{1½}	10^{1}	8^{1½}	8^{nk}	Lovato F Jr	73.25
1Apr95 4Hia^{8}	Reputable Son		3	117	5	9	11	9½	9^{3½}	9^{9}	Chavez J F	9.90
14Jly95 9Bel^{10}	Broadway Joey	b	3	117	8	10	9^{1½}	11	11	10^{2}	Decarlo C P	47.75
17Jun95 1Bel^{11}	Raja Mania	f	3	117	6	5	5^{1½}	8^{1½}	10^{1}	11	Beckner D V	95.75

OFF AT 1:31 Start Good For All But DEMANDING TERMS. Won driving. Time, :22^{2}, :46^{2}, 1:12^{1}, 1:19^{2} Track fast.

$2 Mutuel Prices:				
	11–BIGGIE MUNN	13.40	7.40	5.10
	3–DECIMAL PLACE		10.00	6.10
	1–DAPPER DUTCHMAN			6.30

$2 EXACTA 11–3 PAID $148.00 $2 QUINELLA 3–11 PAID $82.00

Dk. b. or br. g, by Great Neck–Glance At the Hour, by Marshua's Dancer. Trainer Hebert William. Bred by Koerner John H (NY).

BIGGIE MUNN angled to the inside after sprinting clear in the early stages, set the pace under pressure for a half then drew clear under brisk urging. DECIMAL PLACE outrun early, launched a rally between horses leaving the turn, then closed steadily to nip DECIMAL PLACE for the place. DAPPER DUTCHMAN checked slightly and angled to the outside in the early stages, forced the pace outside the winner into upper stretch then weakened in the final eighth. A claim of foul lodged by the rider of DAPPER DUTCHMAN against the winner for interference along the backstretch was disallowed. DEMANDING TERMS trailed early after rearing at the start, rushed up while four wide along the backstretch, moved into contention while four wide on the turn and flattened out. SEARCH MY SOUL chased the leaders from outside to the top of the stretch, then lacked a further response. FOULDRE up close early while saving ground, was finished after going a half. HYPERFLITE failed to threaten while four wide. PLATTKIN never reached contention. REPUTABLE SON was never close while five wide on the turn. BROADWAY JOEY checked early, was never close thereafter. RAJA MANIA showed only brief speed.

Owners— 1, Russo August F; 2, Old Brookside Farm; 3, Bailie Sally A; 4, Boto Stable; 5, O'Bryant Jim & Snyder Ella; 6, Nuesch Felix J; 7, Lenzini John J Jr; 8, Martino Phyllis; 9, Krakower Lawrence J; 10, Campo John P & Nastasi Frank; 11, Anchel Edward

Trainers—1, Hebert William; 2, Contessa Gary C; 3, Bailie Sally A; 4, Kelly Timothy D; 5, Peitz Daniel C; 6, Destasio Richard A; 7, Lenzini John J; 8, Martino Phyllis; 9, Taylor Ronald J; 10, Campo John P; 11, Laboccetta Frank

Biggie Munn broke from the extreme outside but his early pace supremacy allowed him to secure inside position (though he had to survive an objection for angling in a bit too sharply after the start). Meanwhile, his hapless pursuers did their best imitation of the Keystone Cops, giving futile chase. It was over by midstretch.

Not that Biggie Munn needed any extra help, but as luck would have it he caught the most intense gold rail-speed bias of the meet; all seven dirt races were taken by horses on the lead toward the inside, including the sixth — a six and a half furlong maiden special-weight for 2-year-olds.

Since conventional handicapping theory stresses that first time-starters are poor bets unless they attract a lot of attention at the windows, and since most published analysis' of races loaded with first time-starters contain the admonition, "watch the board," I've taken the liberty of penciling in the odds alongside the names of each of the 10 colts so you can factor the "smart money" into your handicapping:

6 **Saratoga**

6½ Furlongs **(1:14^{2}) MAIDEN SPECIAL WEIGHT. Purse $30,000. 2-year-olds. Weight, 118 lbs. (Preference to horses that have not started for a claiming price).**

6½ FURLONGS

START

FINISH

Fortitude 17-1
Own: Harbor View Farm
PEREZ R B (42 2 2 5 .05)

B. c. 2 (Mar)
Sire: Cure The Blues (Stop the Music)
Dam: Outlasting (Seattle Slew)
Br: Harbor View Farm (Ky)
Tr: Jerkens H Allen (22 4 2 3 .18)

118

Lifetime Record :	**1 M 0 0**		**$0**
1995	**1 M 0 0**	**Turf**	**0 0 0 0**
1994	**0 M 0 0**	**Wet**	**0 0 0 0**
Sar	**1 0 0 0**	**Dist**	**0 0 0 0**

22Jly95–2Sar fst 5½f :22^{2} :46^{2} :58^{4} 1:05^{1} Md Sp Wt 27 43 3 8 10^{13} 9^{9} 6^{7½} 6^{9¾} Perez R B 120 18.70 85–07 Sunny Side120^{6} Northern Pursuit120^{nk} Justinthemiddle120^{2} No threat 12

WORKOUTS: Jly 19 Sar 5f fst 1:02^{2} B *5/12* Jly 15 Bel 3f fst :36^{2} H *12/30* Jly 12 Bel 4f fst :49 B *32/60* Jly 8 Bel tr.t 4f fst :51 B *23/29* Jly 2 Bel 3f sly :36^{4} B *1/2*

Dustin's Dream 22-1
Own: Anstu Stable

SANTOS J A (88 6 12 14 .07)

B. c. 2 (Mar)
Sire: Quiet American (Fappiano)
Dam: Wolf Trail (Superbity)
Br: Dizney Donald R (Ky)
Tr: Schulhofer Flint S (25 4 5 5 .16)

118

	Lifetime Record :	0 M 0 0		$0
1995	0 M 0 0		Turf	0 0 0 0
1994	0 M 0 0		Wet	0 0 0 0
Sar	0 0 0 0		Dist	0 0 0 0

WORKOUTS: Aug 4 Bel tr.t 4f fst :49 B 5/20　Jly 30 Bel 4f fst :50⁴ B 40/45　Jly 24 Bel 4f fst :49 B 13/20

Hey You Weasel 5-1
Own: Hough Stanley M & Johnson Kim & Ted

DAVIS R G (88 9 12 18 .10)

B. c. 2 (May)
Sire: Gulch (Mr. Prospector)
Dam: Far Flying (Far North)
Br: Foxfield (Ky)
Tr: Hough Stanley M (10 1 1 1 .10)

118

	Lifetime Record :	1 M 0 1		$3,300
1995	1 M 0 1	$3,300	Turf	0 0 0 0
1994	0 M 0 0		Wet	0 0 0 0
Sar	1 0 0 1	$3,300	Dist	0 0 0 0

29Jly95-2Sar fst 6f :22¹ :45¹ :57² 1:10¹ Md Sp Wt (9⁺ 59 4 4 4³½ 4⁸ 3¹¹ 3¹³ Davis R G 119 f 14.00 71-13 Louis Quatorze119⁵¹ Beefchopper119⁷¹ Hey You Weasel119³½ No rally 9
WORKOUTS: Aug 6 Sar tr.t 3f fst :38 B 2/5　Jly 23 Sar tr.t 4f fst :51² B 16/27　Jly 13 Bel 5f fst 1:02 B 22/30　Jly 7 Bel 4f fst :48¹ Hg8/47　Jun 30 Bel 4f fst :49² B 27/53　Jun 23 Bel 4f gd :48⁴ B 9/38

Scorcherer 40-1
Own: Maycroft Farm

LUZZI M J (61 6 4 5 .10)

Gr/ro c. 2 (May)
Sire: Black Tie Affair (Miswaki)
Dam: Emiress (Damascus)
Br: Maycroft Farm (Ky)
Tr: Serpe Philip M (19 1 0 0 .05)

118

	Lifetime Record :	0 M 0 0		$0
1995	0 M 0 0		Turf	0 0 0 0
1994	0 M 0 0		Wet	0 0 0 0
Sar	0 0 0 0		Dist	0 0 0 0

WORKOUTS: Aug 6 Sar 5f fst 1:05 B 21/21　Jly 31 Sar 4f fst :50 Hg36/54　Jly 26 Sar 5f fst 1:05³ B 45/47　Jly 21 Sar 4f fst :51 B 41/50　Jly 13 Bel 5f fst 1:01 Hg7/30　Jly 7 Bel 4f fst :49⁴ Bg32/47　Jun 30 Bel 4f fst :52 B 46/53　Jun 14 Bel tr.t 4f gd :51⁴ B 15/18

Trail City 5-1
Own: Mott William I

BAILEY J D (97 21 8 13 .22)

Dk. b or br c. 2 (Apr)
Sire: Red Ransom (Roberto)
Dam: Willow Runner (Alydar)
Br: Prestonwood Farm (Ky)
Tr: Mott William I (25 8 4 3 .32)

118

	Lifetime Record :	0 M 0 0		$0
1995	0 M 0 0		Turf	0 0 0 0
1994	0 M 0 0		Wet	0 0 0 0
Sar	0 0 0 0		Dist	0 0 0 0

WORKOUTS: Aug 2 Sar 4f fst :51¹ Bg32/38　Jly 16 Sar TR² 3f fst :37³ Hg4/6　Jly 11 Sar 5f fst 1:03³ B 1/1　Jly 5 Sar tr.t 4f fst :50⁴ B 2/5　●Jun 29 Sar tr.t 4f fst :51² Bg1/5　●Jun 23 Sar tr.t 3f fst :39 B 1/10　Jun 5 Sar tr.t 3f fst :38¹ B 5/16　May 22 Sar 4f fst :41³ B 2/4

Surround Sound 22-1
Own: Humphrey G Watts Jr

PERRET C (22 3 1 5 .14)

Ch. c. 2 (Mar)
Sire: Eastern Echo (Damascus)
Dam: Cherry d'Or (Cassaleria)
Br: Bradyleigh Farms Inc. (Ky)
Tr: Arnold George R II (12 3 1 1 .25)

118

	Lifetime Record :	1 M 0 0		$0
1995	1 M 0 0		Turf	0 0 0 0
1994	0 M 0 0		Wet	0 0 0 0
Sar	1 0 0 0		Dist	0 0 0 0

27Jly95-2Sar fst 6f :22 :45³ :57⁴ 1:10⁴ Md Sp Wt 23⁺ 46 4 12 11¹¹ 10¹¹ 8¹⁰ 7¹⁶½ Perret C 118 40.75 71-12 HonourAndGlory118¹⁰ BlushingJim118⁵³ JettingRobert118ⁿᵏ Broke slowly 12
WORKOUTS: Jly 20 Sar tr.t 4f fst :49³ B 4/28　Jly 14 Bel 5f fst 1:01¹ H 14/32　Jly 9 Bel 3f fst :36³ Hg8/19　Jly 4 Bel 4f fst :49¹ B 23/71　Jun 27 Bel 4f my :50³ B 10/19　Jun 21 Bel 5f fst 1:03¹ H 6/23

Ide 4-1
Own: Willmott Stables

DAY P (86 16 11 11 .19)

Ch. c. 2 (May)
Sire: Forty Niner (Mr. Prospector)
Dam: Maytide (Naskra)
Br: David B. Garvin (Ky)
Tr: Vestal Peter M (10 2 1 2 .20)

118

	Lifetime Record :	0 M 0 0		$0
1995	0 M 0 0		Turf	0 0 0 0
1994	0 M 0 0		Wet	0 0 0 0
Sar	0 0 0 0		Dist	0 0 0 0

WORKOUTS: Aug 5 Sar 5f fst 1:02² Hg3/31　Jly 29 Sar 5f fst 1:01² Hg11/37　Jly 24 Sar 5f gd 1:02 H 3/11　Jly 18 CD 3f fst :37³ B 5/18　Jly 13 CD 4f fst :51 B 15/21　Jly 3 CD 3f fst :35³ H 2/10　Jun 27 CD 3f fst :37² B 8/19

Diligence 9-1
Own: Kinsman Stable

SELLERS S J (49 4 7 6 .08)

Gr/ro c. 2 (Mar)
Sire: Miswaki (Mr. Prospector)
Dam: Honeytab (Al Hattab)
Br: Kinsman Stud Farm (Ky)
Tr: Zito Nicholas P (26 3 3 7 .12)

118

	Lifetime Record :	0 M 0 0		$0
1995	0 M 0 0		Turf	0 0 0 0
1994	0 M 0 0		Wet	0 0 0 0
Sar	0 0 0 0		Dist	0 0 0 0

WORKOUTS: Aug 4 Sar tr.t 4f sly 1:03⁴ B 1/1　Jly 28 Sar 5f fst 1:01³ H 7/22　Jly 14 Bel 4f fst :49⁴ Hg18/39　Jly 8 Bel 3f fst :38 B 17/27

Gold Fever 8-5
Own: Phipps Cynthia

SMITH M E (94 16 12 17 .17)

Ch. c. 2 (Apr)
Sire: Forty Niner (Mr. Prospector)
Dam: Lead Kindly Light (Majestic Light)
Br: Cynthia Phipps (Ky)
Tr: McGaughey Claude III (15 3 2 2 .20)

118

	Lifetime Record :	0 M 0 0		$0
1995	0 M 0 0		Turf	0 0 0 0
1994	0 M 0 0		Wet	0 0 0 0
Sar	0 0 0 0		Dist	0 0 0 0

WORKOUTS: Aug 6 Sar 4f fst :48¹ Hg6/38　Jly 31 Sar tr.t 4f fst :50² B 6/12　Jly 26 Sar 4f fst :48⁴ Hg11/52　Jly 16 Bel 4f fst :49⁴ Bg22/36　Jly 9 Bel 4f fst :50⁴ B 36/48　Jly 4 Bel 4f fst :50¹ Bg55/71　Jun 29 Bel 3f fst :38² Bg27/35

H'Way Three to Six 18-1
Own: Rosenthal Morton

MIGLIORE R (46 4 5 11 .09)

Ch. c. 2 (May)
Sire: Houston (Seattle Slew)
Dam: Stolen Title (Nasty and Bold)
Br: Morton Rosenthal (Ky)
Tr: Brida Dennis J (12 1 1 2 .08)

118

	Lifetime Record :	0 M 0 0		$0
1995	0 M 0 0		Turf	0 0 0 0
1994	0 M 0 0		Wet	0 0 0 0
Sar	0 0 0 0		Dist	0 0 0 0

WORKOUTS: Aug 7 Sar 5f fst 1:02² H 21/40　Aug 2 Sar 4f fst :49² Hg10/30　Jly 28 Sar 5f fst 1:17⁴ B 4/5　Jly 23 Sar tr.t 5f fst 1:03³ B 3/8　Jly 16 Sar tr.t 4f fst :51³ B 3/5　Jly 7 Sar 5f fst 1:03 B 18/30　Jun 26 Bel tr.t 3f gd :39⁴ B 13/14　●Jun 10 Bel 3f fst :37³ Hg1/11　May 31 Bel 3f fst :38² Bg27/34　May 13 Bel tr.t 3f fst :37 B 6/18　Feb 25 HF 1f fst :13 B 7/8

Still unsure? Consider the following information gleaned from *Maiden Stats*:

- Trail City sold for a mere $37,000 as a yearling.
- Ide, a $180,000 yearling, is out of Maytide, a mare who has thrown two prior stakes winners including an $827,000-earner.
- Diligence is a homebred (bred by the owner) out of Honeytab, a mare who has produced four winners including Win Crafty Lady, a stakes-winning sprinter of $304,000. Furthermore, all three of the dam's runners to race at age 2 won:

	SIRE INFO									DAM INFO										SIBLING INFO	
Horse	# wnr/str	2yo wnr/str	% 1st	awd	Mud w%/sts	Turf w%/sts	% 1stT	Spi	prf	Dpl	fls	# wnr/str	sw	2yo wnr/str	awd	Mud w%/sts	Turf w%/sts	Dosage Index	Top Sibling	/Earn
DIJON RIDGE	49/60	19/41	10	7.4	18/174	8/95	11	2.12	w									1.50		
DILEMMA	282/412	103/241	11	7.0	13/526	12/1449	8	2.64	sw	1.09	3	1/2	0	0/1	8.5	0/4	1/2	2.37	Al's Memory	/$ 3
DILIGENCE	282/412	103/241	11	7.0	13/526	12/1449	8	2.64	p	3.77	4	4/4	1	3/3	6.6	0/11	1/2	2.75	Win Crafty Lady	/$30
DILLY OF A LILY	-								w	0.59	1	1/1	0	0/1	7.5	100/1	0/0	2.00	Eastern Red Wing	/$ 1

- Gold Fever, a Phipps-family homebred out of grass-stakes winner Lead Kindly Light, is by the very classy Forty Niner (as is Ide), a Travers winner whose progeny are high-percentage first-out winners.

Based on this pedigree information and the unremarkable first-out performances of three others, the contention seems to boil down to Trail City, Ide, Diligence and Gold Fever. Trail City, a $37,000 purchase, might not 'class up" here, leaving three.

Ide is 4-1, Diligence is 9-1, Gold Fever is 8-5. What to do? The notion that lightly bet newcomers only win once in a blue moon, and that when they do it's a fluke, is utter nonsense. At the 1995 Saratoga meet there were 18 debut winners, as follows:

Horse	Winning Margin	$2 Win Mutual
Crafty But Sweet	neck	$29.40
Sunny Side	6	45.40
Deanna Bee	5	19.80
Honour and Glory	10	3.40
Coxes Fastest	2	14.80
Carrbine Special	5	5.20
Wild 'n' Nasty	8	8.30
Birr	9	10.40
Roar	2	3.90
Jamies First Punch	9	6.80
Sir Cat	3/4	6.60
Diligence	11	21.60
Majestic Dream	2	48.40
Penniless Heiress	11	5.30
Platinum Blonde	1	6.00
Defacto	neck	3.60
Unbridled's Song	8	3.20
Colby	1	10.60

It may once have been true that "insiders" dominated maiden races loaded with first time-starters. But handicappers are much more sophisticated than they used to be, and come armed with a wealth of peripheral information with which to form solid opinions; also, people from all over the country bet on Saratoga's races via simulcast. It's not just backstretch money pouring in through the mutual machines these days, it's money from Las Vegas, from Del Mar, from bettors watching on satellite hook-ups from the comfort of their living rooms.

Note that eight of the 18 debut winners at the Spa, 44.4 percent, returned four-figure mutuels, including four blowouts of five lengths or more. And, to recall, Majestic Dream "figured" on pedigree to the tune of $48.40.

The biggest winning margin was 11 lengths, also known as winning by a pole:

SIXTH RACE **6½ FURLONGS. (1.14^{2}) MAIDEN SPECIAL WEIGHT. Purse $30,000. 2-year-olds. Weight, 118 lbs. (Preference to horses that have not started for a claiming price).**

Saratoga
AUGUST 10, 1995

Value of Race: $30,000 Winner $18,000; second $6,000; third $3,300; fourth $1,800; fifth $900. Mutuel Pool $354,099.00 Exacta Pool $516,574.00

Last Raced	Horse	M/Eqt.	A.Wt	PP	St	¼	½	Str	Fin	Jockey	Odds $1
	Diligence		2 118	8	3	1^{1}	1^{1}	1^{8}	1^{11}	Sellers S J	9.80
	Gold Fever		2 118	9	2	$2^{\frac{1}{2}}$	2^{1}	$2^{1\frac{1}{2}}$	$2^{2\frac{1}{2}}$	Smith M E	1.60
27Jly95 ^{2}Sar^{7}	Surround Sound		2 118	6	7	$9^{\frac{1}{2}}$	$8^{\frac{1}{2}}$	3^{hd}	3^{1}	Perret C	22.20
22Jly95 ^{2}Sar^{6}	Fortitude		2 118	1	8	$7^{2\frac{1}{2}}$	$5^{\frac{1}{2}}$	$4^{\frac{1}{2}}$	4^{2}	Perez R B	17.30
29Jly95 ^{2}Sar^{3}	Hey You Weasel	f	2 118	3	6	$5^{2\frac{1}{2}}$	4^{1}	$5^{1\frac{1}{2}}$	5^{4}	Davis R G	5.50
	Ide		2 118	7	4	8^{2}	9^{8}	7^{1}	$6^{1\frac{1}{2}}$	Day P	4.30
	Trail City		2 118	5	9	$3^{1\frac{1}{2}}$	$3^{1\frac{1}{2}}$	6^{1}	$7^{2\frac{1}{2}}$	Bailey J D	5.80
	Dustin's Dream		2 118	2	5	$6^{1\frac{1}{2}}$	7^{1}	8^{3}	$8^{\frac{1}{2}}$	Santos J A	22.40
	Scorcherer		2 118	4	10	10	10	10	9^{4}	Luzzi M J	39.75
	H'Way Three to Six		2 118	10	1	$4^{\frac{1}{2}}$	$6^{\frac{1}{2}}$	9^{hd}	10	Migliore R	18.10

OFF AT 3:36 Start Good. Won ridden out. Time, :22^{2}, :45^{4}, 1:10^{1}, 1:16^{3} Track fast.

$2 Mutuel Prices:				
	8–DILIGENCE	21.60	7.70	6.20
	9–GOLD FEVER		3.80	3.20
	6–SURROUND SOUND			9.80

$2 EXACTA 8–9 PAID $65.50

Gr/ro c, (Mar), by Miswaki–Honeytab, by Al Hattab. Trainer Zito Nicholas P. Bred by Kinsman Stud Farm (Ky).

DILIGENCE sprinted clear in the early stages, shook off GOLD FEVER in upper stretch, then drew away while being ridden out. GOLD FEVER chased the winner from outside to the top of the stretch, but couldn't stay with that one through the lane. SURROUND SOUND broke slowly, then checked in tight at the start, raced well back for a half, circled five wide into the stretch, then failed to threaten with a mild late rally. FORTITUDE angled four wide while gradually gaining on the turn, then lacked a strong closing bid. HEY YOU WEASEL raced just off the pace while saving ground to the turn and lacked a further response. IDE never reached contention. TRAIL CITY chased the leaders while saving ground to the top of the stretch, then gave way. DUSTIN'S DREAM checked along the backstretch and was never close thereafter. SCORCHERER was outrun after breaking slowly. H'WAY THREE TO SIX showed only brief speed.

Owners— 1, Kinsman Stable; 2, Phipps Cynthia; 3, Humphrey G Watts Jr; 4, Harbor View Farm; 5, Hough Stanley M & Johnson Kim & Ted; 6, Willmott Stables; 7, Mott William I & Verchota Robert; 8, Anstu Stable; 9, Maycroft Farm; 10, Rosenthal Morton

Trainers—1, Zito Nicholas P; 2, McGaughey Claude III; 3, Arnold George R II; 4, Jerkens H Allen; 5, Hough Stanley M; 6, Vestal Peter M; 7, Mott William I; 8, Schulhofer Flint S; 9, Serpe Philip M; 10, Brida Dennis J

Diligence sprinted clear early, and with the aid of the prevailing bias won under wraps. Handicappers doing instant variants when the charts were published the next day knew this would prove to be a key race: compare Diligence's fractions with the Grade 2 Saratoga Special, run later on the card:

NINTH RACE **6½ FURLONGS. (1.14^{2}) 93rd Running of THE SARATOGA SPECIAL. Purse $100,000 Added. Grade II. 2-year-olds. By subscription of $100 each which should accompany the nomination, $500 to pass the entry box, $500 to start, with $100,000 added. The added money and all fees to be divided 60% to the winner, 20% to second, 11% to third, 6% to fourth and 3% to fifth. Weight, 123 lbs. Non-winners of $50,000 twice, allowed 3 lbs. $50,000, 5 lbs. $30,000 twice, 8 lbs. $30,000, 11 lbs. Starters to be named at the closing time of entries. Trophies will be presented to the winning owner, trainer and jockey. Closed Saturday, July 29, with 24 nominations.**

Saratoga
AUGUST 10, 1995

Value of Race: $110,900 Winner $66,540; second $22,180; third $12,199; fourth $6,654; fifth $3,327. Mutuel Pool $372,995.00 Exacta Pool $383,789.00 Triple Pool $352,174.00

Last Raced	Horse	M/Eqt.	A.Wt	PP	St	¼	½	Str	Fin	Jockey	Odds $1
14Jly95 ^{6}Bel^{1}	Bright Launch		2 112	1	6	1^{1}	1^{hd}	1^{2}	1^{nk}	Santos J A	2.05
26Jly95 ^{4}Mth^{1}	Devil's Honor		2 114	5	1	6^{4}	$5^{2\frac{1}{2}}$	$3^{\frac{1}{2}}$	$2^{1\frac{1}{2}}$	Black A S	37.75
24Jly95 ^{2}Sar^{1}	Severe Clear		2 113	6	7	7^{30}	$6^{2\frac{1}{2}}$	$2^{\frac{1}{2}}$	3^{4}	Alvarado F T	23.70
11Jly95 ^{5}Lrl^{2}	Feather Box		2 114	4	4	$5^{1\frac{1}{2}}$	4^{1}	5^{hd}	$4^{\frac{3}{4}}$	Migliore R	21.60
1Jly95 ^{9}CD^{2}	Aggie Southpaw		2 112	3	2	4^{2}	$3^{\frac{1}{2}}$	6^{16}	5^{2}	Day P	1.20
21Jly95 ^{7}Sar^{4}	Editor's Note	b	2 112	8	5	2^{hd}	$2^{2\frac{1}{2}}$	$4^{\frac{1}{2}}$	6^{14}	Barton D M	7.10
7Jly95 ^{2}Bel^{1}	Meadowtime		2 112	7	8	8	8	8	7^{7}	Davis R G	15.10
19Jly95 ^{1}Rkm^{1}	Whiskey Tears		2 114	2	3	$3^{\frac{1}{2}}$	7^{20}	7^{1}	8	Garcia L I	8.40

OFF AT 5:10 Start Good. Won driving. Time, :22, :45^{2}, 1:11^{1}, 1:17^{4} Track fast.

$2 Mutuel Prices:				
	1–BRIGHT LAUNCH	6.10	4.70	4.10
	6–DEVIL'S HONOR		20.20	10.60
	7–SEVERE CLEAR			8.70

$2 EXACTA 1–6 PAID $182.00 $2 TRIPLE 1–6–7 PAID $1,526.00

B. c, (Feb), by Relaunch–Burnished Bright, by Well Decorated. Trainer Lukas D Wayne. Bred by Carrion Jamie S (Ky).

BRIGHT LAUNCH sprinted clear in the early stages, shook off a mild challenge from EDITOR'S NOTE on the turn, opened a clear advantage in upper stretch, drifted out under left hand urging while clinging to a slim lead in deep stretch, then turned back DEVIL'S HONOR under strong handing. DEVIL'S HONOR reserved early, circled six wide to launch his bid at the top of the stretch, rapidly gained to challenge seventy yards out then drifted in to bump with the winner, nearing the wire. SEVERE CLEAR outrun for a half, made a strong run along the inside to threaten in midstretch but couldn't sustain his bid. FEATHER BOX settled in the middle of the pack along the backstretch, gradually gained while four wide to reach contention in upper stretch, then lacked a strong closing bid. AGGIE SOUTHPAW up close early, dropped back slightly nearing the far turn, lodged a bid between horses entering the stretch, checked outside EDITOR'S NOTE in upper stretch and failed to threaten thereafter. EDITOR'S NOTE moved up steadily from outside to contest the pace on the far turn, battled heads apart outside the winner to the top of the stretch, drifted out in upper stretch, then steadily tired thereafter. MEADOWTIME stumbled badly at the start and was never close thereafter. WHISKEY TEARS showed only brief speed.

Owners— 1, Spence James C; 2, Carpenito Noreen; 3, Hettinger William R; 4, Buckland Farm; 5, Moore Christine S; 6, Young William T; 7, Paraneck Stable; 8, Anderson Karen H

Trainers—1, Lukas D Wayne; 2, Reese Cynthia G; 3, Hernandez Ramon M; 4, Cordero Angel Jr; 5, Hauswald Philip M; 6, Lukas D Wayne; 7, Aquilino Joseph; 8, Smith William R

Overweight: Devil's Honor (2), Severe Clear (1), Feather Box (2), Whiskey Tears (2).

Scratched— Sunny Side (22Jly95 ^{2}SAR^{1})

Bright Launch held by a neck thanks to the bias. Although he ran two ticks faster to the half (:45 2/5) than did Diligence, he required :25 4/5 for the third quarter and drifted out through a final sixteenth in :06 3/5, for a come-home time of :32 2/5. Diligence covered the same real estate in sparkling time, :24 2/5, and :06 2/5, coming home in :30 4/5.

Sure enough, it was a key race. Gold Fever came back two weeks later and broke his maiden by nearly nine lengths, he went on to win a minor stakes race at Aqueduct in the fall.

Ide chased Gold Fever to the stretch before weakening in his next attempt, but then reeled off five straight wins climaxed by a pair of Grade 3 stakes at Churchill Downs, and began his 3-year-old campaign at Oaklawn Park the following spring as one of the more highly regarded Triple Crown contenders:

Ide
Own: Willmott Stables

Ch. c. 3 (May)
Sire: Forty Niner (Mr. Prospector)
Dam: Maytide (Naskra)
Br: Garvin David B (Ky)
Tr: Vestal Peter M (—)

Lifetime Record :	7	5	0	1	$243,780						
1995	7	5	0	1	$243,780	Turf	0	0	0	0	
1994	0	M	0	0		Wet	1	1	0	0	$34,040
CD	2	2	0	0	$171,145	Dist	0	0	0	0	

25Nov95-10CD	fst	$1\frac{1}{16}$	:24^2	:48^2	1:12^4	1:44^1	KyJckeyClub-G3	**94**	1	2	2^1	3^1	3^1	1$^{3/4}$	Perret C	122	*1.00	90–08	Ide122$^{3/4}$ Editor's Note119$^{2\frac{1}{2}}$ El Amante113^5	Hard drive	5
5Nov95-8CD	fst	1	:23	:46^2	1:11^2	1:36^4	Iroquois-G3	**89**	1	1	1^1	1$^{1/2}$	1$^{3\frac{1}{2}}$	1^4	Perret C	121	*1.10	93–14	Ide121^4 El Amante116$^{1/2}$ City By Night114^4	Ridden out	8
20Oct95-8Kee	my	7f	:22	:45	1:10	1:22^4	Fort Springs53k	**91**	5	2	2$^{1/2}$	2$^{1/2}$	1$^{3\frac{1}{2}}$	1^8	Perret C	115	*.90	87–18	Ide115^8 Head Minister115$^{1/2}$ Black Tie Dinner115$^{2\frac{1}{2}}$	Ridden out	6
1Oct95-8TP	fst	6f	:22^4	:47	:59^4	1:12^3	Alw 27900N1X	**71**	5	5	4$^{1/2}$	1$^{1\frac{1}{2}}$	1^3	1^5	Perret C	121	*.70	82–19	Ide121^5 Rush Did It118^1 Never Is Never118^1	Ridden out	8
13Sep95-6TP	fst	6½f	:22^3	:46	1:12	1:18^3	Md Sp Wt	**76**	7	4	4$^{1\frac{1}{4}}$	3$^{1/2}$	1$^{2\frac{1}{2}}$	1^9	Perret C	121	*1.30	83–16	Ide121^9 Tax Amour121^{hd} English Gent121^{hd}		10
Came out, bumped start, much the best																					
24Aug95-6Sar	fst	6½f	:22	:45^4	1:11^3	1:18^2	Md Sp Wt	**63**	11	3	6^2	2$^{1/2}$	2^6	3^9	Santos J A	119	21.50	74–18	Gold Fever119$^{8\frac{3}{4}}$ Crafty Friend119^{hd} Ide119$^{1\frac{1}{2}}$	Bid, weakened	12
10Aug95-6Sar	fst	6½f	:22^2	:45^4	1:10^1	1:16^3	Md Sp Wt	**47**	7	4	8^{10}	9^7	7^{12}	6$^{20\frac{1}{2}}$	Day P	118	4.30	71–13	Diligence118^{11} Gold Fever118$^{2\frac{1}{2}}$ Surround Sound118^1	No threat	10

WORKOUTS: ●Feb 26 OP 5f fst 1:00^2 B *1/24* Feb 20 OP 5f my 1:02 B *3/8* Feb 13 OP 4f fst :48^2 B *2/20* Feb 8 OP 3f fst :36^4 B *7/52*

Worth mentioning is Ide's rapid development in terms of speed figures as the distances increased in the fall, from a 47 when unveiled behind Diligence to three figures in the 89-to-94 range by November. This is a routine pattern of development for regally bred juveniles proving themselves to be of stakes caliber. A similar rise to stardom is shown in the past performances of My Flag:

My Flag
Own: Phipps Ogden

Ch. f. 3 (Mar)
Sire: Easy Goer (Alydar)
Dam: Personal Ensign (Private Account)
Br: Phipps Ogden (Ky)
Tr: McGaughey Claude III (—)

Lifetime Record :	7	2	2	2	$634,614						
1996	1	0	1	0	$20,000	Turf	0	0	0	0	
1995	6	2	1	2	$614,614	Wet	2	1	1	0	$570,000
CD	0	0	0	0		Dist	0	0	0	0	

11Feb96-10GP	fst	1^{70}	:23^3	:47^1	1:11^3	1:42	ⒻDavona Dale-G3	**94**	5	8	8$^{8\frac{3}{4}}$	6^5	4^1	3$^{1\frac{1}{2}}$	Bailey J D	118 b	*.70	83–22	Plum Country118$^{3/4}$ [D]Rare Blend114$^{3/4}$ My Flag118^{no}		9
Inside early, angled out str, altered course deep str, tight qtrs Placed second through disqualification.																					
28Oct95-2Bel	my	$1\frac{1}{16}$	:23	:46^2	1:11	1:42^2	ⒻB C Juv Fil-G1	**95**	8	7	7$^{5\frac{1}{2}}$	3$^{2\frac{1}{2}}$	3$^{2\frac{1}{2}}$	1$^{1/2}$	Bailey J D	119 b	3.50	87–08	My Flag119$^{1/2}$ Cara Rafaela119$^{1\frac{1}{2}}$ Golden Attraction119^{17}	Strong finish	8
7Oct95-5Bel	wf	$1\frac{1}{16}$	:23	:46	1:11^1	1:42^4	ⒻFrizette-G1	**98**	2	5	5^8	4^5	2^2	2$^{3/4}$	Bailey J D	119 b	3.10	84–14	Golden Attraction119$^{3/4}$ My Flag119$^{8\frac{1}{2}}$ Flat Fleet Feet119^{12}	Finished well	5
16Sep95-4Bel	fst	1	:22	:44^3	1:09^4	1:36^1	ⒻMatron-G1	**78**	4	8	8^{15}	6^6	4^8	3$^{5\frac{3}{4}}$	Bailey J D	119	13.50	76–09	Golden Attraction119^{nk} Cara Rafaela119$^{5\frac{1}{2}}$ My Flag119^2	Slow start, rallied	8
14Aug95-6Sar	fst	7f	:23	:45^4	1:11^2	1:24^1	ⒻAlw 32000N2L	**77**	5	6	7^5	7$^{7\frac{3}{4}}$	3$^{3\frac{1}{2}}$	3^8	Bailey J D	118	*2.10	77–19	Summer Squeeze115^5 Wild 'n'Nasty112^3 MyFlag118^2	Improved position	9
21Jly95-8Sar	fst	6f	:21^3	:44^3	:57^1	1:10^4	ⒻSchuylrvill-G2	**74**	7	6	8^9	7^7	5^6	4^6	Bailey J D	115	9.60	81–10	GoldenAttraction121$^{2\frac{1}{2}}$ DylightCome112^{hd} WesternDremer121$^{3\frac{1}{2}}$	Mild gain	8
28Jun95-4Bel	fst	5½f	:22^4	:47^3	1:00^2	1:07	ⒻMd Sp Wt	**67**	3	5	5$^{4\frac{1}{2}}$	5^3	2^{hd}	1no	Bailey J D	115	*.85	80–22	My Flag115^{no} Launch At Dawn115^5 Here's London115^2	Five wide, up late	6

WORKOUTS: Feb 26 GP 4f fst :49^1 B *13/29* Feb 21 GP 4f fst :51 B *42/56* Feb 10 GP 3f fst :35^2 B *2/22* Feb 5 GP 5f fst 1:01 H *3/41* Jan 31 GP 5f fst 1:02^3 B *5/28* Jan 25 GP 5f fst 1:02 B *13/23*

A distant third at 2-1 in an allowance while still feeling her way at Saratoga third time out, the daughter of undefeated champion Personal Ensign improved steadily as autumn unfolded. She finished nearly six lengths behind Golden Attraction in the Matron but was less than a length behind the same rival in the Frizette, and finally surpassed her nemesis in the Breeders' Cup Juvenile Fillies with a stirring stretch charge (mom was so proud!).

August 12

ALABAMA SATURDAY is the second-busiest day of the meeting, surpassed only by the Travers. Unfortunately, the Racing Gods must have handicapped for a wet track because one of those quickly-forming thunderstorms that comes out of nowhere deluged the track beginning at around noon.

As first post approached it was still raining cats and dogs, and it was becoming increasingly more apparent that the day's turf races would be washed to the main track, which by now was an absolute sea of slop. One by one, each of the five scheduled grass races was switched to the main track, a late-breaking state of affairs that had Tom Durkin on the horn every few seconds to inform bettors of yet another program scratch.

With the sudden introduction of slop and the quickly changing pace match ups thrown into the mix, the day's races would have to be re-handicapped, and with all due haste. The second race was for 2-year-olds, and originally had been scheduled for a mile and a sixteenth on the Mellon turf course; it would now be run at seven furlongs on a sloppy main track, and the edge would go to whichever runners, if any, could handle the footing. After no less than a dozen scratches, early and late, a field of eight remained — seven colts and one filly:

2 **Saratoga** *7Fs/SLOPPY*

MELLON TURF COURSE 1 1/16 MILES START FINISH

~~1 1/16 MILES.~~ (Turf). (1:38^4) MAIDEN SPECIAL WEIGHT. Purse $32,000. 2-year-olds. Weight, 118 lbs.
~~(Preference to horses that have not started for a claiming price.)~~

Jetting Robert *110/200* *(210)*
Own: N Y Chezam Stable
VELASQUEZ J (39 1 1 6 .03)
Dk. b or br c. 2 (Apr)
Sire: Roman Diplomat (Roberto)
Dam: Jetting Polly (Tri Jet)
Br: Hector Sanchez (Fla)
Tr: Martin Jose (19 1 2 2 .05)
118
Lifetime Record: 1 M 0 1 $3,300
1995 1 M 0 1 $3,300 | Turf 0 0 0 0
1994 0 M 0 0 | Wet 0 0 0 0
Sar Ⓣ 0 0 0 0 | Dist Ⓣ 0 0 0 0
27Jly95-2Sar fst 6f :22 :45^3 :57^4 1:10^4 Md Sp Wt 51 6 2 64¼ 56¼ 57 3^{14} Velasquez J 118 67.00 73-12 HonourAndGlory118^{10} BlushingJim118^{3½} JttngRobrt118^{nk} Checked 7/16 pl 12
WORKOUTS: Aug 7 Sar 5f fst 1:02^3 H *22/40* Jly 25 Sar 3f fst :38 B *16/26* Jly 17 Sar 4f fst :49 Hg*2/13* Jly 9 Bel 5f fst 1:02 Hg*17/26* Jly 4 Bel 4f fst :49^2 Bg*31/71* Jun 28 Bel 5f fst 1:02^4 Hg*27/42*

Vibrations *110/210* *(215)*
Own: Durst Lillian
BAILEY J D (108 23 11 14 .21)
Gr/ro c. 2 (Mar)
Sire: Regal Classic (Vice Regent)
Dam: Floating Taler (Verbatim)
Br: Schickedanz Gustav (Ont-C)
Tr: Manning Dennis J (2 0 1 1 .00)
118
Lifetime Record: 2 M 1 0 $7,500
1995 2 M 1 0 $7,500 | Turf 2 0 1 0 $7,500
1994 0 M 0 0 | Wet 0 0 0 0
Sar Ⓣ 0 0 0 0 | Dist Ⓣ 0 0 0 0
16Jly95-6Bel fm 6f Ⓣ :22^2 :46^2 :58^1 1:10^1 Md Sp Wt 69 8 3 2 1½ 21 22 2 2½ Bailey J D 116 *2.60 82-15 Game's On116^{2½} Vibrations116^1 Cornwall116^{nk} Held place 12
9Jly95-9Mth fm 5f Ⓣ :22 :45^1 :57^2 Gilded Time30k 64 7 1 4 2½ 44 3^5 4 4¼ McCauley W H 114 14.90 83-13 Cold Snap118^{1½} Skip Away112^1 Cobb's Creek121^{1¾} No stretch bid 7
WORKOUTS: Aug 4 Mth 6f fst 1:18^3 B *3/3* Jly 27 Mth 5f fst 1:03^2 B *4/5* Jun 26 Mth 6f gd 1:17^2 Bg*3/4* Jun 17 Mth 5f fst 1:04^2 B *32/41* Jun 10 Mth 6f fst 1:18 Bg*7/7* Jun 3 Mth 5f fst 1:03 Bg*11/24*

Pro Doc
Own: Rosenthal Mrs Morton
SMITH M E (102 19 14 17 .19)
Gr/ro c. 2 (Mar)
Sire: Prospectors Gamble (Crafty Prospector)
Dam: Smile Softly (Prince Tenderfoot)
Br: Morton Rosenthal (Fla)
Tr: Terrill William V (16 0 2 0 .00)
118
Lifetime Record: 1 M 0 0 $0
1995 1 M 0 0 | Turf 0 0 0 0
1994 0 M 0 0 | Wet 0 0 0 0
Sar Ⓣ 0 0 0 0 | Dist Ⓣ 0 0 0 0
29Jly95-6Sar fst 6f :22 :45^4 :58^4 1:11^4 Md Sp Wt — 8 9 9^{12} 9^{19} 9^{29} — Luzzi M J 119 52.00 — 13 El Amante119^{1½} Hashid119^{2¾} Head Minister119^{3½} Trailed, eased 9
WORKOUTS: Aug 5 Sar tr.t 4f fst :51^4 B *13/18* Jly 25 Sar tr.t 4f fst :51^3 B *16/28* Jly 19 Bel 4f fst :48^3 B *24/66* Jly 10 Bel 5f fst 1:02^4 H *18/28* Jly 5 Bel 5f fst 1:03^1 H *17/29* Jun 29 Bel 4f fst :49^3 B *23/49*

Columbia County *110/230* *(225)*
Own: Zaretsky Martin
ALVARADO F T (34 3 4 1 .09)
Dk. b or br c. 2 (Feb)
Sire: Go and Go (Be My Guest)
Dam: Stuttsman County (Damascus)
Br: Jerry Bilinski (NY)
Tr: Bond Harold James (10 5 1 0 .50)
118
Lifetime Record: 0 M 0 0 $0
1995 0 M 0 0 | Turf 0 0 0 0
1994 0 M 0 0 | Wet 0 0 0 0
Sar Ⓣ 0 0 0 0 | Dist Ⓣ 0 0 0 0
WORKOUTS: Aug 9 Sar 5f fst 1:03^3 B *39/47* Aug 3 Sar 6f fst 1:16 Bg*3/6* Jly 24 Sar 5f gd 1:02^2 Hg*5/11* Jly 17 Sar 4f fst :51^1 B *10/13* Jly 7 Bel 5f fst 1:02 Hg*11/30* Jun 29 Bel 4f fst :50 Bg*28/49*
Jun 15 Bel tr.t 4f fst :50^4 B *23/41* Jun 9 Bel tr.t 4f fst :51^1 B *10/17*

Tuning Up *X/230* *(115)*
Own: Phipps Ogden
VELAZQUEZ J R (80 12 10 6 .15)
Ch. c. 2 (May)
Sire: Easy Goer (Alydar)
Dam: Dancing All Night (Nijinsky II)
Br: Phipps Ogden & Ogden Mills (Ky)
Tr: McGaughey Claude III (19 3 3 3 .16)
118
Lifetime Record: 1 M 0 0 $1,800
1995 1 M 0 0 $1,800 | Turf 0 0 0 0
1994 0 M 0 0 | Wet 1 0 0 0 $1,800
Sar Ⓣ 0 0 0 0 | Dist Ⓣ 0 0 0 0
2Jly95-6Bel my 6f ⊗ :23 :47 :59 1:11^1 Md Sp Wt 45 5 4 4 2½ 3 1½ 2^6 3^{12} Velazquez J R 116 4.40 73-13 Ok By Me116^{11} Erskine116^1 DTuning Up116^{¾} Drifted late 8
Disqualified and placed 4th
WORKOUTS: Aug 7 Sar tr.t 4f fst :51^1 B *23/39* Jly 26 Sar 4f fst :49^1 Hg*19/52* Jly 13 Bel 4f fst :50^2 B *45/66* Jly 1 Bel 3f fst :37^2 B *6/21* Jun 27 Bel 4f my :50 B *5/19* Jun 22 Bel 3f sly :37 B *4/7*

Gun Approval *70/220* *(180)*
Own: Live Oak Plantation
GRAELL A (5 0 1 1 .00)
Ch. c. 2 (Mar)
Sire: With Approval (Caro)
Dam: Shot Gun Bonnie (It's Freezing)
Br: Live Oak Stud (Ont-C)
Tr: Kelly Patrick J (19 2 2 2 .11)
118
Lifetime Record: 2 M 0 1 $3,300
1995 2 M 0 1 $3,300 | Turf 0 0 0 0
1994 0 M 0 0 | Wet 0 0 0 0
Sar Ⓣ 0 0 0 0 | Dist Ⓣ 0 0 0 0
29Jly95-6Sar fst 6f :22 :45^4 :58^4 1:11^4 Md Sp Wt 29 4 4 3^1 4 2½ 7^9 6 16¼ Graell A 119 44.75 66-13 El Amante119^{1½} Hashid119^{2¾} Head Minister119^{3½} Broke awkwardly 9
14Jly95-6Bel fst 5f :22 :45^2 :57^1 Md Sp Wt 51 5 4 3^3 4^2 3^4 3 10¾ Graell A 116 47.00 89-07 Bright Launch116^{¾} Hashid116^{10} Gun Approval116^5 No late bid 8
WORKOUTS: Aug 7 Sar 3f fst :38 Bg*17/26* Jly 26 Sar 3f fst :38^1 B *15/19* Jly 21 Sar 3f fst :37^4 B *10/13* Jly 9 Bel 3f fst :36^1 Hg*4/19* Jun 29 Bel 3f fst :37^2 B *18/35* Jun 14 Bel tr.t 3f gd :37^4 B *4/12*

There was no backstretch "action" going on; six entrants were pegged anywhere from 5-2 to 7-1.

Vibrations was the favorite, probably because he was a "double fig" in terms of Beyer figures; but Vibration's two superior figures had been recorded in turf sprints and were out of context in trying to forecast his slop capabilities, just as dirt figures have little predictive value in grass races.

Second choice at 7-2 was Tuning Up, beaten a dozen lengths in his muddy track-debut at Belmont. According to *Mudders & Turfers*, Tuning Up's sire, Easy Goer, rated as an "X" — indicating fewer than 20 starters on the surface, *with little success thus far*.

The intriguing prospect was Spicy Fact, for several reasons. First and foremost was his *M&T* rating of 320, the highest in the field by a considerable margin, as written alongside his past performances. (Sire Known Fact, a son of legendary wet track-sire In Reality, rates at 210, and broodmare sire Raja Baba at 220; the sire's rating, 210, is added to half the broodmare sire's rating, 110, producing the total score)

Spicy Fact's trouble line "carried out green" from his July 22 debut warranted a check of the full chart footnote, which read "...carried out by the loose horse on the turn, lugged in while racing greenly in upper stretch..." The ground loss of 6 3/4 lengths from the pre-stretch call to the wire was deceptive from another angle: wire-to-wire winner Sunny Side had expanded his lead from a head to six lengths during that segment, which meant Spicy Fact had held his ground relative to everyone else in the field (remember our example of this angle from Aqueduct during the transition from winter to spring).

Since that educational experience Spicy Fact had trained strongly, working a best-of-23 half mile over the track July 30, and coming back with a five-furlong move just five days ago that was second-fastest of 40.

With no loose horse to get in his way this time, Spicy Fact steamrolled from last position after a quarter to gain the lead by upper stretch, and he splashed away with authority at nearly 7-1. Vibrations did not handle the footing nearly as well; the favorite took up sharply while jumping puddles along the backstretch and was not persevered with when hopelessly beaten into the lane:

SECOND RACE Saratoga AUGUST 12, 1995 — 7 FURLONGS. (1.202) MAIDEN SPECIAL WEIGHT. Purse $32,000. 2-year-olds. Weight, 118 lbs. (Preference to horses that have not started for a claiming price.)(ORIGINALLY SCHEDULED FOR TURF AT ONE MILE AND SIXTEENTH.)

Value of Race: $32,000 Winner $19,200; second $6,400; third $3,520; fourth $1,920; fifth $960. Mutuel Pool $348,999.00 Exacta Pool $474,037.00 Quinella Pool $107,431.00

Last Raced	Horse	M/Eqt.	A.	Wt	PP	St	¼	½	Str	Fin	Jockey	Odds $1
22Jly95 2Sar8	Spicy Fact		2	118	7	2	8	42	11½	14½	Maple E	6.90
27Jly95 2Sar3	Jetting Robert		2	118	1	3	1½	1½	23½	24	Velasquez J	5.40
2Jly95 6Bel3	Tuning Up		2	118	5	8	51	69	5½	3no	Velazquez J R	3.50
12Jly95 1Bel4	Fasta		2	115	8	7	7hd	52	612	43	Perez R B	4.70
29Jly95 6Sar6	Gun Approval	b	2	118	6	1	21	21½	4hd	54	Graell A	7.90
	Columbia County		2	118	4	6	33½	31	3hd	69½	Alvarado F T	13.40
16Jly95 6Bel2	Vibrations		2	118	2	5	6hd	72	710	723	Bailey J D	2.55
29Jly95 6Sar9	Pro Doc		2	118	3	4	42½	8	8	8	Smith M E	23.80

OFF AT 1:32 Start Good. Won driving. Time, :222, :463, 1:12, 1:251 Track sloppy.

$2 Mutuel Prices:

1–SPICY FACT	15.80	8.00	5.30
3–JETTING ROBERT		6.50	4.20
7–TUNING UP			3.50

$2 EXACTA 1–3 PAID $103.00 $2 QUINELLA 1–3 PAID $47.60

B. c, (Mar), by Known Fact–Curried Favor, by Raja Baba. Trainer Johnson Philip G. Bred by Mary A. Sullivan (Ky).

SPICY FACT outrun early, rapidly gained while four wide on the turn, accelerated to the front in upper stretch, then drew away under pressure. JETTING ROBERT set the pace slightly off the rail into upper stretch, and held well for the place. TUNING UP outrun for a half, failed to threaten while improving his position in the stretch. FASTA never reached contention while five wide. GUN APPROVAL forced the pace from outside to the top of the stretch and tired in the drive. COLUMBIA COUNTY raced in close contention along the inside to the turn and lacked a further response. VIBRATIONS took up sharply after jumping puddles along the backstretch, and was never close thereafter. PRO DOC was finished early.

Owners— 1, Sullimar Stable; 2, N Y Chezam Stable; 3, Phipps Ogden; 4, Paulson Allen E; 5, Live Oak Plantation; 6, Zaretsky Martin; 7, Durst Lillian; 8, Rosenthal Mrs Morton

Trainers—1, Johnson Philip G; 2, Martin Jose; 3, McGaughey Claude III; 4, Mott William I; 5, Kelly Patrick J; 6, Bond Harold James; 7, Manning Dennis J; 8, Terrill William V

Scratched— Firestix (29Jly95 6SAR5), R.S.V.P. Requested, Zordon, Pirate Performer (29Jly95 6SAR4), Officious (14Jly95 6BEL8), Kings Bet, Touch of Honey (31Jly95 2SAR8), Star of Theatrical (13Jly95 6BEL7), Captain Charlie (10Jun95 1CD8), Account of Grace (4Aug95 1RKM3), Dangerous Ground (30Mar95 3HIA10), Tellerico's Fire (22Jly95 2SAR5)

By post time for the sixth race the sun was breaking through the clouds but the damage had been done. The track was ankle-deep chocolate soup, and the overriding handicapping priority was determining who could handle the footing.

The sixth race was another sprint for 2-year-olds — this one carded for the dirt all along. Though I didn't make the winner, I probably should have given him a look, given his 13-1 odds. At the least, he provides a good example of the kind of form reversals players might anticipate when a field of 2-year-olds encounters slop for the first time.

Examine the first three betting choices, Valid Victor, Northern Pursuit, Chimes Castelli, as well as the winner, State Prize:

5½ Furlongs **(1:032) MAIDEN SPECIAL WEIGHT. Purse $30,000. 2-year-olds. Weight, 118 lbs. (Preference to horses that have not started for a claiming price.)**

Coupled – Northern Pursuit and Sole City; Quite a Day and Citified

Northern Pursuit 220/?
Own: Vogel Harvey C Jr
KRONE J A (76 6 13 8 .08)

Ch. c. 2 (Feb)
Sire: Afleet (Mr. Prospector)
Dam: Harvard's Bay (Halpern Bay)
Br: Haras Santa Maria de Araras (Fla)
Tr: Kimmel John C (20 4 6 3 .20)
118

Lifetime Record:	1 M 1 0	$6,000			
1995	1 M 1 0	$6,000	Turf	0 0 0 0	
1994	0 M 0 0		Wet	0 0 0 0	
Sar	1 0 1 0	$6,000	Dist	1 0 1 0	$6,000

22Jly95–2Sar fst 5½f :222 :462 :584 1:051 Md Sp Wt 53 6 2 21 2hd 22 26 Krone J A 120 *.85 89–07 SunnySide1206 NorthernPursuit120nk Justinthemiddl1202 Held 2nd, green 12

WORKOUTS: Aug 5 Sar 5f fst 1:04 B *23/31* Jly 20 Sar 3f fst :362 B *3/11* ●Jly 12 Bel 5f fst 1:00 Hg *1/25* Jly 4 Bel 5f fst 1:011 H *7/30* ●Jun 28 Bel 4f fst :471 Hg *1/58* Jun 16 Bel tr.t 4f fst :483 H *8/44*

Valid Victor 220/190 (315)
Own: Oxenberg Bea
BAILEY J D (108 23 11 14 .21)

B. c. 2 (May)
Sire: Valid Appeal (In Reality)
Dam: Oedipus Rex (Rexson)
Br: Mangurian Harry T Jr (Fla)
Tr: Hough Stanley M (12 2 1 1 .17)
118

Lifetime Record:	0 M 0 0	$0		
1995	0 M 0 0		Turf	0 0 0 0
1994	0 M 0 0		Wet	0 0 0 0
Sar	0 0 0 0		Dist	0 0 0 0

WORKOUTS: Aug 5 Sar tr.t 5f fst 1:044 B *11/16* Jly 28 Sar 5f fst 1:013 Hg *7/28* Jly 23 Sar tr.t 4f fst :512 B *16/27* Jly 17 Bel 3f fst :37 Bg *4/15* Jly 12 Bel 4f fst :474 H *8/60* Jly 5 Bel 3f fst :382 B *14/21* Jun 30 Bel 3f fst :382 Bg *38/44* Jun 23 Bel 3f gd :36 H *4/21*

Chimes Castelli 190/280 (330)
Own: Fares Farm Inc
SMITH M E (102 19 14 17 .19)

Ch. c. 2 (Jun)
Sire: Leo Castelli (Sovereign Dancer)
Dam: Chimes (Mr. Prospector)
Br: Fares Farm Inc (Ky)
Tr: Lukas D Wayne (17 4 4 2 .24)
118

Lifetime Record:	0 M 0 0	$0		
1995	0 M 0 0		Turf	0 0 0 0
1994	0 M 0 0		Wet	0 0 0 0
Sar	0 0 0 0		Dist	0 0 0 0

WORKOUTS: Aug 8 Sar tr.t 5f fst 1:034 B *3/7* Aug 2 Sar tr.t 5f fst 1:041 B *3/8* Jly 26 Sar 5f fst 1:01 Hg *3/47* Jly 20 Sar tr.t 5f fst 1:041 B *7/9* Jly 12 Bel 4f fst :483 H *28/60* ●Jly 5 Bel 4f fst :474 H *1/57* Jun 27 Bel 3f my :39 B *7/12* Jun 19 SA 3f fst :382 H *23/35*

State Prize 200/300 (350)
Own: Hofmann Georgia E
SAMYN J L (20 4 0 2 .20)

B. c. 2 (Feb)
Sire: Houston (Seattle Slew)
Dam: Your Serve (Conquistador Cielo)
Br: Wilmoth Interests Inc (Ky)
Tr: Jerkens H Allen (26 4 3 3 .15)
118

Lifetime Record:	2 M 0 0	$0		
1995	2 M 0 0		Turf	0 0 0 0
1994	0 M 0 0		Wet	0 0 0 0
Sar	1 0 0 0		Dist	1 0 0 0

29Jly95–6Sar fst 6f :22 :454 :584 1:114 Md Sp Wt 27 3 2 1hd 31 68½ 817 Samyn J L 119 b 19.60 65–13 El Amante1191½ Hashid1192¾ Head Minister1193½ Used in pace 9
14Jly95–2Bel fst 5f :23 :46 :583 Md Sp Wt 28 4 6 66 64½ 66½ 710¼ Samyn J L 116 4.80 83–07 Prospector'sPet116½ TomN'Kth1161¾ ImGoodGmble1161 Pinched break 8

WORKOUTS: Aug 8 Sar 4f fst :48 H *2/32* Jly 25 Sar 5f fst 1:021 H *12/28* Jly 19 Sar 5f fst 1:022 B *5/12* Jly 11 Bel tr.t 5f sly 1:02 B *2/2* Jun 28 Bel 3f fst :374 Bg *13/26* Jun 24 Bel 3f fst :364 H *12/38*

All boasted superior wet track-breeding (though a total score on Northern Pursuit could not be reached because his obscure broodmare sire, Halpern Bay, was not listed in *M&T*. Valid Victor (315), Chimes Castelli (330), and State Prize (350) were bred on both sides of their pedigrees to handle the off-going.

Players willing to give State Prize the benefit of the doubt in spite of two less-than-inspiring finishes on fast tracks collected a $29.80 mutual. Aside from a very high score on Tomlinson's mud ratings, *Maiden Stats* suggested as well that State Prize had potential beyond what he had shown thus far:

	SIRE INFO								DAM INFO											SIBLING INFO		YRLG SALES INF	
93 Unnamed Foals Dam's Name, Yob	# wnr/str	2yo wnr/str	% 1st	awd	Mud w%/sts	Turf w%/sts	% 1stT	Spi	prf	Dpi	# fls	# wnr/str	# sw	2yo wnr/str	awd	Mud w%/sts	Turf wnr/str	Dosage Index	Top Sibling	/Earn$	Price/Sire avg	# Rnk/sld
You're Too Special,81	13/ 19	7/ 14	21	5.8	15/ 34	0/ 0	0	0.71	sw	3.70	4	3/ 4	1	1/ 3	7.5	25/ 4	0/ 1	5.00	Wildly Special	/$169k		
Your Eyes Only,82									w	0.60	5	2/ 4	0	1/ 2	8.2	0/ 15	0/ 1	2.60	Sir Valiant	/$ 69k		
Your Serve,86	9/ 41	5/ 35	6	5.3	8/ 13	0/ 7	0	0.72	ur	0.00	1	0/ 1	0	0/ 1	0.0	0/ 0	0/ 0	3.67	[illegible]		$165k/$ 43k	1/ 50
You Tell Me,85	31/ 42	16/ 30	27	6.6	19/ 74	10/ 10	0	1.45	sw	3.03	1	1/ 1	1	1/ 1	7.3	0/ 0	0/ 1	1.15	+Clev Er Irish	/$ 81k		
Yuki,83	222/ 278	80/ 196	6	7.1	16/1105	9/ 470	5	0.82	w	1.64	4	2/ 3	1	0/ 3	5.3	20/ 10	2/ 2	4.00	See Yn In Court	/$162k		

Listed under his dam, Your Serve, State Prize had fetched $165,000 at auction, the highest-priced of 50 yearlings sired by Houston. Considering that Your Serve had been unraced and had produced one undistinguished starter, the bidding had gone exceptionally high; there must have been something about State Prize that potential buyers had been willing to pay top dollar for.

The top bid went to Georgia Hofmann, owner of the remarkably consistent Grade 1 winner, Sky Beauty.

The flash of improved early speed on July 29 suggested the colt was coming around under the patient and experienced hand of Allen Jerkens.

I sat idly by, and watched a very logical exacta combination pay $125.50:

SIXTH RACE **5½ FURLONGS. (1.03^{2}) MAIDEN SPECIAL WEIGHT. Purse $30,000. 2-year-olds. Weight, 118 lbs. (Preference to horses that have not started for a claiming price.)**

Saratoga

AUGUST 12, 1995

Value of Race: $30,000 Winner $18,000; second $6,000; third $3,300; fourth $1,800; fifth $900. Mutuel Pool $505,712.00 Exacta Pool $730,682.00

Last Raced	Horse	M/Eqt.	A.	Wt	PP	St	¼	⅜	Str	Fin	Jockey	Odds $1
29Jly95 6Sar8	State Prize		2	118	4	1	2^{hd}	2½	2^{2}	1^{nk}	Samyn J L	13.90
	Valid Victor		2	118	2	2	1½	1^{2}	1^{2}	2$4^{1}$½	Bailey J D	1.75
22Jly95 2Sar2	Northern Pursuit		2	118	1	5	4^{1}	4^{1}½	3^{2}½	3^{1}	Krone J A	3.20
3Aug95 2Sar5	Lonsdale	b	2	118	5	8	10	8½	8^{1}	4no	Perez R B	34.25
	Clearly Alert	b	2	118	10	4	5^{5}	5^{4}	4^{1}½	5½	Alvarado F T	13.00
	Chimes Castelli		2	118	3	6	9^{2}	9^{hd}	7½	6^{2}½	Smith M E	4.90
	Citified		2	118	9	10	7½	6½	6^{hd}	7^{5}½	Sellers S J	b-5.40
	Quite a Day		2	118	7	3	3^{2}	3^{hd}	5^{1}	8½	Day P	b-5.40
	Rev Owen G		2	118	6	9	8^{2}	10	10	9½	Chavez J F	20.80
	Premium		2	118	8	7	6½	7^{1}½	9^{3}	10	Davis R G	23.30

b–Coupled: Citified and Quite a Day.

OFF AT 3:41 Start Good. Won driving. Time, :21^{4}, :45^{3}, :58^{3}, 1:05^{2} Track sloppy.

$2 Mutuel Prices:			
5–STATE PRIZE	29.80	10.20	5.80
3–VALID VICTOR		4.70	3.30
1–NORTHERN PURSUIT			3.40

$2 EXACTA 5–3 PAID $125.50

B. c, (Feb), by Houston–Your Serve, by Conquistador Cielo. Trainer Jerkens H Allen. Bred by Wilmoth Interests Inc (Ky).

STATE PRIZE raced just behind the leader to the top of the stretch, then finished determindly to get up in the final strides. VALID VICTOR sprinted clear along the backstretch, raced uncontested on the lead into midstretch, maintained a clear lead into deep stretch, but couldn't hold the winner safe. NORTHERN PURSUIT rushed up along the rail, swung out while gaining on the turn, then lacked a strong closing bid. LONSDALE outrun for a half, failed to threaten with a mild late rally. CLEARLY ALERT went evenly while four wide. CHIMES CASTELLI outrun for a half, closed some ground in the lane. CITIFIED never reached contention after breaking slowly. QUITE A DAY raced just outside the winner to the top of the stretch, and gave way. REV OWEN G was outrun after breaking slowly. PREMIUM raced six wide throughout. STATE PRIZE, NORTHERN PURSUIT, LONSDALE, QUITE A DAY and PREMIUM wore mud caulks.

Owners— 1, Hofmann Georgia E; 2, Oxenberg Bea; 3, Vogel Harvey C Jr; 4, Sigel Marshall E; 5, Sommer Viola; 6, Fares Farm Inc; 7, Dogwood Stable; 8, Dogwood Stable; 9, Flynn Pierce J; 10, Harbor View Farm

Trainers—1, Jerkens H Allen; 2, Hough Stanley M; 3, Kimmel John C; 4, Picou James E; 5, Martin Frank; 6, Lukas D Wayne; 7, Alexander Frank A; 8, Zito Nicholas P; 9, Destasio Richard A; 10, Jerkens H Allen

Scratched— Sole City

Shortly afterward, as post for the prestigious Grade 1 Alabama Stakes neared, my friend and colleague from *The Saratogian*, John Pricci, came over and made a case for a filly boasting nothing more than wins at the maiden and preliminary allowance levels.

"I know she doesn't class up to these, but she *did* win in the slop here as a 2-year-old," he remarked with enthusiasm.

"Forget it," I scornfully countered. "I don't care if she's won in the slop here before or not, Pretty Discreet is a tomato can. Her form's been subpar in three races since coming back from the layoff, and even if she improved 20 lengths the only way she'll ever get a mile and a quarter is by hitching a ride. That filly can't possibly win the Alabama."

There's an old proverb in racing: never say anything bad about a horse until it's been dead for 10 years.

Open mouth, insert foot:

Pretty Discreet
Own: Robsham E Paul
SMITH M E (3 0 0 0 .00)

B. f. 3 (Apr)
Sire: Private Account (Damascus)
Dam: Pretty Persuasive (Believe It)
Br: Robsham E Paul (Ky)
Tr: Terrill William V (—)

118

Lifetime Record:	10	3	3	1	$219,998						
1995	4	1	1	0	$128,960	Turf	0	0	0	0	
1994	6	2	2	1	$91,038	Wet	3	2	0	0	$136,800
Bel	6	1	3	1	$81,038	Dist	1	0	0	0	$2,160

12Aug95-8Sar	sly	1¼	:47^{2}	1:11^{3}	1:36^{3}	2:02	ⒻAlabama-G1	108	9	1	$1^{1\frac{1}{2}}$	$1^{4\frac{1}{2}}$	1^{6}	1^{8}	Smith M E	121	42.75	94-12	PrettyDiscreet121^{8} FrindlyButy121^{16} RogusWlk121$^{2\frac{3}{4}}$	Vigorous hand ride	9
29Jly95-3Sar	fst	1⅛	:48	1:12^{2}	1:38^{4}	1:53	ⒻAlw 36000N2X	72	1	3	$3^{1\frac{1}{2}}$	3^{3}	$3^{5\frac{1}{2}}$	4^{9}	Bailey J D	112	*1.20	62-29	Spire117^{6} Time For Allaire111^{3} Very True111^{no}	Drifted, tired	6
13Jly95-8Bel	fst	7f	:22^{4}	:46	1:11	1:24	3↑ ⒻAlw 34000N2X	84	3	4	$4^{2\frac{1}{2}}$	5^{2}	$3^{1\frac{1}{2}}$	$2^{1\frac{1}{4}}$	Bailey J D	112	3.65	80-17	Class Kris112$^{1\frac{1}{4}}$ PrettyDiscreet112$^{1\frac{3}{4}}$ FullAndFancy111$^{\frac{1}{2}}$	Checked 3/8, wide	6
9Jun95-5Bel	fst	6½f	:22^{2}	:45^{4}	1:11	1:17^{3}	3↑ ⒻAlw 34000N2X	41	3	10	6^{4}	$9^{6\frac{1}{2}}$	10^{12}	$10^{24\frac{3}{4}}$	Bailey J D	112	*2.60	62-19	Russian Flight114^{3} Book Of Fortune112$^{2\frac{1}{2}}$ Full And Fancy112^{4}	Tired	10
8Oct94-6Bel	fst	$1\frac{1}{16}$	:23^{1}	:46^{4}	1:12^{1}	1:43^{4}	ⒻFrizette-G1	64	3	4	4^{13}	$4^{4\frac{1}{2}}$	2^{10}	$3^{21\frac{3}{4}}$	Bailey J D	119	9.50	61-17	Flanders119^{21} ChangeForaDollr119$^{\frac{3}{4}}$ PrettyDiscreet119^{10}	Fractious break	4
17Sep94-4Bel	fst	1	:23	:46^{2}	1:11	1:35	ⒻMatron-G1	86	6	6	6^{4}	4^{2}	4^{5}	$3^{7\frac{3}{4}}$	Bailey J D	119	14.50	80-10	Flanders119$^{3\frac{1}{4}}$ Stormy Blues119$^{4\frac{1}{2}}$ Pretty Discreet119$^{\frac{1}{2}}$	Four wide	6
Awarded second purse money																					
19Aug94-6Sar	sly	6½f	:21^{3}	:45^{1}	1:11	1:17^{4}	ⒻAlw 28000N1X	74	7	2	$5^{7\frac{1}{2}}$	$4^{2\frac{1}{2}}$	1^{hd}	1^{2}	Bailey J D	116	3.90	86-09	Pretty Discreet116^{2} Clever Thing116^{no} Grand Charmer116$^{8\frac{1}{4}}$	Wide, driving	8
22Jly94-8Sar	my	6f	:21^{4}	:45^{3}	:58^{4}	1:12^{3}	ⒻSchuylrvill-G2	47	7	3	$5^{1\frac{1}{4}}$	6^{3}	7^{5}	$7^{10\frac{1}{4}}$	Davis R G	114	14.80	68-11	ChangingWys114^{4} Uncceptble119$^{2\frac{1}{4}}$ ArticExperience114^{no}	Bumped, tired	10
7Jly94-3Bel	fst	6f	:23^{2}	:47^{1}	:59	1:11^{2}	ⒻMd Sp Wt	77	2	2	3^{1}	2^{hd}	$1^{1\frac{1}{2}}$	1^{4}	Bailey J D	115	*.90	84-12	Pretty Discreet115^{4} Noble House115$^{1\frac{3}{4}}$ So Cheerful115$^{\frac{3}{4}}$	Driving	6
23Jun94-5Bel	fst	5f	:22^{1}	:46^{1}		:59	ⒻMd Sp Wt	75	5	5	3^{2}	3^{1}	1^{hd}	2^{nk}	Bailey J D	115	2.20	86-16	LoveTunnel115^{nk} PrttyDiscrt115^{2} DncsInGold115^{5}	Broke slowly, gamely	6

WORKOUTS: Aug 30 Bel 4f fst :49^{1} B *23/30* ●Aug 25 Sar tr.t 5f fst 1:03^{3} B *1/7* Aug 20 Sar tr.t 4f fst :52^{3} B *17/21* Aug 7 Sar tr.t 4f fst :50^{1} B *5/40* Jly 24 Sar tr.t 6f fst 1:17^{1} B *1/1* Jly 20 Sar 4f fst :51^{3} B *22/23*

Pretty Discreet, a hopeless case on paper, came out of the gate as if shot from a cannon and quickly opened up on the field. Increasing her lead at each succeeding point of call, she won laughing by eight lengths at 42-1, while even-money favorite Golden Bri, conqueror of the mighty Serena's Song in Belmont's Coaching Club American Oaks in July, floundered in the going like a fish washed up on shore.

Eerily enough, the place horse, 16 lengths clear of the third place-finisher, no less, also seemed overmatched on paper:

Friendly Beauty
Own: Kinsman Stable & Porthampton Farms
KRONE J A (76 6 13 8 .08)

B. f. 3 (Mar)
Sire: Stalwart (Hoist the Flag)
Dam: Fredaq (Raise A Native)
Br: Kinsman Stud Farm (NY)
Tr: Tesher Howard M (17 3 2 2 .18)

121

Lifetime Record:	10	3	0	3	$98,783						
1995	3	0	0	1	$10,588	Turf	1	0	0	0	$1,500
1994	7	3	0	2	$88,195	Wet	4	2	0	2	$43,195
Sar	4	1	0	2	$24,088	Dist	0	0	0	0	

31Jly95-8Sar	fst	7f	:22^{1}	:45^{3}	1:11	1:24^{1}	Ⓕ[S]SagamoreHill55k	77	2	6	7^{10}	8^{11}	$6^{2\frac{3}{4}}$	3^{3}	Day P	115	6.50	82-16	Shebatim's Trick113^{3} Forested112^{no} Friendly Beauty115$^{2\frac{3}{4}}$	Late gain	8
15Jan95-9GP	fst	$1\frac{1}{16}$ ⊗	:23^{4}	:48	1:12	1:45^{3}	ⒻSweetstChant50k	78	3	8	8^{11}	7^{10}	5^{4}	$4^{2\frac{1}{2}}$	Boulanger G	116	3.80	80-24	Mistress S.114^{2} Mia's Hope114^{nk} Clever Thing113^{hd}	Late rally	11
1Jan95-10Crc	fm	$1\frac{1}{16}$ Ⓣ	:22^{3}	:46^{2}	1:11^{1}	1:43^{2}	ⒻTrop Pk Oaks50k	77	2	9	10^{17}	$10^{9\frac{3}{4}}$	7^{6}	$5^{3\frac{1}{2}}$	Boulanger G	117	10.60	79-39	Rose Law Firm119$^{\frac{1}{2}}$ Honolulu Gold122$^{2\frac{1}{2}}$ Polish Spirit117^{nk}		12
Late gain between horses																					
11Dec94-8Aqu	wf	$1\frac{1}{16}$ [•]	:23^{1}	:46	1:12	1:45^{4}	Ⓕ[S]East View54k	77	2	6	6^{11}	$4^{8\frac{1}{2}}$	$4^{6\frac{1}{2}}$	3^{4}	Chavez J F	121	*1.10	72-22	Rogues Walk121$^{1\frac{1}{4}}$ Foxy Scarlet114$^{2\frac{3}{4}}$ Friendly Beauty121^{6}	Mild gain	7
15Oct94-3Bel	fst	$1\frac{1}{16}$	:22^{4}	:46^{2}	1:12^{1}	1:45^{3}	Ⓕ[S]Maid Of Mist75k	82	4	5	$4^{3\frac{1}{2}}$	3^{1}	$1^{\frac{1}{2}}$	1^{5}	Chavez J F	118	4.10	74-21	Friendly Beauty118^{5} Blum Beauty114^{1} Varsity Gold116$^{4\frac{1}{2}}$	Wide, driving	11
27Sep94-5Bel	sly	1	:22^{1}	:45^{2}	1:10^{4}	1:37^{1}	Ⓕ[S]Alw 32000N1X	85	6	—	—	2^{1}	1^{hd}	$1^{2\frac{1}{2}}$	Chavez J F	116	6.10	77-23	Friendly Beauty116$^{2\frac{1}{2}}$ Blum Beauty116^{7} Talcountess116^{no}	Fog, driving	6
11Sep94-7Bel	fst	6f	:22^{3}	:46	:58	1:10^{2}	Ⓕ[S]JosephAGimma55k	66	2	2	$6^{4\frac{3}{4}}$	$7^{6\frac{1}{4}}$	6^{5}	$5^{7\frac{1}{4}}$	Chavez J F	114	28.90	82-08	Sunny Shamrock114^{hd} Blum Beauty114^{6} Talcountess114^{1}	No threat	8
22Aug94-5Sar	sly	[illegible]	:22^{4}	:47^{1}	1:00^{2}	1:13^{3}	Ⓕ[S]Md Sp Wt	50	10	4	2^{2}	$2^{1\frac{1}{2}}$	2^{2}	$1^{3\frac{1}{2}}$	Chavez J F	117	4.70	73-17	Friendly Beauty117$^{3\frac{1}{2}}$ Haviland Road117$^{2\frac{1}{2}}$ Dominated Way117$^{\frac{3}{4}}$	Driving	10
12Aug94-2Sar	fst	6f	:22^{2}	:46^{1}	:59	1:12^{4}	Ⓕ[S]Md Sp Wt	50	5	6	$6^{5\frac{1}{2}}$	7^{7}	8^{9}	5^{5}	Santos J A	117	3.60	72-15	Farewell Embrace117$^{1\frac{1}{4}}$ Wild Wings117$^{1\frac{1}{2}}$ Flannel Sheets117^{nk}	Evenly	13
22Jly94-2Sar	sly	5½f	:22^{3}	:47	:59^{2}	1:06	Ⓕ[S]Md Sp Wt	49	7	6	3^{4}	5^{3}	$5^{3\frac{3}{4}}$	$3^{5\frac{1}{2}}$	Santos J A	117	*2.50	85-11	Castigating117^{5} Pitchunia117$^{\frac{1}{2}}$ Friendly Beauty117$^{1\frac{1}{4}}$	Four wide	8

WORKOUTS: Jly 26 Sar 5f fst 1:01^{4} H *8/47* Jly 17 Bel 4f fst :48^{1} H *8/62* Jly 12 Bel 4f fst :47^{4} B *8/60* Jun 30 Bel [T] 5f gd 1:01 H (d) *3/7* Jun 27 Bel tr.t 4f gd :51^{3} B *15/18*

Friendly Beauty, like Pretty Discreet, really didn't belong in a race like the Alabama. The New York-bred filly had won the restricted Maid Of The Mist some 10 months ago, credentials which hardly qualified her for a second look in this field, and she had been unable to approach even that level of ability in four subsequent starts. Stretched out to a mile and a quarter for what would be just her second start since January, and carrying 121 pounds, her cause seemed hopeless.

But Friendly Beauty had an ace up her sleeve: she was two-for-four on wet tracks, and one of those wins had come in Saratoga slop a year ago.

On this day, horses had to like the footing or they weren't going anywhere. Friendly Beauty liked it enough to grab second money by 16 lengths at 24-1, and linked with Pretty Discreet, the other Spa slop-winner in the field, for an exacta worth $838.

From that day forward, whenever John P. tells me about a horse, I listen, learn, and keep my big mouth shut.

August 13

WITH BOMBS like State Prize and Pretty Discreet in the sequence, it goes without saying that nobody hit the Pick 6 on the Alabama card, and since it hadn't been hit on Friday either, there was a two-day carryover of $199,113 heading into Sunday.

Weather-wise, Sunday was gorgeous, with temperatures in the 80s and relatively little humidity. The main track had received so much rain Saturday, however, that the track was still labeled muddy for the first five races before being upgraded to good from the sixth on. Two of the day's three scheduled grass races were switched to the main track, but the seventh race, a $47,000 classified allowance at a flat mile on the inner course, remained on the turf.

With close to $200,000 already in the pot, another $300,000 would be bet into the Pick 6, which meant that a cool half-million bucks would be up for grabs depending on the outcomes of races 3 through 8.

After the dust (or mud) had settled shortly before five o'clock in the afternoon, there were 29 winning tickets, and each was worth the tidy sum of $20,298 — well above a theoretical $2 win parlay that figured out to $14,946, thanks to the fact that, because of the carryover, the track was paying out more money than it took in.

There should have been 30 winners, but as it was a Sunday and the *Form* doesn't print a New York edition for the dark Tuesday, I was footloose and fancy-free...and on my way to Great Adventure for a Litfin Family outing. At 11 o'clock in the morning, I was the guest handicapper at the *Daily Form*-sponsored seminar hosted by John Pricci and held at Siro's, the trendy restaurant and after-the-races nightlife spot located a stone's throw from the side clubhouse gate...right off what is now Fourstardave Way, to be precise. I mapped out a Pick 6 play as we went over the card race-by-race, and as the seminar was breaking up I reached for my wallet in order to give "Preach" some money to bet for me in the Pick 6.

But 90 percent of success is being in the right place at the right time. Everyone else was walking across the street to the races, but I was getting in the mini-van and driving up the Thruway past Lake George, and on up to the amusement park. And since I like to fill out multiple tickets that depend on getting a certain number of "key" horses home (a methodology described by Barry Meadow in his excellent money management book, *Money Secrets at the Racetrack*), things can get pretty complicated; sometimes I might fill out as many as 40 or 50 tickets, using key contenders a lot, marginal horses a little, and so on. There were sure to be a lot of late scratches, and as it was already almost noon and everyone was waiting, I didn't have time for a complex and involved Pick 6 play — it would have to be one ticket.

"Aw, forget it," I thought, removing my hand from my pocket." "What are the chances of me hitting this Pick 6 on a drying-out muddy track like this...and not even being there?"

The Pick 6 played itself out while I rode the Tilt-A-Whirl and the Steamin' Demon. We arrived back at our rental house just in time to watch the nightly cable show, *Thoroughbred Action*, hosted by the inimitable Harvey Pack.

Observing strict adherence to the immutable law of racing that says: when selections go postward unsupported they must always win, the Pick 6 sequence went off without a hitch, as all the horses I would've used ran like trained seals in the mud.

What follows is the recap. I hope it is as instructive for you as it was cathartic for me...

The first leg of the sequence was a seven-furlong allowance sprint for 2-year-olds which had never won two races. The two betting choices are shown below:

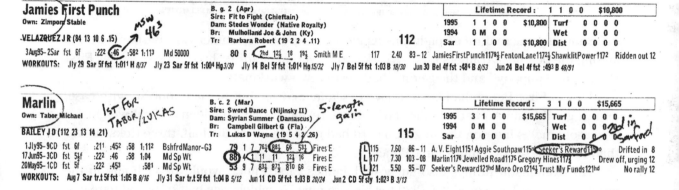

Marlin had earned the field's best Beyer figure (88) in a six-length maiden win. Two weeks later he had gained five lengths in the final quarter of the Bashford Manor, and third place-finisher Seeker's Reward had come back to run second in Saratoga's Sanford Stakes. Following that close-up fifth, the colt had been purchased privately by Michael Tabor and Wayne Lukas, whose most recent 2-year-old purchase the previous fall had been eventual Kentucky Derby-winner and 3-year-old champion Thunder Gulch.

Marlin was 6-5, and Jamies First Punch was 2-1. The gelding was a predictable winner of his August 3 unveiling, winning under a hand ride by a pole. His July 23 workout, 1:00 4/5 from the gate, was third-fastest of 30 at the distance, and those who read the work-tab for that morning's activities noted the following:

SARATOGA — Track Fast

Three Furlongs								
Boulder Drive	:36³ H	Citified	:48³ H	Pleasant Court	:48¹ Hg	Hoop Tattoo	1:01¹ H
Chalk Time	:37 B	Criminal Bundle	:47⁴ H	Pleasurable Miss	:49² Hg	Hooray For Evan	1:01² H
Christmas Cactus	:37¹ B	Currency Arbitrage	:48 Hg	Press Baron	:49¹ B	Is It Worth It	1:01⁴ H
Classic Arbitrage	:36³ H	Dancin At The Haha	:51¹ B	Prettiest Pink	:49 B	Jamies First Punch	1:00⁴ Hg
Contemplation	:35³ Hg,	Dare To Be Me	:50 B	Raising Peas	:49⁴ B	Killer Koupe	1:02⁴ B
Designer Prospect	:36² H	Dazz	:48¹ H	Roger Rooter	:52² B	Laughingtothebank	1:02 Hg
El Alpino	:36³ B	Dream Queen	:50 B	Sacket's Six	:48² H	Medieval Jestress	1:02³ Hg
Girton Gate	:36³ Hg	Easy Edge	:50⁴ B	Secret Society	:48⁴ Hg	Pat N Jac	1:03² B
Guessing Again	:37 H	Falconese	:52 B	Sensuo's	:51⁴ B	Persian King	1:01¹ H
Jets Over Miami	:37¹ B	Forested	:47³ H	She's Good	:48³ H	Ravishing Raven	1:00⁴ H
Quality Speed	:36³ H	French Bundle	:48³ H	Strawberry Clover	:48³ B	Red Pfanet	1:04² B
Rae's Silver Lady	:35² H	Glade	:48³ H	Sweet Sultana	:48⁴ H	Rita Red	1:04 H
Saratoga Bid	:36³ H	Going Too Farr	:49 Hg	Sweetly Risen	:50 B	Ruffed Grouse	:59⁴ H
Sean's Woodman	:37 B	Golden Bri	:49 B	Tellitlikeitis	:47³ H	Sailing Days	1:01¹ H
Sublime Season	:36 H	Hail To The Lion	:48² H	Timberly	:49 B	Sandman Sims	1:01¹ H
Terrorist	:38 B	Halloween Mask	:49³ B	Tri My Patience	:49³ H	Scarlet's Diva	1:02¹ Hg
Thundertheweather	:36² H	Humble Vision	:51 B	Verdant Valley	:47 H	Sophie's Friend	1:02³ H
Timber Fox	:37⁴ B	Hurry Home Halo	:48¹ Hg	Zaza	:50⁴ B	Spa City Slew	1:02 H
Triumph At Dusk	:37³ B	I'm Gifted	:50 B	Five Furlongs	:56³	Sunsational Girl	1:01² H
Won Finicky	:35³ Hg	Kacie's Favor	:48 H	Birdonthewire	1:03 B	Uncharted Waters	1:00 H
Four Furlongs		Larga Vista	:49 B	Cashtown Road	1:01¹ Hg	Six Furlongs	1:08
Angry Cop	:51 B	Lobster Joe T	:49 Hg,	Change Partners	1:02 H	Caress	1:13 H
Artic Experience	:49¹ H	Lois' Flag	:49 B	Comstock Lode	1:00⁴ H	Demon Damon	1:14² H
Bali Magic	:48⁴ H	Lutine	:53 B	Court Jester	1:02⁴ B	Lafitte's Lady	1:12⁴ H
Barbican	:47³ H	Lyric Opera	:47¹ H	Crafty Casa	1:02 B	Outlaw	1:14 H
Binary Light	:49 B	Miss Prospector	:50² B	Dakota's Trick	1:01 H	Rutile	1:18⁴ B
Carter's Vision	:51· B	Montreal Red	:48³ B	Fashion Code	1:03 Hg	Seven Furlongs	1:20²
Charmless	:51 B	Nancy's Way	:51 B	Frisco Gold	1:00⁴ H	Breeze Along	1:32 B
				Go Go Gerver	1:03³ B		

CONTEMPLATION (3f) and WON FINICKY (3f) worked in company. CURRENCY ARBITRAGE (4f) is getting serious. JAMIES FIRST PUNCH (5f) bested CASHTOWN ROAD (5f) and LOBSTER JOE T. (5f). CARESS (6f) went her 1/2 in :48 3/5. LAFITTE'S

Simulating actual race conditions as closely as possible, trainer Bob Barbara, who is among the deadliest trainers in New York with first time-starters, had worked Jamies First Punch "in company," and the gelding had bested two workmates.

Jamies First Punch had beaten maiden-claimers, true, but he had done so with ease, and in good time. A check of the day's charts revealed that a maiden special-weight for 2-year-old males later on the August 3 card had gone :46 3/5 to the half, three ticks slower than the pace set by Jamies First Punch.

The Tomlinson ratings also suggested Jamies First Punch would be at home in the muck and mire. He scored 295 (220 for his sire plus 75, which was half of broodmare sire Native Royalty's 150 rating); Marlin checked in at 215.

THIRD RACE
Saratoga
AUGUST 13, 1995

7 FURLONGS. (1.20²) ALLOWANCE. Purse $32,000. 2–year-olds which have never won two races. Weight, 121 lbs. Non-winners of $21,000, allowed 3 lbs. $18,000, 6 lbs. A race other than claiming, 9

Value of Race: $32,000 Winner $19,200; second $6,400; third $3,520; fourth $1,920; fifth $960. Mutuel Pool $318,166.00 Exacta Pool $437,960.00

Last Raced	Horse	M/Eqt. A.Wt	PP	St	¼	½	Str	Fin	Jockey	Odds $1
3Aug95 2Sar¹	Jamies First Punch	2 112	3	4	3½	3¹	1³	1⁸	Velazquez J R	2.30
21Jly95 7Sar⁶	You'vegotmynumber	b 2 118	2	5	5	4½	2⁵	2⁸	Smith M E	5.30
21Jly95 7Sar⁹	Ok by Me	2 118	1	2	2²	2hd	3¹	33½	Davis R G	3.25
21Jly95 7Sar¹¹	Choice Shift	2 118	5	1	1¹	1²	4²	4nk	Beckner D V	13.80
1Jly95 9CD⁵	Marlin	2 115	4	3	4¹	5	5	5	Bailey J D	1.35

OFF AT 2:04 Start Good. Won driving. Time, :22¹, :46, 1:11³, 1:25¹ Track muddy.

$2 Mutuel Prices:	3–JAMIES FIRST PUNCH	6.60	4.70	2.70
	2–YOU'VEGOTMYNUMBER		5.20	3.30
	1–OK BY ME			3.00

$2 EXACTA 3–2 PAID $32.20

B. g, (Apr), by Fit to Fight–Stedes Wonder, by Native Royalty. Trainer Barbara Robert. Bred by Mulholland Joe & John (Ky).

JAMIES FIRST PUNCH settled in good position for a half, accelerated to the front from outside in upper stretch, then drew away under mild encouragement. YOU'VEGOTMYNUMBER checked slightly along the backstretch, made a run along the rail to challenge at the quarter pole but was no match for the winner. OK BY ME angled out along the backstretch, raced up close while drifting out on the turn, tired. CHOICE SHIFT sprinted clear in the early stages, set the pace to the turn and gave way. MARLIN gave way on the far turn. CHOICE SHIFT wore mud caulks.

Owners— 1, Zimpom Stable; 2, Lester Mary V & William H; 3, Clifton William Jr & Rudlein Stable; 4, Condren William & Cornacchia Joseph; 5, Tabor Michael

Trainers— 1, Barbara Robert; 2, Lukas D Wayne; 3, Bond Harold James; 4, Zito Nicholas P; 5, Lukas D Wayne

Jamies First Punch won under mild urging. Marlin, who looked very competitive on paper, could not handle the going and was beaten by 20 lengths.

The fourth was for maiden fillies and mares, and the race had fallen apart when it was taken off the turf — so much so that Psychic Spirit and Bellazene, originally relegated to the mutual field, were the even-money favorites in a race with only five betting interests.

This was a "spread" race for me, and there was no way I would've thrown out Arunforyourmoney, whose Tomlinson rating was an extraordinarily high 360:

FOURTH RACE
Saratoga
AUGUST 13, 1995

1⅛ MILES. (1.47) MAIDEN SPECIAL WEIGHT. Purse $32,000. Fillies and mares, 3-year-olds and upward. Weights: 3-year-olds, 116 lbs. Older, 121 lbs. (Preference to fillies or mares that have not started for $40,000 or less in their last three starts). (ORIGINALLY SCHEDULED FOR TURF AT ONE MILE AND ONE SIXTEENTH.)

Value of Race: $32,000 Winner $19,200; second $6,400; third $3,520; fourth $1,920; fifth $960. Mutuel Pool $313,989.00 Exacta Pool $393,807.00 Quinella Pool $68,590.00

Last Raced	Horse	M/Eqt.	A.Wt	PP	St	¼	½	¾	Str	Fin	Jockey	Odds $1
17Jly95 ^{1}Bel^{9}	Arunforyourmoney		3 116	1	1	5^{hd}	$5^{1\frac{1}{2}}$	$4^{1\frac{1}{2}}$	2^{8}	$1^{1\frac{1}{2}}$	Sellers S J	7.60
7Jly95 ^{9}Bel^{2}	Theycallmecharlie		3 116	4	3	2^{2}	2^{1}	1^{hd}	1^{hd}	$2^{14\frac{1}{2}}$	Krone J A	2.10
22Jly95 ^{3}Sar^{5}	Psychic Spirit	b	4 121	6	5	4^{2}	$4^{\frac{1}{2}}$	5^{4}	4^{hd}	3^{2}	Day P	f-1.15
17Jly95 ^{6}Bel^{5}	Bellazene		3 116	5	4	$3^{1\frac{1}{2}}$	$3^{\frac{1}{2}}$	3^{2}	3^{1}	$4^{1\frac{1}{2}}$	Bailey J D	f-1.15
27Jly95 ^{4}Sar^{8}	Riverboat Princess		4 116	2	2	$1^{\frac{1}{2}}$	$1^{1\frac{1}{2}}$	2^{1}	5^{10}	$5^{8\frac{1}{2}}$	Belmonte L A^{5}	7.90
7Jly95 ^{9}Bel^{5}	Meet Me In Heaven	b	3 116	3	6	6	6	6	6	6	Migliore R	4.90

f-Mutuel Field: Psychic Spirit and Bellazene.

OFF AT 2:35 Start Good. Won driving. Time, :23^{3}, :48^{3}, 1:14^{1}, 1:40^{2}, 1:53^{2} Track muddy.

$2 Mutuel Prices:				
	3-ARUNFORYOURMONEY	17.20	6.00	2.30
	10-THEYCALLMECHARLIE		4.10	2.20
	13-PSYCHIC SPIRIT (f-field)			2.10

$2 EXACTA 3-10 PAID $51.50 $2 QUINELLA 3-10 PAID $19.20

B. f, (Feb), by Runaway Groom-Princess Valid, by Valid Appeal. Trainer Serpe Philip M. Bred by Dizney Donald R (Ky).

ARUNFORYOURMONEY reserved for for six furlongs while saving ground, rallied along the rail to challenge then outfinished THEYCALLMECHARLIE under brisk urging. THEYCALLMECHARLIE stalked outside for five furlongs, surged to the front on the far turn, drifted out while continuing on the lead in upper stretch, then weakened under pressure in the final eighth. PSYCHIC SPIRIT angled to the inside leaving the first turn, raced within striking distance to the turn, lacked a strong closing bid. BELLAZENE raced in close contention while slightly off the rail to the far turn and gradually tired thereafter. RIVERBOAT PRINCESS set the pace along the inside for nearly six furlongs and tired. MEET ME IN HEAVEN never reached contention. THEYCALLMECHARLIE and PSYCHIC SPIRIT wore mud caulks.

Owners— 1, Vermeire Albert; 2, Albatross Bloodstock; 3, Blasland W V Jr & Bouck W; 4, Paxson Mrs Henry D; 5, Lerman Roy S; 6, G Lack Farms

Trainers—1, Serpe Philip M; 2, Dickinson Michael W; 3, Margotta Anthony Jr; 4, Donk David; 5, Lerman Roy S; 6, Klesaris Robert P

Scratched— Consignment (18Jun95 ^{4}BEL^{7}), Soft Spot (17Jly95 ^{6}BEL^{4}), Callas' Aria (22Jly95 ^{3}SAR^{9}), Majestic Bid (17Jly95 ^{1}BEL^{2}), Priya, By Heart, Summerare (10Aug95 ^{5}SAR^{10}), Rising Reason (17Jly95 ^{6}BEL^{2}), Stella Ballerine, Miner Indiscretion (22Jly95 ^{3}SAR^{13}), My Song (30Jly95 ^{9}SAR^{2}), Verve (24Jly95 ^{4}SAR^{9}), Belle Jour (30Jly95 ^{5}SAR^{3}), Shallows (14Jly95 ^{3}BEL^{3})

The fifth was a contentious $35,000 claiming sprint for older males, and the past performances of the winner looked like this:

Carr Heaven
Own: Bond H James & Payson Virgina Kraft
CHAVEZ J F (111 18 16 6 .16) **$35,000**

B. h. 5
Sire: Carr de Naskra (Star de Naskra)
Dam: Heaven Knows (Quadrangle)
Br: Payson Virginia Kraft (NY)
Tr: Bond Harold James (10 5 1 0 .50)

112

Lifetime Record :	**24 7 5 4**	**$126,388**			
1995	4 0 0 2	$6,706	Turf	0 0 0 0	
1994	11 3 3 2	$37,592	Wet	5 2 1 1	$61,846
Sar	4 1 1 0	$58,410	Dist	0 0 0 0	

4Aug95- 5Sar	my	6f	:21^{2}	:44^{4}	:57^{1}	1:10^{4}	3↑ Clm 35000	85	4	7	$6^{6\frac{1}{4}}$	$7^{7\frac{1}{4}}$	5^{5}	6^{3}	Chavez J F	112 fb	2.95	84-13	Nicks Court112^{no} Love Jazz112^{hd} Unreal Mot113^{1}	No threat	8
22Jly95- 8FL	fst	6f	:22^{1}	:45	:57^{1}	1:10^{1}	3↑ [S]WineCountryH30k	78	7	6	$6^{3\frac{1}{2}}$	3^{6}	4^{8}	$4^{4\frac{3}{4}}$	Dominguez C V	115 fb	3.55	88-18	Chrioteer'sWnd$121^{2\frac{3}{4}}$ Who'sGonnBRite115^{2} Lordofthmountin117^{hd}	Hung	7
11Jun95- 9FL	fst	6f	:21^{4}	:45^{2}	:58^{1}	1:12	3↑ [S]Handicap15k	86	3	5	$6^{6\frac{3}{4}}$	$5^{6\frac{1}{2}}$	$4^{4\frac{1}{2}}$	$3^{\frac{3}{4}}$	Dominguez C V	115 fb	1.95	83-24	Royal Ben116^{nk} Who's Gonna BRite$114^{\frac{1}{2}}$ CarrHeaven$115^{1\frac{3}{4}}$	Stumbled start	6
29May95- 9FL	fst	6f	:21^{3}	:44^{4}	:57^{3}	1:11^{3}	3↑ [S]GeorgeBarker30k	81	6	5	5^{5}	$5^{4\frac{3}{4}}$	$4^{5\frac{1}{2}}$	$3^{3\frac{1}{2}}$	Dominguez C V	113 b	3.95	82-22	Royal Ben$113^{2\frac{3}{4}}$ Top End$115^{\frac{3}{4}}$ Carr Heaven$113^{\frac{3}{4}}$	Rallied 5 wide	8
5Dec94- 12FL	sly	6f	:21^{4}	:44^{2}	:57^{3}	1:11	3↑ [S]Handicap15k	73	7	5	5^{6}	5^{6}	$5^{5\frac{1}{2}}$	3^{5}	Dominguez C V	117 fb	3.85	86-18	Noble Sweetheart114^{1} Spent Shell115^{4} Carr Heaven$117^{2\frac{1}{2}}$	6 wide turn	7
6Nov94- 8FL	fst	6f	:21^{1}	:43^{2}	:57	1:10^{3}	3↑ Handicap10k	83	5	4	4^{9}	4^{8}	$3^{6\frac{1}{2}}$	$4^{1\frac{1}{4}}$	Dominguez C V	118 fb	3.70	92-15	Royal Ben$115^{\frac{1}{2}}$ Tea In My Eye112^{no} Dacha$113^{\frac{3}{4}}$	Rallied rail	6
18Sep94- 9FL	fst	6f	:21^{4}	:45^{2}	:59^{2}	1:11^{4}	3↑ [S]Handicap15k	87	1	4	$4^{5\frac{1}{4}}$	$4^{1\frac{1}{2}}$	1^{4}	$1^{3\frac{3}{4}}$	Dominguez C V	115 fb	7.40	87-23	Carr Heaven$115^{3\frac{3}{4}}$ Strawman$117^{1\frac{1}{2}}$ Who's Gonna B Rite$117^{7\frac{1}{4}}$	Drew off	6
27Aug94- 10FL	fst	6f	:21^{4}	:44^{4}	:57^{2}	1:09^{3}	3↑ [S]Handicap15k	74	5	6	$6^{5\frac{3}{4}}$	$4^{4\frac{1}{4}}$	$4^{\frac{1}{2}}$	$3^{3\frac{3}{4}}$	Dominguez C V	116 fb	4.50	94-08	Strwmn$114^{1\frac{3}{4}}$ Who'sGonnBRite117^{2} CrrHeven$116^{1\frac{3}{4}}$	Hung, drifted out str.	8
9Aug94- 10FL	fst	6f	:22^{3}	:45^{2}	:58^{1}	1:10^{4}	3↑ [S]Alw 12000N3	80	5	3	3^{3}	3^{2}	2^{1}	$1^{1\frac{3}{4}}$	Dominguez C V	116 fb	*1.50	92-18	Carr Heaven$116^{1\frac{3}{4}}$ Dacha$116^{\frac{1}{2}}$ Iron Command$116^{1\frac{1}{2}}$	Drove clear	5
30Jly94- 9FL	fst	6f	:22^{1}	:45^{2}	:57^{2}	1:10^{2}	3↑ [S]Alw 12000N3X	83	2	5	$4^{4\frac{1}{2}}$	2^{3}	2^{2}	$2^{2\frac{1}{2}}$	Dominguez C V	116 fb	3.40	91-16	Royal Ben$116^{2\frac{1}{2}}$ Carr Heaven116^{1} Dacha$116^{\frac{1}{2}}$	Finished well	6

WORKOUTS: Jly 11 FL 6f fst 1:15^{3} H *1/2* Jly 3 FL 5f fst 1:04 B *5/11* ●May 26 FL 3f fst :35^{2} H *1/12* ●May 20 FL 6f fst 1:13^{1} H *1/5*

Carr Heaven had lost by only three lengths in the mud nine days earlier, and his Beyer of 85 was competitive in this field. Trainer Bond, James Bond was having the meeting of his life, sending out winners at an absolutely unconscious .500 batting average. Most of all, Carr Heaven was perfectly at home in Saratoga mud, as only those with a long memory knew:

EIGHTH RACE
Saratoga
AUGUST 26, 1992

6 FURLONGS. (1.08) 17th Running EMPIRE STAKES. Purse $75,000 added. 2-year-olds foaled in New York State and approved by the New York State-bred Registry. By subscription of $150 each which should accompany the nomination, $600 to pass the entry box, $600 to start with $75,000 added. The added money and all fees to be divided 60% to the winner, 22% to second, 12% to third and 6% to fourth. Weight 122 lbs. Non-winners of a sweepstake allowed 3 lbs., of two races other than Maiden or Claiming 5 lbs., of such a race 7 lbs. Starters to be named at the closing time of entries. A perpetual trophy will be on display in the Winner's Circle. Closed Wednesday, August 12, with 27 nominations. Value of race $87,450; value to winner $52,470; second $19,239; third $10,494; fourth $5,247. Mutuel pool $252,435. Triple Pool $232,006 Exacta Pool $314,028

Last Raced	Horse	M/Eqt.A.Wt	PP	St	¼	½	Str	Fin	Jockey	Odds $1
8Aug92 3Sar2	Carr Heaven	2 115	5	6	31	2hd	21	1nk	Bailey J D	3.70
8Aug92 3Sar3	Classi Envoy	2 115	4	2	1½	1hd	1hd	25¼	Carr D	13.70
3Aug92 4Sar1	Dam Shot	2 115	6	3	2hd	32½	32½	33¾	Krone J A	1.90
6Aug92 3Sar1	Similar Star	2 115	3	4	7	68	4½	42½	Smith M E	[illegible]
8Aug92 3Sar5	North Flag	2 115	1	7	41½	4hd	5½	5¾	Cruguet J	a-22.50
13Aug92 4Sar1	Loud Brother	2 115	2	5	5hd	5hd	614	619	Maple E	4.90
30Jun92 7FL1	Mr. Angelino	2 115	7	1	61	7	7	7	Antley C W	a-22.50

a-Coupled: North Flag and Mr. Angelino.

OFF AT 5:00 Start good, Won driving. Time, :22², :45², :57³, 1:10² Track muddy.

$2 Mutuel Prices:

5-(E)-CARR HEAVEN	9.40	4.80	3.80
4-(D)-CLASSI ENVOY		10.60	5.20
6-(F)-DAM SHOT			4.20

As a 2-year-old (while also in Bond's care), he had won the Empire Stakes for New York-breds in the mud. Unquestionably, a horse with back-form such as this in Spa mud belonged in any serious Pick 6 play:

FIFTH RACE
Saratoga
AUGUST 13, 1995

7 FURLONGS. (1.20²) CLAIMING. Purse $24,000. 3-year-olds and upward. Weights: 3-year-olds, 117 lbs. Older, 121 lbs. Non-winners of three races since April 10, allowed 3 lbs. Two races since May 8, 6 lbs. A race since July 15, 9 lbs. Claiming price $35,000. (Races where entered for $25,000 or less not considered.)

Value of Race: $24,000 Winner $14,400; second $4,800; third $2,640; fourth $1,440; fifth $720. Mutuel Pool $461,274.00 Exacta Pool $541,346.00 Triple Pool $447,114.00

Last Raced	Horse	M/Eqt. A.Wt	PP	St	¼	½	Str	Fin	Jockey	Cl'g Pr	Odds $1
4Aug95 5Sar6	Carr Heaven	bf 5 112	6	5	43	42	12½	11¾	Chavez J F	35000	6.10
16Jly95 10Bel7	Concoctor	4 112	8	2	6hd	7hd	22	26	Davis R G	35000	9.60
3Aug95 5Sar1	Giant Leap	bf 7 113	7	1	51½	61	62	3½	Smith M E	35000	2.50
29Jun95 5CD2	Coal Mountain	bf 4 112	3	7	72½	53	5hd	4¾	Day P	35000	2.45
2Aug95 9Rkm7	Crystal Pistol	bf 4 118	4	6	3hd	3hd	41	5½	Luzzi M J	35000	24.75
3Aug95 3Sar5	Blum Gone	b 5 113	1	4	22	2½	31	66½	Maple E	35000	4.30
14Mar94 3GP8	Magic Carr	bf 6 108	5	3	11	1½	71	72	Belmonte L A5	35000	20.20
26Jly95 5Sar7	Lucky Quadrant	4 112	2	8	8	8	8	8	Krone J A	35000	9.10

OFF AT 3:08 Start Good. Won driving. Time, :22³, :46¹, 1:10⁴, 1:23² Track muddy.

$2 Mutuel Prices:

7-CARR HEAVEN	14.20	7.60	5.10
12-CONCOCTOR		9.30	4.50
8-GIANT LEAP			3.40

$2 EXACTA 7-12 PAID $150.00 $2 TRIPLE 7-12-8 PAID $486.50

B. h, by Carr de Naskra-Heaven Knows, by Quadrangle. Trainer Bond Harold James. Bred by Payson Virginia Kraft (NY).

CARR HEAVEN was rated just off the pace while three wide for a half, accelerated to the front leaving the quarter pole, opened a clear advantage in midstretch, then turned back CONCOCTOR under brisk urging. CONCOCTOR outrun early, circled five wide to launch his bid on the turn, closed steadily in the middle of the track to clearly best the others. GIANT LEAP reserved for a half, failed to threaten while improving his position. COAL MOUNTAIN checked while being pinched back at the start, angled four wide while lodging a mild bid on the turn then flattened out. CRYSTAL PISTOL checked in tight while breaking inward at the start, stalked the pace three wide on the turn, gradually tired thereafter. BLUM GONE forced the pace along the inside for a half, gained a brief lead on the turn, then faded in the drive. MAGIC CARR was used up setting the early pace. LUCKY QUADRANT broke slowly and was never close thereafter. CARR HEAVEN and CRYSTAL PISTOL wore mud caulks.

Owners— 1, Bond H James & Payson Virgina Kraft; 2, Hawkins Gregory D; 3, Joques Farm; 4, Dizney Donald R; 5, McDonnell Francis C; 6, Riccio James A; 7, Winbound Farms; 8, Manfuso Robert T

Trainers—1, Bond Harold James; 2, Freeman Willard C; 3, Moschera Gasper S; 4, Hauswald Philip M; 5, Hartley James E; 6, Araya Rene A; 7, Gullo Gary P; 8, Voss Katharine M

Overweight: Giant Leap (1), Blum Gone (1), Magic Carr (1).

Carr Heaven was claimed by Joques Farm; trainer, Moschera Gasper S.,
Coal Mountain was claimed by Haley Terrence W; trainer, Lake Robert P.

Scratched— Flaming Falcon (31Jly95 9SAR11), Chispaviva (24Jly95 5SAR2), Sun Valley Sundae (24Jly95 5SAR3), Concordes Prospect (27Jly95 3SAR7)

The sixth was a gimme:

Gold Sunrise
Own: Al Maktoum Mohammed
BAILEY J D (115 25 14 14 .22)

B. f. 2 (Feb)
Sire: Forty Niner (Mr. Prospector)
Dam: Seattle Dawn (Grey Dawn II)
Br: Dinwiddie Farms Ltd (Va)
Tr: Mott William I (31 9 4 4 .29)

117

Lifetime Record:	2 M 2 0	$12,000			
1995	2 M 2 0	$12,000	Turf	0 0 0 0	
1994	0 M 0 0		Wet	0 0 0 0	
Sar	1 0 1 0	$6,000	Dist	2 0 2 0	$12,000

21Jly95-2Sar	fst	5½f	:21⁴ :45¹	:57²	1:03⁴	ⒻMd Sp Wt	74	6	3	32½	31½	33½	29	Bailey J D	119 b	4.30	93-10	Flat Fleet Feet1199 Gold Sunrise119hd Oxford Scholar1193½ Up for place 6
3Jly95-2Bel	fst	5f	:22¹ :46²		:59¹	ⒻMd Sp Wt	78	2	1	1hd	12	11	2nk	Bailey J D	115 b	2.65	90-14	Bundle Of Gold115nk Gold Sunrise1151¾ Brainless1055 Gamely 8

WORKOUTS: Aug 9 Sar 5f fst 1:03² B 38/48 Aug 2 Sar 4f fst :50 B 18/38 Jly 13 Bel 4f fst :50³ B 50/66 Jun 28 Bel 5f fst 1:01² Bg 17/42 Jun 21 Bel 4f fst :49¹ B 31/71 Jun 16 Bel 3f fst :38² B 25/38

Gold Sunrise had led for every step but the last when nailed on the line in his debut July 3, then had the misfortune to hook a tiger by the tongue-twisting name of Flat Fleet

Feet, who sped the opening fractions in :21 4/5 and :45 1/5, won off by nine lengths, and came back to win the Grade 2 Adirondack Stakes on August 9.

According to *Mudders & Turfers*, Gold Sunrise scored a 290.

SIXTH RACE
Saratoga
AUGUST 13, 1995

5½ FURLONGS. (1.032) MAIDEN SPECIAL WEIGHT. Purse $30,000. Fillies, 2-year-olds. Weight: 117 lbs. (Preference to fillies that have not started for a claiming price.)

Value of Race: $30,000 Winner $18,000; second $6,000; third $3,300; fourth $1,800; fifth $900. Mutuel Pool $441,729.00 Exacta Pool $699,898.00

Last Raced	Horse	M/Eqt. A.Wt	PP	St	¼	¾	Str	Fin	Jockey	Odds $1
21Jly95 2Sar2	Gold Sunrise	b 2 117	4	1	2³	2³	2½	1³	Bailey J D	0.90
	Tricky Priestess	2 117	1	2	1¹	1¹	1hd	2½	Decarlo C P	35.25
21Jly95 6Sar4	Launch At Dawn	2 117	2	7	4¹½	4²	3³	3²½	Day P	7.10
	Sweet Emma Lou	f 2 117	7	4	7²	5hd	5hd	4hd	Lovato F Jr	21.90
28Jly95 2Sar2	Thesky'sthelimit	2 117	5	3	3hd	3½	4¹½	5⁵	Santos J A	7.90
4Aug95 2Sar2	Irma	2 117	6	5	5¹½	6³	6²½	6³½	Davis R G	5.00
	Opening Reality	2 117	3	6	6hd	7¹	7¹	7⁴½	Chavez J F	16.10
	Malley	2 117	9	8	9	8¹½	8¹½	8²	Krone J A	10.80
	Twobuster	2 117	8	9	8¹½	9	9	9	Graell A	22.00

OFF AT 3:41 Start Good. Won driving. Time, :22, :46, :59, 1:05⁴ Track good.

$2 Mutuel Prices:

4-GOLD SUNRISE	3.80	3.20	2.40
1-TRICKY PRIESTESS		14.80	6.60
2-LAUNCH AT DAWN			4.00

$2 EXACTA 4-1 PAID $100.50

B. f, (Feb), by Forty Niner–Seattle Dawn, by Grey Dawn II. Trainer Mott William I. Bred by Dinwiddie Farms Ltd (Va).

GOLD SUNRISE forced the pace from outside into upper stretch, then wore down TRICKY PRIESTESS under brisk urging. TRICKY PRIESTESS sprinted clear in the early stages, led into midstretch then weakened. LAUNCH AT DAWN raced just off the pace while saving ground for a half, then finished willingly for a share. SWEET EMMA LOU unhurried for a half while four wide, failed to threaten with a mild late rally. THESKY'STHELIMIT raced in close contention between horses for a half, tired in the drive. IRMA was never a factor. OPENING REALITY never reached contention after being pinched at the start. MALLEY was never a factor. TWOBUSTER checked while being pinched at the start, and was never close thereafter.

Owners— 1, Al Maktoum Mohammed; 2, Blasland Warren V Jr; 3, Evans Edward P; 4, Schwartz Barry K; 5, Green-Tel Stable & Jay Cee Jay Stb; 6, Paraneck Stable; 7, Shapiro Theodore W; 8, Campbell Alex G Jr; 9, Wilson Charles T Jr

Trainers— 1, Mott William I; 2, Margotta Anthony Jr; 3, Hennig Mark; 4, Hushion Michael E; 5, Destefano John M Jr; 6, Aquilino Joseph; 7, Tesher Howard M; 8, Arnold George R II; 9, Hernandez Ramon M

Scratched— Coming Out Party, Tellitlikeitis (4May95 2BEL6)

The seventh was the one-mile grass race, and it was strictly a two-horse affair:

7 Saratoga

1 MILE. (Inner Turf). (1:34⁴) ALLOWANCE. Purse $47,000. 3-year-olds and upward which have not won a sweepstakes over eight and a half furlongs since August 13. Weights: 3-year-olds, 118 lbs. Older, 123 lbs. Non-winners of $35,000 on the turf since October 28, allowed 3 lbs. $35,000 twice in 1994-95, 6 lbs. $28,800 twice since December 25, 9 lbs.

Dove Hunt
Own: Farish William S
DAY P (102 18 12 14 .18)

B. c. 4
Sire: Danzig (Northern Dancer)
Dam: Hunt's Lark (Knightly Dawn)
Br: Farish W S (Ky)
Tr: Howard Neil J (12 2 0 1 .17)

123

only (on T) worse than 2d came in latest

Lifetime Record: 16 7 3 1 $389,756

1995	8 4 0 1	$163,576	Turf	13 7 2 0	$355,696
1994	2 0 1 0	$8,820	Wet	1 0 0 1	$11,000
Sar ⊤	1 1 0 0	$14,100	Dist ⊤	7 4 2 0	$181,266

4Jly95-40CD fm 1 ⊤ :222 :451 1:092 1:33³ 3+ FirecrackrH-G3   97 1 9 77¾ 52 42¾ 42½ Day P   L 120   *1.20 101–02 Jaggery John113½ Rare Reason115¼ Fly Cry119½   Boxed in 10
29May95-11Mth fm 1 ⊤ :222 :451 1:09 1:33⁴ 3+ Red Bank H-G3   104 2 7 75½ 31½ 11 14½ McCauley W H   L 118   *1.50 101–04 Dove Hunt118⁴½ Rare Reason115¹ Winnetou113¹½   Ridden out 10
26Apr95-8Kee fm 1 ⊤ :231 :462 1:113 1:35⁴ Fort Harrod-G3   98 5 6 62¾ 3nk 11½ 11¾ Santos J A   L 113   5.00 91–10 Dove Hunt113½ Road Of War114¼ Night Silence116½   Hard drive 10
13Apr95-7Kee fm 1 ⊤ :242 :481 1:122 1:37¹ Alw 45550C   95 3 3 3½ 11½ 12½ 11½ Santos J A   L 118   *2.00 84–18 Dove Hunt118¹½ Maxigroom112¹½ Camptown Dancer118²   Driving 7
5Mar95-8GP fm *1⅛ ⊤ :232 :463 1:102 1:41⁴ Alw 37000N4X   80 9 5 52¼ 42¾ 52¾ 56¼ Santos J A   L 119   4.40 93 — Siberian Summer117¹¾ Lassigny117³½ Standing Cast117³½   Faded 10
18Feb95-10GP fm *1⅛ ⊤ :241 :482 1:123 1:42² Alw 30000N3X   90 4 2 2½ 1hd 1hd 12 Santos J A   L 117   *1.70 96 — Dove Hunt117² DHTalb117 DHInside The Beltway117¹½   Driving 10
20Jan95-5GP fm *1¼ ⊗ :48 1:124 1:372 1:50³ Alw 30000N3X   89 8 3 3² 2hd 2hd 44 Santos J A   L 117   *1.40 88–13 Undue Influence117hd Rocket City122¹½ RupertSpringFire119²½   Weakened 10
7Jan95-8GP sly 1⅛ ⊗ :234 :472 1:11 1:42³ 3+ Appleton H-G3   97 4 3 31½ 31½ 35 35¼ Santos J A   L 114   9.10 92–06 Dusty Screen116nk The Vid114⁵ Dove Hunt114⁴   7
   Steadied 1st turn, weakened
24Dec94-9FG fm *1⅛ ⊤ :223 :464 1:123 1:444 WoodchopperH44k   72 9 4 46 910 915 916¼ Sellers S J   L 122   4.20 77–07 Fly Cry121⁵ Finder's Wish113½ Mahogany Hall111³   10
   3-wd 1st turn, clipped heels 2nd turn
20Nov94-6CD fm 1 ⊤ :234 :474 1:12² 1:36⁴ 3+ Alw 42900N$Y   91 7 6 5⁴ 52¼ 5½ 22½ Sellers S J   113   *1.50 86–10 Milt's Overture115²½ Dove Hunt113½ Atomic Power113nk   Bid, 2nd best 10

WORKOUTS: ●Aug 9 Sar 6f fst 1:13³ H 2/11   ●Aug 3 Sar 6f fst 1:13 H 1/6   Jly 28 Sar 5f fst 1:01¹ H 4/28   ●Jly 15 CD 4f fst :48² B 1/21   Jun 27 CD ⊤ 5f yl 1:01² H (d) 1/3   Jun 20 CD ⊤ 6f fm 1:16² B (d) 1/1

Unfinished Symph
Own: Hatcher & Rice & Seawind Stables
ANTLEY C W (—)
  Entered 11Aug95- 8 SAR

B. c. 4
Sire: Aloha Prospector (Native Prospector)
Dam: Accuwoman (Akureyri)
Br: Joselson Stanley I (Md)
Tr: Ward Wesley A (2 0 0 0 .00)

123

scr Darci's Joy (Feux)   *scr Barth (Pri)*   *worked a few days late*   *no challenges '95*

Lifetime Record: 15 6 4 2 $624,700

1995	2 2 0 0	$208,400	Turf	10 4 4 1	$586,100
1994	12 4 4 2	$416,300	Wet	1 0 0 1	$6,150
Sar ⊤	0 0 0 0		Dist ⊤	4 2 1 1	$348,400

10Jun95-8Hol fm 1 ⊤ :231 :453 1:092 1:33 3+ Shoemaker H-G2   111 1 2 11½ 11½ 11½ 11¾ Antley C W   LB 121   *1.00 98–08 Unfinished Symph121¹¾ Rapan Boy118hd Journalism117¹¾   Gamely 9
22Apr95-7GG fm 1 ⊤ :222 :46 1:094 1:34 3+ S F Mile H-G2   110 7 4 11 11 11¾ Antley C W   LB 118   5.00 104–05 Unfinished Symph118²½ Vaudeville119½ Torch Rouge114¹   Closed gamely 9
20Nov94-2Hol fm 1⅛ ⊤ :464 1:102 1:342 1:472 Hol Derby-G1   86 11 7 42 25 109½ Baze G   LB 122   8.60 78–13 River Flyer122¹½ Dare And Go122½ Fadeyev122³½   6-wide 7/8, weakened 13
5Nov94-7CD fm 1⅛ ⊤ :231 :461 1:094 1:342 3+ BC Mile-G1   102 3 1 1hd 1hd 2hd 33 Baze G   L 122   25.20f 98 — Barathea126³ Johann Quatz126hd Unfinished Symph123¹½   Weakened late 14
8Oct94-8Haw yl 1⅛ ⊤ :464 1:104 1:372 1:514 Haw Derby-G3   99 1 9 69¼ 66¼ 13 2hd Baze G   L 122   *1.70 64–36 Chrysalis House115hd Unfinished Symph122¼ Marvin'sFaith122¼   Led late 11
5Sep94-8Dmr fm 1⅛ ⊤ :474 1:114 1:362 1:483 Dmr Dby Inv-G2   99 2 4 42¼ 42½ 52½ 56¼ Pedroza M A   LB 120   6.00 92–08 Ocean Crest122½ Unfinished Symph120½ DEagle Eyed122¹½   Game try 10
14Aug94-8Dmr fm 1⅛ ⊤ :234 :48 1:12 1:42¹ La Jolla H-G3   97 5 3 31½ 3nk 1hd 2no Baze G   LB 120   *1.30 95–07 Marvin's Faith114no Unfinished Symph120hd Ocean Crest114nk   Game try 7
19Jun94-8Hol fm 1⅛ ⊤ :464 1:102 1:334 1:462 + Cinema H-G3   102 3 4 42¾ 31 11½ 12 Baze G   LB 118   3.70 92–11 UnfinishedSymph118² Vaudeville115² FumoDiLondr121no   Clear, driving 8
21May94-8Hol fm 1⅛ ⊤ :464 :46 1:10 1:403 + WillRogers H-G3   99 5 4 42½ 41½ 41½ 13hd Baze G   LB 116   16.80 93–10 UnfinishedSymph116hd SilverMusic118⁵ VlintNtur122²   Game try 8
7May94-8Hol fm 1 ⊤ :23 :462 1:104 1:35 SpotlghtBCH-G3   90 4 5 63¼ 62¾ 43½ 2½ Baze G   LB 116   17.10 86–11 Fumo Di Londra119³ Unfinished Symph116½ Timbalier113no   8
   Bumped, split rivals 1/8

WORKOUTS: Aug 6 Hol ⊤ 6f sf 1:16² B (d) 1/1   Jly 28 Sar ⊤ 6f fm 1:14³ H (d) 1/2   Jly 17 Sar ⊤ 5f fm 1:00⁴ H 1/1   Jly 11 Sar tr.t 5f fst 1:02 H 1/1   Jun 4 Hol ⊤ 5f gd 1:02 B 1/1   ●May 26 Hol ⊤ 6f fm 1:10¹ H (d) 1/8

Dove Hunt and Unfinished Symph were both being groomed toward the Breeders' Cup Mile, but on this day I much preferred Dove Hunt. Both 4-year-old colts owned a similar finishing kick — I calculated the last race for each on Quinn-style turf figures at an identical 113 — but Unfinished Symph had been scratched from the Daryl's Joy Stakes when he spiked a fever earlier in the meet, and he had also scratched out of Friday's Bernard Baruch Handicap. Having had only two races since last November, victories in which he faced no challengers from the pre-stretch call to the finish, and recovering from a fever, it was more than likely that Unfinished Symph would be "short" for this race, which was to be contested over soft, demanding going.

Dove Hunt's only finish worse than second from seven starts at a mile on turf had come last time out, when boxed in through the stretch of Churchill Down's Firecracker Handicap, a bit of bad racing luck that had snapped his three-race winning streak; quite likely, he might have surpassed a 113 finishing figure had he been allowed clear sailing in the stretch.

Dove Hunt had something of a "home court advantage" as well, as he had broken his maiden over an "off" inner course going one mile at Saratoga as a 2-year-old, on the 1993 Travers undercard:

SECOND RACE 1 MILE.(InnerTurf). (1.34⁴) MAIDEN SPECIAL WEIGHT. Purse $23,500. 2-year-olds.
Saratoga Weight, 118 lbs.
AUGUST 21, 1993
Value of race $23,500; value to winner $14,100; second $5,170; third $2,820; fourth $1,410. Mutuel pool $384,394. Exacta Pool $609,567 Quinella Pool $164,669

Last Raced	Horse	M/Eqt.A.Wt	PP St	¼	½	¾	Str	Fin	Jockey	Odds $1
11Aug93 5Sar9	Dove Hunt	2 118	6 7	23½	22	21	25	12	Day P	4.50
22Jly93 5Bel2	Check Ride	2 118	9 8	11	12	11	11	27½	Krone J A	.80
22Jly93 1Bel5	Micromax	2 118	8 9	9	9	9	86	32½	Alvarado F T	48.80
	Hazy	2 118	2 2	3hd	3hd	41	31½	41	McCauley W H	5.00
6Aug93 3Sar7	Boy Terror	b 2 118	7 6	43½	41	3hd	41	52½	Samyn J L	24.00
4Aug93 6Sar2	Ridgewinder	2 118	4 3	73	61	51½	61½	62	Santos J A	4.20
9Aug93 3Sar14	Holiday Stutz	2 118	5 5	52	5½	61	5hd	72½	Toscano P R	56.00
9Aug93 3Sar13	Ruddy Glow	2 118	1 1	6hd	72	71	7hd	84½	Velazquez J R	61.10
23Jun93 5Bel10	Majesty's Power	b 2 118	3 4	83	84	8hd	9	9	Carr D	31.60

OFF AT 1:40 Start good, Won driving. Time, :24³, :49 , 1:14⁴, 1:39³ Course yielding.

$2 Mutuel Prices: 7-(G)-DOVE HUNT 11.00 3.80 3.20
12-(L)-CHECK RIDE 2.60 2.40
11-(K)-MICROMAX 6.40
$2 EXACTA 7-12 PAID $25.00 $2 QUINELLA 7-12 PAID $9.00

B. c, (May), by Danzig—Hunt's Lark, by Knightly Dawn. Trainer Howard Neil J. Bred by Farish W S (Ky).
DOVE HUNT relinquished the lead to CHECK RIDE leaving the first turn settled just behind that one along the backstretch, launched a rally from outside entering the stretch, then wore down CHECK RIDE to win going away.

I was willing to take a stand and "single" Dove Hunt, in order to spread in other legs of the Pick 6.

Unfinished Symph expended valuable energy fending off early pressure from a well-traveled colt named Dumaani, and was a sitting duck when Dove Hunt unleashed an explosive closing burst to win going away:

SEVENTH RACE
Saratoga
AUGUST 13, 1995

1 MILE. (Inner Turf)(1.344) ALLOWANCE. Purse $47,000. 3-year-olds and upward which have not won a sweepstakes over eight and a half furlongs since August 13. Weights: 3-year-olds, 118 lbs. Older, 123 lbs. Non-winners of $35,000 on the turf since October 28, allowed 3 lbs. $35,000 twice in 1994-95, 6 lbs. $28,800 twice since December 25, 9 lbs.

Value of Race: $47,000 Winner $28,200; second $9,400; third $5,170; fourth $2,820; fifth $1,410. Mutuel Pool $375,508.00 Exacta Pool $571,685.00

Last Raced	Horse	M/Eqt.	A.	Wt	PP	St	¼	½	¾	Str	Fin	Jockey	Odds $1
4Jly95 10CD4	Dove Hunt		4	123	1	2	53½	53	41	31	11½	Day P	2.05
10Jun95 8Hol1	Unfinished Symph		4	123	2	1	24	11	11	12	23	Cruguet J	1.05
4Jly95 8Bel6	Dumaani		4	123	3	3	1½	21	23	2½	32½	Smith M E	6.60
14Jun95 8Bel5	L'Hermine-GB	bf	6	114	4	5	6	6	6	53	41¾	Lovato F Jr	16.80
2Jly95 8Bel10	Artema-IR		4	114	6	4	41	42	3½	44	56½	Velasquez J	21.60
4Jly95 8Bel5	Inside The Beltway	b	4	123	5	6	3½	3hd	52½	6	6	Bailey J D	5.80

OFF AT 4:13 Start Good. Won driving. Time, :243, :474, 1:114, 1:362 Course soft.

$2 Mutuel Prices:				
	2-DOVE HUNT	6.10	2.80	2.40
	3-UNFINISHED SYMPH		2.70	2.30
	1A-DUMAANI			2.90

$2 EXACTA 2-3 PAID $13.20

B. c, by Danzig–Hunt's Lark, by Knightly Dawn. Trainer Howard Neil J. Bred by Farish W S (Ky).

DOVE HUNT unhurried for five furlongs, launched a rally three wide leaving the turn, then unleashed a strong late run in the middle of the track to win going away. UNFINISHED SYMPH set or forced the pace along the inside for six furlongs, opened a clear lead in upper stretch, but couldn't withstand the winner's late charge. DUMAANI forced the pace outside UNFINISHED SYMPH to the top of the stretch, and weakened from his early efforts. L'HERMINE outrun for six furlongs while saving ground, failed to threaten while improving his position. ARTEMA raced within striking distance while saving ground for six furlongs then lacked a strong closing bid. INSIDE THE BELTWAY raced just off the pace to the turn and gave way.

Owners— 1, Farish William S; 2, Hatcher & Rice & Seawind Stables; 3, Shadwell Stable; 4, Schwartz Barry K; 5, Gaylord & Hubbard; 6, Beler Constantine P

Trainers—1, Howard Neil J; 2, Ward Wesley A; 3, McLaughlin Kiaran P; 4, Hushion Michael E; 5, Petalino Joe; 6, Sciacca Gary

Scratched— Gabr (8Jly95 8BEL6), Grand Continental (11Aug95 8SAR6), Compadre (11Aug95 8SAR3)

The eighth race was the Grade 1 Ballerina Handicap for fillies and mares, 3 and up, and it was the key to the Pick 6. Inside Information was everybody's stand-alone single on the card. I had written her up as "Best Bet" in my *Form* analysis, but my Sunday analysis has a deadline of 6:15 on Friday afternoon — almost 48 hours in advance. Had I known that a thunderstorm would render the track a sea of mud, I would've given Classy Mirage a great deal more consideration, and I related as much to that morning's seminar audience. Look over the race and judge for yourself:

8 Saratoga

7 Furlongs **(1:202) 17th Running of THE BALLERINA HANDICAP. Purse $150,000 Added. Grade I. Fillies and mares, 3-year-olds and upward. By subscription of $100 each which should accompany the nomination, $500 to pass the entry box, $500 to start. The purse to be divided 60% to the winner, 20% to second, 11% to third, 6% to fourth and 3% to fifth. Weights: Monday, August 7. Starters to be named at the closing time of entries. Trophies will be presented to the winning owner, trainer and jockey. Closed Saturday, July 29, with 23 nominations.**

Laura's Pistolette
Own: Smith Jack III
BAILEY J D (112 23 13 14 .21)

B. f. 4
Sire: Big Pistol (Romeo)
Dam: Lovely Nedra (Irish Tower)
Br: Jones Bartow & Ned Partnership (Ky)
Tr: Johnson Murray W (—)

112

Lifetime Record:	18	6	3	5	$232,196						
1995	5	2	1	1	$129,300	Turf	3	0	0	2	$9,;
1994	10	2	2	4	$72,385	Wet	3	1	1	1	$35,:
Sar	0	0	0	0		Dist	3	1	0	1	$81,(

4Jly95-9Mth	fst	1 1/16	:234	:464	1:101	1:434	3↑ ⓕMolPitcherH-G2	84	1	4	34½	37	49	412¾	Santagata N	L 115	11.50	73-21	Inside Information1246¾ Jade Flush1151¾ Halo America1184¼	Faded driv
4Jun95-7CD	fst	1	:232	:464	1:114	1:36	3↑ ⓕAlw 49700N2m	98	1	1	11½	1½	12	16	Sellers S J	L 123	*1.40	97-07	Laura's Pistolette1236 Clever Bit1203½ Clever Act1232½	Mild hand rid
6May95-6CD	fst	7f	:222	:452	1:10	1:221	ⓕHumanaDstfH-G3	97	4	3	96½	85¼	2½	1no	Nakatani C S	L 114	29.80	98 —	Laura's Pistolette114no Morning Meadow1132½ Traverse City1141½	
7-wide stretch, fully extended																				
30Apr95-9CD	fst	6½f	:224	:463	1:12	1:183	3↑ ⓕAlw 38580N$Y	76	5	2	64¼	44½	2hd	2¾	Sellers S J	L 119 f	2.40	85-14	VenetianFleet115¾ Laura'sPistolette119¾ FlamingStn1151½	Bid, 2nd bes
30Mar95-9TP	fst	6½f	:223	:46	1:113	1:182	ⓕAlw 32800N$Y	82	3	4	55½	44	35	37	Sellers S J	L 122	2.40	77-21	Southern Truce1161 El Pepina1136 Laura'sPistolette1222	No late threa
17Dec94-9TP	my	1 1/16	:224	:454	1:103	1:431	3↑ ⓕMy Charmer47k	94	11	4	32½	21	11½	21	Castanon J L	L 114	19.60	90-20	Sdie'sDrem1191 Lur'sPistoltt1145 BlushingMggi117nk	Good try, 2nd bes
7Dec94-8TP	my	1	:224	:463	1:12	1:374	3↑ ⓕAlw 30290N$Y	88	5	3	32	32½	32	1¾	Arguello F A Jr	L 114 f	*.70	83-20	Laura's Pistolette114¾ Mari'sKey1165 StrawberryOnTop116hd	Hard driv
19Nov94-7CD	fst	1 1/16	:24	:481	1:134	1:46	3↑ ⓕAlw 43500N$Y	87	1	4	45	43	2hd	21½	Gryder A T	L 113	6.40	82-23	G.U.Dncr1161½ Lur'sPistoltt1131½ BlushingMggi1182	Bid, led, second bes
6Nov94-5CD	fm	1 1/16 ⓣ	:233	:473	1:13	1:443	3↑ ⓕAlw 40500N$Y	74	2	4	46½	41	55	46	Martinez W	L 111	12.80	77-16	Ma Guerre114no Adored Slew1144½ Heavenliness1141½	
Steadied, in tight 3/16's, no late response																				
14Oct94-5Kee	my	1 1/16	:232	:472	1:12	1:453	3↑ ⓕAlw 32500N3X	78	9	4	31	3½	21½	32¾	Sellers S J	L 113 f	4.60	78-25	StellaCielo117¾ VenetianRed1142 Laur'sPistolette1132	No late respons

WORKOUTS: ●Aug 10 Sar 3f fst :353 H 1/18 ●Aug 3 CD 4f fst :48 Bg 1/29 ●Jly 28 CD 5f fst 1:01 H 1/18 Jly 17 CDT 4f fst :494 B 2/4 Jun 29 CDT 3f fst :37 B 1/2 Jun 24 CDT tr.t 6f fst 1:15 B 1/2

Classy Mirage
Own: Middletown Stables

B. m. 5
Sire: Storm Bird (Northern Dancer)
Dam: First Mirage (Riva Ridge)
Br: Stavola Joseph & William (NJ)
Tr: Jerkens H Allen (27 4 3 3 .15)

not the highweight this time — *hard duel*

119

Lifetime Record: 21 11 3 4 $539,222

1995	3 2 1 0	$106,545	Turf	0 0 0 0
1994	12 4 1 4	$298,307	Wet	4 0 1 1 $41,232
Sar	3 1 2 0	$88,588	Dist	3 1 1 0 $40,348

KRONE J A (80 7 14 8 .09)

26Jly95-9Sar fst 6f	:213 :443 :564 1:093 3↑	ⒻHonorbleMiss80k	100 1 4 1½ 1½ 1³ 2½	Krone J A	123 b	*.70	92-14	LowKeyAffair115² ClassyMirge123⁹ TwistAfleet120³	Dueled, weakened 5
3Jun95-10Bel fst 6f	:221 :454 :574 1:111 3↑	ⒻGenuinRiskH-G2	93 1 2 1½ 1½ 15 13½	Krone J A	122 b	*.40	85-14	Classy Mirage122³½ Through The Door111½ Lottsa Talc117²	Under wraps 4
13May95-7Bel fst 6f	:223 :453 :572 1:093	ⒻAlw 44000N$Y	105 3 1 12 12 1³ 19	Perez R B⁵	116 b	*.30	93-10	Classy Mirage116⁹ Susan Valley116²½ Miss Prospector116¹	Handily 5
6Nov94-4Aqu wf 7f	:221 :45 1:10 1:23 3↑	ⒻFirstFlghtH-G2	65 6 2 4½ 3½ 7⁸½ 815	Krone J A	122 b	*1.25e	74-17	Twist Afleet117nk Ann Dear117²¾ Incinerate113½	Gave way 6
8Oct94-4Bel fst 6f	:221 1:10 1:361 1:484 3↑	ⒻBeldame-G1	85 4 3 3³½ 2½ 3⁵ 316	Krone J A	123 b	—	71-17	Heavenly Prize119⁶ Educated Risk123¹⁰ Classy Mirage123¹¹	Tired 4
Exhibition Race, No Wagering									
9Sep94-9Med sly 6f	:221 :45 :57 1:093 3↑	ⒻMed Bud BCH-G3	98 6 1 5½ 3nk 3nk 3½	Krone J A	123 b	*.60	93-12	Ann Dear115hd Wild Lady A.112nk Classy Mirage123¹	Needed more 6
19Aug94-9Sar my 6f	:222 :443 1:084 1:214 3↑	ⒻBallerina H-G1	102 3 1 2½ 2hd 2½ 2¹½	Krone J A	123 b	*1.90	95-09	Roamin Rachel118¹½ Classy Mirage123nk Twist Afleet113nk	Gamely 6
29Jly94-8Sar gd 6f	:214 :443 :563 1:093 3↑	ⒻHonorbleMissB1k	104 6 4 41 2½ 1¹ 1¹	Krone J A	122 b	*1.10	93-06	ClassyMirage122³ SpinningRound119½ ForAllSesons117¹½	Wide, clearly 6
13Jly94-7Bel fst 6f	:221 :453 :571 1:093 3↑	ⒻAlw 40000N$Y	112 5 2 3¹½ 1½ 1¹ 1¹½	Krone J A	119 b	*.30	90-05	Classy Mirage121³½ Miss Indy Anna119²½ Educated Risk116⁵½	Ridden out 6
29Apr94-8GS gd 6f	:213 :442 :563 1:094 3↑	ⒻGS Bud BC H-G3	88 2 4 3½½ 3² 3⁶ 34½	Davis R G	119 b	*1.00	88-16	Sister Dell109¹½ Apelia120³½ Classy Mirage119½	No rally 4

WORKOUTS: Aug 11 Sar 4f fst :49¹ B *10/24* Aug 8 Sar 6f fst 1:12² H *1/2* Aug 2 Sar 6f fst 1:13² H *1/8* Jly 22 Sar 5f fst :59³ H *1/12* Jly 19 Sar 4f fst :49 B *5/12* Jly 13 Bel tr.t 3f fst :36¹ H *3/16*

Inside Information
Own: Phipps Ogden Mills

(blew out :36 in mud yesterday)

B. f. 4
Sire: Private Account (Damascus)
Dam: Pure Profit (Key to the Mint)
Br: Phipps Ogden Mills (Ky)
Tr: McGaughey Claude III (19 3 3 3 .16)

runs at any track (and wins)

126

GP MTH DEL KEE AQU

Lifetime Record: 13 11 0 2 $773,529

1995	4 4 0 0	$292,132	Turf	0 0 0 0
1994	7 6 0 1	$462,797	Wet	2 2 0 0 $170,220
Sar	0 0 0 0		Dist	2 2 0 0 $44,422

SMITH M E (104 20 14 17 .19)

4Jly95-9Mth fst 1⅛	:234 :464 1:101 1:434 3↑	ⒻMolPitcherH-G2	106 3 2 2hd 1hd 1⁴ 16½	Smith M E	124	*.30	86-21	Inside Information124⁶½ Jade Flush115½ Halo America118⁴½	Handily 5
3Jun95-10Mth fst 170	:223 :454 1:111 1:414 3↑	ⒻMth Bud BCH-G3	107 2 3 3½ 1hd 1¹½ 12½	Smith M E	123	*.30	93-20	Inside Information123²½ Morning Meadow115⁵ Incinerate116¹⁰	Handily 5
Came in some upper stretch, driving									
20May95-8Bel wf 1	:224 :462 1:102 1:35 3↑	ⒻShuvee H-G1	111 1 2 2hd 1¹ 1³ 15½	Santos J A	119	2.25e	88-24	Inside Information119⁵½ Sky Beauty126¹⁶ Restored Hope115²	Ridden out 4
26Apr95-7Kee fst 7f	:224 :453 1:093 1:213	ⒻAlw 45590N$Y	102 4 2 1½ 12½ 13 14	Smith M E	118	*.30	93-11	InsidInformtion118⁴ TrvrsCty118⁴½ ScoopThGold114½	Ridden out, sharp 6
18Nov94-6Aqu fst 6½f	:224 :454 1:094 1:16 3↑	ⒻAlw 42000N$Y	102 4 5 2½ 1¹½ 15 18	Smith M E	120	*.15	101-14	Inside Information120⁸ LittleBuckles112hd ReachForClever117¹⁰	Handily 5
12Aug94-8Bel fst 1⅛	:451 1:083 1:332 1:462	ⒻMotherGoose-G1	89 2 2 1½ 2hd 33 310½	Smith M E	121	*.70	89-14	Lakewy121¼ CinnmonSugr121⁶ InsideInformtion121nk	Dueled, weakened 6
8May94-8Aqu my 1	:224 :452 1:093 1:341	ⒻAcorn-G1	96 3 1 1¹½ 1½ 16 1¹¹	Smith M E	121	*.50	92-17	InsideInformation121¹¹ CinnamonSugr121½ SovereignKitty121³½	Handily 5
23Apr94-8Kee fst 1⅛	:242 :491 1:14 1:464	ⒻAshland-G1	101 4 2 2½ 1½ 1³ 15½	Smith M E	121	*.80	75-41	Inside Information121⁵½ Bunting112nk Private Status118²	Ridden out 6
5Mar94-10GP fst 1⅛	:231 :491 1:103 1:424	ⒻBonnie Miss-G2	93 6 5 4½ 2hd 1hd 12½	Smith M E	114	3.00	95-06	Inside Information114²½ CinnmonSugr113nk JdeFlush114⁴	Fully extended 10
21Feb94-1GP fst 1⅛	:241 :481 1:122 1:431	ⒻAlw 29000N2x	88 3 1 1¹½ 1¹ 1¹½ 1nk	Smith M E	118	*.60	94-09	Inside Information118nk Cinnamon Sugar121¹¹ True By Two118⁵½	Driving 5

WORKOUTS: Aug 7 Sar tr.t 4f fst :49¹ B *1/39* Aug 3 Sar tr.t 3f fst :35¹ B *1/10* Jly 30 Sar tr.t 4f fst :49¹ B *2/27* Jly 14 Bel 4f fst :49⁴ B *18/39* Jly 3 Bel 3f fst :34³ B *1/11* Jun 27 Bel 5f my :58⁴ H *1/12*

vice table speed

Low Key Affair
Own: Moyglare Stud

TOP

B. f. 4
Sire: Affirmed (Exclusive Native)
Dam: Talking Picture (Speak John)
Br: Moyglare Stud Farm Ltd (Ky)
Tr: Lukas D Wayne (19 5 4 2 .26)

115

Lifetime Record: 11 6 2 2 $253,749

1995	5 2 1 1	$193,005	Turf	7 4 1 1 $65,244
1994	3 2 1 0	$26,806	Wet	1 0 1 0 $30,000
Sar	1 1 0 0	$48,195	Dist	1 1 0 0 $93,840

DAY P (98 17 12 12 .17)

26Jly95-9Sar fst 6f	:213 :443 :564 1:093 3↑	ⒻHonorbleMiss80k	102 5 5 5⁵½ 5⁴½ 2½ 1½	Day P	115	6.00	93-14	Low Key Affair115½ Classy Mirage123⁹ Twist Afleet120³	Going away 5
24Jun95-9AP fst 7f	:223 :46 1:111 1:243 3↑	ⒻChi Bud BCH-G3	95 3 7 5³½ 4²½ 2½ 1½	Gryder A T	113	4.10	83-16	Low Key Affair113½ Morning Meadow115²½ Marina Park120½	Long drive 9
4Jun95-9CD fst 1⅛	:473 1:122 1:38 1:512 3↑	ⒻFleurDeLisH-G3	97 4 5 4²½ 42 23 33	Barton D M	112	10.10	87-20	Fit To Lead117²¾ Pennyhill Park118¼ LowKeyAffair112½	No late response 7
13May95-7Hol fst 1	⒯ :223 :46 1:103 1:343	ⒻAlw 60000N$mY	71 4 3 35½ 42½ 52⅞ 49½	Pincay L Jr	B 117	*1.50	80-13	Ask Anita122⁶ Dezibelle's Star115¹ Private Persuasion115²½	No late bid 6
16Apr95-8SA wf 1	⒯ :23 :46 1:104 1:363 3↑	ⒻSA Bud BCH-G3	96 3-3 3¹⁰ 34½ 2² 2⁴	Pincay L Jr	B 117	1.90	83-16	Jacodi'sDevil115³ LowKeyAffir117⁴ FondlyRemembered116¹⁵	Inside bid 4
13Nov94 Leopardstwn(Ire) sf 7f	⒯LH 1:374 3↑ Knockaire Stakes (Listed) Stk 23300		1³	Shanahan P	130	*1.85		Low Key Affair130³ Vittoria Colonna123no Little Musgrave129¹½	12
								Saved ground,2nd 2f out,bid 1f out,soon led,quickly clear	
29Oct94 Leopardstwn(Ire) yl 7f	⒯LH 1:29² 3↑ Crofton EBF Race Alw 8800		1¹½	Shanahan P	123	*2.25		Low Key Affair123¹½ Persian Creek134¹½ Vittoria Colonna128²	9
								Rated in 4th,2nd 1-1/2f out,led final furlong,driving	
7May94 Leopardstwn(Ire) gd 1	⒯LH 1:412 ⒯Ltown 1000 Guineas Trial(Lstd) Stk 29200		2½	Kinane M J	124	*1.10		Zavaleta124½ Low Key Affair124½ Common Rumpus121²½	11
								Tracked leader,led over 2f out,headed 150y out	
12Sep93 Curragh(Ire) yl 7f	⒯Str 1:272 Moyglare Stud Stakes-G1 Stk 145000		34½	Kinane M J	123	8.00		Lemon Souffle123⁴ Spain Lane123½ Low Key Affair123hd	11
								Rated in 7th,finished well,up for 3rd	
21Aug93 Curragh(Ire) yl 6f	⒯Str 1:162 ⒻEBF Debutante Stakes (Listed) Stk 21000		1½	Kinane M J	124	*.65		Low Key Affair124½ Anna Ralph121nk Jedwa121⁶	6
								Led virtually throughout,won ridden out	

WORKOUTS: Aug 7 Sar tr.t 5f fst 1:02³ H *2/16* Jly 21 Sar tr.t 5f fst 1:02⁴ H *3/12* Jly 12 Bel 4f fst :48² B *24/60* Jly 4 Bel 4f fst :48 B *3/71* Jun 18 CD 5f fst 1:00² B *2/25* Jun 12 CD 4f my :50 B *8/20*

Unlawful Behavior
Own: Sommer Viola

B. m. 5
Sire: Badger Land (Codex)
Dam: Shoplifter (Our Native)
Br: Baker William A & Cheney Mark (Ky)
Tr: Martin Frank (14 3 3 3 .21)

110

Lifetime Record: 48 10 14 6 $202,470

1995	13 4 4 1	$111,570	Turf	6 0 2 0 $14,580
1994	19 3 6 4	$52,455	Wet	3 1 2 0 $35,785
Sar	2 1 0 0	$26,400	Dist	4 0 0 1 $1,865

PEZUA J M (2 1 0 0 .50)

27Jly95-8Sar fst 1⅛	:464 1:12 1:384 1:523 3↑	ⒻAlw 44000N$Y	85 5 1 1² 12 1¹ 1¹	Pezua J M	121 b	2.25	73-27	UnlwfulBehvior121¹ DncAccount118½ BlovdB121no	Repulsed, challenged 5
7Jly95-8Bel fst 1⅛	:461 1:102 1:352 1:484	ⒻAlw 48000N2m	93 3 4 54 34 34 2¹	Pezua J M	115 b	18.00	84-21	LittleBuckles118⁴ UnlawfulBehavior115² CinnamonSugr121¼	Late gain 4
22Jun95-8Bel sly 1	⊗ :221 :444 1:101 1:372	ⒻAlw 46560C	71 3 2 2³ 21½ 2½ 11½	Pezua J M	112 b	8.20	76-22	Unlawful Behavior112½ UnrealCupcake111¹⁴ Tiffany'sTaylor115²⁴	Up late 4
2Jun95-5Bel fm 1⅛ ⒯	:233 :471 1:11 1:42	ⒻClm c-50000	77 6 2 2² 3²½ 5²¾ 45	Alvarado F T	116 b	4.80	81-13	DinnerDimond116² SunshineLindjne112½ EenieMeeniMiny112²½	No rally 7
Claimed from Davis Barbara J, Moschera Gasper S Trainer									
11May95-4Bel my 1⅛	:224 :454 1:103 1:431	ⒻClm c-40000	75 2 5 5³½ 41½ 21 2²	Perez R B⁵	115 b	2.25	81-22	Alkris114² UnlwfulBehvior115⁸ BonnieShoppr114²	Bid inside, weakened 6
Claimed from Pomerantz Lawrence J, Barbara Robert Trainer									
29Apr95-7Aqu fst 1⅛	:48 1:124 1:391 1:523	ⒻAlw 50000NC	78 2 1 12½ 1½ 3¹½ 35½	Perez R B⁵	110 b	26.75	71-19	Incinerate119³½ Sapor113²½ Unlawful Behavior110¹¾	Speed, weakened 5
21Apr95-4Aqu fst 7f	:233 :463 1:111 1:241	ⒻClm 55000	72 4 3 6³½ 65 57 56½	Perez R B⁵	109 b	4.60	77-15	Evi Bee112½ Manor Queen116³½ Personal Girl116nk	Checked 5/16 pl 6
13Apr95-3Aqu fst 1	:231 :453 1:111 1:382	ⒻClm 35000	76 2 7 67½ 62½ 21 1²	Perez R B⁵	111 b	*2.75	85-24	UnlwflBhvor111² Gn'sGryGrl118½ BonnShoppr107³½	Check brk, stead 1/4 8
2Apr95-4Aqu fst 1¼	:492 1:143 1:41 2:074	ⒻClm c-25000	72 4 3 3½ 3½ 2hd 2nk	Luzzi M J	116 b	1.80	70-23	Bounding Believer116nk Unlawful Behavior116½ Cryptical116³	Wide trip 6
Claimed from Arego Frank, Allen A Ferris III Trainer									
22Mar95-8Lrl fst 1⅛	:234 :472 1:13 1:453	ⒻAlw 24000N4X	58 2 3 44 54 66 6⁹½	Johnston M T	L 117 b	2.20	72-22	Distanza117³ Over Fly117nk Festive Star122²¼	Weakened 6

WORKOUTS: Aug 9 Sar 3f fst :35⁴ H *2/16* Jly 17 Bel 4f fst :46 H *1/62* Jly 3 Bel tr.t 4f fst :46¹ H *1/19* Jun 16 Bel tr.t 4f fst :47¹ H *1/44*

Madder Than Mad
Own: Siegel Jan & Mace & Samantha
SELLERS S J (58 6 7 7 .10)

B. f. 4
Sire: Carr de Naskra (Star de Naskra)
Dam: Ackrimony (Ack Ack)
Br: Trowbridge Mr & Mrs Philip J (NY)
Tr: Jerkens H Allen (27 4 3 3 .15)

112

Lifetime Record :	9	4	4	0	$125,000						
1995	7	3	3	0	$104,550	Turf	1	0	1	0	$10,200
1993	2	1	1	0	$20,450	Wet	1	1	0	0	$23,100
Sar	0	0	0	0		Dist	0	0	0	0	

15Jly95-3Hol	fst	6f		:221	:45	:57	1:084	ⒻAlw 54000N3X	101	1	3	2½	2½	2hd	1nk	Pedroza M A	LB 119	2.30	96-10	Madder ThanMad119nk IsleoBebe117no DancingOvation11511	Game on rail	5
22Jun95-8Hol	fm	5½f	Ⓣ	:211	:433	:554	1:014	ⒻAlw 51000N3X	90	2	5	44½	55	44	22¾	Pedroza M A	LB 122	5.90	95-02	Track Gal1202¾ Madder Than Mad122hd Siyah Nara1161	Bobbled start	6
31May95-2Hol	fst	6f		:214	:444	:564	1:092	3↑ ⒻAlw 45000N2X	91	2	3	32	2hd	11	12½	Pedroza M A	LB 119	3.00	93-10	Madder Than Mad1192½ Afleet Floozie1161 Wild Jewel1165	Ridden out	6
16Apr95-6SA	wf	6f		:22	:453	:58	1:101	ⒻAlw 42000N1X	94	2	2	2½	2hd	11	13½	Pedroza M A	LB 120	*.90	86-12	MadderThanMad1203½ Whatawomn1173½ Cee'sMrynne1202½	Clear, driving	5
19Mar95-3SA	fst	6f		:212	:441	:562	1:091	ⒻAlw 42000N1X	95	2	4	44	44½	32½	2hd	Pedroza M A	LB 121	2.70	91-06	MockOrange121hd MadderThnMd121½ Cthy'sDynsty1214½	4 wide into lane	6
15Feb95-7SA	fst	6f		:214	:444	:564	1:091	ⒻAlw 42000N1X	91	7	2	21½	2½	21	22	Pedroza M A	LB 120	7.60	89-12	WildJewel1212 MadderThanMd1202 Tht'llBeFine117no	Not good enough	7
16Jan95-5SA	gd	6f		:22	:452	:574	1:103	ⒻAlw 42000N1X	40	4	6	710	812	816	817¾	Solis A	LB 120	*1.70	66-18	Queen Gen117½ That'll Be Fine1173 Carol1173½	Wide, no threat	9
5Dec93-4Hol	fst	6f		:214	:444	:571	1:092	ⒻMd Sp Wt	89	6	2	43½	45½	21	11¼	Solis A	L 118	*1.00	93-10	Madder Than Mad1181¼ My Fling1188 Tulgey Wood118no	Driving	10
24Oct93-4SA	fst	6f		:214	:45	:571	1:091	ⒻMd Sp Wt	91	4	3	1hd	1hd	3nk	2nk	Solis A	LB 117	8.20	91-12	Lakeway117nk Madder Than Mad1172 Desert Stormette1177½	Inside duel	7

WORKOUTS: Aug 11 Sar 5f fst 1:012 H *9/35* Aug 7 Sar 7f fst 1:273 H *1/3* Aug 2 Sar 6f fst 1:163 B *3/8* Jly 13 SA 3f fst :362 H *6/13* Jly 12 SA 4f fst :533 H *46/46* Jun 18 Hol 3f fst :364 H *18/38*

One thing about the New York bettors: they love their chalk. Classy Mirage had been 7-10 when run down by Low Key Affair in the Honorable Miss. Having disappointed in that race, she was being shunned at 5-1 in this spot while Inside Information was 2-5.

But there were a lot of angles that suggested the difference between the two mares was a lot closer than 2-5 vs. 5-1. Inside Information had sprinted only once since the previous November, and whenever she did sprint, it was more along the lines of a pipe-opener against hopelessly overmatched classified allowance rivals; all her graded stakes assignments had come at a mile or longer. Her wet track record read 2-for-2, but one win had been the Shuvee over a harrowed surface labeled wet-fast; her only experience with mud had come against overmatched rivals in the Acorn in May of her 3-year-old campaign. Furthermore, after winning the Molly Pitcher in a common gallop on July 4, Inside Information, who was being aimed for the Breeders' Cup Distaff at Belmont Park, had been in comparatively light training during the dog days of summer; she had breezed an easy half 10 days after the Molly Pitcher, then had not worked for another 16 days. In this spot, she would be giving, Classy Mirage, perhaps the fastest female sprinter in New York on her best day, seven pounds.

Classy Mirage had been run down by Low Key Affair and Pat Day (The Headwaiter) after a brutal pace duel with Grade 1 winner Twist Afleet through a :44 3/5 half in the Honorable Miss. That had been her first start in eight weeks, and she had since been honed to a fine edge for the Ballerina by Allen Jerkens, who drilled her a bullet six furlongs a week later, and another six furlongs six days after that. Classy Mirage was not conceding weight this time, as she had in the Honorable Miss when forced to shoulder 123 pounds; in the Ballerina she would be *in receipt* of seven pounds from Inside Information, who had gotten used to the comparatively slow-paced tempo of route racing.

The big edge in Classy Mirage's corner was her experience on wet Saratoga dirt. At the 1994 meet, she had won the Honorable Miss on a good track; in a muddy renewal of the Ballerina, she had been run down by the stretch-running Roamin' Rachel, an opportunistic mare trained by Shug McGaughey who overpowered a weakened Classy Mirage in the stretch; Classy Mirage might've held, but for an excruciating pace duel with Twist Afleet (fresh from a win in the sloppy, Grade 1 Test Stakes) in that match up as well.

In this match up, there was no one with the quality sprint-speed of Twist Afleet to soften up Classy Mirage in the early going, as there had been in both Saratoga-starts when she'd settled for second best.

It was conceivable that Classy Mirage might get the jump on Inside Information and kick some mud back in her face:

EIGHTH RACE
Saratoga
AUGUST 13, 1995

7 FURLONGS. (1.20^2) 17th Running of THE BALLERINA HANDICAP. Purse $150,000 Added. Grade I. Fillies and mares, 3-year-olds and upward. By subscription of $100 each which should accompany the nomination, $500 to pass the entry box, $500 to start. The purse to be divided 60% to the winner, 20% to second, 11% to third, 6% to fourth and 3% to fifth. Weights: Monday, August 7. Starters to be named at the closing time of entries. Trophies will be presented to the winning owner, trainer and jockey. Closed Saturday, July 29, with 23 nominations.

Value of Race: $150,000 Winner $90,000; second $30,000; third $16,500; fourth $9,000; fifth $4,500. Mutuel Pool $659,491.00 Exacta Pool $555,581.00 Triple Pool $366,091.00 Minus Show Pool $33,466.51

Last Raced	Horse	M/Eqt.	A.	Wt	PP	St	¼	½	Str	Fin	Jockey	Odds $1
26Jly95 ^{9}Sar^2	Classy Mirage	b	5	119	2	3	1^{hd}	1^{1½}	1^2	1^6	Krone J A	5.40
4Jly95 ^{9}Mth^1	Inside Information		4	126	3	6	5½	2^1	2^4	2^{4½}	Smith M E	0.40
4Jly95 ^{9}Mth^4	Laura's Pistolette		4	112	1	5	6	3^1	3^{2½}	3^5	Bailey J D	13.10
26Jly95 ^{9}Sar^1	Low Key Affair		4	115	4	4	2^1	5^{1½}	4^{2½}	4^{4½}	Day P	6.00
27Jly95 ^{8}Sar^1	Unlawful Behavior	b	5	110	5	2	4^{hd}	6	5½	5^{2½}	Pezua J M	25.25
15Jly95 ^{3}Hol^1	Madder Than Mad		4	112	6	1	3^1	4½	6	6	Sellers S J	11.80

OFF AT 4:50 Start Good For All But INSIDE INFORMATION. Won driving. Time, :22^4, :46, 1:10, 1:22^2 Track good.

$2 Mutuel Prices:				
	2–CLASSY MIRAGE	12.80	3.70	2.10
	3–INSIDE INFORMATION		2.40	2.10
	1–LAURA'S PISTOLETTE			2.10

$2 EXACTA 2–3 PAID $25.80 $2 TRIPLE 2–3–1 PAID $113.50

B. m, by Storm Bird–First Mirage, by Riva Ridge. Trainer Jerkens H Allen. Bred by Stavola Joseph & William (NJ).

CLASSY MIRAGE set the early pace under pressure, shook off LOW KEY AFFAIR to get clear nearing the far turn, dug in when challenged at the quarter pole, drifted out in upper stretch, turned back INSIDE INFORMATION to open a clear lead in midstretch, then drew away under intermittent urging. INSIDE INFORMATION stumbled badly leaving the gate, was unhurried early, gradually gained while four wide leaving the backstretch, drew alongside the winner to threaten at the top of the stretch but couldn't stay with that one through the lane. LAURA'S PISTOLETTE trailed early, closed the gap a bit while saving ground midway on the turn, but couldn't sustain her rally. LOW KEY AFFAIR forced the early pace outside the winner, dropped back on the far turn and was never close thereafter. UNLAWFUL BEHAVIOR was never a serious threat. MADDER THAN MAD showed speed while between horses for a half then gave way. CLASSY MIRAGE and MADDER THAN MAD wore mud caulks.

Owners— 1, Middletown Stables; 2, Phipps Ogden Mills; 3, Smith Jack III; 4, Moyglare Stud; 5, Sommer Viola; 6, Siegel Jan & Mace & Samantha

Trainers—1, Jerkens H Allen; 2, McGaughey Claude III; 3, Johnson Murray W; 4, Lukas D Wayne; 5, Martin Frank; 6, Jerkens H Allen

$2 Pick-3 (4-2-2) Paid $108.50; Pick-3 Pool $214,113. $2 Pick-6 (3-3-7-4-2-2) 6 Correct 29 Tickets Paid $20,298.00 (including $199,113 Carryover); 5 Correct 638 Tickets Paid $203.50; Pick-6 Pool $692,521. $2 Daily Double (2-2) Paid $35.20; Daily Double Pool $264,149.

When Inside Information stumbled badly at the break, the Ballerina was over, and this is the most forceful way I know to drive home the point that betting 2-5 shots to win is absolutely, positively insane: there are so many things beyond a handicapper's control, such as racing luck, that decent odds are a prerequisite for success.

Inside Information, of course, ran the table the rest of the year, winning the Ruffian Handicap (by 11 lengths), the Spinster (by a head after being fractious in the gate), and climaxing a brilliant career with a 13 1/2-length *tour de force* in the Breeders' Cup Distaff that iced her Eclipse as champion filly or mare. Her career wet-track totals read "3-for-3" (all at Belmont Park), including an other-worldly Beyer of 119 for her muddy Distaff, but no matter what those totals say, she went down to defeat in the Ballerina on a good racetrack that was obviously still quite wet, beaten by a classy sprinter with a valuable seasoning edge in the footing.

Inside Information
Own: Phipps Ogden Mills

B. f. 4
Sire: Private Account (Damascus)
Dam: Pure Profit (Key to the Mint)
Br: Phipps Ogden Mills (Ky)
Tr: McGaughey Claude III (—)

Lifetime Record:	17	14	1	2	$1,641,805						
1995	8	7	1	0	$1,160,408	Turf	0	0	0	0	
1994	7	6	0	1	$462,797	Wet	3	3	0	0	$690,220
CSC	0	0	0	0		Dist	0	0	0	0	

28Oct95-4Bel	my	1⅛	:45^4	1:09^2	1:33^2	1:46	3↑ ⒻB C Distaff-G1	119	1	4	1½	1^{1½}	1^6	1^{13½}	Smith M E	123	*.80e	102–08	Inside Information123^{13} Heavenly Prize123^{2¾} Lakeway123^1		10
Bobbled start, hand ride																					
8Oct95-8Kee	fst	1⅛	:48	1:12^1	1:37^1	1:50	3↑ ⒻSpinster-G1	100	4	3	3^{1½}	2^1	1^{hd}	1^{hd}	Smith M E	123	*.50	84–16	Inside Information123^{hd} Jade Flush123^4 Mariah's Storm123^3		4
Fractious gate, broke in tangle, exchanged brushes stretch, driving																					
16Sep95-6Bel	fst	1 1/16	:23^1	:46	1:09^2	1:40^4	3↑ ⒻRuffian H-G1	112	5	2	1½	1^4	1^{10}	1^{11}	Smith M E	125	*.10	95–09	Inside Information125^{11} Unlawful Behavior110^{no} Incinerate112^{1¼}	Easily	6
13Aug95-8Sar	gd	7f	:22^4	:46	1:10	1:22^2	3↑ ⒻBallerina H-G1	98	3	6	5^{2¼}	2^{1½}	2^2	2^6	Smith M E	126	*.40	88–07	ClssyMrg119^6 InsdInformton126^{4½} Lr'sPstltt112^5	Stumbled badly break	6
4Jly95-9Mth	fst	1 1/16	:23^4	:46^4	1:10^1	1:43^4	3↑ ⒻMolPitcherH-G2	106	3	2	2^{hd}	1^{hd}	1^4	1^{6¾}	Smith M E	124	*.30	86–21	Inside Information124^{6¾} Jade Flush115^{1¾} Halo America118^{4¼}	Handily	5
3Jun95-10Mth	fst	1^{70}	:22^4	:46^2	1:11^1	1:41^4	3↑ ⒻMth Bud BCH-G3	107	2	3	3½	1^{hd}	1^{1½}	1^{2¼}	Smith M E	123	*.30	93–20	Inside Information123^{2¼} Morning Meadow115^5 Incinerate116^{10}		5
Came in some upper stretch, driving																					
20May95-8Bel	wf	1	:22^4	:46^2	1:10^2	1:35	3↑ ⒻShuvee H-G1	111	1	2	2^{hd}	1^1	1^3	1^{5½}	Santos J A	119	2.25e	88–24	Inside Information119^{5½} Sky Beauty126^{16} Restored Hope115^2	Ridden out	4
26Apr95-7Kee	fst	7f	:22^4	:45^3	1:09^3	1:21^3	ⒻAlw 45590N$Y	102	4	2	1½	1^{2½}	1^3	1^4	Smith M E	118	*.30	93–11	InsidInformtion118^4 TrvrsCty118^{4½} ScoopThGold114½	Ridden out, sharp	6

"When you look back on her, the striking thing is her record," said Shug McGaughey after Inside Information was voted champion. "She lost one race as a 2-year-old, that on a tiring track at Aqueduct. She was third in the Mother Goose as a 3-year-old and hurt herself that day, and she had the biggest excuse of all in the Ballerina ... It was unfortunate that she nearly fell on her face in the Ballerina, but she ran a good race to get second ... she won everything else."

Not that it mattered, but my Pick 6 ticket would've used two in the Ballerina. If only I had put it in!

August 19

AFTER WATCHING Pretty Discreet pull off an Alabama victory so implausible that it rivaled Upset's defeat of Man O'War in the 1919 Sanford Stakes, and Jim Dandy's 100-1 shocker in the 1930 Travers Stakes, my biggest mistake as a public handicapper during the 1995 season was getting caught up in Saratoga's "Graveyard of Favorites" mystique and picking Composer to win the Travers.

My undoing was similar to the phenomenon that leads many handicappers astray when they analyze the Kentucky Derby: speed figures do not transfer reliably from nine furlongs to the classic distance of a mile and one-quarter. In that tenth and deciding furlong, characteristics other than sheer brilliance are called into play: true champions summon up reserves of stamina, endurance and determination the pretenders to the throne cannot match. It makes all the difference in the world.

In retrospect, the 126th running of the "Midsummer Derby" did not offer players the chance for a monumental score (unless they singled Thunder Gulch in the last leg of the Pick 6; in that case, the haul was $13,352).

But even though a win mutual of $3.50 and an exacta worth $11.20 aren't the stuff of which Saratoga legends are made, the Travers result offers an instructive example of how class and Grade 1 experience supersedes all else in definitive championship races at classic distances:

8 **Saratoga**

1¼ MILES. (2:00) 126th Running of THE TRAVERS. Purse $750,000. Grade I. 3-year-olds. By subscription of $750 each, which should accompany the nomination, $3,500 to pass the entry box, $4,000 to start. The purse to be divided 60% to the winner, 20% to second, 11% to third, 6% to fourth and 3% to fifth. Weight, 126 lbs. Starters to be named at the closing time of entries. The winner shall have its name inscribed on the Man O'War Cup and a gold plated replica will be presented to the winning owner. Trophies will be presented to the winning trainer and jockey. Closed Saturday, August 5, with 16 nominations.

Composer						Lifetime Record :	8 4 2 0	$177,720	

Composer
Own: Dekwiatkowski Henryk
BAILEY J D (142 32 17 17 .23)

B. c. 3 (Feb)
Sire: Easy Goer (Alydar)
Dam: Honoria (Danzig)
Br: Kennelot Stables Ltd (Ky)
Tr: Mott William I (39 13 4 4 .33)

126

		Lifetime Record :	8 4 2 0	$177,720	
1995	7 3 2 0	$160,920	Turf	0 0 0 0	
1994	1 1 0 0	$16,800	Wet	2 2 0 0	$37,200
Sar	1 1 0 0	$82,575	Dist	0 0 0 0	

30Jly95–8Sar	fst 1⅛	:47 1:11² 1:37³ 1:51	Jim Dandy-G2	106 3 4 42½ 42½ 11½ 15	Bailey J D	112	2.25	81–19	Composer112⁵ Malthus112⅝ Pat N Jac112⁵		Wide turn, drew off 7
7Jly95–4Bel	fst 1¹⁄₁₆	:23¹ :46¹ 1:11 1:42¹ 3+	Alw 36000N2X	104 3 3 3³ 1ʰᵈ 1³ 1¹¹	Bailey J D	112	*1.10	88–21	Composer112¹¹ Tymtodyn113ⁿᵒ Da Bull113½		Ridden out 5
10Jun95–9Bel	fst 1½	:50¹ 1:15¹ 2:05² 2:32	Belmont-G1	76 6 5 41½ 67½ 817 821½	Bailey J D	126	10.50	48–25	Thunder Gulch126² Star Standard126³¼ Citadeed126¹½		Bid, flattened out 11
27May95–3Bel	wf 1¹⁄₁₆	:24³ :48 1:12¹ 1:42⁴ 3+	Alw 34000N1X	87 6 4 5³ 3ⁿᵏ 1¹ 1³	Bailey J D	110	*.95	85–18	Composr110³ Bob's Prospct110¹ IsItPossibl112½		Four wide, going away 6
26Mar95–10Tam	fst 1¹⁄₁₆	:23³ :47¹ 1:12 1:45¹	TampaBay Dby150k	85 5 6 55½ 43 11½ 21¼	Bailey J D	116	3.50	95–07	Gadzook116½ Composer116½ Bet Your Bucks116ⁿᵏ		Gamely 10
12Mar95–8GP	fst 1¹⁄₁₆	:23¹ :47⁴ 1:12³ 1:44²	Alw 32000N2L	82 2 1 2½ 2ʰᵈ 1ʰᵈ 2³	Bailey J D	119	5.80	83–21	Evanston122³ Composer119ʰᵈ Gold Facts122¹½		Gamely, inside 8
25Feb95–8GP	fst 7f	:22³ :45² 1:09¹ 1:22⁴	Alw 26500N1X	53 2 9 9³⅜ 118½ 1116 1019½	Smith M E	119	2.40	70–13	Sikkim122½ Fritz119ʰᵈ Blissful State119¾		Showed little 11
24Sep94– 3Bel	my 7f	:22³ :46¹ 1:10³ 1:23¹	Md Sp Wt	79 5 4 5⁴ 3¹ 1½ 12½	Smith M E	118	6.30	87–13	Composer118²½ Nostra113⁴ Leap To Flame189⁹		Driving 5

WORKOUTS: ●Aug 15 Sar 6f fst 1:14³ B *1/5*   ●Aug 9 Sar 6f fst 1:13 H *1/11*   Jly 26 Sar 5f fst 1:03 B *29/47*   Jly 19 Bel 4f fst :51 B *61/66*   Jly 4 Bel 4f fst :50 B *47/71*   ●Jun 28 Bel 6f fst 1:13³ B *1/6*

Pyramid Peak

Own: Oxley John C

Ch. c. 3 (Apr)
Sire: Mt. Livermore (Blushing Groom)
Dam: Way It Should Be (Stalwart)
Br: Oxley John C & Ward Donna C (Ky)
Tr: Ward John T Jr (4 0 1 0 .00)

MCCAULEY W H (2 0 0 0 .00) 126

Lifetime Record:	9 5 1 1	$339,772			
1995	7 3 1 1	$301,700	Turf	0 0 0 0	
1994	2 2 0 0	$38,072	Wet	2 2 0 0	$38,072
Sar	0 0 0 0		Dist	1 0 0 0	

30Jly95-11Mth fst 1⅛ :46 1:10^{2} 1:35^{3} 1:48^{4} HaskellInvH-G1 109 9 8 7^{5}½ 6^{4}½ 2^{3}½ 2¾ McCauley W H 120 6.80 89-09 Serena's Song118¾ Pyramid Peak120^{3}½ Citadeed118^{2} Wide early, gamely 11
8Jly95-9Mth fst 1$\frac{1}{16}$:23^{3} :47 1:11^{3} 1:44 LongBranchBC78k 108 3 1 1^{hd} 2^{hd} 1^{hd} 1¾ McCauley W H 120 1.30 85-20 Pyramid Peak120¾ Suave Prospect120^{7}½ Mighty Magee118^{12} Driving 5
3Jun95-8Bir fst 1⅛ :46^{4} 1:11^{2} 1:37^{3} 1:50^{4} Alabama Dby200k 99 3 3 2^{2} 1½ 2^{1}½ 2^{hd} McCauley W H B 122 1.20 93-13 Dazzling Falls122^{hd} [D]Pyramid Peak122^{2}½ Viking Ship122^{3}½ 9
Lugged out upper stretch Disqualified and placed 4th
6May95-8CD fst 1¼ :45^{4} 1:10^{1} 1:35^{3} 2:01^{1} Ky Derby-G1 89 3 5 8^{5}½ 17^{10} 17^{12} 17^{13} McCauley W H 126 18.00e 93 — Thunder Gulch126^{2}½ Tejano Run126^{hd} Timber Country126¾ Gave way 19
1Apr95-10Hia fst 1⅛ :46^{3} 1:10^{4} 1:35^{3} 1:48 Flamingo-G3 102 1 3 3^{2}½ 4^{1}½ 1^{hd} 1¾ McCauley W H 118 4.00 102-08 Pyramid Peak118¾ Royal Mitch122^{5} Bullet Trained118^{nk} 8
Eight wide top str, drifted inward deep str, fully extended
11Mar95-11GP fst 7f :22^{4} :45^{3} 1:09^{3} 1:22 Swale-G3 98 3 6 5^{3} 3^{2}½ 2^{1} 3^{2}½ Bailey J D 114 2.10 90-11 Mr.Greeley114¾ DeviousCourse119^{1}¾ PyramidPek114^{2} Weakened, inside 6
11Feb95-10GP fst 7f :22^{3} :45^{3} 1:10^{2} 1:23^{3} Alw 27000N2X 92 4 3 2^{1} 2^{hd} 1½ 1^{1}½ Bailey J D 119 2.90 85-14 Pyramid Peak119^{1}½ Koennecker119^{2} Admiralty122^{nk} Driving 8
25Nov94-8CD my 6f :21^{4} :46 :58^{2} 1:11^{2} Alw 34740N2L 90 12 5 3^{nk} 2^{1} 2½ 1^{3}½ Maple S 121 11.00 89-15 Pyramid Peak121^{3}½ Steprock121^{1} Te N Te121^{2}½ Driving clear 12
19Oct94-2Kee sly 6½f :22^{4} :46^{2} 1:12^{1} 1:19 Md Sp Wt 58 4 9 1½ 2^{hd} 1^{1} 1½ Maple S 120 *1.90 81-16 Pyramid Peak120½ Tut120^{3} Make Your Choice120^{3} 10
Slow to start, driving rail, gamely

WORKOUTS: ●Aug 9 Sar 5f fst :59^{4} H *1/48* Jly 20 Sar 4f fst :48^{3} H *9/23* ●Jun 30 Kee 5f fst 1:00^{3} H *1/12* May 26 CD 5f gd 1:03^{3} B *19/29*

Malthus

Own: Perez Robert

Dk. b or br c. 3 (Apr)
Sire: Temperence Hill (Stop the Music)
Dam: Hytania (Buckpasser)
Br: Lynda G Leet (Ky)
Tr: Callejas Alfredo (22 3 2 2 .14)

CHAVEZ J F (137 20 18 9 .15) 126

Lifetime Record:	9 4 3 0	$101,566			
1995	5 2 3 0	$94,885	Turf	0 0 0 0	
1994	4 2 0 0	$6,681	Wet	1 0 1 0	$361
Sar	1 0 1 0	$27,525	Dist	0 0 0 0	

30Jly95-8Sar fst 1⅛ :47 1:11^{2} 1:37^{3} 1:51 Jim Dandy-G2 98 4 7 7^{12} 6^{9}½ 4^{5} 2^{5} Chavez J F 112 43.25 76-19 Composer112^{5} Malthus112½ Pat N Jac112^{5} Wide, up for 2nd 7
2Jly95♦Remon(Pan) fst*1$\frac{1}{16}$ LH 2:14^{4} 3↑ Grn Clsco Pres de la Republica-G1 2^{11} Pedroza M 120 Jed Forest126^{11} Malthus120^{4} El Chacal116^{1}½ 13
Tr: Alberto Paz Rodriguez Stk 286000 *Towards rear,6th halfway,finished well without threatening*
21May95♦Remon(Pan) fst*1⅛ LH 1:56^{2} Invitational Handicap 1^{5} Pedroza M 118 Malthus118^{5} Strong Cat118^{6} Farfallino109^{hd} 10
Hcp 4000 *Rated in 5th,strong run to lead 2f out,drew clear,handily*
14May95♦Remon(Pan) my*1⅛ LH 1:56^{2} Handicap Especial 2^{1}½ Pedroza M 120 Don Juan A117^{1}½ Malthus120½ Lost Talent112½ 7
Hcp 3500 *Held up in 6th,4th halfway,late gain into 2nd*
29Jan95♦Remon(Pan) fst*7f LH 1:29 Clasico Empleados de Establos-G3 1^{1}½ Pedroza M 114 3.30 Malthus114^{1}½ Pana Brass114^{6} Big Prince116^{4}½ 8
Stk 12000 *Well placed in 4th,led over 1f out,driving*
18Dec94♦Remon(Pan) fst*7f LH 1:30^{4} Clasico Felipe E Motta-G2 4^{4} Abrego N 117 El Andarin118 Farallones118^{nk} Recompensalo115^{2} 10
Stk 25000 *Tracked in 3rd,one-paced late*
11Dec94♦Remon(Pan) fst*6f LH 1:15^{1} Especial Handicap 1^{6}½ Abrego N 116 *1.80 Malthus116^{6}½ Lord Falcon113^{1}½ Tadeo II110^{2} 10
Hcp 3500 *Led throughout,quickly clear,easily*
18Sep94♦Remon(Pan) fst*6f LH 1:16^{1} Premio Bulove 5^{8} Velasquez C 116 Doral Park116^{3} El Andarin116^{hd} El Terror116^{3} 11
Alw 10000 *Raced in mid-pack,evenly late.Farallones 4th*
27Aug94♦Remon(Pan) fst*5½f LH 1:10^{2} Maiden Race 1^{2}½ Velasquez C 117 2.60 Malthus117^{2}½ Seven Slew115^{5} Liz Lorena110^{2}½ 5
Maiden 3000 *Tracked in 3rd,led 1f out,handily*

WORKOUTS: Aug 15 Sar 5f fst 1:00 B *2/47* Aug 8 Sar 3f fst :36 H *5/16* Jly 28 Sar 4f fst :50^{2} B *28/39* Jly 22 Sar 4f fst :49 H *6/19*

Rank And File

Own: Am W D Stable & Caputo John

Ch. c. 3 (Feb)
Sire: Forty Niner (Mr. Prospector)
Dam: Princess Accord (D'Accord)
Br: Cheveley Park Stud (Ky)
Tr: Schettino Dominick A (16 1 1 1 .06)

LUZZI M J (87 8 5 7 .09) 126

Lifetime Record:	8 2 0 0	$33,240			
1995	6 2 0 0	$33,240	Turf	3 0 0 0	
1994	2 M 0 0		Wet	3 1 0 0	$20,400
Sar	3 1 0 0	$22,440	Dist	0 0 0 0	

Entered 17Aug95- 8 SAR
5Aug95-6Sar wf 1⅛ :48^{3} 1:13^{2} 1:38^{3} 1:52 Alw 34000N1X 85 2 1 1^{1} 1½ 1^{2} 1^{hd} Bailey J D 112 6.90 76-25 Rank And File112^{hd} Slip112^{1}½ Knackattack117^{1} All out 6
24Jly95-7Sar fst 1⅛ :47^{1} 1:11^{4} 1:37^{3} 1:50^{1} 3↑ Alw 34000N1X 81 2 2 2^{1} 2^{hd} 1½ 4^{4} Bailey J D 112 17.10 81-13 Jo Ran Express112^{1} Law Of The Sea106^{hd} Cresson Springs111^{3} Bid, tired 7
4Jly95-3Bel fst 7f :22^{3} :45^{3} 1:11^{4} 1:25^{3} 3↑ Md 45000 72 3 8 4^{2} 3^{1}½ 1^{hd} 1^{3}½ Bailey J D 112 11.50 73-17 Rank And File112^{3}½ Point Man115^{1}½ Kadrmas115^{1} Altered course 1/4 pl 8
8Jun95-4Bel fm 1¼ [T] :47^{2} 1:12 1:36^{3} 2:00^{4} 3↑ Md Sp Wt 50 7 2 2½ 3^{1}½ 6^{10} 8^{19} Samyn J L 112 51.25 65-17 Menzies112½ Kazan117^{8}½ Banquet114^{3} Dueled, tired 12
21May95-10Bel fm 1$\frac{1}{16}$ [T] :23^{4} :47^{3} 1:12^{1} 1:43^{2} 3↑ Md Sp Wt 64 4 3 3^{1}½ 2^{1} 3^{1}½ 6^{4}¾ Santos J A 114 12.90 74-15 Hypo Runner114^{2} Come Talk To Me113½ Mactou113^{1}½ Bid, flattened 10
6May95-4Bel gd 1 (T) :24^{4} :48 1:13^{4} 1:37^{2} 3↑ Md Sp Wt 49 7 9 10^{6}¾ 5^{4}½ 7^{8} 7^{14}¾ Samyn J L 113 16.60 61-22 Fidgetyfeet113^{1} Forest Thunder114½ Paulo113^{1} Four wide, flattened 12
24Sep94-3Bel my 7f :22^{3} :46^{1} 1:10^{3} 1:23^{1} Md Sp Wt 44 4 3 3^{3}½ 4^{2} 4^{11} 5^{16} Krone J A 118 5.50 71-13 Composer118^{2}½ Nostra113^{4} Leap To Flame118^{9} No factor 5
21Aug94-3Sar sly 7f ⊗ :22^{1} :45^{2} 1:11^{2} 1:25^{3} Md Sp Wt 26 3 5 2^{hd} 2^{3}½ 5^{9}½ 7^{20} Bailey J D 118 8.40 57-20 Manila Thriller118^{1}½ Noble 'n Heart118^{5} Banquet118^{5}½ Brief speed 8

WORKOUTS: Aug 17 Sar 3f fst :36^{1} B *2/13* Jly 17 Bel 4f fst :46^{4} H *2/62* Jly 1 Bel 4f fst :48^{1} H *4/52* Jun 26 Bel 4f gd :51^{2} B *17/19* Jun 5 Bel 4f fst :49 B *19/36* May 30 Bel 3f sly :38^{2} B (d)*2/7*

Thunder Gulch

Own: Tabor Michael

Ch. c. 3 (May)
Sire: Gulch (Mr. Prospector)
Dam: Line of Thunder (Storm Bird)
Br: Brant Peter M (Ky)
Tr: Lukas D Wayne (26 5 5 2 .19)

STEVENS G L (—) 126

Lifetime Record:	13 7 2 2	$2,182,586			
1995	7 5 0 1	$1,911,580	Turf	0 0 0 0	
1994	6 2 2 1	$271,006	Wet	1 0 1 0	$24,288
Sar	0 0 0 0		Dist	2 1 0 1	$776,140

23Jly95-8Hol fst 1⅛ :46^{2} 1:10^{1} 1:35^{3} 1:49 Swaps-G2 101 4 2 2½ 2^{1} 1^{hd} 1^{2} Stevens G L B 126 b *.90 88-09 Thunder Gulch126^{2} Da Hoss118¾ Petionville120¾ Gamely 7
10Jun95-9Bel fst 1½ :50^{1} 1:15^{1} 2:05^{2} 2:32 Belmont-G1 101 10 3 2½ 2½ 1^{hd} 1^{2} Stevens G L 126 b *1.50 70-25 Thunder Gulch126^{2} Star Standard126^{3}½ Citadeed126^{1}½ 11
3 or 4 wide, driving, clear
20May95-10Pim fst 1$\frac{3}{16}$:47^{1} 1:10^{4} 1:35^{2} 1:54^{2} Preakness-G1 105 11 5 5^{3}½ 5^{4} 4¾ 3¾ Stevens G L 126 b 3.80 101-08 Timber Country126½ Oliver's Twist126^{nk} Thunder Gulch126^{4} 11
Wide bid, good try
6May95-8CD fst 1¼ :45^{4} 1:10^{1} 1:35^{3} 2:01^{1} Ky Derby-G1 108 16 6 5^{4} 3^{nk} 1^{1}½ 1^{2}½ Stevens G L 126 b 24.50 106 — ThunderGulch126^{2}½ TejnoRun126^{hd} TimbrCountry126¾ 4-wide, stiff drive 19
15Apr95-7Kee fst 1⅛ :49 1:13^{1} 1:37^{2} 1:49^{1} Blue Grass-G2 101 4 3 3^{1} 3½ 4^{2} 4^{4}½ Day P 121 b *1.30 83-13 Wild Syn121^{2}½ Suave Prospect121^{hd} Tejano Run121^{2} 6
Leaned in, bumped 1st turn, came up empty
11Mar95-10GP fst 1⅛ :47^{1} 1:11^{3} 1:36^{2} 1:49^{3} Fla Derby-G1 101 7 3 3^{1}½ 2^{hd} 2^{1}½ 1no Smith M E 122 b 2.00 89-11 Thunder Gulch122^{no} Suave Prospect122^{5} Mecke122^{2} 10
Forced outward deep str, fully extended
18Feb95-9GP fst 1$\frac{1}{16}$:23^{1} :46^{4} 1:11 1:43^{1} FntnOfYouth-G2 105 9 7 5^{1}½ 3^{nk} 1^{hd} 1^{nk} Smith M E 119 b 4.70 92-16 Thunder Gulch119^{nk} Suave Prospect117^{4} Jambalaya Jazz119^{3}½ 12
Wide bkstr, seven wide top str, fully extended
18Dec94-8Hol fst 1$\frac{1}{16}$:22^{4} :46 1:09^{3} 1:40^{3} Hol Fty-G1 99 1 4 4^{7} 4^{7} 3^{5} 2^{6}½ Nakatani C S B 121 b 3.80 91-04 Afternoon Deelites121^{6}½ Thunder Gulch121^{10} A. J. Jett121½ Second best 5
26Nov94-7Aqu fst 1⅛ :48^{1} 1:14 1:40^{2} 1:53^{4} Remsen-G2 89 9 7 7^{4}½ 4^{1}¾ 2^{1} 1^{nk} Stevens G L 115 5.60 67-28 Thunder Gulch115^{nk} Western Echo119^{3} Mighty Magee114¾ 10
Lugged in, bumped late, driving
11Nov94-8Aqu fst 1 :23 :46^{1} 1:11^{1} 1:37^{2} Nashua-G3 79 6 5 4^{3} 4^{2} 4^{3}½ 4^{4}¾ Bailey J D 112 *1.35 76-21 Devious Course114^{2} Mighty Magee112¾ Old Tascosa122^{no} Saved ground 7

WORKOUTS: Aug 14 Sar tr.t 5f fst 1:03 B *9/35* Aug 7 Sar tr.t 6f fst 1:16^{4} B *1/2* Aug 1 Sar tr.t 5f fst 1:04^{3} B *7/12* ●Jly 17 SA 5f fst 1:00 H *1/14* Jly 10 SA 7f fst 1:25^{1} H *1/1* Jly 3 SA 6f fst 1:15^{3} H *4/8*

Star Standard
Own: Condren W J & Cornacchia J M
DAY P (132 23 15 19 .17)

B. c. 3 (Apr)
Sire: Risen Star (Secretariat)
Dam: Hoist Emy's Flag (Hoist the Flag)
Br: Highclere Inc & Louie Roussel III (Ky)
Tr: Zito Nicholas P (38 6 4 8 .16)

126

Lifetime Record:	14 4 2 1	$345,201			
1995	7 3 1 0	$316,461	Turf	2 0 1 0	$7,740
1994	7 1 1 1	$28,740	Wet	3 2 0 0	$117,882
Sar	3 0 0 1	$7,129	Dist	1 0 0 0	$34,370

30Jly95-8Sar fst 1⅛ :47 1:112 1:373 1:51 Jim Dandy-G2 67 5 1 11 21½ 512 524¼ Krone J A 121 2.35 57-19 Composer1125 Malthus112¾ Pat N Jac1125 Drifted early, tired 7
10Jun95-9Bel fst 1½ :501 1:151 2:052 2:32 Belmont-G1 99 11 1 1½ 1½ 2hd 22 Krone J A 126 6.30 68-25 Thunder Gulch1262 Star Standard1263½ Citadeed1261½ 11
Bore out badly, second best
20May95-10Pim fst 1 3/16 :471 1:104 1:352 1:542 Preakness-G1 99 8 2 2hd 2hd 1hd 44¾ McCarron C J 126 29.50 97-08 Timber Country126½ Oliver's Twist126nk Thunder Gulch1264 11
Bumped start, weakened late
23Apr95-8Kee sly 1 1/16 :224 :462 1:113 1:45 Lexington-G2 97 2 2 2hd 1hd 11½ 12¼ Day P 115 3.70 84-27 Star Standard1152¼ Royal Mitch1183 Guadalcanal1158½ 5
Jumped path on track 1/16, driving
11Mar95-10GP fst 1⅛ :471 1:113 1:362 1:493 Fla Derby-G1 71 4 1 2hd 1hd 917 918½ Boulanger G 122 *1.90e 70-11 Thunder Gulch122no Suave Prospect1225 Mecke1222 Faltered 10
3Feb95-9GP fst 1 1/16 :232 :471 1:113 1:45 Alw 40000NC 92 2 1 11 11 2hd 24 Boulanger G 115 9.70 79-25 [D]Jambalaya Jazz1194 Star Standard1151½ Flitch115nk 8
Checked to avoid clipping heels furlong grounds, gamely Placed first through disqualification.
8Jan95-1GP fst 1⅛ :483 1:133 1:381 1:502 Alw 26000N1X 95 4 1 11½ 1½ 12½ 15½ Boulanger G 117 *1.20 85-22 Star Standard1175½ Country Garrison117no Sonic Signal117no Ridden out 5
23Oct94-8Kee fst 1 1/16 :23 :46 1:114 1:443 BreedersFty-G2 55 6 5 59 108¾ 1015 1019½ Martinez W 121 18.60 66-24 Tejano Run1213 Cinch1213½ Gold Miner1214 Done after 1/2 11
29Sep94-3Bel wf 1 1/16 :24 :48 1:124 1:442 Md Sp Wt 87 2 1 11 12½ 12½ 12¾ Samyn J L 118 *1.20 80-22 StarStandrd1182¾ Mr.Affirmed11817 SeminoleStorm1185 Drifted, driving 6
8Sep94-9Bel fm 1 (T) :233 :464 1:113 1:353 Md Sp Wt 70 2 4 1hd 1hd 31 47¾ Davis R G 118 7.40 76-13 Islamabad118no Claudius1184¾ Noble 'n Heart1183 Dueled inside 11
WORKOUTS: ●Aug 12 Sar tr.t 5f fst 1:01 H *1/14* ●Aug 6 Sar tr.t 5f fst 1:011 H *1/9* ●Jly 22 Sar tr.t 5f fst 1:023 B *1/9* Jly 14 Bel 5f fst 1:02 B *20/32* Jly 6 Bel 5f fst 1:014 B *7/16* Jun 29 Bel 5f fst 1:012 B *6/28*

Citadeed
Own: Allan Ivan
MAPLE E (56 8 8 7 .14)

B. c. 3 (Jan)
Sire: Shadeed (Nijinsky II)
Dam: Johanna Keene (Raise a Cup)
Br: Echo Valley Horse Farm (Ky)
Tr: Violette Richard A Jr (7 2 0 1 .29)

126

Lifetime Record:	10 3 0 3	$235,600			
1995	5 1 0 3	$220,872	Turf	5 1 0 1	$14,413
1994	5 2 0 0	$14,728	Wet	0 0 0 0	
Sar	0 0 0 0		Dist	1 0 0 0	

30Jly95-11Mth fst 1⅛ :46 1:102 1:353 1:484 HaskellInvH-G1 103 6 6 31½ 31½ 33½ 34¼ Maple E L 118 3.50 86-09 Serena's Song118¾ Pyramid Peak1203½ Citadeed1182 Tired 11
10Jun95-9Bel fst 1½ :501 1:151 2:052 2:32 Belmont-G1 94 1 4 52 33½ 35 35½ Maple E 126 6.30 64-25 Thunder Gulch1262 Star Standard1263½ Citadeed1261½ 11
Checked 1st turn, bid far turn, tired
28May95-9Bel fst 1⅛ :453 1:094 1:36 1:50 Peter Pan-G2 99 9 2 43½ 44 31 1½ Maple E 112 6.70 82-22 Citadeed112½ Pat N Jac113nk Treasurer1152½ Wide, determinedly 10
6May95-8CD fst 1¼ :454 1:101 1:353 2:011 Ky Derby-G1 97 19 3 43 72½ 95¼ 97¼ Maple E L 126 11.60f 99 — ThunderGulch1262¼ TejnoRun126hd TimbrCountry126¾ Bid far turn, tired 19
19Apr95♦ Newmarket(GB) gd 7f (T)Str 1:23 European Free Handicap(Listed) Stk 46600 34¼ Eddery Pat 131 16.00 Diffident1311¼ Harayir1333 Citadeed131nk 12
Tr: Peter Chapple-Hyam
Rated in 5th,bid 2f out,finished well under pressure
7Nov94♦ M-Laffitte(Fr) hy *7f (T)Str 1:321 Criterium de Maisons-Laffitte-G2 Stk 114000 53 Reid J 123 6.20 Bishop Of Cashel123nk Bashaayeash1231½ Chequer1231 7
Slowly away,raced in 5th,one-paced final furlong
20Oct94♦ Newbury(GB) yl *7f (T)LH 1:33 Horris Hill Stakes-G3 Stk 63300 43 Darley K 124 12.00 Painter's Row1242½ Bishop Of Cashel124hd Be Mindful124½ 10
Pressed pace in 3rd,led 2-1/2f to 1f out,one-paced final furlong
14Jun94♦ Ascot(GB) gd 6f (T)Str 1:151 Coventry Stakes-G3 Stk 67400 51 Dettori L 125 25.00 Srl Pekan125nk Moon King125no Missel125nk 16
Slowly away,mid-pack halfway,bid over 1f out,not good enough
30May94♦ Doncaster(GB) gd 6f (T)Str 1:133 Toyota Cross & Sons Cndtns Stk Alw 10800 1nk Reid J 127 *1.50 Citadeed127nk Lago Di Varano1255 Lady Davenport1204 5
Never far back,dueled 1f out,led final 50y,driving
14May94♦ Southwell(GB) fst 6f LH 1:164 Freesia Maiden Stakes (dirt) Maiden 7800 13 Whitworth S 126 *.40 Citadeed1263 Shaa Spin1213½ Colombo King1262 10
Tracked in 5th,split horses 2f out,led final furlong,ridden out
WORKOUTS: Aug 14 Sar 5f fst 1:011 H *9/46* Aug 9 Sar 4f fst :50 B *19/26* Jly 25 Sar 5f fst 1:012 B *4/28* Jly 19 Bel 6f fst 1:13 H *1/1* Jly 14 Bel 5f fst 1:00 H *2/32* Jly 8 Bel 4f fst :504 B *41/44*

After running a subpar fourth in his final Kentucky Derby prep, Thunder Gulch drew post 16, in Churchill Downs auxiliary starting gate, and was dismissed at 24-1 in the Run for the Roses. He won it convincingly, finished a close-up third in the Preakness, and won the Belmont Stakes by two lengths, to miss becoming a Triple Crown winner by less than a length. Returned from a six-week freshening in Hollywood Park's Swaps Stakes, historically a tricky race that has upended the likes of Seattle Slew and Sunday Silence, Thunder Gulch picked up right where he left off, driving clear by two lengths to notch his sixth victory of Grade 1 or Grade 2 status.

By James Quinn's definition of class standards described in *The Handicapper's Stakes Festival,* to be considered an authentic Grade 1 winner, a horse should have two such victories to its credit; to qualify as an authentic Grade 2 winner, the same standards apply. By that line of measurement Thunder Gulch is the genuine Grade 1 article, but none of the other six Travers contestants are an authentic *anything.* Composer owns a single Grade 2 win, Pyramid Peak a Grade 3; Star Standard and Citadeed a single Grade 2 apiece.

Moreover, Composer's Jim Dandy was officially classified as a Grade 2 win, but he had run away from six rivals of dubious achievement: runnerup Malthus, as you can see from his Travers past performances, was a Panamanian import of little distinction who was 43-1 for his U.S. debut; third place-finisher Pat N Jac had placed in the Grade 2 Peter Pan but had won nothing more than allowance races; the most accomplished Jim Dandy-horses going in had been Star Standard, Blu Tusmani and Hoolie, who had each won a single Grade 2.

Composer's three victories as a 3-year-old consisted of the Jim Dandy and two conditioned allowances, and he had carried no more than 112 pounds in any of them; he would shoulder scale weight of 126 in the Travers — an impost Thunder Gulch had carried to victory three times, in the Kentucky Derby, the Belmont, and the Swaps.

Pyramid Peak, like Composer, had been far up the track in his only prior tussle with Thunder Gulch, but he has at least run against a legitimate graded stakes winner, albeit a filly, in Monmouth's Grade 1 Haskell when he rallied into the teeth of an inside speed-favoring bias to get second behind another Wayne Lukas-trained winning machine, the remarkable Serena's Song:

Serena's Song
Own: Lewis Beverly J & Robert B
STEVENS G L (—)

B. f. 3 (Apr)
Sire: Rahy (Blushing Groom)
Dam: Imagining (Northfields)
Br: Baker Howard (Ky)
Tr: Lukas D Wayne (15 2 3 6 .13)

118

Lifetime Record:	18	10	3	1	$1,521,435						
1995	8	6	1	0	$924,100	Turf	0	0	0	0	
1994	10	4	2	1	$597,335	Wet	0	0	0	0	
Mth	0	0	0	0		Dist	3	3	0	0	$600,000

8Jly95-9Bel	fst	1¼	:47^{4}	1:12	1:37^{2}	2:03^{4}	ⒻC C Am Oaks-G1	95	4	3	3^{1½}	1^{1½}	1^{½}	2^{1½}	Stevens G L		121	*.20	73-21	GoldenBri121^{1½} Sern'sSong121^{8} ChngForDollr121^{2}	Took lead 9/16, wknd	6
9Jun95-8Bel	fst	1⅛	:46^{3}	1:11^{1}	1:36^{3}	1:50^{1}	ⒻMotherGoose-G1	101	6	1	2^{hd}	1^{½}	1^{3}	1^{3}	Stevens G L		121	*.05	81-24	Serena's Song121^{3} Golden Bri121^{6} Forested121^{12}	Ridden out	6
19May95-10Pim	fst	1⅛	:47	1:11^{2}	1:36	1:48^{2}	ⒻBlackEydSsn-G2	113	6	2	2^{1½}	2^{½}	1^{2}	1^{9}	Stevens G L		122	*.40	96-14	Serena'sSong122^{9} Conquistdoress115^{1¼} RreOpportunity115^{7}	Ridden out	7
6May95-8CD	fst	1¼	:45^{4}	1:10^{1}	1:35^{3}	2:01^{1}	Ky Derby-G1	91	13	1	1^{1½}	1^{hd}	4^{2½}	16^{11½}	Nakatani C S		121	*3.40e	95	—	Thunder Gulch126^{2¼} Tejano Run126^{hd} Timber Country126^{¾}	19
Hard pressed, tired badly																						
1Apr95-11TP	fst	1⅛	:46^{3}	1:11^{1}	1:36^{2}	1:49^{3}	Jim Beam-G2	114	3	1	1^{hd}	1^{1}	1^{4}	1^{3½}	Nakatani C S		116	*.90	95-20	Serena's Song116^{3½} Tejano Run121^{5} Mecke121^{4}	Sharp, ridden out	8
12Mar95-8SA	fst	1$\frac{1}{16}$	:23^{3}	:47^{3}	1:12	1:42^{3}	ⒻS A Oaks-G1	106	4	2	2^{½}	2^{½}	1^{2½}	1^{hd}	Nakatani C S	B	117	*.70	82-23	Serena's Song117^{hd} Urbane117^{14} Mari's Sheba117^{no}	Gamely, just held	5
19Feb95-8SA	fst	1	:22^{4}	:46	1:10	1:35^{2}	ⒻLasVirgenes-G1	108	1	1	1^{hd}	2^{hd}	1^{hd}	1^{1¼}	Nakatani C S	B	122	*.50	92-17	Serena's Song122^{1¼} Cat's Cradle118^{nk} Urbane116^{2}	Very game effort	7
29Jan95-8SA	fst	7f	:22^{3}	:44^{4}	1:08^{3}	1:21^{2}	ⒻSntaYnez BC-G2	102	5	1	1^{hd}	2^{hd}	1^{1½}	1^{2}	Nakatani C S	B	123	1.50	95-09	Serena's Song123^{2} Cat's Cradle121^{2} Call Now121^{4½}	Much the best	5
17Dec94-9Hol	fst	1$\frac{1}{16}$	:23^{3}	:46^{4}	1:10^{4}	1:41^{4}	ⒻHol Starlet-G1	103	5	1	1^{hd}	1^{hd}	1^{1½}	1no	Nakatani C S	B	120	*.40	92-13	Serena's Song120^{no} Urbane120^{3½} Ski Dancer120^{4}	Game on rail	5
5Nov94-5CD	fst	1$\frac{1}{16}$	:23	:46^{1}	1:11^{2}	1:45^{1}	ⒻB C Juv Fil-G1	92	12	3	1^{hd}	1^{½}	2^{hd}	2^{hd}	Nakatani C S		119	7.00	88-07	Flanders119^{hd} Serena's Song119^{4} Stormy Blues119^{½}		13

Exactas with Thunder Gulch on top of both Composer and Pyramid Peak were each paying in the $10-$12 range with a minute or so to post, an improvement on 3-5 in the straight pools but nothing to write home about. The only prudent thing to do was sit back, enjoy watching a champion go about his business, and wait for a more promising wagering opportunity.

EIGHTH RACE
Saratoga
AUGUST 19, 1995

1¼ MILES. (2:00) 126th Running of THE TRAVERS. Purse $750,000. Grade I. 3-year-olds. By subscription of $750 each, which should accompany the nomination, $3,500 to pass the entry box, $4,000 to start. The purse to be divided 60% to the winner, 20% to second, 11% to third, 6% to fourth and 3% to fifth. Weight, 126 lbs. Starters to be named at the closing time of entries. The winner shall have its name inscribed on the Man O'War Cup and a gold plated replica will be presented to the winning owner. Trophies will be presented to the winning trainer and jockey. Closed Saturday, August 5, with 16 nominations.

Value of Race: $750,000 Winner $450,000; second $150,000; third $82,500; fourth $45,000; fifth $22,500. Mutuel Pool $1,866,034.00 Exacta Pool $1,486,748.00 Triple Pool $1,122,281.00

Last Raced	Horse	M/Eqt.	A.	Wt	PP	¼	½	¾	1	Str	Fin	Jockey	Odds $1
23Jly95 8Hol1	Thunder Gulch	b	3	126	5	4^{1}	4^{3½}	4^{2}	1^{hd}	1^{½}	1^{4½}	Stevens G L	0.75
30Jly95 11Mth2	Pyramid Peak		3	126	2	1^{hd}	2^{½}	1^{½}	2^{1½}	2^{2}	2^{2}	McCauley W H	4.10
30Jly95 8Sar2	Malthus		3	126	3	7	7	7	5^{1½}	3^{½}	3^{2½}	Chavez J F	25.00
30Jly95 8Sar1	Composer		3	126	1	5^{½}	5^{1½}	5^{6}	3^{2½}	4^{4}	4^{15}	Bailey J D	4.10
30Jly95 8Sar5	Star Standard		3	126	6	2^{½}	1^{hd}	3^{1}	4^{½}	5^{1½}	5^{2}	Day P	8.50
30Jly95 11Mth3	Citadeed		3	126	7	3^{1½}	3^{1½}	2^{½}	6^{½}	6^{hd}	6^{6}	Maple E	13.60
5Aug95 6Sar1	Rank And File		3	126	4	6^{2}	6^{3}	6^{1½}	7	7	7	Luzzi M J	56.00

OFF AT 4:41 Start Good. Won driving. Time, :23^{2}, :47^{1}, 1:11^{2}, 1:37^{1}, 2:03^{3} Track fast.

$2 Mutuel Prices:				
	5–THUNDER GULCH	3.50	2.70	2.10
	2–PYRAMID PEAK		3.60	2.80
	3–MALTHUS			3.30

$2 EXACTA 5–2 PAID $11.20 $2 TRIPLE 5–2–3 PAID $101.50

Ch. c, (May), by Gulch–Line of Thunder, by Storm Bird. Trainer Lukas D Wayne. Bred by Brant Peter M (Ky).

THUNDER GULCH broke in the air at the start, recovering quickly moved up from outside to settle just off the pace on the first turn, was kept just behind the leaders while seven wide along the backstretch, angled in a bit while launching his bid on the far turn, drew alongside PYRAMID PEAK to challenge on the turn, surged to the front at the quarter pole, battled heads apart from outside into midstretch, shook off PYRAMID PEAK under brisk left hand urging inside the furlong marker, switched to the right hand whip while drifting out briefly in deep stretch, then drew off with authority. PYRAMID PEAK rushed up along the rail to contest the early pace, drifted out carrying out STAR STANDARD on the first turn and into the backstretch, alternated for the lead inside STAR STANDARD while racing in the four path down the backstretch, fought gamely into midstretch but couldn't match strides with the winner in the final eighth. MALTHUS raced far back while trailing for seven furlongs, closed the gap a bit while saving ground on the turn, made a run along the inside to threaten in midstretch but was no match for the top two. COMPOSER unhurried for six furlongs while saving ground, split horses while gaining on the turn, angled to the outside of THUNDER GULCH at the top of the stretch, then lacked a strong closing response. STAR STANDARD was carried out by PYRAMID PEAK while battling heads apart on the first turn, alternated for the lead while five wide on the backstretch, checked slightly and angled to the inside on the far turn, then gradually tired thereafter. CITADEED stalked the early pace while six wide, made a brief run to challenge on the far turn, then gave way abruptly. RANK AND FILE never reached contention. STAR STANDARD wore mud caulks.

Thunder Gulch broke in the air at the start but quickly settled into stride just off the pace, attacked Pyramid Peak on the far turn and drew away from that colt in the all-important tenth and final furlong. Composer moved menacingly approaching the quarter pole, but his run was short-lived and he was exposed as less-than-top quality, at least at this point of his career. "He had run as much as he was going to run when he hit the top of the stretch," said Jerry Bailey afterward.

In the fall, Thunder Gulch was retired to stud after sustaining a condylar fracture of his left front cannon bone in the Jockey Club Gold Cup. The over-achieving son of Gulch, who fetched only $40,000 as a yearling, left the track with nine wins in 16 starts, good for earnings of $2,915,086.

I'll settle for half that.

Finish Lines

IN THE AMOUNT OF TIME it takes to read a book, a year has come and gone. Experiencing, gathering, organizing, and writing the material in *Real-life Handicapping* was something of an eye-opener for me, and I hope you picked up some fresh angles and twists to improve your game.

The most profitable plays in turf races invariably were lightly-raced horses that beckoned with inviting pedigrees, or experienced turf horses that combined a touch of class with a strong finishing kick.

In dirt races, non-numerical aspects of pace came into play frequently: also-rans that recently had "won" demanding pace duels and were subsequently spotted in less taxing match-ups; lone speed-types dropping in class; horses with natural speed turning back from routes to sprints jammed with one-dimensional speedballs. By-the-numbers approaches held the most meaning when instant variants were applied, and through the extrapolation of interior fractions, turn times, and such.

On grass or dirt, trainer patterns are a potent source of overlays. Horses with hidden back-form under the conditions were dynamite as well: horses like Primitive Hall and Tiffany's Taylor, with proven ability to win off the bench, are high-percentage plays handicappers should be looking to exploit.

In reviewing a year's worth of personal action, perhaps the thing that surprised me the most was that adjusted final-time figures, whether the Beyer Speed Figures, or *The Sheets*, or *Thoro-graph*, did not provide the foundation for any memorable scores — although they remain a useful tool for evaluating class moves up and down the ladder. Since most of the crowd's betting action focuses on these numbers almost exclusively, this was indeed a propitious state of affairs — and one I intend to maintain.

Speed figures are used most effectively to detect improving and declining form, but that sort of "condition analysis" was covered extensively in *Expert Handicapping* and would have been repetitive here.

Workouts are a strong, yet underrated predictive tool for evaluating surface switches, as we saw with Golden Plover. They also provide essential information in maiden races, and about horses returning from layoffs. Ironically, though workouts can help handicappers measure horses' form and affinity for a given surface, their usefulness is overrated when it comes to assessing relative abilities in racing's showcase races — precisely when they are scrutinized the most. In the days leading up to the Breeders' Cup or the Triple Crown, in-depth coverage of workouts is reported to horseplayers as if they will have great bearing on the outcome, but most Grade 1 horses routinely train swiftly and impressively to begin with. The fact that "Inside Information came home a strong final quarter and had the clockers nodding in approval" really is much ado about nothing.

I like to supplement the *Daily Racing Form* past performances with its sister companion, *National Charts Weekly*, and with peripheral sources such as *Maiden Stats*, *Mudders & Turfers*, and *Sire Ratings*. They are indispensable tools for making decisions about debuting horses, and those venturing to grass or wet dirt for the first time.

I don't go in much for all the computerized, high-tech mumbo jumbo that has saturated the handicapping marketplace in recent years. Basically, they're just clever ways of shuffling numbers around. This is much more than a numbers game, and there is no substitute for the most powerful computer of all...your brain.

"Statistics are like bikinis...," Mets' baseball announcer Ralph Kiner once observed, "...they show you a lot, but not everything."

Ultimately, successful handicapping is about staying on the right side of the percentages, without getting caught up in a maze of numbers. It's about watching races attentively, examining result charts thoroughly, maintaining a file of back *Forms* diligently, and supporting your opinions at the betting windows creatively.

But alas, there's a limit to what one can accomplish by reading books such as this, which merely chronicle someone else's real-life experiences. As Aristotle said, "What we have to do, we learn by doing." I have the feeling he would've been a damn good horseplayer.

References

Handicapping books:

Brohamer, Tom. *Modern Pace Handicapping*, William Morrow, 1991.

Cramer, Mark. *Thoroughbred Form Cycles*, William Morrow, 1990.
        Kinky Handicapping TBS Publishing, 1993.
        Scared Money, City Miner Books, 1994.

Davidowitz, Steven. *Betting Thoroughbreds*, 2nd Revised Edition., Dutton 1995.

Helm, Mike. *Exploring Pedigree*, City Miner Books, 1994.

Litfin, Dave. *Dave Litfin's Expert Handicapping*, Little, Brown & Co., 1995.

Quinn, James. *Recreational Handicapping*, William Morrow, 1990.
        Figure Handicapping, William Morrow, 1992.
        The Handicapper's Stakes Festival, William Morrow, 1995.

Recommended information resources:

Maiden Stats
Published annually @ $99.95 by Bloodstock Research Information Services,
801 Corporate Drive, Lexington, KY 40503. Tel. 800/354-9206.

Mudders & Turfers
Updated annually @ $49 by Lee Tomlinson. P.O. Box 608, Nanuet, NY 10954.
Tel. 800/272-8039.

Sire Ratings 1996-97
Updated annually @ $35 by Mike Helm. Published by City Miner Books. P.O. Box 176,
Berkeley, CA 94701. Tel: 510/841-1511 • Fax: 510/841-1566.

National Charts Weekly. Published by the *Daily Racing Form* @ $5 per issue.
Complete charts from all major tracks plus Beyer Speed Figures for the winners of each
race. Main offices: 2231 East Camelback Road, Phoenix, Ariz., 85016. Tel. 602/468-6500
or 800/306-3676.

Also Available From City Miner Books:

Mark Cramer
Scared Money, $19.95
Kinkier Handicapping, $29.00

Mike Helm
Exploring Pedigree $29.95
Sire Ratings:1996-1997, $35.00
Bred To Run, $27.50
A Breed Apart, $22.50

Bill Olmsted
Trainer Pattern Pocket Guide:
1996-1997 Edition, $50.00

Lee Tomlinson
Mudders & Turfers, $50.00

ORDERING INFORMATION